SECOND EDITION

iOS 9 Programming Fundamentals with Swift

Swift, Xcode, and Cocoa Basics

Matt Neuburg

Beijing · Boston · Farnham · Sebastopol · Tokyo

iOS 9 Programming Fundamentals with Swift, Second Edition

by Matt Neuburg

Copyright © 2016 Matt Neuburg. All rights reserved.

Printed in the United States of America.

Published by O'Reilly Media, Inc., 1005 Gravenstein Highway North, Sebastopol, CA 95472.

O'Reilly books may be purchased for educational, business, or sales promotional use. Online editions are also available for most titles (*http://safaribooksonline.com*). For more information, contact our corporate/institutional sales department: 800-998-9938 or *corporate@oreilly.com*.

Editor: Rachel Roumeliotis	**Cover Designer:** Karen Montgomery
Production Editor: Kristen Brown	**Interior Designer:** David Futato
Proofreader: O'Reilly Production Services	**Illustrator:** Matt Neuburg
Indexer: Matt Neuburg	

April 2015:   First Edition

October 2015:   Second Edition

Revision History for the Second Edition:

2015-09-23:   First release

See *http://oreilly.com/catalog/errata.csp?isbn=9781491936771* for release details.

ISBN: 978-1-491-93677-1

[LSI]

Table of Contents

Part I. Language

Preface

On June 2, 2014, Apple's WWDC keynote address ended with a shocking announcement: "We have a new programming language." This came as a huge surprise to the developer community, which was accustomed to Objective-C, warts and all, and doubted that Apple could ever possibly relieve them from the weight of its venerable legacy. The developer community, it appeared, had been wrong.

Having picked themselves up off the floor, developers immediately began to examine this new language — Swift — studying it, critiquing it, and deciding whether to use it. My own first move was to translate all my existing iOS apps into Swift; this was enough to convince me that, for all its faults, Swift deserved to be adopted by new students of iOS programming, and that my books, therefore, should henceforth assume that readers are using Swift.

The Swift language is designed from the ground up with these salient features:

Object-orientation
   Swift is a modern, object-oriented language. It is *purely* object-oriented: "Everything is an object."

Clarity
   Swift is easy to read and easy to write, with minimal syntactic sugar and few hidden shortcuts. Its syntax is clear, consistent, and explicit.

Safety
   Swift enforces strong typing to ensure that it knows, and that you know, what the type of every object reference is at every moment.

Economy
   Swift is a fairly small language, providing some basic types and functionalities and no more. The rest must be provided by your code, or by libraries of code that you use — such as Cocoa.

Memory management

Swift manages memory automatically. You will rarely have to concern yourself with memory management.

Cocoa compatibility

The Cocoa APIs are written in C and Objective-C. Swift is explicitly designed to interface with most of the Cocoa APIs.

These features make Swift an excellent language for learning to program iOS.

The alternative, Objective-C, still exists, and you can use it if you like. Indeed, it is easy to write an app that includes both Swift code and Objective-C code; and you may have reason to do so. Objective-C, however, lacks the very advantages that Swift offers. Objective-C agglomerates object-oriented features onto C. It is therefore only partially object-oriented; it has both objects and scalar data types, and its objects have to be slotted into one particular C data type (pointers). Its syntax can be difficult and tricky; reading and writing nested method calls can make one's eyes glaze over, and it invites hacky habits such as implicit nil-testing. Its type checking can be and frequently is turned off, resulting in programmer errors where a message is sent to the wrong type of object and the program crashes. It uses manual memory management; the recent introduction of ARC (automatic reference counting) has alleviated some of the programmer tedium and has greatly reduced the likelihood of programmer error, but errors are still possible, and memory management ultimately remains manual.

Recent revisions and additions to Objective-C — ARC, synthesis and autosynthesis, improved literal array and dictionary syntax, blocks — have made it easier and more convenient, but such patches have also made the language even larger and possibly even more confusing. Because Objective-C must encompass C, there are limits to how far it can be extended and revised. Swift, on the other hand, is a clean start. If you were to dream of *completely* revising Objective-C to create a *better* Objective-C, Swift might be what you would dream of. It puts a modern, rational front end between you and the Cocoa Objective-C APIs.

Therefore, Swift is the programming language used throughout this book. Nevertheless, the reader will also need some awareness of Objective-C (including C). The Foundation and Cocoa APIs, the built-in commands with which your code must interact in order to make anything happen on an iOS device, are still written in C and Objective-C. In order to interact with them, you have to know what those languages would expect. For example, in order to pass a Swift array where an NSArray is expected, you need to know what consitutes an object acceptable as an element of an Objective-C NSArray.

Therefore, in this edition, although I do not attempt to teach Objective-C, I do describe it in enough detail to allow you to read it when you encounter it in the documentation and on the Internet, and I occasionally show some Objective-C code. Part III, on Cocoa, is really all about learning to think the way Objective-C thinks — because the structure and behavior of the Cocoa APIs are fundamentally based on Objective-C. And the book ends with an appendix that details how Swift and Objective-C communicate with one another, as well as detailing how your app can be written partly in Swift and partly in Objective-C.

The Scope of This Book

This book is actually one of a pair with my *Programming iOS 9*, which picks up exactly where this book leaves off. They complement and supplement one another. The two-book architecture should, I believe, render the size and scope of each book tractable for readers. Together, they provide a complete grounding in the knowledge needed to begin writing iOS apps; thus, when you *do* start writing iOS apps, you'll have a solid and rigorous understanding of what you are doing and where you are heading. If writing an iOS program is like building a house of bricks, this book teaches you what a brick is and how to handle it, while *Programming iOS 9* hands you some actual bricks and tells you how to assemble them.

When you have read this book, you'll know about Swift, Xcode, and the underpinnings of the Cocoa framework, and you will be ready to proceed directly to *Programming iOS 9*. Conversely, *Programming iOS 9* assumes a knowledge of this book; it begins, like Homer's *Iliad*, in the middle of the story, with the reader jumping with all four feet into views and view controllers, and with a knowledge of the language and the Xcode IDE already presupposed. If you started reading *Programming iOS 9* and wondered about such unexplained matters as Swift language basics, the UIApplicationMain function, the nib-loading mechanism, Cocoa patterns of delegation and notification, and retain cycles, wonder no longer — I didn't explain them there because I do explain them here.

The three parts of this book teach the underlying basis of all iOS programming:

- Part I introduces the Swift language, from the ground up — I do not assume that you know any other programming languages. My way of teaching Swift is different from other treatments, such as Apple's; it is systematic and Euclidean, with pedagogical building blocks piled on one another in what I regard as the most helpful order. At the same time, I have tried to confine myself to the essentials. Swift is not a big language, but it has some subtle and unusual corners. You don't need to dive deep into all of these, and my discussion will leave many of them unexplored. You will probably never encounter them, and if you do, you will have entered an advanced Swift world outside the scope of this discussion. To give an obvious example, readers may be surprised to find that I never mention Swift playgrounds or the REPL. My focus here is real-life iOS programming, and my explanation of Swift therefore concentrates on those common, practical aspects of the language that, in my experience, actually come into play in the course of programming iOS.

- Part II turns to Xcode, the world in which all iOS programming ultimately takes place. It explains what an Xcode project is and how it is transformed into an app, and how to work comfortably and nimbly with Xcode to consult the documentation and to write, navigate, and debug code, as well as how to bring your app through the subsequent stages of running on a device and submission to the App Store. There is also a very important chapter on nibs and the nib editor (Interface Builder), including outlets and actions as well as the mechanics of nib loading; however, such specialized topics as autolayout constraints in the nib are postponed to the other book.

- Part III introduces the Cocoa Touch framework. When you program for iOS, you take advantage of a suite of frameworks provided by Apple. These frameworks, taken together, constitute Cocoa; the brand of Cocoa that provides the API for programming iOS is Cocoa Touch. Your code will ultimately be almost entirely about communicating with Cocoa. The Cocoa Touch frameworks provide the underlying functionality that any iOS app needs to have. But to use a framework, you have to think the way the framework thinks, put your code where the framework expects it, and fulfill many obligations imposed on you by the framework. To make things even more interesting, Cocoa uses Objective-C, while you'll be using Swift: you need to know how your Swift code will interface with Cocoa's features and behaviors. Cocoa provides important foundational classes and adds linguistic and architectural devices such as categories, protocols, delegation, and notifications, as well as the pervasive responsibilities of memory management. Key–value coding and key–value observing are also discussed here.

The reader of this book will thus get a thorough grounding in the fundamental knowledge and techniques that any good iOS programmer needs. The book itself doesn't show how to write any particularly interesting iOS apps, but it does constantly use my own real apps and real programming situations to illustrate and motivate its explanations. And then you'll be ready for *Programming iOS 9*, of course!

Versions

This book is geared to Swift 2.0, iOS 9, and Xcode 7.

In general, only very minimal attention is given to earlier versions of iOS and Xcode. It is not my intention to embrace in this book any detailed knowledge about earlier versions of the software, which is, after all, readily and compendiously available in my earlier books. The book does contain, nevertheless, a few words of advice about backward compatibility (especially in Chapter 9).

The Swift language included with Xcode 7, Swift 2.0, has changed very significantly from its immediate predecessor, Swift 1.2. If you were using Swift 1.2 previously, you'll almost certainly find that your code won't compile with Swift 2.0 without some thorough revision. Similarly, the code in this book, being written in Swift 2.0, is totally incompatible with Swift 1.2. On the assumption that you might have some prior knowledge of Swift 1.2, I call out, in the course of my discussion, most of the important language features that are new or changed in Swift 2.0. But I do not describe or explain Swift 1.2

at all; if you need to know about it — though I can't imagine why you would — consult the previous edition of this book.

Acknowledgments

My thanks go first and foremost to the people at O'Reilly Media who have made writing a book so delightfully easy: Rachel Roumeliotis, Sarah Schneider, Kristen Brown, Dan Fauxsmith, and Adam Witwer come particularly to mind. And let's not forget my first and long-standing editor, Brian Jepson, who had nothing whatever to do with this edition, but whose influence is present throughout.

As in the past, I have been greatly aided by some fantastic software, whose excellences I have appreciated at every moment of the process of writing this book. I should like to mention, in particular:

- git (*http://git-scm.com*)
- SourceTree (*http://www.sourcetreeapp.com*)
- TextMate (*http://macromates.com*)
- AsciiDoc (*http://www.methods.co.nz/asciidoc*)
- BBEdit (*http://barebones.com/products/bbedit/*)
- Snapz Pro X (*http://www.ambrosiasw.com*)
- GraphicConverter (*http://www.lemkesoft.com*)
- OmniGraffle (*http://www.omnigroup.com*)

The book was typed and edited entirely on my faithful Unicomp Model M keyboard (*http://pckeyboard.com*), without which I could never have done so much writing over so long a period so painlessly. For more about my physical work environment, see *http://matt.neuburg.usesthis.com*.

From the Programming iOS 4 Preface

A programming framework has a kind of personality, an overall flavor that provides an insight into the goals and mindset of those who created it. When I first encountered Cocoa Touch, my assessment of its personality was: "Wow, the people who wrote this are really clever!" On the one hand, the number of built-in interface objects was severely and deliberately limited; on the other hand, the power and flexibility of some of those objects, especially such things as UITableView, was greatly enhanced over their OS X counterparts. Even more important, Apple created a particularly brilliant way (UIView-Controller) to help the programmer make entire blocks of interface come and go and supplant one another in a controlled, hierarchical manner, thus allowing that tiny iPhone display to unfold virtually into multiple interface worlds within a single app without the user becoming lost or confused.

The popularity of the iPhone, with its largely free or very inexpensive apps, and the subsequent popularity of the iPad, have brought and will continue to bring into the fold many new programmers who see programming for these devices as worthwhile and doable, even though they may not have felt the same way about OS X. Apple's own annual WWDC developer conventions have reflected this trend, with their emphasis shifted from OS X to iOS instruction.

The widespread eagerness to program iOS, however, though delightful on the one hand, has also fostered a certain tendency to try to run without first learning to walk. iOS gives the programmer mighty powers that can seem as limitless as imagination itself, but it also has fundamentals. I often see questions online from programmers who are evidently deep into the creation of some interesting app, but who are stymied in a way that reveals quite clearly that they are unfamiliar with the basics of the very world in which they are so happily cavorting.

It is this state of affairs that has motivated me to write this book, which is intended to ground the reader in the fundamentals of iOS. I love Cocoa and have long wished to write about it, but it is iOS and its popularity that has given me a proximate excuse to do so. Here I have attempted to marshal and expound, in what I hope is a pedagogically helpful and instructive yet ruthlessly Euclidean and logical order, the principles and elements on which sound iOS programming rests. My hope, as with my previous books, is that you will both read this book cover to cover (learning something new often enough to keep you turning the pages) and keep it by you as a handy reference.

This book is not intended to disparage Apple's own documentation and example projects. They are wonderful resources and have become more wonderful as time goes on. I have depended heavily on them in the preparation of this book. But I also find that they don't fulfill the same function as a reasoned, ordered presentation of the facts. The online documentation must make assumptions as to how much you already know; it can't guarantee that you'll approach it in a given order. And online documentation is more suitable to reference than to instruction. A fully written example, no matter how well commented, is difficult to follow; it demonstrates, but it does not teach.

A book, on the other hand, has numbered chapters and sequential pages; I can assume you know views before you know view controllers for the simple reason that Part I precedes Part II. And along with facts, I also bring to the table a degree of experience, which I try to communicate to you. Throughout this book you'll find me referring to "common beginner mistakes"; in most cases, these are mistakes that I have made myself, in addition to seeing others make them. I try to tell you what the pitfalls are because I assume that, in the course of things, you will otherwise fall into them just as naturally as I did as I was learning. You'll also see me construct many examples piece by piece or extract and explain just one tiny portion of a larger app. It is not a massive finished program that teaches programming, but an exposition of the thought process that developed that program. It is this thought process, more than anything else, that I hope you will gain from reading this book.

Conventions Used in This Book

The following typographical conventions are used in this book:

Italic
: Indicates new terms, URLs, email addresses, filenames, and file extensions.

`Constant width`
: Used for program listings, as well as within paragraphs to refer to program elements such as variable or function names, databases, data types, environment variables, statements, and keywords.

`Constant width bold`
: Shows commands or other text that should be typed literally by the user.

`Constant width italic`
: Shows text that should be replaced with user-supplied values or by values determined by context.

 This element signifies a tip or suggestion.

 This element signifies a general note.

 This element indicates a warning or caution.

Using Code Examples

Supplemental material (code examples, exercises, etc.) is available for download at *http://github.com/mattneub/Programming-iOS-Book-Examples*.

This book is here to help you get your job done. In general, if example code is offered with this book, you may use it in your programs and documentation. You do not need to contact us for permission unless you're reproducing a significant portion of the code. For example, writing a program that uses several chunks of code from this book does not require permission. Selling or distributing a CD-ROM of examples from O'Reilly books does require permission. Answering a question by citing this book and quoting example code does not require permission. Incorporating a significant amount of example code from this book into your product's documentation does require permission.

We appreciate, but do not require, attribution. An attribution usually includes the title, author, publisher, and ISBN. For example: "*iOS 9 Programming Fundamentals with Swift* by Matt Neuburg (O'Reilly). Copyright 2016 Matt Neuburg, 978-1-491-93677-1."

If you feel your use of code examples falls outside fair use or the permission given above, feel free to contact us at *permissions@oreilly.com*.

Safari® Books Online

 *Safari Books Online* is an on-demand digital library that delivers expert content in both book and video form from the world's leading authors in technology and business.

Technology professionals, software developers, web designers, and business and creative professionals use Safari Books Online as their primary resource for research, problem solving, learning, and certification training.

Safari Books Online offers a range of plans and pricing for enterprise, government, education, and individuals.

Members have access to thousands of books, training videos, and prepublication manuscripts in one fully searchable database from publishers like O'Reilly Media, Prentice Hall Professional, Addison-Wesley Professional, Microsoft Press, Sams, Que, Peachpit Press, Focal Press, Cisco Press, John Wiley & Sons, Syngress, Morgan Kaufmann, IBM Redbooks, Packt, Adobe Press, FT Press, Apress, Manning, New Riders, McGraw-Hill, Jones & Bartlett, Course Technology, and hundreds more. For more information about Safari Books Online, please visit us online.

How to Contact Us

Please address comments and questions concerning this book to the publisher:

O'Reilly Media, Inc.
1005 Gravenstein Highway North
Sebastopol, CA 95472
800-998-9938 (in the United States or Canada)
707-829-0515 (international or local)
707-829-0104 (fax)

We have a web page for this book, where we list errata, examples, and any additional information. You can access this page at *http://bit.ly/ios9-prog-fundamentals*.

To comment or ask technical questions about this book, send email to *bookquestions@oreilly.com*.

For more information about our books, courses, conferences, and news, see our website at *http://www.oreilly.com*.

Find us on Facebook: *http://facebook.com/oreilly*

Follow us on Twitter: *http://twitter.com/oreillymedia*

Watch us on YouTube: *http://www.youtube.com/oreillymedia*

Language

This part of the book teaches the Swift language, from the ground up. The description is rigorous and orderly. Here you'll become sufficiently conversant with Swift to be comfortable with it, so that you can proceed to the practical business of actual programming.

- Chapter 1 surveys the structure of a Swift program, both physically and conceptually. You'll learn how Swift code files are organized, and you'll be introduced to the most important underlying concepts of the object-oriented Swift language: variables and functions, scopes and namespaces, object types and their instances.

- Chapter 2 explores Swift functions. We start with the basics of how functions are declared and called; then we discuss parameters — external parameter names, default parameters, and variadic parameters. Then we dive deep into the power of Swift functions, with an explanation of functions inside functions, functions as first-class values, anonymous functions, functions as closures, and curried functions.

- Chapter 3 starts with Swift variables — their scope and lifetime, and how they are declared and initialized, along with important Swift features such as computed variables and setter observers. Then some important built-in Swift types are introduced, including Booleans, numbers, strings, ranges, tuples, and Optionals.

- Chapter 4 is all about Swift object types — classes, structs, and enums. It explains how these three object types work, and how you declare, instantiate, and use them. Then it proceeds to polymorphism and casting, protocols, generics, and extensions. The chapter concludes with a discussion of Swift's umbrella types, such as AnyObject, and collection types — Array, Dictionary, and Set (including option sets, the new Swift 2.0 way of expressing bitmasks).

- Chapter 5 is a miscellany. We start with Swift's flow control structures for branching, looping, and jumping, including a major new Swift 2.0 feature, error handling. Then I'll explain how to create your own Swift operators. The chapter concludes by describing Swift access control (privacy), introspection (reflection), and memory management.

CHAPTER 1

The Architecture of Swift

It will be useful at the outset for you to have a general sense of how the Swift language is constructed and what a Swift-based iOS program looks like. This chapter will survey the overall architecture and nature of the Swift language. Subsequent chapters will fill in the details.

Ground of Being

A complete Swift command is a *statement*. A Swift text file consists of multiple *lines* of text. Line breaks are meaningful. The typical layout of a program is one statement, one line:

```
print("hello")
print("world")
```

(The `print` command provides instant feedback in the Xcode console.)

You can combine more than one statement on a line, but then you need to put a semicolon between them:

```
print("hello"); print("world")
```

You are free to put a semicolon at the end of a statement that is last or alone on its line, but no one ever does (except out of habit, because C and Objective-C *require* the semicolon):

```
print("hello");
print("world");
```

Conversely, a single statement can be broken into multiple lines, in order to prevent long statements from becoming long lines. But you should try to do this at sensible places so as not to confuse Swift. For example, after an opening parenthesis is a good place:

```
print(
    "world")
```

Comments are everything after two slashes in a line (so-called C++-style comments):

```
print("world") // this is a comment, so Swift ignores it
```

You can also enclose comments in /*...*/, as in C. Unlike C, C-style comments can be nested.

Many constructs in Swift use curly braces as delimiters:

```
class Dog {
    func bark() {
        print("woof")
    }
}
```

By convention, the contents of curly braces are preceded and followed by line breaks and are indented for clarity, as shown in the preceding code. Xcode will help impose this convention, but the truth is that Swift doesn't care, and layouts like this are legal (and are sometimes more convenient):

```
class Dog { func bark() { print("woof") }}
```

Swift is a *compiled* language. This means that your code must *build* — passing through the compiler and being turned from text into some lower-level form that a computer can understand — before it can *run* and actually do the things it says to do. The Swift compiler is very strict; in the course of writing a program, you will often try to build and run, only to discover that you can't even build in the first place, because the compiler will flag some *error*, which you will have to fix if you want the code to run. Less often, the compiler will let you off with a *warning*; the code can run, but in general you should take warnings seriously and fix whatever they are telling you about. The strictness of the compiler is one of Swift's greatest strengths, and provides your code with a large measure of audited correctness even before it ever starts running.

 The Swift compiler's error and warning messages range from the insightful to the obtuse to the downright misleading. You will often know that *something* is wrong with a line of code, but the Swift compiler will not be telling you clearly exactly *what* is wrong or even *where* in the line to focus your attention. My advice in these situations is to pull the line apart into several lines of simpler code until you reach a point where you can guess what the issue is. Try to love the compiler despite the occasional unhelpful nature of its messages. Remember, it knows more than you do, even if it is sometimes rather inarticulate about its knowledge.

Everything Is an Object?

In Swift, "everything is an object." That's a boast common to various modern object-oriented languages, but what does it mean? Well, that depends on what you mean by "object" — and what you mean by "everything."

Let's start by stipulating that an object, roughly speaking, is something you can send a message to. A message, roughly speaking, is an imperative instruction. For example, you can give commands to a dog: "Bark!" "Sit!" In this analogy, those phrases are messages, and the dog is the object to which you are sending those messages.

In Swift, the syntax of message-sending is *dot-notation*. We start with the object; then there's a dot (a period); then there's the message. (Some messages are also followed by parentheses, but ignore them for now; the full syntax of message-sending is one of those details we'll be filling in later.) This is valid Swift syntax:

```
fido.bark()
rover.sit()
```

The idea of *everything* being an object is a way of suggesting that even "primitive" linguistic entities can be sent messages. Take, for example, 1. It appears to be a literal digit and no more. It will not surprise you, if you've ever used any programming language, that you can say things like this in Swift:

```
let sum = 1 + 2
```

But it *is* surprising to find that 1 can be followed by a dot and a message. This is legal and meaningful in Swift (don't worry about what it actually means):

```
let x = 1.successor()
```

But we can go further. Return to that innocent-looking 1 + 2 from our earlier code. It turns out that this is actually a kind of syntactic trickery, a convenient way of expressing and hiding what's really going on. Just as 1 is actually an object, + is actually a message; but it's a message with special syntax (*operator* syntax). In Swift, every noun is an object, and every verb is a message.

Perhaps the ultimate acid test for whether something is an object in Swift is whether you can modify it. An object type can be *extended* in Swift, meaning that you can define your own messages on that type. For example, you can't normally send the sayHello message to a number. But you can change a number type so that you can:

```
extension Int {
    func sayHello() {
        print("Hello, I'm \(self)")
    }
}
1.sayHello() // outputs: "Hello, I'm 1"
```

I rest my case.

In Swift, then, 1 is an object. In some languages, such as Objective-C, it clearly is not; it is a "primitive" or *scalar* built-in data type. The distinction being drawn here, then, when we say that "everything is an object," is between object types on the one hand and scalars on the other. In Swift, there are no scalars; *all* types are ultimately object types. That's what "everything is an object" really means.

Three Flavors of Object Type

If you know Objective-C or some other object-oriented language, you may be surprised by Swift's notion of what *kind* of object 1 is. In many languages, such as Objective-C, an object is a *class* or an instance of a class. Swift has classes and instances, and you can send messages to them; but 1 in Swift is neither of those: it's a *struct*. And Swift has yet another kind of thing you can send messages to, called an *enum*.

So Swift has three kinds of object type: classes, structs, and enums. I like to refer to these as the three *flavors* of object type. Exactly how they differ from one another will emerge in due course. But they are all very definitely object types, and their similarities to one another are far stronger than their differences. For now, just bear in mind that these three flavors exist.

(The fact that a struct or enum is an object type in Swift will surprise you particularly if you know Objective-C. Objective-C has structs and enums, but they are not objects. Swift structs, in particular, are much more important and pervasive than Objective-C structs. This difference between how Swift views structs and enums and how Objective-C views them can matter when you are talking to Cocoa.)

Variables

A variable is a *name* for an object. Technically, it *refers* to an object; it is an object *reference*. Nontechnically, you can think of it as a shoebox into which an object is placed. The object may undergo changes, or it may be replaced inside the shoebox by another object, but the name has an integrity all its own.

In Swift, no variable comes implicitly into existence; all variables must be *declared*. If you need a name for something, you must say "I'm creating a name." You do this with one of two keywords: `let` or `var`. In Swift, declaration is usually accompanied by *initialization* — you use an equal sign to give the variable a *value*, right there as part of the declaration. These are both variable declarations (and initializations):

```
let one = 1
var two = 2
```

Once the name exists, you are free to use it. For example, we can change the value of what's in `two` to be the same as the value of what's in `one`:

```
let one = 1
var two = 2
two = one
```

The last line of that code uses both the name one and the name two declared in the first two lines: the name one, on the right side of the equal sign, is used merely to *refer* to the value inside the shoebox (namely 1); but the name two, on the left side of the equal sign, is used to *replace* the value inside the shoebox. A statement like that, with a variable name on the left side of an equal sign, is called an *assignment*, and the equal sign is the *assignment operator*. The equal sign is not an assertion of equality, as it might be in an algebraic formula; it is a command. It means: "Get the value of what's on the right side of me, and use it to replace the value inside what's on the left side of me."

The two kinds of variable declaration differ in that a name declared with let cannot have its object replaced. A variable declared with let is a *constant*; its value is assigned once and stays. This won't even compile:

```
let one = 1
var two = 2
one = two // compile error
```

It is always possible to declare a name with var to give yourself the most flexibility, but if you know you're never going to replace the initial value of a variable, it's better to use let, as this permits Swift to behave more efficiently — so much more efficiently, in fact, that the Swift compiler will actually call your attention to any case of your using var where you could have used let, offering to change it for you.

Variables also have a *type*. This type is established when the variable is declared and *can never change*. For example, this won't compile:

```
var two = 2
two = "hello" // compile error
```

Once two is declared and initialized as 2, it is a number (properly speaking, an Int) and it must always be so. You can replace its value with 1 because that's also an Int, but you can't replace its value with "hello" because that's a string (properly speaking, a String) — and a String is not an Int.

Variables literally have a life of their own — more accurately, a *lifetime* of their own. As long as a variable exists, it keeps its value alive. Thus, a variable can be not only a way of conveniently *naming* something, but also a way of *preserving* it. I'll have more to say about that later.

 By convention, type names such as String or Int (or Dog or Cat) start with a capital letter; variable names start with a small letter. *Do not violate this convention.* If you do, your code might still compile and run just fine, but I will personally send agents to your house to remove your kneecaps in the dead of night.

Functions

Executable code, like `fido.bark()` or `one = two`, cannot go just anywhere. In general, it must live inside the body of a *function*. A function is a batch of code that can be told, as a batch, to run. Typically, a function has a name, and it gets that name through a function declaration. Function declaration syntax is another of those details that will be filled in later, but here's an example:

```
func go() {
    let one = 1
    var two = 2
    two = one
}
```

That describes a sequence of things to do — declare `one`, declare `two`, change the value of `two` to match the value of `one` — and it gives that sequence a *name*, `go`; but it doesn't *perform* the sequence. The sequence is performed when someone *calls* the function. Thus, we might say, elsewhere:

```
go()
```

That is a command to the `go` function that it should actually run. But again, that command is itself executable code, so it cannot live on its own either. It might live in the body of a different function:

```
func doGo() {
    go()
}
```

But wait! This is getting a little nutty. That, too, is just a function declaration; to run it, someone must call `doGo`, and that's executable code too. This seems like some kind of infinite regression; it looks like none of our code will *ever* run. If all executable code has to live in a function, who will tell *any* function to run? The initial impetus must come from somewhere.

In real life, fortunately, this regression problem doesn't arise. Remember that your goal is ultimately to write an iOS app. Thus, your app will be run on an iOS device (or the Simulator) by a runtime that already wants to call certain functions. So you start by writing special functions that you know the runtime itself will call. That gives your app a way to get started and gives you places to put functions that will be called by the runtime at key moments — such as when the app launches, or when the user taps a button in your app's interface.

 Swift also has a special rule that a file called *main.swift*, exceptionally, can have executable code at its top level, outside any function body, and this is the code that actually runs when the program runs. You can construct your app with a *main.swift* file, but in general you won't need to.

The Structure of a Swift File

A Swift program can consist of one file or many files. In Swift, a file is a meaningful unit, and there are definite rules about the structure of the Swift code that can go inside it. (I'm assuming that we are *not* in a *main.swift* file.) Only certain things can go at the top level of a Swift file — chiefly the following:

Module `import` *statements*

A module is an even higher-level unit than a file. A module can consist of multiple files, and in Swift, the files within a module can all see each other automatically; but a module can't see another module without an `import` statement. For example, that is how you are able to talk to Cocoa in an iOS program: the first line of your file says `import UIKit`.

Variable declarations

A variable declared at the top level of a file is a *global* variable: it lives as long as the program runs.

Function declarations

A function declared at the top level of a file is a *global* function: all code will be able to see and call it, without sending a message to any object.

Object type declarations

The declaration for a class, a struct, or an enum.

For example, this is a legal Swift file containing (just to demonstrate that it can be done) an `import` statement, a variable declaration, a function declaration, a class declaration, a struct declaration, and an enum declaration:

```
import UIKit
var one = 1
func changeOne() {
}
class Manny {
}
struct Moe {
}
enum Jack {
}
```

That's a very silly and mostly empty example, but remember, our goal is to survey the parts of the language and the structure of a file, and the example shows them.

Furthermore, the curly braces for each of the things in that example can all have variable declarations, function declarations, and object type declarations within them! Indeed, *any* structural curly braces can contain such declarations. So, for example, the keyword `if` (which is part of Swift's flow control, discussed in Chapter 5) is followed by structural curly braces, and they can contain variable declarations, function declarations, and object type declarations. This code, while silly, is legal:

```
func silly() {
    if true {
        class Cat {}
        var one = 1
        one = one + 1
    }
}
```

You'll notice that I did *not* say that executable code can go at the top level of a file. That's because it can't! *Only a function body can contain executable code.* It can contain executable code at any depth within itself; in the preceding code, the line one = one + 1, which is executable code, is legal because it is inside the if construct, which is inside a function body. But the line one = one + 1 *cannot* go at the top level of the file; and it *cannot* go directly inside the Cat declaration's curly braces.

Example 1-1 is a legal Swift file, schematically illustrating the structural possibilities. (Ignore the hanky-panky with the name variable declaration inside the enum declaration for Jack; enum top-level variables have some special rules that I'll explain later.)

Example 1-1. Schematic structure of a legal Swift file

```
import UIKit
var one = 1
func changeOne() {
    let two = 2
    func sayTwo() {
        print(two)
    }
    class Klass {}
    struct Struct {}
    enum Enum {}
    one = two
}
class Manny {
    let name = "manny"
    func sayName() {
        print(name)
    }
    class Klass {}
    struct Struct {}
    enum Enum {}
}
struct Moe {
    let name = "moe"
    func sayName() {
        print(name)
    }
    class Klass {}
```

```
        struct Struct {}
        enum Enum {}
    }
}
enum Jack {
    var name : String {
        return "jack"
    }
    func sayName() {
        print(name)
    }
    class Klass {}
    struct Struct {}
    enum Enum {}
}
```

Obviously, we can recurse down as far we like: we could have a class declaration containing a class declaration containing a class declaration…and so on. But there's no point illustrating *that*.

Scope and Lifetime

In a Swift program, things have a *scope*. This refers to their ability to be seen by other things. Things are nested inside of other things, making a nested hierarchy of things. The rule is that things can see things *at their own level and higher*. The levels are:

- A module is a scope.
- A file is a scope.
- An object declaration is a scope.
- Curly braces are a scope.

When something is declared, it is declared at some level within that hierarchy. Its place in the hierarchy — its scope — determines whether it can be seen by other things.

Look again at Example 1-1. Inside the declaration of Manny is a name variable declaration and a sayName function declaration; the code *inside* sayName's curly braces can see things *outside* those curly braces at a higher level, and can therefore see the name variable. Similarly, the code inside the body of the changeOne function can see the one variable declared at the top level of the file; indeed, *everything* throughout this file can see the one variable declared at the top level of the file.

Scope is thus a very important way of *sharing information*. Two different functions declared inside Manny would *both* be able to see the name declared at Manny's top level. Code inside Jack and code inside Moe can *both* see the one declared at the file's top level.

Things also have a *lifetime*, which is effectively equivalent to their scope. A thing lives as long as its surrounding scope lives. Thus, in Example 1-1, the variable one lives as long as the file lives — namely, as long the program runs. It is global *and persistent*. But the variable `name` declared at the top level of Manny exists only so long as Manny exists (I'll talk in a moment about what that means). Things declared at a deeper level live even shorter lifetimes; for example, let's return to this code:

```
func silly() {
    if true {
        class Cat {}
        var one = 1
        one = one + 1
    }
}
```

In that code, the class Cat and the variable one exist only during the brief instant that the path of code execution passes through the if construct. When the function `silly` is called, the path of execution enters the if construct. Here, Cat is declared and comes into existence; then one is declared and comes into existence; then the executable line `one = one + 1` is executed; and then the scope ends and both Cat and one vanish in a puff of smoke.

Object Members

Inside the three object types (class, struct, and enum), things declared at the top level have special names, mostly for historical reasons. Let's use the Manny class as an example:

```
class Manny {
    let name = "manny"
    func sayName() {
        print(name)
    }
}
```

In that code:

- `name` is a variable declared at the top level of an object declaration, so it is called a *property* of that object.

- `sayName` is a function declared at the top level of an object declaration, so it is called a *method* of that object.

Things declared at the top level of an object declaration — properties, methods, and any objects declared at that level — are collectively the *members* of that object. Members have a special significance, because they define the *messages* you are allowed to send to that object!

Namespaces

A *namespace* is a named region of a program. A namespace has the property that the names of things inside it cannot be reached by things outside it without somehow first passing through the barrier of saying that region's name. This is a good thing because it allows the same name to be used in different places without a conflict. Clearly, namespaces and scopes are closely related notions.

Namespaces help to explain the significance of declaring an object at the top level of an object, like this:

```
class Manny {
    class Klass {}
}
```

This way of declaring Klass makes Klass a *nested type*. It effectively "hides" Klass inside Manny. Manny is a namespace! Code *inside* Manny can see (and say) Klass directly. But code outside Manny can't do that. It has to specify the namespace *explicitly* in order to pass through the barrier that the namespace represents. To do so, it must say Manny's name first, followed by a dot, followed by the term Klass. In short, it has to say `Manny.Klass`.

The namespace does not, of itself, provide secrecy or privacy; it's a convenience. Thus, in Example 1-1, I gave Manny a Klass class, and I also gave Moe a Klass class. But they don't conflict, because they are in different namespaces, and I can differentiate them, if necessary, as `Manny.Klass` and `Moe.Klass`.

It will not have escaped your attention that the syntax for diving explicitly into a namespace is the message-sending dot-notation syntax. They are, in fact, the same thing.

In effect, message-sending allows you to see into scopes you can't see into otherwise. Code inside Moe can't *automatically* see the Klass declared inside Manny, but it *can* see it by taking one easy extra step, namely by speaking of `Manny.Klass`. It can do *that* because it *can* see Manny (because Manny is declared at a level that code inside Moe can see).

Modules

The top-level namespaces are *modules*. By default, your app is a module and hence a namespace; that namespace's name is, roughly speaking, the name of the app. For example, if my app is called `MyApp`, then if I declare a class Manny at the top level of a file, that class's *real* name is `MyApp.Manny`. But I don't usually need to use that real name, because my code is already inside the same namespace, and can see the name Manny directly.

Frameworks are also modules, and hence they are also namespaces. For example, Cocoa's Foundation framework, where NSString lives, is a module. When you program iOS, you will say `import Foundation` (or, more likely, you'll say `import UIKit`, which itself imports Foundation), thus allowing you to speak of NSString without saying `Foundation.NSString`. But you *could* say `Foundation.NSString`, and if you were so silly as to declare a different NSString in your own module, you would *have* to say `Foundation.NSString`, in order to differentiate them. You can also create your own frameworks, and these, too, will be modules.

Thus, above and beyond the level of the file, as shown in Example 1-1, are any libraries (modules) that the file imports. Your code *always implicitly imports Swift itself.* You could make this explicit by starting a file with the line `import Swift`; there is no need to do this, but it does no harm either.

That fact is important, because it solves a major mystery: where do things like `print` come from, and why is it possible to use them outside of any message to any object? `print` is in fact a function declared at the top level of the *Swift.h* header file — which your file can see exactly because it imports Swift. It is thus an ordinary top-level function like any other. You could say things like `Swift.print("hello")`, but you probably never will, because there's no name conflict to resolve.

 You can actually *see* the *Swift.h* file and read it and study it, and this can be a useful thing to do. To do so, Command-click the term `print` in your code. Alternatively, explicitly `import Swift` and Command-click the term `Swift`. Behold, there's the Swift header file! You won't see any executable Swift *code* here, but you will see the *declarations* for all the available Swift terms, including top-level functions like `print`, operators like +, and declarations of built-in types such as Int and String (look for `struct Int`, `struct String`, and so on).

Instances

Object types — class, struct, and enum — have an important feature in common: they can be *instantiated*. In effect, when you declare an object type, you are only defining a *type*. To instantiate a type is to make a thing — an *instance* — of that type.

So, for example, I can declare a Dog class, and I can give my class a method:

```
class Dog {
    func bark() {
        print("woof")
    }
}
```

But I don't have actually have any Dog objects in my program yet. I have merely described the *type* of thing a Dog *would* be if I had one. To get an actual Dog, I have to *make* one.

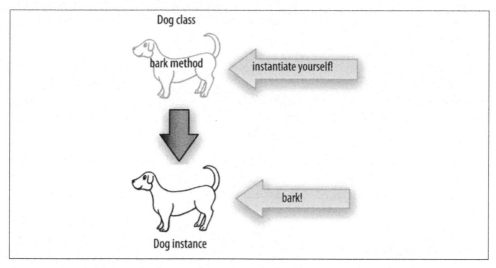

Figure 1-1. Making an instance and calling an instance method

The process of making an actual Dog object whose type is the Dog class is the process of instantiating Dog. The result is a new object — a Dog *instance.*

In Swift, instances can be created by using the object type's name as a function name and calling the function. This involves using parentheses. When you append parentheses to the name of an object type, you are sending a very special kind of message to that object type: Instantiate yourself!

So now I'm going to make a Dog instance:

```
let fido = Dog()
```

There's a lot going on in that code! I did two things. I instantiated Dog, thus causing me to end up with a Dog instance. I also put that Dog instance into a shoebox called `fido` — I declared a variable and initialized the variable by assigning my new Dog instance to it. Now `fido` *is a Dog instance.* (Moreover, because I used `let`, `fido` will always be this same Dog instance. I could have used `var` instead, but even then, initializing `fido` as a Dog instance would have meant `fido` could only be some Dog instance after that.)

Now that I have a Dog instance, I can send *instance messages* to it. And what do you suppose they are? They are Dog's properties and methods! For example:

```
let fido = Dog()
fido.bark()
```

That code is legal. Not only that, it is effective: it actually does cause "woof" to appear in the console. I made a Dog and I made it bark! (See Figure 1-1.)

There's an important lesson here, so let me pause to emphasize it. By default, properties and methods are *instance* properties and methods. You can't use them as messages to the object type itself; you have to have an *instance* to send those messages to. As things stand, this is illegal and won't compile:

```
Dog.bark() // compile error
```

It is possible to declare a function `bark` in such a way that saying `Dog.bark()` *is* legal, but that would be a different kind of function — a *class* function or a *static* function — and you would need to say so when you declare it.

The same thing is true of properties. To illustrate, let's give Dog a `name` property. The only respect in which any Dog has had a name up to now has been the name of the variable to which it is assigned. But that name is not intrinsic to the Dog object *itself*. The `name` property will be:

```
class Dog {
    var name = ""
}
```

That allows me to set a Dog's `name`, but it needs to be an *instance* of Dog:

```
let fido = Dog()
fido.name = "Fido"
```

It is possible to declare a property `name` in such a way that saying `Dog.name` is legal, but that would be a different kind of property — a *class* property or a *static* property — and you would need to say so when you declare it.

Why Instances?

Even if there were no such thing as an instance, an object type is itself an object. We know this because it is possible to send a message to an object type: it is possible to treat an object type as a namespace and to dive explicitly into that namespace (the phrase `Manny.Klass` is a case in point). Moreover, since class and static members exist, it is possible to call a method directly on a class, a struct, or an enum type, and to refer to a property of a class, a struct, or an enum type. Why, then, do instances exist at all?

The answer has mostly to do with the nature of instance properties. The value of an instance property is defined with respect to *a particular instance*. This is where instances get their real usefulness and power.

Consider again our Dog class. I'll give it a `name` property and a `bark` method; remember, these are an instance property and an instance method:

```
class Dog {
    var name = ""
    func bark() {
        print("woof")
    }
}
```

A Dog instance comes into existence with a blank name (an empty string). But its name property is a var, so once we have any Dog instance, we can assign to its name a new String value:

```
let dog1 = Dog()
dog1.name = "Fido"
```

We can also ask for a Dog instance's name:

```
let dog1 = Dog()
dog1.name = "Fido"
print(dog1.name) // "Fido"
```

The important thing is that we can make more than one Dog instance, and that two different Dog instances can have two different name property values (Figure 1-2):

```
let dog1 = Dog()
dog1.name = "Fido"
let dog2 = Dog()
dog2.name = "Rover"
print(dog1.name) // "Fido"
print(dog2.name) // "Rover"
```

Note that a Dog instance's name property has nothing to do with the name of the variable to which a Dog instance is assigned. The variable is just a shoebox. You can pass an instance from one shoebox to another. But the instance itself maintains its own internal integrity:

```
let dog1 = Dog()
dog1.name = "Fido"
var dog2 = Dog()
dog2.name = "Rover"
print(dog1.name) // "Fido"
print(dog2.name) // "Rover"
dog2 = dog1
print(dog2.name) // "Fido"
```

That code didn't change Rover's name; it changed which dog was inside the dog2 shoebox, replacing Rover with Fido.

The full power of object-based programming has now emerged. There is a Dog object type which defines *what it is to be a Dog.* Our declaration of Dog says that a Dog instance — *any* Dog instance, *every* Dog instance — has a name property and a bark method. But *each* Dog instance can have its own name property *value.* They are *different* instances and maintain their own internal *state.* So multiple instances of the same object type

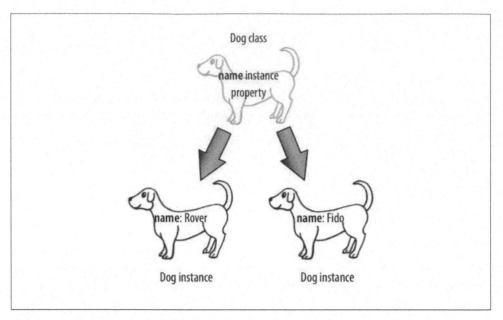

Figure 1-2. Two dogs with different property values

behave alike — both Fido and Rover can bark, and will do so when they are sent the bark message — but they are different instances and can have different property values: Fido's name is "Fido" while Rover's name is "Rover".

(The same thing is true of 1 and 2, though this fact is somewhat more opaque. An Int has a value property. 1 is an Int whose value is 1, and 2 is an Int whose value is 2. However, this fact is of less interest in real life, because obviously you're not going to *change* the value of 1!)

So an instance is a reflection of the instance methods of its type, but that isn't *all* it is; it's also a collection of instance properties. The object type is responsible for *what* properties the instance has, but not necessarily for the *values* of those properties. The values can change as the program runs, and apply only to a particular instance. An instance is a cluster of particular property values.

An instance is responsible not only for the values but also for the *lifetimes* of its properties. Suppose we bring a Dog instance into existence and assign to its name property the value "Fido". Then this Dog instance is keeping the string "Fido" alive just so long as we do not replace the value of its name with some other value *and just so long as this instance lives*.

In short, an instance is both code and data. The code it gets from its type and in a sense is shared with all other instances of that type, but the data belong to it alone. The data can persist as long as the instance persists. The instance has, at every moment, a state — the complete collection of its own personal property values. An instance is a device for maintaining state. It's a box for storage of data.

self

An instance is an object, and an object is the recipient of messages. Thus, an instance needs a way of sending a message to itself. This is made possible by the magic word `self`. This word can be used wherever an instance of the appropriate type is expected.

For example, let's say I want to keep the thing that a Dog says when it barks — namely `"woof"` — in a property. Then in my implementation of `bark` I need to refer to that property. I can do it like this:

```
class Dog {
    var name = ""
    var whatADogSays = "woof"
    func bark() {
        print(self.whatADogSays)
    }
}
```

Similarly, let's say I want to write an instance method `speak` which is merely a synonym for `bark`. My `speak` implementation can consist of simply calling my own `bark` method. I can do it like this:

```
class Dog {
    var name = ""
    var whatADogSays = "woof"
    func bark() {
        print(self.whatADogSays)
    }
    func speak() {
        self.bark()
    }
}
```

Observe that the term `self` in that example appears only in instance methods. When an instance's code says `self`, it is referring to *this* instance. If the expression `self.name` appears in a Dog instance method's code, it means the `name` of *this* Dog instance, the one whose code is running at that moment.

It turns out that every use of the word `self` I've just illustrated is completely optional. You can omit it and all the same things will happen:

```
class Dog {
    var name = ""
    var whatADogSays = "woof"
    func bark() {
        print(whatADogSays)
```

```
    }
    func speak() {
        bark()
    }
}
```

The reason is that if you omit the message recipient and the message you're sending can be sent to `self`, the compiler supplies `self` as the message's recipient under the hood. However, I *never* do that (except by mistake). As a matter of style, I like to be *explicit* in my use of `self`. I find code that omits `self` harder to read and understand. And there are situations where you *must* say `self`, so I prefer to use it whenever I'm allowed to.

Privacy

Earlier, I said that a namespace is not, of itself, an insuperable barrier to accessing the names inside it. But it *can* act as a barrier if you want it to. For example, not all data stored by an instance is intended for alteration by, or even visibility to, another instance. And not every instance method is intended to be called by other instances. Any decent object-based programming language needs a way to endow its object members with *privacy* — a way of making it harder for other objects to see those members if they are not supposed to be seen.

Consider, for example:

```
class Dog {
    var name = ""
    var whatADogSays = "woof"
    func bark() {
        print(self.whatADogSays)
    }
    func speak() {
        print(self.whatADogSays)
    }
}
```

Here, other objects can come along and change my property `whatADogSays`. Since that property is used by both `bark` and `speak`, we could easily end up with a Dog that, when told to `bark`, says `"meow"`. This seems somehow undesirable:

```
let dog1 = Dog()
dog1.whatADogSays = "meow"
dog1.bark() // meow
```

You might reply: Well, silly, why did you declare `whatADogSays` with `var`? Declare it with `let` instead. Make it a constant! Now no one can change it:

```
class Dog {
    var name = ""
    let whatADogSays = "woof"
    func bark() {
```

```
        print(self.whatADogSays)
    }
    func speak() {
        print(self.whatADogSays)
    }
}
```

That is a good answer, but it is not quite good enough. There are two problems. Suppose I want a Dog instance itself to be able to change `self.whatADogSays`. Then `whatADog-Says` *has* to be a `var`; otherwise, even the instance itself can't change it. Also, suppose I don't want any other object to *know* what this Dog says, except by calling `bark` or `speak`. Even when declared with `let`, other objects can still *read* the value of `whatADog-Says`. Maybe I don't like that.

To solve this problem, Swift provides the `private` keyword. I'll talk later about all the ramifications of this keyword, but for now it's enough to know that it solves the problem:

```
class Dog {
    var name = ""
    private var whatADogSays = "woof"
    func bark() {
        print(self.whatADogSays)
    }
    func speak() {
        print(self.whatADogSays)
    }
}
```

Now `name` is a public property, but `whatADogSays` is a private property: it can't be seen by other objects. A Dog instance can speak of `self.whatADogSays`, but a *different* object with a reference to a Dog instance as, say, `dog1` cannot say `dog1.whatADogSays`.

The important lesson here is that object members are public by default, and if you want privacy, you have to ask for it. The class declaration defines a namespace; this namespace requires that other objects use an extra level of dot-notation to refer to what's inside the namespace, but other objects *can* still refer to what's inside the namespace; the namespace does not, in and of itself, close any doors of visibility. The `private` keyword lets you close those doors.

Design

You now know what an object is, and what an instance is. But what object types will your program need, what methods and properties should they have, when and how will they be instantiated, and what should you do with those instances when you have them? Unfortunately I can't tell you that; it's an art — the art of object-based programming. What I *can* tell you is what your chief considerations are going to be as you design and implement an object-based program — the process that I call *growing a program*.

Object-based program design must be founded upon a secure understanding of the nature of objects. You want to design object types that encapsulate the right sort of functionality (methods) accompanied by the right set of data (properties). Then, when you instantiate those object types, you want to make sure that your instances have the right lifetimes, sufficient exposure to one another, and an appropriate ability to communicate with one another.

Object Types and APIs

Your program files will have very few, if any, top-level functions and variables. Methods and properties of object types — in particular, instance methods and instance properties — will be where most of the action is. Object types give each actual instance its specialized abilities. They also help to organize your program's code meaningfully and maintainably.

We may summarize the nature of objects in two phrases: encapsulation of functionality, and maintenance of state. (I first used this summary many years ago in my book *REALbasic: The Definitive Guide*.)

Encapsulation of functionality

Each object does its own job, and presents to the rest of the world — to other objects, and indeed in a sense to the programmer — an opaque wall whose only entrances are the methods to which it promises to respond and the actions it promises to perform when the corresponding messages are sent to it. The details of how, behind the scenes, it actually implements those actions are secreted within itself; no other object needs to know them.

Maintenance of state

Each individual instance is a bundle of data that it maintains. Often that data is private, so it's encapsulated as well; no other object knows what that data is or in what form it is kept. The only way to discover from outside what private data an object is maintaining is if there's a public method or property that reveals it.

As an example, imagine an object whose job is to implement a stack — it might be an instance of a Stack class. A *stack* is a data structure that maintains a set of data in LIFO order (last in, first out). It responds to just two messages: push and pop. Push means to add a given piece of data to the set. Pop means to remove from the set the piece of data that was most recently pushed and hand it out. It's like a stack of plates: plates are placed onto the top of the stack or removed from the top of the stack one by one, so the first plate to go onto the stack can't be retrieved until all other subsequently added plates have been removed (Figure 1-3).

The stack object illustrates encapsulation of functionality because the outside world knows nothing of how the stack is actually implemented. It might be an array, it might be a linked list, it might be any of a number of other implementations. But a client object

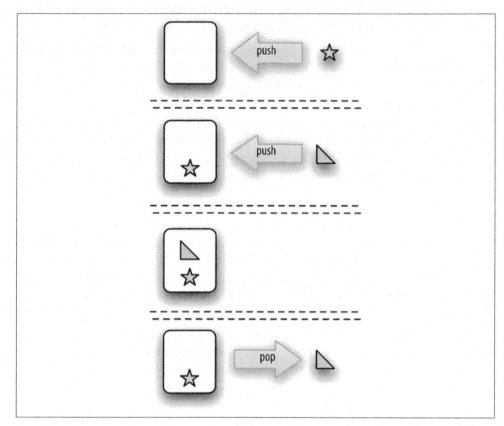

Figure 1-3. A stack

— an object that actually sends a push or pop message to the stack object — knows nothing of this and cares less, provided the stack object adheres to its contract of behaving like a stack. This is also good for the programmer, who can, as the program develops, safely substitute one implementation for another without harming the vast machinery of the program as a whole. And just the other way round, the stack object knows nothing and cares less about who is telling it to push or to pop, and why. It just hums along and does its job in its reliable little way.

The stack object illustrates maintenance of state because it isn't just the gateway to the stack data — it *is* the stack data. Other objects can get access to that data, but only by virtue of having access to the stack object itself, and only in the manner that the stack object permits. The stack data is effectively inside the stack object; no one else can see it. All that another object can do is push or pop. If a certain object is at the top of our stack object's stack right now, then whatever object sends the pop message to this stack object will receive that object in return. If no object sends the pop message to this stack object, then the object at the top of the stack will just sit there, waiting.

The sum total of messages that each object type is eligible to be sent by other objects — its *API* (application programming interface) — is like a list or menu of things you can ask this type of object to do. Your object types divide up your code; their APIs form the basis of communication between those divisions.

In real life, when you're programming iOS, the vast majority of object types you'll be working with will not be yours but Apple's. Swift itself comes with a few useful object types, such as String and Int; you'll also import UIKit, which includes a *huge* number of object types, all of which spring to life in your program. You didn't create any of those object types, so to learn to use them, you consult the published APIs, also known as the *documentation*. Apple's own Cocoa documentation consists largely of pages where each page lists and describes the properties and methods supplied by one object type. For example, to know what messages you can send to an NSString instance, you'd start by studying the NSString class documentation. That page is really just a big list of properties and methods, so it tells you what an NSString object can do. That isn't everything in the world there is to know about an NSString, but it's a big percentage of it.

Thus, in real life, the "wise programmer" of whom I spoke a moment ago will be, in large part, Apple. *Your* wisdom will lie not in creating new object types but in *using* the object types that Apple has already given you. You can *also* create new object types, and you will do so, but proportionately you will do this vastly less than you will use the object types that exist already.

Instance Creation, Scope, and Lifetime

The important moment-to-moment entities in a Swift program are mostly instances. Object types define what *kinds* of instances there can be and how each kind of instance behaves. But the actual instances of those types are the state-carrying individual "things" that the program is all about, and instance methods and properties are messages that can be sent to instances. So there need to *be* instances in order for the program to *do* anything.

By default, however, there are *no* instances! Looking back at Example 1-1, we defined some object types, but we made no instances of them. If we were to run this program, our object types would exist from the get-go, but that's all that would exist. We've created a world of pure potentiality — some types of object that *might* exist. In that world, nothing would actually *happen*.

Instances do not come into being by magic. You have to instantiate a type in order to obtain an instance. Much of the action of your program, therefore, will consist of instantiating types. And of course you will want those instances to persist, so you will also assign each newly created instance to a variable as a shoebox to hold it, name it, and give it a lifetime. The instance will *persist* according to the lifetime of the variable that refers to it. And the instance will be *visible* to other instances according to the scope of the variable that refers to it.

Much of the art of object-based programming turns out to be exactly here, in giving instances a sufficient lifetime and making them visible to one another. You will often put an instance into a particular shoebox — assigning it to a particular variable, declared at a certain scope — exactly so that, thanks to the rules of variable lifetime and scope, this instance will *persist* long enough to keep being useful to your program while it will still be needed, and so that other code can *get a reference* to this instance and talk to it later.

Planning how you're going create instances, and working out the lifetimes and communication between those instances, may sound daunting. Fortunately, in real life, when you're programming iOS, the Cocoa framework itself will once again provide an initial scaffolding for you.

For example, you'll know from the start that, for an iOS app, you need an app delegate type and a view controller type, and in fact when you create an iOS app project, Xcode will give them to you. Moreover, as your app launches, the runtime will instantiate those object types for you, and will place those instances into a fixed and useful relationship. The runtime will make an app delegate instance and assign it in such a way that it lives for the lifetime of the app; it will create a window instance and assign it to a property of the app delegate; and it will create a view controller instance and assign it to a property of the window. Finally, the view controller instance has a view, which automatically appears in the window.

Thus, without your doing any work at all, you already have some objects that will persist for the lifetime of the app, including one that is the basis of your visible interface. Just as important, you have well-defined globally available ways of referring to all these objects. This means that, without writing any code, you already have access to some important objects, and you have an initial place to put any other objects with long lifetimes and any other visible bits of interface that your app may need.

Summary and Conclusion

As we imagine constructing an object-based program for performing a particular task, we bear in mind the nature of objects. There are types and instances. A type is a set of methods describing what all instances of that type can do (encapsulation of functionality). Instances of the same type differ only in the value of their properties (maintenance of state). We plan accordingly. Objects are an organizational tool, a set of boxes for encapsulating the code that accomplishes a particular task. They are also a conceptual tool. The programmer, being forced to think in terms of discrete objects, must divide the goals and behaviors of the program into discrete tasks, each task being assigned to an appropriate object.

At the same time, no object is an island. Objects can cooperate with one another, namely by communicating with one another — that is, by sending messages to one another. The ways in which appropriate lines of communication can be arranged are innumerable. Coming up with an appropriate arrangement — an *architecture* — for the cooperative and orderly relationship between objects is one of the most challenging aspects of object-based programming. In iOS programming, you get a boost from the Cocoa framework, which provides an initial set of object types and a practical basic architectural scaffolding.

Using object-based programming effectively to make a program do what you want it to do while keeping it clear and maintainable is itself an art; your abilities will improve with experience. Eventually, you may want to do some further reading on effective planning and construction of the architecture of an object-based program. I recommend in particular two classic, favorite books. *Refactoring*, by Martin Fowler (Addison-Wesley, 1999), describes why you might need to rearrange what methods belong to what classes (and how to conquer your fear of doing so). *Design Patterns*, by Erich Gamma, Richard Helm, Ralph Johnson, and John Vlissides (also known as "the Gang of Four"), is the bible on architecting object-based programs, listing all the ways you can arrange objects with the right powers and the right knowledge of one another (Addison-Wesley, 1994).

CHAPTER 2

Functions

Nothing is so characteristic of Swift syntax as the way you declare and call functions. Probably nothing is so important, either! As I said in Chapter 1, all your code is going to be in functions; they are where the action is.

Function Parameters and Return Value

A function is like one of those pseudoscientific machines for processing miscellaneous stuff that you probably drew in your math textbook in elementary school. You know the ones I mean: with a funnel-like "hopper" at the top, and then a bunch of gears and cranks, and then a tube at the bottom where something is produced. A function is a machine like that: you feed some stuff in, the stuff is processed in accordance with what this particular machine does, and something is produced.

The stuff that goes in is the input; what comes out is the output. More technically, a function that expects input has *parameters*; a function that produces output has a *result*. For example, here's a very silly but perfectly valid function that expects two Int values, adds them together, and produces that sum:

```
func sum (x:Int, _ y:Int) -> Int {
    let result = x + y
    return result
}
```

The syntax here is very strict and well-defined, and you can't use Swift unless you understand it perfectly. Let's pause to appreciate it in full detail; I'll break the first line into pieces so that I can call them out individually:

```
func sum ❶
   (x:Int, _ y:Int) ❷❸
   -> Int { ❹
       let result = x + y ❺
       return result ❻
}
```

❶ The declaration starts with the keyword func, followed by the *name* of this
   function; here, it's sum. This is the name that must be used in order to *call* the
   function — that is, in order to run the code that the function contains.

❷ The name of the function is followed by its *parameter list*. It consists, minimally,
   of parentheses. If this function takes parameters (input), they are listed inside
   the parentheses, separated by comma. Each parameter has a strict format: the
   name of the parameter, a colon, and the *type* of the parameter. Here, our sum
   function expects two parameters — an Int, to which it gives the name x, and
   another Int, to which it gives the name y.

   Observe that these names, x and y, are arbitrary and purely local (*internal*) to
   this function. They are different from any other x and y that may be used in
   other functions or at a higher level of scope. These names are defined so that
   the parameter values will have names by which they can be referred to in the
   code within the function body. The parameter declaration is, indeed, a kind of
   variable declaration: we are declaring variables x and y for use inside this
   function.

❸ This particular function declaration also has an underscore (_) and a space
   before the name of the second parameter in the parameter list. *I'm not going to
   explain that underscore yet.* I need it for the example, so just trust me for now.

❹ After the parentheses is an arrow operator ->, followed by the type of value that
   this function will return. Then we have curly braces enclosing the *body* of the
   function — its actual code.

❺ Within the curly braces, in the function body, the variables defined as the
   parameter names have sprung to life, with the types specified in the parameter
   list. We know that this code won't run unless this function is called and is actually
   passed values in its parameters.

   Here, the parameters are called x and y, so we can confidently use those values,
   referring to them by those names, secure in the knowledge that such values will
   exist and that they will be Int values, as specified by our parameter list. Not only
   the programmer, but also the compiler can be sure about this.

❻ If the function is to return a value, it must do so with the keyword return
   followed by that value. And, not surprisingly, the type of that value must match
   the type declared earlier for the return value (after the arrow operator).

Here, I return a variable called `result`; it was created by adding two Int values together, so it is an Int, which is what this function is supposed to produce. If I tried to return a String (`return "howdy"`), or if I were to omit the `return` statement altogether, the compiler would stop me with an error.

Note that the keyword `return` actually does *two* things. It returns the accompanying value, and it also halts execution of the function. It is permitted for more lines of code to follow a `return` statement, but the compiler will warn if this means that those lines of code can never be executed.

The function declaration, then, before the curly braces, is a contract about what kinds of values will be used as input and about what kind of output will be produced. According to this contract, the function *expects* a certain number of parameters, each of a certain type, and *yields* a certain type of result. Everything must correspond to this contract. The function body, inside the curly braces, can use the parameters as local variables. The returned value must match the declared return type.

The same contract applies to code elsewhere that *calls* this function. Here's some code that calls our `sum` function:

```
let z = sum(4,5)
```

Focus your attention on the right side of the equal sign — `sum(4,5)`. That's the function call. How is it constructed? It uses the *name* of the function; that name is followed by *parentheses*; and inside those parentheses, separated by comma, are the *values* to be passed to each of the function's parameters. Technically, these values are called *arguments*. Here, I'm using literal Int values, but I'm perfectly free to use Int variables instead; the only requirement is that I use things that have the correct type:

```
let x = 4
let y = 5
let z = sum(y,x)
```

In that code, I purposely used the names x and y for the variables whose values are passed as arguments, and I purposely reversed them in the call, to emphasize that these names have *nothing to do* with the names x and y inside the function parameter list and the function body. These names do not magically make their way to the function. Their *values* are all that matter; their values are the arguments.

What about the value returned by the function? That value is magically *substituted* for the function call, at the point where the function call is made. It happens that in the preceding code, the result is 9. So the last line is exactly as if I had said:

```
let z = 9
```

The programmer and the compiler both know exactly what type of thing this function returns, so they also know where it is and isn't legal to call this function. It's fine to call this function as the initialization part of the declaration of the variable z, just as it would be to use 9 as the initialization part of that declaration: in both cases, we have an Int, and so z ends up being declared as an Int. But it would not be legal to write this:

```
let z = sum(4,5) + "howdy" // compile error
```

Because sum returns an Int, that's the same as trying to add an Int to a String — and by default, you can't do that in Swift.

Observe that it is legal to ignore the value returned from a function call:

```
sum(4,5)
```

That code is legal; it causes neither a compile error nor a runtime error. It is also sort of silly in this particular situation, because we have made our sum function go to all the trouble of adding 4 and 5 for us and we have then thrown away the answer without capturing or using it. However, there are lots of situations where it is perfectly reasonable to ignore the value returned from a function call; in particular, the function may do other things (technically called *side effects*) in addition to returning a value, and the purpose of your call to that function may be those other things.

If you can call sum wherever you can use an Int, and if the parameters of sum have to be Int values, doesn't that mean you can call sum inside a call to sum? Of course it does! This is perfectly legal (and reasonable):

```
let z = sum(4,sum(5,6))
```

The only argument against writing code like that is that you might confuse yourself and that it might make things harder to debug later. But, technically, it's quite normal.

Void Return Type and Parameters

Let's return to our function declaration. With regard to a function's parameters and return type, there are two degenerate cases that allow us to express a function declaration more briefly:

A function without a return type

No law says that a function *must* return a value. A function may be declared to return *no* value. In that case, there are three ways to write the declaration: you can write it as returning Void; you can write it as returning (), an empty pair of parentheses; or you can omit the arrow operator and the return type entirely. These are all legal:

```
func say1(s:String) -> Void { print(s) }
func say2(s:String) -> () { print(s) }
func say3(s:String) { print(s) }
```

If a function returns no value, then its body need not contain a `return` statement. If it does contain a `return` statement, its purpose will be purely to end execution of the function at that point.

This `return` statement will usually consist of `return` and nothing else. However, `Void` (the type returned by a function that returns no value) is an actual type in Swift, and a function that returns no value technically *does* in fact return a value of this type, which may be expressed as the literal `()`. (I'll explain in Chapter 3 what the literal `()` really represents.) Thus, it is legal for such a function to say `return ()`; whether it says that or not, `()` is what it returns. Writing `return ()` — or `return;`, with a semicolon — can be useful to disambiguate in case Swift thinks I'm trying to return whatever is on the next line.

A call to a function that returns no value is made purely for the function's side effects; it has no useful return value that can be made part of a larger expression, so it will usually be the only thing in its line of code, with the `()` value that it returns being ignored. Nevertheless, it is legally possible to capture that value in a variable typed as `Void`; for example:

```
let pointless : Void = say1("howdy")
```

A function without any parameters

No law says that a function *must* take any parameters. If it doesn't, the parameter list in the function declaration can be completely empty. But you can't omit the parameter list parentheses themselves! They will be present in the function declaration, after the function's name:

```
func greet1() -> String { return "howdy" }
```

Obviously a function can lack both a return value and parameters; these are all ways of expressing the same thing:

```
func greet1() -> Void { print("howdy") }
func greet2() -> () { print("howdy") }
func greet3() { print("howdy") }
```

Just as you cannot omit the parentheses (the parameter list) from a function declaration, you cannot omit the parentheses from a function call. Those parentheses will be empty if the function takes no parameters, but they must be present. For example:

```
greet1()
```

Notice the parentheses!

Function Signature

If we ignore for a moment the parameter names in the function declaration, we can completely characterize a function by the types of its inputs and its output, using an expression like this:

```
(Int, Int) -> Int
```

That in fact is a legal expression in Swift. It is the *signature* of a function. In this case, it's the signature of our `sum` function. Of course, there can be other functions that take two Int parameters and return an Int — and that's just the point. This signature characterizes *all* functions that have this number of parameters, of these types, and that return a result of this type. A function's signature is, in effect, *its* type — the type *of the function.* The fact that functions have types will be of great importance later on.

The signature of a function must include both the parameter list (without parameter names) and the return type, even if one or both of those is empty; so, the signature of a function that takes no parameters and returns no value may be written in any of four equivalent ways, including `Void -> Void` and `() -> ()`.

External Parameter Names

A function can *externalize* the names of its parameters. The external names must then appear in a call to the function as *labels* to the arguments. There are several reasons why this is a good thing:

- It clarifies the purpose of each argument; each argument label can give a clue as to how that argument contributes to the behavior of the function.

- It distinguishes one function from another; two functions can have the same name and signature but different externalized parameter names.

- It helps Swift to interface with Objective-C and Cocoa, where method parameters nearly always have externalized names.

To externalize a parameter name, put the external name before the internal parameter name, separated by a space, in the function declaration. The external name can be the same as the internal name, or different. Externalized parameter names are so standard in Swift, however, that there's a rule: *all* parameter names *except for the first parameter* are externalized *automatically* by default. Thus, if you want a parameter name to be externalized, and if this is *not* the first parameter, and if you want the externalized name to be the same as the internal name, *do nothing* — that will happen all by itself.

Here's the declaration for a function that concatenates a string with itself a given number of times:

```
func repeatString(s:String, times:Int) -> String {
    var result = ""
    for _ in 1...times { result += s }
    return result
}
```

That function's first parameter has an internal name only, but its second parameter has an external name, which will be the same as its internal name, namely `times`. And here's how to call it:

```
let s = repeatString("hi", times:3)
```

In the call, as you can see, the external name precedes the argument as a label, separated by a colon.

As I've already said, a parameter's external name can be different from its internal name. Let's say that in our `repeatString` function we prefer to use `times` purely as an external name, with a different name — say, n — as the internal name. Then the declaration would look like this:

```
func repeatString(s:String, times n:Int) -> String {
    var result = ""
    for _ in 1...n { result += s}
    return result
}
```

In the body of that function, there is now no `times` variable available; `times` is purely an external name, for use in the call. The internal name is n, and that's the name the code refers to.

 The existence of external names doesn't mean that the call can use a different parameter order from the declaration. For example, our `repeatString` expects a String parameter and an Int parameter, *in that order*. The order can't be different in the call, even though the label might appear to disambiguate which argument goes with which parameter. (Later, though, I'll give an apparent exception to this rule.)

Our `repeatString` function demonstrates the default rule that the first parameter has no external name, while the others do. Why is this the default? One reason is that the first parameter often doesn't need an external name, because the function name usually clarifies sufficiently what the first parameter is for — as it does in the case of `repeatString` (it repeats a *string*, which the first parameter should provide). Another reason — much more important in real life — is that this convention allows Swift functions to interface with Objective-C methods, which typically work this way.

For example, here's the Objective-C declaration for a Cocoa NSString method:

```
- (NSString *)stringByReplacingOccurrencesOfString:(NSString *)target
                          withString:(NSString *)replacement
```

This method takes two NSString parameters and returns an NSString. The external name of the second parameter is obvious — it's withString. But it's a bit less obvious what the name of the first parameter is. On the one hand, you could argue that it's stringByReplacingOccurrencesOfString. On the other hand, that's not really the name of the *parameter*; it's more the name of the *method*. Actually, the formal name of the method is the whole thing: stringByReplacingOccurrencesOfString:withString:. But Swift function call syntax has parentheses distinguishing the function name from the external parameter names. So when Swift wants to call this Objective-C method, the first thing-before-a-colon becomes the name of the *function*, before the parentheses, and the second thing-before-a-colon becomes the label of the *second argument*, inside the parentheses. A Swift String and a Cocoa NSString are automatically bridged to one another, so you can actually call this Cocoa method on a Swift String, like this:

```
let s = "hello"
let s2 = s.stringByReplacingOccurrencesOfString("ell", withString:"ipp")
// s2 is now "hippo"
```

If a function is your own function — that is, if you declare it — and if it is not a method that Objective-C will ever call (so that there is no need to conform to Objective-C's expectations), then you are free to depart from the default behavior. You can do any of the following in your function declaration:

Externalize the name of the first parameter
> If you want to externalize the name of the first parameter, put the external name before the internal name. The two names can be the same.

Change the name of a nonfirst parameter
> If you want to change the external name of a parameter other than the first parameter, put the desired external name before the internal name.

Suppress the externalization of a nonfirst parameter
> To suppress a nonfirst parameter's external name, precede it with an underscore and a space:

```
func say(s:String, _ times:Int) {
```

Now this method would have to be called without labeling the second parameter:

```
let d = Dog()
d.say("woof", 3)
```

(That explains my declaration func sum (x:Int, _ y:Int) -> Int at the start of this chapter: I was suppressing the externalization of the second parameter name, so as not to have to explain argument labels at the outset.)

Overloading

In Swift, function overloading is legal (and common). This means that two functions with exactly the same name (including their external parameter names) can coexist as long as they have different signatures.

Thus, for example, these two functions can coexist:

```
func say (what:String) {
}
func say (what:Int) {
}
```

The reason overloading works is that Swift has strict typing. A String is not an Int. Swift can tell them apart in the declaration, and Swift can tell them apart in a function call. Thus, Swift knows unambiguously that `say("what")` is different from `say(1)`.

Overloading works for the return type as well. Two functions with the same name and parameter types can have different return types. But the context of the call must disambiguate; that is, it must be clear what return type the caller is expecting.

For example, these two functions can coexist:

```
func say() -> String {
    return "one"
}
func say() -> Int {
    return 1
}
```

But now you can't call `say` like this:

```
let result = say() // compile error
```

The call is ambiguous, and the compiler tells you so. The call must be used in a context where the expected return type is clear. For example, suppose we have another function that is not overloaded, and that expects a String parameter:

```
func giveMeAString(s:String) {
    print("thanks!")
}
```

Then giveMeAString(say()) is legal, because only a String can go in this spot, so we must be calling the say that returns a String. Similarly:

```
let result = say() + "two"
```

Only a String can be "added" to a String, so this say() must be a String.

The legality of overloading in Swift is particularly striking if you're coming from Objective-C, where overloading is *not* legal. If you tried to declare two overloaded versions of the same method in Objective-C, you'd get a "Duplicate declaration" compile error. And indeed, if you try to declare two overloaded methods in Swift, but in a place where Objective-C can see them (see Appendix A for what that means), you'll get a Swift compile error, because such overloading is incompatible with Objective-C.

 Two functions with the same signature but different external parameter names do *not* constitute a case of overloading; the functions have different external parameter names, so they are simply two different functions with two different names.

Default Parameter Values

A parameter can have a default value. This means that the caller can omit the parameter entirely, supplying no argument for it; the value will then be the default.

To provide a default value, append = and the default value after the parameter type in the declaration:

```
class Dog {
    func say(s:String, times:Int = 1) {
        for _ in 1...times {
            print(s)
        }
    }
}
```

In effect, there are now *two* functions — say plain and simple, and say(times:). If you just want to say something once, you can call say plain and simple, and a times: parameter value of 1 will be supplied for you:

```
let d = Dog()
d.say("woof") // same as saying d.say("woof", times:1)
```

If you want repetition, call say(times:):

```
let d = Dog()
d.say("woof", times:3)
```

If parameters with external names have default values, the requirement that they be called in order is lifted. For example, if a function is declared like this:

```
func doThing (a a:Int = 0, b:Int = 3) {}
```

then it is legal to call it like this:

```
doThing(b:5, a:10)
```

However, this might be an oversight — with Swift, it's always hard to know, and certainly it would be illegal to call it like that if either parameter lacked a default value — so I would recommend that you not do that sort of thing: keep your call's arguments ordered like the parameters in the declaration.

Variadic Parameters

A parameter can be *variadic*. This means that the caller can supply as many values of this parameter's type as desired, separated by comma; the function body will receive these values as an array.

To indicate that a parameter is variadic, follow it by three dots, like this:

```
func sayStrings(arrayOfStrings:String ...) {
    for s in arrayOfStrings { print(s) }
}
```

And here's how to call it:

```
sayStrings("hey", "ho", "nonny nonny no")
```

In earlier versions of Swift, a variadic parameter had to be the last parameter; but that limitation has been lifted in Swift 2.0. The limitation is now only that a function can declare a maximum of one variadic parameter (because otherwise it might be impossible to determine where the list of values ends). For example:

```
func sayStrings(arrayOfStrings:String ..., times:Int) {
    for _ in 1...times {
        for s in arrayOfStrings { print(s) }
    }
}
```

And here's how to call it:

```
sayStrings("Mannie", "Moe", "Jack", times:3)
```

The global print function takes a variadic first parameter, so you can output multiple values with a single command:

```
print("Mannie", 3, true) // Mannie 3 true
```

Default parameters dictate further details of the output. The default `separator:` is a space (when you provide multiple values), and the default `terminator:` is a newline; you can change either or both:

```
print("Mannie", "Moe", separator:", ", terminator: ", ")
print("Jack")
// output is "Mannie, Moe, Jack" on one line
```

 Unfortunately, there's a hole in the Swift language: there's no way to convert an array into a comma-separated list of arguments (comparable to splatting in Ruby). If what you're starting with is an array of some type, you can't use it where a variadic of that type is expected.

Ignored Parameters

A parameter whose local name is an underscore is ignored. The caller must supply an argument, but it has no name within the function body and cannot be referred to there. For example:

```
func say(s:String, times:Int, loudly _:Bool) {
```

No `loudly` parameter makes its way into the function body, but the caller must still provide the third parameter:

```
say("hi", times:3, loudly:true)
```

The declaration needn't have an externalized name for the ignored parameter:

```
func say(s:String, times:Int, _:Bool) {
```

But the caller must still supply it:

```
say("hi", times:3, true)
```

What's the purpose of this feature? It isn't to satisfy the compiler, because the compiler doesn't complain if a parameter is never referred to in the function body. I use it primarily as a kind of note to myself, a way of saying, "Yes, I know there is a parameter here, and I am deliberately not using it for anything."

Modifiable Parameters

In the body of a function, a parameter is essentially a local variable. By default, it's a variable implicitly declared with `let`. You can't assign to it:

```
func say(s:String, times:Int, loudly:Bool) {
    loudly = true // compile error
}
```

If your code needs to assign to a parameter name within the body of a function, declare the parameter name explicitly with `var`:

```
func say(s:String, times:Int, var loudly:Bool) {
    loudly = true // no problem
}
```

In that code, the parameter `loudly` is still just a local variable. Assigning to it doesn't change the value of any variable outside the function body. However, it is also possible to configure a parameter in such a way that it *does* modify the value of a variable outside the function body! One typical use case is that you want your function to return more than one result. For example, here I'll write a rather advanced function that removes all occurrences of a given character from a given string and returns the number of occurrences that were removed:

```
func removeFromString(var s:String, character c:Character) -> Int {
    var howMany = 0
    while let ix = s.characters.indexOf(c) {
        s.removeRange(ix...ix)
        howMany += 1
    }
    return howMany
}
```

And you call it like this:

```
let s = "hello"
let result = removeFromString(s, character:Character("l")) // 2
```

That's nice, but we forgot one little thing: the original string, `s`, is still `"hello"`! In the function body, we removed all occurrences of the character from the *local* copy of the String parameter, but this change didn't affect the *original* string.

If we want our function to alter the *original* value of an argument passed to it, we must make three changes:

- The parameter we intend to modify must be declared `inout`.
- At the point of the call, the variable holding the value we intend to tell the function to modify must be declared with `var`, not `let`.
- Instead of passing the variable as an argument, we pass its *address*. This is done by preceding its name with an ampersand (&).

Let's make those changes. The declaration of `removeFromString` now looks like this:

```
func removeFromString(inout s:String, character c:Character) -> Int {
```

Our call to `removeFromString` now looks like this:

```
var s = "hello"
let result = removeFromString(&s, character:Character("l"))
```

After the call, `result` is 2 *and* `s` is `"heo"`. Notice the ampersand before name of `s` as the first argument in our function call! I like this requirement, because it forces us to acknowledge explicitly to the compiler, and to ourselves, that we're about to do something potentially dangerous: we're letting this function, as a side effect, modify a value outside of itself.

 When a function with an `inout` parameter is called, the variable whose address was passed as argument to that parameter is *always* set, even if the function makes no changes to that parameter.

You will often encounter variations on this pattern when you're using Cocoa. The Cocoa APIs are written in C and Objective-C, so you probably won't see the Swift term `inout`. You'll probably see some mysterious type such as UnsafeMutablePointer. From your point of view as the caller, however, it's the same thing. You'll prepare a `var` variable and pass its address.

For instance, consider the Core Graphics function `CGRectDivide`. A CGRect is a struct representing a rectangle. You call `CGRectDivide` when you want to slice a rectangle into two rectangles. `CGRectDivide` needs to tell you what both resulting rectangles are. So it needs to return *two* CGRects. Its strategy for doing this is to return *no* value as a result of the function; instead, it says, "You hand me two CGRects *as arguments*, and I will modify them for you so that they are the results of this operation."

Here's how the declaration for `CGRectDivide` appears in Swift:

```
func CGRectDivide(rect: CGRect,
    _ slice: UnsafeMutablePointer<CGRect>,
    _ remainder: UnsafeMutablePointer<CGRect>,
    _ amount: CGFloat,
    _ edge: CGRectEdge)
```

The second and third parameters are each an UnsafeMutablePointer to a CGRect. Here's actual code from one of my apps where I call this function; look at how I treat the second and third arguments:

```
var arrow = CGRectZero
var body = CGRectZero
CGRectDivide(rect, &arrow, &body, Arrow.ARHEIGHT, .MinYEdge)
```

I have to create two `var` CGRect variables beforehand, and they have to have *some* value even though that value will immediately be replaced by the call to `CGRectDivide`, so I assign them `CGRectZero` as a placeholder.

Swift extends CGRect to provide a divide method. This method, being a Swift method, does something that a Cocoa C function cannot do — it returns two values (as a tuple, see Chapter 3)! Thus, you could avoid calling CGRectDivide in the first place. Still, you *can* call CGRectDivide, so it's worth knowing how.

Sometimes, Cocoa will call *your* function with an UnsafeMutablePointer parameter, and *you* will want to change its value. To do this, you cannot assign directly to it, as we did with the inout variable s in our implementation of removeFromString. You're talking to Objective-C, not to Swift, and this is an UnsafeMutablePointer, not an inout parameter. The technique here is to assign to the UnsafeMutablePointer's memory property. Here (without further explanation) is an example from my own code:

```
func popoverPresentationController(
    popoverPresentationController: UIPopoverPresentationController,
    willRepositionPopoverToRect rect: UnsafeMutablePointer<CGRect>,
    inView view: AutoreleasingUnsafeMutablePointer<UIView?>) {
        view.memory = self.button2
        rect.memory = self.button2.bounds
}
```

There is one very common situation where your function can modify a parameter *without* declaring it as inout — namely, when the parameter is an *instance of a class*. This is a special feature of classes, as opposed to the other two object type flavors, enum and struct. String isn't a class; it's a struct. That's why we had to use inout in order to modify a String parameter. So I'll illustrate by declaring a Dog class with a name property:

```
class Dog {
    var name = ""
}
```

Here's a function that takes a Dog instance parameter and a String, and sets that Dog instance's name to that String. Notice that no inout is involved:

```
func changeNameOfDog(d:Dog, to tostring:String) {
    d.name = tostring
}
```

Here's how to call it. There's no inout, so we pass a Dog instance *directly*:

```
let d = Dog()
d.name = "Fido"
print(d.name) // "Fido"
changeNameOfDog(d, to:"Rover")
print(d.name) // "Rover"
```

Observe that we were able to change a property of our Dog instance d, even though it wasn't passed as an inout parameter, and even though it was declared originally with let, not var. This appears to be an exception to the rules about modifying parameters — but it isn't. It's a feature of class instances, namely that they are themselves mutable.

In changeNameOfDog, we didn't actually attempt to modify the *parameter itself*. To do that, we would have had to *substitute a different Dog instance*. That is *not* what we tried to do, and if we did want to do it, the Dog parameter *would* need to be declared inout (and d would have to be declared with var and we would have to pass its address as argument).

 Technically, we say that classes are *reference types*, whereas the other object type flavors are *value types*. When you pass an instance of a struct as an argument to a function, you effectively wind up with a *separate copy* of the struct instance. But when you pass an instance of a class as an argument to a function, you pass a reference to the class instance *itself*. I'll discuss this topic in more detail in Chapter 4.

Function In Function

A function can be declared anywhere, including inside the body of a function. A function declared in the body of a function (also called a *local function*) is available to be called by later code within the same scope, but is completely invisible outside its scope.

This feature is an elegant architecture for functions whose sole purpose is to assist another function. If only function A ever needs to call function B, function B might as well be packaged inside function A.

Here's a typical example from one of my apps (I've omitted everything except the structure):

```
func checkPair(p1:Piece, and p2:Piece) -> Path? {
    // ...
    func addPathIfValid(midpt1:Point, _ midpt2:Point) {
        // ...
    }
    for y in -1..._yct {
        addPathIfValid((pt1.x,y),(pt2.x,y))
    }
    for x in -1..._xct {
        addPathIfValid((x,pt1.y),(x,pt2.y))
    }
    // ...
}
```

What I'm doing in the first for loop (for y) and what I'm doing in the second for loop (for x) are the same — but with a different set of starting values. We could write out the functionality in full inside each for loop, but that would be an unnecessary and confusing repetition. (Such a repetition would violate the principle often referred to as *DRY*, for "Don't Repeat Yourself.") To prevent that repetition, we could refactor the repeated code into an instance method to be called by both for loops, but that exposes this functionality more broadly than we need, as it is called *only* by these two for loops inside checkPair. A local function is the perfect compromise.

Sometimes, it's worth using a local function even when that function will be called in only *one* place. Here's another example from my code (it's actually another part of the same function):

```swift
func checkPair(p1:Piece, and p2:Piece) -> Path? {
    // ...
    if arr.count > 0 {
        func distance(pt1:Point, _ pt2:Point) -> Double {
            // utility to learn physical distance between two points
            let deltax = pt1.0 - pt2.0
            let deltay = pt1.1 - pt2.1
            return sqrt(Double(deltax * deltax + deltay * deltay))
        }
        for thisPath in arr {
            var thisLength = 0.0
            for ix in 0..<(thisPath.count-1) {
                thisLength += distance(thisPath[ix],thisPath[ix+1])
            }
            // ...
        }
    }
    // ...
}
```

Again, the structure is clear (even though the code uses some Swift features I haven't discussed yet). Deep inside the function checkPair, a moment comes when I have an array (arr) of paths, and I need to know the length of every path. Each path is itself an array of points, so to learn its length, I need to sum the distances between each pair of points. To get the distance between a pair of points, I use the Pythagorean theorem. I could apply the Pythagorean theorem and express the calculation right there inside the for loop (for ix). Instead, I've expressed it as a separate function, distance, and inside the for loop I call that function.

There is no savings whatever in the number of lines of code; in fact, declaring distance makes my code longer! Nor, strictly speaking, am I in danger of repeating myself; the application of the Pythagorean theorem is repeated many times, but it occurs at only one spot in my code, namely inside this one for loop. Nevertheless, abstracting the code into a more general distance-calculation utility makes my code much clearer: in effect, I announce in general form what I'm about to do ("Look! I'm going to calculate distances between points now!"), and then I do it. The function name, distance, gives my code *meaning*; it is more understandable and maintainable than if I had directly written out the steps of the distance calculation inline.

Local functions are really local variables with function values (a notion that I'll explain later in this chapter). Therefore, a local function can't have the same name as a local variable in the same scope, and two local functions can't have the same name as one another in the same scope.

Recursion

A function can call itself. This is called *recursion*. Recursion seems a little scary, rather like jumping off a cliff, because of the danger of creating an infinite loop; but if you write the function correctly, you will always have a "stopper" condition that handles the degenerate case and prevents the loop from being infinite:

```
func countDownFrom(ix:Int) {
    print(ix)
    if ix > 0 { // stopper
        countDownFrom(ix-1) // recurse!
    }
}
```

 Before Swift 2.0, Swift imposed a restriction on recursion: a function-in-function (a local function) could not call itself. In Swift 2.0, this restriction is gone.

Function As Value

If you've never used a programming language where functions are first-class citizens, perhaps you'd better sit down now, because what I'm about to tell you might make you feel a little faint: In Swift, a function *is* a first-class citizen. This means that a function can be used wherever a value can be used. For example, a function can be assigned to a variable; a function can be passed as an argument in a function call; a function can be returned as the result of a function.

Swift has strict typing. You can only assign a value to a variable or pass a value into or out of a function if it is the right *type* of value. In order for a function to be used as a value, it needs to *have* a type. And indeed it does! Have you guessed what it is? A function's *signature* is its type.

The chief purpose of using a function as a value is so that this function can later be called without a definite knowledge of *what* function it is.

Here's the world's simplest (and silliest) example, just to show the syntax and structure:

```
func doThis(f:()->()) {
    f()
}
```

That is a function doThis that takes one parameter (and returns no value). The parameter, f, is itself a function; we know this because the type of the parameter is not given as Int or String or Dog, but is a function signature, ()->(), meaning (as you know) a function that takes no parameters and returns no value. The function doThis then *calls* the function f that it received as its parameter — that (as you know) is the meaning of the parentheses after the name of the parameter in the function body.

How would you call the function doThis? To do so, you'd need to pass it a function as argument. One way to do that is to use the name of a function as the argument, like this:

```
func whatToDo() {
    print("I did it")
}
doThis(whatToDo)
```

First, we declare a function *of the proper type* — a function that takes no parameters and returns no value. Then, we call doThis, passing as argument *the name of the function*. Notice that we are not *calling* whatToDo here; we are *passing* it. You know this because there are *no parentheses* after its name. Sure enough, this works: we pass whatToDo as argument to doThis; doThis calls the function that it receives as its parameter; and the string "I did it" appears in the console.

But what's the point of being able to do *that*? If our goal is to call whatToDo, why don't we just call it? What's useful about being able to tell some *other* function to call it? In the example I just gave, there is *nothing* useful about it; I was just showing you the syntax and structure. But in real life, this is a very valuable thing to do, because the other function may call the parameter function in some special way. For example, it might call it after doing other things, or at some later time.

For example, one reason for encapsulating function-calling in a function is that it can reduce repetition and opportunity for error. Here's a case from my own code. A common thing to do in Cocoa is to draw an image, directly, in code. This involves four steps:

```
let size = CGSizeMake(45,20)
UIGraphicsBeginImageContextWithOptions(size, false, 0) ❶
let p = UIBezierPath(
    roundedRect: CGRectMake(0,0,45,20), cornerRadius: 8)
p.stroke() ❷
let result = UIGraphicsGetImageFromCurrentImageContext() ❸
UIGraphicsEndImageContext() ❹
```

❶ Open an image context.

❷ Draw into the context.

❸ Extract the image.

❹ Close the image context.

That's terribly ugly. The sole purpose of all that code is to obtain `result`, the image; but that purpose is buried in all the other code. At the same time, the entire structure is boilerplate; every time I do this in any app, step 1, step 3, and step 4 are exactly the same. Moreover, I live in mortal fear of forgetting a step; for example, if I were to omit step 4 by mistake, the universe would explode.

The only thing that's different every time I draw is step 2. Thus, step 2 is the only part I should have to write out! The entire problem is solved by writing a utility function expressing the boilerplate:

```
func imageOfSize(size:CGSize, _ whatToDraw:() -> ()) -> UIImage {
    UIGraphicsBeginImageContextWithOptions(size, false, 0)
    whatToDraw()
    let result = UIGraphicsGetImageFromCurrentImageContext()
    UIGraphicsEndImageContext()
    return result
}
```

My `imageOfSize` utility is so useful that I declare it at the top level of a file, where all my files can see it. To make an image, I perform step 2 (the actual drawing) in a function and pass that function as argument to the `imageOfSize` utility:

```
func drawing() {
    let p = UIBezierPath(
        roundedRect: CGRectMake(0,0,45,20), cornerRadius: 8)
    p.stroke()
}
let image = imageOfSize(CGSizeMake(45,20), drawing)
```

Now *that* is a beautifully expressive and clear way to turn drawing instructions into an image.

The Cocoa API is full of situations where you'll pass a function to be called by the runtime in some special way or at some later time. For example, when one view controller presents another, the method you'll call takes three parameters — the view controller to be presented; a Bool stating whether you want the presentation to be animated; and a function that is to be called *after* the presentation has finished:

```
let vc = UIViewController()
func whatToDoLater() {
    print("I finished!")
}
self.presentViewController(vc, animated:true, completion:whatToDoLater)
```

The Cocoa documentation will often describe such a function as a *handler*, and will refer it as a *block*, because that's the Objective-C syntactic construct needed here; in Swift, it's a function, so just think of it as a function and pass a function.

Some common Cocoa situations even involve passing *two* functions to a function. For instance, when you perform view animation, you'll often pass one function prescribing the action to be animated and another function saying what to do afterwards:

```
func whatToAnimate() { // self.myButton is a button in the interface
    self.myButton.frame.origin.y += 20
}
func whatToDoLater(finished:Bool) {
    print("finished: \(finished)")
}
UIView.animateWithDuration(
    0.4, animations: whatToAnimate, completion: whatToDoLater)
```

That means: Change the frame origin (that is, the position) of this button in the interface, but do it over time (four-tenths of a second); and then, when that's finished, print a log message in the console saying whether the animation was performed or not.

 To make function type specifiers clearer, take advantage of Swift's typealias feature to create a type alias giving a function type a name. The name can be descriptive, and the possibly confusing arrow operator notation is avoided. For example, if you say typealias VoidVoidFunction = () -> (), you can then say VoidVoidFunction wherever you need to specify a function type with that signature.

Anonymous Functions

Consider again the preceding example:

```
func whatToAnimate() { // self.myButton is a button in the interface
    self.myButton.frame.origin.y += 20
}
func whatToDoLater(finished:Bool) {
    print("finished: \(finished)")
}
UIView.animateWithDuration(
    0.4, animations: whatToAnimate, completion: whatToDoLater)
```

There's a slight bit of ugliness in that code. I'm declaring functions whatToAnimate and whatToDoLater, just because I want to pass those functions in the last line. I don't really need the *names* whatToAnimate and whatToDoLater for anything, except to refer to them in the last line; neither the names nor the functions will ever be used again. Therefore, it would be nice to be able to pass just the *body* of those functions *without* a declared name.

That's called an *anonymous* function, and it's legal and common in Swift. To form an anonymous function, you do two things:

1. Create the function body itself, including the surrounding curly braces, but with no function declaration.

2. If necessary, express the function's parameter list and return type as the first line *inside* the curly braces, followed by the keyword in.

Let's practice by transforming our named function declarations into anonymous functions. Here's the named function declaration for whatToAnimate:

```
func whatToAnimate() {
    self.myButton.frame.origin.y += 20
}
```

Here's an anonymous function that does the same thing. Notice how I've moved the parameter list and return type inside the curly braces:

```
{
    () -> () in
    self.myButton.frame.origin.y += 20
}
```

Here's the named function declaration for whatToDoLater:

```
func whatToDoLater(finished:Bool) {
    print("finished: \(finished)")
}
```

Here's an anonymous function that does the same thing:

```
{
    (finished:Bool) -> () in
    print("finished: \(finished)")
}
```

Now that we know how to make anonymous functions, let's use them. The point where we need the functions is the point where we're passing arguments to animateWith-Duration. We can create and pass anonymous functions *right at that point*, like this:

```
UIView.animateWithDuration(0.4, animations: {
    () -> () in
    self.myButton.frame.origin.y += 20
    }, completion: {
        (finished:Bool) -> () in
        print("finished: \(finished)")
})
```

We can make the same improvement in the way we call the imageOfSize function from the preceding section. Earlier, we called that function like this:

```
func drawing() {
    let p = UIBezierPath(
        roundedRect: CGRectMake(0,0,45,20), cornerRadius: 8)
    p.stroke()
}
let image = imageOfSize(CGSizeMake(45,20), drawing)
```

We now know, however, that we don't need to declare the drawing function separately. We can call `imageOfSize` with an anonymous function:

```
let image = imageOfSize(CGSizeMake(45,20), {
    let p = UIBezierPath(
        roundedRect: CGRectMake(0,0,45,20), cornerRadius: 8)
    p.stroke()
})
```

Anonymous functions are very commonly used in Swift, so make sure you can read and write that code! Anonymous functions, in fact, are *so* common and *so* important, that some shortcuts for writing them are provided:

Omission of the return type

If the anonymous function's return type is known to the compiler, you can omit the arrow operator and the specification of the return type:

```
UIView.animateWithDuration(0.4, animations: {
    () in
    self.myButton.frame.origin.y += 20
}, completion: {
    (finished:Bool) in
    print("finished: \(finished)")
})
```

Omission of the in *line when there are no parameters*

If the anonymous function takes no parameters, and if the return type can be omitted, the `in` line itself can be omitted entirely:

```
UIView.animateWithDuration(0.4, animations: {
    self.myButton.frame.origin.y += 20
}, completion: {
    (finished:Bool) in
    print("finished: \(finished)")
})
```

Omission of the parameter types

If the anonymous function takes parameters and their types are known to the compiler, the types can be omitted:

```
UIView.animateWithDuration(0.4, animations: {
    self.myButton.frame.origin.y += 20
}, completion: {
    (finished) in
    print("finished: \(finished)")
})
```

Omission of the parentheses

If the parameter types are omitted, the parentheses around the parameter list can be omitted:

```
UIView.animateWithDuration(0.4, animations: {
    self.myButton.frame.origin.y += 20
    }, completion: {
        finished in
        print("finished: \(finished)")
})
```

Omission of the in *line even when there are parameters*

If the return type can be omitted, and if the parameter types are known to the compiler, you can omit the in line and refer to the parameters directly within the body of the anonymous function by using the magic names $0, $1, and so on, in order:

```
UIView.animateWithDuration(0.4, animations: {
    self.myButton.frame.origin.y += 20
    }, completion: {
        print("finished: \($0)")
})
```

Omission of the parameter names

If the anonymous function body doesn't need to refer to a parameter, you can substitute an underscore for its name in the parameter list in the in line; in fact, if the anonymous function body doesn't need to refer to *any* of the parameters, you can substitute *one* underscore for *the entire parameter list*:

```
UIView.animateWithDuration(0.4, animations: {
    self.myButton.frame.origin.y += 20
    }, completion: {
        _ in
        print("finished!")
})
```

 But note that if the anonymous function takes parameters, you *must* acknowledge them somehow. You can omit the in line and use the parameters by the magic names $0 and so on, or you can keep the in line and ignore the parameters with an underscore, but you can't omit the in line altogether *and* not use the parameters by their magic names! If you do, your code won't compile.

Omission of the function argument label

If, as will just about always be the case, your anonymous function is the *last* argument being passed in this function call, you can close the function call with a right parenthesis *before* this last argument, and then put just the anonymous function body *without a label* (this is called a *trailing function*):

```
UIView.animateWithDuration(0.4, animations: {
    self.myButton.frame.origin.y += 20
    }) {
        _ in
        print("finished!")
}
```

Omission of the calling function parentheses

If you use the trailing function syntax, and if the function you are calling takes no parameters other than the function you are passing to it, you can omit the empty parentheses from the call. This is the *only* situation in which you can omit the parentheses from a function call! To illustrate, I'll declare and call a different function:

```
func doThis(f:()->()) {
    f()
}
doThis { // no parentheses!
    print("Howdy")
}
```

Omission of the keyword `return`

If the anonymous function body consists of *exactly one statement* and that statement consists of returning a value with the keyword `return`, the keyword `return` can be omitted. To put it another way, in a context that expects a function that returns a value, if an anonymous function body consists of exactly one statement, Swift *assumes* that this statement is an expression whose value is to be returned from the anonymous function:

```
func sayHowdy() -> String {
    return "Howdy"
}
func performAndPrint(f:()->String) {
    let s = f()
    print(s)
}
performAndPrint {
    sayHowdy() // meaning: return sayHowdy()
}
```

When writing anonymous functions, you will frequently find yourself taking advantage of all the omissions you are permitted. In addition, you'll often shorten the *layout* of the code (though not the code itself) by putting the whole anonymous function together with the function call *on one line*. Thus, Swift code involving anonymous functions can be extremely compact.

Here's a typical example. We start with an array of Int values and generate a new array consisting of all those values multiplied by 2, by calling the `map` instance method. The `map` method of an array takes a function that takes one parameter, and returns a value, of the same type as the array's elements; here, our array is made of Int values, so we need to pass to the map method a function that takes one Int parameter and returns an Int. We could write out the whole function, like this:

```
let arr = [2, 4, 6, 8]
func doubleMe(i:Int) -> Int {
    return i*2
}
let arr2 = arr.map(doubleMe) // [4, 8, 12, 16]
```

That, however, is not very Swifty. We don't need the name doubleMe for anything else, so this may as well be an anonymous function. Its return type is known, so we don't need to specify that. Its parameter type is known, so we don't need to specify that. There's just one parameter and we are going to use it, so we don't need the in line as long we refer to the parameter as $0. Our function body consists of just one statement, and it is a return statement, so we can omit return. And map doesn't take any other parameters, so we can omit the parentheses and follow the name directly with a trailing function:

```
let arr = [2, 4, 6, 8]
let arr2 = arr.map {$0*2}
```

Define-and-Call

A pattern that's surprisingly common in Swift is to define an anonymous function and call it, all in one move:

```
{
    // ... code goes here
}()
```

Notice the parentheses after the curly braces. The curly braces define an anonymous function body; the parentheses call that anonymous function.

Why would anyone do such a thing? If you want to run some code, you can just run it; why would you embed it in a deeper level as a function body, only to turn around and run that function body immediately?

For one thing, an anonymous function can be a good way to make your code less imperative and more, well, functional: an action can be taken at the point where it is needed, rather than in a series of preparatory steps. Here's a common Cocoa example: we create and configure an NSMutableParagraphStyle and then use it as an argument in a call to addAttribute:value:range: (content is an NSMutableAttributedString):

```
let para = NSMutableParagraphStyle()
para.headIndent = 10
para.firstLineHeadIndent = 10
// ... more configuration of para ...
content.addAttribute(
    NSParagraphStyleAttributeName,
    value:para, range:NSMakeRange(0,1))
```

I find that code ugly. We don't need para except to pass it as the value: argument within the call to addAttribute:value:range, so it would be much nicer to create and configure it right there within the call, as the value: argument. Swift lets us do just that. I much prefer this way of writing the same code:

```
content.addAttribute(
    NSParagraphStyleAttributeName,
    value: {
        let para = NSMutableParagraphStyle()
        para.headIndent = 10
        para.firstLineHeadIndent = 10
        // ... more configuration of para ...
        return para
    }(),
    range:NSMakeRange(0,1))
```

I'll demonstrate some further uses of define-and-call in Chapter 3.

Closures

Swift functions are *closures*. This means they can *capture* references to external variables in scope within the body of the function. What do I mean by that? Well, recall from Chapter 1 that code in curly braces constitutes a scope, and this code can "see" variables and functions declared in a surrounding scope:

```
class Dog {
    var whatThisDogSays = "woof"
    func bark() {
        print(self.whatThisDogSays)
    }
}
```

In that code, the body of the function bark refers to a variable whatThisDogSays. That variable is *external* to the body of the function, because it is declared outside the body of the function. It is *in scope* for the body of the function, because the code inside the body of the function can see it. And the code inside the body of the function *refers* to it — it says, explicitly, whatThisDogSays.

So far, so good; but we now know that the function bark can be passed as a value. In effect, it can travel from one environment to another! When it does, what happens to that reference to whatThisDogSays? Let's find out:

```
func doThis(f : Void -> Void) {
    f()
}
let d = Dog()
d.whatThisDogSays = "arf"
let f = d.bark
doThis(f) // arf
```

We run that code, and `"arf"` appears in the console.

Perhaps that result doesn't seem very surprising to you. But think about it. We do not directly *call* bark. We make a Dog instance and *pass* its bark function as a value into the function doThis. There, it is called. Now, whatThisDogSays is an instance property of a particular Dog. Inside the function doThis there is no whatThisDogSays. Indeed, inside the function doThis there is no Dog instance! Nevertheless the call f() still works. The function d.bark, as it is passed around, can *still* see that variable whatThisDog-Says, declared *outside* itself, even though it is *called* in an environment where there is no longer any Dog instance and no longer any instance property whatThisDogSays.

The bark function, it appears, as it is passed around, is carrying its environment with it — even when it isn't called until it has been passed into some other environment entirely. So, by "capture" I mean that when a function is passed around as a value, it carries along its internal references to external variables. That is what makes a function a closure.

You'll probably take advantage of the fact that functions are closures without even being conscious of it. Recall this earlier example, where we animate the repositioning of a button in our interface:

```
UIView.animateWithDuration(0.4, animations: {
    self.myButton.frame.origin.y += 20
}) {
    _ in
    print("finished!")
}
```

That code seems innocent enough; but concentrate on the second line, the anonymous function passed as argument to the animations: parameter. You should be saying: Really? Way off in the land of Cocoa, when this anonymous function is executed at some future time to start the animation, Cocoa is going to be able to find myButton, an object referred to as a property of self, way back over here in my code? Yes, Cocoa will be able to do that, because a function is a closure. The reference to this property is captured and maintained by the anonymous function; thus, when the anonymous function is actually called, it works and the button moves.

How Closures Improve Code

Once you understand that functions are closures, you can take advantage of this fact to improve your code's syntax. Closures can help make your code more general, and hence more useful. Here, once again, is my earlier example of a function that accepts drawing instructions and performs them to generate an image:

```
func imageOfSize(size:CGSize, _ whatToDraw:() -> ()) -> UIImage {
    UIGraphicsBeginImageContextWithOptions(size, false, 0)
    whatToDraw()
    let result = UIGraphicsGetImageFromCurrentImageContext()
    UIGraphicsEndImageContext()
    return result
}
```

We can call `imageOfSize` with a trailing anonymous function:

```
let image = imageOfSize(CGSizeMake(45,20)) {
    let p = UIBezierPath(
        roundedRect: CGRectMake(0,0,45,20), cornerRadius: 8)
    p.stroke()
}
```

That code, however, contains an annoying repetition. This is a call to create an image of a given size consisting of a rounded rectangle of that size. We are repeating the size; the pair of numbers `45,20` appears twice. That's silly. Let's prevent the repetition by putting the size into a variable at the outset:

```
let sz = CGSizeMake(45,20)
let image = imageOfSize(sz) {
    let p = UIBezierPath(
        roundedRect: CGRect(origin:CGPointZero, size:sz), cornerRadius: 8)
    p.stroke()
}
```

The variable `sz`, declared outside our anonymous function at a higher level, is visible inside it. Thus we can refer to it inside the anonymous function — and we do so. The anonymous function is a function. Therefore it is a closure. Therefore the anonymous function captures that reference, and carries it on into the call to `imageOfSize`. When `imageOfSize` calls `whatToDraw` and `whatToDraw` refers to a variable `sz`, there's no problem, even though there is no `sz` anywhere in the neighborhood of `imageOfSize`.

Now let's go further. So far, we've been hard-coding the size of the desired rounded rectangle. Imagine, though, that creating images of rounded rectangles of various sizes is something we do often. It would make sense to package this code up as a function, where `sz` is not a fixed value but a parameter; the function will then return the image:

```
func makeRoundedRectangle(sz:CGSize) -> UIImage {
    let image = imageOfSize(sz) {
        let p = UIBezierPath(
            roundedRect: CGRect(origin:CGPointZero, size:sz),
```

```
            cornerRadius: 8)
        p.stroke()
    }
    return image
}
```

Observe that our code still works. Here, sz in the anonymous function refers to the sz parameter that arrives into the surrounding function makeRoundedRectangle. A parameter of the surrounding function is a variable external to and in scope within the anonymous function. The anonymous function is a closure, so it captures the reference to that parameter as it is passed to imageOfSize.

Our code is becoming beautifully compact. To call makeRoundedRectangle, supply a size; an image is returned. Thus, I can perform the call, obtain the image, and put that image into my interface, all in one move, like this:

```
self.myImageView.image = makeRoundedRectangle(CGSizeMake(45,20))
```

Function Returning Function

But now let's go even further! Instead of returning an image, our function can return *a function* that makes rounded rectangles *of the specified size*. If you've never seen a function returned as a value from a function, you may now be gasping for breath. But a function, after all, can be used as a value. We have already passed a function *into* a function as an argument in the function call; now we are going to receive a function *from* a function call as its result:

```
func makeRoundedRectangleMaker(sz:CGSize) -> () -> UIImage { ❶
    func f () -> UIImage { ❷
        let im = imageOfSize(sz) {
            let p = UIBezierPath(
                roundedRect: CGRect(origin:CGPointZero, size:sz),
                cornerRadius: 8)
            p.stroke()
        }
        return im
    }
    return f ❸
}
```

Let's analyze that code slowly:

❶   The declaration is the hardest part. What on earth is the type (signature) of this function makeRoundedRectangleMaker? It is (CGSize) -> () -> UIImage. That expression has *two* arrow operators. To understand it, keep in mind that everything after each arrow operator is the type of a returned value. So make-RoundedRectangleMaker is a function that takes a CGSize parameter and returns a () -> UIImage. Okay, and what's a () -> UIImage? We already know that: it's a function that takes no parameters and returns a UIImage. So makeRounded-

RectangleMaker is a function that takes a CGSize parameter and returns *a function* — a function that itself, when called with *no* parameters, will return a UIImage.

❷ Now here we are in the body of the function makeRoundedRectangleMaker, and our first step is to declare a function (a function-in-function, or local function) of precisely the type we intend to return, namely, one that takes no parameters and returns a UIImage. Here, we're naming this function f. The way this function works is simple and familiar: it calls imageOfSize, passing it an anonymous function that makes an image of a rounded rectangle (im) — and then it returns the image.

❸ Finally, we *return* the function we just made (f). We have thus fulfilled our contract: we said we would return a function that takes no parameters and returns a UIImage, and we do so.

But perhaps you are still gazing open-mouthed at makeRoundedRectangleMaker, wondering how you would ever call it and what you would get if you did. Let's try it:

```
let maker = makeRoundedRectangleMaker(CGSizeMake(45,20))
```

What is the variable maker after that code runs? It's a *function* — a function that takes no parameters and that, when called, produces the image of a rounded rectangle of size 45,20. You don't believe me? I'll prove it — by *calling* the function that is now the value of maker:

```
let maker = makeRoundedRectangleMaker(CGSizeMake(45,20))
self.myImageView.image = maker()
```

Now that you've gotten over your stunned surprise at the notion of a function that produces a function as its result, turn your attention once again to the implementation of makeRoundedRectangleMaker and let's analyze it again, a different way. Remember, I didn't write that function to show you that a function can produce a function. I wrote it to illustrate closures! Let's think about how the environment gets captured:

```
func makeRoundedRectangleMaker(sz:CGSize) -> () -> UIImage {
    func f () -> UIImage {
        let im = imageOfSize(sz) { // *
            let p = UIBezierPath(
                roundedRect: CGRect(origin:CGPointZero, size:sz), // *
                cornerRadius: 8)
            p.stroke()
        }
        return im
    }
    return f
}
```

The function f takes no parameters. Yet, twice within the function body of f (I've marked the places with asterisk comments), there are references to a size value sz. The body of the function f can see sz, the incoming parameter to the surrounding function make-RoundedRectangleMaker, because it is in a surrounding scope. The function f *captures* the reference to sz at the time makeRoundedRectangleMaker is called, and *keeps* that reference when f is returned and assigned to maker:

```
let maker = makeRoundedRectangleMaker(CGSizeMake(45,20))
```

That is why maker is now a function that, when it is called, creates and returns an image of the particular size 45,20 even though it itself will be called *with no parameters*. We have *baked* the knowledge of what size of image to produce into maker.

Looking at it another way, makeRoundedRectangleMaker is a *factory* for creating a whole family of functions similar to maker, each of which produces an image of one particular size. That's a dramatic illustration of the power of closures.

Before I leave makeRoundedRectangleMaker, I'd like to rewrite it in a Swiftier fashion. Within f, there is no need to create im and then return it; we can return the result of calling imageOfSize directly:

```
func makeRoundedRectangleMaker(sz:CGSize) -> () -> UIImage {
    func f () -> UIImage {
        return imageOfSize(sz) {
            let p = UIBezierPath(
                roundedRect: CGRect(origin:CGPointZero, size:sz),
                cornerRadius: 8)
            p.stroke()
        }
    }
    return f
}
```

But there is no need to declare f and then return it either; it can be an anonymous function and we can return it directly:

```
func makeRoundedRectangleMaker(sz:CGSize) -> () -> UIImage {
    return {
        return imageOfSize(sz) {
            let p = UIBezierPath(
                roundedRect: CGRect(origin:CGPointZero, size:sz),
                cornerRadius: 8)
            p.stroke()
        }
    }
}
```

But our anonymous function consists of just one statement, returning the result of the call to imageOfSize. (The anonymous function parameter to imageOfSize is written over multiple lines, but the `imageOfSize` call itself is still just one Swift statement.) Thus there is no need to say `return`:

```
func makeRoundedRectangleMaker(sz:CGSize) -> () -> UIImage {
    return {
        imageOfSize(sz) {
            let p = UIBezierPath(
                roundedRect: CGRect(origin:CGPointZero, size:sz),
                cornerRadius: 8)
            p.stroke()
        }
    }
}
```

Closure Setting a Captured Variable

The power that a closure gets through its ability to capture its environment is even greater than I've shown so far. If a closure captures a reference to a variable outside itself, and if that variable is settable, *the closure can set the variable.*

For example, let's say I've declared this simple function. All it does is to accept a function that takes an Int parameter, and to call that function with an argument of 100:

```
func pass100 (f:(Int)->()) {
    f(100)
}
```

Now, look closely at this code and try to guess what will happen when we run it:

```
var x = 0
print(x)
func setX(newX:Int) {
    x = newX
}
pass100(setX)
print(x)
```

The first `print(x)` call obviously produces 0. The second `print(x)` call produces 100! The `pass100` function has reached into my code and changed the value of my variable x! That's because the function that I passed to `pass100` contains a reference to x; not only does it contain it, but it captures it; not only does it capture it, but it sets its value. That x *is my* x. Thus, `pass100` was able to set my x just as readily as I would have set it by calling `setX` directly.

Closure Preserving Its Captured Environment

When a closure captures its environment, it *preserves* that environment *even if nothing else does.* Here's an example calculated to blow your mind — a function that modifies a function:

```
func countAdder(f:()->()) -> () -> () {
    var ct = 0
    return {
        ct = ct + 1
        print("count is \(ct)")
        f()
    }
}
```

The function countAdder accepts a function as its parameter and returns a function as its result. The function that it returns calls the function that it accepts, with a little bit added: it increments a variable and reports the result. So now try to guess what will happen when we run this code:

```
func greet () {
    print("howdy")
}
let countedGreet = countAdder(greet)
countedGreet()
countedGreet()
countedGreet()
```

What we've done here is to take a function greet, which prints "howdy", and pass it through countAdder. What comes out the other side of countAdder is a new function, which we've named countedGreet. We then call countedGreet three times. Here's what appears in the console:

```
count is 1
howdy
count is 2
howdy
count is 3
howdy
```

Clearly, countAdder has added to the functionality of the function that was passed into it *the ability to report how many times it is called.* Now ask yourself: Where on earth is the variable that maintains this count? Inside countAdder, it was a local variable ct. But it isn't declared inside the anonymous function that countAdder returns. That's deliberate! If it *were* declared inside the anonymous function, we would be setting ct to 0 every time countedGreet is called — we wouldn't be counting. Instead, ct is initialized to 0 once *and then captured* by the anonymous function. Thus, this variable is preserved as part of the *environment* of countedGreet — it is *outside* countedGreet in some mysterious environment-preserving world, so that it can be incremented every time countedGreet is called. That's the power of closures.

That example, with its maintenance of environmental state, can also help us to demonstrate that functions are *reference types*. To show what I mean, I'll start with a contrasting situation. Two *separate* calls to a function factory method produce two *different* functions, as you would expect:

```
let countedGreet = countAdder(greet)
let countedGreet2 = countAdder(greet)
countedGreet() // count is 1
countedGreet2() // count is 1
```

The two functions countedGreet and countedGreet2, in that code, are maintaining
their counts separately. But mere assignment or parameter passing results in a new
reference to the *same* function, as I shall now prove:

```
let countedGreet = countAdder(greet)
let countedGreet2 = countedGreet
countedGreet() // count is 1
countedGreet2() // count is 2
```

Curried Functions

Return once more to makeRoundedRectangleMaker:

```
func makeRoundedRectangleMaker(sz:CGSize) -> () -> UIImage {
    return {
        imageOfSize(sz) {
            let p = UIBezierPath(
                roundedRect: CGRect(origin:CGPointZero, size:sz),
                cornerRadius: 8)
            p.stroke()
        }
    }
}
```

There's something I don't like about this method: the size of the rounded rectangle that
it creates is a parameter (sz), but the cornerRadius of the rounded rectangle is hard-
coded as 8. I'd like the ability to specify a value for the corner radius as well. I can think
of two ways to do it. One is to give makeRoundedRectangleMaker itself another parameter:

```
func makeRoundedRectangleMaker(sz:CGSize, _ r:CGFloat) -> () -> UIImage {
    return {
        imageOfSize(sz) {
            let p = UIBezierPath(
                roundedRect: CGRect(origin:CGPointZero, size:sz),
                cornerRadius: r)
            p.stroke()
        }
    }
}
```

And we would then call it like this:

```
let maker = makeRoundedRectangleMaker(CGSizeMake(45,20), 8)
```

But there's another way. The function that we are returning from makeRounded-
RectangleMaker takes no parameters. Instead, *it* could take the extra parameter:

```
func makeRoundedRectangleMaker(sz:CGSize) -> (CGFloat) -> UIImage {
    return {
        r in
        imageOfSize(sz) {
            let p = UIBezierPath(
                roundedRect: CGRect(origin:CGPointZero, size:sz),
                cornerRadius: r)
            p.stroke()
        }
    }
}
```

Now `makeRoundedRectangleMaker` returns a function that, itself, takes one parameter, so we must remember to supply that when we call it:

```
let maker = makeRoundedRectangleMaker(CGSizeMake(45,20))
self.myImageView.image = maker(8)
```

If we don't need to conserve `maker` for anything, we can of course do all that in one line — a function call that yields a function which we immediately call to obtain our image:

```
self.myImageView.image = makeRoundedRectangleMaker(CGSizeMake(45,20))(8)
```

When a function returns a function that takes a parameter in this way, it is called a *curried* function (after the computer scientist Haskell Curry). It turns out that there's a Swift shorthand for writing the declaration of a curried function. You can omit the first arrow operator *and the top-level anonymous function*, like this:

```
func makeRoundedRectangleMaker(sz:CGSize)(_ r:CGFloat) -> UIImage {
    return imageOfSize(sz) {
        let p = UIBezierPath(
            roundedRect: CGRect(origin:CGPointZero, size:sz),
            cornerRadius: r)
        p.stroke()
    }
}
```

The expression `(sz:CGSize)(_ r:CGFloat)` — two parameter lists in a row, with no arrow operator between them — means "Swift, please curry this function for me." Swift here does all the work of dividing our function into two functions, one (`makeRounded-RectangleMaker`) taking a CGSize parameter and another (the anonymous result) taking a CGFloat. Our code looks as if `makeRoundedRectangleMaker` returns a UIImage, but it actually returns a function that returns a UIImage just as before. And we can call it in exactly the same two ways as before.

CHAPTER 3

Variables and Simple Types

This chapter goes into detail about declaration and initialization of variables. It then discusses all the primary built-in Swift simple types. (I mean "simple" as opposed to collections; the primary built-in collection types are discussed at the end of Chapter 4.)

Variable Scope and Lifetime

Recall, from Chapter 1, that a variable is a named shoebox of a single well-defined type. Every variable must be explicitly and formally declared. To put an object into the shoebox, thus causing the variable name to *refer* to that object, you *assign* the object to the variable. (As we now know from Chapter 2, a function, too, has a type, and can be assigned to a variable.)

Aside from the convenience of giving a reference a name, a variable, by virtue of the place where it is declared, endows its referent with a particular *scope* (visibility) and *lifetime*; assigning something to a variable is a way of ensuring that it can be *seen* by code that needs to see it and that it *persists* long enough to serve its purpose.

In the structure of a Swift file (see Example 1-1), a variable can be declared virtually anywhere. It will be useful to distinguish several levels of variable scope and lifetime:

Global variables

A global variable, or simply a *global*, is a variable declared at the top level of a Swift file. (In Example 1-1, the variable one is a global.)

A global variable lives as long as the file lives. That means it lives forever. Well, not strictly forever, but as long as the program runs.

A global variable is visible everywhere — that's what "global" means. It is visible to all code within the *same* file, because it is at top level, so any other code in the same file must be at the same level or at a lower contained level of scope. Moreover, it is visible (by default) to all code within any *other* file in the same module, because Swift files in the same module can automatically see one another, and hence can see one another's top levels.

Properties

A *property* is a variable declared at the top level of an object type declaration (an enum, struct, or class; in Example 1-1, the three name variables are properties). There are two kinds of properties: instance properties and static/class properties.

Instance properties

By default, a property is an *instance* property. Its value can differ for each instance of this object type. Its lifetime is the same as the lifetime of the instance. Recall from Chapter 1 that an instance comes into existence when it is created (by instantiation); the subsequent lifetime of the instance depends on the lifetime of the variable to which the instance itself is assigned.

Static/class properties

A property is a static/class property if its declaration is preceded by the keyword static or class. (I'll go into detail about those terms in Chapter 4.) Its lifetime is the same as the lifetime of the object type. If the object type is declared at the top level of a file, or at the top level of another object type that is declared at top level, that means it lives forever (as long as the program runs).

A property is visible to all code *inside* the object declaration. For example, an object's methods can see that object's properties. Such code can refer to the property using dot-notation with self, and I always do this as a matter of style, but self can usually be omitted except for purposes of disambiguation.

An instance property is also visible (by default) to other code, provided the other code has a reference to this instance; in that case, the property can be referred to through dot-notation with the instance reference. A static/class property is visible (by default) to other code that can see the name of this object type; in that case, it can be referred to through dot-notation with the object type.

Local variables

A local variable is a variable declared inside a function body. (In Example 1-1, the variable two is a local variable.) A local variable lives only as long as its surrounding curly-brace scope lives: it comes into existence when the path of execution passes into the scope and reaches the variable declaration, and it goes out of existence when the path of execution exits the scope. Local variables are sometimes called *automatic*, to signify that they come into and go out of existence automatically.

A local variable can be seen only by *subsequent* code within the same scope (including a subsequent deeper scope within the same scope).

Variable Declaration

As I explained in Chapter 1, a variable is declared with `let` or `var`:

- With `let`, the variable becomes a *constant* — its value can never be changed after the first assignment of a value (*initialization*).
- With `var`, the variable is a true variable, and its value can be changed by subsequent assignment.

A variable's *type*, however, can *never* be changed. A variable declared with `var` can be given a different value, but that value must conform to the variable's type. Thus, when a variable is declared, it must be *given* a type, which it will have forever after. You can give a variable a type explicitly or implicitly:

Explicit variable type declaration

After the variable's name in the declaration, add a colon and the name of the type:

```
var x : Int
```

Implicit variable type by initialization

If you initialize the variable as part of the declaration, and if you provide no explicit type, Swift will *infer* its type, based on the value with which it is initialized:

```
var x = 1 // and now x is an Int
```

It is perfectly possible to declare a variable's type explicitly *and* assign it an initial value, all in one move:

```
var x : Int = 1
```

In that example, the explicit type declaration is superfluous, because the type (Int) would have been inferred from the initial value. Sometimes, however, providing an explicit type, even while also assigning an initial value, is *not* superfluous. Here are the main situations where that's the case:

Swift's inference would be wrong

A very common case in my own code is when I want to provide the initial value as a numeric literal. Swift will infer either Int or Double, depending on whether the literal contains a decimal point. But there are a lot of other numeric types! When I mean one of those, I will provide the type explicitly, like this:

```
let separator : CGFloat = 2.0
```

Swift can't infer the type

In this situation, the explicit variable type is what allows Swift to infer the type of the initial value. A very common case involves option sets (discussed in Chapter 4). This won't compile:

```
var opts = [.Autoreverse, .Repeat] // compile error
```

The problem is that the names `.Autoreverse` and `.Repeat` are shortcuts for `UIView-AnimationOptions.Autoreverse` and `UIViewAnimationOptions.Repeat`, but Swift doesn't know that unless we tell it:

```
let opts : UIViewAnimationOptions = [.Autoreverse, .Repeat]
```

The programmer can't infer the type

I frequently include a superfluous explicit type declaration as a kind of note to myself. Here's an example from my own code:

```
let duration : CMTime = track.timeRange.duration
```

In that code, `track` is an AVAssetTrack. Swift knows perfectly well that the `duration` property of an AVAssetTrack's `timeRange` property is a CMTime. But I don't! In order to remind myself of that fact, I've shown the type explicitly.

Because explicit variable typing is possible, a variable doesn't have to be initialized when it is declared. It is legal to write this:

```
let x : Int
```

Now x is an empty shoebox — an Int variable without an initial value. I strongly urge you, however, not to do that with a local variable if you can possibly avoid it. It isn't a disaster — the Swift compiler will stop you from trying to use a variable that has never been assigned a value — but it's not a good habit.

The exception that proves the rule is what we might call *conditional initialization*. Sometimes, we don't *know* a variable's initial value until we've performed some sort of conditional test. The variable itself, however, can be declared only once; so it must be declared in advance and conditionally initialized afterwards. This sort of thing is not unreasonable (though there are other, possibly better ways to write it):

```
let timed : Bool
if val == 1 {
    timed = true
} else {
    timed = false
}
```

When a variable's *address* is to be passed as argument to a function, the variable must be declared *and initialized* beforehand, even if the initial value is fake. Recall this real-life example from Chapter 2:

```
var arrow = CGRectZero
var body = CGRectZero
CGRectDivide(rect, &arrow, &body, Arrow.ARHEIGHT, .MinYEdge)
```

After that code runs, our two `CGRectZero` values will have been replaced; they were just momentary placeholders, to satisfy the compiler.

On rare occasions, you'll want to call a Cocoa method that returns a value immediately and later uses that value in a function passed to that same method. For example, Cocoa has a UIApplication instance method declared like this:

```
func beginBackgroundTaskWithExpirationHandler(handler: (() -> Void)?)
    -> UIBackgroundTaskIdentifier
```

That function returns a number (a UIBackgroundTaskIdentifier is just an Int), and will later call the function passed to it (handler) — a function in which you will want to *use* the number that was returned at the outset. Swift's safety rules won't let you declare the variable that holds this number and use it in an anonymous function all in the same line:

```
let bti = UIApplication.sharedApplication()
    .beginBackgroundTaskWithExpirationHandler({
        UIApplication.sharedApplication().endBackgroundTask(bti)
    }) // error: variable used within its own initial value
```

Therefore, you need to declare the variable beforehand; but then Swift has another complaint:

```
var bti : UIBackgroundTaskIdentifier
bti = UIApplication.sharedApplication()
    .beginBackgroundTaskWithExpirationHandler({
        UIApplication.sharedApplication().endBackgroundTask(bti)
    }) // error: variable captured by a closure before being initialized
```

The solution is to declare the variable beforehand and give it a fake initial value as a placeholder:

```
var bti : UIBackgroundTaskIdentifier = 0
bti = UIApplication.sharedApplication()
    .beginBackgroundTaskWithExpirationHandler({
        UIApplication.sharedApplication().endBackgroundTask(bti)
    })
```

 Instance properties of an object (at the top level of an enum, struct, or class declaration) can be initialized in the object's initializer function rather than by assignment in their declaration. It is legal and common for both constant instance properties (let) and variable instance properties (var) to have an explicit type and no directly assigned initial value. I'll have more to say about that in Chapter 4.

Computed Initializer

Sometimes, you'd like to run several lines of code in order to compute a variable's initial value. A simple and compact way to express this is with an anonymous function that you call immediately (see "Define-and-Call" on page 52). I'll illustrate by rewriting an earlier example:

```
let timed : Bool = {
    if val == 1 {
        return true
    } else {
        return false
    }
}()
```

You can do the same thing when you're initializing an instance property. In this class, there's an image (a UIImage) that I'm going to need many times later on. It makes sense to create this image in advance as a constant instance property of the class. To create it means to draw it. That takes several lines of code. So I declare and initialize the property by defining and calling an anonymous function, like this (for my `imageOfSize` utility, see Chapter 2):

```
class RootViewController : UITableViewController {
    let cellBackgroundImage : UIImage = {
        return imageOfSize(CGSizeMake(320,44)) {
            // ... drawing goes here ...
        }
    }()
}
```

Indeed, a define-and-call anonymous function is often the *only* legal way to compute an instance property's initial value with multiple lines of code. The reason is that, when you're initializing an instance property, you can't call an instance method, because there is no instance yet — the instance, after all, is what you are in the process of creating.

Computed Variables

The variables I've been describing so far in this chapter have all been *stored* variables. The shoebox analogy applies. The variable is a name, like a shoebox; a value can be put into the shoebox, by assigning to the variable, and it then sits there and can be retrieved later, by referring to the variable, for as long the variable lives.

Alternatively, a variable can be *computed*. This means that the variable, instead of having a value, has *functions*. One function, the *setter*, is called when the variable is assigned to. The other function, the *getter*, is called when the variable is referred to. Here's some code illustrating schematically the syntax for declaring a computed variable:

```
var now : String { ❶
    get { ❷
        return NSDate().description ❸
    }
    set { ❹
        print(newValue) ❺
    }
}
```

❶ The variable must be a var (not a let). Its type must be declared explicitly. The type is followed *immediately* by curly braces.

❷ The getter function is called get. Note that there is no formal function declaration; the word get is simply followed immediately by a function body in curly braces.

❸ The getter function *must* return a value of the same type as the variable.

❹ The setter function is called set. There is no formal function declaration; the word set is simply followed immediately by a function body in curly braces.

❺ The setter behaves like a function taking one parameter. By default, this parameter arrives into the setter function body with the local name newValue.

Here's some code that illustrates the use of our computed variable. You don't treat it any differently than any other variable! To assign to the variable, assign to it; to use the variable, use it. Behind the scenes, though, the setter and getter functions are called:

```
now = "Howdy" // Howdy ❶
print(now) // 2015-06-26 17:03:30 +0000 ❷
```

❶ Assigning to now calls its setter. The argument passed into this call is the assigned value; here, that's "Howdy". That value arrives in the set function as newValue. Our set function prints newValue to the console.

❷ Fetching now calls its getter. Our get function obtains the current date-time and translates it into a string, and returns the string. Our code then prints that string to the console.

Observe that when we set now to "Howdy" in the first line, the string "Howdy" wasn't stored anywhere. It had no effect, for example, on the value of now in the second line. A set function *can* store a value, but it can't store it in this computed variable; a computed variable isn't storage! It's a shorthand for calling its getter and setter functions.

There are a couple of variants on the basic syntax I've just illustrated:

- The name of the set function parameter doesn't have to be newValue. To specify a different name, put it in parentheses after the word set, like this:

    ```
    set (val) { // now you can use "val" inside the setter function body
    ```

- There doesn't have to be a setter. If the setter is omitted, this becomes a *read-only* variable. Attempting to assign to it is a compile error. A computed variable with no setter is the *primary* way to create a read-only variable in Swift.

- There must always be a getter! However, if there is no setter, the word get and the curly braces that follow it can be omitted. Thus, this is a legal declaration of a read-only variable:

```
var now : String {
    return NSDate().description
}
```

A computed variable can be useful in many ways. Here are the ones that occur most frequently in my real programming life:

Read-only variable

A computed variable is the simplest way to make a read-only variable. Just omit the setter from the declaration. Typically, the variable will be a global variable or a property; there probably wouldn't be much point in a local read-only variable.

Façade for a function

When a value can be readily calculated by a function each time it is needed, it often makes for simpler syntax to express it as a read-only calculated variable. Here's an example from my own code:

```
var mp : MPMusicPlayerController {
    return MPMusicPlayerController.systemMusicPlayer()
}
```

It's no bother to call `MPMusicPlayerController.systemMusicPlayer()` every time I want to refer to this object, but it's more compact to refer to it by a simple name, `mp`. And since `mp` represents a thing, rather than the performance of an action, it's nicer for `mp` to appear as a variable, so that to all appearances it *is* the thing, rather than as a function, which *returns* the thing.

Façade for other variables

A computed variable can sit in front of one or more stored variables, acting as a gatekeeper on how those stored variables are set and fetched. This is comparable to an accessor method in Objective-C. In the extreme case, a public computed variable is backed by a private stored variable:

```
private var _p : String = ""
var p : String {
    get {
        return self._p
    }
    set {
        self._p = newValue
    }
}
```

That's a silly example, because we're not *doing* anything interesting with our accessors: we are just setting and getting the private stored variable directly, so there's no effective difference between p and _p. But based on that template, you could now add functionality so that something useful happens during setting and getting.

As the preceding example demonstrates, a computed instance property function can refer to other instance properties; it can also call instance methods. This is important, because in general the initializer for a stored property can do neither of those things. The reason this is legal for a computed property is that its functions won't be called until the instance actually exists.

Here's a practical example of a computed variable used as a façade for storage. My class has an instance property holding a very large stored piece of data, which can alternatively be nil (it's an Optional, as I'll explain later):

```
var myBigDataReal : NSData! = nil
```

When my app goes into the background, I want to reduce memory usage (because iOS kills backgrounded apps that use too much memory). So I plan to save the data of myBig-DataReal as a file to disk, and then set the variable itself to nil, thus releasing its data from memory. Now consider what should happen when my app comes back to the front and my code tries to fetch myBigDataReal. If it isn't nil, we just fetch its value. But if it *is* nil, this might be because we saved its value to disk. So now I want to restore its value by reading it from disk, and *then* fetch its value. This is a perfect use of a computed variable façade:

```
var myBigData : NSData! {
    set (newdata) {
        self.myBigDataReal = newdata
    }
    get {
        if myBigDataReal == nil {
            // ... get a reference to file on disk, f ...
            self.myBigDataReal = NSData(contentsOfFile: f)
            // ... erase the file ...
        }
        return self.myBigDataReal
    }
}
```

Setter Observers

Computed variables are not needed as a stored variable façade as often as you might suppose. That's because Swift has *another* brilliant feature, which lets you inject functionality into the setter of a stored variable — setter observers. These are functions that are called just before and just after other code *sets* a stored variable.

The syntax for declaring a variable with a setter observer is very similar to the syntax for declaring a computed variable; you can write a willSet function, a didSet function, or both:

```
var s = "whatever" { ❶
    willSet { ❷
        print(newValue) ❸
    }
    didSet { ❹
        print(oldValue) ❺
        // self.s = "something else"
    }
}
```

❶ The variable must be a `var` (not a `let`). It can be assigned an initial value. It is then followed *immediately* by curly braces.

❷ The `willSet` function, if there is one, is the word `willSet` followed immediately by a function body in curly braces. It is called when other code sets this variable, just *before* the variable actually receives its new value.

❸ By default, the `willSet` function receives the incoming new value as `newValue`. You can change this name by writing a different name in parentheses after the word `willSet`. The old value is still sitting in the stored variable, and the `willSet` function can access it there.

❹ The `didSet` function, if there is one, is the word `didSet` followed immediately by a function body in curly braces. It is called when other code sets this variable, just *after* the variable actually receives its new value.

❺ By default, the `didSet` function receives the old value, which has already been replaced as the value of the variable, as `oldValue`. You can change this name by writing a different name in parentheses after the word `didSet`. The new value is already sitting in the stored variable, and the `didSet` function can access it there. Moreover, it is legal for the `didSet` function to *set the stored variable to a different value.*

Setter observer functions are *not* called when the stored variable is initialized or when the `didSet` function changes the stored variable's value. That would be circular!

In practice, I find myself using setter observers, rather than a computed variable, in the vast majority of situations where I would have used a setter override in Objective-C. Here's an example from Apple's own code (the Master–Detail Application template) illustrating a typical use case — changing the interface as a consequence of a property being set:

```
var detailItem: AnyObject? {
    didSet {
        // Update the view.
        self.configureView()
    }
}
```

This is an instance property of a view controller class. Every time this property changes, we need to change the interface, because the job of the interface is, in part, to display the value of this property. So we simply call an instance method every time the property is set. The instance method reads the property's value and sets the interface accordingly.

In this example from my own code, not only do we change the interface, but also we "clamp" the incoming value within a fixed limit:

```
var angle : CGFloat = 0 {
    didSet {
        // angle must not be smaller than 0 or larger than 5
        if self.angle < 0 {
            self.angle = 0
        }
        if self.angle > 5 {
            self.angle = 5
        }
        // modify interface to match
        self.transform = CGAffineTransformMakeRotation(self.angle)
    }
}
```

 A computed variable can't have setter observers. But it doesn't need them! There's a setter function, so anything additional that needs to happen during setting can be programmed directly into that setter function.

Lazy Initialization

The term *lazy* is not a pejorative ethical judgment; it's a formal description of an important behavior. If a stored variable is assigned an initial value as part of its declaration, and if it uses lazy initialization, then the initial value is not actually evaluated and assigned until running code accesses the variable's value.

There are three types of variable that can be initialized lazily in Swift:

Global variables

Global variables are *automatically lazy*. This makes sense if you ask yourself when they should be initialized. As the app launches, files and their top-level code are encountered. It would make no sense to initialize globals now, because the app isn't even running yet. Thus global initialization must be postponed to some moment that *does* make sense. Therefore, a global variable's initialization doesn't happen until other code first refers to that global. Under the hood, this behavior is protected with `dispatch_once`; this makes initialization both singular (it can happen only once) and thread-safe.

Static properties

Static properties behave exactly like global variables, and for basically the same reason. (There are no stored class properties in Swift, so class properties can't be initialized and thus can't have lazy initialization.)

Instance properties

An instance property is not lazy by default, but it may be made lazy by marking its declaration with the keyword `lazy`. This property must be declared with `var`, not `let`. The initializer for such a property might *never* be evaluated, namely if code assigns the property a value before any code fetches the property's value.

Lazy initialization is often used to implement *singleton*. Singleton is a pattern where all code is able to get access to a single shared instance of a certain class:

```
class MyClass {
    static let sharedMyClassSingleton = MyClass()
}
```

Now other code can obtain a reference to MyClass's singleton by saying `MyClass.shared-MyClassSingleton`. The singleton instance is not created until the first time other code says this; subsequently, no matter how many times other code may say this, the instance returned is always that same instance. (Observe that that is *not* what would happen if this were a computed read-only property whose getter calls `MyClass()` and returns that instance; do you see why?)

Now let's talk about lazy initialization of instance properties. Why might you want this? One reason is obvious: the initial value might be expensive to generate, so you'd like to avoid generating it until and unless it is actually needed. But there's another reason that might not occur to you at first, but that turns out to be even more important: a lazy initializer can do things that a normal initializer can't. In particular, it can *refer to the instance*. A normal initializer can't do that, because the instance doesn't yet exist at the time that a normal initializer would need to run (*ex hypothesi*, we're in the middle of creating the instance, so it isn't ready yet). A lazy initializer, by contrast, won't run until some time after the instance has fully come into existence, so referring to the instance is fine. For example, this code would be illegal if the `arrow` property weren't declared `lazy`:

```
class MyView : UIView {
    lazy var arrow : UIImage = self.arrowImage()
    func arrowImage () -> UIImage {
        // ... big image-generating code goes here ...
    }
}
```

A very common idiom is to initialize a lazy instance property with a define-and-call anonymous function:

```
lazy var prog : UIProgressView = {
    let p = UIProgressView(progressViewStyle: .Default)
    p.alpha = 0.7
    p.trackTintColor = UIColor.clearColor()
    p.progressTintColor = UIColor.blackColor()
    p.frame = CGRectMake(0, 0, self.view.bounds.size.width, 20)
    p.progress = 1.0
    return p
}()
```

There are some minor holes in the language: lazy instance properties can't have setter observers, and there's no `lazy let` (so you can't readily make a lazy instance property read-only). But these restrictions are not terribly serious, because `lazy` arguably isn't doing very much that you couldn't do with a calculated property backed by a stored property, as Example 3-1 shows.

Example 3-1. Implementing a lazy property by hand

```
private var lazyOncer : dispatch_once_t = 0
private var lazyBacker : Int = 0
var lazyFront : Int {
    get {
        dispatch_once(&self.lazyOncer) {
            self.lazyBacker = 42 // expensive initial value
        }
        return self.lazyBacker
    }
    set {
        dispatch_once(&self.lazyOncer) {}
        // will set
        self.lazyBacker = newValue
        // did set
    }
}
```

In Example 3-1, the idea is that only `lazyFront` is accessed publicly; `lazyBacker` is its underlying storage, and `lazyOncer` makes everything happen the right number of times. Since `lazyFront` is now an ordinary computed property, we can observe it during setting (put additional code into its setter function, at the points I've marked by "will set" and "did set"), or we can make it read-only (delete the setter entirely).

Built-In Simple Types

Every variable, and every value, must have a type. But what types are there? Up to this point, I've assumed the existence of some types, such as Int and String, without formally telling you about them. Here's a survey of the primary simple types provided by Swift, along with some instance methods, global functions, and operators that apply to them. (Collection types will be discussed at the end of Chapter 4.)

Bool

The Bool object type (a struct) has only two values, commonly regarded as true and false (or yes and no). You can represent these values using the literal keywords true and false, and it is natural to think of a Bool value as *being* either true or false:

```
var selected : Bool = false
```

In that code, selected is a Bool variable initialized to false; it can subsequently be set to false or true, and to no other values. Because of its simple yes-or-no state, a Bool variable of this kind is often referred to as a *flag*.

Cocoa methods very often expect a Bool parameter or return a Bool value. For example, when your app launches, Cocoa calls a method in your code declared like this:

```
func application(application: UIApplication,
    didFinishLaunchingWithOptions launchOptions: [NSObject: AnyObject]?)
    -> Bool
```

You can do anything you like in that method; often, you will do nothing. But you must return a Bool! And in real life, that Bool will always be true. A minimal implementation thus looks like this:

```
func application(application: UIApplication,
    didFinishLaunchingWithOptions launchOptions: [NSObject: AnyObject]?)
    -> Bool {
        return true
}
```

A Bool is useful in conditions; as I'll explain in Chapter 5, when you say if *something*, the *something* is the condition, and is a Bool — or an expression that evaluates to a Bool. For example, when you compare two values with the equality comparison operator ==, the result is a Bool — true if they are equal to each other, false if they are not:

```
if meaningOfLife == 42 { // ...
```

(I'll talk more about equality comparison in a moment, when we come to discuss types that can be compared, such as Int and String.)

When preparing a condition, you will sometimes find that it enhances clarity to store the Bool value in a variable beforehand:

```
let comp = self.traitCollection.horizontalSizeClass == .Compact
if comp { // ...
```

Observe that, when employing that idiom, we use the Bool variable *directly* as the condition. It is silly — and arguably wrong — to say if comp == true, because if comp already *means* "if `comp` is `true`." There is no need to test explicitly whether a Bool equals `true` or `false`; the conditional expression *itself* is already testing that.

Since a Bool can be used as a condition, a call to a function that returns a Bool can be used as a condition. Here's an example from my own code. I've declared a function that returns a Bool to say whether the cards the user has selected constitute a correct answer to the puzzle:

```
func evaluate(cells:[CardCell]) -> Bool { // ...
```

Thus, elsewhere I can say this:

```
if self.evaluate(cellsToTest) { // ...
```

Unlike many computer languages, nothing else in Swift is implicitly coerced to or treated as a Bool. For example, in C, a boolean is actually a number, and 0 is false. But in Swift, nothing is false but `false`, and nothing is true but `true`.

The type name, Bool, comes from the English mathematician George Boole; Boolean algebra provides operations on logical values. Bool values are subject to these same operations:

!

> Not. The ! unary operator reverses the truth value of the Bool to which it is applied as a prefix. If `ok` is `true`, `!ok` is `false` — and *vice versa*.

&&

> Logical-and. Returns `true` only if both operands are `true`; otherwise, returns `false`. If the first operand is `false`, the second operand is not even evaluated (thus avoiding possible side effects).

||

> Logical-or. Returns `true` if either operand is `true`; otherwise, returns `false`. If the first operand is `true`, the second operand is not even evaluated (thus avoiding possible side effects).

If a logical operation is complicated or elaborate, parentheses around subexpressions can help clarify both the logic and the order of operations.

Numbers

The main numeric types are Int and Double, meaning that, left to your own devices, these are the types you'll use. Other numeric types exist mostly for compatibility with the C and Objective-C APIs that Swift needs to be able to talk to when you're programming iOS.

Int

The Int object type (a struct) represents an integer between `Int.max` and `Int.min` inclusive. The actual values of those limits might depend on the platform and architecture under which the app runs, so don't count on them to be absolute; in my testing at this moment, they are 2^{63}-1 and -2^{63} respectively (64-bit words).

The easiest way to represent an Int value is as a numeric literal. A simple numeric literal without a decimal point is taken as an Int by default. Internal underscores are legal; this is useful for making long numbers readable. Leading zeroes are legal; this is useful for padding and aligning values in your code.

You can write an Int literal using binary, octal, or hexadecimal digits. To do so, start the literal with `0b`, `0o`, or `0x` respectively. Thus, for example, `0x10` is decimal 16.

Double

The Double object type (a struct) represents a floating-point number to a precision of about 15 decimal places (64-bit storage).

The easiest way to represent a Double value is as a numeric literal. Any numeric literal containing a decimal point is taken as a Double by default. Internal underscores and leading zeroes are legal.

A Double literal may *not* begin with a decimal point! If the value to be represented is between 0 and 1, start the literal with a leading `0`. (I stress this because it is significantly different from C and Objective-C.)

You can write a Double literal using scientific notation. Everything after the letter `e` is the exponent of 10. You can omit the decimal point if the fractional digits would be zero. For example, `3e2` is 3 times 10^2 (300).

You can write a Double literal using hexadecimal digits. To do so, start the literal with `0x`. You can use exponentiation here too (and again, you can omit the decimal point); everything after the letter `p` is the exponent of 2. For example, `0x10p2` is decimal 64, because you are multiplying 16 by 2^2.

There's a static property `Double.infinity` and an instance property `isZero`, among others.

Coercion

Coercion is the conversion of a value from one numeric type to another. Swift doesn't really have explicit coercion, but it has something that serves the same purpose — instantiation. To convert an Int explicitly into a Double, instantiate Double with an Int in the parentheses. To convert a Double explicitly into an Int, instantiate Int with a Double in the parentheses; this will truncate the original value (everything after the decimal point will be thrown away):

```
let i = 10
let x = Double(i)
print(x) // 10.0, a Double
let y = 3.8
let j = Int(y)
print(j) // 3, an Int
```

When numeric values are assigned to variables or passed as arguments to a function, Swift will perform implicit coercion *of literals only*. This code is legal:

```
let d : Double = 10
```

But this code is not legal, because what you're assigning is a *variable* (not a literal) of a different type; the compiler will stop you:

```
let i = 10
let d : Double = i // compile error
```

The solution is to *coerce explicitly* as you assign or pass the variable:

```
let i = 10
let d : Double = Double(i)
```

The same rule holds when numeric values are combined by an arithmetic operation. Swift will perform implicit coercion *of literals only*. The usual situation is an Int combined with a Double; the Int is treated as a Double:

```
let x = 10/3.0
print(x) // 3.33333333333333
```

But *variables* of different numeric types *must be coerced explicitly* so that they are the *same* type if you want to combine them in an arithmetic operation. Thus, for example:

```
let i = 10
let n = 3.0
let x = i / n // compile error; you need to say Double(i)
```

These rules are evidently a consequence of Swift's strict typing; but (as far as I am aware) they constitute very unusual treatment of numeric values for a modern computer language, and will probably drive you mad in short order. The examples I've given so far were easily solved, but things can become more complicated if an arithmetic expression is longer, and the problem is compounded by the existence of other numeric types that are needed for compatibility with Cocoa, as I shall now proceed to explain.

Other numeric types

If you weren't programming iOS — if you were using Swift in some isolated, abstract world — you could probably do all necessary arithmetic with Int and Double alone. Unfortunately, to program iOS you need Cocoa, which is full of other numeric types; and Swift has types that match every one of them. Thus, in addition to Int, there are signed integers of various sizes — Int8, Int16, Int32, Int64 — plus the unsigned integer UInt along with UInt8, UInt16, UInt32, and UInt64. In addition to Double, there is the lower-precision Float (32-bit storage, about 6 or 7 decimal places of precision) and the extended-precision Float80; plus, in the Core Graphics framework, CGFloat (whose size can be that of Float or Double, depending on the bitness of the architecture).

You may also encounter a C numeric type when trying to interface with a C API. These types, as far as Swift is concerned, are just type aliases, meaning that they are alternate names for another type; for example, a CDouble (corresponding to C's `double`) is just a Double by another name, a CLong (C's `long`) is an Int, and so on. Many other numeric type aliases will arise in various Cocoa frameworks; for example, an NSTimeInterval is merely a type alias for Double.

Here's the problem. I have just finished telling you that you can't assign, pass, or combine values of different numeric types using variables; you have to coerce those values explicitly to the correct type. But now it turns out that you're being flooded by Cocoa with numeric values of many types! Cocoa will often hand you a numeric value that is neither an Int nor a Double — and you won't necessarily realize this, until the compiler stops you dead in your tracks for some sort of type mismatch. You must then figure out what you've done wrong and coerce everything to the same type.

Here's a typical example from one of my apps. We have a UIImage, we extract its CGImage, and now we want to express the size of that CGImage as a CGSize:

```
let mars = UIImage(named:"Mars")!
let marsCG = mars.CGImage
let szCG = CGSizeMake( // compile error
    CGImageGetWidth(marsCG),
    CGImageGetHeight(marsCG)
)
```

The trouble is that `CGImageGetWidth` and `CGImageGetHeight` return Ints, but `CGSizeMake` expects CGFloats. This is not an issue in C or Objective-C, where there is implicit coercion from the former to the latter. But in Swift, *you* have to coerce explicitly:

```
var szCG = CGSizeMake(
    CGFloat(CGImageGetWidth(marsCG)),
    CGFloat(CGImageGetHeight(marsCG))
)
```

Here's another real-life example. A slider, in the interface, is a UISlider, whose `minimumValue` and `maximumValue` are Floats. In this code, `s` is a UISlider, `g` is a UIGestureRecognizer, and we're trying to use the gesture recognizer to move the slider's "thumb" to wherever the user tapped within the slider:

```
let pt = g.locationInView(s)
let percentage = pt.x / s.bounds.size.width
let delta = percentage * (s.maximumValue - s.minimumValue) // compile error
```

That won't compile. `pt` is a CGPoint, and therefore `pt.x` is a CGFloat. Luckily, `s.bounds.size.width` is also a CGFloat, so the second line compiles; `percentage` is

```
                                              Quick Help

                                              Declaration let percentage: CGFloat
    let percentage = pt.x / s.bounds.size.width      Declared In  MySlider.swift
```

Figure 3-1. Quick Help displays a variable's type

now inferred to be a CGFloat. In the third line, however, we try to combine `percentage` with `s.maximumValue` and `s.minimumValue` — and they are Floats, not CGFloats. We must coerce explicitly:

```
let delta = Float(percentage) * (s.maximumValue - s.minimumValue)
```

The good news here — perhaps the only good news — is that if you can get enough of your code to compile, Xcode's Quick Help feature will tell you what type Swift has inferred for a variable (Figure 3-1). This can assist you in tracking down your issues with numeric types.

 In the rare circumstance where you need to assign or pass an integer type where another integer type is expected and you don't actually know what that other integer type is, you can get Swift to coerce dynamically by calling `numericCast`. For example, if `i` and `j` are previously declared variables of different integer types, `i = numericCast(j)` coerces `j` to the integer type of `i`.

Arithmetic operations

Swift's arithmetic operators are as you would expect; they are familiar from other computer languages as well as from real arithmetic:

+

Addition operator. Add the second operand to the first and return the result.

-

Subtraction operator. Subtract the second operand from the first and return the result. A different operator (unary minus), used as a prefix, looks the same; it returns the additive inverse of its single operand. (There is, in fact, also a unary plus operator, which returns its operand unchanged.)

*

Multiplication operator. Multiply the first operand by the second and return the result.

/

Division operator. Divide the first operand by the second and return the result.

As in C, division of one Int by another Int yields an Int; any remaining fraction is stripped away. 10/3 is 3, not 3-and-one-third.

%

Remainder operator. Divide the first operand by the second and return the remainder. The result can be negative, if the first operand is negative; if the second operand is negative, it is treated as positive. Floating-point operands are legal.

Integer types can be treated as binary bitfields and subjected to binary bitwise operations:

&

Bitwise-and. A bit in the result is 1 if and only if that bit is 1 in both operands.

|

Bitwise-or. A bit in the result is 0 if and only if that bit is 0 in both operands.

^

Bitwise-or, exclusive. A bit in the result is 1 if and only if that bit is not identical in both operands.

~

Bitwise-not. Precedes its single operand; inverts the value of each bit and returns the result.

<<

Shift left. Shift the bits of the first operand leftward the number of times indicated by the second operand.

>>

Shift right. Shift the bits of the first operand rightward the number of times indicated by the second operand.

 Technically, the shift operators perform a logical shift if the integer is unsigned, and an arithmetic shift if the integer is signed.

Integer overflow or underflow — for example, adding two Int values so as to exceed Int.max — is a runtime error (your app will crash). In simple cases the compiler will stop you, but you can get away with it easily enough:

```
let i = Int.max - 2
let j = i + 12/2 // crash
```

Under certain circumstances you might want to force such an operation to succeed, so special overflow/underflow methods are supplied. These methods return a tuple; I'll show you an example even though I haven't discussed tuples yet:

```
let i = Int.max - 2
let (j, over) = Int.addWithOverflow(i,12/2)
```

Now j is `Int.min + 3` (because the value has wrapped around from `Int.max` to `Int.min`) and `over` is `true` (to report the overflow).

If you don't care to hear about whether or not there was an overflow/underflow, special arithmetic operators let you suppress the error: `&+`, `&-`, `&*`.

You will frequently want to combine the value of an existing variable arithmetically with another value and store the result in the same variable. Remember that to do so, you will need to have declared the variable as a `var`:

```
var i = 1
i = i + 7
```

As a shorthand, operators are provided that perform the arithmetic operation and the assignment all in one move:

```
var i = 1
i += 7
```

The shorthand (*compound*) assignment arithmetic operators are `+=`, `-=`, `*=`, `/=`, `%=`, `&=`, `|=`, `^=`, `~=`, `<<=`, `>>=`.

It is often desirable to increase or decrease a numeric value by 1, so there are unary increment and decrement operators `++` and `--`. These differ depending on whether they are prefixed or postfixed. If prefixed (`++i`, `--i`) the value is incremented (or decremented), stored back in the same variable, and then used within the surrounding expression; if postfixed (`i++`, `i--`), the *current* value of the variable is used within the surrounding expression, and *then* the value is incremented (or decremented) and stored back in the same variable. Obviously, the variable must be declared with `var`.

Operation precedence is largely intuitive: for example, `*` has a higher precedence than `+`, so `x+y*z` multiplies y by z first, and then adds the result to x. Use parentheses to disambiguate when in doubt; for example, `(x+y)*z` performs the addition first.

Global functions include `abs` (absolute value), `max`, and `min`:

```
let i = -7
let j = 6
print(abs(i)) // 7
print(max(i,j)) // 6
```

Other mathematical functions, such as square roots, rounding, pseudorandom numbers, trigonometry, and so forth, come from the C standard libraries that are visible because you've imported UIKit. You still have to be careful about numeric types, and there is no implicit coercion, even for literals.

For example, `sqrt` expects a C `double`, which is a CDouble, which is a Double. So you can't say `sqrt(2)`; you have to say `sqrt(2.0)`. Similarly, `arc4random` returns a UInt32. So if `n` is an Int and you want to get a random number between between 0 and `n-1`, you can't say `arc4random()%n`; you have to coerce the result of calling `arc4random` to an Int.

Comparison

Numbers are compared using the comparison operators, which return a Bool. For example, the expression `i==j` tests whether `i` and `j` are equal; when `i` and `j` are numbers, "equal" means numerically equal. So `i==j` is `true` only if `i` and `j` are "the same number," in exactly the sense you would expect.

The comparison operators are:

`==`

> Equality operator. Returns `true` if its operands are equal.

`!=`

> Inequality operator. Returns `false` if its operands are equal.

`<`

> Less-than operator. Returns `true` if the first operand is less than the second operand.

`<=`

> Less-than-or-equal operator. Returns `true` if the first operand is less than or equal to the second operand.

`>`

> Greater-than operator. Returns `true` if the first operand is greater than the second operand.

`>=`

> Greater-than-or-equal operator. Returns `true` if the first operand is greater than or equal to the second operand.

Keep in mind that, because of the way computers store numbers, equality comparison of Double values may not succeed where you would expect. To test whether two Doubles are effectively equal, it can be more reliable to compare the difference between them to a very small value (usually called an *epsilon*):

```
let isEqual = abs(x - y) < 0.000001
```

String

The String object type (a struct) represents text. The easiest way to represent a String value is with a literal, which is delimited by double quotes:

```
let greeting = "hello"
```

A Swift string is thoroughly modern; under the hood, it's Unicode, and you can include any character directly in a string literal. If you don't want to bother typing a Unicode character whose codepoint you know, use the notation \u{...}, where what's between the curly braces is up to eight hex digits:

```
let leftTripleArrow = "\u{21DA}"
```

The backslash in that string representation is the *escape* character; it means, "I'm not really a backslash; I indicate that the next character gets special treatment." Various nonprintable and ambiguous characters are entered as escaped characters; the most important are:

\n
> A Unix newline character

\t
> A tab character

\"
> A quotation mark (escaped to show that this is not the end of the string literal)

\\
> A backslash (escaped because a lone backslash is the escape character)

One of Swift's coolest features is *string interpolation*. This permits you to embed any value that can be output with print inside a literal string *as a string*, even if it is not itself a string. The notation is escaped parentheses: \(...). For example:

```
let n = 5
let s = "You have \(n) widgets."
```

Now s is the string "You have 5 widgets." The example is not very compelling, because we know what n is and could have typed 5 directly into our string; but imagine that we *don't* know what n is! Moreover, the stuff in escaped parentheses doesn't have to be the name of a variable; it can be almost any expression that evaluates as legal Swift. If you don't know how to add, this example is more compelling:

```
let m = 4
let n = 5
let s = "You have \(m + n) widgets."
```

One thing that *can't* go inside escaped parentheses is double quotes. This is disappointing, but it's not much of a hurdle; just assign to a variable and use the variable instead. For example, you can't say this:

```
let ud = NSUserDefaults.standardUserDefaults()
let s = "You have \(ud.integerForKey("widgets")) widgets." // compile error
```

Escaping the double quotes doesn't help. You have to write it as multiple lines, like this:

```
let ud = NSUserDefaults.standardUserDefaults()
let n = ud.integerForKey("widgets")
let s = "You have \(n) widgets."
```

To combine (concatenate) two strings, the simplest approach is to use the + operator (and its += assignment shortcut):

```
let s = "hello"
let s2 = " world"
let greeting = s + s2
```

This convenient notation is possible because the + operator is *overloaded*: it does one thing when the operands are numbers (numeric addition) and another when the operands are strings (concatenation). As I'll explain in Chapter 5, *all* operators can be overloaded, and you can overload them to operate in some appropriate way on your own types.

As an alternative to +=, you can call the appendContentsOf instance method:

```
var s = "hello"
let s2 = " world"
s.appendContentsOf(s2) // or: s += s2
```

Another way of concatenating strings is with the joinWithSeparator method. You start with an array (yes, I know we haven't gotten to arrays yet) of strings to be concatenated, and hand it the string that is to be inserted between all of them:

```
let s = "hello"
let s2 = "world"
let space = " "
let greeting = [s,s2].joinWithSeparator(space)
```

The comparison operators are also overloaded so that they all work with String operands. Two String values are equal (==) if they are, in the natural sense of the words, "the same text." A String is less than another if it is alphabetically prior.

A few additional convenient instance methods and properties are provided. isEmpty returns a Bool reporting whether this string is the empty string (""). hasPrefix and hasSuffix report whether this string starts or ends with another string; for example, "hello".hasPrefix("he") is true. The uppercaseString and lowercaseString properties provide uppercase and lowercase versions of the original string.

Coercion between a String and an Int is possible. To make a string that represents an Int, it is sufficient to use string interpolation; alternatively, use the Int as a String initializer, just as if you were coercing between numeric types:

```
let i = 7
let s = String(i) // "7"
```

Your string can also represent an Int in some other base; supply a radix: argument expressing the base:

```
let i = 31
let s = String(i, radix:16) // "1f"
```

A String that might represent a number can be coerced to a numeric type; an integer type will accept a radix: argument expressing the base. The coercion might fail, though, because the String might *not* represent a number of the specified type; so the result is not a number but an Optional wrapping a number (I haven't talked about Optionals yet, so you'll have to trust me for now; failable initializers are discussed in Chapter 4):

```
let s = "31"
let i = Int(s) // Optional(31)
let s2 = "1f"
let i2 = Int(s2, radix:16) // Optional(31)
```

 Coercion to String is in fact the basis of string interpolation, and of representation in the console with print. You can make *any* object coercible to String, by making it conform to any of three protocols: Streamable, CustomStringConvertible, and CustomDebugStringConvertible. I'll give an example when I explain what a protocol is, in Chapter 4.

The length of a String, in characters, is given by the count method of its characters property:

```
let s = "hello"
let length = s.characters.count // 5
```

Why isn't there simply a length property of a String? It's because a String doesn't really have a simple length. The String is stored as a sequence of Unicode codepoints, but multiple Unicode codepoints can combine to form a character; so, in order to know how many characters are represented by such a sequence, we actually have to walk through the sequence and resolve it into the characters that it represents.

You, too, can walk through a String's characters. The simplest way is with the for...in construct (see Chapter 5). What you get when you do this are Character objects; I'll talk more about Character objects later:

```
let s = "hello"
for c in s.characters {
    print(c) // print each Character on its own line
}
```

At an even deeper level, you can decompose a String into its UTF-8 codepoints or its UTF-16 codepoints, using the utf8 and utf16 properties:

```
let s = "\u{BF}Qui\u{E9}n?"
for i in s.utf8 {
    print(i) // 194, 191, 81, 117, 105, 195, 169, 110, 63
}
for i in s.utf16 {
    print(i) // 191, 81, 117, 105, 233, 110, 63
}
```

There is also a unicodeScalars property representing a collection of the String's UTF-32 codepoints expressed as UnicodeScalar structs. To compose a string from numeric codepoints, instantiate a UnicodeScalar from a number and append it to a String. To illustrate, here's a utility function that turns a two-letter country abbreviation into an emoji representation of its flag:

```
func flag(country:String) -> String {
    let base : UInt32 = 127397
    var s = ""
    for v in country.unicodeScalars {
        s.append(UnicodeScalar(base + v.value))
    }
    return s
}
// and here's how to use it:
let s = flag("DE")
```

The curious thing is that there aren't more methods for standard string manipulation. How, for example, do you capitalize a string, or find out whether a string contains a given substring? Most modern programming languages have a compact, convenient way of doing things like that; Swift doesn't. The reason appears to be that missing features are provided by the Foundation framework, to which you'll always be linked in real life (importing UIKit imports Foundation). A Swift String is bridged to a Foundation NSString. This means that, to a large extent, Foundation NSString methods magically spring to life whenever you are using a Swift String. For example:

```
let s = "hello world"
let s2 = s.capitalizedString // "Hello World"
```

The capitalizedString property comes from the Foundation framework; it's provided by Cocoa, not by Swift. It's an NSString property; it appears tacked on to String "for free." Similarly, here's how to locate a substring of a string:

```
let s = "hello"
let range = s.rangeOfString("ell") // Optional(Range(1..<4))
```

I haven't explained yet what an Optional is or what a Range is (I'll talk about them later in this chapter), but that innocent-looking code has made a remarkable round-trip from Swift to Cocoa and back again: the Swift String s becomes an NSString, the NSString `rangeOfString` method is called, a Foundation NSRange struct is returned, and the NSRange is converted to a Swift Range and wrapped up in an Optional.

It will often happen, however, that you don't want this round-trip conversion. For various reasons, you might want to stay in the Foundation world and receive the answer as a Foundation NSRange. To accomplish that, you have to cast your string explicitly to an NSString, using the `as` operator (I'll discuss casting formally in Chapter 4):

```
let s = "hello"
let range = (s as NSString).rangeOfString("ell") // (1,3), an NSRange
```

Here's another example, also involving NSRange. Suppose you want to derive the string `"ell"` from `"hello"` by its range — the second, third, and fourth characters. Foundation's NSString method `substringWithRange:` requires that you supply a range — meaning an NSRange. You can readily form the NSRange directly, using a Foundation function; but when you do, your code doesn't compile:

```
let s = "hello"
let ss = s.substringWithRange(NSMakeRange(1,3)) // compile error
```

The reason for the compile error is that Swift has absorbed NSString's `substringWithRange:`, and expects you to supply a Swift Range here. I'll explain in a moment how to do that, but you may find it simpler to tell Swift to stay in the Foundation world, by casting:

```
let s = "hello"
let ss = (s as NSString).substringWithRange(NSMakeRange(1,3)) // "ell"
```

Character

The Character object type (a struct) represents a single Unicode grapheme cluster — what you would naturally think of as one character of a string. A String object can be decomposed into a sequence of Character objects by taking its `characters` property. Formally, this is a `String.CharacterView` struct; but I'll call it simply a *character sequence*. As I mentioned earlier, you can walk through a character sequence with `for...in` to obtain the String's Characters, one by one:

```
let s = "hello"
for c in s.characters {
    print(c) // print each Character on its own line
}
```

It isn't common to encounter Character objects outside of some character sequence of which they are a part. There isn't even a way to write a literal Character. To make a Character from scratch, initialize it from a single-character String:

The String–NSString Element Mismatch

Swift and Cocoa have different ideas of what the elements of a string are. The Swift conception involves characters. The NSString conception involves UTF-16 codepoints. Each approach has its advantages. The NSString way makes for great speed and efficiency in comparison to Swift, which must walk the string to investigate how the characters are constructed; but the Swift way gives what you would intuitively think of as the right answer. To emphasize this difference, a nonliteral Swift string has no `length` property; its analog to an NSString's `length` is the `count` of its `utf16` property.

Fortunately, the element mismatch doesn't arise very often in practice; but it can arise. Here's a good test case:

```
let s = "Ha\u{030A}kon"
print(s.characters.count) // 5
let length = (s as NSString).length // or: s.utf16.count
print(length) // 6
```

We've created our string (the Norwegian name Håkon) using a Unicode codepoint that combines with the previous codepoint to form a character with a ring over it. Swift walks the whole string, so it normalizes the combination and reports five characters. Cocoa just sees at a glance that this string contains six 16-bit codepoints.

```
let c = Character("h")
```

By the same token, you can initialize a String from a Character:

```
let c = Character("h")
let s = (String(c)).uppercaseString
```

Characters can be compared for equality; "less than" means what you would expect it to mean.

A character sequence has many properties and methods that can come in handy. By virtue of being a collection (a CollectionType), it has a `first` and `last` property; these are Optionals, because the string might be empty:

```
let s = "hello"
let c1 = s.characters.first // Optional("h")
let c2 = s.characters.last // Optional("o")
```

The `indexOf` method locates the first occurrence of a given character within the sequence and returns its index. Again, this is an Optional, because the character might be absent:

```
let s = "hello"
let firstL = s.characters.indexOf("l") // Optional(2)
```

All Swift indexes are numbered starting with 0, so 2 means the third character. The index value here, however, is not an Int; I'll explain in a moment what it is and what it's good for.

By virtue of being a sequence (a SequenceType), a character sequence has a `contains` method that returns a Bool, reporting whether a certain character is present:

```
let s = "hello"
let ok = s.characters.contains("o") // true
```

Alternatively, `contains` can take a function that takes a Character and returns a Bool. (The `indexOf` method can do this too.) This code reports whether the target string contains a vowel:

```
let s = "hello"
let ok = s.characters.contains {"aeiou".characters.contains($0)} // true
```

The `filter` method takes a function that takes a Character and returns a Bool, effectively eliminating those characters for which `false` is returned. The result is a character sequence, but you can coerce that to a String. Thus, here's how to delete all consonants from a String:

```
let s = "hello"
let s2 = String(s.characters.filter {"aeiou".characters.contains($0)}) // "eo"
```

The `dropFirst` and `dropLast` methods return (in effect) a new character sequence without the first or last character, respectively:

```
let s = "hello"
let s2 = String(s.characters.dropFirst()) // "ello"
```

`prefix` and `suffix` extract the character sequence of a given length from the start or end of the original character sequence:

```
let s = "hello"
let s2 = String(s.characters.prefix(4)) // "hell"
```

`split` breaks a character sequence up into an array, according to a function that takes a Character and returns a Bool. In this example, I obtain the words of a String, where a "word" is simplemindedly defined as a run of Characters other than a space:

```
let s = "hello world"
let arr = s.characters.split{$0 == " "}
```

The result, however, is an array of rather curious SubSlice objects; to get String objects, we need to apply the `map` function and coerce them all to Strings. I'll talk about `map` in Chapter 4, so you'll have to trust me for now:

```
let s = "hello world"
let arr = split(s.characters){$0 == " "}.map{String($0)} // ["hello", "world"]
```

A String — in reality, its underlying character sequence — can also be manipulated similarly to an array. For example, you can use subscripting to obtain the character at a certain position. Unfortunately, this isn't as easy as it might be. For example, what's the second character of "hello"? This doesn't compile:

```
let s = "hello"
let c = s[1] // compile error
```

The reason is that the indexes on a String (which are actually indexes on its character sequence) are a special nested type, a `String.Index` (which is actually a type alias for `String.CharacterView.Index`). To make an object of this type is rather tricky. Start with a String's (or a character sequence's) `startIndex` or `endIndex`, or with the return value from the `indexOf` method; you can then call the `advancedBy` method to derive the index you want:

```
let s = "hello"
let ix = s.startIndex
let c = s[ix.advancedBy(1)] // "e"
```

The reason for this clumsy circumlocution is that Swift doesn't know where the characters of a character sequence actually are until it walks the sequence; calling `advancedBy` is how you make Swift do that.

In addition to the `advancedBy` method, you can increment or decrement an index value with ++ and --, and you can obtain the next or preceding index value with the `successor` and `predecessor` methods. Thus, I could have written the preceding example like this:

```
let s = "hello"
var ix = s.startIndex
let c = s[++ix] // "e"
```

Or like this:

```
let s = "hello"
let ix = s.startIndex
let c = s[ix.successor()] // "e"
```

Once you've obtained a desired character index value, you can use it to modify the String. For example, the `insertContentsOf(at:)` method inserts a character sequence — not a String! — into a String:

```
var s = "hello"
let ix = s.characters.startIndex.advancedBy(1)
s.insertContentsOf("ey, h".characters, at: ix) // s is now "hey, hello"
```

Similarly, `removeAtIndex` deletes a single character (and returns that character).

(Manipulations involving longer character stretches require use of a Range, which is the subject of the next section.)

Note that a character sequence can be coerced directly to an Array of Character objects — for example, `Array("hello".characters)`. It could be worth your while to do that, because array indexes *are* Ints, and are thus easy to work with. Once you've manipulated the array of Characters, you can coerce it directly to a String. I'll give an example in the next section (and I'll discuss arrays, and say more about collections and sequences, in Chapter 4).

Range

The Range object type (a struct) represents a pair of endpoints. There are two operators for forming a Range literal; you supply a start value and an end value, with one of the Range operators between them:

`...`

Closed interval operator. The notation `a...b` means "everything from `a` up to `b`, *including* `b`."

`..<`

Half-open interval operator. The notation `a..<b` means "everything from `a` up to but *not* including `b`."

Spaces around a Range operator are legal.

 There are no reverse Ranges: the start value of a Range can't be greater than the end value (the compiler won't stop you, but you'll crash at runtime).

The types of a Range's endpoints will typically be some kind of number — most often, Ints:

```
let r = 1...3
```

If the end value is a negative literal, it has to be enclosed in parentheses:

```
let r = -1000...(-1)
```

A very common use of a Range is to loop through numbers with `for...in`:

```
for ix in 1 ... 3 {
    print(ix) // 1, then 2, then 3
}
```

You can also use a Range's `contains` instance method to test whether a value falls within given limits; a range used in this way is actually an interval (strictly, an IntervalType):

```
let ix = // ... an Int ...
if (1...3).contains(ix) { // ...
```

For purposes of testing containment, a Range's endpoints can be Doubles:

```
let d = // ... a Double ...
if (0.1...0.9).contains(d) { // ...
```

Another common use of a Range is to index into a sequence. For example, here's one way to get the second, third, and fourth characters of a String. As I suggested at the end of the preceding section, we coerce the String's characters to an Array; we can then use an Int Range as an index into that array, and coerce back to a String:

```
let s = "hello"
let arr = Array(s.characters)
let result = arr[1...3]
let s2 = String(result) // "ell"
```

Alternatively, you can use a Range to index directly into a String (or its underlying character sequence), but then it has to be a Range of String.Index, which, as I've already pointed out, is rather clumsy to obtain. One way to get one is to let Swift convert the NSRange that you get back from a Cocoa method call into a Swift Range for you:

```
let s = "hello"
let r = s.rangeOfString("ell") // a Swift Range (wrapped in an Optional)
```

You can also generate your Range endpoints as index values — for example, by using advancedBy from the String's startIndex, as I showed earlier. Once you have a Range of the proper type, you can extract a substring by subscripting:

```
let s = "hello"
let ix1 = s.startIndex.advancedBy(1)
let ix2 = ix1.advancedBy(2)
let s2 = s[ix1...ix2] // "ell"
```

An elegant shortcut is to start with a sequence's indices property, which returns a half-open Range between the sequence's startIndex and its endIndex; you can then modify the Range and use it:

```
let s = "hello"
var r = s.characters.indices
r.startIndex++
r.endIndex--
let s2 = s[r] // "ell"
```

The replaceRange method splices into a range, thus modifying the string:

```
var s = "hello"
let ix = s.startIndex
let r = ix.advancedBy(1)...ix.advancedBy(3)
s.replaceRange(r, with: "ipp") // s is now "hippo"
```

Similarly, you can delete a stretch of characters with the removeRange method:

```
var s = "hello"
let ix = s.startIndex
let r = ix.advancedBy(1)...ix.advancedBy(3)
s.removeRange(r) // s is now "ho"
```

A Swift Range and a Cocoa NSRange are constructed very differently from one another. A Swift Range is defined by two endpoints. A Cocoa NSRange is defined by a starting point and a length. But you can coerce a Swift Range whose endpoints are Ints to an NSRange, and you can convert from an NSRange to a Swift Range with the `toRange` method (which returns an Optional wrapping a Range).

Sometimes, Swift goes even further. For example, when we say `"hello".rangeOf-String("ell")`, Swift bridges between Range and NSRange for us, correctly taking account of the fact that Swift and Cocoa interpret characters and string length differently, as well as the fact that an NSRange's values are Ints, while the endpoints of a Range describing a Swift substring are `String.Index`.

Tuple

A *tuple* is a lightweight custom ordered collection of multiple values. As a type, it is expressed by surrounding the types of the contained values with parentheses and separating them by commas. For example, here's a declaration for a variable whose type is a tuple of an Int and a String:

```
var pair : (Int, String)
```

The literal value of a tuple is expressed in the same way — the contained values, surrounded with parentheses and separated by commas:

```
var pair : (Int, String) = (1, "One")
```

Those types can be inferred, so there's no need for the explicit type in the declaration:

```
var pair = (1, "One")
```

Tuples are a pure Swift language feature; they are not compatible with Cocoa and Objective-C, so you'll use them only for values that Cocoa never sees. Within Swift, however, they have many uses. For example, a tuple is an obvious solution to the problem that a function can return only one value; a tuple *is* one value, but it *contains* multiple values, so using a tuple as the return type of a function permits that function to return multiple values.

Tuples come with numerous linguistic conveniences. You can assign to a tuple of variable names as a way of assigning to multiple variables simultaneously:

```
var ix: Int
var s: String
(ix, s) = (1, "One")
```

That's such a convenient thing to do that Swift lets you do it in one line, declaring and initializing multiple variables simultaneously:

```
var (ix, s) = (1, "One") // can use let or var here
```

Assigning variable values to one another through a tuple swaps them safely:

```
var s1 = "hello"
var s2 = "world"
(s1, s2) = (s2, s1) // now s1 is "world" and s2 is "hello"
```

 There's also a global function swap that swaps values in a more general way.

To ignore one of the assigned values, use an underscore to represent it in the receiving tuple:

```
let pair = (1, "One")
let (_, s) = pair // now s is "One"
```

The enumerate method lets you walk a sequence with for...in and receive, on each iteration, each successive element's index number along with the element itself; this double result comes to you as — you guessed it — a tuple:

```
let s = "hello"
for (ix,c) in s.characters.enumerate() {
    print("character \(ix) is \(c)")
}
```

I also pointed out earlier that numeric instance methods such as addWithOverflow return a tuple.

You can refer to the individual elements of a tuple directly, in two ways. The first way is by index number, using a *literal number* (not a variable value) as the name of a message sent to the tuple with dot-notation:

```
let pair = (1, "One")
let ix = pair.0 // now ix is 1
```

If your reference to a tuple isn't a constant, you can assign into it by the same means:

```
var pair = (1, "One")
pair.0 = 2 // now pair is (2, "One")
```

The second way to access tuple elements is to give them names. The notation is like that of function parameters, and must appear as part of the explicit or implicit type declaration. Thus, here's one way to establish tuple element names:

```
let pair : (first:Int, second:String) = (1, "One")
```

And here's another way:

```
let pair = (first:1, second:"One")
```

The names are now part of the type of this value, and travel with it through subsequent assignments. You can then use them as literal message names, just like (and together with) the numeric literals:

```
var pair = (first:1, second:"One")
let x = pair.first // 1
pair.first = 2
let y = pair.0 // 2
```

You can assign from a tuple without names into a corresponding tuple with names (and *vice versa*):

```
let pair = (1, "One")
let pairWithNames : (first:Int, second:String) = pair
let ix = pairWithNames.first // 1
```

You can also pass, or return from a function, a tuple without names where a corresponding tuple with names is expected:

```
func tupleMaker() -> (first:Int, second:String) {
    return (1, "One") // no names here
}
let ix = tupleMaker().first // 1
```

If you're going to be using a certain type of tuple consistently throughout your program, it might be useful to give it a type name. To do so, use Swift's `typealias` keyword. For example, in my LinkSame app I have a Board class describing and manipulating the game layout. The board is a grid of Piece objects. I needed a way to describe positions of the grid. That's a pair of integers, so I define my own type as a tuple:

```
class Board {
    typealias Point = (Int,Int)
    // ...
}
```

The advantage of that notation is that it now becomes easy to use Points throughout my code. For example, given a Point, I can fetch the corresponding Piece:

```
func pieceAt(p:Point) -> Piece? {
    let (i,j) = p
    // ... error-checking goes here ...
    return self.grid[i][j]
}
```

The obvious similarity between a tuple with element names and a function parameter list is not a coincidence. A parameter list *is* a tuple! The truth is that *every function takes one tuple parameter and returns one tuple*. Thus, you can pass a single tuple to a function that takes multiple parameters. For example, suppose you have a function like this:

```
func f (i1:Int, _ i2:Int) -> () {}
```

The parameter list of `f` is a tuple. Thus, we can call `f` with a single tuple as argument:

```
let tuple = (1,2)
f(tuple)
```

In that example, f has no external parameter names. If a function does have external parameter names, you can pass it a tuple with named elements. Here is such a function:

```
func f2 (i1 i1:Int, i2:Int) -> () {}
```

You can call it like this:

```
let tuple = (i1:1, i2:2)
f2(tuple)
```

However, for reasons that are not entirely clear to me, tuples passed as function parameters in this way must be *constants*. This code won't compile:

```
var tuple = (i1:1, i2:2)
f2(tuple) // compile error
```

Similarly, Void, the type of value returned by a function that doesn't return a value, is actually a type alias for an empty tuple. That's why it is also notated as ().

Optional

The Optional object type (an enum) wraps another object of any type. A single Optional object can wrap only *one* object. Alternatively, an Optional object might wrap *no* other object. This is what makes an Optional optional: it *might* wrap another object, but then again it might not. Think of an Optional as being itself a kind of shoebox — a shoebox which can quite legally be empty.

Let's start by creating an Optional that does wrap an object. Suppose we want an Optional wrapping the String "howdy". One way to create it is with the Optional initializer:

```
var stringMaybe = Optional("howdy")
```

If we log stringMaybe to the console with print, we'll see an expression identical to the corresponding initializer: Optional("howdy").

After that declaration and initialization, stringMaybe is typed, not as a String, nor as an Optional plain and simple, but as an Optional wrapping a String. This means that any other Optional wrapping a String can be assigned to it — but not an Optional wrapping some other type. This code is legal:

```
var stringMaybe = Optional("howdy")
stringMaybe = Optional("farewell")
```

This code, however, is not legal:

```
var stringMaybe = Optional("howdy")
stringMaybe = Optional(123) // compile error
```

Optional(123) is an Optional wrapping an Int, and you can't assign an Optional wrapping an Int where an Optional wrapping a String is expected.

Optionals are so important to Swift that special syntax for working with them is baked into the language. The usual way to make an Optional is not to use the Optional initializer (though you can certainly do that), but to assign or pass a value of some type to a reference that is already typed as an Optional wrapping that type. For example, once `stringMaybe` is typed as an Optional wrapping a String, it is legal to assign a String directly to it. This seems as if it should not be legal — but it is. The outcome is that the assigned String is wrapped in an Optional for us, automatically:

```
var stringMaybe = Optional("howdy")
stringMaybe = "farewell" // now stringMaybe is Optional("farewell")
```

We also need a way of typing something *explicitly* as an Optional wrapping a String. Otherwise, we cannot declare a variable with an Optional type, and we cannot declare a parameter with an Optional type. Formally, an Optional is a generic, so an Optional wrapping a String is an `Optional<String>` (I'll explain that syntax in Chapter 4). However, you don't have to write that. The Swift language supports syntactic sugar for expressing an Optional type: use the name of the wrapped type followed by a question mark. For example:

```
var stringMaybe : String?
```

Thus I don't need to use the Optional initializer at all. I can type the variable as an Optional wrapping a String and assign a String into it for wrapping, all in one move:

```
var stringMaybe : String? = "howdy"
```

That, in fact, is the normal way to make an Optional in Swift.

Once you've got an Optional wrapping a particular type, you can use it wherever an Optional wrapping that type is expected — just like any other value. If a function expects an Optional wrapping a String as its parameter, you can pass `stringMaybe` as argument to that parameter:

```
func optionalExpecter(s:String?) {}
let stringMaybe : String? = "howdy"
optionalExpecter(stringMaybe)
```

Moreover, where an Optional wrapping a certain type of value is expected, you can pass a value of that wrapped type instead. That's because parameter passing is just like assignment: an unwrapped value will be wrapped implicitly for you. For example, if a function expects an Optional wrapping a String, you can pass a String argument, which will be wrapped into an Optional in the received parameter:

```
func optionalExpecter(s:String?) {
    // ... here, s will be an Optional wrapping a String ...
    print(s)
}
optionalExpecter("howdy") // console prints: Optional("howdy")
```

But you cannot do the opposite — you cannot use an Optional wrapping a type where the wrapped type is expected. This won't compile:

```
func realStringExpecter(s:String) {}
let stringMaybe : String? = "howdy"
realStringExpecter(stringMaybe) // compile error
```

The error message reads: "Value of optional type `Optional<String>` not unwrapped; did you mean to use ! or ??" You're going to be seeing that sort of message a lot in Swift, so get used to it! As that message suggests, if you want to use an Optional where the type of thing it wraps is expected, you must *unwrap* the Optional — that is, you must reach inside it and *retrieve* the actual thing that it wraps. Now I'm going to talk about how to do that.

Unwrapping an Optional

We have seen more than one way to wrap an object in an Optional. But what about the opposite procedure? How do we unwrap an Optional to get at the object wrapped inside it? One way is to use the *unwrap operator* (or *forced unwrap operator*), which is a post-fixed exclamation mark. For example:

```
func realStringExpecter(s:String) {}
let stringMaybe : String? = "howdy"
realStringExpecter(stringMaybe!)
```

In that code, the `stringMaybe!` syntax expresses the operation of reaching inside the Optional `stringMaybe`, grabbing the wrapped value, and substituting it at that point. Since `stringMaybe` is an Optional wrapping a String, the thing inside it is a String. That is exactly what the `realStringExpecter` function wants as its parameter! Thus, we are able to pass the unwrapped Optional as argument to `realStringExpecter`. `stringMaybe` is an Optional *wrapping* the String `"howdy"`, but `stringMaybe!` *is* the String `"howdy"`.

If an Optional wraps a certain type, you cannot send it a message expected by that type. You must unwrap it first. For example, let's try to get an uppercase version of `stringMaybe`:

```
let stringMaybe : String? = "howdy"
let upper = stringMaybe.uppercaseString // compile error
```

The solution is to unwrap `stringMaybe` to get at the String inside it. We can do this directly, in place, using the unwrap operator:

```
let stringMaybe : String? = "howdy"
let upper = stringMaybe!.uppercaseString
```

If an Optional is to be used several times where the unwrapped type is expected, and if you're going to be unwrapping it with the unwrap operator each time, your code can quickly start to look like the dialog from a 1960s Batman comic. For example, in iOS programming, an app's window is an Optional UIWindow property of the app delegate (`self.window`):

```
// self.window is an Optional wrapping a UIWindow
self.window = UIWindow()
self.window!.rootViewController = RootViewController()
self.window!.backgroundColor = UIColor.whiteColor()
self.window!.makeKeyAndVisible()
```

That sort of thing soon gets old (or silly). One obvious alternative is to assign the unwrapped value *once* to a variable of the wrapped type and then use that variable:

```
// self.window is an Optional wrapping a UIWindow
self.window = UIWindow()
let window = self.window!
// now window (not self.window) is a UIWindow, not an Optional
window.rootViewController = RootViewController()
window.backgroundColor = UIColor.whiteColor()
window.makeKeyAndVisible()
```

However, there's another way, as I shall now explain.

Implicitly unwrapped Optional

Swift provides another way of using an Optional where the wrapped type is expected: you can declare the Optional *type* as being *implicitly unwrapped*. This is actually a separate type — ImplicitlyUnwrappedOptional. An ImplicitlyUnwrappedOptional is an Optional, but the compiler permits some special magic associated with it: its value can be used *directly* where the wrapped type is expected. You *can* unwrap an ImplicitlyUnwrappedOptional explicitly, but you don't have to, because it is already implicitly unwrapped (hence the name). For example:

```
func realStringExpecter(s:String) {}
var stringMaybe : ImplicitlyUnwrappedOptional<String> = "howdy"
realStringExpecter(stringMaybe) // no problem
```

As with Optional, Swift provides syntactic sugar for expressing an implicitly unwrapped Optional type. Just as an Optional wrapping a String can be expressed as `String?`, an implicitly unwrapped Optional wrapping a String can be expressed as `String!`. Thus, we can rewrite the preceding code like this (and this is how you would in fact write it):

```
func realStringExpecter(s:String) {}
var stringMaybe : String! = "howdy"
realStringExpecter(stringMaybe)
```

Bear in mind that *an implicitly unwrapped Optional is still an Optional*. It's just a convenience. By declaring something as an implicitly unwrapped Optional, you are asking the compiler, if you happen to use this value where the wrapped type is expected, to forgive you and to unwrap the value for you.

As far as their types are concerned, a normal Optional wrapping a certain type (such as a `String?`) and an implicitly unwrapped Optional wrapping that same type (such as a `String!`) are considered interchangeable: you can pass either one where either one is expected.

The magic word nil

I have talked so far about Optionals that contain a wrapped value. But what about an Optional that *doesn't* contain any wrapped value? Such an Optional is, as I've already said, a perfectly legal entity; that, indeed, is the whole point of Optionals.

You are going to need a way to *ask* whether an Optional contains a wrapped value, and a way to *specify* an Optional *without* a wrapped value. Swift makes both of those things easy, through the use of a special keyword, `nil`:

To learn whether an Optional contains a wrapped value
> Test the Optional for equality against `nil`. If the test succeeds, the Optional is empty. An empty Optional is also reported in the console as `nil`.

To specify an Optional with no wrapped value
> Assign or pass `nil` where the Optional type is expected. The result is an Optional of the expected type, containing no wrapped value.

For example:

```
var stringMaybe : String? = "Howdy"
print(stringMaybe) // Optional("Howdy")
if stringMaybe == nil {
    print("it is empty") // does not print
}
stringMaybe = nil
print(stringMaybe) // nil
if stringMaybe == nil {
    print("it is empty") // prints
}
```

The magic word `nil` lets you express the concept "An Optional wrapping the appropriate type, but not actually containing any object of that type." Clearly, that's very convenient magic; you'll want to take advantage of it. It is very important to understand, however, that it *is* magic: `nil` in Swift is *not* a thing and is *not* a value. *It is a shorthand.* It is natural to think and speak as if this shorthand were real. For example, I will say that something "is `nil`." But in reality, nothing "is `nil`"; `nil` isn't a thing. What I really mean is that this thing is equatable with `nil` (because it is an Optional not wrapping anything).

The *real* value of an Optional that contains no wrapped object is `Optional.None`, and the *real* value of an Optional wrapping a String that contains no wrapped String is `Optional<String>.None`. But you'll probably never actually need to say those things in your code, because it's so much easier to say `nil`. I'll explain in Chapter 4 what those expressions signify.

Because a variable typed as an Optional can be `nil`, Swift follows a special initialization rule: a variable (`var`) typed as an Optional *is* `nil`, automatically. This is legal:

```
func optionalExpecter(s:String?) {}
var stringMaybe : String?
optionalExpecter(stringMaybe)
```

That code is interesting because it looks as if it should be illegal. We declared a variable `stringMaybe`, but we never assigned it a value. Nevertheless we are now passing it around as if it were an actual thing. That's because it *is* an actual thing. This variable has been *implicitly initialized* — to `nil`. A variable (`var`) typed as an Optional is the *only* sort of variable that gets implicit initialization in Swift.

We come now to perhaps the most important rule in all of Swift: You *cannot unwrap an Optional containing nothing* (an Optional equatable with `nil`). Such an Optional contains nothing; there's nothing to unwrap. Like Oakland, there's no there there. In fact, explicitly unwrapping an Optional containing nothing will *crash your program* at runtime:

```
var stringMaybe : String?
let s = stringMaybe! // crash
```

The crash message reads: "Fatal error: unexpectedly found `nil` while unwrapping an Optional value." Get used to it, because you're going to be seeing it a lot. This is an easy mistake to make. Unwrapping an Optional that contains no value is, in fact, probably the most common way to crash a Swift program. You should look upon this kind of crash as a blessing. Very often, in fact, you will *want* to crash if your Optional contains no value, because it *should* contain a value, and the fact that it doesn't indicates that you've made a mistake elsewhere.

To eliminate such a crash, you need to ensure that your Optional contains a value, and *don't* unwrap it if it doesn't. One obvious way to do that is to test against `nil` first:

```
var stringMaybe : String?
// ... stringMaybe might be assigned a real value here ...
if stringMaybe != nil {
    let s = stringMaybe!
    // ...
}
```

Optional chains

A common situation is that you want to send a message to the value wrapped inside an Optional. To do so, you can unwrap the Optional in place. I gave an example earlier:

```
let stringMaybe : String? = "howdy"
let upper = stringMaybe!.uppercaseString
```

That form of code is called an *Optional chain*. In the middle of a chain of dot-notation, you have unwrapped an Optional.

You *cannot* send a message to an Optional *without* unwrapping it. Optionals themselves don't respond to any messages. (Well, they do respond to some messages, but very few, and you are unlikely to use them — and in any case they are not the messages to which the thing inside them responds.) If you try to send to an Optional a message intended for the thing inside it, you will get an error message from the compiler:

```
let stringMaybe : String? = "howdy"
let upper = stringMaybe.uppercaseString // compile error
```

We have already seen, however, that if you unwrap an Optional that contains no wrapped object, you'll crash. So what if you're *not sure* whether this Optional contains a wrapped object? How can you send a message to an Optional in that situation? Swift provides a special shorthand for exactly this purpose. To send a message *safely* to an Optional that might be empty, you can *unwrap the Optional optionally*. To do so, unwrap the Optional with the question mark postfix operator instead of the exclamation mark:

```
var stringMaybe : String?
// ... stringMaybe might be assigned a real value here ...
let upper = stringMaybe?.uppercaseString
```

That's an Optional chain in which you used a question mark to unwrap the Optional. By using that notation, you have unwrapped the Optional optionally — meaning conditionally. The condition in question is one of safety; a test for nil is performed for us. Our code means: "If stringMaybe contains a String, unwrap it and send it the uppercase-String message. If it doesn't (that is, if it equates to nil), *do not* unwrap it and *do not* send it any messages!"

Such code is a double-edged sword. On the one hand, if stringMaybe is nil, you won't crash at runtime. On the other hand, if stringMaybe is nil, that line of code won't do anything useful — you won't get any uppercase string.

But now there's a new question. In that code, we initialized a variable upper to an expression that involves sending the uppercaseString message. Now it turns out that the uppercaseString message might or not even be sent. So what, exactly, is upper initialized *to*?

To handle this situation, Swift has a special rule. If an Optional chain contains an optionally unwrapped Optional, and if this Optional chain produces a value, that value is itself *wrapped in an Optional*. Thus, `upper` is typed as an Optional wrapping a String. This works brilliantly, because it covers both possible cases. Let's say, first, that `string-Maybe` contains a String:

```
var stringMaybe : String?
stringMaybe = "howdy"
let upper = stringMaybe?.uppercaseString // upper is a String?
```

After that code, `upper` is *not* a String; it is *not* `"HOWDY"`. It is an Optional wrapping `"HOWDY"`! On the other hand, if the attempt to unwrap the Optional fails, the Optional chain can return `nil` instead:

```
var stringMaybe : String?
let upper = stringMaybe?.uppercaseString // upper is a nil String?
```

Unwrapping an Optional optionally in this way is elegant and safe; but consider the consequences. On the one hand, even if `stringMaybe` is `nil`, we won't crash at runtime. On the other hand, we're no better off than we were before: we've ended up with yet another Optional on our hands! Whether `stringMaybe` is `nil` or not, `upper` is typed as an Optional wrapping a String, and in order to use that String, we're going to have to unwrap `upper`. And we don't know whether `upper` is `nil`, so we have exactly the same problem we had before — we need to make sure that we unwrap `upper` safely, and that we don't accidentally unwrap an empty Optional.

Longer Optional chains are legal. They work just as you would expect: no matter how many Optionals are unwrapped in the course of the chain, if any of them is unwrapped optionally, the entire expression produces an Optional wrapping the type it would have produced if the Optionals were unwrapped normally, and is free to fail safely at any point along the way. For example:

```
// self.window is a UIWindow?
let f = self.window?.rootViewController?.view.frame
```

The `frame` property of a view is a CGRect. But after that code, `f` is *not* a CGRect. It's an Optional wrapping a CGRect. If *any* of the optional unwrapping along the chain fails (because the Optional we propose to unwrap is `nil`), the *entire* chain can return `nil` to indicate failure.

 Observe that the preceding code does not end up nesting Optionals; it doesn't produce a CGRect wrapped in an Optional wrapped in an Optional, merely because there are two Optionals being optionally unwrapped in the chain. However, it is possible, for other reasons, to end up with an Optional wrapped in an Optional. I'll give an example in Chapter 4.

If an Optional chain involving optional unwrapping produces a result, you can learn whether all the Optionals in the chain were safely unwrapped by examining that result:

if it isn't `nil`, everything was unwrapped successfully. But what if an Optional chain containing optional unwrapping produces *no* result? For example:

```
self.window?.rootViewController = UIViewController()
```

Now we're in a quandary. It's true that we won't crash; if `self.window` is `nil`, it won't be unwrapped, so we're safe. But if `self.window` is `nil`, we didn't succeed in giving our window a root view controller either! It would be nice to know whether the unwrapping in *this* Optional chain succeeded. Fortunately, there's a trick for finding out. Every statement in Swift that doesn't otherwise return a value returns `Void`. Therefore, an assignment into an Optional chain with optional unwrapping returns an Optional wrapping `Void` — and you can capture that Optional. That means you can test the Optional against `nil`; if it isn't `nil`, the assignment worked. For example:

```
let ok : Void? = self.window?.rootViewController = UIViewController()
if ok != nil {
    // it worked
}
```

Naturally, you don't need to capture the Optional wrapping `Void` explicitly in a variable; you can capture and test it against `nil` in a single move:

```
if (self.window?.rootViewController = UIViewController()) != nil {
    // it worked
}
```

If a function call returns an Optional, you can unwrap the result and use it. You don't necessarily have to capture the result in order to do that; you can unwrap it in place, by putting an exclamation mark or a question mark after the function call (that is, after the closing parenthesis). That's really no different from what we've been doing all along, except that instead of an Optional property or variable, this is a function call that returns an Optional. For example:

```
class Dog {
    var noise : String?
    func speak() -> String? {
        return self.noise
    }
}
let d = Dog()
let bigname = d.speak()?.uppercaseString
```

After that, don't forget, `bigname` is not a String — it's an Optional wrapping a String.

 I'll discuss some additional Swift syntax for checking whether an Optional is `nil` when I come to flow control in Chapter 5.

The ! and ? postfix operators, which respectively unconditionally and conditionally unwrap an Optional, have basically *nothing* to do with the ! and ? used with type names as syntactic sugar for expressing Optional types (such as String? to mean an Optional wrapping a String, and String! to mean an implicitly unwrapped Optional wrapping a String). The outward similarity has confused many a beginner.

Comparison with Optional

In a comparison with something other than nil, an Optional gets special treatment: the wrapped value, not the Optional itself, is compared. So, for example, this works:

```
let s : String? = "Howdy"
if s == "Howdy" { // ... they _are_ equal!
```

That shouldn't work, but it does — mercifully so, since it would be maddening to have to unwrap an Optional just to compare its wrapped value with something (especially as you'd have to check first whether the Optional is nil). Instead of comparing the Optional itself with "Howdy", Swift automagically (and safely) compares its wrapped value (if there is one) with "Howdy", and the comparison succeeds. If the wrapped value is not "Howdy", the comparison fails. If there is *no* wrapped value (s is nil), the comparison fails too — safely! Thus, you can compare s to nil or to a String, and the comparison works correctly in all cases.

In the same way, if an Optional wraps a type of value that can be compared using the greater-than and less-than operators, those operators can be applied directly to the Optional:

```
let i : Int? = 2
if i < 3 { // ... it _is_ less!
```

Why Optionals?

Now that you know how to use an Optional, you are probably wondering *why* to use an Optional. Why does Swift have Optionals at all? What are they good for?

One very important purpose of Optionals is to provide *interchange of object values with Objective-C*. In Objective-C, *any* object reference can be nil. You thus need a way to send nil to Objective-C and to receive nil from Objective-C. Swift Optionals provide your only way to do that.

Swift will typically assist you by a judicious use of appropriate types in the Cocoa APIs. For example, consider a UIView's backgroundColor property. It's a UIColor, but it can be nil, and you are allowed to set it to nil. Thus, it is typed as a UIColor?. You don't need to work directly with Optionals in order to *set* such a value! Remember, assigning the wrapped type to an Optional is legal, as the assigned value will be wrapped for you.

Thus, you can set myView.backgroundColor to a UIColor — or to nil! But if you *get* a UIView's backgroundColor, you now have an Optional wrapping a UIColor, *and you must be conscious of this fact*, for all the reasons I've already discussed: if you're not, surprising things can happen:

```
let v = UIView()
let c = v.backgroundColor
let c2 = c.colorWithAlphaComponent(0.5) // compile error
```

You're trying to send the colorWithAlphaComponent message to c, as if it were a UIColor. It *isn't* a UIColor. It's an Optional wrapping a UIColor. Xcode will brilliantly and desperately try to help you in this situation; if you use code completion to enter the name of the colorWithAlphaComponent method, Xcode will insert a question mark after c, thus (optionally) unwrapping the Optional and giving you legal code:

```
let v = UIView()
let c = v.backgroundColor
let c2 = c?.colorWithAlphaComponent(0.5)
```

In the vast majority of situations, however, a Cocoa object type will *not* be marked as an Optional. That's because, although in *theory* it *could* be nil (because any Objective-C object reference can be nil), in practice it won't be. Swift thus saves you a step by treating the value as the object type itself. This magic is performed by hand-tweaking the Cocoa APIs (also called *auditing*). In the very first public version of Swift (in June of 2014), *all* object values received from Cocoa were in fact typed as Optionals (usually implicitly unwrapped Optionals). But then Apple embarked on the massive project of hand-tweaking the APIs to eliminate Optionals that didn't need to be Optionals.

In a few cases, you may still encounter implicitly unwrapped Optionals in a Cocoa API. For example, as of this writing, the API for the NSBundle method loadNib-Named:owner:options: looks like this:

```
func loadNibNamed(name: String!,
    owner: AnyObject!,
    options: [NSObject : AnyObject]!)
    -> [AnyObject]!
```

Those implicitly unwrapped Optionals show that this header hasn't yet been hand-tweaked. They don't represent the situation accurately — you'll *never* pass nil as the first parameter, for example — but they do no serious harm.

Another important use of Optionals is to defer initialization of an instance property. If a variable (declared with var) is typed as an Optional, it has a value even if you don't initialize it — namely nil. That comes in very handy in situations where you know something *will* have a value, but not right away. A typical example in real-life iOS programming is an outlet, which is a reference to something in your interface such as a button:

```
class ViewController: UIViewController {
    @IBOutlet var myButton: UIButton!
    // ...
}
```

Ignore, for now, the @IBOutlet designation, which is an internal hint to Xcode (as I'll explain in Chapter 7). The important thing is that this property, myButton, won't have a value when our ViewController instance first comes into existence, but shortly thereafter the view controller's view will be loaded and myButton will be set so that it points to an actual UIButton object in the interface. Therefore, the variable is typed as an implicitly unwrapped Optional. It's an Optional because we need a placeholder value for myButton when the ViewController instance first comes into existence. It's implicitly unwrapped so that in our code we can just treat self.myButton as a reference to an actual UIButton, passing through the Optional without noticing that it *is* an Optional.

A closely related situation is when a variable, again typically an instance property, represents data that will take time to acquire. For example, in my Albumen app, as we launch, I create an instance of my root view controller. I also want to gather a bunch of data about the user's music library and store that data in instance properties of the root view controller instance. But gathering that data will take time. Therefore I must instantiate the root view controller *first* and gather the data *later*, because if we pause to gather the data *before* instantiating the root view controller, the app will take too long to launch — the delay will be perceptible, and we might even crash (because iOS forbids long launch times). Therefore the data properties are all typed as Optionals; they are nil until the data are gathered, at which time they are assigned their "real" values:

```
class RootViewController : UITableViewController {
    var albums : [MPMediaItemCollection]! // initialized to nil
    // ...
```

Finally, one of the most important uses of Optionals is to permit a value to be marked as empty or erroneous. The preceding code is a good illustration. When my Albumen app launches, it displays a table listing all the user's music albums. At launch time, however, that data has not yet been gathered. My table-display code tests albums to see whether it's nil and, if it is, displays an empty table. After gathering the data, I tell my table to display its data *again*. This time, the table-display code finds that albums is *not* nil, but rather consists of actual data — and it now displays that data. The use of an Optional allows one and the same value, albums, to store the data or to state that there is no data.

Many built-in Swift functions use an Optional in a similar way. I mentioned earlier that you can coerce a String to an Int:

```
let s = "31"
let i = Int(s) // Optional(31)
```

Initializing an Int from a String returns an Optional because the conversion can fail. If s is "howdy", it isn't a number. Thus the type returned cannot be an Int, because there is no Int that can be taken to mean, "I didn't find any Int." Returning an Optional solves the problem neatly: nil means "I didn't find any Int," and otherwise the actual Int result is sitting there wrapped up in the Optional.

Swift is cleverer than Objective-C in this regard. If a reference is an object, Objective-C can return nil to report failure; but not everything in Objective-C is an object. Thus, many important Cocoa methods return a special value to indicate failure, and you have to know this and remember to test for it. For example, NSString's rangeOfString: might not find the given substring in the target string; in that case, it returns an NSRange whose length is zero and whose location (index) is a special value, NSNotFound, which is actually just a very large negative number. Fortunately, a knowledge of this special value is built into the Swift bridge to the Cocoa API: Swift types the returned value as an Optional wrapping a Range, and if rangeOfString: does return an NSRange whose location is NSNotFound, Swift expresses it as nil!

Not every part of the Swift–Cocoa bridge is so helpful, however. If you call NSArray's indexOfObject:, the result is an Int, not an Optional wrapping an Int; that result can be NSNotFound, and you have to remember to test for this:

```
let arr = [1,2,3]
let ix = (arr as NSArray).indexOfObject(4)
if ix == NSNotFound { // ...
```

An alternative in this case might be to stay in Swift and call the indexOf method, which returns an Optional:

```
let arr = [1,2,3]
let ix = arr.indexOf(4)
if ix == nil { // ...
```

CHAPTER 4

Object Types

In the preceding chapter, I discussed some built-in object types. But I have not yet explained object types themselves. As I mentioned in Chapter 1, Swift object types come in three flavors: enum, struct, and class. What are the differences between them? And how would you create your own object type? That's what this chapter is about.

I'll describe object types in general, and then each of the three flavors. Then I'll explain three Swift ways of giving an object type greater flexibility: protocols, generics, and extensions. Finally, the survey of Swift's built-in types will conclude with three umbrella types and three collection types.

Object Type Declarations and Features

Object types are declared with the flavor of the object type (`enum`, `struct`, or `class`), the name of the object type (which should start with a capital letter), and curly braces:

```
class Manny {
}
struct Moe {
}
enum Jack {
}
```

An object type declaration can appear anywhere: at the top level of a file, at the top level of another object type declaration, or in the body of a function. The visibility (*scope*), and hence the usability, of this object type by other code depends upon where it appears (see Chapter 1):

- Object types declared at the top level of a file will, by default, be visible to all files in your project (module). This is the usual place for object type declarations.
- Sometimes it's useful to declare a type inside the declaration of another type, thus giving it a namespace. This is called a *nested type*.

- An object type declared within the body of a function will exist only inside the scope of the curly braces that surround it; such declarations are legal but rare.

Declarations for any object type may contain within their curly braces the following things:

Initializers

An object type is merely the *type* of an object. The purpose of declaring an object type will usually (though not always) be so that you can make an actual object — an *instance* — that *has* this type. An initializer is a special function, declared and called in a special way, allowing you to do that.

Properties

A variable declared at the top level of an object type declaration is a *property*. By default, it is an *instance property*. An instance property is scoped to an instance: it is accessed through a particular instance of this type, and its value can be different for every instance of this type.

Alternatively, a property can be a *static/class property*. For an enum or struct, it is declared with the keyword `static`; for a class, it may instead be declared with the keyword `class`. Such a property belongs to the object type itself: it is accessed through the type, and it has just one value, associated with the type.

Methods

A function declared at the top level of an object type declaration is a *method*. By default, it is an *instance method*: it is called by sending a message to a particular instance of this type. Inside an instance method, `self` is the instance.

Alternatively, a function can be a *static/class method*. For an enum or struct, it is declared with the keyword `static`; for a class, it may be declared instead with the keyword `class`. It is called by sending a message to the type. Inside a static/class method, `self` is the type.

Subscripts

A subscript is a special kind of instance method. It is called by appending square brackets to an instance reference.

Object type declarations

An object type declaration can contain an object type declaration — a nested type. From inside the containing object type, the nested type is in scope; from outside the containing object type, the nested type must be referred to through the containing object type. Thus, the containing object type is a namespace for the nested type.

Initializers

An *initializer* is a function called in order to bring an instance of an object type into existence. Strictly speaking, it is a static/class method, because it is called by talking to the object type. It is usually called using special syntax: the name of the type is followed directly by parentheses, as if the type itself were a function. When an initializer is called, a new instance is created and returned as a result. You will usually do something with the returned instance, such as assigning it to a variable, in order to preserve it and work with it in subsequent code.

For example, suppose we have a Dog class:

```
class Dog {
}
```

Then we can make a Dog instance like this:

```
Dog()
```

That code, however, though legal, is silly — so silly that it warrants a warning from the compiler. We have created a Dog instance, but there is no reference to that instance. Without such a reference, the Dog instance comes into existence and then immediately vanishes in a puff of smoke. The usual sort of thing is more like this:

```
let fido = Dog()
```

Now our Dog instance will persist as long as the variable `fido` persists (see Chapter 3) — and the variable `fido` gives us a reference to our Dog instance, so that we can use it.

Observe that `Dog()` calls an initializer even though our Dog class doesn't declare any initializers! The reason is that object types may have *implicit initializers*. These are a convenience that save you from the trouble of writing your own initializers. But you *can* write your own initializers, and you will often do so.

An initializer is kind of function, and its declaration syntax is rather like that of a function. To declare an initializer, you use the keyword `init` followed by a parameter list, followed by curly braces containing the code. An object type can have multiple initializers, distinguished by their parameters. The parameter names, *including the first parameter*, are externalized by default (though of course you can prevent this by putting an underscore before a parameter name). A frequent use of the parameters is to set the values of instance properties.

For example, here's a Dog class with two instance properties, `name` (a String) and `license` (an Int). We give these instance properties default values that are effectively placeholders — an empty string and the number zero. Then we declare three initializers, so that the caller can create a Dog instance in three different ways: by supplying a name, by supplying a license number, or by supplying both. In each initializer, the parameters supplied are used to set the values of the corresponding properties:

```
class Dog {
    var name = ""
    var license = 0
    init(name:String) {
        self.name = name
    }
    init(license:Int) {
        self.license = license
    }
    init(name:String, license:Int) {
        self.name = name
        self.license = license
    }
}
```

Observe that in that code, in each initializer, I've given each parameter the same name as the property to which it corresponds. There's no reason to do that apart from stylistic clarity. In the code for each initializer, I can distinguish the parameter from the property by using self to access the property.

The result of that declaration is that I can create a Dog in three different ways:

```
let fido = Dog(name:"Fido")
let rover = Dog(license:1234)
let spot = Dog(name:"Spot", license:1357)
```

What I *can't* do is to create a Dog with *no* initializer parameters. I wrote initializers, so my implicit initializer went away. This code is no longer legal:

```
let puff = Dog() // compile error
```

Of course, I could *make* that code legal by explicitly declaring an initializer with no parameters:

```
class Dog {
    var name = ""
    var license = 0
    init() {
    }
    init(name:String) {
        self.name = name
    }
    init(license:Int) {
        self.license = license
    }
    init(name:String, license:Int) {
        self.name = name
        self.license = license
    }
}
```

Now, the truth is that we don't need those four initializers, because an initializer is a function, and a function's parameters can have default values. Thus, I can condense all that code into a single initializer, like this:

```
class Dog {
    var name = ""
    var license = 0
    init(name:String = "", license:Int = 0) {
        self.name = name
        self.license = license
    }
}
```

I can still make an actual Dog instance in four different ways:

```
let fido = Dog(name:"Fido")
let rover = Dog(license:1234)
let spot = Dog(name:"Spot", license:1357)
let puff = Dog()
```

Now comes the really interesting part. In my property declarations, I can *eliminate* the assignment of default initial values (as long as I declare explicitly the *type* of each property):

```
class Dog {
    var name : String // no default value!
    var license : Int // no default value!
    init(name:String = "", license:Int = 0) {
        self.name = name
        self.license = license
    }
}
```

That code is legal (and common) — because an initializer initializes! In other words, I don't have to give my properties initial values in their declarations, *provided I give them initial values in all initializers.* That way, I am guaranteed that all my instance properties have values when the instance comes into existence, which is what matters. Conversely, an instance property without an initial value when the instance comes into existence *is illegal.* A property *must* be initialized either as part of its declaration or by every initializer, and the compiler will stop you otherwise.

The Swift compiler's insistence that all instance properties be properly initialized is a valuable feature of Swift. (Contrast Objective-C, where instance properties can go uninitialized — and often do, leading to mysterious errors later.) Don't fight the compiler; work with it. The compiler will help you by giving you an error message ("Return from initializer without initializing all stored properties") until *all* your initializers initialize *all* your instance properties:

```
class Dog {
    var name : String
    var license : Int
    init(name:String = "") {
        self.name = name // compile error
    }
}
```

Because setting an instance property in an initializer counts as initialization, it is legal even if the instance property is a constant declared with let:

```
class Dog {
    let name : String
    let license : Int
    init(name:String = "", license:Int = 0) {
        self.name = name
        self.license = license
    }
}
```

In our artificial examples, we have been very generous with our initializer: we are letting the caller instantiate a Dog without supplying a name argument or a license argument. Usually, however, the purpose of an initializer is just the opposite: we want to *force* the caller to supply *all* needed information at instantiation time. Thus, in real life, it is much more likely that our Dog class would look like this:

```
class Dog {
    let name : String
    let license : Int
    init(name:String, license:Int) {
        self.name = name
        self.license = license
    }
}
```

In that code, our Dog has a name and a license, and values for these *must* be supplied at instantiation time (there are no default values), and those values can never be changed thereafter (these properties are constants). In this way, we enforce a rule that every Dog must have a meaningful name and license. There is now only *one* way to make a Dog:

```
let spot = Dog(name:"Spot", license:1357)
```

Optional properties

Sometimes, there is no meaningful default value that can be assigned to an instance property during initialization. For example, perhaps the initial value of this property will not be obtained until some time has elapsed *after* this instance has come into existence. This situation conflicts with the requirement that all instance properties be initialized either in their declaration or through an initializer. You could, of course, just circumvent the problem by assigning a default initial value anyway; but this fails to communicate to your own code the fact that this isn't a "real" value.

A sensible and common solution, as I explained in Chapter 3, is to declare your instance property as a var having an Optional type. An Optional has a value, namely nil, signifying that no "real" value has been supplied; and an Optional var is initialized to nil automatically. Thus, your code can test this instance property against nil and, if it is nil, it won't use the property. Later, the property will be given its "real" value. Of course, that value is now wrapped in an Optional; but if you declare this property as an implicitly unwrapped Optional, you have the additional advantage of being able to use the wrapped value directly, without explicitly unwrapping it — as if this weren't an Optional at all — once you're sure it is safe to do so:

```
// this property will be set automatically when the nib loads
@IBOutlet var myButton: UIButton!
// this property will be set after time-consuming gathering of data
var albums : [MPMediaItemCollection]!
```

Referring to self

Except in order to set an instance property, an initializer may not refer to self, explicitly or implicitly, until all instance properties have been initialized. This rule guarantees that the instance is fully formed before it is used. This code, for example, is illegal:

```
struct Cat {
    var name : String
    var license : Int
    init(name:String, license:Int) {
        self.name = name
        meow() // too soon - compile error
        self.license = license
    }
    func meow() {
        print("meow")
    }
}
```

The call to the instance method meow is implicitly a reference to self — it means self.meow(). The initializer can say that, but not until it has fulfilled its primary contract of initializing all uninitialized properties. The call to the instance method meow simply needs to be moved down one line, so that it comes *after* both name and license have been initialized.

Delegating initializers

Initializers within an object type can call one another by using the syntax self.init(...). An initializer that calls another initializer is called a *delegating initializer*. When an initializer delegates, the other initializer — the one that it delegates to — must completely initialize the instance first, and then the delegating initializer can work with the fully initialized instance, possibly setting again a var property that was already set by the initializer that it delegated to.

A delegating initializer appears to be an exception to the rule against saying `self` too early. But it isn't, because it is saying `self` in order to delegate — and delegating will cause all instance properties to be initialized. In fact, the rules about a delegating initializer saying `self` are even more stringent: a delegating initializer cannot refer to `self`, *not even* to set a property, until after the call to the other initializer. For example:

```
struct Digit {
    var number : Int
    var meaningOfLife : Bool
    init(number:Int) {
        self.number = number
        self.meaningOfLife = false
    }
    init() { // this is a delegating initializer
        self.init(number:42)
        self.meaningOfLife = true
    }
}
```

Moreover, a delegating initializer cannot set an immutable property (a `let` variable) at all. That is because it cannot refer to the property until after it has called the other initializer, and at that point the instance is fully formed — initialization proper is over, and the door for initialization of immutable properties has closed. Thus, the preceding code would be illegal if `meaningOfLife` were declared with `let`, because the second initializer is a delegating initializer and cannot set an immutable property.

Be careful not to delegate recursively! If you tell an initializer to delegate to itself, or if you create a vicious circle of delegating initializers, the compiler won't stop you (I regard that as a bug), but your running app will hang. For example, don't say this:

```
struct Digit { // do not do this!
    var number : Int = 100
    init(value:Int) {
        self.init(number:value)
    }
    init(number:Int) {
        self.init(value:number)
    }
}
```

Failable initializers

An initializer can return an Optional wrapping the new instance. In this way, `nil` can be returned to signal failure. An initializer that behaves this way is a *failable initializer*. To mark an initializer as failable when declaring it, put a question mark (or, for an implicitly unwrapped Optional, an exclamation mark) after the keyword `init`. If your failable initializer needs to return `nil`, explicitly write `return nil`. It is up to the caller to test the resulting Optional for equivalence with `nil`, unwrap it, and so forth, as with any Optional.

Here's a version of Dog with an initializer that returns an implicitly unwrapped Optional, returning `nil` if the `name:` or `license:` arguments are invalid:

```
class Dog {
    let name : String
    let license : Int
    init!(name:String, license:Int) {
        self.name = name
        self.license = license
        if name.isEmpty {
            return nil
        }
        if license <= 0 {
            return nil
        }
    }
}
```

The resulting value is typed as `Dog!` — the Optional is implicitly unwrapped — so the caller who instantiates a Dog in this way can use the result directly as if it were simply a Dog instance. But if `nil` was returned, any attempt on the caller's part to access members of the Dog instance will result in a crash at runtime:

```
let fido = Dog(name:"", license:0)
let name = fido.name // crash
```

Cocoa and Objective-C conventionally return `nil` from initializers to signal failure; the API for such initializers has been hand-tweaked as a Swift failable initializer if initialization really might fail. For example, the UIImage initializer `init?(named:)` is a failable initializer, because there might be no image with the given name. It is not implicitly unwrapped, so the resulting value is a `UIImage?` and must be unwrapped before you can use it. (Most Objective-C initializers, however, are *not* bridged as failable initializers, even though in theory *any* Objective-C initializer might return `nil`.)

Properties

A *property* is a variable — one that happens to be declared at the top level of an object type declaration. This means that everything said about variables in Chapter 3 applies. A property has a fixed type; it can be declared with `var` or `let`; it can be stored or computed; it can have setter observers. An instance property can also be declared `lazy`.

A stored instance property must be given an initial value. But, as I explained a moment ago, this doesn't have to be through assignment in the declaration; it can be through an initializer instead. Setter observers are not called during initialization of properties.

Code that initializes a property cannot fetch an instance property or call an instance method. Such behavior would require a reference, explicit or implicit, to `self`; and during initialization, there is no `self` yet — `self` is exactly what we are in the process of initializing. Making this mistake can result in some of Swift's most perplexing compile error messages. For example, this is illegal (and removing the explicit references to self doesn't make it legal):

```
class Moi {
    let first = "Matt"
    let last = "Neuburg"
    let whole = self.first + " " + self.last // compile error
}
```

One solution in that situation would be to make whole a computed property:

```
class Moi {
    let first = "Matt"
    let last = "Neuburg"
    var whole : String {
        return self.first + " " + self.last
    }
}
```

That's legal because the computation won't actually be performed until after self exists. Another solution is to declare whole as lazy:

```
class Moi {
    let first = "Matt"
    let last = "Neuburg"
    lazy var whole : String = self.first + " " + self.last
}
```

Again, that's legal because the reference to self won't be performed until after self exists. Similarly, a property initializer can't call an instance method, but a computed property can, and so can a lazy property.

As I demonstrated in Chapter 3, a variable's initializer can consist of multiple lines of code if you write it as a define-and-call anonymous function. If this variable is an instance property, and if that code is to refer to other instance properties or instance methods, the variable must be declared lazy:

```
class Moi {
    let first = "Matt"
    let last = "Neuburg"
    lazy var whole : String = {
        var s = self.first
        s.appendContentsOf(" ")
        s.appendContentsOf(self.last)
        return s
    }()
}
```

If a property is an instance property (the default), it can be accessed only through an instance, and its value is separate for each instance. For example, let's start once again with a Dog class:

```
class Dog {
    let name : String
    let license : Int
    init(name:String, license:Int) {
        self.name = name
        self.license = license
    }
}
```

Our Dog class has a name instance property. Then we can make two different Dog instances with two different name values, and we can access each Dog instance's name through the instance:

```
let fido = Dog(name:"Fido", license:1234)
let spot = Dog(name:"Spot", license:1357)
let aName = fido.name // "Fido"
let anotherName = spot.name // "Spot"
```

A static/class property, on the other hand, is accessed through the type, and is scoped to the type, which usually means that it is global and unique. I'll use a struct as an example:

```
struct Greeting {
    static let friendly = "hello there"
    static let hostile = "go away"
}
```

Now code elsewhere can fetch the values of Greeting.friendly and Greeting.hostile. That example is neither artificial nor trivial; immutable static/class properties are a convenient and effective way to supply your code with nicely name-spaced constants.

Unlike instance properties, static properties can be initialized with reference to one another; the reason is that static property initializers are lazy (see Chapter 3):

```
struct Greeting {
    static let friendly = "hello there"
    static let hostile = "go away"
    static let ambivalent = friendly + " but " + hostile
}
```

Notice the lack of self in that code. In static/class code, self means the type itself. I like to use self explicitly wherever it would be implicit, but here I can't use it without arousing the ire of the compiler (I regard this as a bug). To clarify the status of the terms friendly and hostile, I can use the name of the type, just as any other code would do:

```
struct Greeting {
    static let friendly = "hello there"
    static let hostile = "go away"
    static let ambivalent = Greeting.friendly + " but " + Greeting.hostile
}
```

On the other hand, if I write `ambivalent` as a computed property, I *can* use `self`:

```
struct Greeting {
    static let friendly = "hello there"
    static let hostile = "go away"
    static var ambivalent : String {
        return self.friendly + " but " + self.hostile
    }
}
```

On the other other hand, I'm not allowed to use `self` when the initial value is set by a define-and-call anonymous function (again, I regard this as a bug):

```
struct Greeting {
    static let friendly = "hello there"
    static let hostile = "go away"
    static var ambivalent : String = {
        return self.friendly + " but " + self.hostile // compile error
    }()
}
```

Methods

A *method* is a function — one that happens to be declared at the top level of an object type declaration. This means that everything said about functions in Chapter 2 applies.

By default, a method is an instance method. This means that it can be accessed only through an instance. Within the body of an instance method, `self` is the instance. To illustrate, let's continue to develop our Dog class:

```
class Dog {
    let name : String
    let license : Int
    let whatDogsSay = "Woof"
    init(name:String, license:Int) {
        self.name = name
        self.license = license
    }
    func bark() {
        print(self.whatDogsSay)
    }
    func speak() {
        self.bark()
        print("I'm \(self.name)")
    }
}
```

Now I can make a Dog instance and tell it to speak:

```
let fido = Dog(name:"Fido", license:1234)
fido.speak() // Woof I'm Fido
```

In my Dog class, the speak method calls the instance method bark by way of self, and obtains the value of the instance property name by way of self; and the bark instance method obtains the value of the instance property whatDogsSay by way of self. This is because instance code can use self to refer to this instance. Such code can omit self if the reference is unambiguous; thus, for example, I could have written this:

```
func speak() {
    bark()
    print("I'm \(name)")
}
```

But I *never* write code like that (except by accident). Omitting self, in my view, makes the code harder to read and maintain; the loose terms bark and name seem mysterious and confusing. Moreover, sometimes self cannot be omitted. For example, in my implementation of init(name:license:), I *must* use self to disambiguate between the parameter name and the property self.name.

A static/class method is accessed through the type, and self means the type. I'll use our Greeting struct as an example:

```
struct Greeting {
    static let friendly = "hello there"
    static let hostile = "go away"
    static var ambivalent : String {
        return self.friendly + " but " + self.hostile
    }
    static func beFriendly() {
        print(self.friendly)
    }
}
```

And here's how to call the static beFriendly method:

```
Greeting.beFriendly() // hello there
```

There is a kind of conceptual wall between static/class members, on the one hand, and instance members on the other; even though they may be declared within the same object type declaration, they inhabit different worlds. A static/class method can't refer to "the instance" because there is no instance; thus, a static/class method cannot directly refer to any instance properties or call any instance methods. An instance method, on the other hand, can refer to the type by name, and can thus access static/class properties and can call static/class methods. (I'll talk later in this chapter about another way in which an instance method can refer to the type.)

For example, let's return to our Dog class and grapple with the question of what dogs say. Presume that all dogs say the same thing. We'd prefer, therefore, to express whatDogsSay not at instance level but at class level. This would be a good use of a static property. Here's a simplified Dog class that illustrates:

```
class Dog {
    static var whatDogsSay = "Woof"
    func bark() {
        print(Dog.whatDogsSay)
    }
}
```

Now we can make a Dog instance and tell it to bark:

```
let fido = Dog()
fido.bark() // Woof
```

Subscripts

A *subscript* is an instance method that is called in a special way — by appending square brackets to an instance reference. The square brackets can contain arguments to be passed to the subscript method. You can use this feature for whatever you like, but it is suitable particularly for situations where this is an object type with *elements* that can be appropriately accessed by key or by index number. I have already described (in Chapter 3) the use of this syntax with strings, and it is familiar also from dictionaries and arrays; you can use square brackets with strings and dictionaries and arrays exactly because Swift's String and Dictionary and Array types declare subscript methods.

The syntax for declaring a subscript method is somewhat like a function declaration and somewhat like a computed property declaration. That's no coincidence! A subscript is like a function in that it can take parameters: arguments can appear in the square brackets when a subscript method is called. A subscript is like a computed property in that the call is used like a reference to a property: you can fetch its value or you can assign into it.

To illustrate, I'll write a struct that treats an integer as if it were a string, returning a digit that can be specified by an index number in square brackets; for simplicity, I'm deliberately omitting any sort of error-checking:

```
struct Digit {
    var number : Int
    init(_ n:Int) {
        self.number = n
    }
    subscript(ix:Int) -> Int { ❶ ❷
        get { ❸
            let s = String(self.number)
            return Int(String(s[s.startIndex.advancedBy(ix)]))!
        }
    }
}
```

❶ After the keyword `subscript` we have a parameter list stating what parameters are to appear inside the square brackets; by default, their names are *not* externalized.

❷ Then, after the arrow operator, we have the type of value that is passed out (when the getter is called) or in (when the setter is called); this is parallel to the type declared for a computed property, even though the syntax with the arrow operator is like the syntax for the returned value in a function declaration.

❸ Finally, we have curly braces whose contents are exactly like those of a computed property. You can have `get` and curly braces for the getter, and `set` and curly braces for the setter. If there's a getter and no setter, the word `get` and its curly braces can be omitted. The setter receives the new value as `newValue`, but you can change that name by supplying a different name in parentheses after the word `set`.

Here's an example of calling the getter; the instance with appended square brackets containing the arguments is used just as if you were getting a property value:

```
var d = Digit(1234)
let aDigit = d[1] // 2
```

Now I'll expand my Digit struct so that its subscript method includes a setter (and again I'll omit error-checking):

```
struct Digit {
    var number : Int
    init(_ n:Int) {
        self.number = n
    }
    subscript(ix:Int) -> Int {
        get {
            let s = String(self.number)
            return Int(String(s[s.startIndex.advancedBy(ix)]))!
        }
        set {
            var s = String(self.number)
            let i = s.startIndex.advancedBy(ix)
            s.replaceRange(i...i, with: String(newValue))
            self.number = Int(s)!
        }
    }
}
```

And here's an example of calling the setter; the instance with appended square brackets containing the arguments is used just as if you were setting a property value:

```
var d = Digit(1234)
d[0] = 2 // now d.number is 2234
```

An object type can declare multiple subscript methods, provided their signatures distinguish them as different functions.

Nested Object Types

An object type may be declared inside an object type declaration, forming a nested type:

```
class Dog {
    struct Noise {
        static var noise = "Woof"
    }
    func bark() {
        print(Dog.Noise.noise)
    }
}
```

A nested object type is no different from any other object type, but the rules for referring to it from the outside are changed; the surrounding object type acts as a namespace, and must be referred to explicitly in order to access the nested object type:

```
Dog.Noise.noise = "Arf"
```

The Noise struct is thus namespaced inside the Dog class. This namespacing provides clarity: the name Noise does not float free, but is explicitly associated with the Dog class to which it belongs. Namespacing also allows more than one Noise struct to exist, without any clash of names. Swift built-in object types often take advantage of namespacing; for example, the String struct is one of several structs that contain an Index struct, with no clash of names.

(It is also possible, through Swift's privacy rules, to hide a nested object type, in such a way that it cannot be referenced from the outside at all. This is useful for organization and encapsulation when one object type needs a second object type as a helper, but no *other* object type needs to know about the second object type. Privacy is discussed in Chapter 5.)

Instance References

On the whole, the names of object types will be global, and you will be able to refer to them simply by using their names. Instances, however, are another story. Instances must be deliberately created, one by one. That is what instantiation is for. Once you have created an instance, you can cause that instance to persist, by storing the instance in a variable with sufficient lifetime; using that variable as a reference, you can send instance messages to that instance, accessing instance properties and calling instance methods.

Direct instantiation of an object type is the act of creating a *brand new* instance of that type, *directly, yourself*. It involves *you* calling an initializer. In many cases, though, some *other* object will create or provide the instance for you.

A simple example is what happens when you manipulate a String, like this:

```
let s = "Hello, world"
let s2 = s.uppercaseString
```

In that code, we end up with two String instances. The first one, s, we created using a string literal. The second one, s2, was created for us when we accessed the first string's uppercaseString property. Thus we have two instances, and they will persist independently as long as our references to them persist; but we didn't get either of them by calling an initializer.

In other cases, the instance you are interested in will *already* exist in some persistent fashion; the problem will then be to find a way of *getting a reference* to that instance.

Let's say, for example, that this is a real-life iOS app. You will certainly have a root view controller, which will be an instance of some type of UIViewController. Let's say it's an instance of the ViewController class. Once your app is up and running, this instance already exists. It would then be utterly counterproductive to attempt to speak to the root view controller by *instantiating* the ViewController class:

```
let theVC = ViewController()
```

All that code does is to make a *second, different* instance of the ViewController class, and your messages to that instance will be wasted, as it is not *the particular already existing instance* that you wanted to talk to. That is a very common beginner mistake; don't make it.

Getting a reference to an already existing instance can be, of itself, an interesting problem. Instantiation is definitely not how to do it. But how *do* you do it? Well, it depends. In this particular situation, the goal is to obtain, from any code, a reference to your app's root view controller instance. I'll describe, just for the sake of the example, how you would do it.

Getting a reference always starts with something you already have a reference to. Often, this will be a class. In iOS programming, the app itself is an instance, and there is a class that holds a reference to that instance and will hand it to you whenever you ask for it. That class is the UIApplication class, and the way to get a reference to the app instance is to call its `sharedApplication` class method:

```
let app = UIApplication.sharedApplication()
```

Now we have a reference to the application instance. The application instance has a `keyWindow` property:

```
let window = app.keyWindow
```

Now we have a reference to our app's key window. That window owns the root view controller, and will hand us a reference to it, as its own `rootViewController` property; the app's `keyWindow` is an Optional, so to get at its `rootViewController` we must unwrap the Optional:

```
let vc = window?.rootViewController
```

And voilà, we have a reference to our app's root view controller. To obtain the reference to this persistent instance, we created, in effect, a chain of method calls and properties leading from the known to the unknown, from a globally available class to the particular desired instance:

```
let app = UIApplication.sharedApplication()
let window = app.keyWindow
let vc = window?.rootViewController
```

Clearly, we can write that chain as an actual chain, using repeated dot-notation:

```
let vc = UIApplication.sharedApplication().keyWindow?.rootViewController
```

You don't *have* to chain your instance messages into a single line — chaining through multiple `let` assignments is completely efficient, possibly more legible, and certainly easier to debug — but it's a handy formulaic convenience and is particularly characteristic of dot-notated object-oriented languages like Swift.

The general problem of getting a reference to a particular already existing instance is so interesting and pervasive that I will devote much of Chapter 13 to it.

Enums

An *enum* is an object type whose instances represent *distinct predefined alternative values*. Think of it as a list of known possibilities. An enum is the Swift way to express a set of constants that are alternatives to one another. An enum declaration includes case statements. Each case is the name of one of the alternatives. An instance of an enum will represent exactly one alternative — one case.

For example, in my Albumen app, different instances of the same view controller can list any of four different sorts of music library contents: albums, playlists, podcasts, or audiobooks. The view controller's behavior is slightly different in each case. So I need a sort of four-way switch that I can set once when the view controller is instantiated, saying which sort of contents this view controller is to display. That sounds like an enum!

Here's the basic declaration for that enum; I call it Filter, because each case represents a different way of filtering the contents of the music library:

```
enum Filter {
    case Albums
    case Playlists
    case Podcasts
    case Books
}
```

That enum doesn't have an initializer. You *can* write an initializer for an enum, as I'll demonstrate in a moment; but there is a default mode of initialization that you'll probably use most of the time — the name of the enum followed by dot-notation and one of the cases. For example, here's how to make an instance of Filter representing the Albums case:

```
let type = Filter.Albums
```

As a shortcut, if the type is known in advance, you can omit the name of the enum; the bare case must still be preceded by a dot. For example:

```
let type : Filter = .Albums
```

You can't say `.Albums` just anywhere out of the blue, because Swift doesn't know what enum it belongs to. But in that code, the variable is explicitly declared as a Filter, so Swift knows what `.Albums` means. A similar thing happens when passing an enum instance as an argument in a function call:

```
func filterExpecter(type:Filter) {}
filterExpecter(.Albums)
```

In the second line, I create an instance of Filter and pass it, all in one move, without having to include the name of the enum. That's because Swift knows from the function declaration that a Filter is expected here.

In real life, the space savings when omitting the enum name can be considerable — especially because, when talking to Cocoa, the enum type names are often long. For example:

```
let v = UIView()
v.contentMode = .Center
```

A UIView's `contentMode` property is typed as a UIViewContentMode enum. Our code is neater and simpler because we don't have to include the name UIViewContentMode explicitly here; `.Center` is nicer than `UIViewContentMode.Center`. But either is legal.

Code *inside* an enum declaration can use a case name *without* dot-notation. The enum is a namespace; code inside the declaration is inside the namespace, so it can see the case names directly.

Instances of an enum with the same case are regarded as equal. Thus, you can compare an enum instance for equality against a case. Again, the type of enum is known from the first term in the comparison, so the second term can omit the enum name:

```
func filterExpecter(type:Filter) {
    if type == .Albums {
        print("it's albums")
    }
}
filterExpecter(.Albums) // "it's albums"
```

Case With Fixed Value

Optionally, when you declare an enum, you can add a type declaration. The cases then all carry with them a fixed (constant) value of that type. If the type is an integer numeric type, the values can be implicitly assigned, and will start at zero by default. In this code, `.Mannie` carries a value of 0, `.Moe` carries of a value of 1, and so on:

```
enum PepBoy : Int {
    case Mannie
    case Moe
    case Jack
}
```

If the type is String, the implicitly assigned values are the string equivalents of the case names. In this code, `.Albums` carries a value of `"Albums"`, and so on:

```
enum Filter : String {
    case Albums
    case Playlists
    case Podcasts
    case Books
}
```

Regardless of the type, you can assign values explicitly as part of the case declarations:

```
enum Filter : String {
    case Albums = "Albums"
    case Playlists = "Playlists"
    case Podcasts = "Podcasts"
    case Books = "Audiobooks"
}
```

The types attached to an enum in this way are limited to numbers and strings, and the values assigned must be literals. The values carried by the cases are called their *raw values*. An instance of this enum has just one case, so it has just one fixed raw value, which can be retrieved with its `rawValue` property:

```
let type = Filter.Albums
print(type.rawValue) // Albums
```

Having each case carry a fixed raw value can be quite useful. In my Albumen app, the Filter cases really do have those String values, and so when the view controller wants to know what title string to put at the top of the screen, it simply retrieves the current type's `rawValue`.

The raw value associated with each case must be unique within this enum; the compiler will enforce this rule. Therefore, the mapping works the other way: given a raw value, you can derive the case. For example, you can instantiate an enum that has raw values by using its `rawValue:` initializer:

```
let type = Filter(rawValue:"Albums")
```

However, the attempt to instantiate the enum in this way might fail, because you might supply a raw value corresponding to no case; therefore, this is a failable initializer, and the value returned is an Optional. In that code, `type` is not a Filter; it's an Optional wrapping a Filter. This might not be terribly important, however, because the thing you are most likely to want to do with an enum is to compare it for equality with a case of the enum; you can do that with an Optional without unwrapping it. This code is legal and works correctly:

```
let type = Filter(rawValue:"Albums")
if type == .Albums { // ...
```

Case With Typed Value

The raw values discussed in the preceding section are fixed in advance: a given case carries with it a certain raw value, and that's that. Alternatively, you can construct a case whose constant value can be set *when the instance is created*. To do so, do not declare any type for the enum as a whole; instead, append a tuple type to the name of the case. There will usually be just one type in this tuple, so what you'll write will look like a type name in parentheses. Any type may be declared. Here's an example:

```
enum Error {
    case Number(Int)
    case Message(String)
    case Fatal
}
```

That code means that, at instantiation time, an Error instance with the `.Number` case must be assigned an Int value, an Error instance with the `.Message` case must be assigned a String value, and an Error instance with the `.Fatal` case can't be assigned any value. Instantiation with assignment of a value is really a way of calling an initialization function, so to supply the value, you pass it as an argument in parentheses:

```
let err : Error = .Number(4)
```

The attached value here is called an *associated value*. What you are supplying here is actually a tuple, so it can contain literal values or value references; this is legal:

```
let num = 4
let err : Error = .Number(num)
```

The tuple can contain more than one value, with or without names; if the values have names, they must be used at initialization time:

```
enum Error {
    case Number(Int)
    case Message(String)
    case Fatal(n:Int, s:String)
}
let err : Error = .Fatal(n:-12, s:"Oh the horror")
```

An enum case that declares an associated value is actually an initialization function, so you can capture a reference to that function and call the function later:

```
let fatalMaker = Error.Fatal
let err = fatalMaker(n:-1000, s:"Unbelievably bad error")
```

I'll explain how to *extract* the associated value from an actual instance of such an enum in Chapter 5.

At the risk of sounding like a magician explaining his best trick, I will now reveal how an Optional works. An Optional is simply an enum with two cases: `.None` and `.Some`. If it is `.None`, it carries no associated value, and it equates to `nil`. If it is `.Some`, it carries the wrapped value *as its associated value.*

Enum Initializers

An explicit enum initializer must do what default initialization does: it must return a particular case of this enum. To do so, set `self` to the case. In this example, I'll expand my Filter enum so that it can be initialized with a numeric argument:

```
enum Filter : String {
    case Albums = "Albums"
    case Playlists = "Playlists"
    case Podcasts = "Podcasts"
    case Books = "Audiobooks"
    static var cases : [Filter] = [Albums, Playlists, Podcasts, Books]
    init(_ ix:Int) {
        self = Filter.cases[ix]
    }
}
```

Now there are three ways to make a Filter instance:

```
let type1 = Filter.Albums
let type2 = Filter(rawValue:"Playlists")!
let type3 = Filter(2) // .Podcasts
```

In that example, we'll crash in the third line if the caller passes a number that's out of range (less than 0 or greater than 3). If we want to avoid that, we can make this a failable initializer and return nil if the number is out of range:

```
enum Filter : String {
    case Albums = "Albums"
    case Playlists = "Playlists"
    case Podcasts = "Podcasts"
    case Books = "Audiobooks"
    static var cases : [Filter] = [Albums, Playlists, Podcasts, Books]
    init!(_ ix:Int) {
        if !(0...3).contains(ix) {
            return nil
        }
        self = Filter.cases[ix]
    }
}
```

An enum can have multiple initializers. Enum initializers can delegate to one another by saying self.init(...). The only requirement is that, at some point in the calling chain, self must be set to a case; if that doesn't happen, your enum won't compile.

In this example, I improve my Filter enum so that it can be initialized with a String raw value without having to say rawValue: in the call. To do so, I declare a failable initializer with a string parameter that delegates to the built-in failable rawValue: initializer:

```
enum Filter : String {
    case Albums = "Albums"
    case Playlists = "Playlists"
    case Podcasts = "Podcasts"
    case Books = "Audiobooks"
    static var cases : [Filter] = [Albums, Playlists, Podcasts, Books]
    init!(_ ix:Int) {
        if !(0...3).contains(ix) {
            return nil
        }
```

```
        self = Filter.cases[ix]
    }
    init!(_ rawValue:String) {
        self.init(rawValue:rawValue)
    }
}
```

Now there are four ways to make a Filter instance:

```
let type1 = Filter.Albums
let type2 = Filter(rawValue:"Playlists")
let type3 = Filter(2) // .Podcasts
let type4 = Filter("Playlists")
```

Enum Properties

An enum can have instance properties and static properties, but there's a limitation: an enum instance property can't be a stored property. This makes sense, because if two instances of the same case could have different stored instance property values, they would no longer be equal to one another — which would undermine the nature and purpose of enums.

Computed instance properties are fine, however, and the value of the property can vary by rule in accordance with the case of self. In this example from my real code, I've associated a search function with each case of my Filter enum, suitable for fetching the songs of that type from the music library:

```
enum Filter : String {
    case Albums = "Albums"
    case Playlists = "Playlists"
    case Podcasts = "Podcasts"
    case Books = "Audiobooks"
    var query : MPMediaQuery {
        switch self {
        case .Albums:
            return MPMediaQuery.albumsQuery()
        case .Playlists:
            return MPMediaQuery.playlistsQuery()
        case .Podcasts:
            return MPMediaQuery.podcastsQuery()
        case .Books:
            return MPMediaQuery.audiobooksQuery()
        }
    }
}
```

If an enum instance property is a computed variable with a setter, other code can assign to this property. However, that code's reference to the enum instance must be a variable (var), not a constant (let). If you try to assign to an enum instance property through a let reference, you'll get a compile error.

Enum Methods

An enum can have instance methods (including subscripts) and static methods. Writing an enum method is straightforward. Here's an example from my own code. In a card game, the cards draw themselves as rectangles, ellipses, or diamonds. I've abstracted the drawing code into an enum that draws itself as a rectangle, an ellipse, or a diamond, depending on its case:

```
enum ShapeMaker {
    case Rectangle
    case Ellipse
    case Diamond
    func drawShape (p: CGMutablePath, inRect r : CGRect) -> () {
        switch self {
        case Rectangle:
            CGPathAddRect(p, nil, r)
        case Ellipse:
            CGPathAddEllipseInRect(p, nil, r)
        case Diamond:
            CGPathMoveToPoint(p, nil, r.minX, r.midY)
            CGPathAddLineToPoint(p, nil, r.midX, r.minY)
            CGPathAddLineToPoint(p, nil, r.maxX, r.midY)
            CGPathAddLineToPoint(p, nil, r.midX, r.maxY)
            CGPathCloseSubpath(p)
        }
    }
}
```

An enum instance method that modifies the enum itself must be marked as `mutating`. For example, an enum instance method might assign to an instance property of `self`; even though this is a computed property, such assignment is illegal unless the method is marked as `mutating`. An enum instance method can even change the case of `self`, by assigning to `self`; but again, the method must be marked as `mutating`. The caller of a mutating instance method must have a variable reference to the instance (`var`), not a constant reference (`let`).

In this example, I add an `advance` method to my Filter enum. The idea is that the cases constitute a sequence, and the sequence can cycle. By calling `advance`, I transform a Filter instance into an instance of the next case in the sequence:

```
enum Filter : String {
    case Albums = "Albums"
    case Playlists = "Playlists"
    case Podcasts = "Podcasts"
    case Books = "Audiobooks"
    static var cases : [Filter] = [Albums, Playlists, Podcasts, Books]
    mutating func advance() {
        var ix = Filter.cases.indexOf(self)!
```

```
        ix = (ix + 1) % 4
        self = Filter.cases[ix]
    }
}
```

And here's how to call it:

```
var type = Filter.Books
type.advance() // type is now Filter.Albums
```

(A subscript setter is always considered `mutating` and does not have to be specially marked.)

Why Enums?

An enum is a switch whose states have names. There are many situations where that's a desirable thing. You could implement a multistate value yourself; for example, if there are five possible states, you could use an Int whose values can be 0 through 4. But then you would have to provide a lot of additional overhead — making sure that no other values are used, and interpreting those numeric values correctly. A list of five named cases is much better! Even when there are only *two* states, an enum is often better than, say, a mere Bool, because the enum's states have names. With a Bool, you have to know what `true` and `false` signify in a particular usage; with an enum, the name of the enum and the names of its cases *tell* you its significance. Moreover, you can store extra information in an enum's associated value or raw value; you can't do that with a mere Bool.

For example, in my LinkSame app, the user can play a real game with a timer or a practice game without a timer. At various places in the code, I need to know which type of game this is. The game types are the cases of an enum:

```
enum InterfaceMode : Int {
    case Timed = 0
    case Practice = 1
}
```

The current game type is stored in an instance property `interfaceMode`, whose value is an InterfaceMode. Thus, it's easy to set the game type by case name:

```
// ... initialize new game ...
self.interfaceMode = .Timed
```

And it's easy to examine the game type by case name:

```
// notify of high score only if user is not just practicing
if self.interfaceMode == .Timed { // ...
```

So what are the raw value integers for? That's the really clever part. They correspond to the segment indexes of a UISegmentedControl in the interface! Whenever I change the `interfaceMode` property, a setter observer also selects the corresponding segment of the UISegmentedControl (`self.timedPractice`), simply by fetching the `rawValue` of the current enum case:

```
var interfaceMode : InterfaceMode = .Timed {
    willSet (mode) {
        self.timedPractice?.selectedSegmentIndex = mode.rawValue
    }
}
```

Structs

A *struct* is the Swift object type *par excellence*. An enum, with its fixed set of cases, is a reduced, specialized kind of object. A class, at the other extreme, will often turn out to be overkill; it has some features that a struct lacks, but if you don't need those features, a struct may be preferable.

Of the numerous object types declared in the Swift header, only four are classes (and you are unlikely to encounter any of them consciously). On the contrary, nearly all the built-in object types provided by Swift itself are structs. A String is a struct. An Int is a struct. A Range is a struct. An Array is a struct. And so on. That shows how powerful a struct can be.

Struct Initializers, Properties, and Methods

A struct that doesn't have an explicit initializer and that doesn't *need* an explicit initializer — because it has no stored properties, or because all its stored properties are assigned default values as part of their declaration — automatically gets an implicit initializer with no parameters, `init()`. For example:

```
struct Digit {
    var number = 42
}
```

That struct can be initialized by saying `Digit()`. But if you add any explicit initializers of your own, you lose that implicit initializer:

```
struct Digit {
    var number = 42
    init(number:Int) {
        self.number = number
    }
}
```

Now you can say `Digit(number:42)`, but you can't say `Digit()` any longer. Of course, you can add an explicit initializer that does the same thing:

```
struct Digit {
    var number = 42
    init() {}
    init(number:Int) {
        self.number = number
    }
}
```

Now you can say `Digit()` once again, as well as `Digit(number:42)`.

A struct that has stored properties and that doesn't have an explicit initializer automatically gets an implicit initializer derived from its instance properties. This is called the *memberwise initializer*. For example:

```
struct Digit {
    var number : Int // can use "let" here
}
```

That struct is legal — indeed, it is legal even if the `number` property is declared with `let` instead of `var` — even though it seems we have not fulfilled the contract requiring us to initialize all stored properties in their declaration or in an initializer. The reason is that this struct automatically has a memberwise initializer which *does* initialize all its properties. In this case, the memberwise initializer is called `init(number:)`.

The memberwise initializer exists even for `var` stored properties that are assigned a default value in their declaration; thus, this struct has a memberwise initializer `init(number:)`, in addition to its implicit `init()` initializer:

```
struct Digit {
    var number = 42
}
```

But if you add any explicit initializers of your own, you lose the memberwise initializer (though of course you can write an explicit initializer that does the same thing).

If a struct has any explicit initializers, then they must fulfill the contract that all stored properties must be initialized either by direct initialization in the declaration or by all initializers. If a struct has multiple explicit initializers, they can delegate to one another by saying `self.init(...)`.

A struct can have instance properties and static properties, and they can be stored or computed variables. If other code wants to set a property of a struct instance, its reference to that instance must be a variable (`var`), not a constant (`let`).

A struct can have instance methods (including subscripts) and static methods. If an instance method sets a property, it must be marked as `mutating`, and the caller's reference to the struct instance must be a variable (`var`), not a constant (`let`). A mutating instance method can even replace this instance with another instance, by setting `self` to a different instance of the same struct. (A subscript setter is always considered `mutating` and does not have to be specially marked.)

Struct As Namespace

I very often use a degenerate struct as a handy namespace for constants. I call such a struct "degenerate" because it consists entirely of static members; I don't intend to use this object type to make any instances. Nevertheless, there is absolutely nothing wrong with this use of a struct.

For example, let's say I'm going to be storing user preference information in Cocoa's NSUserDefaults. NSUserDefaults is a kind of dictionary: each item is accessed through a key. The keys are typically strings. A common programmer mistake is to write out these string keys literally every time a key is used; if you then misspell a key name, there's no penalty at compile time, but your code will mysteriously fail to work correctly. The proper approach is to embody these keys as constant strings and use the names of the strings; that way, if you make a mistake typing the name of a string, the compiler can catch you. A struct with static members is a great way to define those constant strings and clump their names into a namespace:

```
struct Default {
    static let Rows = "CardMatrixRows"
    static let Columns = "CardMatrixColumns"
    static let HazyStripy = "HazyStripy"
}
```

That code means that I can now refer to an NSUserDefaults key with a name, such as `Default.HazyStripy`.

If a struct declares static members whose values are instances of the same struct type, you can omit the struct name when supplying a static member where an instance of this struct type is expected — as if the struct were an enum:

```
struct Thing {
    var rawValue : Int = 0
    static var One : Thing = Thing(rawValue:1)
    static var Two : Thing = Thing(rawValue:2)
}
let thing : Thing = .One // no need to say Thing.One here
```

The example is artificial, but the situation is not; many Objective-C enums are bridged to Swift as this kind of struct (and I'll talk about them later in this chapter).

Classes

A *class* is similar to a struct, with the following key differences:

Reference type

Classes are reference types. This means, among other things, that a class instance has two remarkable features that are not true of struct instances or enum instances:

Mutability

A class instance is mutable in place. Even if your reference to an instance of a class is a constant (`let`), you can change the value of an instance property through that reference. An instance method of a class never has to be marked `mutating` (and cannot be).

Multiple references

When a given instance of a class is assigned to multiple variables or passed as argument to a function, you get multiple references to *one and the same object*.

Inheritance

A class can have a superclass. A class that has a superclass is a *subclass* of that superclass. Class types can thus form a hierarchical tree.

In Objective-C, classes are the only object type. Some built-in Swift struct types are magically bridged to Objective-C class types, but your custom struct types don't have that magic. Thus, when programming iOS with Swift, a primary reason for declaring a class, rather than a struct, is as a form of interchange with Objective-C and Cocoa.

Value Types and Reference Types

A major difference between enums and structs, on the one hand, and classes, on the other hand, is that enums and structs are *value types*, whereas classes are *reference types*.

A value type is *not mutable in place*. In practice, this means that you can't change the value of an instance property of a value type. It *looks* like you can do it, but in reality, you can't. For example, consider a struct. A struct is a value type:

```
struct Digit {
    var number : Int
    init(_ n:Int) {
        self.number = n
    }
}
```

Now, it *looks* as if you can change a Digit's `number` property. That, after all, is the whole purpose of declaring that property as a `var`; and Swift's syntax of assignment would certainly lead us to believe that changing a Digit's `number` is possible:

```
var d = Digit(123)
d.number = 42
```

But in reality, in that code, we are *not* changing the number property of *this* Digit instance; we are, in fact, making a *different* Digit instance and replacing the first one. To see that this is true, add a setter observer:

```
var d : Digit = Digit(123) {
    didSet {
        print("d was set")
    }
}
d.number = 42 // "d was set"
```

In general, then, when you change an instance value type, you are actually *replacing* that instance with another instance. That explains why it is impossible to mutate a value type instance if the reference to that instance is declared with let. As you know, an initialized variable declared with let cannot be assigned to. If that variable refers to a value type instance, and that value type instance has a property, and we try to assign to that property, even if the property is declared with var, the compiler will stop us:

```
struct Digit {
    var number : Int
    init(_ n:Int) {
        self.number = n
    }
}
let d = Digit(123)
d.number = 42 // compile error
```

The reason is that this change would require us to replace the Digit instance inside the d shoebox. But we *can't* replace the Digit instance pointed to by d with another Digit instance, because that would mean assigning into d — which the let declaration forbids.

That, in turn, is why an instance method of a struct or enum that sets a property of the instance must be marked explicitly with the mutating keyword. For example:

```
struct Digit {
    var number : Int
    init(_ n:Int) {
        self.number = n
    }
    mutating func changeNumberTo(n:Int) {
        self.number = n
    }
}
```

Without the mutating keyword, that code won't compile. The mutating keyword assures the compiler that you understand what's really happening here: if that method is called, it replaces the instance. The result is that this method can be called only on a reference declared with var, not let:

```
let d = Digit(123)
d.changeNumberTo(42) // compile error
```

None of what I've just said, however, applies to class instances! Class instances are reference types, not value types. An instance property of a class, to be settable, must be declared with var, obviously; but the reference to a class instance does *not* have to be declared with var in order to set that property through that reference:

```
class Dog {
    var name : String = "Fido"
}
let rover = Dog()
rover.name = "Rover" // fine
```

In the last line of that code, the class instance pointed to by rover is being *mutated in place.* No implicit assignment to rover is involved, and so the let declaration is powerless to prevent the mutation. A setter observer on a Dog variable is *not* called when a property is set:

```
var rover : Dog = Dog() {
    didSet {
        print("did set rover")
    }
}
rover.name = "Rover" // nothing in console
```

The setter observer would be called if we were to set rover explicitly (to another Dog instance), but it is not called merely because we change a property of the Dog instance already pointed to by rover.

Those examples involve a declared variable reference. Exactly the same difference between a value type and a reference type may be seen with a parameter of a function call. The compiler will stop us in our tracks if we try to assign into an enum parameter's instance property or a struct parameter's instance property. This doesn't compile:

```
func digitChanger(d:Digit) {
    d.number = 42 // compile error
}
```

To make that code compile, we must declare the parameter with var:

```
func digitChanger(var d:Digit) {
    d.number = 42
}
```

But this compiles even without the var declaration:

```
func dogChanger(d:Dog) {
    d.name = "Rover"
}
```

The underlying reason for these differences between value types and reference types is that, with a reference type, there is in effect a concealed level of indirection between your reference to the instance and the instance itself; the reference actually refers to a *pointer* to the instance. This, in turn, has another important implication: it means that when a class instance is assigned to a variable or passed as an argument to a function, you can wind up with *multiple references to the same object*. That is not true of structs and enums. When an enum instance or a struct instance is assigned to a variable, or passed to or from a function, what is assigned or passed is essentially a *new copy* of that instance. But when a class instance is assigned to a variable, or passed to or from a function, what is assigned or passed is a reference to the *same* instance.

To prove it, I'll assign one reference to another and then mutate the second reference — and then I'll examine what happened to the first reference. Let's start with the struct:

```
var d = Digit(123)
print(d.number) // 123
var d2 = d // assignment!
d2.number = 42
print(d.number) // 123
```

In that code, we changed the `number` property of d2, a struct instance; but nothing happened to the `number` property of d. Now let's try the class:

```
var fido = Dog()
print(fido.name) // Fido
var rover = fido // assignment!
rover.name = "Rover"
print(fido.name) // Rover
```

In that code, we changed the `name` property of `rover`, a class instance — and the `name` property of `fido` was changed as well! That's because, after the assignment in the third line, `fido` and `rover` refer to *one and the same instance*. When an enum or struct instance is assigned, it is effectively *copied*; a fresh, separate instance is created. But when a class instance is assigned, you get a new reference to the *same* instance.

The same thing is true of parameter passing. Let's start with the struct:

```
func digitChanger(var d:Digit) {
    d.number = 42
}
var d = Digit(123)
print(d.number) // 123
digitChanger(d)
print(d.number) // 123
```

We passed our Digit struct instance d to the function `digitChanger`, which set the `number` property of its local parameter d to 42. Nevertheless, the `number` property of *our* Digit d remains 123. That's because the Digit that arrives inside `digitChanger` is quite literally *a different Digit*. The act of passing a Digit as a function argument creates a *separate copy*. But with a class instance, what is passed is a reference to the *same* instance:

```
func dogChanger(d:Dog) { // no "var" needed
    d.name = "Rover"
}
var fido = Dog()
print(fido.name) // "Fido"
dogChanger(fido)
print(fido.name) // "Rover"
```

The change made to d inside the function dogChanger affected *our* Dog instance fido! Handing a class instance to a function does *not* copy that instance; it is more like *lending* that instance to the function.

The ability to generate multiple references to the same instance is significant particularly in a world of object-based programming, where objects persist and can have properties that persist along with them. If object A and object B are both long-lived objects, and if they both have a Dog property (where Dog is a class), and if they have each been handed a reference to one and the same Dog instance, then either object A or object B can mutate its Dog, and this mutation will affect the other's Dog. You can thus be holding on to an object, only to discover that it has been mutated by someone else behind your back. The problem is even more acute in a multithreaded app, where one and the same object can be mutated differently, in place, by two different threads. None of these issues arise with a value type; this difference can, indeed, be an important reason for preferring a struct to a class when you're designing an object type.

The fact that class instances are reference types can thus be bad. But it is also good! It's good because it means that passing a class instance is simple: all you're doing is passing a pointer. No matter how big and complicated a class instance may be, no matter how many properties it may have containing vast amounts of data, passing the instance is incredibly fast and efficient, because no new data is generated. Moreover, the extended lifetime of a class instance, as it passed around, can be crucial to its functionality and its integrity; a UIViewController needs to be a class, not a struct, because an individual UIViewController instance, no matter how it gets passed around, must continue to represent the same single real and persistent view controller in your running app's view controller hierarchy.

Subclass and Superclass

Two classes can be *subclass* and *superclass* of one another. For example, we might have a class Quadruped and a class Dog and make Quadruped the superclass of Dog. A class may have many subclasses, but a class can have only one immediate superclass. I say "immediate" because that superclass might itself have a superclass, and so on in a rising chain, until we get to the ultimate superclass, called the *base class*, or *root class*. Because a class can have many subclasses but only one superclass, there is a hierarchical tree of subclasses, each branching from its superclass, and so on, with a single class, the base class, at the top.

Another consequence of the difference between value types and reference types is that a value type cannot be structurally recursive: an instance property of a value type cannot be an instance of the same type. This code won't compile:

```
struct Dog { // compile error
    var puppy : Dog?
}
```

More complex circular chains, such as a Dog with a Puppy property and a Puppy with a Dog property, are similarly illegal. But if Dog is a class instead of a struct, there's no error. This is a consequence of the nature of memory management of value types as opposed to reference types. (I'll talk more about reference type memory management in Chapter 5, and Chapter 12 will be entirely devoted to it.)

In Swift 2.0 an enum case's associated value can be an instance of that enum, provided the case (or the entire enum) is marked indirect:

```
enum Node {
    case None(Int)
    indirect case Left(Int, Node)
    indirect case Right(Int, Node)
    indirect case Both(Int, Node, Node)
}
```

As far as the Swift language itself is concerned, there is no requirement that a class should have any superclass, or, if it does have a superclass, that it should ultimately be descended from any particular base class. Thus, a Swift program can have many classes that have no superclass, and it can have many independent hierarchical subclass trees, each descended from a different base class.

Cocoa, however, doesn't work that way. In Cocoa, there is effectively just one base class — NSObject, which embodies all the functionality necessary for a class to *be* a class in the first place — and all other classes are subclasses, at some level, of that one base class. Cocoa thus consists of one huge tree of hierarchically arranged classes, even before you write a single line of code or create any classes of your own. We can imagine diagramming this tree as an outline. And in fact Xcode will *show* you this outline (Figure 4-1): in an iOS project window, choose View → Navigators → Show Symbol Navigator and click Hierarchical, with the first and third icons in the filter bar selected (blue). The Cocoa classes are the part of the tree descending from NSObject.

The reason for having a superclass–subclass relationship in the first place is to allow related classes to *share functionality*. Suppose, for example, we have a Dog class and a Cat class, and we are considering declaring a walk method for both of them. We might reason that both a dog and a cat walk in pretty much the same way, by virtue of both

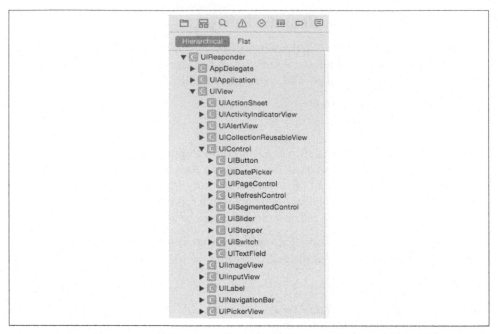

Figure 4-1. Part of the Cocoa class hierarchy as shown in Xcode

being quadrupeds. So it might make sense to declare walk as a method of the Quadruped class, and make both Dog and Cat subclasses of Quadruped. The result is that both Dog and Cat can be sent the walk message, even if neither of them has a walk method, because each of them has a superclass that *does* have a walk method. We say that a subclass *inherits* the methods of its superclass.

To declare that a certain class is a subclass of a certain superclass, add a colon and the superclass name after the class's name in its declaration. So, for example:

```
class Quadruped {
    func walk () {
        print("walk walk walk")
    }
}
class Dog : Quadruped {}
class Cat : Quadruped {}
```

Now let's prove that Dog has indeed inherited walk from Quadruped:

```
let fido = Dog()
fido.walk() // walk walk walk
```

Observe that, in that code, the `walk` message can be sent to a Dog instance just as if the `walk` instance method were declared in the Dog class, even though the `walk` instance method is in fact declared in a superclass of Dog. That's inheritance at work.

The purpose of subclassing is not *merely* so that a class can inherit another class's methods; it's so that it can also declare methods *of its own*. Typically, a subclass consists of the methods inherited from its superclass *and then some*. If Dog has no methods of its own, after all, it's hard to see why it should exist separately from Quadruped. But if a Dog knows how to do something that not every Quadruped knows how to do — let's say, bark — then it makes sense as a separate class. If we declare bark in the Dog class, and `walk` in the Quadruped class, and make Dog a subclass of Quadruped, then Dog inherits the ability to walk from the Quadruped class *and also* knows how to bark:

```
class Quadruped {
    func walk () {
        print("walk walk walk")
    }
}
class Dog : Quadruped {
    func bark () {
        print("woof")
    }
}
```

Again, let's prove that it works:

```
let fido = Dog()
fido.walk() // walk walk walk
fido.bark() // woof
```

Within a class, it is a matter of indifference whether that class has an instance method because that method is declared in that class or because the method is declared in a superclass and inherited. A message to `self` works equally well either way. In this code, we have declared a `barkAndWalk` instance method that sends two messages to `self`, without regard to where the corresponding methods are declared (one is native to the subclass, one is inherited from the superclass):

```
class Quadruped {
    func walk () {
        print("walk walk walk")
    }
}
class Dog : Quadruped {
    func bark () {
        print("woof")
    }
    func barkAndWalk() {
```

```
        self.bark()
        self.walk()
    }
}
```

And here's proof that it works:

```
let fido = Dog()
fido.barkAndWalk() // woof walk walk walk
```

It is also permitted for a subclass to *redefine* a method inherited from its superclass. For example, perhaps some dogs bark differently from other dogs. We might have a class NoisyDog, for instance, that is a subclass of Dog. Dog declares bark, but NoisyDog also declares bark, and defines it differently from how Dog defines it. This is called *overriding*. The very natural rule is that if a subclass overrides a method inherited from its superclass, then when the corresponding message is sent to an instance of that subclass, it is the subclass's version of that method that is called.

In Swift, when you override something inherited from a superclass, you must explicitly acknowledge this fact by preceding its declaration with the keyword override. So, for example:

```
class Quadruped {
    func walk () {
        print("walk walk walk")
    }
}
class Dog : Quadruped {
    func bark () {
        print("woof")
    }
}
class NoisyDog : Dog {
    override func bark () {
        print("woof woof woof")
    }
}
```

And let's try it:

```
let fido = Dog()
fido.bark() // woof
let rover = NoisyDog()
rover.bark() // woof woof woof
```

Observe that a subclass function by the same *name* as a superclass's function is not necessarily, of itself, an override. Recall that Swift can distinguish two functions with the same name, provided they have different *signatures*. Those are different functions, and so an implementation of one in a subclass is not an override of the other in a superclass. An override situation exists only when the subclass redefines the *same* function that it inherits from a superclass — using the same name, including the external parameter names, and the same signature.

It often happens that we want to override something in a subclass and yet access the thing overridden in the superclass. This is done by sending a message to the keyword super. Our bark implementation in NoisyDog is a case in point. What NoisyDog really does when it barks is the same thing Dog does when *it* barks, but more times. We'd like to express that relationship in our implementation of NoisyDog's bark. To do so, we have NoisyDog's bark implementation send the bark message, not to self (which would be circular), but to super; this causes the search for a bark instance method implementation to start in the superclass rather than in our own class:

```
class Dog : Quadruped {
    func bark () {
        print("woof")
    }
}
class NoisyDog : Dog {
    override func bark () {
        for _ in 1...3 {
            super.bark()
        }
    }
}
```

And it works:

```
let fido = Dog()
fido.bark() // woof
let rover = NoisyDog()
rover.bark() // woof woof woof
```

A subscript function is a method. If a superclass declares a subscript, the subclass can declare a subscript with the same signature, provided it designates it with the override keyword. To call the superclass subscript implementation, the subclass can use square brackets after the keyword super (e.g. super[3]).

Along with methods, a subclass also inherits its superclass's properties. Naturally, the subclass may also declare additional properties of its own. It is possible to override an inherited property (with some restrictions that I'll talk about later).

A class declaration can prevent the class from being subclassed by preceding the class declaration with the final keyword. A class declaration can prevent a class member from being overridden by a subclass by preceding the member's declaration with the final keyword.

Class Initializers

Initialization of a class instance is considerably more complicated than initialization of a struct or enum instance, because of the existence of class inheritance. The chief task of an initializer is to ensure that all properties have an initial value, thus making the instance well-formed as it comes into existence; and an initializer may have other tasks to perform that are essential to the initial state and integrity of this instance. A class, however, may have a superclass, which may have properties and initializers of its own. Thus we must somehow ensure that when a subclass is initialized, its superclass's properties are initialized and the tasks of its initializers are performed in good order, in addition to initializing the properties and performing the initializer tasks of the subclass itself.

Swift solves this problem coherently and reliably — and ingeniously — by enforcing some clear and well-defined rules about what a class initializer must do.

Kinds of class initializer

The rules begin with a distinction between the kinds of initializer that a class can have:

Implicit initializer
> A class with no stored properties, or with stored properties all of which are initialized as part of their declaration, and that has *no* explicit initializers, has an *implicit* initializer `init()`.

Designated initializer
> A class initializer, by default, is a *designated* initializer. A class with any stored properties that are *not* initialized as part of their declaration *must* have at least one designated initializer, and when the class is instantiated, exactly one of its designated initializers must be called, and must see to it that all stored properties are initialized. A designated initializer may *not* delegate to another initializer in the same class; it is *illegal* for a designated initializer to use the phrase `self.init(...)`.

Convenience initializer
> A *convenience* initializer is marked with the keyword `convenience`. It is a delegating initializer; it *must* contain the phrase `self.init(...)`. Moreover, a convenience initializer must delegate to a designated initializer: when it says `self.init(...)`, it must call a designated initializer in the same class — or else it must call another convenience initializer in the same class, thus forming a chain of convenience initializers which ends by calling a designated initializer in the same class.

Here are some examples. This class has no stored properties, so it has an implicit `init()` initializer:

```
class Dog {
}
let d = Dog()
```

This class's stored properties have default values, so it has an implicit `init()` initializer too:

```
class Dog {
    var name = "Fido"
}
let d = Dog()
```

This class has stored properties without default values; it has a designated initializer, and all of those properties are initialized in that designated initializer:

```
class Dog {
    var name : String
    var license : Int
    init(name:String, license:Int) {
        self.name = name
        self.license = license
    }
}
let d = Dog(name:"Rover", license:42)
```

This class is similar to the previous example, but it also has two convenience initializers. The caller doesn't have to supply any parameters, because a convenience initializer with no parameters calls through a chain of convenience initializers ending with a designated initializer:

```
class Dog {
    var name : String
    var license : Int
    init(name:String, license:Int) {
        self.name = name
        self.license = license
    }
    convenience init(license:Int) {
        self.init(name:"Fido", license:license)
    }
    convenience init() {
        self.init(license:1)
    }
}
let d = Dog()
```

Note that the rules about what else an initializer can say and when it can say it, as I described them earlier in this chapter, are still in force. A designated initializer cannot, except in order to initialize a property, say `self` until *all* of this class's properties have been initialized. A convenience initializer is a delegating initializer, so it cannot say `self` until after it has called, directly or indirectly, a designated initializer (and cannot set an immutable property at all).

Subclass initializers

Having defined and distinguished between designated initializers and convenience initializers, we are ready for the rules about what happens with regard to initializers when a class is itself a subclass of some other class:

No declared initializers
> If a subclass doesn't have to have any initializers of its own, and if it declares no initializers of its own, then its initializers consist of the initializers inherited from its superclass.

Convenience initializers only
> If a subclass doesn't have to have any initializers of its own, it is eligible to declare convenience initializers, and these work exactly as convenience initializers always do, because inheritance supplies `self` with the designated initializers that the convenience initializers must call.

Designated initializers
> If a subclass declares any designated initializers of its own, the entire game changes drastically. Now, no initializers are inherited! The existence of an explicit designated initializer *blocks initializer inheritance*. The only initializers the subclass now has are the initializers that you explicitly write. (However, there's an exception, which I'll come to in a moment.)

Every designated initializer in the subclass now has an extra requirement: it must call one of the *superclass's designated initializers*, by saying `super.init(...)`. Moreover, the rules about saying `self` continue to apply. A subclass designated initializer must do things in this order:

1. It must ensure that all properties of *this* class (the subclass) are initialized.
2. It must call `super.init(...)`, and the initializer that it calls must be a designated initializer.
3. Only then may this initializer say `self` for any other reason — to call an instance method, say, or to access an inherited property.

Convenience initializers in the subclass are still subject to the rules I've already outlined. They must call `self.init(...)`, calling a designated initializer directly or (through a chain of convenience initializers) indirectly. In the absence of inherited initializers, the initializer that a convenience initializer calls must be explicitly present in the subclass.

If a designated initializer doesn't call `super.init(...)`, then `super.init()` is called implicitly if possible. This code is legal:

```
class Cat {
}
class NamedCat : Cat {
    let name : String
    init(name:String) {
        self.name = name
    }
}
```

In my view, this feature of Swift is a mistake: Swift should not indulge in secret behavior, even if that behavior might be considered "helpful." I believe that that code should not compile; a designated initializer should *always* have to call `super.init(...)` explicitly.

Override initializers

Superclass initializers can be overridden in the subclass, in accordance with these restrictions:

- An initializer whose signature matches a convenience initializer of the superclass must be a convenience initializer and is not marked `override`.

- An initializer whose signature matches a designated initializer of the superclass can be a designated initializer or a convenience initializer, and must be marked `override`. The superclass designated initializer that an override designated initializer calls with `super.init(...)` can be the one that it overrides.

Generally, if a subclass has *any* designated initializers, *no* initializers are inherited. But if a subclass overrides *all* of its superclass's *designated* initializers, then the subclass *does* inherit the superclass's *convenience* initializers.

Failable initializers

A failable designated initializer cannot say `return nil` until after it has completed all of its own initialization duties. Thus, for example, a failable subclass designated initializer must see to it that all the subclass's properties are initialized and must call `super.init(...)` before it can say `return nil`. (There is a certain delicious irony here: before it can tear the instance down, the initializer must finish building the instance up. But this is necessary in order to ensure that the superclass is given a coherent opportunity to do its own initialization.)

If an initializer called by a failable initializer is failable, the calling syntax does not change, and no additional test is needed — if a called failable initializer fails, the whole initialization process will fail (and will be aborted) immediately.

A failable initializer that returns an implicitly unwrapped Optional (`init!`) is treated just like a normal initializer (`init`) for purposes of overriding and delegation.

For a failable initializer that returns an ordinary Optional (init?), there are some additional restrictions:

- init can override init?, but not *vice versa*.
- init? can call init.
- init can call init? by saying init and unwrapping the result (with an exclamation mark, because if the init? fails, you'll crash).

Here's a meaningless example, just to show the legal syntax:

```
class A:NSObject {
    init?(ok:Bool) {
        super.init()          // init? can call init
    }
}
class B:A {
    override init(ok:Bool) { // init can override init?
        super.init(ok:ok)!   // init can call init? using "!"
    }
}
```

 At no time can a subclass initializer set a constant (let) property of a superclass. This is because, by the time the subclass is allowed to do anything other than initialize its own properties and call another initializer, the superclass has finished its own initialization and the door for initializing its constants has closed.

Here are some basic examples. We start with a class whose subclass has no explicit initializers of its own:

```
class Dog {
    var name : String
    var license : Int
    init(name:String, license:Int) {
        self.name = name
        self.license = license
    }
    convenience init(license:Int) {
        self.init(name:"Fido", license:license)
    }
}
class NoisyDog : Dog {
}
```

Given that code, you can make a NoisyDog like this:

```
let nd1 = NoisyDog(name:"Fido", license:1)
let nd2 = NoisyDog(license:2)
```

That code is legal, because NoisyDog inherits its superclass's initializers. However, you can't make a NoisyDog like this:

```
let nd3 = NoisyDog() // compile error
```

That code is illegal. Even though a NoisyDog has no properties of its own, it has no implicit init() initializer; its initializers are its inherited initializers, and its superclass, Dog, has no implicit init() initializer to inherit.

Now here is a class whose subclass's only explicit initializer is a convenience initializer:

```
class Dog {
    var name : String
    var license : Int
    init(name:String, license:Int) {
        self.name = name
        self.license = license
    }
    convenience init(license:Int) {
        self.init(name:"Fido", license:license)
    }
}
class NoisyDog : Dog {
    convenience init(name:String) {
        self.init(name:name, license:1)
    }
}
```

Observe how NoisyDog's convenience initializer fulfills its contract by calling self.init(...) to call a designated initializer — which it happens to have inherited. Given that code, there are three ways to make a NoisyDog, just as you would expect:

```
let nd1 = NoisyDog(name:"Fido", license:1)
let nd2 = NoisyDog(license:2)
let nd3 = NoisyDog(name:"Rover")
```

Next, here is a class whose subclass declares a designated initializer:

```
class Dog {
    var name : String
    var license : Int
    init(name:String, license:Int) {
        self.name = name
        self.license = license
    }
    convenience init(license:Int) {
        self.init(name:"Fido", license:license)
    }
}
class NoisyDog : Dog {
```

```
    init(name:String) {
        super.init(name:name, license:1)
    }
}
```

NoisyDog's explicit initializer is now a designated initializer. It fulfills its contract by calling a designated initializer in super. NoisyDog has now *cut off inheritance* of all initializers; the *only* way to make a NoisyDog is like this:

```
let nd1 = NoisyDog(name:"Rover")
```

Finally, here is a class whose subclass overrides its designated initializers:

```
class Dog {
    var name : String
    var license : Int
    init(name:String, license:Int) {
        self.name = name
        self.license = license
    }
    convenience init(license:Int) {
        self.init(name:"Fido", license:license)
    }
}
class NoisyDog : Dog {
    override init(name:String, license:Int) {
        super.init(name:name, license:license)
    }
}
```

NoisyDog has overridden *all* of its superclass's designated initializers, so it inherits its superclass's convenience initializers. There are thus two ways to make a NoisyDog:

```
let nd1 = NoisyDog(name:"Rover", license:1)
let nd2 = NoisyDog(license:2)
```

Those examples illustrate the main rules that you should keep in your head. You probably don't need to memorize the remaining rules, because the compiler will enforce them, and will keep slapping you down until you get them right.

Required initializers

There's one more thing to know about class initializers: a class initializer may be preceded by the keyword `required`. This means that a subclass may not lack it. This, in turn, means that if a subclass implements designated initializers, thus blocking inheritance, it *must* override this initializer. Here's a (rather pointless) example:

```
class Dog {
    var name : String
    required init(name:String) {
        self.name = name
    }
}
```

```
class NoisyDog : Dog {
    var obedient = false
    init(obedient:Bool) {
        self.obedient = obedient
        super.init(name:"Fido")
    }
} // compile error
```

That code won't compile. `init(name:)` is marked `required`; thus, our code won't compile unless we inherit or override `init(name:)` in NoisyDog. But we cannot inherit it, because, by implementing the NoisyDog designated initializer `init(obedient:)`, we have blocked inheritance. Therefore we must override it:

```
class Dog {
    var name : String
    required init(name:String) {
        self.name = name
    }
}
class NoisyDog : Dog {
    var obedient = false
    init(obedient:Bool) {
        self.obedient = obedient
        super.init(name:"Fido")
    }
    required init(name:String) {
        super.init(name:name)
    }
}
```

Observe that our overridden required intializer is not marked with `override`, but *is* marked with `required`, thus guaranteeing that the requirement continues drilling down to any further subclasses.

I have explained what declaring an initializer as `required` does, but I have not explained *why* you'd need to do it. I'll give examples later in this chapter.

Surprises from Cocoa

The initializer inheritance rules can cause some rude surprises to pop up when you're subclassing one of Cocoa's classes. For example, when programming iOS, you will surely declare a UIViewController subclass. Let's say you give your subclass a designated initializer. A designated initializer in the superclass, UIViewController, is `init(nibName:bundle:)`, so, in obedience to the rules, you call that from your designated initializer:

```
class ViewController: UIViewController {
    init() {
        super.init(nibName:"MyNib", bundle:nil)
    }
}
```

So far, so good; but you are then surprised to find that code elsewhere that makes a ViewController instance no longer compiles:

```
let vc = ViewController(nibName:"MyNib", bundle:nil) // compile error
```

That code was legal until you wrote your designated initializer; now it isn't. The reason is that by implementing a designated initializer in your subclass, you have blocked initializer inheritance! Your ViewController class used to inherit the init(nib-Name:bundle:) initializer from UIViewController; now it doesn't. You need to override that initializer as well, even if all your implementation does is to call the overridden initializer:

```
class ViewController: UIViewController {
    init() {
        super.init(nibName:"MyNib", bundle:nil)
    }
    override init(nibName: String?, bundle: NSBundle?) {
        super.init(nibName:nibName, bundle:bundle)
    }
}
```

The code that instantiates ViewController now does indeed compile:

```
let vc = ViewController(nibName:"MyNib", bundle:nil) // fine
```

But now there's a further surprise: ViewController *itself* doesn't compile! The reason is that there is also a required initializer being imposed upon ViewController, and you must implement that as well. You didn't know about this before, because, when View-Controller had no explicit initializers, you were inheriting the required initializer; now you've blocked inheritance. Fortunately, Xcode's Fix-It feature offers to supply a stub implementation; it doesn't do anything (in fact, it crashes if called), but it satisfies the compiler:

```
required init?(coder aDecoder: NSCoder) {
    fatalError("init(coder:) has not been implemented")
}
```

I'll explain later in this chapter how this required initializer is imposed.

Class Deinitializer

A class, and only a class (not the other flavors of object type), can have a deinitializer. This is a function declared with the keyword deinit followed by curly braces containing the function body. You never call this function yourself; it is called by the runtime when an instance of this class goes out of existence. If a class has a superclass, the subclass's deinitializer (if any) is called before superclass's deinitializer (if any).

The idea of a deinitializer is that you might want to perform some cleanup, or just log to the console to prove to yourself that your instance is going out of existence in good order. I'll take advantage of deinitializers when I discuss memory management issues in Chapter 5.

Class Properties and Methods

A subclass can override its inherited properties. The override must have the same name and type as the inherited property, and must be marked with override. (A property cannot have the same name as an inherited property but a different type, as there is no way to distinguish them.) The following additional rules apply:

- If the superclass property is writable (a stored property or a computed property with a setter), the subclass's override may consist of adding setter observers to this property.
- Alternatively, the subclass's override may be a computed variable. In that case:
  - If the superclass property is stored, the subclass's computed variable override must have both a getter and a setter.
  - If the superclass property is computed, the subclass's computed variable override must reimplement all the accessors that the superclass implements. If the superclass property is read-only (it has just a getter), the override can add a setter.

The overriding property's functions may refer to — and may read from and write to — the inherited property, through the super keyword.

A class can have static members, marked static, just like a struct or an enum. It can also have class members, marked class. Both static and class members are inherited by subclasses (as static and class members).

The chief difference between static and class methods from the programmer's point of view is that a static method cannot be overridden; it is as if static were a synonym for class final.

Here, for example, I'll use a static method to express what dogs say:

```
class Dog {
    static func whatDogsSay() -> String {
        return "woof"
    }
    func bark() {
        print(Dog.whatDogsSay())
    }
}
```

A subclass now inherits `whatDogsSay`, but can't override it. No subclass of Dog may contain any implementation of a class method or a static method `whatDogsSay` with this same signature.

Now I'll use a class method to express what dogs say:

```
class Dog {
    class func whatDogsSay() -> String {
        return "woof"
    }
    func bark() {
        print(Dog.whatDogsSay())
    }
}
```

A subclass inherits `whatDogsSay`, and *can* override it, either as a class function or as a static function:

```
class NoisyDog : Dog {
    override class func whatDogsSay() -> String {
        return "WOOF"
    }
}
```

The difference between static properties and class properties is similar, but with an additional, rather dramatic qualification: static properties can be stored, but class properties can only be computed.

Here, I'll use a static class property to express what dogs say:

```
class Dog {
    static var whatDogsSay = "woof"
    func bark() {
        print(Dog.whatDogsSay)
    }
}
```

A subclass inherits `whatDogsSay`, but can't override it; no subclass of Dog can declare a class or static property `whatDogsSay`.

Now I'll use a class property to express what dogs say. It cannot be a stored property, so I'll have to use a computed property instead:

```
class Dog {
    class var whatDogsSay : String {
        return "woof"
    }
    func bark() {
        print(Dog.whatDogsSay)
    }
}
```

A subclass inherits `whatDogsSay` and can override it either as a class property or as a static property. But even as a static property the subclass's override cannot be a stored property, in keeping with the rules of property overriding that I outlined earlier:

```swift
class NoisyDog : Dog {
    override static var whatDogsSay : String {
        return "WOOF"
    }
}
```

Polymorphism

When a computer language has a hierarchy of types and subtypes, it must resolve the question of what such a hierarchy means for the relationship between the type of an *object* and the declared type of a *reference* to that object. Swift obeys the principles of *polymorphism*. In my view, it is polymorphism that turns an object-based language into a full-fledged object-oriented language. We may summarize Swift's polymorphism principles as follows:

Substitution
Wherever a certain type is expected, a subtype of that type may be used instead.

Internal identity
An object's type is a matter of its internal nature, regardless of how the object is referred to.

To see what these principles mean in practice, imagine we have a Dog class, along with its subclass, NoisyDog:

```swift
class Dog {
}
class NoisyDog : Dog {
}
let d : Dog = NoisyDog()
```

The substitution rule says that the last line is legal: we can assign a NoisyDog instance to a reference, d, that is typed as a Dog. The internal identity rule says that, under the hood, d now *is* a NoisyDog.

You may be asking: How is the internal identity rule manifested? If a reference to a NoisyDog is typed as a Dog, in what sense is this "really" a NoisyDog? To illustrate, let's examine what happens when a subclass overrides an inherited method. Let me redefine Dog and NoisyDog to demonstrate:

```swift
class Dog {
    func bark() {
        print("woof")
    }
}
```

```
class NoisyDog : Dog {
    override func bark() {
        super.bark(); super.bark()
    }
}
```

Now look at this code and tell me whether it compiles and, if so, what happens when it runs:

```
func tellToBark(d:Dog) {
    d.bark()
}
var d = NoisyDog()
tellToBark(d)
```

That code does compile. We create a NoisyDog instance and pass it to a function that expects a Dog parameter. This is permitted, because NoisyDog is a Dog subclass (substitution). A NoisyDog can be used wherever a Dog is expected. Typologically, a NoisyDog *is* a kind of Dog.

But when the code actually runs, *how* does the object referred to by the local variable d inside the tellToBark function react to being told to bark? On the one hand, d is *typed* as Dog, and a Dog barks by saying "woof" once. On the other hand, in our code, when tellToBark is called, what is *really* passed is a NoisyDog instance, and a NoisyDog barks by saying "woof" twice. What will happen? Let's find out:

```
func tellToBark(d:Dog) {
    d.bark()
}
var d = NoisyDog()
tellToBark(d) // woof woof
```

The result is "woof woof". The internal identity rule says that what matters when a message is sent is not how the recipient of that message is *typed* through this or that *reference*, but what that recipient actually *is*. What arrives inside tellToBark is a NoisyDog, regardless of the type of variable that holds it; thus, the bark message causes this object to say "woof" *twice*. It is a NoisyDog!

Here's another important consequence of polymorphism — the meaning of the keyword self. It means the actual instance, and thus its meaning depends upon the type of the actual instance — even if the word self *appears* in a superclass's code. For example:

```
class Dog {
    func bark() {
        print("woof")
    }
    func speak() {
        self.bark()
    }
}
```

```
class NoisyDog : Dog {
    override func bark() {
        super.bark(); super.bark()
    }
}
```

What happens when we tell a NoisyDog to speak? Let's try it:

```
let d = NoisyDog()
d.speak() // woof woof
```

The speak method is declared in Dog, the superclass — not in NoisyDog. The speak method calls the bark method. It does this by way of the keyword self. (I could have omitted the explicit reference to self here, but self would still be involved implicitly, so I'm not cheating by making self explicit.) There's a bark method in Dog, and an override of the bark method in NoisyDog. Which bark method will be called?

The word self is encountered within the Dog class's implementation of speak. But what matters is not *where* the word self *appears* but what it *means*. It means *this instance*. And the internal identity principle tells us that this instance is a NoisyDog! Thus, it is NoisyDog's override of bark that is called.

Thanks to polymorphism, you can take advantage of subclasses to add power and customization to existing classes. This is important particularly in the world of iOS programming, where most of the classes are defined by Cocoa and don't belong to you. The UIViewController class, for example, is defined by Cocoa; it has lots of built-in methods that Cocoa will call, and these methods perform various important tasks — but in a generic way. In real life, you'll make a UIViewController *subclass* and *override* those methods to do the tasks appropriate to your particular app. This won't bother Cocoa in the slightest, because (substitution principle) wherever Cocoa expects to receive or to be talking to a UIViewController, it will accept without question an instance of your UIViewController subclass. And this substitution will also work as expected, because (internal identity principle) whenever Cocoa calls one of those UIViewController methods on your subclass, it is your subclass's override that will be called.

 Polymorphism is cool, but it is also slow. It requires *dynamic dispatch*, meaning that the runtime has to *think* about what a message to a class instance means. This is another reason for preferring a struct over a class where possible: structs don't need dynamic dispatch. Alternatively, you can reduce the need for dynamic dispatch by declaring a class or a class member final or private, or by turning on Whole Module Optimization (see Chapter 6).

Casting

The Swift compiler, with its strict typing, imposes severe restrictions on what messages can be sent to an object reference. The messages that the compiler will permit to be sent to an object reference are those permitted by the reference's *declared* type, including its inheritance.

This means that, thanks to the internal identity principle of polymorphism, an object may be capable of receiving messages that the compiler won't permit us to send. This puts us in a serious bind. For example, let's give NoisyDog a method that Dog doesn't have:

```
class Dog {
    func bark() {
        print("woof")
    }
}
class NoisyDog : Dog {
    override func bark() {
        super.bark(); super.bark()
    }
    func beQuiet() {
        self.bark()
    }
}
```

In that code, we configure a NoisyDog so that we can tell it to beQuiet. Now look at what happens when we try to tell an object typed as a Dog to be quiet:

```
func tellToHush(d:Dog) {
    d.beQuiet() // compile error
}
let d = NoisyDog()
tellToHush(d)
```

Our code doesn't compile. We can't send the beQuiet message to this object, even though it is in fact a NoisyDog and has a beQuiet method. That's because the reference d inside the function body is typed as a Dog — and a Dog has no beQuiet method. There is a certain irony here: for once, we know more than the compiler does! We know that our code would run correctly — because d really is a NoisyDog — if only we could get our code to compile in the first place. We need a way to say to the compiler, "Look, compiler, just trust me: this thing is going to turn out to be a NoisyDog when the program actually runs, so let me send it this message."

There is in fact a way to do this — *casting*. To cast, you use a form of the keyword as followed by the name of the type you claim something really is. Swift will not let you cast just any old type to any old other type — for example, you can't cast a String to an Int — but it will let you cast a superclass to a subclass. This is called *casting down*. When you cast down, the form of the keyword as that you must use is as! with an exclamation mark. The exclamation mark reminds you that you are *forcing* the compiler to do something it would rather not do:

```
func tellToHush(d:Dog) {
    (d as! NoisyDog).beQuiet()
}
let d = NoisyDog()
tellToHush(d)
```

That code compiles, and works. A useful way to rewrite the example is like this:

```
func tellToHush(d:Dog) {
    let d2 = d as! NoisyDog
    d2.beQuiet()
    d2.beQuiet()
}
let d = NoisyDog()
tellToHush(d)
```

The reason that way of rewriting the code is useful is in case we have *other* NoisyDog messages to send to this object. Instead of casting *every time* we want to send a message to it, we cast the object *once* to its internal identity type, and assign it to a variable. Now that variable's type — inferred, in this case, from the cast — *is* that internal identity type, and we can send multiple messages to the variable.

A moment ago, I said that the as! operator's exclamation mark reminds you that you are forcing the compiler's hand. It also serves as a warning: your code can now crash! The reason is that you might be lying to the compiler. Casting down is a way of telling the compiler to relax its strict type checking and to let you call the shots. If you use casting to make a false claim, the compiler may permit it, but you will crash when the app runs:

```
func tellToHush(d:Dog) {
    (d as! NoisyDog).beQuiet() // compiles, but prepare to crash...!
}
let d = Dog()
tellToHush(d)
```

In that code, we told the compiler that this object would turn out to be a NoisyDog, and the compiler obediently took its hands off and allowed us to send the beQuiet message to it. But in fact, this object was a Dog when our code ran, and so we ultimately crashed when the cast failed because this object was *not* a NoisyDog.

To prevent yourself from lying accidentally, you can *test* the type of an instance at runtime. One way to do this is with the keyword is. You can use is in a condition; if the condition passes, *then* cast, in the knowledge that your cast is safe:

```
func tellToHush(d:Dog) {
    if d is NoisyDog {
        let d2 = d as! NoisyDog
        d2.beQuiet()
    }
}
```

The result is that we won't cast d to a NoisyDog unless it really *is* a NoisyDog.

An alternative way to solve the same problem is to use Swift's `as?` operator. This casts down, but with the option of failure; therefore what it casts to is (you guessed it) an Optional — and now we are on familiar ground, because we know how to deal safely with an Optional:

```
func tellToHush(d:Dog) {
    let noisyMaybe = d as? NoisyDog // an Optional wrapping a NoisyDog
    if noisyMaybe != nil {
        noisyMaybe!.beQuiet()
    }
}
```

That doesn't look much cleaner or shorter than our previous approach. But remember that we can safely send a message to an Optional by optionally unwrapping the Optional! Thus we can skip the assignment and condense to a single line:

```
func tellToHush(d:Dog) {
    (d as? NoisyDog)?.beQuiet()
}
```

First we use the `as?` operator to obtain an Optional wrapping a NoisyDog (or `nil`). Then we optionally unwrap that Optional and send a message to it. If d isn't a NoisyDog, the Optional will be `nil` and the message won't be sent. If d *is* a NoisyDog, the Optional will be unwrapped and the message will be sent. Thus, that code is safe.

Recall from Chapter 3 that comparison operators applied to an Optional are automatically applied to the object wrapped by the Optional. The `as!`, `as?`, and `is` operators work the same way. Consider an Optional d wrapping a Dog (that is, d is a Dog? object). This might, in actual fact, be wrapping either a Dog or a NoisyDog; the substitution principle applies to Optional types, because it applies to the type of thing wrapped by the Optional. To find out which it is, you might be tempted to use `is`. But can you? After all, an Optional is neither a Dog nor a NoisyDog — it's an Optional! Well, the good news is that Swift knows what you mean; when the thing on the left side of `is` is an Optional, Swift pretends that it's the value wrapped in the Optional. Thus, this works just as you would hope:

```
let d : Dog? = NoisyDog()
if d is NoisyDog { // it is!
```

When using `is` with an Optional, the test fails in good order if the Optional is `nil`. Thus our `is` test really does *two* things: it checks whether the Optional is `nil`, and if it is not, it then checks whether the wrapped value is the type we specify.

What about casting? You can't really cast an Optional to anything. But you can use the `as!` operator with an Optional, because Swift knows what you mean; when the thing on the left side of `as!` is an Optional, Swift treats it as the wrapped type. Moreover, the consequence of applying the `as!` operator is that two things happen: Swift unwraps first, and then casts. This code works, because d is unwrapped to give us d2, which is a Noisy-Dog:

```
let d : Dog? = NoisyDog()
let d2 = d as! NoisyDog
d2.beQuiet()
```

That code, however, is not safe. You shouldn't cast like that, without testing first, unless you are very sure of your ground. If d were `nil`, you'd crash in the second line because you're trying to unwrap a `nil` Optional. And if d were a Dog, not a NoisyDog, you'd *still* crash in the second line when the cast fails. That's why there's also an `as?` operator, which *is* safe — but yields an Optional:

```
let d : Dog? = NoisyDog()
let d2 = d as? NoisyDog
d2?.beQuiet()
```

Another way you'll use casting is during a value interchange between Swift and Objective-C when two types are *equivalent*. For example, you can cast a Swift String to a Cocoa NSString, and *vice versa*. That's not because one is a subclass of the other, but because they are *bridged* to one another; in a very real sense, they are the same type. When you cast from String to NSString, you're not casting down, and what you're doing is not dangerous, so you use the `as` operator, with no exclamation mark. I gave an example, in Chapter 3, of a situation where you might need to do that:

```
let s = "hello"
let range = (s as NSString).rangeOfString("ell") // (1,3), an NSRange
```

The cast from String to NSString tells Swift to stay in the Cocoa world as it calls `range-OfString`, and thus causes the result to be the Cocoa result, an NSRange, rather than a Swift Range.

A number of common classes are bridged in this way between Swift and Objective-C. Often, you won't need to cast as you cross the bridge from Swift to Objective-C, because Swift will automatically cast for you. For example, a Swift Int and a Cocoa NSNumber are two very different things; nevertheless, you can often use an Int where an NSNumber is expected, without casting, like this:

```
let ud = NSUserDefaults.standardUserDefaults()
ud.setObject(1, forKey: "Test")
```

In that code, we used an Int, namely 1, where Objective-C expects an NSObject instance. An Int is *not* an NSObject instance; it isn't even a class instance (it's a struct instance). But Swift sees that an NSObject is expected, decides that an NSNumber would best represent an Int, and crosses the bridge for you. Thus, what winds up being stored in NSUserDefaults is an NSNumber.

Coming back the other way, however, when you call `objectForKey:`, Swift has no information about what this value really is, so you have to cast explicitly if you want an Int — and now you are casting down (as I'll explain in more detail later):

```
let i = ud.objectForKey("Test") as! Int
```

That cast works because `ud.objectForKey("Test")` yields an NSNumber wrapping an integer, and casting that to a Swift Int is permitted — the types are bridged. But if `ud.objectForKey("Test")` were *not* an NSNumber (or if it were `nil`), you'd crash. If you're not sure of your ground, use `is` or `as?` to be safe.

Type Reference

It can be useful for an instance to refer to its own type — for example, to send a message to that type. In an earlier example, a Dog instance method fetched a Dog class property by sending a message to the Dog type explicitly — by using the word `Dog`:

```
class Dog {
    class var whatDogsSay : String {
        return "Woof"
    }
    func bark() {
        print(Dog.whatDogsSay)
    }
}
```

The expression `Dog.whatDogsSay` seems clumsy and inflexible. Why should we have to hard-code into Dog a knowledge of what class it is? It *has* a class; it should just *know* what it is.

In Objective-C, you may be accustomed to using the `class` instance method to deal with this situation. In Swift, an instance might not have a class (it might be a struct instance or an enum instance); what a Swift instance has is a *type*. The instance method that Swift provides for this purpose is the `dynamicType` method. An instance can access its type through this method. Thus, if you don't like the notion of a Dog instance calling a Dog class method by saying `Dog` explicitly, there's another way:

```
class Dog {
    class var whatDogsSay : String {
        return "Woof"
    }
```

```
    func bark() {
        print(self.dynamicType.whatDogsSay)
    }
}
```

An important thing about using `dynamicType` instead of hard-coding a class name is that it obeys polymorphism:

```
class Dog {
    class var whatDogsSay : String {
        return "Woof"
    }
    func bark() {
        print(self.dynamicType.whatDogsSay)
    }
}
class NoisyDog : Dog {
    override class var whatDogsSay : String {
        return "Woof woof woof"
    }
}
```

Now watch what happens:

```
let nd = NoisyDog()
nd.bark() // Woof woof woof
```

If we tell a NoisyDog instance to `bark`, it says `"Woof woof woof"`. The reason is that `dynamicType` means, "The type that this instance actually is, right now." That's what makes this type *dynamic*. We send the `bark` message to a NoisyDog instance. The `bark` implementation refers to `self.dynamicType`; `self` means this instance, which is a NoisyDog, and so `self.dynamicType` is the NoisyDog class, and it is NoisyDog's version of `whatDogsSay` that is fetched.

 You can also use `dynamicType` for learning the name of an object's type, as a string — typically for debugging purposes. When you say `print(myObject.dynamic-Type)`, you'll see the type name in the console.

In some situations, you may want to pass an object type as a value. That is legal; an object type is itself an object. Here's what you need to know:

- To *declare* that an object type is acceptable — for example, as the type of a variable or parameter — use dot-notation with the name of the type and the keyword `Type`.

- To *use* an object type as a value — for example, to assign a type to a variable or pass it to a function — use a reference to the type (the type's name, or some instance's `dynamicType`), possibly followed by the keyword `self` using dot-notation.

For example, here's a function that accepts a Dog type as its parameter:

```
func typeExpecter(whattype:Dog.Type) {
}
```

And here's an example of calling that function:

```
typeExpecter(Dog) // or: typeExpecter(Dog.self)
```

Or you could call it like this:

```
let d = Dog() // or: let d = NoisyDog()
typeExpecter(d.dynamicType) // or: typeExpecter(d.dynamicType.self)
```

Why might you want to do something like that? A typical situation is that your function is a factory for instances: given a type, it creates an instance of that type, possibly prepares it in some way, and returns it. You can use a variable reference to a type to make an instance of that type, by explicitly sending it an init(...) message.

For example, here's a Dog class with an init(name:) initializer, and its NoisyDog subclass:

```
class Dog {
    var name : String
    init(name:String) {
        self.name = name
    }
}
class NoisyDog : Dog {
}
```

And here's a factory method that creates a Dog or a NoisyDog, as specified by its parameter, gives it a name, and returns it:

```
func dogMakerAndNamer(whattype:Dog.Type) -> Dog {
    let d = whattype.init(name:"Fido") // compile error
    return d
}
```

As you can see, since whattype refers to a type, we can call its initializer to make an instance of that type. However, there's a problem. The code doesn't compile. The reason is that the compiler is in doubt as to whether the init(name:) initializer is implemented by every possible subtype of Dog. To reassure it, we must declare that initializer with the required keyword:

```
class Dog {
    var name : String
    required init(name:String) {
        self.name = name
    }
}
class NoisyDog : Dog {
}
```

I promised I'd tell you why you might need to declare an initializer as `required`; now I'm fulfilling that promise! The `required` designation reassures the compiler; every subclass of Dog must inherit or reimplement `init(name:)`, so it's legal to send the `init(name:)` message to a type reference that might refer to Dog or some subclass of Dog. Now our code compiles, and we can call our function:

```
let d = dogMakerAndNamer(Dog) // d is a Dog named Fido
let d2 = dogMakerAndNamer(NoisyDog) // d2 is a NoisyDog named Fido
```

In a class method, `self` stands for the class — polymorphically. This means that, in a class method, you can send a message to `self` to call an initializer polymorphically. Here's an example. Let's say we want to move our instance factory method into Dog itself, as a class method. Let's call this class method `makeAndName`. We want this class method to create and return a named Dog of whatever class we send the `makeAndName` message to. If we say `Dog.makeAndName()`, we should get a Dog. If we say `NoisyDog.make-AndName()`, we should get a NoisyDog. That type is the polymorphic `self` class, so our `makeAndName` class method initializes `self`:

```
class Dog {
    var name : String
    required init(name:String) {
        self.name = name
    }
    class func makeAndName() -> Dog {
        let d = self.init(name:"Fido")
        return d
    }
}
class NoisyDog : Dog {
}
```

It works as expected:

```
let d = Dog.makeAndName() // d is a Dog named Fido
let d2 = NoisyDog.makeAndName() // d2 is a NoisyDog named Fido
```

But there's a problem. Although d2 is in fact a NoisyDog, it is *typed* as a Dog. This is because our `makeAndName` class method is declared as returning a Dog. That isn't what we meant to say. What we want to say is that this method returns an instance of the same type as the class to which the `makeAndName` message was originally sent. In other words, we need a polymorphic type declaration! That type is `Self` (notice the capitalization). It is used as a return type in a method declaration to mean "an instance of whatever type this is at runtime." Thus:

```
class Dog {
    var name : String
    required init(name:String) {
        self.name = name
    }
```

```
    class func makeAndName() -> Self {
        let d = self.init(name:"Fido")
        return d
    }
}
class NoisyDog : Dog {
}
```

Now when we call `NoisyDog.makeAndName()` we get a NoisyDog typed as a NoisyDog.

`Self` also works for instance method declarations. Therefore, we can write an instance method version of our factory method. Here, we start with a Dog or a NoisyDog and tell it to have a puppy of the same type as itself:

```
class Dog {
    var name : String
    required init(name:String) {
        self.name = name
    }
    func havePuppy(name name:String) -> Self {
        return self.dynamicType.init(name:name)
    }
}
class NoisyDog : Dog {
}
```

And here's some code to test it:

```
let d = Dog(name:"Fido")
let d2 = d.havePuppy(name:"Fido Junior")
let nd = NoisyDog(name:"Rover")
let nd2 = nd.havePuppy(name:"Rover Junior")
```

As expected, `d2` is a Dog, but `nd2` is a NoisyDog typed as a NoisyDog.

All this terminology can get a bit confusing, so here's a quick summary:

`.dynamicType`
: In code, sent to an instance: the polymorphic (internal) type of this instance, re-gardless of how the instance reference is typed. Static/class members are accessible through an instance's `dynamicType`.

`.Type`
: In declarations, sent to a type: the polymorphic type (as opposed to an instance of the type). For example, in a function declaration, `Dog` means a Dog instance is expected (or an instance of one its subclasses), but `Dog.Type` means that the Dog type itself is expected (or the type of one of its subclasses).

`.self`

In code, sent to a type: the type. For example, to pass the Dog type where `Dog.Type` is expected, you can pass `Dog.self`. (It is not illegal to send `.self` to an instance, but it is pointless.)

`self`

In instance code, this instance, polymorphically.

In static/class code, this type, polymorphically; `self.init(...)` instantiates the type.

`Self`

In a method declaration, when specifying the return type, this class or this instance's class, polymorphically.

Protocols

A *protocol* is a way of expressing commonalities between otherwise unrelated types. For example, a Bee object and a Bird object might need to have certain features in common by virtue of the fact that both a bee and a bird can fly. Thus, it might be useful to define a Flier type. The question is: In what sense can both Bee and Bird be Fliers?

One possibility, of course, is class inheritance. If Bee and Bird are both classes, there's a class hierarchy of superclasses and subclasses. So Flier could be the superclass of both Bee and Bird. The problem is that there may be other reasons why Flier *can't* be the superclass of both Bee and Bird. A Bee is an Insect; a Bird isn't. Yet they both have the power of flight — independently. We need a type that cuts across the class hierarchy somehow, tying remote classes together.

Moreover, what if Bee and Bird are *not* both classes? In Swift, that's a very real possibility. Important and powerful objects can be structs instead of classes. But there is no struct hierarchy of superstructs and substructs! That, after all, is one of the major differences between structs and classes. Yet structs need the ability to possess and express formal commonalities every bit as much as classes do. How can a Bee struct and a Bird struct both be Fliers?

Swift solves this problem through the use of protocols. Protocols are tremendously important in Swift; the Swift header defines over 70 of them! Moreover, Objective-C has protocols as well; Swift protocols correspond roughly to these, and can interchange with them. Cocoa makes heavy use of protocols.

A protocol is an object *type*, but there are no protocol *objects* — you can't instantiate a protocol. A protocol is much more lightweight than that. A protocol declaration is just a list of properties and methods. The properties have no values, and the methods have no code! The idea is that a "real" object type can formally declare that it belongs to a protocol type; this is called *adopting* or *conforming to* the protocol. An object type that adopts a protocol is signing a contract stating that it actually implements the properties and methods listed by the protocol.

For example, let's say that being a Flier consists of no more than implementing a `fly` method. Then a Flier protocol could specify that there must be a `fly` method; to do so, it lists the `fly` method *with no function body*, like this:

```
protocol Flier {
    func fly()
}
```

Any type — an enum, a struct, a class, or even another protocol — can then adopt this protocol. To do so, it lists the protocol after a colon after its name in its declaration. (If the adopter is a class with a superclass, the protocol comes after a comma after the superclass specification.)

Let's say Bird is a struct. Then it can adopt Flier like this:

```
struct Bird : Flier {
} // compile error
```

So far, so good. But that code won't compile. The Bird struct has made a promise to implement the features listed in the Flier protocol. Now it must keep that promise! The `fly` method is the only requirement of the Flier protocol. To satisfy that requirement, I'll just give Bird an empty `fly` method:

```
protocol Flier {
    func fly()
}
struct Bird : Flier {
    func fly() {
    }
}
```

That's all there is to it! We've defined a protocol, and we've made a struct adopt that protocol. Of course, in real life you'll probably want to make the adopter's implementation of the protocol's methods *do* something; but the protocol says nothing about that.

 New in Swift 2.0, a protocol can declare a method *and provide its implementation*, thanks to protocol extensions, which I'll discuss later in this chapter.

Why Protocols?

Perhaps at this point you're scratching your head over *why* this is a useful thing to do. We made a Bird a Flier, but so what? If we wanted a Bird to know how to fly, why didn't we just give Bird a `fly` method *without* adopting any protocol? The answer has to do with types. Don't forget, a protocol is a type. Our protocol, Flier, is a type. Therefore, I can use Flier wherever I would use a type — to declare the type of a variable, for example, or the type of a function parameter:

```
func tellToFly(f:Flier) {
    f.fly()
}
```

Think about that code for a moment, because it embodies the entire point of protocols. A protocol is a type — so *polymorphism applies.* Protocols give us another way of expressing the notion of type and subtype. This means that, by the substitution principle, a Flier here could be an instance of any object type — an enum, a struct, or a class. It doesn't matter *what* object type it is, *as long as it adopts the Flier protocol.* If it adopts the Flier protocol, then it must have a `fly` method, because that's exactly what it *means* to adopt the Flier protocol! Therefore the compiler is willing to let us send the `fly` message to this object. A Flier is, by definition, an object that can be told to `fly`.

The converse, however, is not true: an object with a `fly` method is *not* automatically a Flier. It isn't enough to *obey* the requirements of a protocol; the object type must *adopt* the protocol. This code won't compile:

```
struct Bee {
    func fly() {
    }
}
let b = Bee()
tellToFly(b) // compile error
```

A Bee *can* be sent the `fly` message, *qua* Bee. But `tellToFly` doesn't take a Bee parameter; it takes a Flier parameter. Formally, a Bee is *not* a Flier. To make a Bee a Flier, simply declare formally that Bee adopts the Flier protocol. This code does compile:

```
struct Bee : Flier {
    func fly() {
    }
}
let b = Bee()
tellToFly(b)
```

Enough of birds and bees; we're ready for a real-life example! As I've already said, Swift is chock full of protocols already. Let's make one of our own object types adopt one. One of the most useful Swift protocols is CustomStringConvertible. The CustomString-Convertible protocol requires that we implement a `description` String property. If we do that, a wonderful thing happens: when an instance of this type is used in string interpolation or `print` (or the `po` command in the console), the `description` property value is used automatically to represent it.

Recall, for example, the Filter enum, from earlier in this chapter. I'll add a `description` property to it:

```
enum Filter : String {
    case Albums = "Albums"
    case Playlists = "Playlists"
    case Podcasts = "Podcasts"
    case Books = "Audiobooks"
    var description : String { return self.rawValue }
}
```

But that isn't enough, in and of itself, to give Filter the power of the CustomStringCon-vertible protocol; to do that, we also need to *adopt* the CustomStringConvertible pro-tocol formally. There is already a colon and a type in the Filter declaration, so an adopted protocol comes after a comma:

```
enum Filter : String, CustomStringConvertible {
    case Albums = "Albums"
    case Playlists = "Playlists"
    case Podcasts = "Podcasts"
    case Books = "Audiobooks"
    var description : String { return self.rawValue }
}
```

We have now made Filter formally adopt the CustomStringConvertible protocol. The CustomStringConvertible protocol requires that we implement a `description` String property; we *do* implement a `description` String property, so our code compiles. Now we can hand a Filter to `print`, or interpolate it into a string, and its `description` will appear automatically:

```
let type = Filter.Albums
print(type) // Albums
print("It is \(type)") // It is Albums
```

Behold the power of protocols. You can give *any* object type the power of string con-version in exactly the same way.

Note that a type can adopt more than one protocol! For example, the built-in Double type adopts CustomStringConvertible, Hashable, Comparable, and other built-in pro-tocols. To declare adoption of multiple protocols, list each one after the first protocol in the declaration, separated by comma. For example:

```
struct MyType : CustomStringConvertible, Hashable, Comparable {
    // ...
}
```

(Of course, that code won't compile unless I also declare the required methods in My-Type, so that MyType really *does* adopt those protocols.)

Protocol Type Testing and Casting

A protocol is a type, and an adopter of a protocol is its subtype. Polymorphism applies. Therefore, the operators for mediating between an object's declared type and its real type work when the object is declared as a protocol type. For example, given a protocol Flier that is adopted by both Bird and Bee, we can use the `is` operator to test whether a particular Flier is in fact a Bird:

```
func isBird(f:Flier) -> Bool {
    return f is Bird
}
```

Similarly, `as!` and `as?` can be used to cast an object declared as a protocol type down to its actual type. This is important to be able to do, because the adopting object will typically be able to receive messages that the protocol can't receive. For example, let's say that a Bird can get a worm:

```
struct Bird : Flier {
    func fly() {
    }
    func getWorm() {
    }
}
```

A Bird can `fly` *qua* Flier, but it can `getWorm` only *qua* Bird. Thus, you can't tell just any old Flier to get a worm:

```
func tellGetWorm(f:Flier) {
    f.getWorm() // compile error
}
```

But if this Flier is a Bird, clearly it *can* get a worm. That is exactly what casting is all about:

```
func tellGetWorm(f:Flier) {
    (f as? Bird)?.getWorm()
}
```

Declaring a Protocol

Protocol declaration can take place only at the top level of a file. To declare a protocol, use the keyword `protocol` followed by the name of the protocol, which, being an object type, should start with a capital letter. Then come curly braces which may contain the following:

Properties

A property declaration in a protocol consists of `var` (not `let`), the property name, a colon, its type, and curly braces containing the word `get` or the words `get set`. In the former case, the adopter's implementation of this property *can* be writable, while in the latter case, it *must* be: the adopter may not implement a `get set` property as a read-only computed property or as a constant (`let`) stored property.

To declare a static/class property, precede it with the keyword `static`. A class adopter is free to implement this as a class property.

Methods

A method declaration in a protocol is a function declaration without a function body — that is, it has no curly braces and thus it has no code. Any object function type is legal, including `init` and `subscript`. (The syntax for declaring a subscript in a protocol is the same as the syntax for declaring a subscript in an object type, except that there will be no function bodies, so the curly braces, like those of a property declaration in a protocol, will contain `get` or `get set`.)

To declare a static/class method, precede it with the keyword `static`. A class adopter is free to implement this as a class method.

If a method, as implemented by an enum or struct, might need to be declared `mutating`, the protocol must specify the `mutating` designation; the adopter cannot add `mutating` if the protocol lacks it. However, the adopter may omit `mutating` if the protocol has it.

Type alias

A protocol can introduce a local synonym for a type that it mentions in its declarations by declaring a type alias. For example, `typealias Time = Double` allows the Time type to be referred to inside the protocol's curly braces; elsewhere (such as in an adopting object type), the Time type doesn't exist, but the Double type is a match for it.

There are other ways to use a type alias in a protocol, which I'll discuss later.

Protocol adoption

A protocol can itself adopt one or more protocols; the syntax is just as you would expect — a colon after the protocol's name in the declaration, followed by a comma-separated list of the protocols it adopts. In effect, this gives you a way to create an entire secondary hierarchy of types! The Swift headers make heavy use of this.

A protocol that adopts another protocol may repeat the contents of the adopted protocol's curly braces, for clarity; but it doesn't have to, as this repetition is implicit. An object type that adopts such a protocol must satisfy the requirements of this protocol and all protocols that the protocol adopts.

 If the only purpose of a protocol would be to combine other protocols by adopting all of them, without adding any new requirements, and if this combination is used in just one place in your code, you can avoid formally declaring the protocol in the first place by creating the combining protocol on the fly. To do so, use a type name `protocol<...,...>`, where the contents of the angle brackets is a comma-separated list of protocols.

Optional Protocol Members

In Objective-C, a protocol member can be declared optional, meaning that this member doesn't have to be implemented by the adopter, but it may be. For compatibility with Objective-C, Swift allows optional protocol members, but only in a protocol explicitly bridged to Objective-C by preceding its declaration with the @objc attribute. In such a protocol, an optional member — meaning a method or property — is declared by preceding its declaration with the keyword optional:

```
@objc protocol Flier {
    optional var song : String {get}
    optional func sing()
}
```

Only a class can adopt such a protocol, and this feature will work only if the class is an NSObject subclass, or the optional member is marked with the @objc attribute:

```
class Bird : Flier {
    @objc func sing() {
        print("tweet")
    }
}
```

An optional member is not guaranteed to be implemented by the adopter, so Swift doesn't know whether it's safe to send a Flier either the song message or the sing message.

In the case of an optional property like song, Swift solves the problem by wrapping its value in an Optional. If the Flier adopter doesn't implement the property, the result is nil and no harm done:

```
let f : Flier = Bird()
let s = f.song // s is an Optional wrapping a String
```

 This is one of those rare situations where you can wind up with a double-wrapped Optional. For example, if the value of the optional property song were a String?, then fetching its value from a Flier would yield a String??.

 An optional property can be declared {get set} by its protocol, but there is no legal syntax for setting such a property in an object of that protocol type. For example, if f is a Flier and song is declared {get set}, you can't set f.song. I regard this as a bug in the language.

In the case of an optional method like sing, things are more elaborate. If the method is not implemented, we must not be permitted to call it in the first place. To handle this situation, the method *itself* is automatically typed as an Optional version of its declared type. To send the `sing` message to a Flier, therefore, you must unwrap it. The safe approach is to unwrap it optionally, with a question mark:

```
let f : Flier = Bird()
f.sing?()
```

That code compiles — and it also runs safely. The effect is to send the `sing` message to f *only if this Flier adopter implements* `sing`. If this Flier adopter *doesn't* implement `sing`, nothing happens. You could have force-unwrapped the call — `f.sing!()` — but then your app would crash if the adopter doesn't implement `sing`.

If an optional method returns a value, that value is wrapped in an Optional as well. For example:

```
@objc protocol Flier {
    optional var song : String {get}
    optional func sing() -> String
}
```

If we now call `sing?()` on a Flier, the result is an Optional wrapping a String:

```
let f : Flier = Bird()
let s = f.sing?() // s is an Optional wrapping a String
```

If we force-unwrap the call — `sing!()` — the result is either a String (if the adopter implements `sing`) or a crash (if it doesn't).

Many Cocoa protocols have optional members. For example, your iOS app will have an app delegate class that adopts the UIApplicationDelegate protocol; this protocol has many methods, all of them optional. That fact, however, will have no effect on how you implement those methods; you don't need to mark them in any special way. Your app delegate class is already a subclass of NSObject, so this feature just works. Either you implement a method or you don't. Similarly, you will often make your UIViewController subclass adopt a Cocoa delegate protocol with optional members; again, this is an NSObject subclass, so you'll just implement the methods you want to implement, with no special marking. (I'll talk more about Cocoa protocols in Chapter 10, and about delegate protocols in Chapter 11.)

Class Protocol

A protocol declared with the keyword `class` after the colon after its name is a *class protocol*, meaning that it can be adopted only by class object types:

```
protocol SecondViewControllerDelegate : class {
    func acceptData(data:AnyObject!)
}
```

(There is no need to say `class` if this protocol is already marked `@objc`; the `@objc` attribute implies that this is also a class protocol.)

A typical reason for declaring a class protocol is to take advantage of special memory management features that apply only to classes. I haven't discussed memory management yet, but I'll continue the example anyway (and I'll repeat it when I do talk about memory management, in Chapter 5):

```
class SecondViewController : UIViewController {
    weak var delegate : SecondViewControllerDelegate?
    // ...
}
```

The keyword `weak` marks the `delegate` property as having special memory management. Only a class instance can participate in this kind of special memory management. The `delegate` property is typed as a protocol, and a protocol might be adopted by a struct or an enum type. So to satisfy the compiler that this object *will* in fact be a class instance, and *not* a struct or enum instance, the protocol is declared as a class protocol.

Implicitly Required Initializers

Suppose that a protocol declares an initializer. And suppose that a class adopts this protocol. By the terms of this protocol, this class and any subclass it may ever have must implement this initializer. Therefore, the class must not only implement the initializer, but it must also mark it as `required`. An initializer declared in a protocol is thus *implicitly required*, and the class is forced to make that requirement explicit.

Consider this simple example, which won't compile:

```
protocol Flier {
    init()
}
class Bird : Flier {
    init() {} // compile error
}
```

That code generates an elaborate but perfectly informative compile error message: "Initializer requirement `init()` can only be satisfied by a `required` initializer in non-final class Bird." To compile our code, we must designate our initializer as `required`:

```
protocol Flier {
    init()
}
class Bird : Flier {
    required init() {}
}
```

The alternative, as the compile error message informs us, would be to mark the Bird class as `final`. This would mean that it *cannot have any subclasses* — thus guaranteeing that the problem will never arise in the first place. If Bird were marked `final`, there would be no need to mark its `init` as `required`.

In the above code, Bird is *not* marked as final, and its init *is* marked as required. This, as I've already explained, means in turn that any subclass of Bird that implements any designated initializers — and thus loses initializer inheritance — must implement the required initializer and mark it required as well.

That fact is responsible for a strange and annoying feature of real-life iOS programming with Swift that I mentioned earlier in this chapter. Let's say you subclass the built-in Cocoa class UIViewController — something that you are extremely likely to do. And let's say you give your subclass an initializer — something that you are also extremely likely to do:

```
class ViewController: UIViewController {
    init() {
        super.init(nibName: "ViewController", bundle: nil)
    }
}
```

That code won't compile. The compile error says: "required initializer init(coder:) must be provided by subclass of UIViewController."

We are now in a position to understand what's going on. It turns out that UIView-Controller adopts a protocol, NSCoding. And this protocol requires an initializer init(coder:). None of that is your doing; UIViewController and NSCoding are declared by Cocoa, not by you. But that doesn't matter! This is the same situation I was just describing. Your UIViewController subclass must either inherit init(coder:) or must explicitly implement it and mark it required. Well, your subclass has implemented a designated initializer of its own — thus cutting off initializer inheritance. Therefore it must implement init(coder:) and mark it required.

But that makes no sense if you are not expecting init(coder:) ever to be *called* on your UIViewController subclass. You are being forced to write an initializer for which you can provide no meaningful functionality! Fortunately, Xcode's Fix-It feature will offer to write the initializer for you, like this:

```
required init?(coder aDecoder: NSCoder) {
    fatalError("init(coder:) has not been implemented")
}
```

That code satisfies the compiler. (I'll explain in Chapter 5 why it's a legal initializer even though it doesn't fulfill an initializer's contract.) It also deliberately crashes if it is ever called.

If you *do* have functionality for this initializer, you will delete the fatalError line and insert your own functionality in its place. A minimum meaningful implementation would be super.init(coder:aDecoder), but of course if your class has properties that need initialization, you will need to initialize them first.

Not only UIViewController but *lots* of built-in Cocoa classes adopt NSCoding. You will encounter this problem if you subclass *any* of those classes and implement your own initializer. It's just something you'll have to get used to.

Literal Convertibles

One of the wonderful things about Swift is that so many of its features, rather than being built-in and accomplished by magic, are implemented *in* Swift and are exposed to view in the Swift header. Literals are a case in point. The reason you can say 5 to make an Int whose value is 5, instead of formally initializing Int by saying Int(5), is not because of magic (or at least, not entirely because of magic). It's because Int adopts a protocol, IntegerLiteralConvertible. Not only Int literals, but *all* literals work this way. The following literal convertible protocols are declared in the Swift header:

- NilLiteralConvertible
- BooleanLiteralConvertible
- IntegerLiteralConvertible
- FloatLiteralConvertible
- StringLiteralConvertible
- ExtendedGraphemeClusterLiteralConvertible
- UnicodeScalarLiteralConvertible
- ArrayLiteralConvertible
- DictionaryLiteralConvertible

Your own object type can adopt a literal convertible protocol as well. This means that a literal can appear where an instance of your object type is expected! For example, here we declare a Nest type that contains some number of eggs (its eggCount):

```
struct Nest : IntegerLiteralConvertible {
    var eggCount : Int = 0
    init() {}
    init(integerLiteral val: Int) {
        self.eggCount = val
    }
}
```

Because Nest adopts IntegerLiteralConvertible, we can pass an Int where a Nest is expected, and our init(integerLiteral:) will be called automatically, causing a new Nest object with the specified eggCount to come into existence at that moment:

```
func reportEggs(nest:Nest) {
    print("this nest contains \(nest.eggCount) eggs")
}
reportEggs(4) // this nest contains 4 eggs
```

Generics

A *generic* is a sort of placeholder for a type, into which an actual type will be slotted later. This is useful because of Swift's strict typing. Without sacrificing that strict typing, there are situations where you can't or don't want to specify too precisely in a certain region of your code what the exact type of something is going to be.

It is important to understand that generics do not in any way relax Swift's strict typing. In particular, they do not postpone resolution of a type until runtime. When you use a generic, your code will still specify its real type; that real type is known with complete specificity at compile time! The particular region of your code where the type is *expected* uses a generic so that *it* doesn't have to specify the type fully, but at the point where that code is *used* by other code, the type *is* specified. The placeholder is generic, but it is *resolved* to an actual specific type whenever the generic is used.

An Optional is a good example. Any type of value can be wrapped up in an Optional. Yet you are never in any doubt as to what type is wrapped up in a *particular* Optional. How can this be? It's because Optional is a generic type. Here's how an Optional works.

I have already said that an Optional is an enum, with two cases: .None and .Some. If an Optional's case is .Some, it has an associated value — the value that is wrapped by this Optional. But what is the type of that associated value? On the one hand, one wants to say that it can be any type; that, after all, is why anything can be wrapped up in an Optional. On the other hand, any given Optional that wraps a value wraps a value of some specific type. When you unwrap an Optional, that unwrapped value needs to be typed as what it is, so that it can be sent messages appropriate for that type.

The solution to this sort of problem is a Swift generic. The declaration for the Optional enum in the Swift header starts like this:

```
enum Optional<Wrapped> {
    // ...
}
```

That syntax means: "In the course of this declaration, I'm going to be using a made-up type — a type *placeholder* — that I call Wrapped. It's a real and individual type, but I'm not going to say more about it right now. All you need to know is that whenever I say Wrapped, I mean this one particular type. When an actual Optional is created, it will be perfectly clear what type Wrapped stands for, and then, wherever I say Wrapped, you should substitute the type that it stands for."

Let's look at more of the Optional declaration:

```
enum Optional<Wrapped> {
    case None
    case Some(Wrapped)
    init(_ some: Wrapped)
    // ...
}
```

Having declared that Wrapped is a placeholder, we proceed to use it. There's a case .None. There's also a case .Some, which has an associated value — of type Wrapped. We also have an initializer, which takes a parameter — of type Wrapped. Thus, the type with which we are initialized — whatever type that may be — *is* type Wrapped, and thus is the type of value that is associated with the .Some case.

It is this identity between the type of the initializer parameter and the type of the .Some associated value that allows the latter to be resolved. In the declaration of the Optional enum, Wrapped is a placeholder. But in real life, when an actual Optional is created, it will be initialized with an actual value of some definite type. Usually, we'll use the question-mark syntactic sugar (type String?) and the initializer will be called for us behind the scenes, but let's call the initializer explicitly for the sake of clarity:

```
let s = Optional("howdy")
```

That code resolves the type of Wrapped for this particular Optional instance! Obviously, "howdy" is a String. As a result, the compiler knows that for this *particular* Optional<Wrapped>, Wrapped is String. Under the hood, wherever Wrapped appears in the declaration of the Optional enum, the compiler substitutes String. Thus, the declaration for the *particular* Optional referred to by the variable s looks, in the compiler's mind, like this:

```
enum Optional<String> {
    case None
    case Some(String)
    init(_ some: String)
    // ...
}
```

That is the pseudocode declaration of an Optional whose Wrapped placeholder has been replaced everywhere with the String type. We can summarize this by saying that s is an Optional<String>. In fact, that is legal syntax! We can create the same Optional like this:

```
let s : Optional<String> = "howdy"
```

A great many of the built-in Swift types involve generics. In fact, this feature of the language seems to be designed with the Swift types in mind; generics exist exactly so that the Swift types can do what they need to do.

Generic Declarations

Here's a list of the places where generics, in one form or another, can be declared in Swift:

Generic protocol with `Self`

In a protocol, use of the keyword `Self` (note the capitalization) turns the protocol into a generic. `Self` is a placeholder meaning the *type of the adopter*. For example, here's a Flier protocol that declares a method that takes a `Self` parameter:

```
protocol Flier {
    func flockTogetherWith(f:Self)
}
```

That means that if the Bird object type were to adopt the Flier protocol, its implementation of `flockTogetherWith` would need to declare its f parameter as a Bird.

Generic protocol with empty type alias

A protocol can declare a type alias *without defining* what the type alias stands for — that is, the `typealias` statement doesn't include an equal sign. This turns the protocol into a generic; the alias name, called an *associated type*, is a placeholder. For example:

```
protocol Flier {
    typealias Other
    func flockTogetherWith(f:Other)
    func mateWith(f:Other)
}
```

An adopter will declare some particular type where the generic uses the type alias name, thus resolving the placeholder. If the Bird struct adopts the Flier protocol and declares the f parameter of `flockTogetherWith` as a Bird, that declaration resolves Other to Bird for this particular adopter — and now Bird must declare the f parameter for `mateWith` as a Bird as well:

```
struct Bird : Flier {
    func flockTogetherWith(f:Bird) {}
    func mateWith(f:Bird) {}
}
```

 This form of generic protocol is ultimately the same as the previous form; where I've written f:Other, Swift understands this to mean f:Self.Other, and in fact it is legal (and possibly clearer) to write that.

Generic functions

A function declaration can use a generic placeholder type for any of its parameters, for its return type, and within its body. Declare the placeholder name in angle brackets after the function name:

```
func takeAndReturnSameThing<T> (t:T) -> T {
    return t
}
```

The caller will use some particular type where the placeholder appears in the function declaration, thus resolving the placeholder:

```
let thing = takeAndReturnSameThing("howdy")
```

Here, the type of the argument "howdy" used in the call resolves T to String; therefore this call to takeAndReturnSameThing will also return a String, and the variable capturing the result, thing, is inferred to String as well.

Generic object types

An object type declaration can use a generic placeholder type anywhere within its curly braces. Declare the placeholder name in angle brackets after the object type name:

```
struct HolderOfTwoSameThings<T> {
    var firstThing : T
    var secondThing : T
    init(thingOne:T, thingTwo:T) {
        self.firstThing = thingOne
        self.secondThing = thingTwo
    }
}
```

A user of this object type will use some particular type where the placeholder appears in the object type declaration, thus resolving the placeholder:

```
let holder = HolderOfTwoSameThings(thingOne:"howdy", thingTwo:"getLost")
```

Here, the type of the thingOne argument, "howdy", used in the initializer call, resolves T to String; therefore thingTwo must also be a String, and the properties firstThing and secondThing are Strings as well.

For generic functions and object types, which use the angle bracket syntax, the angle brackets may contain multiple placeholder names, separated by comma. For example:

```
func flockTwoTogether<T, U>(f1:T, _ f2:U) {}
```

The two parameters of flockTwoTogether can now be resolved to two different types (though they do not *have* to be different).

Type Constraints

All our examples so far have permitted any type to be substituted for the placeholder. Alternatively, you can limit the types that are eligible to be used for resolving a particular placeholder. This is called a *type constraint*. The simplest form of type constraint is to put a colon and a type name after the placeholder's name when it first appears. The type name after the colon can be a class name or a protocol name.

For example, let's return to our Flier and its `flockTogetherWith` function. Suppose we want to say that the parameter of `flockTogetherWith` should be declared by the adopter as a type that adopts Flier. You would *not* do that by declaring the type of that parameter as Flier in the protocol:

```
protocol Flier {
    func flockTogetherWith(f:Flier)
}
```

That code says: You can't adopt this protocol unless you declare a function `flockTogetherWith` whose f parameter is declared as Flier:

```
struct Bird : Flier {
    func flockTogetherWith(f:Flier) {}
}
```

That isn't what we want to say! We want to say that Bird should be able to adopt Flier while declaring f as being of *some Flier adopter type*, such as Bird. The way to say that is to use a placeholder constrained as a Flier. For example, we could do it like this:

```
protocol Flier {
    typealias Other : Flier
    func flockTogetherWith(f:Other)
}
```

Unfortunately, that's illegal: a protocol can't use itself as a type constraint. The workaround is to declare an extra protocol that Flier itself will adopt, and constrain Other to that protocol:

```
protocol Superflier {}
protocol Flier : Superflier {
    typealias Other : Superflier
    func flockTogetherWith(f:Other)
}
```

Now Bird can be a legal adopter like this:

```
struct Bird : Flier {
    func flockTogetherWith(f:Bird) {}
}
```

In a generic function or a generic object type, the type constraint appears in the angle brackets. For example:

```
func flockTwoTogether<T:Flier>(f1:T, _ f2:T) {}
```

Now you can't call `flockTwoTogether` with two String parameters, because a String is not a Flier. Moreover, if Bird and Insect both adopt Flier, `flockTwoTogether` can be called with two Bird parameters or with two Insect parameters — but not with a Bird and an Insect, because T is just one placeholder, signifying one Flier adopter type.

A type constraint on a placeholder is often useful as a way of assuring the compiler that some message can be sent to an instance of the placeholder type. For example, let's say we want to implement a function `myMin` that returns the smallest from a list of the same type. Here's a promising implementation as a generic function, but there's one problem — it doesn't compile:

```
func myMin<T>(things:T...) -> T {
    var minimum = things[0]
    for ix in 1..<things.count {
        if things[ix] < minimum { // compile error
            minimum = things[ix]
        }
    }
    return minimum
}
```

The problem is the comparison `things[ix] < minimum`. How does the compiler know that the type T, the type of `things[ix]` and `minimum`, will be resolved to a type that can in fact be compared using the less-than operator in this way? It doesn't, and that's exactly why it rejects that code. The solution is to promise the compiler that the resolved type of T *will* in fact work with the less-than operator. The way to do that, it turns out, is to constrain T to Swift's built-in Comparable protocol; adoption of the Comparable protocol exactly guarantees that the adopter *does* work with the less-than operator:

```
func myMin<T:Comparable>(things:T...) -> T {
```

Now `myMin` compiles, because it cannot be called except by resolving T to an object type that adopts Comparable and hence can be compared with the less-than operator. Naturally, built-in object types that you think should be comparable, such as Int, Double, String, and Character, do in fact adopt the Comparable protocol! If you look in the Swift headers, you'll find that the built-in `min` global function is declared in just this way, and for just this reason.

A generic protocol (a protocol whose declaration mentions `Self` or has an associated type) can be used as a type only in a generic, as a type constraint. This won't compile:

```
protocol Flier {
    typealias Other
    func fly()
}
```

```
func flockTwoTogether(f1:Flier, _ f2:Flier) { // compile error
    f1.fly()
    f2.fly()
}
```

To use a generic Flier protocol as a type, we must write a generic and use Flier as a type constraint. For example:

```
protocol Flier {
    typealias Other
    func fly()
}
func flockTwoTogether<T1:Flier, T2:Flier>(f1:T1, _ f2:T2) {
    f1.fly()
    f2.fly()
}
```

Explicit Specialization

In the examples so far, the user of a generic resolves the placeholder's type through inference. But there's another way to perform resolution: the user can resolve the type manually. This is called *explicit specialization*. In some situations, explicit specialization is mandatory — namely, if the placeholder type cannot be resolved through inference. There are two forms of explicit specialization:

Generic protocol with associated type

The adopter of a protocol can resolve the protocol's associated type manually through a **typealias** declaration using the protocol's alias name with an explicit type assignment. For example:

```
protocol Flier {
    typealias Other
}
struct Bird : Flier {
    typealias Other = String
}
```

Generic object type

The user of a generic object type can resolve the object's placeholder type(s) manually using the same angle bracket syntax used to declare the generic in the first place, with actual type names in the angle brackets. For example:

```
class Dog<T> {
    var name : T?
}
let d = Dog<String>()
```

(That explains the Optional<String> type used earlier in this chapter and in Chapter 3.)

You cannot explicitly specialize a generic function. You can, however, declare a generic type with a nongeneric function that uses the generic type's placeholder; explicit specialization of the generic type resolves the placeholder, and thus resolves the function:

```
protocol Flier {
    init()
}
struct Bird : Flier {
    init() {}
}
struct FlierMaker<T:Flier> {
    static func makeFlier() -> T {
        return T()
    }
}
let f = FlierMaker<Bird>.makeFlier() // returns a Bird
```

When a class is generic, you can subclass it, provided you resolve the generic. (This is new in Swift 2.0.) You can do this either through a matching generic subclass or by resolving the superclass generic explicitly. For example, here's a generic Dog:

```
class Dog<T> {
    var name : T?
}
```

You can subclass it as a generic whose placeholder matches that of the superclass:

```
class NoisyDog<T> : Dog<T> {}
```

That's legal because the resolution of the NoisyDog placeholder T will resolve the Dog placeholder T. The alternative is to subclass an explicitly specialized Dog:

```
class NoisyDog : Dog<String> {}
```

Associated Type Chains

When a generic placeholder is constrained to a generic protocol with an associated type, the associated type name can be chained with dot-notation to the placeholder name to specify that type.

Here's an example. Imagine that in a game program, soldiers and archers are enemies of one another. I'll express this by subsuming a Soldier struct and an Archer struct under a Fighter protocol that has an Enemy associated type, which is itself constrained to be a Fighter (again, I'll need an extra protocol that Fighter adopts):

```
protocol Superfighter {}
protocol Fighter : Superfighter {
    typealias Enemy : Superfighter
}
```

I'll resolve that associated type manually for both structs:

```
struct Soldier : Fighter {
    typealias Enemy = Archer
}
struct Archer : Fighter {
    typealias Enemy = Soldier
}
```

Now I'll create a generic struct to express the opposing camps of these fighters:

```
struct Camp<T:Fighter> {
}
```

Now suppose that a camp may contain a spy from the opposing camp. What is the type of that spy? Well, if this is a Soldier camp, it's an Archer; and if it's an Archer camp, it's a Soldier. More generally, since T is a Fighter, it's the type of the Enemy of this adopter of Fighter. I can express that neatly by chaining the associated type name to the place-holder name:

```
struct Camp<T:Fighter> {
    var spy : T.Enemy?
}
```

The result is that if, for a particular Camp, T is resolved to Soldier, `T.Enemy` means Fighter — and *vice versa*. We have created a correct and inviolable rule for the type that a Camp's `spy` must be. This won't compile:

```
var c = Camp<Soldier>()
c.spy = Soldier() // compile error
```

We've tried to assign an object of the wrong type to this Camp's `spy` property. But this does compile:

```
var c = Camp<Soldier>()
c.spy = Archer()
```

Longer chains of associated type names are possible — in particular, when a generic protocol has an associated type which is itself constrained to a generic protocol with an associated type.

For example, let's give each type of Fighter a characteristic weapon: a soldier has a sword, while an archer has a bow. I'll make a Sword struct and a Bow struct, and I'll unite them under a Wieldable protocol:

```
protocol Wieldable {
}
struct Sword : Wieldable {
}
struct Bow : Wieldable {
}
```

I'll add a Weapon associated type to Fighter, which is constrained to be a Wieldable, and once again I'll resolve it manually for each type of Fighter:

```
protocol Superfighter {
    typealias Weapon : Wieldable
}
protocol Fighter : Superfighter {
    typealias Enemy : Superfighter
}
struct Soldier : Fighter {
    typealias Weapon = Sword
    typealias Enemy = Archer
}
struct Archer : Fighter {
    typealias Weapon = Bow
    typealias Enemy = Soldier
}
```

Now let's say that every Fighter has the ability to steal his enemy's weapon. I'll give the Fighter generic protocol a `steal(weapon:from:)` method. How can the Fighter generic protocol express the parameter types in a way that causes its adopter to declare this method with the proper types?

The `from:` parameter type is this Fighter's Enemy. We already know how to express that: it's the placeholder plus dot-notation with the associated type name. Here, the placeholder is the adopter of this protocol — namely, `Self`. So the `from:` parameter type is `Self.Enemy`. And what about the `weapon:` parameter type? That's the Weapon of that Enemy! So the `weapon:` parameter type is `Self.Enemy.Weapon`:

```
protocol Fighter : Superfighter {
    typealias Enemy : Superfighter
    func steal(weapon:Self.Enemy.Weapon, from:Self.Enemy)
}
```

(That code will compile, and will mean the same thing, if we omit `Self`. But `Self` would still be the implicit start of the chain, and I think it makes the meaning of the code clearer.)

The result is that the following declarations for Soldier and Archer correctly adopt the Fighter protocol, and the compiler approves:

```
struct Soldier : Fighter {
    typealias Weapon = Sword
    typealias Enemy = Archer
    func steal(weapon:Bow, from:Archer) {
    }
}
struct Archer : Fighter {
    typealias Weapon = Bow
    typealias Enemy = Soldier
    func steal (weapon:Sword, from:Soldier) {
    }
}
```

The example is artificial (though, I hope, sufficiently vivid); but the concept is not. The Swift headers make heavy use of associated type chains; the associated type chain `Generator.Element` is particularly common, because it expresses the type of the element of a sequence. The SequenceType generic protocol has an associated type Generator, which is constrained to be an adopter of the generic GeneratorType protocol, which in turn has an associated type Element.

Additional Constraints

A simple type constraint limits the types eligible for resolving a placeholder to a single type. Sometimes, you want to limit the eligible resolving types still further: you want additional constraints.

In a generic protocol, the colon in a type alias constraint is effectively the same as the colon that appears in a type declaration. Thus, it can be followed by multiple protocols, or by a superclass and multiple protocols:

```
class Dog {
}
class FlyingDog : Dog, Flier {
}
protocol Flier {
}
protocol Walker {
}
protocol Generic {
    typealias T : Flier, Walker
    typealias U : Dog, Flier
}
```

In the Generic protocol, the associated type T can be resolved only as a type that adopts the Flier protocol *and* the Walker protocol, and the associated type U can be resolved only as a type that is a Dog (or a subclass of Dog) *and* that adopts the Flier protocol.

In the angle brackets of a generic function or object type, that syntax is illegal; instead, you can append a `where` clause, consisting of one or more comma-separated additional constraints on a declared placeholder:

```
func flyAndWalk<T where T:Flier, T:Walker> (f:T) {}
func flyAndWalk2<T where T:Flier, T:Dog> (f:T) {}
```

A `where` clause can also impose additional constraints on the associated type of a generic protocol that already constrains a placeholder, using an associated type chain (described in the preceding section). This pseudocode shows what I mean; I've omitted the content of the `where` clause, to focus on what the `where` clause will be constraining:

```
protocol Flier {
    typealias Other
}
func flockTogether<T:Flier where T.Other /*???*/ > (f:T) {}
```

As you can see, the placeholder T is already constrained to be a Flier. Flier is itself a generic protocol, with an associated type Other. Thus, whatever type resolves T will resolve Other. The where clause constrains further the types eligible to resolve T, by restricting the types eligible to resolve Other.

So what sort of restriction are we allowed to impose on our associated type chain? One possibility is the same sort of restriction as in the preceding example — a colon followed by a protocol that it must adopt, or by a class that it must descend from. Here's an example with a protocol:

```
protocol Flier {
    typealias Other
}
struct Bird : Flier {
    typealias Other = String
}
struct Insect : Flier {
    typealias Other = Bird
}
func flockTogether<T:Flier where T.Other:Equatable> (f:T) {}
```

Both Bird and Insect adopt Flier, but they are not both eligible as the argument in a call to the flockTogether function. The flockTogether function can be called with a Bird argument, because a Bird's Other associated type is resolved to String, which adopts the built-in Equatable protocol. But flockTogether can't be called with an Insect argument, because an Insect's Other associated type is resolved to Bird, which *doesn't* adopt the Equatable protocol:

```
flockTogether(Bird()) // okay
flockTogether(Insect()) // compile error
```

Here's an example with a class:

```
protocol Flier {
    typealias Other
}
class Dog {
}
class NoisyDog : Dog {
}
struct Pig : Flier {
    typealias Other = NoisyDog // or Dog
}
func flockTogether<T:Flier where T.Other:Dog> (f:T) {}
```

The flockTogether function can be called with a Pig argument, because Pig adopts Flier and resolves Other to a Dog or a subclass of Dog:

```
flockTogether(Pig()) // okay
```

Instead of a colon, we can use an equality operator == followed by a type. The type at the end of the associated type chain must then *be* this exact type — not merely an adopter or subclass. For example:

```
protocol Flier {
    typealias Other
}
protocol Walker {
}
struct Kiwi : Walker {
}
struct Bird : Flier {
    typealias Other = Kiwi
}
struct Insect : Flier {
    typealias Other = Walker
}
func flockTogether<T:Flier where T.Other == Walker> (f:T) {}
```

The flockTogether function can be called with an Insect argument, because Insect adopts Flier and resolves Other to Walker. But it can't be called with a Bird argument. Bird adopts Flier, and it resolves Other to *an adopter of* Walker, namely Kiwi — but that isn't good enough to satisfy the == restriction.

The same sort of thing would be true if we had said == Dog in the previous example. A Pig argument would no longer be acceptable if Pig resolves Other to NoisyDog; Pig must resolve Other to Dog *itself* in order to be acceptable as an argument.

The type on the right side of the == operator can itself be an associated type chain. The resolved types at the ends of the two chains must then be identical. For example:

```
protocol Flier {
    typealias Other
}
struct Bird : Flier {
    typealias Other = String
}
struct Insect : Flier {
    typealias Other = Int
}
func flockTwoTogether<T:Flier, U:Flier where T.Other == U.Other>
    (f1:T, _ f2:U) {}
```

The flockTwoTogether function can be called with a Bird and a Bird, and it can be called with an Insect and an Insect, but it can't be called with an Insect and a Bird, because they don't resolve the Other associated type to the same type.

The Swift header makes extensive use of where clauses with an == operator, especially as a way of restricting a sequence type. For example, the String `appendContentsOf` method is declared twice, like this:

```
mutating func appendContentsOf(other: String)
mutating func appendContentsOf<S : SequenceType
    where S.Generator.Element == Character>(newElements: S)
```

I mentioned in Chapter 3 that `appendContentsOf` can concatenate a String to a String. But that's not the only kind of thing that `appendContentsOf` can concatenate to a String! A character sequence is legal too:

```
var s = "hello"
s.appendContentsOf(" world".characters) // "hello world"
```

And so is an array of Character:

```
s.appendContentsOf(["!" as Character])
```

Those are both sequences *of characters* — and the generic in the second `appendContentsOf` method declaration is how you specify that. It's a sequence, because it's a type that adopts the SequenceType protocol. But it's not just any old sequence; its `Generator.Element` associated type chain must be resolved to Character. The `Generator.Element` chain, as I mentioned earlier, is Swift's way of expressing the notion of a sequence's element type.

The Array struct has an `appendContentsOf` method too, but it's declared a little differently:

```
mutating func appendContentsOf<S : SequenceType
    where S.Generator.Element == Element>(newElements: S)
```

A sequence must be of just one type. If a sequence consists of String elements, you can add more elements to it, but only String elements; you can't add a sequence of Int elements to a sequence of String elements. An array is a sequence; it is a generic whose Element placeholder is the type of its elements. So the Array struct uses the == operator in its `appendContentsOf` method declaration to enforce this rule: the element type of the argument sequence must be *the same as* the element type of the existing array.

Extensions

An *extension* is a way of injecting your own code into an object type that has already been declared elsewhere; you are *extending* an existing object type. You can extend your own object types; you can also extend one of Swift's object types or one of Cocoa's object types, in which case you are *adding functionality* to a type that doesn't belong to you!

Extension declaration can take place only at the top level of a file. To declare an extension, put the keyword extension followed by the name of an existing object type, then optionally a colon plus the names of any protocols you want to add to the list of those adopted by this type, and finally curly braces containing the usual things that go inside an object type declaration — with the following restrictions:

- An extension can't override an existing member (but it can overload an existing method).
- An extension can't declare a stored property (but it can declare a computed property).
- An extension of a class can't declare a designated initializer or a deinitializer (but it can declare a convenience initializer).

Extending Object Types

In my real programming life, I sometimes extend a built-in Swift or Cocoa type just to encapsulate some missing functionality by expressing it as a property or method. Here are some examples from actual apps.

In a card game, I need to shuffle the deck, which is stored in an array. I extend Swift's built-in Array type to give it a shuffle method:

```
extension Array {
    mutating func shuffle () {
        for i in (0..<self.count).reverse() {
            let ix1 = i
            let ix2 = Int(arc4random_uniform(UInt32(i+1)))
            (self[ix1], self[ix2]) = (self[ix2], self[ix1])
        }
    }
}
```

Cocoa's Core Graphics framework has many useful functions associated with the CGRect struct, and Swift already extends CGRect to add some helpful properties and methods; but there's no shortcut for getting the center point (a CGPoint) of a CGRect, something that in practice one very often needs. I extend CGRect to give it a center property:

```
extension CGRect {
    var center : CGPoint {
        return CGPointMake(self.midX, self.midY)
    }
}
```

An extension can declare a static or class method; since an object type is usually globally available, this can often be an excellent way to slot a global function into an appropriate namespace. For example, in one of my apps, I find myself frequently using a certain color (a UIColor). Instead of creating that color repeatedly, it makes sense to encapsulate the instructions for generating it in a global function. But instead of making that function *completely* global, I make it — appropriately enough — a class method of UIColor:

```
extension UIColor {
    class func myGoldenColor() -> UIColor {
        return self.init(red:1.000, green:0.894, blue:0.541, alpha:0.900)
    }
}
```

Now I can use that color throughout my code simply by saying `UIColor.myGolden-Color()`, completely parallel to built-in class methods such as `UIColor.redColor()`.

Another good use of an extension is to make built-in Cocoa classes work with your private data types. For example, in my Zotz app, I've defined an enum whose raw values are the key strings to be used when archiving or unarchiving a property of a Card:

```
enum Archive : String {
    case Color = "itsColor"
    case Number = "itsNumber"
    case Shape = "itsShape"
    case Fill = "itsFill"
}
```

The only problem is that in order to use this enum when archiving, I have to take its `rawValue` each time:

```
coder.encodeObject(s1, forKey:Archive.Color.rawValue)
coder.encodeObject(s2, forKey:Archive.Number.rawValue)
coder.encodeObject(s3, forKey:Archive.Shape.rawValue)
coder.encodeObject(s4, forKey:Archive.Fill.rawValue)
```

That's just ugly. An elegant fix (suggested in a WWDC 2015 video) is to teach NSCoder, the class of `coder`, what to do when the `forKey:` argument is an Archive instead of a String. In an extension, I overload the `encodeObject:forKey:` method:

```
extension NSCoder {
    func encodeObject(objv: AnyObject?, forKey key: Archive) {
        self.encodeObject(objv, forKey:key.rawValue)
    }
}
```

In effect, I've moved the `rawValue` call out of my code and into NSCoder's code. Now I can archive a Card without saying `rawValue`:

```
coder.encodeObject(s1, forKey:Archive.Color)
coder.encodeObject(s2, forKey:Archive.Number)
coder.encodeObject(s3, forKey:Archive.Shape)
coder.encodeObject(s4, forKey:Archive.Fill)
```

Extensions on one's own object types can help to organize one's code. A frequently used convention is to add an extension for each protocol one's object type needs to adopt, like this:

```
class ViewController: UIViewController {
    // ... UIViewController method overrides go here ...
}
extension ViewController : UIPopoverPresentationControllerDelegate {
    // ... UIPopoverPresentationControllerDelegate methods go here ...
}
extension ViewController : UIToolbarDelegate {
    // ... UIToolbarDelegate methods go here ...
}
```

An extension on your own object type is also a way to spread your definition of that object type over multiple files, if you feel that several shorter files are better than one long file.

When you extend a Swift struct, a curious thing happens with initializers: it becomes possible to declare an initializer and keep the implicit initializers:

```
struct Digit {
    var number : Int
}
extension Digit {
    init() {
        self.init(number:42)
    }
}
```

That code means that you can instantiate a Digit by calling the explicitly declared initializer — Digit() — or by calling the implicit memberwise initializer — Digit(number:7). Thus, the explicit declaration of an initializer through an extension did not cause us to lose the implicit memberwise initializer, as would have happened if we had declared the same initializer inside the original struct declaration.

Extending Protocols

New in Swift 2.0, you can extend a protocol. When you do, you can add methods and properties to the protocol, just as for any object type. Unlike a protocol declaration, these methods and properties are not mere requirements, to be fulfilled by the adopter of the protocol; they are actual methods and properties, to be *inherited* by the adopter of the protocol! For example:

```
protocol Flier {
}
extension Flier {
    func fly() {
        print("flap flap flap")
    }
}
struct Bird : Flier {
}
```

Observe that Bird can now adopt Flier without implementing the `fly` method. Even if we were to add `func fly()` as a requirement in the Flier protocol declaration, Bird could *still* adopt Flier without implementing the `fly` method. That's because the Flier protocol extension *supplies* the `fly` method! Bird thus *inherits* an implementation of `fly`:

```
let b = Bird()
b.fly() // flap flap flap
```

An adopter *can* implement a method inherited from a protocol extension, thus overriding that method:

```
struct Insect : Flier {
    func fly() {
        print("whirr")
    }
}
let i = Insect()
i.fly() // whirr
```

But be warned: this kind of inheritance is *not polymorphic*. The adopter's implementation is not an override; it is merely another implementation. The internal identity rule does *not* apply; it matters how a reference is typed:

```
let f : Flier = Insect()
f.fly() // flap flap flap
```

Even though f is internally an Insect (as we can discover with the `is` operator), the `fly` message is being sent to an object reference typed as a Flier, so it is Flier's implementation of the `fly` method that is called, not Insect's implementation.

To get something that looks like polymorphic inheritance, we must declare `fly` as a requirement *in the original protocol*:

```
protocol Flier {
    func fly() // *
}
extension Flier {
    func fly() {
        print("flap flap flap")
    }
}
struct Insect : Flier {
    func fly() {
        print("whirr")
    }
}
```

Now an Insect maintains its internal integrity:

```
let f : Flier = Insect()
f.fly() // whirr
```

This difference makes sense, because adoption of a protocol does not (and must not) introduce the overhead of dynamic dispatch. Therefore the compiler must make a *static* decision. If the method is declared as a requirement in the original protocol, we are guaranteed that the adopter implements it, and so we can (and do) call the adopter's implementation. But if the method exists only in the protocol extension, then deciding whether the adopter reimplements it would require dynamic dispatch at runtime, and that would defeat the nature of protocols — so the compiler messages the protocol extension.

The chief benefit of protocol extensions is that they allow code to be moved to an appropriate scope. Here's an example from my Zotz app. I have four enums, each representing an attribute of a Card: Fill, Color, Shape, and Number. They all have an Int raw value. I was tired of having to say `rawValue:` every time I initialized one of these enums from its raw value, so I gave each enum a delegating initializer with no externalized parameter name, that calls the built-in `init(rawValue:)` initializer:

```
enum Fill : Int {
    case Empty = 1
    case Solid
    case Hazy
    init?(_ what:Int) {
        self.init(rawValue:what)
    }
}
enum Color : Int {
    case Color1 = 1
    case Color2
    case Color3
    init?(_ what:Int) {
        self.init(rawValue:what)
    }
}
// ... and so on ...
```

I didn't like the repetition of my initializer declaration, but in Swift 1.2 and before, there was nothing I could do about that. In Swift 2.0, I can move that declaration into a protocol extension. It turns out that an enum with a raw value automatically adopts the built-in generic RawRepresentable protocol, where the raw value type is a type alias called RawValue. So I can shoehorn my initializer into the RawRepresentable protocol:

```
extension RawRepresentable {
    init?(_ what:RawValue) {
        self.init(rawValue:what)
    }
}
enum Fill : Int {
    case Empty = 1
    case Solid
    case Hazy
```

```
    }
    enum Color : Int {
        case Color1 = 1
        case Color2
        case Color3
    }
    // ... and so on ...
```

In the Swift standard library, protocol extensions have meant that many global functions can be recast as methods. For example, in Swift 1.2 and earlier, enumerate (see Chapter 3) was a global function:

```
func enumerate<Seq:SequenceType>(base:Seq) -> EnumerateSequence<Seq>
```

It was a global function because it had to be. This is a function that is to apply only to sequences — adopters of the SequenceType protocol. Prior to Swift 2.0, how could that be expressed? An enumerate method might have been declared as a *requirement* of the SequenceType protocol, but this would mean merely that every adopter of Sequence-Type must implement it; it wouldn't *provide* an implementation. The only way to do that was as a global function, with the sequence as parameter, using a generic constraint to guard the door, so to speak, so that *only* a sequence could be passed as argument.

In Swift 2.0, however, enumerate is a method, declared in an extension to the Sequence-Type protocol:

```
    extension SequenceType {
        func enumerate() -> EnumerateSequence<Self>
    }
```

Now there's no need for a generic constraint. There's no need for a generic. There's no need for a parameter! This is a method *of* SequenceType; the sequence to be enumerated is the sequence to which the enumerate message is sent.

That example could be greatly multiplied; a *lot* of Swift standard library global functions were turned into methods in Swift 2.0. This change effectively transforms the feel of the language.

Extending Generics

When you extend a generic type, the placeholder type names are visible to your extension declaration. That's good, because you might need to use them; but it can make your code a little mystifying, because you seem to be using an undefined type name out of the blue. It might be a good idea to add a comment, to remind yourself what you're up to:

```
    class Dog<T> {
        var name : T?
    }
    extension Dog {
```

```
    func sayYourName() -> T? { // T is the type of self.name
        return self.name
    }
}
```

New in Swift 2.0, a generic type extension can include a where clause. This has the same effect as any generic constraint: it limits which resolvers of the generic can call the code injected by this extension, and assures the compiler that your code is legal for those resolvers.

As with protocol extensions, this means that a global function can be turned into a method. Recall this example from earlier in this chapter:

```
func myMin<T>(things:T...) -> T {
    var minimum = things[0]
    for ix in 1..<things.count {
        if things[ix] < minimum { // compile error
            minimum = things[ix]
        }
    }
    return minimum
}
```

Why did I make that a global function? Because before Swift 2.0, I had to. Let's say I wanted to make this a method of Array. In Swift 1.2 and before, you could extend Array, and your extension could *refer to* Array's generic placeholder; but it couldn't *constrain* that placeholder further. Thus, there was no way to inject a method into Array while guaranteeing that the placeholder would be a Comparable — and so the compiler wouldn't permit the use of the < operator on an element of the array. In Swift 2.0, I *can* constrain the generic placeholder further, and so I *can* make this a method of Array:

```
extension Array where Element:Comparable { // Element is the element type
    func min() -> Element {
        var minimum = self[0]
        for ix in 1..<self.count {
            if self[ix] < minimum {
                minimum = self[ix]
            }
        }
        return minimum
    }
}
```

That method can be called only on an array of Comparable elements; it isn't injected into other kinds of arrays, so the compiler won't permit it to be called:

```
let m = [4,1,5,7,2].min() // 1
let d = [Digit(12), Digit(42)].min() // compile error
```

The second line doesn't compile, because I haven't made my Digit struct adopt the Comparable protocol.

Once again, this change in the Swift language has resulted in a major wholesale reorganization of the Swift standard library, allowing global functions to be moved into struct extensions and protocol extensions as methods. For example, the global find function from Swift 1.2 and before has become, in Swift 2.0, the CollectionType index-Of method; it is constrained so that the collection's elements are Equatables, because you can't find a needle in a haystack unless you have a way of identifying the needle when you see it:

```
extension CollectionType where Generator.Element : Equatable {
    func indexOf(element: Self.Generator.Element) -> Self.Index?
}
```

That's a protocol extension, and it is also a generic extension constrained with a where clause — neither of which was possible before Swift 2.0.

Umbrella Types

Swift provides a few built-in types as general umbrella types, capable of embracing multiple real types under a single heading.

AnyObject

The umbrella type most commonly encountered in real-life iOS programming is Any-Object. It is actually a protocol; as a protocol, it is completely empty, requiring no properties or methods. It has the special feature that *all class types* conform to it automatically. Thus, it is possible to assign or pass any class instance where an AnyObject is expected, and to cast in either direction:

```
class Dog {
}
let d = Dog()
let any : AnyObject = d
let d2 = any as! Dog
```

Certain Swift types, which are *not* class types — such as String and the basic numeric types — are bridged to Objective-C types, which *are* class types, defined by the Foundation framework. This means that, in the presence of the Foundation framework, a Swift bridged type can be assigned, passed, or cast to an AnyObject, even if it is not a class type — because it will be cast first to its Objective-C bridged class type automatically, behind the scenes — and an AnyObject can be cast down to a Swift bridged type. For example:

```
let s = "howdy"
let any : AnyObject = s // implicitly casts to NSString
let s2 = any as! String
let i = 1
let any2 : AnyObject = i // implicitly casts to NSNumber
let i2 = any2 as! Int
```

The common way to encounter an AnyObject is in the course of interchange with Objective-C. Swift's ability to cast any class type to and from an AnyObject parallels Objective-C's ability to cast any class type to and from an id. In effect, AnyObject *is* the Swift version of id.

NSUserDefaults, NSCoding, and key–value coding (Chapter 10), for example, all allow you to retrieve an object of indeterminate class by a string key name; such an object will arrive into Swift as an AnyObject — in particular, as an Optional wrapping an AnyObject, because there might be no such key, in which case Cocoa needs to be able to return nil. In general, however, an AnyObject will be of little use to you; you'll want to let Swift know what sort of object this *really* is. Unwrapping the Optional and casting down from AnyObject is up to you. If you're perfectly sure of your ground, you can force-unwrap and force-cast with the as! operator:

```
required init ( coder decoder: NSCoder ) {
    let s = decoder.decodeObjectForKey(Archive.Color) as! String
    // ...
}
```

Of course, you'd better be telling the truth when you cast down an AnyObject with as!, or you will crash when the code runs and the cast turns out to be impossible. You can use the is and as? operators, if you're in doubt, to make sure your cast is safe.

Suppressing type checking

A surprising feature of AnyObject is that it can be used to suspend the compiler's judgment as to whether a certain message can be sent to an object — similar to Objective-C, where typing something as an id causes the compiler to suspend judgment about what messages can be sent to it. Thus, you can send a message to an AnyObject without bothering to cast to its real type. (Nevertheless, if you *know* the object's real type, you probably *will* cast to that type.)

You can't send just any old message to an AnyObject; the message must correspond to a class member that meets one of the following criteria:

- It is a member of an Objective-C class.
- It is a member of your own Swift subclass (or extension) of an Objective-C class.
- It is a member of a Swift class, and is marked @objc (or dynamic).

This feature is fundamentally parallel to optional protocol members, which I discussed earlier in this chapter — with some slight differences. Let's start with two classes:

```
class Dog {
    @objc var noise : String = "woof"
    @objc func bark() -> String {
        return "woof"
    }
}
class Cat {}
```

The Dog property `noise` and the Dog method `bark` are marked `@objc`, so they are visible as potential messages to be sent to an AnyObject. To prove it, I'll type a Cat as an AnyObject and send it one of these messages. Let's start with the `noise` property:

```
let c : AnyObject = Cat()
let s = c.noise
```

That code, amazingly, compiles. Moreover, it doesn't crash when the code runs! The `noise` property has been typed as an Optional wrapping its original type. Here, that's an Optional wrapping a String. If the object typed as AnyObject doesn't implement `noise`, the result is `nil` and no harm done. Moreover, unlike an optional protocol property, the Optional in question is implicitly unwrapped. Therefore, if the AnyObject turns out to have a `noise` property (for example, if it had been a Dog), the resulting implicitly unwrapped String can be treated directly as a String.

Now let's try it with a method call:

```
let c : AnyObject = Cat()
let s = c.bark?()
```

Again, that code compiles and is safe. If the Object typed as AnyObject doesn't implement `bark`, no `bark()` call is performed; the method result type has been wrapped in an Optional, so s is typed as `String?` and has been set to `nil`. If the AnyObject turns out to have a `bark` method (for example, if it had been a Dog), the result is an Optional wrapping the returned String. If you call `bark!()` on the AnyObject instead, the result will be a String, but you'll crash if the AnyObject doesn't implement `bark`. Unlike an optional protocol member, you can even send the message *with no unwrapping*. This is legal:

```
let c : AnyObject = Cat()
let s = c.bark()
```

That's just like force-unwrapping the call: the result is a String, but it's possible to crash.

Object identity and type identity

Sometimes, what you want to know is not what *type* an object is, but whether an object itself is the *particular object* you think it is. This problem can't arise with a value type, but it can arise with a reference type, where there can be more than one distinct reference to one and the same object. A class is a reference type, so the problem can arise with class instances.

Swift's solution is the identity operator (===). This operator is available for instances of object types that adopt the AnyObject protocol — like classes! It compares one object reference with another. It is not a comparison of values for equality, like the equality operator (==); you're asking whether two object references refer to one and the same object. There is also a negative version of the identity operator (!==).

A typical use case is that a class instance arrives from Cocoa, and you need to know whether it is in fact a particular object to which you already have a reference. For example, an NSNotification has an `object` property that helps identify the notification (usually, it is the original sender of the notification); Cocoa is agnostic about its underlying type, so this is another of those situations where you'll receive an AnyObject wrapped in an Optional. Like ==, the === operator works seamlessly on an Optional, so you can use it to make sure that a notification's `object` property is the object you expect:

```swift
func changed(n:NSNotification) {
    let player = MPMusicPlayerController.applicationMusicPlayer()
    if n.object === player {
        // ...
    }
}
```

AnyClass

AnyClass is the class of AnyObject. It corresponds to the Objective-C `Class` type. It arises typically in declarations where a Cocoa API wants to say that a class is expected.

For example, the UIView `layerClass` class method is declared, in its Swift translation, like this:

```swift
class func layerClass() -> AnyClass
```

That means: if you override this method, implement it to return a class. This will presumably be a CALayer subclass. To return an actual class in your implementation, send the `self` message to the name of the class:

```swift
override class func layerClass() -> AnyClass {
    return CATiledLayer.self
}
```

A reference to an AnyClass object behaves much like a reference to an AnyObject object. You can send it any Objective-C message that Swift knows about — any Objective-C *class* message. To illustrate, once again I'll start with two classes:

```swift
class Dog {
    @objc static var whatADogSays : String = "woof"
}
class Cat {}
```

Objective-C can see whatADogSays, and it sees it as a class property. Therefore you can send whatADogSays to an AnyClass reference:

```
let c : AnyClass = Cat.self
let s = c.whatADogSays
```

A reference to a class, such as you can obtain by sending dynamicType to an instance reference, or by sending self to the type name, is of a type that adopts AnyClass, and you can compare references to such types with the === operator. In effect, this is a way of finding out whether two references to classes refer to the same class. For example:

```
func typeTester(d:Dog, _ whattype:Dog.Type) {
    if d.dynamicType === whattype {
        // ...
    }
}
```

The condition is true only if d and whattype are *the same* type (without regard to polymorphism); for example, if Dog has a subclass NoisyDog, then the condition is true if the parameters are Dog() and Dog.self or NoisyDog and NoisyDog.self, but not if they are NoisyDog() and Dog.self. This is valuable, despite the lack of polymorphism, because you can't use the is operator when the thing on the right side is a type reference — it has to be a literal type name.

Any

The Any type is a type alias for an empty protocol that is automatically adopted by all types. Thus, where an Any object is expected, absolutely any object can be passed:

```
func anyExpecter(a:Any) {}
anyExpecter("howdy")       // a struct instance
anyExpecter(String)        // a struct
anyExpecter(Dog())         // a class instance
anyExpecter(Dog)           // a class
anyExpecter(anyExpecter) // a function
```

An object typed as Any can be tested against, or cast down to, any object or function type. To illustrate, here's a protocol with an associated type, and two adopters who explicitly resolve it:

```
protocol Flier {
    typealias Other
}
struct Bird : Flier {
    typealias Other = Insect
}
struct Insect : Flier {
    typealias Other = Bird
}
```

Now here's a function that takes a Flier along with a second parameter typed as Any, and tests whether that second parameter's type is the same as the Flier's resolved Other type; the test is legal because Any can be tested against any type:

```
func flockTwoTogether<T:Flier>(flier:T, _ other:Any) {
    if other is T.Other {
        print("they can flock together")
    }
}
```

If we call flockTwoTogether with a Bird and an Insect, the console says "they can flock together." If we call it with a Bird and an object of any other type, it doesn't.

Collection Types

Swift, in common with most modern computer languages, has built-in collection types Array and Dictionary, along with a third type, Set. Array and Dictionary are sufficiently important that the language accommodates them with some special syntax. At the same time, like most Swift types, they are quite thinly provided with related functions; some missing functionality is provided by Cocoa's NSArray and NSDictionary, to which they are respectively bridged. The Set collection type is bridged to Cocoa's NSSet.

Array

An array (Array, a struct) is an ordered collection of object instances (the *elements* of the array) accessible by index number, where an index number is an Int numbered from 0. Thus, if an array contains four elements, the first has index 0 and the last has index 3. A Swift array cannot be sparse: if there is an element with index 3, there is also an element with index 2 and so on.

The most salient feature of Swift arrays is their strict typing. Unlike some other computer languages, a Swift array's elements must be *uniform* — that is, the array must consist solely of elements of the same definite type. Even an empty array must have a definite element type, despite the fact that it happens to lack elements at this moment. An array is itself typed in accordance with its element type. Arrays whose elements are of different types are considered, themselves, to be of two different types: an array of Int elements is of a different type from an array of String elements. Array types are polymorphic in accordance with their element types: if NoisyDog is a subclass of Dog, then an array of NoisyDog can be used where an array of Dog is expected. If all this reminds you of Optionals, it should. Like an Optional, a Swift array is a generic. It is declared as Array<Element>, where the placeholder Element is the type of a particular array's elements.

The uniformity restriction is not as severe as it might seem at first glance. An array must have elements of just one type, but types are very flexible. By a clever choice of type, you can have an array whose elements are of different types *internally*. For example:

- If there's a Dog class with a NoisyDog subclass, an array of Dog can contain both Dog objects and NoisyDog objects.
- If both Bird and Insect adopt the Flier protocol, an array of Flier can contain both Bird objects and Insect objects.
- An array of AnyObject can contain instances of any class and of any Swift bridged type — such as an Int, a String, and a Dog.
- A type might itself be a carrier of different possible types. My Error enum, earlier in this chapter, is an example; its associated value might be an Int or it might be a String, so an array of Error elements can carry both Int values and String values within itself.

To declare or state the type of a given array's elements, you could explicitly resolve the generic placeholder; an array of Int elements would thus be an `Array<Int>`. However, Swift offers syntactic sugar for stating an array's element type, using square brackets around the name of the element type, like this: `[Int]`. That's the syntax you'll use most of the time.

A literal array is represented as square brackets containing a list of its elements separated by comma (and optional spaces): for example, `[1,2,3]`. The literal for an empty array is empty square brackets: `[]`.

An array's default initializer `init()`, called by appending empty parentheses to the array's type, yields an empty array of that type. Thus, you can create an empty array of Int like this:

```
var arr = [Int]()
```

Alternatively, if a reference's type is known in advance, the empty array `[]` can be inferred to that type. Thus, you can also create an empty array of Int like this:

```
var arr : [Int] = []
```

If you're starting with a literal array containing elements, you won't usually need to declare the array's type, because Swift will infer it by looking at the elements. For example, Swift will infer that `[1,2,3]` is an array of Int. If the array element types consist of a class and its subclasses, like Dog and NoisyDog, Swift will infer the common superclass as the array's type. Even `[1, "howdy"]` is a legal array literal; it is inferred to be an array of NSObject. However, in some cases you will need to declare an array reference's type explicitly even while assigning a literal to that array:

```
let arr : [Flier] = [Insect(), Bird()]
```

An array also has an initializer whose parameter is a sequence. This means that if a type is a sequence, you can split an instance of it into the elements of an array. For example:

- `Array(1...3)` generates the array of Int `[1,2,3]`.
- `Array("hey".characters)` generates the array of Character `["h","e","y"]`.
- `Array(d)`, where d is a Dictionary, generates an array of tuples of the key–value pairs of d.

Another array initializer, `init(count:repeatedValue:)`, lets you populate an array with the same value. In this example, I create an array of 100 Optional strings initialized to `nil`:

```
let strings : [String?] = Array(count:100, repeatedValue:nil)
```

That's the closest you can get in Swift to a sparse array; we have 100 slots, each of which might or might not contain a string (and to start with, none of them do).

Array casting and type testing

When you assign, pass, or cast one array type to another array type, you are operating on the individual elements of the array. Thus, for example:

```
let arr : [Int?] = [1,2,3]
```

That code is actually a shorthand: to treat an array of Int as an array of Optionals wrapping Int means that each individual Int in the original array must be wrapped in an Optional. And that is exactly what happens:

```
let arr : [Int?] = [1,2,3]
print(arr) // [Optional(1), Optional(2), Optional(3)]
```

Similarly, suppose we have a Dog class and its NoisyDog subclass; then this code is legal:

```
let dog1 : Dog = NoisyDog()
let dog2 : Dog = NoisyDog()
let arr = [dog1, dog2]
let arr2 = arr as! [NoisyDog]
```

In third line, we have an array of Dog. In the fourth line, we cast this array down to an array of NoisyDog, meaning that we cast each individual Dog in the first array to a NoisyDog (and we won't crash when we do that, because each element of the first array really *is* a NoisyDog).

You can test all the elements of an array with the `is` operator by testing the array itself. For example, given the array of Dog from the previous code, you can say:

```
if arr is [NoisyDog] { // ...
```

That will be `true` if each element of the array is in fact a NoisyDog.

Similarly, the `as?` operator will cast an array to an Optional wrapping an array, which will be `nil` if the underlying cast cannot be performed:

```
let dog1 : Dog = NoisyDog()
let dog2 : Dog = NoisyDog()
let dog3 : Dog = Dog()
let arr = [dog1, dog2]
let arr2 = arr as? [NoisyDog] // Optional wrapping an array of NoisyDog
let arr3 = [dog2, dog3]
let arr4 = arr3 as? [NoisyDog] // nil
```

The reason for casting down an array is exactly the same as the reason for casting down any value — it's so that you can send appropriate messages to the elements of that array. If NoisyDog declares a method that Dog doesn't have, you can't send that message to an element of an array of Dog. Somehow, you need to cast that element down to a NoisyDog so that the compiler will let you send it that message. You can cast down an individual element, or you can cast down the entire array; you'll do whichever is safe and makes sense in a particular context.

Array comparison

Array equality works just as you would expect: two arrays are equal if they contain the same number of elements and all the elements are pairwise equal in order:

```
let i1 = 1
let i2 = 2
let i3 = 3
if [1,2,3] == [i1,i2,i3] { // they are equal!
```

Two arrays don't have to be of the same type to be compared against one another for equality, but the test won't succeed unless they do in fact contain objects that are equal to one another. Here, I compare a Dog array against a NoisyDog array; they are in fact equal because the dogs they contain are the same dogs in the same order:

```
let nd1 = NoisyDog()
let d1 = nd1 as Dog
let nd2 = NoisyDog()
let d2 = nd2 as Dog
if [d1,d2] == [nd1,nd2] { // they are equal!
```

Arrays are value types

Because an array is a struct, it is a value type, not a reference type. This means that every time an array is assigned to a variable or passed as argument to a function, it is effectively copied. I do not mean to imply, however, that merely assigning or passing an array is expensive, or that a lot of actual copying takes place every time. If the reference to an array is a constant, clearly no copying is actually necessary; and even operations that yield a new array derived from another array, or that mutate an array, may be quite efficient. You just have to trust that the designers of Swift have thought about these problems and have implemented arrays efficiently behind the scenes.

Although an array itself is a value type, its elements are treated however those elements would normally be treated. In particular, an array of class instances, assigned to multiple variables, results in multiple references to the same instances.

Array subscripting

The Array struct implements subscript methods to allow access to elements using square brackets after a reference to an array. You can use an Int inside the square brackets. For example, in an array consisting of three elements, if the array is referred to by a variable arr, then arr[1] accesses the second element.

You can also use a Range of Int inside the square brackets. For example, if arr is an array with three elements, then arr[1...2] signifies the second and third elements. Technically, an expression like arr[1...2] yields something called an ArraySlice. However, an ArraySlice is very similar to an array; for example, you can subscript an ArraySlice in just the same ways you would subscript an array, and an ArraySlice can be passed where an array is expected. In general, therefore, you will probably pretend that an ArraySlice *is* an array.

If the reference to an array is mutable (var, not let), then a subscript expression can be assigned to. This alters what's in that slot. Of course, what is assigned must accord with the type of the array's elements:

```
var arr = [1,2,3]
arr[1] = 4 // arr is now [1,4,3]
```

If the subscript is a range, what is assigned must be an array. This can change the length of the array being assigned to:

```
var arr = [1,2,3]
arr[1..<2] = [7,8] // arr is now [1,7,8,3]
arr[1..<2] = [] // arr is now [1,8,3]
arr[1..<1] = [10] // arr is now [1,10,8,3] (no element was removed!)
```

It is a runtime error to access an element by a number larger than the largest element number or smaller than the smallest element number. If arr has three elements, speaking of arr[-1] or arr[3] is not illegal linguistically, but your program will crash.

Nested arrays

It is legal for the elements of an array to be arrays. For example:

```
let arr = [[1,2,3], [4,5,6], [7,8,9]]
```

That's an array of arrays of Int. Its type declaration, therefore, is [[Int]]. (No law says that the contained arrays have to be the same length; that's just something I did for clarity.)

To access an individual Int inside those nested arrays, you can chain subscript operations:

```
let arr = [[1,2,3], [4,5,6], [7,8,9]]
let i = arr[1][1] // 5
```

If the outer array reference is mutable, you can also write into a nested array:

```
var arr = [[1,2,3], [4,5,6], [7,8,9]]
arr[1][1] = 100
```

You can modify the inner arrays in other ways as well; for example, you can insert additional elements into them.

Basic array properties and methods

An array is a collection (CollectionType protocol), which is itself a sequence (Sequence-Type protocol). If those terms have a familiar ring, they should: the same is true of a String's characters, which I called a character sequence in Chapter 3. For this reason, an array has a striking similarity to a character sequence.

As a collection, an array's count read-only property reports the number of elements it contains. If an array's count is 0, its isEmpty property is true.

An array's first and last read-only properties return its first and last elements, but they are wrapped in an Optional because the array might be empty and so these properties would need to be nil. This is one of those rare situations in Swift where you can wind up with an Optional wrapping an Optional. For example, consider an array of Optionals wrapping Ints, and what happens when you get the last property of such an array.

An array's largest accessible index is one *less* than its count. You may find yourself calculating index values with reference to the count; for example, to refer to the last two elements of arr, you can say:

```
let arr = [1,2,3]
let arr2 = arr[arr.count-2...arr.count-1] // [2,3]
```

Swift doesn't adopt the modern convention of letting you use negative numbers as a shorthand for that calculation. On the other hand, for the common case where you want the last n elements of an array, you can use the suffix method:

```
let arr = [1,2,3]
let arr2 = arr.suffix(2) // [2,3]
```

Both `suffix` and its companion `prefix` have the remarkable feature that there is no penalty for going out of range:

```
let arr = [1,2,3]
let arr2 = arr.suffix(10) // [1,2,3] (and no crash)
```

Instead of describing the size of the suffix or prefix by its count, you can express the limit of the suffix or prefix by its index:

```
let arr = [1,2,3]
let arr2 = arr.suffixFrom(1)    // [2,3]
let arr3 = arr.prefixUpTo(1)    // [1]
let arr4 = arr.prefixThrough(1) // [1,2]
```

An array's `startIndex` property is 0, and its `endIndex` property is its `count`. Moreover, an array's `indices` property is a half-open range whose endpoints are its `startIndex` and `endIndex` — that is, a range accessing the entire array. If you start with a mutable reference to this range, you can modify *its* `startIndex` and `endIndex` to derive a new range. We did the same thing with a character sequence in Chapter 3; but an array's index values are Ints, so you can use ordinary arithmetic operations:

```
let arr = [1,2,3]
var r = arr.indices
r.startIndex = r.endIndex-2
arr2 = arr[r] // [2,3]
```

The `indexOf` method reports the index of the first occurrence of an element in an array, but it is wrapped in an Optional so that `nil` can be returned if the element doesn't appear in the array. If the array consists of Equatables, the comparison uses == to identify the element being sought:

```
let arr = [1,2,3]
let ix = arr.indexOf(2) // Optional wrapping 1
```

Even if the array *doesn't* consist of Equatables, you can supply your own function that takes an element type and returns a Bool, and you'll get back the first element for which that Bool is `true`. In this example, my Bird struct has a `name` String property:

```
let aviary = [Bird(name:"Tweety"), Bird(name:"Flappy"), Bird(name:"Lady")]
let ix = aviary.indexOf {$0.name.characters.count < 5} // Optional(2)
```

As a sequence, an array's `contains` method reports whether it contains an element. Again, you can rely on the == operator if the elements are Equatables, or you can supply your own function that takes an element type and returns a Bool:

```
let arr = [1,2,3]
let ok = arr.contains(2) // true
let ok2 = arr.contains {$0 > 3} // false
```

The `startsWith` method reports whether an array's starting elements match the elements of a given sequence of the same type. Once more, you can rely on the == operator for Equatables, or you can supply a function that takes two values of the element type and returns a Bool stating whether they match:

```
let arr = [1,2,3]
let ok = startsWith(arr, [1,2]) // true
let ok2 = arr.startsWith([1,-2]) {abs($0) == abs($1)} // true
```

The `elementsEqual` method is the sequence generalization of array comparison: the two sequences must be of the same length, and either their elements must be Equatables or you can supply a matching function.

The `minElement` and `maxElement` methods return the smallest or largest element in an array, wrapped in an Optional in case the array is empty. If the array consists of Comparables, you can let the < operator do its work; alternatively, you can supply a function that returns a Bool stating whether the smaller of two given elements is the first:

```
let arr = [3,1,-2]
let min = arr.minElement() // Optional(-2)
let min2 = arr.minElement {abs($0)<abs($1)} // Optional(1)
```

If the reference to an array is mutable, the `append` and `appendContentsOf` instance methods add elements to the end of it. The difference between them is that append takes a single value of the element type, while `appendContentsOf` takes a sequence of the element type. For example:

```
var arr = [1,2,3]
arr.append(4)
arr.appendContentsOf([5,6])
arr.appendContentsOf(7...8) // arr is now [1,2,3,4,5,6,7,8]
```

The + operator is overloaded to behave like `appendContentsOf` (not append!) when the left-hand operand is an array, except that it generates a new array, so it works even if the reference to the array is a constant. If the reference to the array is mutable, you can extend it in place with the += operator. Thus:

```
let arr = [1,2,3]
let arr2 = arr + [4] // arr2 is now [1,2,3,4]
var arr3 = [1,2,3]
arr3 += [4] // arr3 is now [1,2,3,4]
```

If the reference to an array is mutable, the instance method `insert(atIndex:)` inserts a single element at the given index. To insert multiple elements at once, use assignment into a range-subscripted array, as I described earlier (and there is also an `insertContentsOf(at:)` method).

If the reference to an array is mutable, the instance method `removeAtIndex` removes the element at that index; the instance method `removeLast` removes the last element, and `removeFirst` removes the first element. These methods also *return* the value that was removed from the array; you can ignore the returned value if you don't need it.

These methods do not wrap the returned value in an Optional, and accessing an out-of-range index will crash your program. Another form of removeFirst lets you specify how many elements to remove, but returns no value; it, too, can crash if there aren't that many elements.

On the other hand, popFirst and popLast do wrap the returned value in an Optional, and are thus safe even if the array is empty. If the reference is *not* mutable, you can use the dropFirst and dropLast methods to return an array (actually, a slice) with the end element removed.

The joinWithSeparator instance method starts with an array of arrays. It extracts their individual elements, and interposes between each sequence of extracted elements the elements of its parameter array. The result is an intermediate sequence called a Join-Sequence, and might have to be coerced further to an Array if that's what you were after. For example:

```
let arr = [[1,2], [3,4], [5,6]]
let arr2 = Array(arr.joinWithSeparator([10,11]))
// [1, 2, 10, 11, 3, 4, 10, 11, 5, 6]
```

Calling joinWithSeparator with an empty array as parameter is thus a way to flatten an array of arrays:

```
let arr = [[1,2], [3,4], [5,6]]
let arr2 = Array(arr.joinWithSeparator([]))
// [1, 2, 3, 4, 5, 6]
```

There's also a flatten instance method that does the same thing. Again, it returns an intermediate sequence (or collection), so you might want to coerce to an Array:

```
let arr = [[1,2], [3,4], [5,6]]
let arr2 = Array(arr.flatten())
// [1, 2, 3, 4, 5, 6]
```

The reverse instance method yields a new array whose elements are in the opposite order from the original.

The sortInPlace and sort instance methods respectively sort the original array (if the reference to it is mutable) and yield a new sorted array based on the original. Once again, you get two choices: if this is an array of Comparables, you can let the < operator dictate the new order; alternatively, you can supply a function that takes two parameters of the element type and returns a Bool stating whether the first parameter should be ordered before the second (just like minElement and maxElement). For example:

```
var arr = [4,3,5,2,6,1]
arr.sortInPlace() // [1, 2, 3, 4, 5, 6]
arr.sortInPlace {$0 > $1} // [6, 5, 4, 3, 2, 1]
```

In that last line, I provided an anonymous function. Alternatively, of course, you can pass as argument the name of a declared function. In Swift, comparison operators *are* the names of functions! Therefore, I can do the same thing more briefly, like this:

```
var arr = [4,3,5,2,6,1]
arr.sortInPlace(>) // [6, 5, 4, 3, 2, 1]
```

The split instance method breaks an array into an array of arrays at the elements that pass a specified test, which is a function that takes a value of the element type and returns a Bool; the elements passing the test are eliminated:

```
let arr = [1,2,3,4,5,6]
let arr2 = arr.split {$0 % 2 == 0} // split at evens: [[1], [3], [5]]
```

Array enumeration and transformation

An array is a sequence, and so you can enumerate it, inspecting or operating with each element in turn. The simplest way is by means of a for...in loop; I'll have more to say about this construct in Chapter 5:

```
let pepboys = ["Manny", "Moe", "Jack"]
for pepboy in pepboys {
    print(pepboy) // prints Manny, then Moe, then Jack
}
```

Alternatively, you can use the forEach instance method. Its parameter is a function that takes an element of the array (or other sequence) and returns no value. Think of it as the functional equivalent of the imperative for...in loop:

```
let pepboys = ["Manny", "Moe", "Jack"]
pepboys.forEach {print($0)} // prints Manny, then Moe, then Jack
```

If you need the index numbers as well as the elements, call the enumerate instance method and loop on the result; what you get on each iteration is a tuple:

```
let pepboys = ["Manny", "Moe", "Jack"]
for (ix,pepboy) in pepboys.enumerate() {
    print("Pep boy \(ix) is \(pepboy)") // Pep boy 0 is Manny, etc.
}
// or:
pepboys.enumerate().forEach {print("Pep boy \($0.0) is \($0.1)")}
```

Swift also provides three powerful array transformation instance methods. Like for-Each, these methods all enumerate the array for you, so that the loop is buried implicitly inside the method call, making your code tighter and cleaner.

Let's start with the map instance method. It yields a new array, each element of which is the result of passing the corresponding element of the old array through a function that you supply. This function accepts a parameter of the element type and returns a result which may be of some other type; Swift can usually infer the type of the resulting array elements by looking at the type returned by the function.

For example, here's how to multiply every element of an array by 2:

```
let arr = [1,2,3]
let arr2 = arr.map {$0 * 2} // [2,4,6]
```

Here's another example, to illustrate the fact that map can yield an array with a different element type:

```
let arr = [1,2,3]
let arr2 = arr.map {Double($0)} // [1.0, 2.0, 3.0]
```

Here's a real-life example showing how neat and compact your code can be when you use map. In order to remove all the table cells in a section of a UITableView, I have to specify the cells as an array of NSIndexPath objects. If sec is the section number, I can form those NSIndexPath objects individually like this:

```
let path0 = NSIndexPath(forRow:0, inSection:sec)
let path1 = NSIndexPath(forRow:1, inSection:sec)
// ...
```

Hmmm, I think I see a pattern here! I could generate my array of NSIndexPath objects by looping through the row values using for...in. But with map, there's a much tighter way to express the same loop (ct is the number of rows in the section):

```
let paths = Array(0..<ct).map {NSIndexPath(forRow:$0, inSection:sec)}
```

Actually, map is a CollectionType instance method — and a Range is itself a Collection-Type. Therefore, I don't need the cast to an array:

```
let paths = (0..<ct).map {NSIndexPath(forRow:$0, inSection:sec)}
```

The filter instance method also yields a new array. Each element of the new array is an element of the old array, in the same order; but some of the elements of the old array may be omitted — they were filtered out. What filters them out is a function that you supply; it accepts a parameter of the element type and returns a Bool stating whether this element should go into the new array.

For example:

```
let pepboys = ["Manny", "Moe", "Jack"]
let pepboys2 = pepboys.filter{$0.hasPrefix("M")} // [Manny, Moe]
```

Finally, we come to the reduce instance method. If you've learned LISP or Scheme, you're probably accustomed to reduce; otherwise, it can be a bit mystifying at first. It's a way of *combining* all the elements of an array (actually, a sequence) into a single value. This value's type — the result type — doesn't have to be the same as the array's element type. You supply a function that takes two parameters; the first is of the result type, the second is of the element type, and the result is the combination of those two parameters, as the result type. The result of each iteration becomes the first parameter in the *next* iteration, along with the next element of the array as the second parameter. Thus, the output of combining pairs accumulates, and the final accumulated value is the final output of the reduce function. However, that doesn't explain where the first parameter for the *first* iteration comes from. The answer is that you have to supply it as the first argument of the reduce call.

That will all be easier to understand with a simple example. Let's assume we've got an array of Int. Then we can use reduce to sum all the elements of the array. Here's some pseudocode where I've left out the first argument of the reduce call, so that you can think about what it needs to be:

```
let sum = arr.reduce(/*???*/) {$0 + $1}
```

Each pair of parameters will be added together to get the first parameter on the next iteration. The second parameter on every iteration is an element of the array. So the question is, what should the first element of the array be added to? We want the actual sum of all the elements, no more and no less; so clearly the first element of the array should be added to 0! So here's actual working code:

```
let arr = [1, 4, 9, 13, 112]
let sum = arr.reduce(0) {$0 + $1} // 139
```

Once again, we can write that code more briefly, because the + operator is the name of a function of the required type:

```
let sum = arr.reduce(0, combine:+)
```

In my real iOS programming life, I depend heavily on these methods, often using two or even all three of them together, nested or chained or both. Here's an example; it's rather elaborate, but it's very typical of how neatly you can do things with arrays using Swift, so bear with me. I have a table view that displays data divided into sections. Under the hood, the data is an array of arrays of String — a [[String]] — where each subarray represents the rows of a section. Now I want to filter that data to eliminate all strings that don't contain a certain substring. I want to keep the sections intact, but if removing strings removes *all* of a section's strings, I want to eliminate that section array entirely.

The heart of the action is the test for whether a string contains a substring. I'm going to use Cocoa methods for that, in part because they allow me to do a case-insensitive search. If s is a string from my array, and target is the substring we're looking for, then the code for looking to see whether s contains target case-insensitively is as follows:

```
let options = NSStringCompareOptions.CaseInsensitiveSearch
let found = s.rangeOfString(target, options: options)
```

Recall the discussion of rangeOfString in Chapter 3. If found is not nil, the substring was found. Here, then, is the actual code, preceded by some sample data for exercising it:

```
let arr = [["Manny", "Moe", "Jack"], ["Harpo", "Chico", "Groucho"]]
let target = "m"
let arr2 = arr.map {
    $0.filter {
        let options = NSStringCompareOptions.CaseInsensitiveSearch
        let found = $0.rangeOfString(target, options: options)
        return (found != nil)
    }
}.filter {$0.count > 0}
```

After the first two lines, setting up the sample data, what remains is a *single command* — a map call, whose function consists of a filter call, with a filter call chained to it. If that code doesn't prove to you that Swift is cool, nothing will.

Swift Array and Objective-C NSArray

When you're programming iOS, you import the Foundation framework (or UIKit, which imports Foundation) and thus the Objective-C NSArray type. Swift's Array type is bridged to Objective-C's NSArray type. However, such bridging is possible only if the types of the elements *in* the array can be bridged. Objective-C's rules for what can be an element of an NSArray are both looser and tighter than Swift's. On the one hand, the elements of an NSArray do not all have to be of the same type. On the other hand, an element of an NSArray must be an *object,* as Objective-C understands that term. In general, a type is bridged to Objective-C if it can be cast up to AnyObject — meaning that it is a class type, or else a specially bridged struct such as Int, Double, or String.

Passing a Swift array to Objective-C is thus usually easy. If your Swift array consists of things that can be cast up to AnyObject, you'll just pass the array, either by assignment or as an argument in a function call:

```
let arr = [UIBarButtonItem(), UIBarButtonItem()]
self.navigationItem.leftBarButtonItems = arr
self.navigationItem.setLeftBarButtonItems(arr, animated: true)
```

To call an NSArray method on a Swift array, you may have to cast to NSArray:

```
let arr = ["Manny", "Moe", "Jack"]
let s = (arr as NSArray).componentsJoinedByString(", ")
// s is "Manny, Moe, Jack"
```

A Swift Array seen through a var reference is mutable, but an NSArray isn't mutable no matter how you see it. For mutability in Objective-C, you need an NSMutableArray, a subclass of NSArray. You can't cast, assign, or pass a Swift array to an NSMutableArray; you have to coerce. The best way is to call the NSMutableArray initializer init(array:), to which you can pass a Swift array directly:

```
let arr = ["Manny", "Moe", "Jack"]
let arr2 = NSMutableArray(array:arr)
arr2.removeObject("Moe")
```

To convert back from an NSMutableArray to a Swift array, you can cast; if you want an array of the original Swift type, you'll need to cast *twice* in order to quiet the compiler:

```
var arr = ["Manny", "Moe", "Jack"]
let arr2 = NSMutableArray(array:arr)
arr2.removeObject("Moe")
arr = arr2 as NSArray as! [String]
```

If a Swift object type can't be cast up to AnyObject, it isn't bridged to Objective-C, and the compiler will stop you if you try to pass an Array containing an instance of that type where an NSArray is expected. In such a situation, you'll need to "bridge" the array elements *yourself*.

Here, for example, I have a Swift array of CGPoint. That's perfectly fine in Swift, but CGPoint is a struct, which Objective-C doesn't see as an object, so you can't put one in an NSArray. If I try to pass this array where an NSArray is expected, I'll get a compiler error: "[CGPoint] is not convertible to NSArray." The solution is to wrap each CGPoint in an NSValue, an Objective-C object type specifically designed to act as a carrier for nonobject types; now we have a Swift array of NSValue, which can subsequently be handed to Objective-C:

```
let arrNSValues = arrCGPoints.map { NSValue(CGPoint:$0) }
```

Another case in point is a Swift array of Optionals. An Objective-C collection can't contain nil (because, in Objective-C, nil isn't an object). Therefore you can't put an Optional in an NSArray. You'll have to do something with those Optionals before passing the array where an NSArray is expected. If an Optional wraps a value, you can unwrap it. But if an Optional wraps *no* value (it is nil), you *can't* unwrap it. One solution is to do what you would do in Objective-C. An Objective-C NSArray can't contain nil, so Cocoa provides a special class, NSNull, whose singleton instance, NSNull(), can stand in for nil where an object is needed. Thus, if I have an array of Optionals wrapping Strings, I can unwrap those that aren't nil and substitute NSNull() for those that are:

```
let arr2 : [AnyObject] =
    arr.map{if $0 == nil {return NSNull()} else {return $0!}}
```

(In Chapter 5, I'll write that code much more compactly.)

Now let's talk about what happens when an NSArray arrives from Objective-C into Swift. There won't be any problem crossing the bridge: the NSArray will arrive safely as a Swift Array. But a Swift Array *of what?* Of itself, an NSArray carries no information about what type of element it contains. The default, therefore, is that an Objective-C NSArray will arrive as a Swift array of AnyObject.

Fortunately, you won't encounter this default anywhere near as often as in the past. Starting in Xcode 7, the Objective-C language has been modified so that the declaration of an NSArray, NSDictionary, or NSSet — the three collection types that are bridged to Swift — can include element type information. (Objective-C calls this a *lightweight generic.*) In iOS 9, the Cocoa APIs have been revised so that they *do* include this information. Thus, for the most part, the arrays you receive from Cocoa will be correctly typed.

For example, this elegant code was previously impossible:

```
let arr = UIFont.familyNames().map {
    UIFont.fontNamesForFamilyName($0)
}
```

The result is an array of arrays of String, listing all available fonts grouped by family. That code is possible because both of those UIFont class methods are now seen by Swift as returning an array of String. Previously, those arrays were untyped — they were arrays of AnyObject — and casting down to an array of String was up to *you*.

It is still perfectly possible, though far less likely, that you will receive an array of Any-Object from Objective-C. If that happens, then usually you *will* want to cast it down or otherwise transform it into an array of some specific Swift type. Here's an Objective-C class containing a method whose return type of NSArray hasn't been marked up with an element type:

```
@implementation Pep
- (NSArray*) boys {
    return @[@"Mannie", @"Moe", @"Jack"];
}
@end
```

To call that method and do anything useful with the result, it will be necessary to cast that result down to an array of String. If I'm sure of my ground, I can force the cast:

```
let p = Pep()
let boys = p.boys() as! [String]
```

As with any cast, though, be sure you don't lie! An Objective-C array can contain more than one type of object. Don't force such an array to be cast down to a type to which not all the elements can be cast, or you'll crash when the cast fails; you'll need a more deliberate strategy for eliminating or otherwise transforming the problematic elements.

Dictionary

A dictionary (Dictionary, a struct) is an unordered collection of object pairs. In each pair, the first object is the *key*; the second object is the *value*. The idea is that you use a key to access a value. Keys are usually strings, but they don't have to be; the formal requirement is that they be types that adopt the Hashable protocol, meaning that they adopt Equatable and also have a hashValue property (an Int) such that two equal keys have equal hash values and two unequal keys do not. Thus, the hash values can be used behind the scenes for rapid key access. Swift numeric types, strings, and enums are Hashables.

As with arrays, a given dictionary's types must be uniform. The key type and the value type don't have to be the same type, and they often will not be. But within any dictionary, all keys must be of the same type, and all values must be of the same type. Formally, a dictionary is a generic, and its placeholder types are ordered key type, then value type: `Dictionary<Key,Value>`. As with arrays, however, Swift provides syntactic sugar for expressing a dictionary's type, which is what you'll usually use: `[Key: Value]`. That's square brackets containing a colon (and optional spaces) separating the key type from the value type. This code creates an empty dictionary whose keys (when they exist) will be Strings and whose values (when they exist) will be Strings:

```
var d = [String:String]()
```

The colon is used also between each key and value in the literal syntax for expressing a dictionary. The key–value pairs appear between square brackets, separated by comma, just like an array. This code creates a dictionary by describing it literally (and the dictionary's type of `[String:String]` is inferred):

```
var d = ["CA": "California", "NY": "New York"]
```

The literal for an empty dictionary is square brackets containing just a colon: `[:]`. This notation can be used provided the dictionary's type is known in some other way. Thus, this is another way to create an empty `[String:String]` dictionary:

```
var d : [String:String] = [:]
```

If you try to fetch a value through a nonexistent key, there is no error, but Swift needs a way to report failure; therefore, it returns `nil`. This, in turn, implies that the value returned when you successfully access a value through a key must be an Optional wrapping the real value!

Access to a dictionary's contents is usually by subscripting. To fetch a value by key, subscript the key to the dictionary reference:

```
let d = ["CA": "California", "NY": "New York"]
let state = d["CA"]
```

Bear in mind, however, that after that code, `state` is not a String — it's an Optional wrapping a String! Forgetting this is a common beginner mistake.

If the reference to a dictionary is mutable, you can also assign into a key subscript expression. If the key already exists, its value is replaced. If the key doesn't already exist, it is created and the value is attached to it:

```
var d = ["CA": "California", "NY": "New York"]
d["CA"] = "Casablanca"
d["MD"] = "Maryland"
// d is now ["MD": "Maryland", "NY": "New York", "CA": "Casablanca"]
```

Alternatively, call `updateValue(forKey:)`; it has the advantage that it returns the old value wrapped in an Optional, or `nil` if the key wasn't already present.

By a kind of shorthand, assigning `nil` into a key subscript expression removes that key–value pair if it exists:

```
var d = ["CA": "California", "NY": "New York"]
d["NY"] = nil // d is now ["CA": "California"]
```

Alternatively, call `removeValueForKey`; it has the advantage that it returns the removed value before it removes the key–value pair. The removed value is returned wrapped in an Optional, so a `nil` result tells you that this key was never in the dictionary to begin with.

As with arrays, a dictionary type is legal for casting down, meaning that the individual elements will be cast down. Typically, only the value types will differ:

```
let dog1 : Dog = NoisyDog()
let dog2 : Dog = NoisyDog()
let d = ["fido": dog1, "rover": dog2]
let d2 = d as! [String : NoisyDog]
```

As with arrays, `is` can be used to test the actual types in the dictionary, and `as?` can be used to test and cast safely. Dictionary equality, like array equality, works as you would expect.

Basic dictionary properties and enumeration

A dictionary has a `count` property reporting the number of key–value pairs it contains, and an `isEmpty` property reporting whether that number is 0.

A dictionary has a `keys` property reporting all its keys, and a `values` property reporting all its values. They are effectively opaque structs (a LazyForwardCollection, if you must know), but when you enumerate them with `for...in`, you get the expected type:

```
var d = ["CA": "California", "NY": "New York"]
for s in d.keys {
    print(s) // s is a String
}
```

 A dictionary is unordered! You can enumerate it (or its keys, or its values), but do not expect the elements to arrive in any particular order.

You can extract all a dictionary's keys or values at once, by coercing the `keys` or `values` property to an array:

```
var d = ["CA": "California", "NY": "New York"]
var keys = Array(d.keys)
```

You can also enumerate a dictionary itself. As you might expect from what I've already said, each iteration provides a key–value tuple:

```
var d = ["CA": "California", "NY": "New York"]
for (abbrev, state) in d {
    print("\(abbrev) stands for \(state)")
}
```

You can extract a dictionary's entire contents at once as an array (of key–value tuples) by coercing the dictionary to an array:

```
var d = ["CA": "California", "NY": "New York"]
let arr = Array(d) // [("NY", "New York"), ("CA", "California")]
```

Like an array, a dictionary and its keys property and its values property are collections (CollectionType) and sequences (SequenceType). Therefore, everything I said about arrays as collections and sequences in the previous section is applicable! For example, if a dictionary d has Int values, you can sum them with the reduce instance method:

```
let sum = d.values.reduce(0, combine:+)
```

You can obtain its smallest value (wrapped in an Optional):

```
let min = d.values.minElement()
```

You can list the values that match some criterion:

```
let arr = Array(d.values.filter{$0 < 2})
```

(The coercion to Array is needed because the sequence resulting from filter is lazy: there isn't really anything in it until we enumerate it or collect it into an array.)

Swift Dictionary and Objective-C NSDictionary

The Foundation framework dictionary type is NSDictionary, and Swift's Dictionary type is bridged to it. Considerations for passing a dictionary across the bridge are parallel to those I've already discussed for arrays. The untyped bridged API characterization of an NSDictionary will be [NSObject:AnyObject], using the Objective-C Foundation object base class for the keys; there are various reasons for this choice, but from Swift's point of view the main one is that AnyObject is not a Hashable. NSObject, on the other hand, is extended by the Swift APIs to adopt Hashable; and since NSObject is the base class for Cocoa classes, any Cocoa class type will be Hashable. Thus, any NSDictionary can cross the bridge.

Like NSArray, NSDictionary key and value types can now be marked in Objective-C. The most common key type in a real-life Cocoa NSDictionary is NSString, so you might well receive an NSDictionary as a [String:AnyObject]. Specific typing of an NSDictionary's *values*, however, is much rarer; dictionaries that you pass to and receive from Cocoa will *very* often have values of different types. It is not at all surprising to have a dictionary whose keys are strings but whose values include a string, a number, a color, and an array. For this reason, you will usually *not* cast down the entire dictionary's type; instead, you'll work with the dictionary as having AnyObject values, and cast when fetching an *individual value* from the dictionary. Since the value returned from subscripting a key is itself an Optional, you will typically unwrap and cast the value as a standard single move.

Here's an example. A Cocoa NSNotification object comes with a `userInfo` property. It is an NSDictionary that might itself be `nil`, so the Swift API characterizes it like this:

```
var userInfo: [NSObject : AnyObject]? { get }
```

Let's say I'm expecting this dictionary to be present and to contain a `"progress"` key whose value is an NSNumber containing a Double. My goal is to extract that NSNumber and assign the Double that it contains to a property, `self.progress`. Here's one way to do that safely, using optional unwrapping and optional casting (`n` is the NSNotification object):

```
let prog = (n.userInfo?["progress"] as? NSNumber)?.doubleValue
if prog != nil {
    self.progress = prog!
}
```

That's an optional chain that ends by fetching an NSNumber's `doubleValue` property, so `prog` is implicitly typed as an Optional wrapping a Double. The code is safe, because if there is no `userInfo` dictionary, or if it doesn't contain a `"progress"` key, or if that key's value isn't an NSNumber, nothing happens, and `prog` will be `nil`. I then test `prog` to see whether it *is* `nil`; if it isn't, I know that it's safe to force-unwrap it, and that the unwrapped value is the Double I'm after.

(In Chapter 5 I'll describe another syntax for accomplishing the same goal, using conditional binding.)

Conversely, here's a typical example of creating a dictionary and handing it off to Cocoa. This dictionary is a mixed bag: its values are a UIFont, a UIColor, and an NSShadow. Its keys are all strings, which I obtain as constants from Cocoa. I form the dictionary as a literal and pass it, all in one move, with no need to cast anything:

```
UINavigationBar.appearance().titleTextAttributes = [
    NSFontAttributeName : UIFont(name: "ChalkboardSE-Bold", size: 20)!,
    NSForegroundColorAttributeName : UIColor.darkTextColor(),
    NSShadowAttributeName : {
        let shad = NSShadow()
        shad.shadowOffset = CGSizeMake(1.5,1.5)
        return shad
    }()
]
```

As with NSArray and NSMutableArray, if you want Cocoa to mutate a dictionary, you must coerce to NSMutableDictionary. In this example, I want to do a join between two dictionaries, so I harness the power of NSMutableDictionary, which has an addEntries-FromDictionary: method:

```
var d1 = ["NY":"New York", "CA":"California"]
let d2 = ["MD":"Maryland"]
let mutd1 = NSMutableDictionary(dictionary:d1)
mutd1.addEntriesFromDictionary(d2)
d1 = mutd1 as NSDictionary as! [String:String]
// d1 is now ["MD": "Maryland", "NY": "New York", "CA": "California"]
```

That sort of thing is needed quite often, because there's no native method for adding the elements of one dictionary to another dictionary. Indeed, native utility methods involving dictionaries in Swift are disappointingly thin on the ground: there really aren't any. Still, Cocoa and the Foundation framework are right there, so perhaps Apple feels there's no point duplicating in the Swift standard library the functionality that already exists in Foundation. If having to drop into Cocoa bothers you, you can write your own library; for example, addEntriesFromDictionary: is easily reimplemented as a Swift Dictionary instance method through an extension:

```
extension Dictionary {
    mutating func addEntriesFromDictionary(d:[Key:Value]) { // generic types
        for (k,v) in d {
            self[k] = v
        }
    }
}
```

Set

A set (Set, a struct) is an unordered collection of unique objects. It is thus rather like the keys of a dictionary! Its elements must be all of one type; it has a count and an isEmpty property; it can be initialized from any sequence; you can cycle through its elements with for...in. But the order of elements is not guaranteed, and you should make no assumptions about it.

The uniqueness of set elements is implemented by constraining their type to adopt the Hashable protocol, just like the keys of a Dictionary. Thus, the hash values can be used behind the scenes for rapid access. Checking whether a set contains a given element, which you can do with the contains instance method, is *very* efficient — far more efficient than doing the same thing with an array. Therefore, if element uniqueness is acceptable (or desirable) and you don't need indexing or a guaranteed order, a set can be a much better choice of collection than an array.

The fact that a set's elements are Hashables means that they must also be Equatables. This makes sense, because the notion of uniqueness depends upon being able to answer the question of whether a given object is already in the set.

There are no set literals in Swift, but you won't need them because you can pass an array literal where a set is expected. There is no syntactic sugar for expressing a set type, but the Set struct is a generic, so you can express the type by explicitly specializing the generic:

```
let set : Set<Int> = [1, 2, 3, 4, 5]
```

In that particular example, however, there was no need to specialize the generic, as the Int type can be inferred from the array.

It sometimes happens (more often than you might suppose) that you want to examine one element of a set as a kind of sample. Order is meaningless, so it's sufficient to obtain *any* element, such as the first element. For this purpose, use the `first` instance property; it returns an Optional, just in case the set is empty and has no first element.

The distinctive feature of a set is the uniqueness of its objects. If an object is added to a set and that object is already present, it isn't added a second time. Conversion from an array to a set and back to an array is thus a quick and reliable way of *uniquing* the array — though of course order is not preserved:

```
let arr = [1,2,1,3,2,4,3,5]
let set = Set(arr)
let arr2 = Array(set) // [5,2,3,1,4], perhaps
```

A set is a collection (CollectionType) and a sequence (SequenceType), so it is analogous to an array or a dictionary, and what I have already said about those types generally applies to a set as well. For example, Set has a `map` instance method; it returns an array, but of course you can turn that right back into a set if you need to:

```
let set : Set = [1,2,3,4,5]
let set2 = Set(set.map {$0+1}) // {6, 5, 2, 3, 4}, perhaps
```

If the reference to a set is mutable, a number of instance methods spring to life. You can add an object with `insert`; if the object is already in the set, nothing happens, but there is no penalty. You can remove an object and return it by specifying the object itself (or something equatable to it), with the `remove` method; it returns the object wrapped in an Optional, or `nil` if the object was not present. You can remove and return the first object (whatever "first" may mean) with `removeFirst`; it crashes if the set is empty, so take precautions (or use `popFirst`, which is safe).

Equality comparison (==) is defined for sets as you would expect; two sets are equal if every element of each is also an element of the other.

If the notion of a set brings to your mind visions of Venn diagrams from elementary school, that's good, because sets have instance methods giving you all those set operations you remember so fondly. The parameter can be a set, or it can be any sequence, which will be converted to a set; for example, it might be an array, a range, or even a character sequence:

`intersect`, `intersectInPlace`
> Yields the elements of this set that also appear in the parameter.

`union`, `unionInPlace`
> Yields the elements of this set along with the (unique) elements of the parameter.

`exclusiveOr`, `exclusiveOrInPlace`
> Yields the elements of this set that don't appear in the parameter, plus the (unique) elements of the parameter that don't appear in this set.

`subtract`, `subtractInPlace`
> Yields the elements of this set except for those that appear in the parameter.

`isSubsetOf`, `isStrictSubsetOf`
`isSupersetOf`, `isStrictSupersetOf`
> Returns a Bool reporting whether the elements of this set are respectively embraced by or embrace the elements of the parameter. The "strict" variant yields `false` if the two sets consist of the same elements.

`isDisjointWith`
> Returns a Bool reporting whether this set and the parameter have no elements in common.

Here's a real-life example of elegant Set usage from one of my apps. I have a lot of numbered pictures, of which we are to choose one randomly. But I don't want to choose a picture that has recently been chosen. Therefore, I keep a list of the numbers of all recently chosen pictures. When it's time to choose a new picture, I convert the list of all possible numbers to a Set, convert the list of recently chosen picture numbers to a Set, and `subtract` to get a list of unused picture numbers! Now I choose a picture number at random and add it to the list of recently chosen picture numbers:

```
let ud = NSUserDefaults.standardUserDefaults()
var recents = ud.objectForKey(RECENTS) as? [Int]
if recents == nil {
    recents = []
}
var forbiddenNumbers = Set(recents!)
let legalNumbers = Set(1...PIXCOUNT).subtract(forbiddenNumbers)
let newNumber = Array(legalNumbers)[
    Int(arc4random_uniform(UInt32(legalNumbers.count)))
]
forbiddenNumbers.insert(newNumber)
ud.setObject(Array(forbiddenNumbers), forKey:RECENTS)
```

Option sets

An *option set* (technically, an OptionSetType) is Swift's way of treating as a struct a certain type of enumeration commonly used in Cocoa. It is not, strictly speaking, a Set;

but it is deliberately set-like, sharing common features with Set through the SetAlgebra-Type protocol. Thus, an option set has `contains`, `insert`, and `remove` methods, along with all the various set operation methods.

The purpose of option sets is to help you grapple with Objective-C *bitmasks*. A bitmask is an integer whose bits are used as switches when multiple options are to be specified simultaneously. Such bitmasks are very common in Cocoa. In Objective-C, and in Swift prior to Swift 2.0, bitmasks are manipulated through the arithmetic bitwise-or and bitwise-and operators. Such manipulation can be mysterious and error-prone. Thanks to option sets, Swift 2.0 allows bitmasks to be manipulated through set operations instead.

For example, when specifying how a UIView is to be animated, you are allowed to pass an `options:` argument whose value comes from the UIViewAnimationOptions enumeration, whose definition (in Objective-C) begins as follows:

```
typedef NS_OPTIONS(NSUInteger, UIViewAnimationOptions) {
    UIViewAnimationOptionLayoutSubviews         = 1 << 0,
    UIViewAnimationOptionAllowUserInteraction   = 1 << 1,
    UIViewAnimationOptionBeginFromCurrentState  = 1 << 2,
    UIViewAnimationOptionRepeat                 = 1 << 3,
    UIViewAnimationOptionAutoreverse            = 1 << 4,
    // ...
};
```

Pretend that an NSUInteger is 8 bits (it isn't, but let's keep things simple and short). Then this enumeration means that (in Swift) the following name–value pairs are defined:

```
UIViewAnimationOptions.LayoutSubviews          0b00000001
UIViewAnimationOptions.AllowUserInteraction    0b00000010
UIViewAnimationOptions.BeginFromCurrentState   0b00000100
UIViewAnimationOptions.Repeat                  0b00001000
UIViewAnimationOptions.Autoreverse             0b00010000
```

These values can be combined into a single value — a *bitmask* — that you pass as the `options:` argument for your animation. All Cocoa has to do to understand your intentions is to look to see which bits in the value that you pass are set to 1. So, for example, `0b00011000` would mean that `UIViewAnimationOptions.Repeat` and `UIView-AnimationOptions.Autoreverse` are both true (and that the others, by implication, are all false).

The question is how to *form* the value `0b00011000` in order to pass it. You could form it directly as a literal and set the `options:` argument to `UIViewAnimationOptions(raw-Value:0b00011000)`; but that's not a very good idea, because it's error-prone and makes your code incomprehensible. In Objective-C, you'd use the arithmetic bitwise-or operator, analogous to this Swift code:

```
let val =
    UIViewAnimationOptions.Autoreverse.rawValue |
    UIViewAnimationOptions.Repeat.rawValue
let opts = UIViewAnimationOptions(rawValue: val)
```

In Swift 2.0, however, the UIViewAnimationOptions type is an option set struct (because it is marked as NS_OPTIONS in Objective-C), and therefore can be treated much like a Set. For example, given a UIViewAnimationOptions value, you can add an option to it using `insert`:

```
var opts = UIViewAnimationOptions.Autoreverse
opts.insert(.Repeat)
```

Alternatively, you can start with an array literal, just as if you were initializing a Set:

```
let opts : UIViewAnimationOptions = [.Autoreverse, .Repeat]
```

 To indicate that no options are to be set, pass an empty option set ([]). This is a major change from Swift 1.2 and earlier, where the convention was to pass nil — illogically, since this value was never an Optional.

The inverse situation is that Cocoa hands *you* a bitmask, and you want to know whether a certain bit is set. In this example from a UITableViewCell subclass, the cell's `state` comes to us as a bitmask; we want to know about the bit indicating that the cell is showing its edit control. In the past, it was necessary to extract the raw values and use the bitwise-and operator:

```
override func didTransitionToState(state: UITableViewCellStateMask) {
    let editing = UITableViewCellStateMask.ShowingEditControlMask.rawValue
    if state.rawValue & editing != 0 {
        // ... the ShowingEditControlMask bit is set ...
    }
}
```

That's a tricky formula, all too easy to get wrong. In Swift 2.0, this is an option set, so the `contains` method tells you the answer:

```
override func didTransitionToState(state: UITableViewCellStateMask) {
    if state.contains(.ShowingEditControlMask) {
        // ... the ShowingEditControlMask bit is set ...
    }
}
```

Swift Set and Objective-C NSSet

Swift's Set type is bridged to Objective-C NSSet. The untyped medium of interchange is Set<NSObject>, because NSObject is seen as Hashable. Of course, the same rules apply as for arrays. An Objective-C NSSet expects its elements to be class instances, and Swift will help by bridging where it can. In real life, you'll probably start with an array and coerce it to a set or pass it where a set is expected, as in this example from my own code:

```
let types : UIUserNotificationType = [.Alert, .Sound] // a bitmask
let category = UIMutableUserNotificationCategory()
category.identifier = "coffee"
let settings = UIUserNotificationSettings( // second parameter is an NSSet
    forTypes: types, categories: [category])
```

Coming back from Objective-C, you'll get a Set of NSObject if Objective-C doesn't know what this is a set of, and in that case you would probably cast down as needed. As with NSArray, however, NSSet can now be marked up to indicate its element type; many Cocoa APIs *have* been marked up, and no casting will be necessary:

```
override func touchesBegan(touches: Set<UITouch>, withEvent event: UIEvent?) {
    let t = touches.first // an Optional wrapping a UITouch
    // ...
}
```

CHAPTER 5

Flow Control and More

This chapter presents the miscellaneous remaining aspects of the Swift language. I'll start by describing the syntax of Swift's flow control constructs for branching, looping, and jumping. Then I'll talk about how to override operators and how to create your own operators. The chapter ends with a survey of Swift's privacy and introspection features and some specialized modes of reference type memory management.

Flow Control

A computer program has a *path of execution* through its code statements. Normally, this path follows a simple rule: execute each statement in succession. But there is another possibility. Flow control can be used to make the path of execution skip some code statements, or repeat some code statements. Flow control is what makes a computer program "intelligent," and not merely a simple fixed sequence of steps. By testing the truth value of a *condition* — an expression that evaluates to a Bool and is thus `true` or `false` — the program decides *at that moment* how to proceed. Flow control based on testing a condition may be divided into two general types:

Branching
> The code is divided into alternative chunks, like roads that diverge in a wood, and the program is presented with a choice of possible ways to go: the truth of a condition is used to determine which chunk will actually be executed.

Looping
> A chunk of code is marked off for possible repetition: the truth of a condition is used to determine whether the chunk should be executed, and then whether it should be executed again. Each repetition is called an *iteration*. Typically, some feature of the environment (such as the value of a variable) is changed on each iteration, so that the repetitions are not identical, but are successive stages in progressing through an overall task.

The chunks of code in flow control, which I refer to as *blocks*, are demarcated by curly braces. These curly braces constitute a scope. New local variables can be declared here, and go out of existence automatically when the path of execution exits the curly braces. For a loop, this means that local variables come into existence and go out of existence on each iteration. As with any scope, code inside the curly braces can see the surrounding higher scope.

Swift flow control is fairly simple, and by and large is similar to flow control in C and related languages. There are two fundamental syntactic differences between Swift and C, both of which make Swift simpler and clearer: in Swift, a condition *does not have to be wrapped in parentheses*, and the curly braces *can never be omitted*. Moreover, Swift adds some specialized flow control features to help you grapple more conveniently with Optionals, and boasts a particularly powerful form of switch statement.

Branching

Swift has two forms of branching: the if construct, and the switch statement. I'll also discuss conditional evaluation, a compact form of if construct.

If construct

The Swift branching construct with `if` is similar to C. Many examples of if constructs have appeared already in this book. The construct may be formally summarized as shown in Example 5-1.

Example 5-1. The Swift if construct

```
if condition {
    statements
}

if condition {
    statements
} else {
    statements
}

if condition {
    statements
} else if condition {
    statements
} else {
    statements
}
```

The third form, containing `else if`, can have as many `else if` blocks as needed, and the final `else` block may be omitted.

Here's a real-life if construct that lies at the heart of one of my apps:

```
// okay, we've tapped a tile; there are three cases
if self.selectedTile == nil { // no selected tile: select and play this tile
    self.selectTile(tile)
    self.playTile(tile)
} else if self.selectedTile == tile { // selected tile tapped: deselect it
    self.deselectAll()
    self.player?.pause()
} else { // there was a selected tile, another tile tapped: swap them
    self.swap(self.selectedTile, with:tile, check:true, fence:true)
}
```

Conditional binding

In Swift, `if` can be followed immediately by a variable declaration and assignment — that is, by `let` or `var` and a new local variable name, possibly followed by a colon and a type declaration, then an equal sign and a value. This syntax, called a *conditional binding*, is actually a shorthand for conditionally unwrapping an Optional. The assigned value is expected to be an Optional — the compiler will stop you if it isn't — and this is what happens:

- If the Optional is `nil`, the condition fails and the block is not executed.
- If the Optional is *not* `nil`, then:

  1. The Optional is unwrapped.
  2. The unwrapped value is assigned to the declared local variable.
  3. The block is executed with the local variable in scope.

Thus, a conditional binding is a convenient shorthand for safely passing an unwrapped Optional into a block. The Optional is unwrapped, and the block is executed, only if the Optional *can* be unwrapped.

It is perfectly reasonable for the local variable in a conditional binding to have the same name as an existing variable in the surrounding scope. It can even have the same name as the Optional being unwrapped! There is then no need to make up a new name, and inside the block the unwrapped value of the Optional overshadows the original Optional, which thus cannot be accessed accidentally.

Here's an example of a conditional binding. Recall this code from Chapter 4, where I optionally unwrap an NSNotification's userInfo dictionary, attempt to fetch a value from the dictionary using the "progress" key, and proceed only if that value turns out to be an NSNumber:

```
let prog = (n.userInfo?["progress"] as? NSNumber)?.doubleValue
if prog != nil {
    self.progress = prog!
}
```

We can rewrite that code as a conditional binding:

```
if let prog = (n.userInfo?["progress"] as? NSNumber)?.doubleValue {
    self.progress = prog
}
```

It is also possible to nest conditional bindings. To illustrate, I'll rewrite the previous example to use a separate conditional binding for every Optional in the chain:

```
if let ui = n.userInfo {
    if let prog : AnyObject = ui["progress"] {
        if let prog = prog as? NSNumber {
            self.progress = prog.doubleValue
        }
    }
}
```

The result is somewhat more verbose and the nest is rather deeply indented — Swift programmers like to call this the "pyramid of doom" — but in my view it is also considerably more legible, because the structure reflects perfectly the successive stages of testing. To help avoid the indentation, successive conditional bindings can be combined into a list, separated by comma:

```
if let ui = n.userInfo, prog = ui["progress"] as? NSNumber {
    self.progress = prog.doubleValue
}
```

A binding in the list can even be followed by a where clause folding yet another condition into the line. And the entire list can start with a condition, before the word let or var is encountered. Here's a real life example from my own code (which I'll explain further in Chapter 11). The "pyramid of doom" consists of four nested conditions:

```
override func observeValueForKeyPath(keyPath: String?,
    ofObject object: AnyObject?, change: [String : AnyObject]?,
    context: UnsafeMutablePointer<()>) {
        if keyPath == "readyForDisplay" {
            if let obj = object as? AVPlayerViewController {
                if let ok = change?[NSKeyValueChangeNewKey] as? Bool {
                    if ok {
                        // ...
                    }
                }
            }
        }
}
```

Alternatively, those four conditions can be combined into a single list:

```
override func observeValueForKeyPath(keyPath: String?,
    ofObject object: AnyObject?, change: [String : AnyObject]?,
    context: UnsafeMutablePointer<()>) {
        if keyPath == "readyForDisplay",
        let obj = object as? AVPlayerViewController,
        let ok = change?[NSKeyValueChangeNewKey] as? Bool where ok {
            // ...
        }
}
```

But whether the second version is more legible is an open question.

New in Swift 2.0, you can express the chain of conditions as a series of guard statements (see "Guard" on page 264); I think I like this idiom best:

```
override func observeValueForKeyPath(keyPath: String?,
    ofObject object: AnyObject?, change: [String : AnyObject]?,
    context: UnsafeMutablePointer<()>) {
        guard keyPath == "readyForDisplay" else {return}
        guard let obj = object as? AVPlayerViewController else {return}
        guard let ok = change?[NSKeyValueChangeNewKey] as? Bool else {return}
        guard ok else {return}
        // ...
}
```

Switch statement

A switch statement is a neater way of writing an extended if...else if...else construct. In C (and Objective-C), a switch statement contains hidden traps; Swift eliminates those traps, and adds power and flexibility. As a result, switch statements are commonly used in Swift (whereas they are relatively rare in my Objective-C code).

In a switch statement, the condition consists in the comparison of different possible values, called *cases*, against a single value, called the *tag*. The case comparisons are performed *successively in order*. As soon as a case comparison succeeds, that case's code is executed and the entire switch statement is exited. The schema is shown in

Example 5-2; there can be as many cases as needed, and the `default` case can be omitted (subject to restrictions that I'll explain in a moment).

Example 5-2. The Swift switch statement

```
switch tag {
case pattern1:
    statements
case pattern2:
    statements
default:
    statements
}
```

Here's an actual example:

```
switch i {
case 1:
    print("You have 1 thingy!")
case 2:
    print("You have 2 thingies!")
default:
    print("You have \(i) thingies!")
}
```

In that code, a variable `i` functions as the tag. The value of `i` is first compared to the value 1. If it *is* 1, that case's code is executed and that's all. If it is *not* 1, it is compared to the value 2. If it *is* 2, *that* case's code is executed and that's all. If the value of `i` matches neither of those, the `default` case's code is executed.

In Swift, a switch statement must be *exhaustive*. This means that *every* possible value of the tag must be covered by a case. The compiler will stop you if you try to violate this rule. The rule makes intuitive sense when a value's type allows only a limited number of possibilities; the usual example is an enum, which itself has a small, fixed set of cases as its possible values. But when, as in the preceding example, the tag is an Int, there is an infinite number of possible individual cases. Thus, a "mop-up" case *must* appear, to mop up all the cases that you didn't write explicitly. A common way to write a "mop-up" case is to use a `default` case.

Each case's code can consist of multiple lines; it doesn't have to be a single line, as the cases in the preceding example happen to be. However, it must consist of *at least* a single line; it is illegal for a Swift switch case to be completely empty. It is legal for the first (or only) line of a case's code to appear on the same line as the case, after the colon; thus, I could have written the preceding example like this:

```
switch i {
case 1: print("You have 1 thingy!")
case 2: print("You have 2 thingies!")
default: print("You have \(i) thingies!")
}
```

The minimum single line of case code is the keyword break; used in this way, break acts as a placeholder meaning, "Do nothing." It is very common for a switch statement to include a default (or other "mop-up" case) consisting of nothing but the keyword break; in this way, you exhaust all possible values of the tag, but if the value is one that no case explicitly covers, you do nothing.

Now let's focus on the comparison between the tag value and the case value. In the preceding example, it works like an equality comparison (==); but that isn't the only possibility. In Swift, a case value is actually a special expression called a *pattern*, and the pattern is compared to the tag value using a "secret" pattern-matching operator, ~=. The more you know about the syntax for constructing a pattern, the more powerful your case values and your switch statements will be.

A pattern can include an underscore (_) to absorb all values without using them. An underscore case is thus an alternative form of "mop-up" case:

```
switch i {
case 1:
    print("You have 1 thingy!")
case _:
    print("You have many thingies!")
}
```

A pattern can include a declaration of a local variable name (an unconditional binding) to absorb all values and use the actual value. This is another alternative form of "mop-up" case:

```
switch i {
case 1:
    print("You have 1 thingy!")
case let n:
    print("You have \(n) thingies!")
}
```

When the tag is a Comparable, a case can include a Range; the test involves sending the Range the contains message:

```
switch i {
case 1:
    print("You have 1 thingy!")
case 2...10:
    print("You have \(i) thingies!")
default:
    print("You have more thingies than I can count!")
}
```

When the tag is an Optional, a case can test it against nil. Thus, a possible way to unwrap an Optional safely is to test against nil *first* and then unwrap in a subsequent case, since we'll never reach the unwrapping if the nil test succeeds. In this example, i is an Optional wrapping an Int:

```
switch i {
case nil: break
default:
    switch i! {
    case 1:
        print("You have 1 thingy!")
    case let n:
        print("You have \(n) thingies!")
    }
}
```

That seems a bit clumsy, however, so Swift 2.0 introduces a new syntax: appending ? to a case pattern safely unwraps an Optional tag. Thus, we can rewrite that example like this:

```
switch i {
case 1?:
    print("You have 1 thingy!")
case let n?:
    print("You have \(n) thingies!")
case nil: break
}
```

When the tag is a Bool, a case can test it against a condition. Thus, by a clever perversion, you can use the cases to test *any* conditions you like — by using true as the tag! A switch statement thus becomes a genuine substitute for an extended if...else if construct. In this example from my own code, I could have used if...else if, but each case is just one line, so a switch statement seems clearer:

```
func positionForBar(bar: UIBarPositioning) -> UIBarPosition {
    switch true {
    case bar === self.navbar:  return .TopAttached
    case bar === self.toolbar: return .Bottom
    default:                   return .Any
    }
}
```

A pattern can include a where clause adding a condition to limit the truth value of the case. This is often, though not necessarily, used in combination with a binding; the condition can refer to the variable declared in the binding:

```
switch i {
case let j where j < 0:
    print("i is negative")
case let j where j > 0:
    print("i is positive")
case 0:
    print("i is 0")
default:break
}
```

A pattern can include the `is` operator to test the tag's type. In this example, assume that we have a Dog class and its NoisyDog subclass, and that d is typed as Dog:

```
switch d {
case is NoisyDog:
    print("You have a noisy dog!")
case _:
    print("You have a dog.")
}
```

A pattern can include a cast with the `as` (not `as?`) operator. Typically, you'll combine this with a binding that declares a local variable; despite the use of unconditional `as`, the value is conditionally cast and, if the cast succeeds, the local variable carries the cast value into the case code. Assume that Dog implements `bark` and that NoisyDog implements `beQuiet`:

```
switch d {
case let nd as NoisyDog:
    nd.beQuiet()
case let d:
    d.bark()
}
```

You can also use `as` (not `as!`) to cast down the tag (and possibly unwrap it) conditionally as part of a test against a specific match; in this example, i might be an AnyObject or an Optional wrapping an AnyObject:

```
switch i {
case 0 as Int:
    print("It is 0")
default:break
}
```

You can perform multiple tests at once by expressing the tag as a tuple and wrapping the corresponding tests in a tuple. The case passes only if every test in the test tuple succeeds against the corresponding member of the tag tuple. In this example, we start with a dictionary d typed as `[String:AnyObject]`. Using a tuple, we can safely attempt to extract and cast two values at once:

```
switch (d["size"], d["desc"]) {
case let (size as Int, desc as String):
    print("You have size \(size) and it is \(desc)")
default:break
}
```

When a tag is an enum, the cases can be cases of the enum. A switch statement is thus an excellent way to handle an enum. Here's an enum:

```
enum Filter {
    case Albums
    case Playlists
    case Podcasts
    case Books
}
```

And here's a switch statement, where the tag, type, is a Filter:

```
switch type {
case .Albums:
    print("Albums")
case .Playlists:
    print("Playlists")
case .Podcasts:
    print("Podcasts")
case .Books:
    print("Books")
}
```

No "mop-up" is needed, because I exhausted the cases. (In that example, the dot before the case names is needed. But if the code is *inside* the enum's declaration, the dot can be omitted.)

A switch statement provides a way to extract an associated value from an enum case. Recall this enum from Chapter 4:

```
enum Error {
    case Number(Int)
    case Message(String)
    case Fatal
}
```

To extract the error number from an Error whose case is .Number, or the message string from an Error whose case is .Message, I can use a switch statement. Recall that the associated value is actually a tuple. A tuple of patterns after the matched case name is applied to the associated value. If a pattern is a binding variable, it captures the associated value. The let (or var) can appear inside the parentheses or after the case keyword; this code illustrates both alternatives:

```
switch err {
case .Number(let theNumber):
    print("It is a .Number: \(theNumber)")
case let .Message(theMessage):
    print("It is a .Message: \(theMessage)")
case .Fatal:
    print("It is a .Fatal")
}
```

If the let (or var) appears after the case keyword, I can add a where clause:

```
switch err {
case let .Number(n) where n > 0:
    print("It's a positive error number \(n)")
case let .Number(n) where n < 0:
    print("It's a negative error number \(n)")
case .Number(0):
    print("It's a zero error number")
default:break
}
```

If I don't want to extract the error number but just want to match against it, I can use some other pattern inside the parentheses:

```
switch err {
case .Number(1..<Int.max):
    print("It's a positive error number")
case .Number(Int.min...(-1)):
    print("It's a negative error number")
case .Number(0):
    print("It's a zero error number")
default:break
}
```

This same pattern also gives us yet another way to deal with an Optional tag. An Optional, as I explained in Chapter 4, is in fact an enum. It has two cases, .None and .Some, where the wrapped value is the .Some case's associated value. But now we know how to extract the associated value! Thus we can rewrite yet again the earlier example where i is an Optional wrapping an Int:

```
switch i {
case .None: break
case .Some(1):
    print("You have 1 thingy!")
case .Some(let n):
    print("You have \(n) thingies!")
}
```

New in Swift 2.0, the lightweight if case construct lets you use in a condition the same sort of pattern syntax you'd use in a case of a switch statement. Where a switch case pattern is compared against a previously stated tag, an if case pattern is followed by an equal sign and the tag. In practice, this is useful primarily for performing a single conditional binding to extract an associated value from an enum (err is our Error enum once again):

```
if case let .Number(n) = err {
    print("The error number is \(n)")
}
```

You can even append a where clause, just as in a switch case:

```
if case let .Number(n) = err where n < 0 {
    print("The negative error number is \(n)")
}
```

To combine case tests (with an implicit logical-or), separate them with a comma:

```
switch i {
case 1,3,5,7,9:
    print("You have a small odd number of thingies.")
case 2,4,6,8,10:
    print("You have a small even number of thingies.")
default:
    print("You have too many thingies for me to count.")
}
```

In this example, i is declared as an AnyObject:

```
switch i {
case is Int, is Double:
    print("It's some kind of number.")
default:
    print("I don't know what it is.")
}
```

But you can't use a comma to combine patterns that declare binding variables, presumably because it isn't clear what variable should be set to what value.

Another way of combining cases is to fall through from one case to the next by using a fallthrough statement. It is not uncommon for a case to consist entirely of a fallthrough statement, though it is perfectly legal for a case to execute some code and then fall through:

```
switch pep {
case "Manny": fallthrough
case "Moe": fallthrough
case "Jack":
    print("\(pep) is a Pep boy")
default:
    print("I don't know who \(pep) is")
}
```

Note that fallthrough evades the test of the next case; it simply starts executing the next case's code, directly. Therefore, the next case can't declare any binding variables, because they would never be set.

Conditional evaluation

An interesting problem arises when you'd like to decide what value to use — for example, what value to assign to a variable. This seems like a good use of a branching construct. You can, of course, declare the variable first without initializing it, and then set it from within a subsequent branching construct. It would be nice, however, to use a branching construct *as* the variable's value. Here, for example, I try (and fail) to write a variable assignment where the equal sign is followed directly by a branching construct:

```
let title = switch type { // compile error
case .Albums:
    "Albums"
case .Playlists:
    "Playlists"
case .Podcasts:
    "Podcasts"
case .Books:
    "Books"
}
```

There are languages that let you talk that way, but Swift is not one of them. However, an easy workaround does exist — use a define-and-call anonymous function:

```
let title : String = {
    switch type {
    case .Albums:
        return "Albums"
    case .Playlists:
        return "Playlists"
    case .Podcasts:
        return "Podcasts"
    case .Books:
        return "Books"
    }
}()
```

In the special case where a value can be decided by a two-pronged condition, Swift provides the C ternary operator (:?). Its scheme is as follows:

```
condition ? exp1 : exp2
```

If the condition is true, the expression *exp1* is evaluated and the result is used; otherwise, the expression *exp2* is evaluated and the result is used. Thus, you can use the ternary operator while performing an assignment, using this schema:

```
let myVariable = condition ? exp1 : exp2
```

What myVariable gets initialized to depends on the truth value of the condition. I use the ternary operator heavily in my own code. Here's an example:

```
cell.accessoryType =
    ix.row == self.currow ? .Checkmark : .DisclosureIndicator
```

The context needn't be an assignment; here, we're deciding what value to pass as a function argument:

```
CGContextSetFillColorWithColor(
    context, self.hilite ? purple.CGColor : beige.CGColor)
```

In the version of C used by modern Objective-C, there's a collapsed form of the ternary operator that allows you to test a value against nil. If it is nil, you get to supply a substitute value. If it *isn't* nil, the tested value itself is used. In Swift, the analogous operation would involve testing an Optional: if the tested Optional is nil, use the substitute value; if it *isn't* nil, *unwrap* the Optional and use the unwrapped value. Swift has such an operator — the ?? operator (called the *nil-coalescing* operator).

Recall this example from Chapter 4, where arr is a Swift array of Optional strings and I'm converting it to a form that can be handed over to Objective-C as an NSArray:

```
let arr2 : [AnyObject] =
    arr.map {if $0 == nil {return NSNull()} else {return $0!}}
```

We can write the same thing much more neatly using the ternary operator:

```
let arr2 = arr.map { $0 != nil ? $0! : NSNull() }
```

And the nil-coalescing operator is even neater:

```
let arr2 = arr.map { $0 ?? NSNull() }
```

Expressions using ?? can be chained:

```
let someNumber = i1 as? Int ?? i2 as? Int ?? 0
```

That code tries to cast i1 to an Int and use that Int. If that fails, it tries to cast i2 to an Int and use *that* Int. If *that* fails, it gives up and uses 0.

Loops

The usual purpose of a loop is to repeat a block of code with some simple difference on each iteration. This difference will typically serve also as a signal for when to stop the loop. Swift provides two basic loop structures: while loops and for loops.

While loops

A while loop comes in two forms, schematized in Example 5-3.

Example 5-3. The Swift while loop

```
while condition {
    statements
}

repeat {
    statements
} while condition
```

The chief difference between the two forms is the timing of the test. In the second form, the condition is tested after the block has executed — meaning that the block will be executed at least once.

Usually, the code inside the block will change something that alters both the environment and the condition, thus eventually bringing the loop to an end. Here's a typical example from my own code (movenda is an array):

```
while self.movenda.count > 0 {
    let p = self.movenda.removeLast()
    // ...
}
```

Each iteration removes an element from movenda, so eventually its count falls to 0 and the loop is no longer executed; execution then proceeds to the next line after the closing curly braces.

The condition in the first form of while loop can be a conditional binding of an Optional. This provides a compact way of safely unwrapping an Optional and looping until the Optional is nil; the local variable containing the unwrapped Optional is in scope inside the curly braces. Thus, my code can be rewritten more compactly:

```
while let p = self.movenda.popLast() {
    // ...
}
```

Another common use of while loops in my code is to walk my way up or down a hierarchy. In this example, I start with a subview (textField) of some table view cell, and I want to know *which* table view cell it is a subview of. So I keep walking up the view hierarchy, investigating each superview in turn, until I reach a table view cell:

```
var v : UIView = textField
repeat { v = v.superview! } while !(v is UITableViewCell)
```

After that code, v *is* the desired table view cell. Nevertheless, that code is dangerous: we'll crash if we don't encounter a UITableViewCell before reaching the top of the view hierarchy — a view whose superview is nil. Here is a safe way to write the same code:

```
var v : UIView = textField
while let vv = v.superview where !(vv is UITableViewCell) {v = vv}
if let c = v.superview as? UITableViewCell { // ...
```

Similar to the if case construct, while case lets you use a switch case pattern. In this rather artificial example, we have an array of various Error enums:

```
let arr : [Error] = [
    .Message("ouch"), .Message("yipes"), .Number(10), .Number(-1), .Fatal
]
```

We can extract the .Message associated string values from the start of the array, like this:

```
var i = 0
while case let .Message(message) = arr[i++]  {
    print(message) // "ouch", then "yipes"; then the loop stops
}
```

For loops

A Swift for loop comes in two forms, as schematized in Example 5-4.

Example 5-4. The Swift for loop

```
for variable in sequence {
    statements
}

for before-all; condition; after-each {
    statements
}
```

The first form — the for...in construct — is similar to Objective-C's for...in construct. In Objective-C, this syntax is available whenever a class conforms to the NSFast-Enumeration protocol. In Swift, it is available whenever a type adopts the SequenceType protocol.

In the for...in construct, the variable is implicitly declared with let on each iteration; it is thus immutable by default. (If you need to assign to the variable within the block, write for var.) The variable is also local to the block. On each iteration, a successive element of the sequence is used to initialize the variable, which is then in scope inside block. This is the form of for loop you'll use most often, especially because it is so easy in Swift to create a sequence on the fly if you don't have one already. In C, for example, the way to iterate through the numbers 1 to 5 is to use the second form, and you can certainly do the same in Swift:

```
for var i = 1; i < 6; i++ {
    print(i)
}
```

But in Swift, you can create a sequence of the numbers 1 through 5 on the fly — a Range — and that's what you'll usually do:

```
for i in 1...5 {
    print(i)
}
```

A SequenceType has a generate method which yields a "generator" object which, itself, has a mutating next method that returns the next object in the sequence wrapped in an Optional, or nil if there is no next object. Under the hood, therefore, for...in is actually a kind of while loop:

```
var g = (1...5).generate()
while let i = g.next() {
    print(i)
}
```

Sometimes you may find that writing out the while loop explicitly in that way makes the loop easier to control and to customize.

The sequence will often be an existing value. It might be a character sequence, in which case the variable values are the successive Characters. It might be an array, in which case the variable values are the successive elements of the array. It might be a dictionary, in which case the variable values are a key–value tuple, and you will probably express the variable as a tuple of two names in order to capture them. Many examples have already appeared in earlier chapters.

As I explained in Chapter 4, you may encounter an array coming from Objective-C whose elements will need to be cast down from AnyObject. It is quite typical to do this as part of the sequence specification:

```
let p = Pep()
for boy in p.boys() as! [String] {
    // ...
}
```

The sequence enumerate method yields a sequence of tuples preceding each element of the original sequence with its index number:

```
for (i,v) in self.tiles.enumerate() {
    v.center = self.centers[i]
}
```

If you need to skip some values of the sequence, Swift 2.0 allows you to append a where clause:

```
for i in 0...10 where i % 2 == 0 {
    print(i) // 0, 2, 4, 6, 8, 10
}
```

Like if case and while case, there's also for case. Return to our example of an array of Error enums:

```
let arr : [Error] = [
    .Message("ouch"), .Message("yipes"), .Number(10), .Number(-1), .Fatal
]
```

Here we cycle through the whole array, extracting just the .Number associated values:

```
for case let .Number(i) in arr {
    print(i) // 10, then -1
}
```

A sequence also has instance methods, such as map, filter, and reverse; in this example, I count backward by even numbers:

```
let range = (0...10).reverse().filter{$0 % 2 == 0}
for i in range {
    print(i) // 10, 8, 6, 4, 2, 0
}
```

Yet another approach is to generate the sequence by calling the `stride` method. It's an instance method of the Strideable protocol, which is adopted by numeric types and anything else that can be incremented and decremented. It has two forms:

- `stride(through:by:)`
- `stride(to:by:)`

Which form you use depends on whether you want the sequence to include the final value or not. The `by:` argument can be negative:

```
for 10.stride(through: 0, by: -2) {
    print(i) // 10, 8, 6, 4, 2, 0
}
```

You can cycle through two sequences simultaneously using the global `zip` function, which takes two sequences and yields a Zip2 struct, which is itself a sequence. The value on each iteration through a Zip2 is a tuple of the corresponding elements from both original sequences; if one of the original sequences is longer than the other, the extra elements are ignored:

```
let arr1 = ["CA", "MD", "NY", "AZ"]
let arr2 = ["California", "Maryland", "New York"]
var d = [String:String]()
for (s1,s2) in zip(arr1,arr2) {
    d[s1] = s2
} // now d is ["MD": "Maryland", "NY": "New York", "CA": "California"]
```

The second form of for loop is a clone of the C for loop (refer to Example 5-4). The idea here is usually to increment or decrement a counter. The *before-all* statement is executed once as the for loop is first encountered and is usually used for initialization of the counter. The condition is then tested, and if `true`, the block is executed; the condition will usually test whether the counter has reached some limit. The *after-each* statement is then executed, and will usually increment or decrement the counter; the condition is then immediately tested again. Thus, to execute a block using integer values 1, 2, 3, 4, and 5 for `i`, the standard formula (if you're going to use this kind of for loop) is:

```
var i : Int
for i = 1; i < 6; i++ {
    print(i)
}
```

To limit the scope of the counter to the inside of the curly braces, declare it as part of the *before-all* statement:

```
for var i = 1; i < 6; i++ {
    print(i)
}
```

No law says, however, that this kind of for loop must be about counting or incrementing. Recall this earlier example of a while loop, where we cycle up the view hierarchy looking for a table view cell:

```
var v : UIView = textField
repeat { v = v.superview! } while !(v is UITableViewCell)
```

Here's another way to express that, using a for loop whose block is empty:

```
var v : UIView
for v = textField; !(v is UITableViewCell); v = v.superview! {}
```

As in C, each statement in the declaration (separated by semicolon) may consist, itself, of more than one code statement (separated by comma). This can be a handy, elegant way to clarify your intentions. In this example from my own code, I declare *two* variables in the *before-all* statement, and change *both* of them in the *after-each* statement; there are other ways to accomplish this same end, certainly, but this seems cleanest and clearest:

```
var values = [0.0]
for (var i = 20, direction = 1.0; i < 60; i += 5, direction *= -1) {
    values.append( direction * M_PI / Double(i) )
}
```

Jumping

Although branching and looping constitute the bulk of the decision-making flow of code execution, sometimes even they are insufficient to express the logic of what needs to happen next. On rare occasions, it is useful to be able to interrupt your code's progress completely and *jump* to a different place within it.

The most general way to jump from anywhere to anywhere is the goto command, common in early programming languages, but now notoriously "considered harmful." Swift doesn't have a goto command, but it does provide a repertory of controlled ways of jumping, which will, in practice, cover any real-life situation. Swift's modes of jumping are all forms of *early exit* from the current flow of code.

You are familiar already with one of the most important forms of early exit: return, which brings the current function to an immediate end and resumes at the point where the function was called. Thus, return may be considered a form of jumping.

Shortcircuiting and labels

Swift has several ways of shortcircuiting the flow of branch and loop constructs:

fallthrough
    A fallthrough statement in a switch case aborts execution of the current case code and immediately begins executing the code of the next case. There must *be* a next case or the compiler will stop you.

`continue`

A `continue` statement in a loop construct aborts execution of the current iteration and proceeds to the next iteration:

- In a while loop, `continue` means to perform immediately the conditional test.

- In a for loop of the first type (`for...in`), `continue` means to proceed immediately to the next iteration if there is one.

- In a for loop of the second type (C for loop), `continue` means to perform immediately the *after-each* statement and then the conditional test.

`break`

A `break` statement aborts the current construct:

- In a loop, `break` aborts the loop completely.

- In the code of a switch case, `break` aborts the entire switch construct.

When constructs are nested, you may need to specify which construct you want to `continue` or `break`. Therefore, Swift permits you to put a *label* before the start of a do block, an if construct, a switch statement, a while loop, or a for loop. The label is an arbitrary name followed by a colon. You can then use that label name as a second term in a `continue` or `break` statement within the labeled construct at any depth, to specify that this is the construct you are referring to.

Here's an artifical example to illustrate the syntax. First, I'll nest two for loops with no label:

```
for i in 1...5 {
    for j in 1...5 {
        print("\(i), \(j);")
        break
    }
}
// 1, 1; 2, 1; 3, 1; 4, 1; 5, 1;
```

As you can see from the output, that code keeps aborting the inner loop after one iteration, while the outer loop proceeds normally through all five iterations. But what if you wanted to abort the entire nested construct? The solution is a label:

```
outer: for i in 1...5 {
    for j in 1...5 {
        print("\(i), \(j);")
        break outer
    }
}
// 1, 1;
```

New in Swift 2.0, you can put a label before the word `if`, and you can also `break` with a label name within the code of an `if` or `else` block; similarly, you can put a label before the word `do` and you can `break` with a label name in a `do` block. With these additions, Swift's shortcircuiting capabilities may be considered feature-complete.

Throwing and catching errors

Sometimes a situation arises where further coherent progress is impossible: the entire operation in which we are engaged has failed. It can then be desirable to abort the current scope, and possibly the current function, and possibly even the function that called it, and so on, exiting to a point where we can acknowledge this failure and proceed in good order in some other way.

For this purpose, Swift 2.0 provides a mechanism for *throwing and catching errors*. In keeping with its usual insistence on safety and clarity, Swift imposes certain strict conditions on the use of this mechanism, and the compiler will ensure that you adhere to them.

An *error*, in this sense, is a kind of message, presumably specifying what went wrong. This message is passed up the nest of scopes and function calls as part of the error-handling process, and the code that recovers from the failure can, if desired, read the message and determine how to proceed. In Swift, an error must be an object of a type that adopts the ErrorType protocol, which has just two requirements: a String _domain property and an Int _code property. In practice, that's likely to mean one of the following:

NSError
> NSError is Cocoa's class for communicating the nature of a problem. If your call to a Cocoa method generates a failure, Cocoa will send you an NSError instance. You can also create your own NSError instance by calling its designated initializer, `init(domain:code:userInfo:)`.

A Swift type that adopts ErrorType
> As soon as a type adopts the ErrorType protocol, it is ready to be used as an error object; the protocol requirements are magically fulfilled for you, behind the scenes. Typically, this type will be an enum, which will communicate its message by means of its cases: different cases will distinguish different kinds of possible failure, perhaps with raw values or associated types to carry further information.

There are two stages of the error mechanism to consider: throwing an error, and catching an error. Throwing an error aborts the current path of execution and hands an error object to the error-handling mechanism. Catching an error receives that error object and responds in good order, with the path of execution resuming after the point of catching. In effect, we have *jumped* from the throwing point to the catching point.

To *throw an error*, use the keyword `throw` followed by an error object. This causes the current block of code to be aborted and the error-handling mechanism to kick in. To ensure that the `throw` command is used coherently, Swift imposes a rule that you can say `throw` only in one of the following two places:

In the do block of a `do...catch` *construct*

> A `do...catch` construct consists of (at least) two blocks, the do block and the catch block. The point of the construct is that a catch block can be fed any errors thrown from within the do block. Thus, such an error can be handled coherently — it can be *caught*. I'll describe the `do...catch` construct in more detail in a moment.

In a function marked `throws`

> If an error is thrown *not* inside the do block of a `do...catch` construct, or if an error is thrown inside the do block but the catch block fails to catch it, the error message travels right up and out of the current function. You are thus relying on some *other* function — the function that called this function, or the function that called that function, and so on up the call stack — to catch the error. To signal to any callers (and to the compiler) that this can happen, your function must include the keyword `throws` in its declaration.

To *catch an error*, use a `do...catch` construct. An error thrown from within the do block can be caught by a catch block that accompanies it. The `do...catch` construct's schema looks like Example 5-5.

Example 5-5. The Swift `do...catch` *construct*

```
do {
    statements // a throw can happen here
} catch errortype {
    statements
} catch {
    statements
}
```

A single do block can be accompanied by multiple catch blocks. Catch blocks are like the cases of a switch statement, and will usually have the same logic: first, you might have specialized catch blocks, each of which is designed to handle some limited set of possible errors; finally, you might have a general catch block that acts as the default, mopping up any errors that were not caught by any of the specialized catch blocks.

In fact, the *syntax* used by a catch block to specify what sorts of error it catches *is* the pattern syntax used by a case in a switch statement! Imagine that this *is* a switch statement, and that the tag is the error object. Then the matching of that error object to a particular catch block is performed just as if you had written `case` instead of `catch`. Typically, when the ErrorType is an enum, a specialized catch block will state at least the enum that it catches, and possibly also the case of that enum; it can have a binding, to capture the enum or its associated type; and it can have a `where` clause to limit the possibilities still further.

To illustrate, I'll start by defining a couple of errors:

```
enum MyFirstError : ErrorType {
    case FirstMinorMistake
    case FirstMajorMistake
    case FirstFatalMistake
}
enum MySecondError : ErrorType {
    case SecondMinorMistake(i:Int)
    case SecondMajorMistake(s:String)
    case SecondFatalMistake
}
```

Now here's a do...catch construct designed to demonstrate some of the different ways we can catch different errors in different catch blocks:

```
do {
    // throw can happen here
} catch MyFirstError.FirstMinorMistake {
    // catches MyFirstError.FirstMinorMistake
} catch let err as MyFirstError {
    // catches all other cases of MyFirstError
} catch MySecondError.SecondMinorMistake(let i) where i < 0 {
    // catches e.g. MySecondError.SecondMinorMistake(i:-3)
} catch {
    // catches everything else
}
```

In a catch block with an accompanying pattern, it is up to you to capture in the pattern any desired information about the error. For example, if you want the error itself to travel as a variable into the catch block, you'll need a binding in the pattern. In a catch block with *no* accompanying pattern, the error object arrives into the block as a variable called error.

If a line of code in a function says throw, and this is *not* in a do block that has a "mop-up" catch block, then *the function itself* must be marked with throws — because if not every possible error is caught, and an error is thrown, that error can travel right out of the enclosing function. The syntax is that the keyword throws will appear immediately after the parameter list (and before the arrow operator, if there is one). For example:

```
enum NotLongEnough : ErrorType {
    case ISaidLongIMeantLong
}
func giveMeALongString(s:String) throws {
    if s.characters.count < 5 {
        throw NotLongEnough.ISaidLongIMeantLong
    }
    print("thanks for the string")
}
```

The addition of `throws` to a function declaration creates a new function type. The type of `giveMeALongString` is not `(String) -> ()`, but rather `(String) throws -> ()`. If a function receives as parameter a function that can throw, that parameter's type needs to be specified accordingly:

```
func receiveThrower(f:(String) throws -> ()) {
    // ...
}
```

That function can now be called with `giveMeALongString` as argument:

```
func callReceiveThrower() {
    receiveThrower(giveMeALongString)
}
```

An anonymous function, if necessary, can include the keyword `throws` in its `in` line, in the same place where it would appear in a normal function declaration. But this is not necessary if, as is usually the case, the anonymous function's type is known by inference:

```
func callReceiveThrower() {
    receiveThrower {
        s in
        if s.characters.count < 5 {
            throw NotLongEnough.ISaidLongIMeantLong
        }
        print("thanks for the string")
    }
}
```

Swift also imposes a requirement on the *caller* of a `throws` function: the caller must precede the call with the keyword `try`. This keyword acknowledges, to the programmer and to the compiler, that we understand that this function can throw. It also imposes a further requirement: this call must take place where throwing is legal! A function called with `try` can throw, so saying `try` is just like saying `throw`: you must say it either in the do block of a `do...catch` construct or in a function marked `throws`.

So, for example:

```
func stringTest() {
    do {
        try giveMeALongString("is this long enough for you?")
    } catch {
        print("I guess it wasn't long enough: \(error)")
    }
}
```

If, however, you are very sure that a function that can throw will in fact *not* throw, then you can call it with the keyword `try!` instead of `try`. This relieves you of all further responsibility: you can say `try!` *anywhere*, without catching the possible throw. But be warned: if you're wrong, and this function *does* throw when your program runs, your program can crash at that moment, because you have allowed an error to proceed, uncaught, all the way up to the top of the calling chain.

Thus, this is legal but dangerous:

```
func stringTest() {
    try! giveMeALongString("okay")
}
```

In between `try` and `try!` is `try?`. This has the advantage that, like `try!`, you can use it anywhere, without catching the possible throw. In addition, it won't crash if there *is* a throw; instead, it returns `nil`. Thus, `try?` is useful particularly in situations where its expression returns a value. If there's no throw, it wraps that value in an Optional. Commonly, you'll unwrap that Optional safely in the same line with a conditional binding. I'll give an example in a moment.

A function that receives a `throws` function parameter, and that calls that function (with `try`), and that doesn't throw for any *other* reason, may itself be marked as `rethrows` instead of `throws`. The difference is that when a `rethrows` function is called, the caller can pass as argument a function that does *not* throw, and in that case the call doesn't have to be marked with `try` (and the calling function doesn't have to be marked with `throws`):

```
func receiveThrower(f:(String) throws -> ()) rethrows {
    try f("ok?")
}
func callReceiveThrower() { // no throws needed
    receiveThrower { // no try needed
        s in
        print("thanks for the string!")
    }
}
```

Now let's talk about how Swift's error-handling mechanism relates to Cocoa and Objective-C. A common Cocoa pattern is that a method will return `nil` to indicate failure, and will take an `NSError**` parameter as a way of communicating an error to the caller outside of the method result. Swift types such a parameter as an NSError-Pointer, meaning a pointer to an Optional wrapping an NSError. For example, NSString has an initializer declared in Objective-C like this:

```
- (instancetype)initWithContentsOfFile:(NSString *)path
    encoding:(NSStringEncoding)enc
    error:(NSError **)error;
```

Prior to Swift 2.0, the Swift translation of that declaration looked like this:

```
convenience init?(contentsOfFile path: String,
    encoding enc: UInt,
    error: NSErrorPointer)
```

And you would call it by passing, as the last argument, the address of an Optional wrapping an NSError:

```
var err : NSError?
let s = String(contentsOfFile: f, encoding: NSUTF8StringEncoding, error: &err)
```

The idea is that after that call, s is either a String (wrapped in an Optional) or nil. If it's nil, the call has failed, and you can examine err, which has been set by indirection, to find out why.

In Swift 2.0, however, that Objective-C method is automatically recast to take advantage of the error-handling mechanism. The error: parameter is removed from the Swift translation of the declaration, and is replaced by a throws marker:

```
init(contentsOfFile path: String, encoding enc: NSStringEncoding) throws
```

Thus there is no need to declare an NSError variable beforehand, and no need to receive the NSError by indirection. Instead, you just call the method, within the controlled conditions dictated by Swift: you have to say try, in a place where throwing is legal. The result can never be nil, and so it is no longer a String wrapped in an Optional; it's a String, plain and simple, because if the initialization fails, the call will throw and no result will arrive at all:

```
do {
    let f = // path to some file, maybe
    let s = try String(contentsOfFile: f, encoding: NSUTF8StringEncoding)
    // ... if successful, do something with s ...
} catch {
    print((error as NSError).localizedDescription)
}
```

If you're very sure the initialization won't fail, you can skip the do...catch construct and use try! instead:

```
let f = // path to some file, maybe
let s = try! String(contentsOfFile: f, encoding: NSUTF8StringEncoding)
```

But even if you're in doubt, you can skip the do...catch construct and still proceed safely by using try?, in which case the value returned *is* an Optional — which you'll probably unwrap safely at the same time, like this:

```
let f = // path to some file, maybe
if let s = try? String(contentsOfFile: f, encoding: NSUTF8StringEncoding) {
    // ...
}
```

Objective-C NSError and Swift ErrorType are bridged to one another. Thus, in a catch block a moment ago, I cast the error variable to NSError and examined it using an NSError property. However, you don't have to do that; instead of treating the caught error as an NSError, you can treat it *as a Swift enum.*

For common Cocoa error types, the name of the bridged enum is the name of the NSError domain, with "Domain" deleted from its name. Let's say there is no such file, the call throws, and we catch the error. This NSError's domain is "NSCocoaError-Domain", so Swift can see it as an NSCocoaError enum. Moreover, its code is 260, which is expressed in Objective-C as NSFileReadNoSuchFileError and in Swift as the File-ReadNoSuchFileError enum case. Thus we can catch the same error like this:

```
do {
    let f = // path to some file, maybe
    let s = try String(contentsOfFile: f, encoding: NSUTF8StringEncoding)
    // ... if successful, do something with s ...
} catch NSCocoaError.FileReadNoSuchFileError {
    print("no such file")
} catch {
    print(error)
}
```

 See the *FoundationError.h* header file in Objective-C to learn about Cocoa's built-in standard error domains.

The same sort of thing is true in reverse. As I said earlier, a Swift type that adopts ErrorType automatically implements its requirements behind the scenes: in particular, its _domain is the name of the type, and, if this is an enum, its _code is the index number of its case (otherwise, the _code is 1). If an ErrorType is used where an NSError is expected (or is simply cast to an NSError), those become the NSError's domain and code values.

Defer

The purpose of the defer statement, new in Swift 2.0, is to *ensure* that a certain block of code will be executed at the time the path of execution flows out of the current scope, no matter how.

A defer statement applies to the scope in which it appears, such as a function body, a while block, an if construct, and so on. Wherever you say defer, curly braces surround it; the defer block will be executed when the path of execution leaves those curly braces. Leaving the curly braces can involve reaching the last line of code within the curly braces, or any of the forms of early exit described earlier in this section.

To see why this is useful, consider the following pair of commands:

UIApplication.sharedApplication().beginIgnoringInteractionEvents()
    Stops all user touches from reaching any view of the application.

UIApplication.sharedApplication().endIgnoringInteractionEvents()
    Restores the ability of user touches to reach views of the application.

It can be valuable to turn off user interactions at the start of some slightly time-consuming operation and then turn them back on after that operation, especially when, *during* the operation, the interface or the app's logic will be in some state where the user's tapping a button, say, could cause things to go awry. Thus, it is not uncommon for a method to be constructed like this:

```
func doSomethingTimeConsuming() {
    UIApplication.sharedApplication().beginIgnoringInteractionEvents()
    // ... do stuff ...
    UIApplication.sharedApplication().endIgnoringInteractionEvents()
}
```

All well and good — *if* we can guarantee that the only path of execution out of this function will be by way of that last line. But what if we need to return early from this function? Our code now looks like this:

```
func doSomethingTimeConsuming() {
    UIApplication.sharedApplication().beginIgnoringInteractionEvents()
    // ... do stuff ...
    if somethingHappened {
        return
    }
    // ... do more stuff ...
    UIApplication.sharedApplication().endIgnoringInteractionEvents()
}
```

Ooops! We've just made a terrible mistake. By providing an additional path out of our doSomethingTimeConsuming function, we've created the possibility that our code might never encounter the call to endIgnoringInteractionEvents(). We might leave our function by way of the return statement — and the user will then be left unable to interact with the interface. Obviously, we need to add another endIgnoring... call inside the if construct, just before the return statement. But as we continue to develop our code, we must remember, if we add *further* ways out of this function, to add *yet another* endIgnoring... call for *each* of them. This is madness!

The defer statement solves the problem. It lets us specify *once* what should happen when we leave this scope, *no matter how*. Our code now looks like this:

```
func doSomethingTimeConsuming() {
    UIApplication.sharedApplication().beginIgnoringInteractionEvents()
    defer {
        UIApplication.sharedApplication().endIgnoringInteractionEvents()
    }
    // ... do stuff ...
    if somethingHappened {
        return
    }
    // ... do more stuff ...
}
```

The endIgnoring... call in the defer block will be executed, not where it appears, but before the return statement, or before the last line of the method — whichever path of execution ends up leaving the function. The defer statement says: "Eventually, and as late as possible, be sure to execute this code." We have thus ensured the necessary balance between turning off user interactions and turning them back on again. Most uses of the defer statement will probably come under this same rubric: you'll use it to balance a command or restore a disturbed state.

 If the current scope has multiple defer blocks pending, they will be called in the reverse of the order in which they originally appeared. In effect, there is a defer *stack*; each successive defer statement pushes its code onto the top of the stack, and exiting the scope in which a defer statement appeared pops that code and executes it.

Aborting

Aborting is an extreme form of flow control; the program stops dead in its tracks. In effect, you have deliberately crashed your own program. This is an unusual thing to do, but it can be useful as a way of raising a very red flag: you don't really *want* to abort, so if you *do* abort, things must be so bad that you've no choice.

One way to abort is by calling the global function fatalError. It takes a String parameter permitting you to provide a message to appear in the console. I've already given this example:

```
required init?(coder aDecoder: NSCoder) {
    fatalError("init(coder:) has not been implemented")
}
```

That code says, in effect, that execution should *never* reach this point. We have no real implementation of init(coder:), and we do not expect to be initialized this way. If we *are* initialized this way, something has gone very wrong, and we *want* to crash, because our program has a serious bug.

An initializer containing a fatalError call does not have to initialize any properties. This is because fatalError is declared with the @noreturn attribute, which causes the compiler to abandon any contextual requirements. Similarly, a function that returns a value does not have to return any value if a fatalError call is encountered.

You can also abort conditionally by calling the assert function. Its first parameter is a condition — something that evaluates as a Bool. If the condition is false, we will abort; the second parameter is a String message to appear in the console if we *do* abort. The idea here is that you are making a bet (an *assertion*) that the condition is true — a bet that you feel so strongly about that if the condition is false, there's a serious bug in your program and you want to crash so you can learn of this bug and fix it.

By default, `assert` works only when you're developing your program. When your program is to be finalized and made public, you throw a different build switch, telling the compiler that `assert` should be ignored. In effect, the conditions in your `assert` calls are then disregarded; they are all seen as `true`. This means that you can safely leave `assert` calls in your code. By the time your program ships, of course, none of your assertions should be failing; any bugs that caused them to fail should already have been ironed out.

The disabling of assertions in shipping code is performed in an interesting way. The condition parameter is given an extra layer of indirection by declaring it as an `@autoclosure` function. This means that, even though the parameter is *not* in fact a function, the compiler will wrap it in a function; thus, the runtime needn't call that function unless it has to. In shipping code, the runtime will *not* call that function. This mechanism averts expensive and unnecessary evaluation: an `assert` condition test may involve side effects, but the test won't even be performed when assertions are turned off in your shipping program.

 Alternatively, Swift provides the `precondition` function. It is similar to `assert`, except that it remains operative even in a shipping program.

Guard

If the need for jumping might arise, you will probably want to test a condition that decides whether to jump. Swift 2.0 provides a special syntax for this situation — the guard statement. In effect, a guard statement is an if statement where you *must* exit early in response to failure of the condition. Its form is shown in Example 5-6.

Example 5-6. The Swift guard statement

```
guard condition else {
    statements
    exit
}
```

A guard statement, as you can see, consists solely of a condition and an `else` block. The `else` block *must* jump out of the current scope, by any of the means that Swift provides, such as `return`, `break`, `continue`, `throw`, or `fatalError` — anything that guarantees to the compiler that, in case of failure of the condition, execution absolutely will not proceed within the block that contains the guard statement.

An elegant consequence of this architecture is that, because the guard statement guarantees an exit on failure of the condition, the compiler knows that the condition has succeeded after the guard statement if we do *not* exit. Thus, a conditional binding in the condition *is in scope after the guard statement*, without introducing a further nested scope. For example:

```
guard let s = optionalString else {return}
// s is now a String (not an Optional)
```

That construct, as I demonstrated earlier, can be a nice alternative to the "pyramid of doom." It will also come in handy in conjunction with `try?`. Let's presume we can't proceed unless `String(contentsOfFile:encoding:)` succeeds. Then we can rewrite our earlier example like this:

```
let f = // path to some file, maybe
guard let s = try? String(contentsOfFile: f, encoding: NSUTF8StringEncoding)
    else {return}
// s is now a String (not an Optional)
```

There is also a `guard case` construct, forming the logical inverse of `if case`. To illustrate, we'll use our Error enum once again:

```
guard case let .Number(n) = err else {return}
// n is now the extracted number
```

Note that a guard statement's conditional binding can't use a name already declared in the same scope on the left side of the equal sign. This is illegal:

```
let s = // ... some Optional
guard let s = s else {return} // compile error
```

The reason is that `guard let`, unlike `if let` and `while let`, doesn't declare the bound variable for a nested scope; it declares it for *this* scope. Thus, we can't declare s here because s has already been declared in the same scope.

Operators

Swift operators such as + and > are not magically baked into the language. They are, in fact, functions; they are explicitly declared and implemented just like any other function. That is why, as I pointed out in Chapter 4, the term + can be passed as the last parameter in a `reduce` call; `reduce` expects a function taking two parameters and returning a value whose type matches that of the first parameter, and + *is* in fact the name of such a function. It also explains how Swift operators can be overloaded for different value types. You can use + with numbers, strings, or arrays — with a different meaning in each case — because two functions with the same name but different parameter types (different signatures) are two *different* functions; from the parameter types, Swift is able to determine *which* + function you are calling.

These facts are not merely an intriguing behind-the-scenes implementation detail. They have practical implications for you and your code. You are free to overload existing operators to apply to *your* object types. You can even invent *new* operators! In this section, we'll do both.

First, we must talk about how operators are declared. Clearly there is some sort of syntactical hanky-panky (a technical computer science term), because you don't *call* an operator function in the same way as a normal function. You don't say +(1,2); you say 1+2. Even so, 1 and 2 in that second expression *are* the parameters to a + function call. How does Swift know that the + function uses this special syntax?

To see the answer, look in the Swift header:

```
infix operator + {
    associativity left
    precedence 140
}
```

That is an operator declaration. An operator declaration announces that this symbol *is* an operator, and tells how many parameters it has and what the usage syntax will be in relation to those parameters. The really important part is the stuff before the curly braces: the keyword `operator`, preceded by an operator *type* — here, `infix` — and followed by the name of the operator. The types are:

infix
   This operator takes two parameters and appears between them.

prefix
   This operator takes one parameter and appears before it.

postfix
   This operator takes one parameter and appears after it.

An operator is also a function, so you also need a function declaration stating the type of the parameters and the result type of the function. Again, the Swift header shows us an example:

```
func +(lhs: Int, rhs: Int) -> Int
```

That is one of many declarations for the + function in the Swift header. In particular, it is the declaration for when the parameters are both Int. In that situation, the result is itself an Int. (The local parameter names `lhs` and `rhs`, which don't affect the special calling syntax, presumably stand for "left-hand side" and "right-hand side.")

Both an operator declaration and its corresponding function declaration(s) must appear at the top level of a file. If the operator is a `prefix` or `postfix` operator, the function declaration must start with the word `prefix` or `postfix`; the default is `infix` and can therefore be omitted.

We now know enough to override an operator to work with an object type of our own! As a simple example, imagine a Vial full of bacteria:

```
struct Vial {
    var numberOfBacteria : Int
    init(_ n:Int) {
        self.numberOfBacteria = n
    }
}
```

When two Vials are combined, you get a Vial with all the bacteria from both of them. So the way to add two Vials is to add their bacteria:

```
func +(lhs:Vial, rhs:Vial) -> Vial {
    let total = lhs.numberOfBacteria + rhs.numberOfBacteria
    return Vial(total)
}
```

And here's code to test our new + operator override:

```
let v1 = Vial(500_000)
let v2 = Vial(400_000)
let v3 = v1 + v2
print(v3.numberOfBacteria) // 900000
```

In the case of a compound assignment operator, the first parameter is the thing being assigned to. Therefore, to implement such an operator, the first parameter must be declared inout. Let's do that for our Vial class:

```
func +=(inout lhs:Vial, rhs:Vial) {
    let total = lhs.numberOfBacteria + rhs.numberOfBacteria
    lhs.numberOfBacteria = total
}
```

Here's code to test our += override:

```
var v1 = Vial(500_000)
let v2 = Vial(400_000)
v1 += v2
print(v1.numberOfBacteria) // 900000
```

It might be useful also to override the equality comparison operator == for our Vial class. This satisfies the requirement for Vial to adopt the Equatable protocol, but of course it won't actually adopt it unless we tell it to:

```
func ==(lhs:Vial, rhs:Vial) -> Bool {
    return lhs.numberOfBacteria == rhs.numberOfBacteria
}
extension Vial:Equatable{}
```

Now that Vial is an Equatable, it becomes a candidate for use with methods such as indexOf:

```
let v1 = Vial(500_000)
let v2 = Vial(400_000)
let arr = [v1,v2]
let ix = arr.indexOf(v1) // Optional wrapping 0
```

What's more, the complementary inequality operator != has sprung to life for Vials automatically! That's because it's already defined for *any* Equatable in terms of the == operator. By the same token, if we now override < for Vial and tell it to adopt Comparable, the other three comparison operators spring to life automatically.

Next, let's invent a completely new operator. As an example, I'll inject an operator into Int that raises one number to the power of another. As my operator symbol, I'll use ^^ (I'd like to use ^ but it's already in use for something else). For simplicity, I'll omit error-checking for edge cases (such as exponents less than 1):

```
infix operator ^^ {
}
func ^^(lhs:Int, rhs:Int) -> Int {
    var result = lhs
    for _ in 1..<rhs {result *= lhs}
    return result
}
```

That's all it takes! Here's some code to test it:

```
print(2^^2) // 4
print(2^^3) // 8
print(3^^3) // 27
```

When defining an operator, you'll add precedence and associativity specifications if you're concerned about how this operator interacts in expressions containing other operators. I'm not going to go into the details; see the Swift manual if you need to. The manual also lists the special characters that can be used as part of a custom operator name:

```
/ = - + ! * % < > & | ^ ? ~
```

An operator name can also contain many other symbol characters (that is, characters that can't be mistaken for some sort of alphanumeric) that are harder to type; see the manual for a formal list.

Privacy

Privacy (also known as *access control*) refers to the explicit modification of the normal scope rules. I gave an example in Chapter 1:

```
class Dog {
    var name = ""
    private var whatADogSays = "woof"
    func bark() {
        print(self.whatADogSays)
    }
}
```

The intention here is to limit how other objects can see the Dog property whatADog-Says. It is a private property, intended primarily for the Dog class's own internal use: a Dog can speak of self.whatADogSays, but other objects should not be aware that it even exists.

Swift has three levels of privacy:

internal
> The default rule is that declarations are *internal*, meaning that they are globally visible to *all code in all files within the containing module*. That is why Swift files within the same module can see one another's top-level contents *automatically*, with no effort on your part. (That's different from C and Objective-C, where files can't see each other at all unless you explicitly show them to one another through include or import statements.)

private *(narrower than* internal*)*
> A thing declared private is visible *only within its containing file*. The formulation of this rule may not be quite what you were expecting from the notion of privacy. In some languages, private means private to an object declaration. In Swift, private is not as private as that; two classes in the same file can see one another even if both are declared private. This could be a good reason for breaking your code into multiple files, following the usual convention of one class per file.

public *(wider than* internal*)*
> A thing declared public is visible *even outside its containing module*. Another module must first import this module before it can see anything at all. But once another module *has* imported this module, it still won't be able to see anything in this module that hasn't been explicitly declared public. If you don't write any modules, you might never need to declare anything public. If you do write a module, you *must* declare *something* public, or your module is useless.

Private Declaration

By declaring object members private, you specify by inversion what the public API of this object is. Here's an example from my own code:

```
class CancelableTimer: NSObject {
    private var q = dispatch_queue_create("timer",nil)
    private var timer : dispatch_source_t!
    private var firsttime = true
    private var once : Bool
    private var handler : () -> ()
    init(once:Bool, handler:()->()) {
        // ...
    }
    func startWithInterval(interval:Double) {
        // ...
```

```
    }
    func cancel() {
        // ...
    }
}
```

The initializer init(once:handler:) and the startWithInterval: and cancel methods, which are *not* marked private, are this class's public API. They say, "Please feel
free to call me!" The properties, however, are all private; no other code (that is, no code
outside this file) can see them, either to get them or to set them. They are purely for the
internal use of the methods of this class. They maintain state, but it is not a state that
any other code needs to know about.

It's worth emphasizing that privacy can be restricted only to the level of the current file.
For example:

```
class Cat {
    private var secretName : String?
}
class Dog {
    func nameCat(cat:Cat) {
        cat.secretName = "Lazybones"
    }
}
```

Why is that code legal? I said that a Cat's secretName was private, so why is a Dog allowed
to come along and change it? It's because privacy is not at the level of the individual
object type; it's at the level of the file. I've defined Cat and Dog in the same file, so they
(if you'll pardon the expression) can see one another's private members.

It happens that a convenient real-life convention is to define each class in its own file.
In fact, the file is very often named after the class that's defined within it; a file containing
the declaration for the ViewController class will typically be named *View-
Controller.swift*. But there is no rule governing any of that. File names are not meaningful
in Swift, and Swift files within the same module can all see inside one another automatically, without being told one another's names. File names are mostly a convenience
for the *programmer*: in Xcode, I see a list of my program's files, so it's helpful, when I
want to find the declaration for the ViewController class, to see the name *View-
Controller.swift* giving me a hint as to which file to look in.

The *formal* reason for dividing your code into files is to make privacy work. Let's say I
have two files, *Cat.swift* and *Dog.swift*:

```
// Cat.swift:
class Cat {
    private var secretName : String?
}

// Dog.swift:
class Dog {
```

```
    func nameCat(cat:Cat) {
        cat.secretName = "Lazybones" // compile error
    }
}
```

Now *that* code won't compile: the compiler says, "Cat does not have a member named secretName." Cat *does* have a member named secretName, but not as far as code in a different file is concerned. And Dog now *is* in a different file, so privacy works.

It may be that on some occasions you will want to draw a distinction between the privacy of a variable regarding setting and its privacy regarding getting. To draw this distinction, place the word set in parentheses after its own privacy declaration. Thus, private(set) var myVar means that the *setting* of this variable is restricted to code within this same file. It says nothing about restricting the *getting* of this variable, which is left at the default. Similarly, you can say public private(set) var myVar to make getting this variable public, while setting this variable is kept private. (You can use this same syntax with a subscript function.)

Public Declaration

If you write a module, you'll need to specify at least some object declarations as public, or code that imports your module won't be able to see it. Other declarations that are not declared public are internal, meaning that they are private to the module. Thus, judicious use of public declarations configures the public API of your module.

For example, in my Zotz app, which is a card game, the object types for creating and portraying cards and for combining them into a deck are bundled into a framework called ZotzDeck. Many of these types, such as Card and Deck, are declared public. Many utility object types, however, are not; the classes within the ZotzDeck module can see and use them, but code outside the module doesn't need to be aware of them at all.

The members of a public object type are not, themselves, automatically public. If you want a method to be public, you have to declare it public. This is an excellent default behavior, because it means that these members are not shared outside the module unless you want them to be. (As Apple puts it, you must "opt in to publishing" object members.)

For example, in my ZotzDeck module, the Card class is declared public but its initializer is not. Why? Because it doesn't need to be. The way you (meaning the importer of the ZotzDeck module) get cards is by initializing a Deck; the initializer for Deck *is* declared public, so you can do that. There is never any reason to make a card independently of a Deck, and thanks to the privacy rules, you can't.

Privacy Rules

It took time for Apple to add access control to Swift in the early months of the language's release, mostly because the compiler had to be taught an extensive set of rules for ensuring that the privacy level of related things is coherent. For example:

- A variable can't be public if its type is private, because other code wouldn't be able to use such a variable.
- A subclass can't be public unless the superclass is public.
- A subclass can change an overridden member's access level, but it cannot even *see* its superclass's private members unless they are declared in the same file together.

And so on. I could proceed to list all the rules, but I won't. There is no need for me to enunciate them formally. They are spelled out in great detail in the Swift manual, which you can consult if you need to. In general, you probably won't need to; they make intuitive sense, and you can rely on the compiler to help you with useful error messages if you violate one.

Introspection

Swift provides limited ability to *introspect* an object, letting an object display the names and values of its properties. This feature is intended for debugging, not for use in your program's logic. For example, you can use it to modify the way your object is displayed in the Xcode Debug pane.

To introspect an object, use it as the `reflecting` parameter when you instantiate a Mirror. The Mirror's `children` will then be name–value tuples describing the original object's properties. Here, for example, is a Dog class with a `description` property that takes advantage of introspection. Instead of hard-coding a list of the class's instance properties, we introspect the instance to obtain the names and values of the properties. This means that we can later add more properties without having to modify our `description` implementation:

```
struct Dog : CustomStringConvertible {
    var name = "Fido"
    var license = 1
    var description : String {
        var desc = "Dog ("
        let mirror = Mirror(reflecting:self)
        for (k,v) in mirror.children {
            desc.appendContentsOf("\(k!): \(v), ")
        }
        let c = desc.characters.count
        return String(desc.characters.prefix(c-2)) + ")"
    }
}
```

If we now instantiate Dog and pass that instance to `print`, this is what we see in the console:

```
Dog (name: Fido, license: 1)
```

 If your object type adopts both the CustomStringConvertible protocol (`description` property) and the CustomDebugStringConvertible protocol (`debugDescription` property), the `description` will be preferred, but you can output the debug-Description with the `debugPrint` function.

By adopting the CustomReflectable protocol, we can take charge of what a Mirror's `children` are. To do so, we implement the `customMirror` method to return our own custom Mirror object whose `children` property we have configured as a collection of name–value tuples.

In this (silly) example, we implement `customMirror` to supply altered names for our properties:

```
struct Dog : CustomReflectable {
    var name = "Fido"
    var license = 1
    func customMirror() -> Mirror {
        let children : [Mirror.Child] = [
            ("ineffable name", self.name),
            ("license to kill", self.license)
        ]
        let m = Mirror(self, children:children)
        return m
    }
}
```

The outcome is that when we po a Dog instance in the Xcode Debug pane console, our custom property names are displayed:

```
- ineffable name : "Fido"
- license to kill : 1
```

Memory Management

Swift memory management is handled automatically, and you will usually be unaware of it. Objects come into existence when they are instantiated and go out of existence as soon as they are no longer needed. Memory management of reference type objects, however, is quite tricky under the hood; I'll devote Chapter 12 to a discussion of the underlying mechanism. Even for the Swift user, things can occasionally go wrong in this regard. (Value types do not require the sort of complex memory management that reference types do, so no memory management issues can arise for them.)

Trouble typically arises when two class instances have references to one another. When that's the case, you can have a *retain cycle* which will result in a *memory leak*, meaning that the two instances *never* go out of existence. Some computer languages solve this sort of problem with a periodic "garbage collection" phase that detects retain cycles and cleans them up, but Swift doesn't do that; you have to fend off retain cycles manually.

The way to test for and observe a memory leak is to implement a class's `deinit`. This method is called when the instance goes out of existence. If the instance never goes out of existence, `deinit` is never called. That's a bad sign, if you were expecting that the instance *should* go out of existence.

Here's an example. First, I'll make two class instances and watch them go out of existence:

```
func testRetainCycle() {
    class Dog {
        deinit {
            print("farewell from Dog")
        }
    }
    class Cat {
        deinit {
            print("farewell from Cat")
        }
    }
    let d = Dog()
    let c = Cat()
}
testRetainCycle() // farewell from Cat, farewell from Dog
```

When we run that code, both "farewell" messages appear in the console. We created a Dog instance and a Cat instance, but the only references to them are automatic (local) variables inside the `testRetainCycle` function. When execution of that function's body comes to an end, all automatic variables are destroyed; that is what it means to be an automatic variable. There are no other references to our Dog and Cat instances that might make them persist, and so they are destroyed in good order.

Now I'll change that code by giving the Dog and Cat objects references to each other:

```
func testRetainCycle() {
    class Dog {
        var cat : Cat?
        deinit {
            print("farewell from Dog")
        }
    }
    class Cat {
        var dog : Dog?
        deinit {
            print("farewell from Cat")
        }
    }
```

```
        let d = Dog()
        let c = Cat()
        d.cat = c // create a...
        c.dog = d // ...retain cycle
    }
    testRetainCycle() // nothing in console
```

When we run that code, *neither* "farewell" message appears in the console. The Dog and Cat objects have references to one another. Those are *persisting* references (also called *strong* references). A persisting reference sees to it that, for example, as long as our Dog has a reference to a particular Cat, that Cat will not be destroyed. That's a good thing, and is a fundamental principle of sensible memory management. The bad thing is that the Dog and the Cat have persisting references *to one another*. That's a retain cycle! Neither the Dog instance nor the Cat instance can be destroyed, because neither of them can "go first" — it's like Alphonse and Gaston who can never get through the door because each requires the other to precede him. The Dog can't be destroyed first because the Cat has a persisting reference to him, and the Cat can't be destroyed first because the Dog has a persisting reference to him.

These objects are therefore now *leaking*. Our code is over; both d and c are gone. There are *no* further references to either of these objects; neither object can ever be referred to again. No code can mention them; no code can reach them. But they live on, floating, useless, and taking up memory.

Weak References

One solution to a retain cycle is to mark the problematic reference as weak. This means that the reference is *not* a persisting reference. It is a *weak reference*. The object referred to can now go out of existence even while the referrer continues to exist. Of course, this presents a terrible danger, because now the object referred to may be destroyed behind the referrer's back. But Swift has a solution for that, too: only an Optional reference can be marked as weak. That way, if the object referred to *is* destroyed behind the referrer's back, the referrer will see something coherent, namely nil. Also, the reference must be a var reference, precisely because it can change spontaneously to nil.

Thus, this code breaks the retain cycle and prevents the memory leak:

```
func testRetainCycle() {
    class Dog {
        weak var cat : Cat?
        deinit {
            print("farewell from Dog")
        }
    }
    class Cat {
        weak var dog : Dog?
        deinit {
            print("farewell from Cat")
```

```
        }
    }
    let d = Dog()
    let c = Cat()
    d.cat = c
    c.dog = d
}
testRetainCycle() // farewell from Cat, farewell from Dog
```

I've gone overboard in that code. To break the retain cycle, there's no need to make *both* Dog's `cat` and Cat's `dog` weak references; making just *one* of the two a weak reference is sufficient to break the cycle. That, in fact, is the usual solution when a retain cycle threatens. One of the pair will be more of an "owner" than the other; the one that is *not* the "owner" will have a weak reference to its "owner."

Although, as I mentioned earlier, value types are not subject to the same memory management issues as reference types, a value type can still be *involved* in a retain cycle with a class instance. In my retain cycle example, if Dog is a class and Cat is a struct, we still get a retain cycle. The solution is the same: make Cat's `dog` a weak reference. (You can't make Dog's `cat` a weak reference if Cat is a struct; only a reference to a class type can be declared `weak`.)

Do *not* use weak references unless you have to! Memory management is not to be toyed with lightly. Nevertheless, there are real-life situations in which weak references are the right thing to do, even when no retain cycle appears to threaten. For example, a view controller's references to *subviews of its own view* are usually weak, because the view itself already has persisting references to those subviews, and we would not typically want those subviews to persist in the absence of the view itself:

```
class HelpViewController: UIViewController {
    weak var wv : UIWebView?
    override func viewWillAppear(animated: Bool) {
        super.viewWillAppear(animated)
        let wv = UIWebView(frame:self.view.bounds)
        // ... further configuration of wv here ...
        self.view.addSubview(wv)
        self.wv = wv
    }
    // ...
}
```

In that code, `self.view.addSubview(wv)` causes the UIWebView `wv` to persist; our own reference to it, `self.wv`, can thus be weak.

Unowned References

There's another Swift solution for retain cycles. Instead of marking a reference as `weak`, you can mark it as `unowned`. This approach is useful in special cases where one object absolutely cannot exist without a reference to another, but where this reference need not be a persisting reference.

For example, let's pretend that a Boy may or may not have a Dog, but every Dog must have a Boy — and so I'll give Dog an init(boy:) initializer. The Dog needs a reference to its Boy, and the Boy needs a reference to his Dog if he has one; that's potentially a retain cycle:

```
func testUnowned() {
    class Boy {
        var dog : Dog?
        deinit {
            print("farewell from Boy")
        }
    }
    class Dog {
        let boy : Boy
        init(boy:Boy) { self.boy = boy }
        deinit {
            print("farewell from Dog")
        }
    }
    let b = Boy()
    let d = Dog(boy: b)
    b.dog = d
}
testUnowned() // nothing in console
```

We can solve this by declaring Dog's boy property unowned:

```
func testUnowned() {
    class Boy {
        var dog : Dog?
        deinit {
            print("farewell from Boy")
        }
    }
    class Dog {
        unowned let boy : Boy // *
        init(boy:Boy) { self.boy = boy }
        deinit {
            print("farewell from Dog")
        }
    }
    let b = Boy()
    let d = Dog(boy: b)
    b.dog = d
}
testUnowned() // farewell from Boy, farewell from Dog
```

An advantage of an unowned reference is that it doesn't have to be an Optional — in fact, it *cannot* be an Optional — and it can be a constant (let). But an unowned reference is also dangerous, because the object referred to can go out of existence behind the referrer's back, and an attempt to use that reference will cause a crash, as I can demonstrate by this rather forced code:

```
var b = Optional(Boy())
let d = Dog(boy: b!)
b = nil // destroy the Boy behind the Dog's back
print(d.boy) // crash
```

Thus, you should use unowned only if you are absolutely certain that the object referred to will outlive the referrer.

Weak and Unowned References in Anonymous Functions

A subtle variant of a retain cycle arises when an instance property's value is a function referring to the instance:

```
class FunctionHolder {
    var function : (Void -> Void)?
    deinit {
        print("farewell from FunctionHolder")
    }
}
func testFunctionHolder() {
    let f = FunctionHolder()
    f.function = {
        print(f)
    }
}
testFunctionHolder() // nothing in console
```

Oooops! I've created a retain cycle, by referring, inside the anonymous function, to the object that is holding a reference to it. Because functions are closures, the Function-Holder f, declared outside the anonymous function, is captured by the anonymous function as a persisting reference. But the function property of this FunctionHolder contains this anonymous function, and that's a persisting reference too. So that's a retain cycle: the FunctionHolder persistently refers to the function, which persistently refers to the FunctionHolder.

In this situation, I *cannot* break the retain cycle by declaring the function property as weak or unowned. Only a reference to a class type can be declared weak or unowned, and a function is not a class. Thus, I must declare the captured value f *inside the anonymous function* as weak or unowned instead.

Swift provides an ingenious syntax for doing that. At the very start of the anonymous function body, where the in line would go (and before the in line if there is one), you put square brackets containing a comma-separated list of any problematic class type references that will be captured from the surrounding environment, each reference preceded by weak or unowned. This list is called a *capture list*. If you have a capture list, you must follow it by the keyword in if you are not already including the keyword in for other reasons:

```
class FunctionHolder {
    var function : (Void -> Void)?
    deinit {
        print("farewell from FunctionHolder")
    }
}
func testFunctionHolder() {
    let f = FunctionHolder()
    f.function = {
        [weak f] in // *
        print(f)
    }
}
testFunctionHolder() // farewell from FunctionHolder
```

This syntax solves the problem. But marking a reference as weak in a capture list has a mild side effect that you will need to be aware of: such a reference passes into the anonymous function as an Optional. This is good, because it means that if the object referred to goes out of existence behind our back, the value of the Optional is nil. But of course you must also adjust your code accordingly, unwrapping the Optional as needed in order to use it. The usual technique is to perform the *weak–strong dance*: you unwrap the Optional once, right at the start of the function, in a conditional binding:

```
class FunctionHolder {
    var function : (Void -> Void)?
    deinit {
        print("farewell from FunctionHolder")
    }
}
func testFunctionHolder() {
    let f = FunctionHolder()
    f.function = { // here comes the weak-strong dance
        [weak f] in // weak
        guard let f = f else { return }
        print(f) // strong
    }
}
testFunctionHolder() // farewell from FunctionHolder
```

The conditional binding let f = f accomplishes two goals. First, it unwraps the Optional version of f that arrived into the anonymous function. Second, it declares another f that is a normal (strong) reference. So if the unwrapping succeeds, this new f will persist for the rest of this scope.

In that particular example, there is no way on earth that this FunctionHolder instance, f, can go out of existence while the anonymous function lives on. There are no other references to the anonymous function; it persists only as a property of f. Therefore I can avoid some behind-the-scenes bookkeeping overhead, as well as the weak–strong dance, by declaring f as unowned in my capture list instead.

In real life, my own most frequent use of unowned is precisely in this context. Very often, the reference marked as unowned in the capture list will be self. Here's an example from my own code:

```
class MyDropBounceAndRollBehavior : UIDynamicBehavior {
    let v : UIView
    init(view v:UIView) {
        self.v = v
        super.init()
    }
    override func willMoveToAnimator(anim: UIDynamicAnimator!) {
        if anim == nil { return }
        let sup = self.v.superview!
        let grav = UIGravityBehavior()
        grav.action = {
            [unowned self] in
            let items = anim.itemsInRect(sup.bounds) as! [UIView]
            if items.indexOf(self.v) == nil {
                anim.removeBehavior(self)
                self.v.removeFromSuperview()
            }
        }
        self.addChildBehavior(grav)
        grav.addItem(self.v)
        // ...
    }
    // ...
}
```

There's a potential (and rather elaborate) retain cycle here: self.addChild-Behavior(grav) causes a persistent reference to grav, grav has a persistent reference to grav.action, and the anonymous function assigned to grav.action refers to self. To break the retain cycle, I declare the reference to self as unowned in the anonymous function's capture list.

 Don't panic! Beginners have a tendency to backstop *all* their anonymous functions with [weak self]. That's unnecessary and wrong. Only a retained function can raise even the possibility of a retain cycle. Merely passing a function does *not* introduce such a possibility, especially if the function being passed will be called immediately. Always confirm that you actually *have* a retain cycle before concerning yourself with how to prevent a retain cycle.

Memory Management of Protocol-Typed References

Only a reference to an instance of a class type can be declared `weak` or `unowned`. A reference to an instance of a struct or enum type cannot be so declared, because its memory management doesn't work the same way (and is not subject to retain cycles).

A reference that is declared as a protocol type, therefore, has a problem. A protocol might be adopted by a struct or an enum. Therefore you cannot wantonly declare such a reference `weak` or `unowned`. You can only declare a protocol-typed reference `weak` or `unowned` if it is a class protocol — that is, if it is marked with `@objc` or `class`.

In this code, SecondViewControllerDelegate is a protocol that I've declared. This code won't compile unless SecondViewControllerDelegate is declared as a class protocol:

```
class SecondViewController : UIViewController {
    weak var delegate : SecondViewControllerDelegate?
    // ...
}
```

Here's the actual declaration of SecondViewControllerDelegate; it *is* declared as a class protocol, and that's why the preceding code is legal:

```
protocol SecondViewControllerDelegate : class {
    func acceptData(data:AnyObject!)
}
```

A protocol declared in Objective-C is implicitly marked as `@objc` and is a class protocol. Thus, this declaration from my real-life code is legal:

```
weak var delegate : WKScriptMessageHandler?
```

WKScriptMessageHandler is a protocol declared by Cocoa (in particular, by the Web Kit framework). Thus, it is implicitly marked `@objc`; only a class can adopt WKScript-MessageHandler, and so the compiler is satisfied that the `delegate` variable will be an instance of a class, and thus the reference can be treated as `weak`.

PART II

IDE

By now, you're doubtless anxious to jump in and start writing an app. To do that, you need a solid grounding in the tools you'll be using. The heart and soul of those tools can be summed up in one word: Xcode. In this part of the book we explore Xcode, the *IDE* (integrated development environment) in which you'll be programming iOS. Xcode is a big program, and writing an app involves coordinating a lot of pieces; this part of the book will help you become comfortable with Xcode. Along the way, we'll generate a simple working app through some hands-on tutorials.

- Chapter 6 tours Xcode and explains the architecture of the *project*, the collection of files from which an app is generated.

- Chapter 7 is about nibs. A *nib* is a file containing a drawing of your interface. Understanding nibs — knowing how they work and how they relate to your code — is crucial to your use of Xcode and to proper development of just about any app.

- Chapter 8 pauses to discuss the Xcode documentation and other sources of information on the API.

- Chapter 9 explains editing your code, testing and debugging your code, and the various steps you'll take on the way to submitting your app to the App Store. You'll probably want to skim this chapter quickly at first, returning to it as a detailed reference later while developing and submitting an actual app.

CHAPTER 6

Anatomy of an Xcode Project

Xcode is the application used to develop an iOS app. An Xcode *project* is the source for an app; it's the entire collection of files and settings used to construct the app. To create, develop, and maintain an app, you must know how to manipulate and navigate an Xcode project. So you must know something about Xcode, and you must know something about the nature and structure of Xcode projects and how Xcode shows them to you. That's the subject of this chapter.

 The term "Xcode" is used in two ways. It's the name of the application in which you edit and build your app, and it's the name of an entire suite of utilities that accompanies it — in the latter sense, Instruments and the Simulator are part of Xcode. This ambiguity should generally present little difficulty.

Xcode is a powerful, complex, and extremely large program. My approach in introducing Xcode is to suggest that you adopt a kind of deliberate tunnel vision: if you don't understand something, don't worry about it — don't even look at it, and don't touch it, because you might change something important. Our survey of Xcode will chart a safe, restricted, and essential path, focusing on aspects of Xcode that you most need to understand immediately, and resolutely ignoring everything else.

For full information, study Apple's own documentation (choose Help → Xcode Overview); it may seem overwhelming at first, but what you need to know is probably in there somewhere. There are also entire books devoted to describing and explaining Xcode.

New Project

Even before you've written any code, an Xcode project is quite elaborate. To see this, let's make a new, essentially "empty" project; you'll find that it isn't empty at all.

1. Start up Xcode and choose File → New → Project.

2. The "Choose a template" dialog appears. The *template* is your project's initial set of files and settings. When you pick a template, you're really picking an existing folder full of files; basically, it will be one of the folders inside *Xcode.app/Contents/Developer/Platforms/iPhoneOS.platform/Developer/Library/Xcode/Templates/ Project Templates/iOS/Application*. This template folder will essentially be copied, and a few values will be filled in, in order to create your project.

    So, in this case, on the left, under iOS, choose Application. On the right, select Single View Application. Click Next.

3. You are now asked to provide a name for your project (Product Name). Let's call our new project *Empty Window*.

    In a real project, you should give some thought to the project's name, as you're going to be living in close quarters with it. As Xcode copies the template folder, it's going to use the project's name to "fill in the blank" in several places, including the name of the app. Thus, whatever you type at this moment is something you'll be seeing throughout your project. You are not locked into the name of your project forever, though, and there's a separate setting allowing you to change at any time the name of the app that it produces. I'll talk later about name changes ("Renaming Parts of a Project" on page 324).

    It's fine to use spaces in a project name. Spaces are legal in the project name, the app name, and the various names of files and folders that Xcode will generate automatically; and in the few places where spaces are problematic (such as the bundle identifier, discussed in the next paragraph), the name you type as the Product Name will have its spaces converted to hyphens. But do *not* use any other punctuation in your project name! Such punctuation can cause Xcode features to break in subtle ways.

4. Note the Organization Identifier field. The first time you create a project, this field will be blank, and you should fill it in. The goal here is to create a unique string identifying you or your organization. The convention is to start the organization identifier with `com.` and to follow it with a string (possibly with multiple dot-components) that no one else is likely to use. For example, I use `com.neuburg.matt`. Every app on a device or submitted to the App Store needs a unique bundle identifier. Your app's bundle identifier, which is shown in gray below the organization identifier, will consist of the organization identifier plus a version of the project's name; if you give every project a unique name within your personal world, the bundle identifier will uniquely identify this project and the app that it produces (or you can change the bundle identifier manually later if necessary).

5. The Language pop-up menu lets you choose between Swift and Objective-C. This choice is not positively binding; it dictates the initial structure and code of the project template, but you are free to add Swift files to an Objective-C project, or

Objective-C files to a Swift project. You can even start with an Objective-C project and decide later to convert it completely to Swift. (See "Bilingual Targets" on page 558.) For now, choose Swift.

6. Make sure the Devices pop-up menu is set to iPhone. Again, this choice is not positively binding; but for now, let's assume that our app is to run on iPhone only.

7. Make sure Use Core Data, Include Unit Tests, and Include UI Tests are *not* checked. Click Next.

8. You've now told Xcode how to construct your project. Basically, it's going to copy the *Single View Application.xctemplate* folder from within the *Project Templates* folder I mentioned earlier. But you need to tell it where to copy this template folder *to*. That's why Xcode is now presenting a Save dialog. You are to specify the location of a folder that is about to be created — the *project folder* for this project. The project folder can go just about anywhere, and you can move it after creating it. I usually create new projects on the Desktop.

9. Xcode also offers to create a git repository for your project. In real life, this can be a great convenience (see Chapter 9), but for now, uncheck that checkbox. Click Create.

10. The *Empty Window* project folder is created on disk (on the Desktop, if that's the location you just specified), and the project window for the Empty Window project opens in Xcode.

The project we've just created is a working project; it really does build an iOS app called Empty Window. To see this, make sure that the scheme and destination in the project window's toolbar are listed as Empty Window → iPhone 6. (The scheme and destination are actually pop-up menus, so you can click on them to change their values if needed.) Choose Product → Run. After some delay, the iOS Simulator application eventually opens and displays your app running — an empty white screen.

 To *build* a project is to compile its code and assemble the compiled code, together with various resources, into the actual app. Typically, if you want to know whether your code compiles and your project is consistently and correctly constructed, you'll build the project (Product → Build). Alternatively, you can compile an individual file (choose Product → Perform Action → Compile [Filename]). To *run* a project is to launch the built app, in the Simulator or on a connected device; if you want to know whether your code works as expected, you'll run the project (Product → Run), which automatically builds first if necessary.

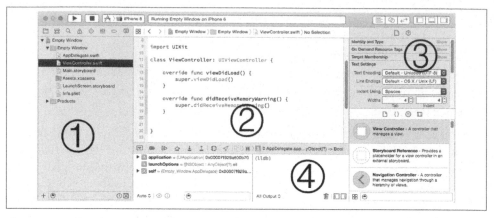

Figure 6-1. The project window

The Project Window

An Xcode project embodies a lot of information about what files constitute the project and how they are to be used when building the app, such as:

- The source files (your code) that are to be compiled

- Any *.storyboard* or *.xib* files, graphically expressing interface objects to be instantiated as your app runs

- Any resources, such as icons, images, or sound files, that are to be part of the app

- All settings (instructions to the compiler, to the linker, and so on) that are to be obeyed as the app is built

- Any frameworks that the code will need when it runs

A single Xcode project window presents all of this information, as well as letting you access, edit, and navigate your code, plus reporting the progress and results of such procedures as building or debugging an app and more. This window displays a lot of information and embodies a lot of functionality! A project window is powerful and elaborate; learning to navigate and understand it takes time. Let's pause to explore this window and see how it is constructed.

A project window has four main parts (Figure 6-1):

1. On the left is the Navigator pane. Show and hide it with View → Navigators → Show/Hide Navigator (Command-0) or with the first View button at the right end of the toolbar.

2. In the middle is the Editor pane (or simply "editor"). This is the main area of a project window. A project window nearly always displays an Editor pane, and can display multiple Editor panes simultaneously.

3. On the right is the Utilities pane. Show and hide it with View → Utilities → Show/ Hide Utilities (Command-Option-0) or with the third View button at the right end of the toolbar.

4. At the bottom is the Debug pane. Show and hide it with View → Debug Area → Show/Hide Debug Area (Command-Shift-Y) or with the second View button at the right end of the toolbar.

 All Xcode keyboard shortcuts can be customized; see the Key Bindings pane of the Preferences window. Keyboard shortcuts that I cite are the defaults.

The Navigator Pane

The Navigator pane is the column of information at the left of the project window. Among other things, it's your primary mechanism for controlling what you see in the main area of the project window (the editor). An important use pattern for Xcode is: you select something in the Navigator pane, and that thing is displayed in the editor.

It is possible to toggle the visibility of the Navigator pane (View → Navigators → Hide/ Show Navigator, or Command-0); for example, once you've used the Navigator pane to reach the item you want to see or work on in the editor, you might hide the Navigator pane temporarily to maximize your screen real estate (especially on a smaller monitor). You can change the Navigator pane's width by dragging the vertical line at its right edge.

The Navigator pane itself can display eight different sets of information; thus, there are actually eight navigators. These are represented by the eight icons across its top; to switch among them, use these icons or their keyboard shortcuts (Command-1, Command-2, and so on). If the Navigator pane is hidden, pressing a navigator's keyboard shortcut both shows the Navigator pane and switches to that navigator.

Depending on your settings in the Behaviors pane of Xcode's preferences, a navigator might show itself automatically when you perform a certain action. For example, by default, when you build your project, if warning messages or error messages are generated, the Issue navigator will appear. This automatic behavior will not prove troublesome, because it is generally precisely the behavior you want, and if it isn't, you can change it; plus you can easily switch to a different navigator at any time.

Let's begin experimenting immediately with the various navigators:

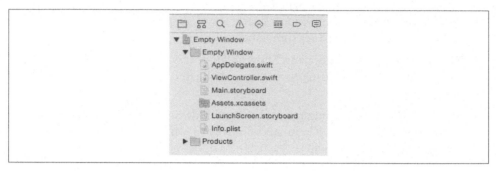

Figure 6-2. The Project navigator

Project navigator (Command-1)

Click here for basic navigation through the files that constitute your project. For example, in the Empty Window folder (these folder-like things in the Project navigator are actually called *groups*), click *AppDelegate.swift* to view its code in the editor (Figure 6-2).

At the top level of the Project navigator, with a blue Xcode icon, is the Empty Window project itself; click it to view the settings associated with your project and its targets. Don't change anything here without knowing what you're doing! I'll talk later in this chapter about what these settings are for.

The filter bar at the bottom of the Project navigator lets you limit what files are shown; when there are many files, this is great for quickly reaching a file with a known name. For example, try typing "delegate" in the filter bar search field. Don't forget to remove your filter when you're done experimenting.

 Once you've filtered a navigator, it stays filtered until you remove the filter — even if you close the project! A common mistake is to filter a navigator, forget that you've done so, fail to notice the filter (because you're looking at the navigator itself, not down at the bottom where the filter bar is), and wonder, "Hey, where did all my files go?"

Symbol navigator (Command-2)

A *symbol* is a name, typically the name of a class or method. Among other things, this can be useful for navigating your code. For example, highlight the first two icons in the filter bar (the first two are blue, the third is dark), and see how quickly you can reach the definition of AppDelegate's `applicationDidBecomeActive:` method.

Try highlighting the filter bar icons in various ways to see how the contents of the Symbol navigator change. Type in the search field in the filter bar to limit what

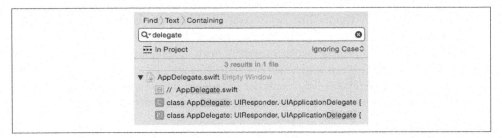

Figure 6-3. The Find navigator

appears in the Symbol navigator; for example, try typing "active" in the search field, and see what happens.

 When the second filter icon is not highlighted, you are shown all symbols, including those defined by Swift and those defined by Cocoa (Figure 4-1). This is a great way to learn what object types exist, and to reach the headers where those types are declared (an important form of documentation: see Chapter 8).

Find navigator (Command-3)

This is a powerful search facility for finding text globally in your project. You can also summon the Find navigator with Find → Find in Project (Command-Shift-F). The words above the search field show what options are currently in force; they are pop-up menus, so click one to change the options. Try searching for "delegate" (Figure 6-3). Click a search result to jump to it in your code.

Below the search field, at the left, is the current *search scope*. This limits what files will be searched. Click it to see the Search Scopes panel. You can limit the search to a group (folder) within your project. You can also define a new scope: click New Scope to summon the scope configuration popover, where you can examine your options. Scopes are defined per user, not per project; scopes that you create here will appear in other projects.

You can type in the other search field, the one in the filter bar at the bottom, to limit further which search results are displayed. (I'm going to stop calling your attention to the filter bar now, but every navigator has it in some form.)

Issue navigator (Command-4)

You'll need this navigator primarily when your code has issues. This doesn't refer to emotional instability; it's Xcode's term for warning and error messages emitted when you build your project.

To see the Issue navigator in action, you'll need to give your code an issue. Navigate (as you already know how to do, in at least three different ways) to the file *App-*

Delegate.swift, and in the blank line after the last comment at the top of the file's contents, above the import line, type howdy. Build the project (Command-B). The Issue navigator will display some error messages, showing that the compiler is unable to cope with this illegal word appearing in an illegal place. Click an issue to see it within its file. In your code, issue "balloons" may appear to the right of lines containing issues; if you're distracted or hampered by these, toggle their visibility with Editor → Issues → Hide/Show All Issues (Command-Control-M).

Now that you've made Xcode miserable, select "howdy" and delete it; save and build again, and your issues will be gone. If only real life were this easy!

Test navigator (Command-5)
   This navigator lists test files and individual test methods and permits you to run your tests and see whether they succeeded or failed. A test is code that isn't part of your app; rather, it calls a bit of your app's code to see whether it behaves as expected. I'll talk more about tests in Chapter 9.

Debug navigator (Command-6)
   By default, this navigator will appear when your code is paused while you're debugging it. There is not a strong distinction in Xcode between running and debugging; the milieu is the same. The difference is mostly a matter of whether breakpoints are obeyed (more about that, and about debugging in general, in Chapter 9).

   To see the Debug navigator in action, you'll need to give your code a breakpoint. Navigate once more to the file *AppDelegate.swift*, select in the line that says return true, and choose Debug → Breakpoints → Add Breakpoint at Current Line to make a blue breakpoint arrow appear on that line. Run the project. By default, as the breakpoint is encountered, the Navigator pane switches to the Debug navigator, and the Debug pane appears at the bottom of the window. This overall layout (Figure 6-4) will rapidly become familiar as you debug your projects.

   The Debug navigator starts with several numeric and graphical displays of profiling information (at a minimum, you'll see CPU, Memory, Disk, and Network); click one to see extensive graphical information in the editor. This information allows you to track possible misbehavior of your app as you run it, without the added complexity of running the Instruments utility (discussed in Chapter 9). To toggle the visibility of the profiling information at the top of the Debug navigator, click the "gauge" icon (to the right of the process's name).

   The Debug navigator also displays the call stack, with the names of the nested methods in which a pause occurs; as you would expect, you can click on a method name to navigate to it. You can shorten or lengthen the list with the first button in the filter bar at the bottom of the navigator. The second icon to the right of the process's name lets you toggle between display by thread and display by queue.

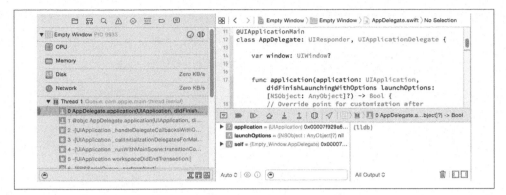

Figure 6-4. The Debug layout

The Debug pane, which can be shown or hidden at will (View → Debug Area → Hide/Show Debug Area, or Command-Shift-Y), consists of two subpanes:

The variables list (on the left)
It is populated with the variables in scope for the selected method in the call stack.

The console (on the right)
Here the debugger displays text messages; that's how you learn of exceptions thrown by your running app, plus you can have your code deliberately send you log messages describing your app's progress and behavior. Such messages are important, so keep an eye on the console as your app runs. You can also use the console to enter commands to the debugger. This can often be a better way to explore values during a pause than the variables list.

Either the variables list or the console can be hidden using the two buttons at the bottom right of the pane. The console can also be summoned by choosing View → Debug Area → Activate Console.

 View debugging displays, and allows you to explore, your app's view hierarchy. To switch to view debugging, choose Debug → View Debugging → Capture View Hierarchy (or click the Debug View Hierarchy button in the bar at the top of the Debug pane).

Breakpoint navigator (Command-7)
This navigator lists all your breakpoints. At the moment you've only one, but when you're actively debugging a large project with many breakpoints, you'll be glad of this navigator. Also, this is where you create special breakpoints (such as symbolic

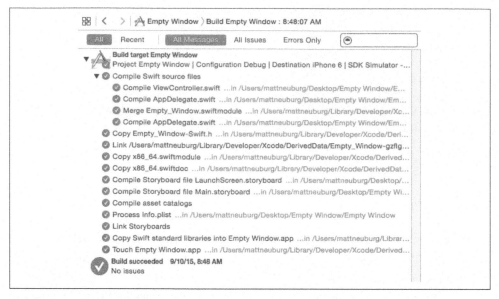

Figure 6-5. Viewing a report

breakpoints), and in general it's your center for managing existing breakpoints. We'll return to this topic in Chapter 9.

Report navigator (Command-8)

This navigator lists your recent major actions, such as building or running (debugging) your project. Click a listing to see (in the editor) the report generated when you performed that action. The report might contain information that isn't displayed in any other way, and also it lets you dredge up console messages from the recent past ("What was that exception I got while debugging a moment ago?").

For example, by clicking on the listing for a successful build, and by choosing to display All and All Messages using the filter switches at the top of the report, we can see the steps by which a build takes place (Figure 6-5). To reveal the full text of a step, click on that step and then click the Expand Transcript button that appears at the far right (and see also the menu items in the Editor menu).

When navigating by clicking in the Navigator pane, modifications to your click can determine where navigation takes place. By default, Option-click navigates in an assistant pane (discussed later in this chapter), double-click navigates by opening a new window, and Option-Shift-click summons a little heads-up pane where you can specify where to navigate (a new window, a new tab, or a new assistant pane). For the settings that govern these click modifications, see the Navigation pane of Xcode's preferences.

The Utilities Pane

The Utilities pane is the column at the right of the project window. It contains inspectors that provide information about the current selection or its settings; if those settings can be changed, this is where you change them. It also contains libraries that function as a source of objects you may need while editing your project. The Utilities pane's importance emerges mostly when you're editing a *storyboard* or *.xib* file (Chapter 7). But it can be useful also while editing code, because Quick Help, a form of documentation (Chapter 8), is displayed here as well, plus the Utilities pane is the source of code snippets (Chapter 9). To toggle the visibility of the Utilities pane, choose View → Utilities → Hide/Show Utilities (Command-Option-0). You can change the Utilities pane's width by dragging the vertical line at its left edge.

The Utilities pane consists of numerous palettes, which are clumped into multiple sets, which are themselves divided into two major groups: the top half of the pane and the bottom half of the pane. You can change the relative heights of these two halves by dragging the horizontal line that separates them.

The top half

What appears in the top half of the Utilities pane depends on what's selected in the current editor. There are four main cases:

A code file is being edited

The top half of the Utilities pane shows either the File inspector or Quick Help. Toggle between them with the icons at the top of this half of the Utilities pane, or with their keyboard shortcuts (Command-Option-1, Command-Option-2). The File inspector is rarely needed, but Quick Help can be useful because it displays documentation (Chapter 8). The File inspector consists of multiple sections, each of which can be expanded or collapsed by clicking its header.

A .storyboard or .xib file is being edited

The top half of the Utilities pane shows, in addition to the File inspector and Quick Help, the Identity inspector (Command-Option-3), the Attributes inspector (Command-Option-4), the Size inspector (Command-Option-5), and the Connections inspector (Command-Option-6). These can consist of multiple sections, each of which can be expanded or collapsed by clicking its header.

An asset catalog is being edited

In addition to the File inspector and Quick Help, the Attributes inspector displays more information about the selected resource set or resource. It lets you determine which variants of the selected resource set are listed and set its on-demand resource tags; if the selected resource is an image, you can see and configure additional information about it.

The view hierarchy is being debugged

> In addition to the File inspector and Quick Help, the Object inspector describes the currently selected view, and the Size inspector displays the currently selected view's size, position, and constraints.

The bottom half

> The bottom half of the Utilities pane shows one of four libraries. Toggle between them with the icons at the top of this half of the Utilities pane, or with their keyboard shortcuts. They are the File Template library (Command-Option-Control-1), the Code Snippet library (Command-Option-Control-2), the Object library (Command-Option-Control-3), and the Media library (Command-Option-Control-4). The Object library is the most important; you'll use it heavily when editing a *.storyboard* or *.xib* file.

> To see a help pop-up describing the currently selected item in a library, press Spacebar.

The Editor

In the middle of the project window is the *editor*. This is where you get actual work done, reading and writing your code (Chapter 9), or designing your interface in a *.storyboard* or *.xib* file (Chapter 7). The editor is the core of the project window. You can hide the Navigator pane, the Utilities pane, and the Debug pane, but there is no such thing as a project window without an editor (though you can cover the editor completely with the Debug pane).

The editor provides its own form of navigation, the *jump bar* across the top. Not only does the jump bar show you hierarchically what file is currently being edited, but also it allows you to switch to a different file. In particular, each path component in the jump bar is also a pop-up menu. These pop-up menus can be summoned by clicking on a path component, or by using keyboard shortcuts (shown in the second section of the View → Standard Editor submenu). For example, Control-4 summons a hierarchical pop-up menu, which can be navigated entirely with the keyboard, allowing you to choose a different file in your project to edit. Moreover, each pop-up menu in the jump bar also has a filter field; to see it, summon a pop-up menu from the jump bar and start typing. Thus you can navigate your project even if the Project navigator isn't showing.

The symbol at the left end of the jump bar (Control-1) summons a hierarchical menu (the Related Items menu) allowing navigation to files related to the current one. What appears here depends not only on what file is currently being edited but on the current selection within that file. This is an extremely powerful and convenient menu, and you should take time to explore it. You can navigate to related class files and header files (Superclasses, Subclasses, and Siblings; siblings are classes with the same superclass); you can view methods called by the currently selected method, and that call the currently selected method. New in Xcode 7, choose Generated Interface to view the public API of a Swift file or Objective-C header file as seen by Swift.

The editor remembers the history of things it has displayed, and you can return to previously viewed content with the Back button in the jump bar, which is also a pop-up menu from which you can choose. Alternatively, choose Navigate → Go Back (Command-Control-Left).

It is likely, as you develop a project, that you'll want to edit more than one file simultaneously, or obtain multiple views of a single file so that you can edit two areas of it simultaneously. This can be achieved in three ways: assistants, tabs, and secondary windows.

Assistants

You can split the editor into multiple editors by summoning an *assistant* pane. To do so, click the second Editor button in the toolbar ("Show the Assistant editor"), or choose View → Assistant Editor → Show Assistant Editor (Command-Option-Return). Also, by default, adding the Option key to navigation opens an assistant pane; for example, Option-click in the Navigator pane, or Option-choose in the jump bar, to navigate by opening an assistant pane (or to navigate in an existing assistant pane if there is one). To remove the assistant pane, click the first Editor button in the toolbar, or choose View → Standard Editor → Show Standard Editor (Command-Return), or click the X button at the assistant pane's top right.

You can determine how assistant panes are to be arranged. To do so, choose from the View → Assistant Editor submenu. I usually prefer All Editors Stacked Vertically, but it's purely a matter of taste. Once you've summoned an assistant pane, you can split it further into additional assistant panes. To do so, click the Plus button at the top right of an assistant pane. To dismiss an assistant pane, click the X button at its top right.

What makes an assistant pane an assistant, and not just a form of split-pane editing, is that it can bear a special relationship to the primary editor pane. The primary editor pane is the one whose contents, by default, are determined by what you click on in the Navigator pane; an assistant pane, meanwhile, can respond to what file is being edited in the primary editor pane by changing intelligently what file it (the assistant pane) is editing. This is called *tracking*. To configure the tracking behavior of an assistant pane, use the first component in its jump bar (Control-4). This is the Tracking menu; it's like the Related Items menu that I discussed a moment ago, but selecting a category determines automatic tracking behavior. If a category has multiple files, a pair of arrow buttons appears at the right end of the assistant's jump bar, with which you can navigate between them (or use the second jump bar component, Control-5). You can turn off tracking by setting the assistant's first jump bar component to Manual.

If you want to close the assistant pane but continue to edit its contents without any assistant pane present, move the assistant pane's contents to the main editor pane first (Navigate → Open In Primary Editor).

Tabs

You can embody the entire project window interface as a tab. To do so, choose File → New → Tab (Command-T), revealing the tab bar (just below the toolbar) if it wasn't showing already. Use of a tabbed interface will likely be familiar from applications such as Safari. You can switch between tabs by clicking on a tab, or with Command-Shift-}. At first, your new tab will look largely identical to the original window from which it was spawned. But then you can make changes in a tab — change what panes are showing or what file is being edited, for example — without affecting any other tabs. Thus you can get multiple views of your project. You can assign a descriptive name to a tab: double-click on a tab name to make it editable.

Secondary windows

A secondary project window is similar to a tab, but it appears as a separate window instead of a tab in the same window. To create one, choose File → New → Window (Command-Shift-T). Alternatively, you can promote a tab to be a window by dragging it right out of its current window.

There isn't a strong difference between a tab and a secondary window; which you use, and for what, will be a matter of taste and convenience. I find that the advantage of a secondary window is that you can see it at the same time as the main window, and that it can be small. Thus, when I have a file I frequently want to refer to, I often spawn off a secondary window displaying that file, sized fairly small and without any panes other than the editor.

Tabs and windows come in handy in connection with custom behaviors. For example, as I mentioned before, it's important to be able to view the console while debugging; I like to see it at the full size of the project window, but I also want to be able to switch back to viewing my code. So I've created a custom behavior (click the Plus button at the bottom of the Behaviors pane of the Preferences window) that performs two actions: Show tab named Console in active window, and Show debugger with Console View. Moreover, I've given that behavior a keyboard shortcut. Thus at any time I can press my keyboard shortcut, and we switch to the Console tab (creating it if it doesn't exist), displaying nothing but the console. This is just a tab, so I can switch between it and my code with Command-Shift-}.

 There are many ways to change what appears in an editor, and the navigators don't automatically stay in sync with those changes. To select in the Project navigator the file displayed in the current editor, choose Navigate → Reveal in Project Navigator.

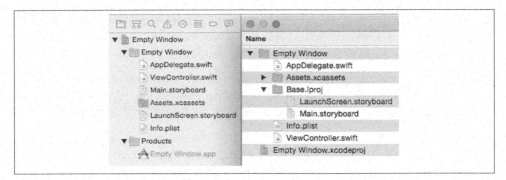

Figure 6-6. The Project navigator and the project folder

The Project File and Its Dependents

The first item in the Project navigator (Command-1) represents the project itself. (In the Empty Window project that we created earlier in this chapter, it is called Empty Window.) Hierarchically dependent upon it are items that contribute to the building of the project. Many of these items, as well as the project itself, correspond to items on disk in the project folder.

To survey this correspondence, let's examine the project folder in the Finder simultaneously with the Xcode project window. Select the project listing in the Project navigator and choose File → Show in Finder. The Finder displays the contents of your project folder (Figure 6-6).

 Never, never, *never* touch anything in a project folder by way of the Finder, except for double-clicking the project file to open the project. Don't put anything directly into a project folder. Don't remove anything from a project folder. Don't rename anything in a project folder. Don't touch anything in a project folder! Do all your interaction with the project through the project window in Xcode. (When you're an Xcode power user, you'll know when you can disobey this rule. Until then, just obey it blindly.)

The reason is that the project expects things in the project folder to be a certain way. If you make any alterations to the project folder directly in the Finder, behind the project's back, you can upset those expectations and break the project. When you work in the project window, it is Xcode itself that makes any necessary changes in the project folder, and all will be well.

The most important thing in the project folder is *Empty Window.xcodeproj*. This is the *project file*, corresponding to the project listed in the Project navigator. All Xcode's knowledge about your project — what files it consists of and how to build the project

— is stored in this file. To open a project from the Finder, double-click the project file. Alternatively, you can drag the project folder onto Xcode's icon (in the Finder, in the Dock, or in the application switcher) and Xcode will locate the project file and open it for you; thus, you might never need to open the project folder at all!

Let's consider how the groups and files displayed hierarchically down from the project in the Project navigator correspond to reality on disk as portrayed in the Finder (Figure 6-6). Recall that *group* is the technical term for the folder-like objects shown in the Project navigator:

- The Empty Window group corresponds directly to the *Empty Window* folder on disk. Groups in the Project navigator don't necessarily correspond to folders on disk in the Finder, and folders on disk in the Finder don't necessarily correspond to groups in the Project navigator. But in this case, there is such a correspondence!

- Files within the Empty Window group, such as *AppDelegate.swift*, correspond to real files on disk that are inside the *Empty Window* folder. If you were to create additional code files (which, in real life, you would almost certainly do in the course of developing your project), you would likely put them in the Empty Window group in the Project navigator, and they, too, would then be in the *Empty Window* folder on disk. (That, however, is not a requirement; your files can live anywhere and your project will still work fine.)

- Two files in the Empty Window group, *Main.storyboard* and *LaunchScreen.storyboard*, appear in the Finder inside a folder that doesn't visibly correspond to anything in the Project navigator, called *Base.lproj*. This arrangement has to do with *localization*, which I'll discuss in Chapter 9.

- The item *Assets.xcassets* in the Project navigator corresponds to a specially structured folder *Assets.xcassets* on disk. This is an *asset catalog*; you add resources to the asset catalog in Xcode, which maintains that folder on disk for you. I'll talk more about the asset catalog later in this chapter, and in Chapter 9.

You may be tempted to find all this confusing. Don't! Remember what I said about not involving yourself with the project folder on disk in the Finder. You've seen it; you know that it has contents; you know that they bear some relation to the Project navigator; now forget about them. Keep your attention on the Project navigator, make your modifications to the project there, and all will be well.

Feel free, as you develop your project and add files to it, to add further groups to the Project navigator. The purpose of groups is to make the Project navigator work well for you! They don't affect how the app is built, and by default they don't correspond to any folder on disk; they are just an organizational convenience within the Project navigator. To make a new group, choose File → New → Group. To rename a group, select it in the Project navigator and press Return to make the name editable. For example, if some of your code files have to do with a login screen that your app sometimes presents, you might clump them together in a Login group. If your app is to contain some sound files, you might put them into a Sounds group. And so on.

The Products group and its contents don't correspond to anything in the project folder. Xcode generates a reference to the executable bundle generated by building each target in your project, and by convention these references appear in the Products group.

Another conventional group is the Frameworks group, listing frameworks on which your code depends. Your code does depend on some frameworks, but by default they are not listed in the Project navigator, and the Project navigator has no Frameworks group, because these frameworks are not explicitly linked into your build; instead, your code uses *modules*, which means that the import statements at the top of your files are sufficient to cause linkage to take place implicitly. However, if you were to link *explicitly* to a framework, it would be listed in the Project navigator, and you might then create a Frameworks group, just to give that listing a nice place to live. I'll discuss frameworks later in this chapter.

The Target

A *target* is a collection of parts along with rules and settings for how to build a product from them. Whenever you build, what you're really building is a target (possibly more than one target).

Select the Empty Window project at the top of the Project navigator, and you'll see two things on the left side of the editor (Figure 6-7): the project itself, and a list of your targets. Our Empty Window project comes with one target — the *app target*, called Empty Window (just like the project itself). The app target is the target that you use to build and run your app. Its settings are the settings that tell Xcode how your app is to be built; its product is the app itself.

Under certain circumstances, you might add further targets to a project:

- You might want to perform unit tests or interface tests; to do so, you'd add a target. (I'll talk more about testing in Chapter 9.)

- You might write a framework as part of your iOS app; with a custom framework, you can factor common code into a single locus, and you can configure its privacy details as a namespace. A custom framework needs to be built, so it, too, is a target. (I'll talk more about frameworks later in this chapter.)

- You might write an application extension, such as a today extension (content to appear in the notification center) or a photo editing extension (custom photo editing interface to appear in the Photos app). Those, too, are targets.

The project name and the list of targets can appear in two ways (Figure 6-7): either as a column on the left side of the editor, or, if that column is collapsed to save space, as a

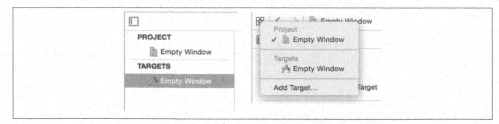

Figure 6-7. Two ways of showing the project and targets

Figure 6-8. The app target's build phases

pop-up menu at the top left of the editor. If, in the column or pop-up menu, you select the *project*, you *edit the project*; if you select a *target*, you *edit the target*. I'll use those expressions a lot in later instructions.

Build Phases

Edit the app target and click Build Phases at the top of the editor (Figure 6-8). These are the stages by which your app is built. The *build phases* are both a report to you on how the target will be built and a set of instructions to Xcode on how to build the target; if you change the build phases, you change the build process. Click each build phase to see a list of the files in your target to which that build phase will apply.

Two of the build phases have contents. The meanings of these build phases are pretty straightforward:

Compile Sources

Certain files (your code) are compiled, and the resulting compiled code is copied into the app.

This build phase typically applies to all of the target's *.swift* files; those are the code files that constitute the target. Sure enough, it currently contains *ViewController.swift* and *AppDelegate.swift*. If you add a new Swift file to your project (typically in order to declare another class), you'll specify that it should be part of the app target, and it will automatically be added to the Compile Sources build phase.

Copy Bundle Resources

Certain files are copied into the app, so that your code or the system can find them there when the app runs.

This build phase currently applies to the asset catalog; any resources you add to the asset catalog will be copied into your app as part of the catalog. It also currently lists your launch storyboard file, *LaunchScreen.storyboard*, and your app's interface storyboard file, *Main.storyboard*.

Copying doesn't necessarily mean making an identical copy. Certain types of file are automatically treated in special ways as they are copied into the app bundle. For example, copying the asset catalog means that icons in the catalog are written out to the top level of the app bundle, and the asset catalog itself is transformed into a *.car* file; copying a *.storyboard* file means that it is transformed into a *.storyboardc* file, which is itself a bundle containing nib files.

You can alter these lists manually, and sometimes you may need to do so. For instance, if something in your project, such as a sound file, was not in Copy Bundle Resources and you wanted it copied into the app during the build process, you would drag it from the Project navigator into the Copy Bundle Resources list, or (easier) click the Plus button beneath the Copy Bundle Resources list to get a helpful dialog listing everything in your project. Conversely, if something in your project was in Copy Bundle Resources and you *didn't* want it copied into the app, you would delete it from the list; this would not delete it from your project, from the Project navigator, or from the Finder, but only from the list of things to be copied into your app.

It is possible that you might need to alter the Link Binary With Libraries build phase. Certain libraries, usually frameworks, are linked to the compiled code (now referred to, following compilation, as the *binary*), thus telling your code to expect those libraries to be present on the device when the app runs. Our Empty Window project does link to some frameworks, but it doesn't use this build phase to do it; instead, it imports the frameworks as modules and the frameworks are linked automatically. However, in some cases you would need to link the binary with additional frameworks explicitly; I'll talk about that later in this chapter.

Figure 6-9. Target build settings

A useful trick is to add a Run Script build phase, which runs a custom shell script late in the build process. To do so, choose Editor → Add Build Phase → Add Run Script Build Phase. Open the newly added Run Script build phase to edit the custom shell script. A minimal shell script might read:

```
echo "Running the Run Script build phase"
```

The "Show environment variables in build log" checkbox causes the build process's environment variables and their values to be listed in the build report during the Run Script build phase. This alone can be a reason to add a Run Script build phase; you can learn a lot about how the build process works by examining the environment variables.

Build Settings

Build phases are only one aspect of how a target knows how to build the app. The other aspect is *build settings.* To see them, edit the target and click Build Settings at the top of the editor (Figure 6-9). Here you'll find a long list of settings, most of which you'll never touch. Xcode examines this list in order to know what to do at various stages of the build process. Build settings are the reason your project compiles and builds the way it does.

You can determine what build settings are displayed by clicking Basic or All. The settings are combined into categories, and you can close or open each category heading to save room. If you know something about a setting you want to see, such as its name, you can use the search field at the top right to filter what settings are shown.

You can determine how build settings are displayed by clicking Combined or Levels; in Figure 6-9, I've clicked Levels, in order to discuss what levels are. It turns out that not only does a *target* contain values for the build settings, but the *project* also contains values for the same build settings; furthermore, Xcode has certain built-in default build setting values. The Levels display shows all of these levels at once, so you can understand the derivation of the actual values used for every build setting.

To understand the chart, read from right to left. For example, the iOS default for the Build Active Architecture Only setting's Debug configuration (far right) is No. But then the project comes along (second column from the right) and sets it to Yes. The target (third column from the right) doesn't change that setting, so the result (fourth column from the right) is that the setting resolves to Yes.

You will rarely have occasion to manipulate build settings directly, as the defaults are usually acceptable. Nevertheless, you *can* change build setting values, and this is where you would do so. You can change a value at the project level or at the target level. You can select a build setting and show Quick Help in the Utilities pane to learn more about it. For further details on what the various build settings are, consult Apple's documentation, especially the *Xcode Build Setting Reference*.

Configurations

There are actually multiple lists of build setting values — though only one such list applies when a particular build is performed. Each such list is called a *configuration*. Multiple configurations are needed because you build in different ways at different times for different purposes, and thus you'll want certain build settings to take on different values under different circumstances.

By default, there are two configurations:

Debug
> This configuration is used throughout the development process, as you write and run your app.

Release
> This configuration is used for late-stage testing, when you want to check performance on a device, and for archiving the app to be submitted to the App Store.

Configurations exist at all because the project says so. To see where the project says so, edit the project and click Info at the top of the editor (Figure 6-10). Note that these configurations are just names. You can make additional configurations, and when you do, you're just adding to the list of names. The importance of configurations emerges only when those names are coupled with build setting values. Configurations can affect build setting values both at the project level and at the target level.

For example, return to the target build settings (Figure 6-9) and type "Optim" into the search field. Now you can look at the Optimization Level build setting (Figure 6-11). The Debug configuration value for Optimization Level is None: while you're developing your app, you build with the Debug configuration, so your code is just compiled line by line in a straightforward way. The Release configuration value for Optimization Level is Fast; when your app is ready to ship, you build it with the Release configuration, so the resulting binary is optimized for speed, which is great for your users running the

Figure 6-10. Configurations

Figure 6-11. How configurations affect build settings

app on a device, but would be no good while you're developing the app because break-points and stepping in the debugger wouldn't work properly.

An even better choice as the Release configuration Optimization Level setting might be Fast, Whole Module Optimization. This allows the Swift compiler to survey all your code files at once. Compilation may take considerably longer, but the resulting optimization can be better; for example, the compiler may be able to deduce that certain class members don't need dynamic dispatch, thus making your code even faster.

Schemes and Destinations

So far, I have not said how Xcode knows *which* configuration to use during a particular build. This is determined by a scheme.

A *scheme* unites a target (or multiple targets) with a build configuration, with respect to the purpose for which you're building. A new project comes by default with a single scheme, named after the project. Thus the Empty Window project's single scheme is currently called Empty Window. To see it, choose Product → Scheme → Edit Scheme. The scheme editor dialog opens (Figure 6-12).

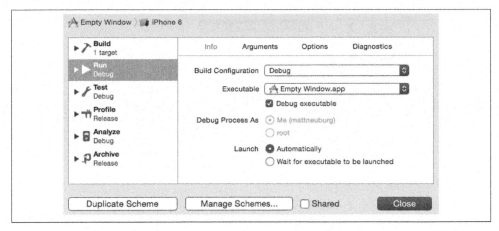

Figure 6-12. The scheme editor

On the left side of the scheme editor are listed various actions you might perform from the Product menu. Click an action to see its corresponding settings in this scheme.

The first action, the Build action, is different from the other actions, because it is common to all of them — the other actions all implicitly involve building. The Build action merely determines what target(s) will be built when each of the other actions is performed. For our project this means that the app target is always to be built, regardless of the action you perform.

The second action, the Run action, determines the settings that will be used when you build and run. The Build Configuration pop-up menu (in the Info pane) is set to Debug. That explains where the current build configuration comes from: at the moment, whenever you build and run (Product → Run, or click the Run button in the toolbar), you're using the Debug build configuration and the build setting values that correspond to it, because you're using this scheme, and that's what this scheme says to do when you build and run.

You can edit an existing scheme, though it is not likely that you would need to do so. Another possibility is that you might create an additional scheme. One way to do this is by choosing Manage Schemes from the Scheme pop-up menu in the project window toolbar (Figure 6-13).

The Scheme pop-up menu is something you're going to be using a lot. Your schemes are all listed here, and thus you can easily switch between them before you build and run. Hierarchically appended to each scheme are the destinations. A *destination* is effectively a machine that can run your app. On any given occasion, you might want to run the app on a physical device or in the Simulator — and, if in the Simulator, you

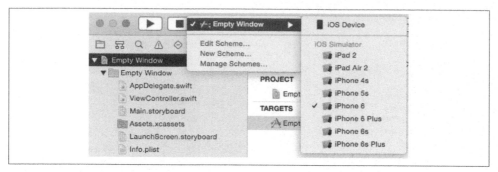

Figure 6-13. The Scheme pop-up menu

might want to specify that a particular type of device should be simulated. To make that choice, pick a destination in the Scheme pop-up menu.

Destinations and schemes have nothing to do with one another. The presence of destinations in the Scheme pop-up menu is intended as a convenience, allowing you to use this one pop-up menu to choose either a scheme or a destination, or both, in a single move. To switch easily among destinations without changing schemes, click the destination name in the Scheme pop-up menu. To switch among schemes, possibly also determining the destination (as shown in Figure 6-13), click the scheme name in the Scheme pop-up menu.

Each simulated device has a system version that is installed on that device. At the moment, all our simulated devices are running iOS 9.0; thus, there is no distinction to be drawn, and the system version is not shown. However, you can download additional SDKs (systems) in Xcode's Downloads preference pane. If you do, and if your app can run under more than one system version, you might also see a system version listed in the Scheme pop-up menu as part of a Simulator destination name. For example, if you've installed the iOS 8.4 SDK, and if your project's deployment target (see Chapter 9) is 8.0, the Scheme pop-up menu in the project window toolbar might say "iOS 9.0" or "iOS 8.4" after the destination name.

 If you have downloaded additional SDKs, and if your app is configured to run on multiple systems, and you still don't see, among the destinations, any simulated devices with those systems, choose Window → Device to summon the Devices window. This is where you manage what simulated devices exist. Here you can create, delete, and rename simulated devices, and specify whether a simulated device actually appears as a destination in the Scheme pop-up menu.

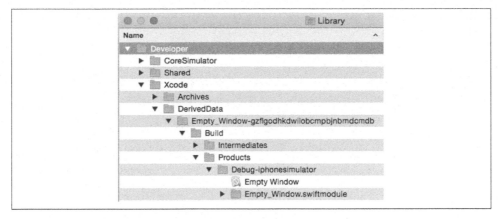

Figure 6-14. The built app, in the Finder

From Project to Running App

An app file is really a special kind of folder called a *package* (and a special kind of package called a *bundle*). The Finder normally disguises a package as a file and does not dive into it to reveal its contents to the user, but you can bypass this protection and investigate an app bundle with the Show Package Contents command. By doing so, you can study the internal structure of your built app bundle.

We'll use the Empty Window app that we built earlier as a sample minimal app to investigate. You'll have to locate it in the Finder; by default, it should be somewhere in your user *Library/Developer/Xcode/DerivedData* folder, as shown in Figure 6-14.

In the Finder, Control-click the Empty Window app, and choose Show Package Contents from the contextual menu. Here you can see the results of the build process (Figure 6-15).

Think of the app bundle as a transformation of the project folder:

Empty Window
> Our app's compiled code. The build process has compiled *ViewController.swift* and *AppDelegate.swift* into this single file, our app's binary. This is the heart of the app, its actual executable material. When the app is launched, the binary is linked to the various frameworks, and the code begins to run. (Later in this chapter, I'll explain in detail what "begins to run" involves.)

Main.storyboardc
> Our app's interface storyboard file. The project's *Main.storyboard* is where our app's interface comes from — in this case, an empty white view occupying the entire window. The build process has compiled *Main.storyboard* (using the `ibtool` command-line tool) into a tighter format, resulting in a *.storyboardc* file, which is

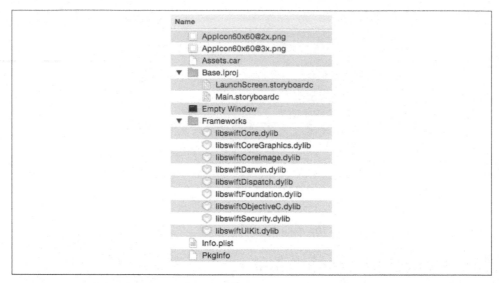

Figure 6-15. Contents of the app package

actually a bundle of nib files to be loaded as required while the app runs. One of these nib files, loaded as our app launches, will be the source of the white view displayed in the interface. *Main.storyboardc* occupies the same subfolder location (inside *Base.lproj*) as *Main.storyboard* does in the project folder; as I said earlier, this folder structure has to do with localization (to be discussed in Chapter 9).

LaunchScreen.storyboardc
Our app's launch screen file. This file, the compiled version of *LaunchScreen.storyboard*, contains the interface that will be displayed briefly during the time it takes for our app to launch.

Assets.car, AppIcon60x60@2x.png, AppIcon60x60@3x.png
An asset catalog and a pair of icon files. In preparation for this build, I added some icon images and some other image resources to the original asset catalog, *Assets.xcassets*. This file has been processed (using the `actool` command-line tool), resulting in a compiled asset catalog file (*.car*) containing any resources that have been added to the catalog. At the same time, the icon files have been written out to the top level of the app bundle, where the system can find them.

Info.plist
A configuration file in a strict text format (a *property list* file). It is derived from, but is not identical to, the project's *Info.plist*. It contains instructions to the system about how to treat and launch the app. For example, the project's *Info.plist* has a calculated bundle name derived from the product name, `$(PRODUCT_NAME)`; in the

built app's *Info.plist*, this calculation has been performed, and the value reads `Empty Window`. Also, in conjunction with the asset catalog writing out our icon files to the app bundle's top level, a setting has been added to the built app's *Info.plist* telling the system the name of those icon files.

Frameworks

A number of frameworks have been added to the built app. Our app uses Swift; these frameworks contain the entirety of the Swift language! Other frameworks used by our app are built into the system, but not Swift. This packaging of the Swift frameworks into the app bundle permits Apple to evolve the Swift language rapidly and independently of any system version, and allows Swift to be backward compatible to older systems. The downside is that these frameworks increase the size of our app; but this is a small price to pay for the power and flexibility of Swift. (Perhaps in the future, when the Swift language has settled down, it will be built into the system instead of the individual app, and Swift-based apps will become smaller.)

PkgInfo

A tiny text file reading `APPL????`, signifying the type and creator codes for this app. The *PkgInfo* file is something of a dinosaur; it isn't really necessary for the functioning of an iOS app and is generated automatically. You'll never need to touch it.

In real life, an app bundle may contain more files, but the difference will be mostly one of degree, not kind. For example, our project might have additional *.storyboard* or *.xib* files, additional frameworks, or additional resources such as sound files. All of these would make their way into the app bundle. In addition, an app bundle built to run on a device will contain some security-related files.

You are now in a position to appreciate, in a general sense, how the components of a project are treated and assembled into an app, and what responsibilities accrue to you, the programmer, in order to ensure that the app is built correctly. The rest of this section outlines what goes into the building of an app from a project, as well as how the constituents of that app are used at launch time to get the app up and running.

Build Settings

We have already talked about how build settings are determined. Xcode itself, the project, and the target all contribute to the resolved build setting values, some of which may differ depending on the build configuration. Before building, you, the programmer, will have specified a scheme; the scheme determines the build configuration, meaning the specific set of build setting values that will apply as this build proceeds.

Property List Settings

Your project contains a property list file that will be used to generate the built app's *Info.plist* file. The file in the project does not have to be named *Info.plist*! The app target knows what file it is because it is specified in the Info.plist File build setting. For example, in our project, the value of the app target's Info.plist File build setting has been set to *Empty Window/Info.plist*. (Take a look at the build settings and see!)

The property list file is a collection of key–value pairs. You can edit it, and you may need to do so. There are three main ways to edit your project's *Info.plist*:

- Select the *Info.plist* file in the Project navigator and edit in the editor. By default, the key names (and some of the values) are displayed descriptively, in terms of their functionality; for example, it says "Bundle name" instead of the actual key, which is CFBundleName. But you can view the actual keys: click in the editor and then choose Editor → Show Raw Keys & Values, or use the contextual menu.

  In addition, you can see and edit the *Info.plist* file in its true XML form: Control-click the *Info.plist* file in the Project navigator and choose Open As → Source Code from the contextual menu. (But editing an *Info.plist* as raw XML is risky, because if you make a mistake you can invalidate the XML, causing things to break with no warning.)

- Edit the target, and switch to the Info pane. The Custom iOS Target Properties section shows effectively the same information as editing the *Info.plist* in the editor.

- Edit the target, and switch to the General pane. Some of the settings here are effectively ways of editing the *Info.plist*. For example, when you click a Device Orientation checkbox here, you are changing the value of the "Supported interface orientations" key in the *Info.plist*. (Other settings here are effectively ways of editing build settings. For example, when you change the Deployment Target here, you are changing the value of the iOS Deployment Target build setting.)

Some values in the project's *Info.plist* are processed to transform them into their final values in the built app's *Info.plist*. This step is performed late in the build process. For example, the "Executable file" key's value in the project's *Info.plist* is $(EXECUTABLE_NAME); for this will be substituted the value of the EXECUTABLE_NAME build environment variable (which, as I mentioned earlier, you can discover by means of a Run Script build phase). Also, some additional key–value pairs are injected into the *Info.plist* during processing.

For a complete list of the possible keys and their meanings, consult Apple's document *Information Property List Key Reference*. I'll talk more in Chapter 9 about *Info.plist* settings that you're particularly likely to edit.

Nib Files

A nib file is a description of a piece of user interface in a compiled format contained in a file with the extension *.nib*. Every app that you write is likely to contain at least one nib file. You prepare these nib files by editing a *.storyboard* or *.xib* file graphically in Xcode; in effect, you are designing some objects that you want instantiated when the app runs and the nib file loads.

A nib file is generated during the build process by compilation (using the `ibtool` command-line tool) either from a *.xib* file, which results in a single nib file, or from a *.storyboard* file, which results in a *.storyboardc* bundle containing multiple nib files. This compilation takes place by virtue of the *.storyboard* or *.xib* file being listed in the app target's Copy Bundle Resources build phase.

Our Empty Window project generated from the Single View Application template contains an interface *.storyboard* file called *Main.storyboard*. This one file is subject to special treatment as the app's main storyboard, not because of its name, but because it is pointed to in the *Info.plist* file by the key "Main storyboard file base name" (`UIMain-StoryboardFile`), using its name ("Main") without the *.storyboard* extension — edit the *Info.plist* file and see! The result is that as the app launches, the first nib generated from this *.storyboard* file is loaded automatically to help create the app's initial interface.

I'll talk more about the app launch process and the main storyboard later in this chapter. See Chapter 7 for more about editing *.storyboard* and *.xib* files and how they create instances when your code runs.

Additional Resources

Resources are ancillary files embedded in your app bundle, to be fetched as needed when the app runs, such as images you want to display or sounds you want to play. A real-life app is likely to involve many such additional resources. Making such resources available when your app runs will usually be up to your code (or to the code implied by the loading of a nib file): basically, the runtime simply reaches into your app bundle and pulls out the desired resource. In effect, your app bundle is being treated as a folder full of extra stuff.

There are two places to add resources to your project, corresponding to two different places where they will end up in your app bundle:

The Project navigator

> If you add a resource to the Project navigator, also ensuring that it appears in the Copy Bundle Resources build phase, it is copied by the build process to the top level of your app bundle. In Figure 6-15, that's the same level as the icon image files, such as *AppIcon60x60@2x.png*.

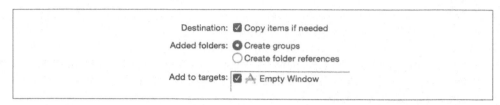

Figure 6-16. Options when adding a resource to a project

An asset catalog
> If you add a resource to an asset catalog, then when the asset catalog is copied and compiled by the build process to the top level of your app bundle (like *Assets.car* in Figure 6-15), the resource will be inside it.

I'll describe both ways of adding resources to your project.

Resources in the Project navigator

To add a resource to your project through the Project navigator, choose File → Add Files to [Project], or drag the resource from the Finder into the Project navigator. A dialog appears (Figure 6-16) in which you make the following settings:

Destination
> You should almost certainly check this checkbox ("Copy items if needed"). Doing so causes the resource to be copied into the project folder. If you leave this checkbox unchecked, your project will be relying on a file that's outside the project folder, where you might delete or change it unintentionally. Keeping everything your project needs inside the project folder is far safer.

Added folders
> This choice matters only if what you're adding to the project is a folder; the difference is in how the project references the folder contents:

> *Create groups*
> > The folder name becomes the name of an ordinary group within the Project navigator; the folder contents appear in this group, but they are listed individually in the Copy Bundle Resources build phase, so by default they will all be copied individually into the top level of the app bundle.

> *Create folder references*
> > The folder is shown in blue in the Project navigator (a *folder reference*); moreover, it is listed as a folder in the Copy Bundle Resources build phase, meaning that the build process will copy *the entire folder and its contents* into the app bundle. This means that the resources inside the folder won't be at the top level of the app bundle, but in a subfolder within it. Such an arrangement can be valuable if you have many resources and you want to separate them into cate-

gories (rather than clumping them all at the top level of the app bundle) or if the folder hierarchy among resources is meaningful to your app. The downside of this arrangement is that the code you write for accessing a resource will have to be specific about what subfolder of the app bundle contains that resource.

Add to targets

Checking the checkbox for a target causes the resource to be added to that target's Copy Bundle Resources build phase. Thus you will almost certainly want to check it for the app target; why else would you be adding this resource to the project? If this checkbox accidentally goes unchecked and you realize later that a resource listed in the Project navigator needs to be added to the Copy Bundle Resources build phase for a particular target, you can add it manually, as I described earlier.

Resources in an asset catalog

Prior to Xcode 7, asset catalogs were intended only for image files. Other resources, such as sound files, could be added only in the Project navigator. New in Xcode 7, asset catalogs can accommodate any kind of data file. Asset catalogs also allow you to specify different versions of a resource to be supplied for different hardware configurations — the device's screen resolution, for example (in the case of an image), or iPhone vs. iPad (for any type of resource).

In the case of image files, asset catalogs allow you to draw easily a distinction that otherwise would depend upon special conventions involving the *name* of the image file. For example, because iOS 9 can run on single-resolution, double-resolution, and triple-resolution devices, you need up to three sizes of every image. In order to work properly with the framework's image-loading methods, such resources employ a special naming convention — for example, *listen.png*, *listen@2x.png*, and *listen@3x.png*. The resulting proliferation of image files in the Project navigator can be overwhelming and error-prone. Asset catalogs alleviate the problem.

Instead of tediously naming the multiple versions of *listen.png* manually as I add them to my project, I can let an asset catalog help me. I edit the asset catalog, click the Plus button at the bottom of the first column, and choose New Image Set. The result is an image set called *Image* with slots for three images at three different sizes. I drag the images from the Finder into their proper slots. The names of the original image files don't matter! The images are automatically copied into the project folder (inside the asset catalog folder), and there is no need for me to specify the target membership of these image files, because they are part of an asset catalog which already has correct target membership. I can rename the image set to something more descriptive than *Image* — let's call it *listen*. The result is that my code can now load the correct image for the current screen resolution by referring to it as "listen", without regard to the original name (or extension) of the images.

The image entries in an asset catalog can be inspected by selecting an image and using the Attributes inspector (Command-Option-4). This shows the original name and (more important) the pixel size of the image.

New in Xcode 7, a parallel procedure applies to resources of other kinds. Let's say I want to add to my app bundle a sound file called *Theme.mp3*. I edit the asset catalog, click the Plus button, and choose New Data Set. A data set called Data appears, with a single Universal slot into which I can now drag my sound file. I rename the data set — let's call it *theme* — and now my code can access this resource by the name "theme" (by means of the NSDataAsset class, new in iOS 9).

Moreover, folders in the asset catalog can be used to provide namespaces: for example, if my *theme* data set is inside an asset catalog folder called *music*, and if I've checked Provides Namespace in the Attributes inspector for that folder, then the data set can be accessed by the name "music/theme".

Thus, the sheer organizational convenience of asset catalogs is, all by itself, an incentive to use them, rather than cluttering the Project navigator and the app bundle's top level with resource files.

 New in Xcode 7, resources in your app can be stored on Apple's servers instead of being included in the app bundle that the user downloads initially from the App Store. Your code subsequently downloads, in the background, any stored resources that the user is likely to need, and can purge them when they are no longer needed. For more information, see Apple's *On-Demand Resources Guide*.

Code Files and the App Launch Process

The build process knows what code files to compile to form the app's binary because they are listed in the app target's Compile Sources build phase. In the case of our Empty Window project, these are *ViewController.swift* and *AppDelegate.swift*. As development of your app proceeds, you will probably add further code files to the project, and you will ensure that they are part of the target and thus that they, too, are listed in its Compile Sources build phase. What typically happens is that you want to add a new object type declaration to your code; you will often do so by adding a new file to the project, because this makes your object type declaration easier to find, and because Swift privacy depends upon code being isolated in individual files (Chapter 5).

When you choose File → New → File to create a new file, you can specify either the Cocoa Touch Class template or the Swift File template. The Swift File template is little more than a blank file: it imports the Foundation framework and that's all. If your goal is to subclass a Cocoa class, the Cocoa Touch Class template will usually be more suitable; it imports the UIKit framework, plus Xcode will write the initial class declaration for you, and in the case of some commonly subclassed superclasses, such as UIView-Controller and UITableViewController, it even provides stub declarations of some of that class's methods.

When the app launches, the system knows where to find the binary inside the app's bundle because the app bundle's *Info.plist* file has an "Executable file" key (`CFBundle-Executable`) whose value is the name of the binary; by default, the binary's name comes from the `EXECUTABLE_NAME` environment variable (such as "Empty Window").

The entry point

The trickiest part of the app launch process is getting started. Having located and loaded the binary, the system must call into it. But where? If this app were an Objective-C program, the answer would be clear. Objective-C is C, so the entry point is the `main` function. Our project would have a *main.m* file containing the `main` function, like this:

```
int main(int argc, char *argv[]) {
    @autoreleasepool {
        return UIApplicationMain(argc, argv, nil,
            NSStringFromClass([AppDelegate class]));
    }
}
```

The `main` function does just two things:

- It sets up a memory management environment — the `@autoreleasepool` and the curly braces that follow it.

- It calls the `UIApplicationMain` function, which does the heavy lifting of helping your app pull itself up by its bootstraps and get running.

Our app, however, is a Swift program. It has no `main` function! Instead, Swift has a special attribute: `@UIApplicationMain`. If you look in the *AppDelegate.swift* file, you can see it, attached to the declaration of the AppDelegate class:

```
@UIApplicationMain
class AppDelegate: UIResponder, UIApplicationDelegate {
```

This attribute essentially does everything that the Objective-C *main.m* file was doing: it creates an entry point that calls `UIApplicationMain` to get the app started.

Under certain circumstances, you might like to remove the `@UIApplicationMain` attribute and substitute a *main* file. You are free to do this. Your file can be an Objective-C file or a Swift file. Let's say it's to be a Swift file. You would create a *main.swift* file and make sure it is added to the app target. The name is crucial, because a file called *main.swift* gets a special dispensation: it is allowed to put executable code at the top level of the file. The file should contain essentially the Swift equivalent of the Objective-C call to `UIApplicationMain`, like this:

```
import UIKit
UIApplicationMain(
    Process.argc, Process.unsafeArgv, nil, NSStringFromClass(AppDelegate))
```

Why might you do that sort of thing? Presumably, it would be because you want to do other things in the *main.swift* file, or because you want to customize the call to `UIApplicationMain`.

UIApplicationMain

Regardless of whether you write your own *main.swift* file or you rely on the Swift `@UIApplicationMain` attribute, you are calling `UIApplicationMain`. This one function call is the primary thing your app does. Your entire app is really nothing but a single gigantic call to `UIApplicationMain`! Moreover, `UIApplicationMain` is responsible for solving some tricky problems as your app gets going. Where will your app get its initial instances? What instance methods will initially be called on those instances? Where will your app's initial interface come from? Let's pause to understand what `UIApplication-Main` does:

1. `UIApplicationMain` creates your app's *first instance* — the shared application instance, which subsequently is to be accessible in code by calling `UIApplication.sharedApplication()`. The third argument in the call to `UIApplicationMain` specifies, as a string, what class the shared application instance should be an instance of. If this argument is `nil`, which will usually be the case, the default class is UIApplication. If, however, you needed to subclass UIApplication, you would specify that subclass here, by substituting an explicit value, such as `NSStringFromClass(MyApplicationSubclass)` (depending on what the subclass is called) as the third argument in the call to `UIApplicationMain`.

2. `UIApplicationMain` also creates your app's *second instance* — the application instance's *delegate*. Delegation is an important and pervasive Cocoa pattern, described in detail in Chapter 11. It is crucial that every app you write have an app delegate instance. The fourth argument in the call to `UIApplicationMain` specifies, as a string, what class the app delegate instance should be. In our manual version of *main.swift*, that specification is `NSStringFromClass(AppDelegate)`. If we use the `@UIApplicationMain` attribute, that attribute is attached, by default, to the App-Delegate class declaration in *AppDelegate.swift*; the attribute means: "*This* is the application delegate class!"

3. If the *Info.plist* file specifies a main storyboard file, `UIApplicationMain` loads it and looks inside it to find the view controller that is designated as this storyboard's *initial view controller* (or *storyboard entry point*); it instantiates this view controller, thus creating your app's *third instance*. In the case of our Empty Window project, as constructed for us from the Single View Application template, that view con-

troller will be an instance of the class called ViewController; the code file defining this class, *ViewController.swift*, was also created by the template.

4. If there was a main storyboard file, `UIApplicationMain` now creates your app's *window* — this is your app's *fourth instance*, an instance of UIWindow (or your app delegate can substitute an instance of a UIWindow subclass). It assigns this window instance as the app delegate's `window` property; it also assigns the initial view controller instance as the window instance's `rootViewController` property. This view is now the app's *root view controller*.

5. `UIApplicationMain` now turns to the app delegate instance and starts calling some of its code, such as `application:didFinishLaunchingWithOptions:`. This is an opportunity for your own code to run! `application:didFinishLaunchingWith-Options:` is a good place to put your code that initializes values and performs start-up tasks; but you don't want anything time-consuming to happen here, because your app's interface still hasn't appeared.

6. If there was a main storyboard, `UIApplicationMain` now causes your app's interface to appear. It does this by calling the UIWindow instance method `makeKeyAnd-Visible`.

7. The window is now about to appear. This, in turn, causes the window to turn to the root view controller and tell it to obtain its main view, which will occupy and appear in the window. If this view controller gets its view from a *.storyboard* or *.xib* file, that view nib file is now loaded; its objects are instantiated and initialized, and they become the objects of the initial interface: the view is placed into the window, where it and its subviews are visible to the user. Your view controller's `viewDidLoad` is also called at this time — another early opportunity for your code to run.

The app is now launched and running! It has an initial set of instances — at a minimum, the shared application instance, the window, the initial view controller, and the initial view controller's view and whatever interface objects it contains. Some of your code has run, and we are now off to the races: `UIApplicationMain` is still running (like Charlie on the M.T.A., `UIApplicationMain` never returns), and is just sitting there, watching for the user to do something, maintaining the *event loop*, which will respond to user actions as they occur.

App without a storyboard

In my description of the app launch process, I used several times the phrase "if there is a main storyboard." In the Xcode 7 app templates, such as the Single View Application template that we used to generate the Empty Window project, there *is* a main storyboard. It is possible, though, *not* to have a main storyboard. In that case, things like creating a window instance, giving it a root view controller, assigning it to the app delegate's `window` property, and calling `makeKeyAndVisible` on the window to show the interface, must be done by your code.

To see what I mean, make a new iPhone project starting with the Single View Application template; let's call it Truly Empty. Now follow these steps:

1. Edit the target. In the General pane, select "Main" in the Main Interface field and delete it (and press Tab to set this change).
2. Delete *Main.storyboard* and *ViewController.swift* from the project.
3. Select and delete the entire code content of *AppDelegate.swift*.

You now have a project with an app target but no storyboard and no code! To make a minimal working app, you need to edit *AppDelegate.swift* in such a way as to recreate the AppDelegate class with just enough code to create and show the window, as shown in Example 6-1.

Example 6-1. An App Delegate class with no storyboard

```
import UIKit
@UIApplicationMain
class AppDelegate : UIResponder, UIApplicationDelegate {
    var window : UIWindow?
    func application(application: UIApplication,
        didFinishLaunchingWithOptions launchOptions: [NSObject: AnyObject]?)
        -> Bool {
            self.window = UIWindow()
            self.window!.rootViewController = UIViewController()
            self.window!.backgroundColor = UIColor.whiteColor()
            self.window!.makeKeyAndVisible()
            return true
    }
}
```

The result is a minimal working app with an empty white window; you can prove to yourself that your code is creating the window by changing the value assigned to the window's `backgroundColor` to something else (such as `UIColor.redColor()`) and running the app again.

This is a working app, but it's kind of useless. It doesn't do anything, and it *can't* really do much of anything, because its root view controller is a generic UIViewController. What we need here is an instance of our *own* view controller — one that can contain our own code, with a view that we can configure in a nib. So let's now make a UIView-Controller subclass along with a *.xib* file containing its view:

1. Choose File → New → File. In the "Choose a template" dialog, under iOS, click Source on the left and select Cocoa Touch Class. Click Next.

2. Name the class MyViewController and specify that it is a subclass of UIView-Controller. *Check* the "Also create XIB file" checkbox! Specify Swift as the language. Click Next.

3. The Save dialog appears. Make sure you are saving into the Truly Empty folder, that the Group pop-up menu is set to Truly Empty as well, and that the Truly Empty target is *checked* — we want these files to be part of the app target. Click Create.

   Xcode has created *two* files for us: *MyViewController.swift*, defining MyView-Controller as a subclass of UIViewController, and *MyViewController.xib*, the source of the nib from which a MyViewController instance will obtain its view.

4. Now go back to the app delegate's `application:didFinishLaunchingWith-Options:`, in *AppDelegate.swift*, and change the root view controller's class to My-ViewController, associating it with its nib, like this:

```
self.window!.rootViewController =
    MyViewController(nibName:"MyViewController", bundle:nil)
```

We have now created a perfectly usable minimal app project without a storyboard. Our code does some of the work that is done automatically by `UIApplicationMain` when there is a main storyboard: we instantiate UIWindow, we set the window instance as the app delegate's `window` property, we instantiate an initial view controller, we set that view controller instance as the window's `rootViewController` property, and we cause the window to appear. Moreover, the appearance of the window automatically causes the MyViewController instance to fetch its view from the nib that has been compiled from *MyViewController.xib*; thus, we can use *MyViewController.xib* to customize the app's initial interface. Besides illustrating explicitly what it is that `UIApplicationMain` does for you implicitly, this is also a perfectly reasonable way to construct an app.

Frameworks and SDKs

A *framework* is a library of compiled code used by your code. Most of the frameworks you are likely to use when programming iOS will be Apple's built-in frameworks. These frameworks are already part of the system on the device where your app will run; they live in */System/Library/Frameworks* on the device, though you can't tell that on an iPhone or iPad because there's no way (normally) to inspect the file hierarchy directly.

Your compiled code also needs to be connected to those frameworks when the project is being built and run on your computer. To make this possible, the iOS device's *System/Library/Frameworks* is duplicated on your computer, inside Xcode itself. This duplicated subset of the device's system is called an *SDK* (for "software development kit"). Which SDK is used depends upon what destination you're building for.

Linking is the process of hooking up your compiled code with the frameworks that it needs, even though those frameworks are in one place at build time and in another place at runtime. Thus, for example:

When you build your code to run on a device
> A copy of any needed frameworks is used. This copy lives in *System/Library/ Frameworks* inside the iPhone SDK, which is located at *Xcode.app/Contents/Developer/Platforms/iPhoneOS.platform/Developer/SDKs/iPhoneOS.sdk.*

When your code runs on a device
> The code, as it starts running, looks in the device's top-level */System/Library/ Frameworks* folder for the frameworks that it needs.

Used in this way, the frameworks are part of an ingenious mechanism whereby Apple's code is effectively incorporated dynamically into your app when the app runs. The frameworks are the locus of all the stuff that every app might need to do; they are Cocoa. That's a lot of stuff, and a lot of compiled code. Your app gets to share in the goodness and power of the frameworks because it is linked to them. Your code works as if the framework code were incorporated into it. Yet your app is relatively tiny; it's the frameworks that are huge.

Linking takes care of connecting your compiled code to any needed frameworks, but it isn't sufficient to allow your code to compile in the first place. The frameworks are full of classes (such as NSString) and methods (such as `rangeOfString:`) that your code will call. To satisfy the compiler, the frameworks publish their API in header files, which your code can import. Thus, for example, your code can speak of NSString and can call `rangeOfString:` because it imports the *NSString* header. Actually, what your code imports is the *UIKit* header, which in turn imports the *Foundation* header, which in turn imports the *NSString* header. And you can see this happening at the top of any of your own code's header files:

```
import UIKit
```

If you Command-click `UIKit`, you are taken to Swift's rendering of the *UIKit* header. There at the top is `import Foundation`. If you look at the *Foundation* header and scroll down, you'll see `import Foundation.NSString`. And if you look in the *NSString* header, you'll see the declaration of the `rangeOfString:` method.

Thus, using a framework is a two-part process:

Import the framework's header
> Your code needs this information in order to *compile* successfully. Your code imports a framework's header by using the `import` keyword, specifying either that framework or a framework that itself imports the desired framework. In Swift, you specify a framework by using its module name.

Link to the framework
> The compiled executable binary needs to be connected to the frameworks it will use while running, effectively incorporating the compiled code from those frame-

works. As your code is built, it is linked to any needed frameworks, in accordance with the list of frameworks in the target's Link Binary With Libraries build phase.

Our project, however, does not do any explicit linking. If you look in the app target's Link Binary With Libraries build phase, it is empty. This is because Swift uses *modules*, and modules can perform *autolinking*. In Objective-C, both those features are optional, and are governed by build settings. But in Swift, use of modules and autolinking is automatic.

Modules are cached information stored on your computer at *Library/Developer/Xcode/DerivedData/ModuleCache*. Merely opening a Swift project causes any imported modules to be cached here. If you drill down into the *ModuleCache* folder, you'll see the modules for over a dozen frameworks and headers (*.pcm* files). Swift's use of modules simplifies the importing and linking process, and improves compilation times.

Modules are ingenious and convenient, but it is sometimes necessary to link to a framework manually. For example, let's say you want to use an MKMapView (Map Kit View) in your interface. You can configure this in a *.storyboard* or *.xib* file, but when you build and run your app, it crashes, complaining: "Could not instantiate class named MKMapView." The reason is that the nib, as it loads, finds that it contains an MKMapView but doesn't know what an MKMapView *is*. MKMapView is defined in the MapKit framework, but the nib doesn't know that.

Adding `import MapKit` at the top of your code doesn't solve the problem; you need to do that if your *code* wants to talk to the MKMapView, but it doesn't help the *nib* understand what an MKMapView is when it loads. The solution is to link to the MapKit framework manually:

1. Edit the target and look at the Build Phases pane.
2. Under Link Binary With Libraries, click the Plus button.
3. A list of available frameworks appears (along with dynamic libraries). Scroll down to *MapKit.framework*, select it, and click Add.

This solves the problem; your app now builds and runs.

You can also create your own framework as part of your project. A framework is a module, so this can be a useful way to structure your code, as I described in Chapter 5 when discussing Swift privacy. To make a new framework:

1. Edit the target and choose Editor → Add Target.
2. On the left of the dialog, under iOS, select Framework & Library; on the right, select Cocoa Touch Framework. Click Next.
3. Give your framework a name; let's call it Coolness. You can pick a language, but I'm not sure this makes any difference, as no code files will be created. The Project and

Embed in Application pop-up menus should be correctly set by default. Click Finish.

A new Coolness framework target is created in your project. If you now add a *.swift* file to the Coolness target, and inside it define an object type *and declare it* `public`, then, back in one of your main app target's files, such as *AppDelegate.swift*, your code can `import Coolness` and will then be able to see that object type and its public members.

Renaming Parts of a Project

The name assigned to your project at creation time is used in many places throughout the project, leading beginners to worry that they can never rename a project without breaking something. But fear not!

First of all, you don't usually *need* to rename the project. Typically, what you want to change is the name of the *app* — the name that the user sees on the device, associated with this app's icon. The project name is *not* that name! Indeed, the project name is not a name that users will *ever* see. If all you want to do is change the name that appears visibly associated with the app on the device, change (or create) the "Bundle Display Name" in the *Info.plist*.

Still, you *can* rename a project, and it's easy to do: select the project listing at the top of the Project navigator, press Return to make its name editable, type the new name, and press Return again. Xcode presents a dialog proposing to change some other names to match, including the app target and the built app — and, by implication, various relevant build settings. You should feel free to accept.

Changing the project name (or target name) does not automatically change the scheme name to match. There is no particular need to do so, but you can change a scheme name freely; choose Product → Manage Schemes and click on the scheme name to make it editable.

Changing the project name (or target name) does not automatically change the main group name to match. There is no particular need to do so, but you can freely change the name of a group in the Project navigator, because these names are arbitrary; they have no effect on the build settings or the build process. However, the main group is special, because (as I've already said) it corresponds to a real folder on disk, the folder that sits beside your project file at the top level of the project folder. It's fine to change the group name, but beginners should not change the name of that folder *on disk*, as it is hard-coded into several build settings.

You can change the name of the project folder in the Finder at any time, and you can move the project folder in the Finder at will, because all build setting references to file and folder items in the project folder are relative.

CHAPTER 7

Nib Management

In Chapter 4, I talked about ways of obtaining an instance. You can directly instantiate an object type:

```
let v = UIView()
```

Or you can obtain a reference to an already existing instance:

```
let v = self.view.subviews[0]
```

But there is a third way: you can *load a nib*. A *nib* is a file, in a special format, filled with instructions for creating and configuring instances. To load a nib means, in effect, to tell that nib to follow those instructions: it *does* create and configure those instances.

My example of a UIView instance is apt, because a UIView is just the kind of instance a nib is likely to create. Nibs are edited in Xcode using a graphical interface, much like a drawing program. The idea is that you are designing some interface objects — mostly instances of UIView and UIView subclasses — that you want to use in your app when it runs. When your app does run, and when the moment comes where you actually need those interface objects (typically because you're about to display them in your visible interface), you load the nib, the nib-loading process creates and configures the instances, and you receive the instances and insert them into your app's actual interface.

You do not *have* to use nibs to create your interface objects. The loading of a nib does nothing that you could not have done directly, in code. You can instantiate a UIView or UIView subclass, you can configure it, you can construct a hierarchy of views, you can place that view hierarchy into your interface — manually, step by step, entirely in code. A nib is just a device for making that process simpler and more convenient. You design the nib beforehand, graphically; when the app runs, your code doesn't have to instantiate or configure any views. It has merely to load the nib and retrieve the resulting instances and put them into your interface. And in fact, because you'll mostly be using view controllers (UIViewController), which are themselves designed with nibs in mind, you won't even have to do that! The view controller will load the nib and retrieve the resulting instances and put them into your interface for you, *automatically*.

Nibs are a simple and ingenious device for making the process of designing and configuring your app's interface simpler and more convenient than it would be if you had to do the same thing in code. But they are also probably the least understood aspect of iOS programming. Many beginners discover nibs the first day they start programming iOS, and proceed to use nibs for years, without knowing what they really are or how they really work. This is a huge mistake. Nibs are *not magic*. They are not hard to understand. It is crucial that you know what nibs are, how they work, and how to manipulate them in your code. Failure to understand nibs opens you up to all kinds of elementary, confusing mistakes that can be avoided or corrected merely by grasping a few basic facts. Those facts are the subject of this chapter.

 The name *nib*, or *nib file*, has nothing to do with fountain pens or bits of chocolate. The graphical nib-design aspect of Xcode, which I call the *nib editor*, used to be (up through Xcode 3.2.x) a separate application called Interface Builder. (The nib editor environment within Xcode is still often referred to as Interface Builder.) The files created by Interface Builder were given the *.nib* file extension, which was an acronym for "NeXTStep Interface Builder." Nowadays, the file you edit directly in the nib editor will be either a *.storyboard* file or a *.xib* file; when the app is built, they are compiled into nib files (see Chapter 6).

The Nib Editor Interface

Let's explore Xcode's nib editor interface. In Chapter 6, we created a simple iPhone project, Empty Window, directly from the Single View Application template; it contains

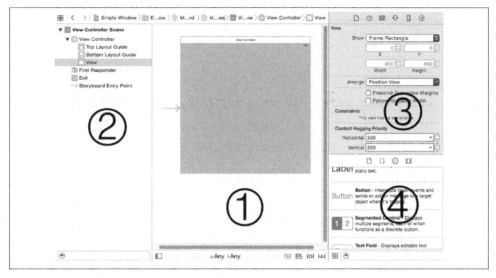

Figure 7-1. Editing a nib file

a storyboard file, so we'll use that. In Xcode, open the Empty Window project, locate *Main.storyboard* in the Project navigator, and click to edit it.

Figure 7-1 shows the project window after selecting *Main.storyboard*. (I've made some additional adjustments to make the screenshot fit on the page.) The interface may be considered in four pieces:

1. The bulk of the editor is devoted to the *canvas*, where you physically design your app's interface. The canvas portrays views in your app's interface and things that can contain views. A *view* is an interface object, which draws itself into a rectangular area. The phrase "things that can contain views" is my way of including view controllers, which are represented in the canvas even though they are not drawn in your app's interface; a view controller isn't a view, but it *has* a view (and controls it).

2. At the left of the editor is the *document outline*, listing the storyboard's contents hierarchically by name. It can be hidden by dragging its right edge or by clicking the button at the bottom left corner of the canvas.

3. The inspectors in the Utilities pane let you edit details of the currently selected object.

4. The libraries in the Utilities pane, especially the Object library, are your source of interface objects to be added to the nib.

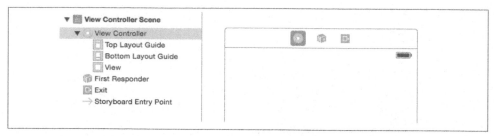

Figure 7-2. A view controller selected in a storyboard

Document Outline

The document outline portrays hierarchically the relationships between the objects in the nib. This structure differs slightly depending on whether you're editing a *.storyboard* file or a *.xib* file.

In a storyboard file, the primary constituents are *scenes*. A scene is, roughly speaking, a single view controller, along with some ancillary material; every scene has a single view controller at its top level.

A view controller isn't an interface object, but it manages an interface object, namely its view (or *main view*). A view controller in a nib doesn't have to have its main view in the same nib, but it usually does, and in that case, in the nib editor, the view usually appears inside the view controller in the canvas. Thus, in Figure 7-1, the large highlighted rectangle in the canvas is a view controller's main view, and is actually inside a view controller.

The view controller itself can be readily seen and selected in the document outline. It is also represented as an icon in the *scene dock*, which appears above the view controller in the canvas when anything in this scene is selected (Figure 7-2). Each view controller in a storyboard file constitutes one scene. In the document outline, this scene is portrayed as a hierarchical collection of names. At the top level of the document outline are the scenes themselves. At the top level of each scene are (more or less) the same objects that appear in the view controller's scene dock: the view controller itself, along with two *proxy objects*, the First Responder token and the Exit token. These objects — the ones displayed as icons in the scene dock, and shown at the top level of the scene in the document outline — are the scene's *top-level objects*.

Objects listed in the document outline are of two kinds:

Nib objects

> The view controller, along with its main view and any subviews that we care to place in that view, are real objects — potential objects that will be turned into actual instances when the nib is loaded by the running app. Such real objects to be instantiated from the nib are also called *nib objects*.

Proxy objects

The proxy objects (here, the First Responder and Exit tokens) do *not* represent instances that will come from the nib when it is loaded. Rather, they represent other objects, and are present to facilitate communication between nib objects and other objects (I'll give examples later in this chapter). You can't create or delete a proxy object; the nib editor shows them automatically.

(Also present in the document outline is the Storyboard Entry Point. This isn't an object of any kind; it's just an indication that this view controller is the storyboard's initial view controller — in its Attributes inspector, Is Initial View Controller is checked — and corresponds to the right-pointing arrow at the left of this view controller in the canvas.)

Most nib objects listed in a storyboard's document outline will depend hierarchically upon a scene's view controller. For example, in Figure 7-2, the view controller has a main view; that view is listed as hierarchically dependent on the view controller. That makes sense, because this view belongs to this view controller. Moreover, any further interface objects that we drag into the main view in the canvas will be listed in the document outline as hierarchically dependent on the view. That makes sense, too. A view can contain other views (its *subviews*) and can be contained by another view (its *superview*). One view can contain many subviews, which might themselves contain subviews. But each view can have only one immediate superview. Thus there is a hierarchical tree of subviews contained by their superviews with a single object at the top. The document outline portrays that tree as an outline — hence the name.

In a *.xib* file, there are no scenes. What would be, in a *.storyboard* file, the top-level objects of a scene become, in a *.xib* file, the top-level objects of the nib itself. Nor is there any requirement that one of these top-level objects be a view controller; it can be, but more often the top-level interface object of a *.xib* file is a view. It might well be a view that is to serve as a view controller's main view, but that's not a requirement either. Figure 7-3 shows a *.xib* with a structure parallel to the single scene of Figure 7-2.

The document outline in Figure 7-3 lists three top-level objects. Two of them are proxy objects, termed Placeholders in the document outline: the File's Owner, and the First Responder. The third is a real object, a view; it will be instantiated when the nib is loaded as the app runs. The document outline in a *.xib* file can't be completely hidden; instead, it is collapsed into a set of icons representing the nib's top-level objects, similar to a scene dock in a storyboard file, and often referred to simply as the *dock* (Figure 7-4).

At present, the document outline may seem unnecessary, because there is very little hierarchy; all objects in Figures 7-2 and 7-3 are readily accessible in the canvas. But when a storyboard contains many scenes, and when a view contains many levels of hierarchically arranged objects (along with their autolayout constraints), you're going to be very glad of the document outline, which lets you survey the contents of the nib in a nice hierarchical structure, and where you can locate and select the object you're after. You can also rearrange the hierarchy here; for example, if you've made an object

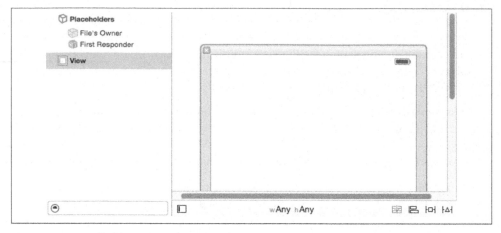

Figure 7-3. A .xib file containing a view

Figure 7-4. The dock in a .xib file

a subview of the wrong view, you can reposition it within this outline by dragging its name.

If the names of nib objects in the document outline seem generic and uninformative, you can change them. The name is technically a *label*, and has no special meaning, so feel free to assign nib objects labels that are useful to you. Select a nib object's label in the document outline and press Return to make it editable, or select the object and edit the Label field in the Document section of the Identity inspector.

Canvas

The canvas provides a graphical representation of a top-level interface nib object along with its subviews, similar to what you're probably accustomed to in any drawing program. The canvas is scrollable and automatically accommodates however many graphical representations it contains; a storyboard canvas can also be zoomed (choose Editor → Canvas → Zoom, or use the contextual menu).

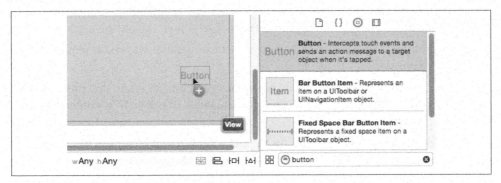

Figure 7-5. Dragging a button into a view

(In a *.xib* file, you can remove the canvas representation of a top-level nib object, without deleting the object, by clicking the X at its top left — see Figure 7-3 — and you can restore the graphical representation to the canvas by clicking that nib object in the document outline.)

Our simple Empty Window project's *Main.storyboard* contains just one scene, so it represents graphically in the canvas just one top-level nib object — the scene's view controller. Inside this view controller, and generally indistinguishable from it in the canvas, is its main view. It happens that this view controller will become our app's window's root view controller when the app runs; therefore its view will occupy the entire window, and will effectively be our app's initial interface (see Chapter 6). That gives us an excellent opportunity to experiment: any visible changes we make within this view should be visible when we subsequently build and run the app. To prove this, let's add a subview:

1. Start with the nib editor looking more or less like Figure 7-1.

2. Look at the Object library (Command-Option-Control-3). If it's in icon view (a grid of icons without text), click the button at the left of the filter bar to put it into list view. Click in the filter bar (or choose Edit → Filter → Filter in Library, Command-Option-L) and type "button" so that only button objects are shown in the list. The Button object is listed first.

3. Drag the Button object from the Object library into the view controller's main view in the canvas (Figure 7-5), and let go of the mouse.

A button is now present in the view in the canvas. The move we've just performed — dragging from the Object library into the canvas — is extremely characteristic; you'll do it often as you design your interface.

Much as in a drawing program, the nib editor provides features to aid you in designing your interface. Here are some things to try:

- Select the button: resizing handles appear. (If you accidentally select it twice and the resizing handles disappear, select the view and then the button again.)

- Using the resizing handles, resize the button to make it wider: dimension information appears.

- Drag the button near an edge of the view: a guideline appears, showing standard spacing. Similarly, drag the button near the center of the view: a guideline shows you when the button is centered.

- With the button selected, hold down the Option key and hover the mouse outside the button: arrows and numbers appear showing the distance between the button and the edges of the view. (If you accidentally clicked and dragged while you were holding Option, you'll now have two buttons. That's because Option-dragging an object duplicates it. Select the unwanted button and press Delete to remove it.)

- Control-Shift-click on the button: a menu appears, letting you select the button or whatever's behind it (in this case, the view, as well as the view controller because the view controller acts as a sort of top-level background to everything we're doing here).

- Double-click the button's title. The title becomes editable. Give it a new title, such as "Howdy!" Hit Return to set the new title.

To prove that we really are designing our app's interface, we'll run the app:

1. Drag the button to a position near the *top left* corner of the canvas. (If you don't do this, the button could be off the screen when the app runs.)

2. Examine the Debug → Activate / Deactivate Breakpoints menu item. If it says Deactivate Breakpoints, choose it; we don't want to pause at any breakpoints you may have created while reading the previous chapter.

3. Make sure the destination in the Scheme pop-up menu is iPhone 6.

4. Choose Product → Run (or click the Run button in the toolbar).

After a heart-stopping pause, the iOS Simulator opens, and presto, our empty window is empty no longer (Figure 7-6); it contains a button! You can tap this button with the mouse, emulating what the user would do with a finger; the button highlights as you tap it.

Inspectors and Libraries

Four inspectors appear in conjunction with the nib editor, and apply to whatever object is selected in the document outline, dock, or canvas:

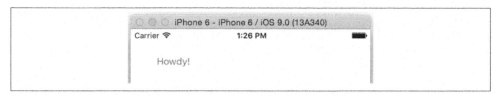

Figure 7-6. The Empty Window app's window is empty no longer

Identity inspector (Command-Option-3)
The first section of this inspector, Custom Class, is the most important. Here you learn, and can change, the selected object's class. Some situations in which you'll need to change the class of an object in the nib appear later in this chapter.

Attributes inspector (Command-Option-4)
Settings here correspond to properties and methods that you might use to configure the object in code. For example, selecting our view and choosing from the Background pop-up menu in the Attributes inspector corresponds to setting the view's backgroundColor property in code. Similarly, selecting our button and typing in the Title field is like calling the button's setTitle:forState: method.

The Attributes inspector has sections corresponding to the selected object's class inheritance. For example, the UIButton Attributes inspector has three sections: in addition to a Button section, there's a Control section (because a UIButton is also a UIControl) and a View section (because a UIControl is also a UIView).

Size inspector (Command-Option-5)
The X, Y, Width, and Height fields determine the object's position and size within its superview, corresponding to its frame property in code; you can equally do this in the canvas by dragging and resizing, but numeric precision can be desirable.

If autolayout is turned on (the default for new *.storyboard* and *.xib* files), the rest of the Size inspector has to do with the selected object's autolayout constraints, plus the buttons at the lower right of the canvas help you manage alignment, positioning, and constraints.

Connections inspector (Command-Option-6)
I'll discuss and demonstrate use of the Connections inspector later in this chapter.

Two libraries are of particular importance when you're editing a nib:

Object library (Command-Option-Control-3)
This library is your source for objects that you want to add to the nib.

Media library (Command-Option-Control-4)
> This library lists media in your project, such as images that you might want to drag into a UIImageView — or directly into your interface, in which case a UIImageView is created for you.

 I've now mentioned autolayout and constraints a couple of times, but I'm not going to explain here what they are. Nor am I going to discuss size classes and conditional constraints (the "Any" buttons at the bottom of the canvas). These are large topics having to do with views and view controllers, and are outside the scope of this book. I deal with these matters in full detail, including how to work with constraints and size classes in the nib editor, in *Programming iOS 9*.

Nib Loading

A nib file is a collection of potential instances — its nib objects. Those instances become real only if, while your app is running, the nib is *loaded*. At that moment, the nib objects contained in the nib are transformed into instances that are available to your app.

This architecture is a source of great efficiency. A nib usually contains interface; interface is relatively heavyweight stuff. A nib isn't loaded until it is needed; indeed, it might never be loaded. Thus this heavyweight stuff won't come into existence until and unless it is needed. In this way, memory usage is kept to a minimum, which is important because memory is at a premium in a mobile device. Also, loading a nib takes time, so loading fewer nibs at launch time — enough to generate just the app's initial interface — makes launching faster.

There's no such thing as "unloading" a nib. The job of the nib-loading process is to deliver some instances; when those instances are delivered, the nib's work, for that moment, is done. Henceforward it's up to the running app to decide what to do with the instances that just sprang to life. It must hang on to them for as long as it needs them, and will let them go out of existence when they are no longer needed.

Think of the nib file as a set of instructions for generating instances; whenever the nib is loaded, those instructions are followed. The same nib file can thus be *loaded multiple times*, generating a new set of instances each time. For example, a nib file might contain a piece of interface that you intend to use in several different places in your app. A nib file representing a single row of a table might be loaded a dozen times in order to generate a dozen visible rows of that table.

When Nibs Are Loaded

Here are some of the chief circumstances under which a nib file is commonly loaded while an app is running:

A view controller is instantiated from a storyboard

A storyboard is a collection of scenes. Each scene starts with a view controller. When that view controller is needed, it is instantiated from the storyboard. This means that a nib containing the view controller is loaded.

A view controller may be instantiated from a storyboard *automatically*. For example, as your app launches, if it has a main storyboard, the runtime looks for that storyboard's *initial view controller* (entry point) and instantiates it (see Chapter 6). Similarly, a storyboard typically contains several scenes connected by segues; when a segue is performed, the destination scene's view controller is instantiated.

It is also possible for your code to instantiate a view controller from a storyboard *manually*. To do so, you start with a UIStoryboard instance, and then:

- You can instantiate the storyboard's initial view controller by calling `instantiateInitialViewController`.

- You can instantiate any view controller whose scene is named within the storyboard by an identifier string by calling `instantiateViewControllerWithIdentifier:`.

A view controller loads its main view from a nib

A view controller has a main view. But a view controller is a lightweight object (it's just some code), whereas its main view is a relatively heavyweight object. Therefore, a view controller, when it is instantiated, lacks its main view. It generates its main view later, when that view is needed because it is to be placed into the interface. A view controller can obtain its main view in several ways; one way is to load its main view from a nib.

If a view controller belongs to a scene in a storyboard, and if, as will usually be the case, it contains its view in that storyboard's canvas (as in our Empty Window example project), then there are *two* nibs involved: the nib containing the view controller, and the nib containing its main view. The nib containing the view controller was loaded in order to instantiate the view controller, as I just described; now, when that view controller instance needs its main view, the main view nib is loaded *automatically*, and the whole interface connected with that view controller springs to life.

In the case of a view controller instantiated in some other way, there may be a *.xib*-generated nib file associated with it, containing its main view. Once again, the view controller will *automatically* load this nib and extract the main view when it's needed. This association between a view controller and its main view nib file is made through the nib file's name. In Chapter 6, we configured this association in code using the UIViewController initializer `init(nibName:bundle:)`, when we said this:

```
self.window!.rootViewController =
    MyViewController(nibName:"MyViewController", bundle:nil)
```

That code caused the view controller to set its own nibName property to "MyView-Controller". This, in turn, means that when the view controller needs its view, it gets it by loading the nib that comes from *MyViewController.xib*.

Your code explicitly loads a nib file

If a nib file comes from a *.xib* file, your code can load it *manually*, by calling one of these methods:

loadNibNamed:owner:options:

An NSBundle instance method. Usually, you'll direct it to NSBundle.main-Bundle().

instantiateWithOwner:options:

A UINib instance method. The nib in question was specified when UINib was instantiated and initialized with init(nibName:bundle:).

To specify a nib file while the app is running actually requires two pieces of information — its name and the bundle containing it. A view controller has not only a nibName property but also a nibBundle property, and the methods for specifying a nib, such as init(nibName:bundle:), have a bundle: parameter. In real life, however, the bundle will be the app bundle (or NSBundle.mainBundle(), which is the same thing); this is the default, so there will be no need to specify a bundle; you'll pass nil instead of supplying an explicit bundle.

Manual Nib Loading

In real life, you'll probably configure your app so that most nib loading takes place automatically, in accordance with the various mechanisms and situations I've just outlined. But in order to understand the nib-loading process, it will be useful for you to practice loading a nib manually. Let's do that.

First we'll create and configure a *.xib* file in our Empty Window project:

1. In the Empty Window project, choose File → New → File and specify iOS → User Interface → View. This will be a *.xib* file containing a UIView instance. Click Next.

2. In the Save dialog, accept the default name, View, for the new *.xib* file. Click Create.

3. We are now back in the Project navigator; our *View.xib* file has been created and selected, and we're looking at its contents in the editor. Those contents consist of a single UIView. It's too large, so select it and, in the Attributes inspector, change the Size pop-up menu, under Simulated Metrics, to Freeform. Handles appear around the view in the canvas; drag them to make the view smaller.

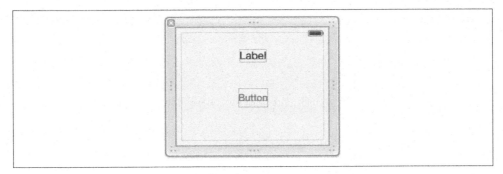

Figure 7-7. Designing a view in a .xib file

4. Populate the view with some arbitrary subviews, dragging them into it from the Object library. You can also configure the view itself; for example, in the Attributes inspector, change its background color (Figure 7-7).

Our goal now is to *load* this nib file, manually, in code, when the app runs. Edit *View-Controller.swift* and, in the `viewDidLoad` method body, insert this line of code:

```
NSBundle.mainBundle().loadNibNamed("View", owner: nil, options: nil)
```

Build and run the app. Hey, what happened? Where's the designed view from *View.xib*? Did our nib fail to load?

No. Our nib did *not* fail to load. We loaded it! But we've omitted two further steps. Remember, there are *three* tasks you have to perform when you load a nib:

1. Load the nib.
2. Obtain the instances that it creates as it loads.
3. Do something with those instances.

We performed the *first* task — we loaded the nib — but we didn't obtain any instances from it. Thus, those instances were created *and then vanished in a puff of smoke!* In order to prevent that, we need to *capture* those instances somehow. The call to `loadNib-Named:owner:options:` returns an array of the top-level nib objects instantiated from the loading of the nib. Those are the instances we need to capture! We have only one top-level nib object — the UIView — so it is sufficient to capture the first (and only) element of this array. Rewrite our code to look like this:

```
let arr = NSBundle.mainBundle().loadNibNamed("View", owner: nil, options: nil)
let v = arr[0] as! UIView
```

We have now performed the *second* task: we've captured the instances that we created by loading the nib. The variable v now refers to a brand-new UIView instance.

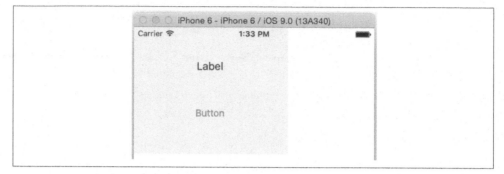

Figure 7-8. A nib-loaded view appears in our interface

But *still* nothing seems to happen when we build and run the app, because we aren't *doing* anything with that UIView. That's the *third* task. Let's fix that by doing something clear and dramatic with the UIView: we'll put it into our interface! Rewrite our code once again:

```
let arr = NSBundle.mainBundle().loadNibNamed("View", owner: nil, options: nil)
let v = arr[0] as! UIView
self.view.addSubview(v)
```

Build and run the app. There's our view! This proves that our loading of the nib worked: we can *see*, in our running app's interface, the view that we designed in the nib (Figure 7-8).

Connections

A *connection* is something in a nib file. It unites two nib objects, running from one to the other. The connection has a direction: that's why I use the words "from" and "to" to describe it. I'll call the two objects the *source* and the *destination* of the connection.

There are two kinds of connection: outlet connections and action connections. The rest of this section describes them, explains how to create and configure them, and discusses the nature of the problems that they are intended to solve.

Outlets

When a nib loads and its instances come into existence, there's a problem: those instances are useless unless you can get a reference to them. In the preceding section, we solved that problem by capturing the array of top-level objects instantiated by the loading of the nib. But there's another way: use an outlet. This approach is more complicated — it requires some advance configuration, which can easily go wrong. But it is also more common, especially when nibs are loaded automatically.

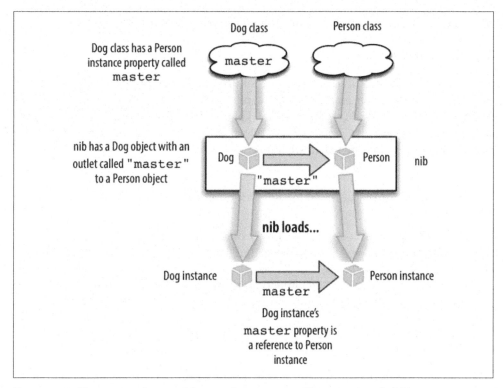

Figure 7-9. How an outlet provides a reference to a nib-instantiated object

An *outlet* is a connection that has a *name*, which is effectively just a string. When the nib loads, something unbelievably clever happens. The source object and the destination object are no longer just potential objects in a nib; they are now real, full-fledged instances. The outlet's name is now immediately used to locate an *instance property* with that same name in the outlet's source object, and *the destination object is assigned to that property*. The source object now has a reference to the destination object!

For example, suppose there's a Dog object and a Person object in a nib, and suppose a Dog has a master instance property. Then if we make an outlet from the Dog object to the Person object in the nib, and if that outlet is named "master", then when the nib loads and the Dog instance and the Person instance are created, that Person instance will be assigned as the value of that Dog instance's master property (Figure 7-9).

The nib-loading mechanism can't magically *create* an instance property — that is, it doesn't cause the source object, once instantiated, to have an instance property of the correct name if it didn't have one before. The class of the source object has to have been defined with this instance property *already*. Thus, for an outlet to work, preparation must be performed in *two different places*: in the class of the source object, and in the nib. This is a bit tricky; Xcode does try to help you get it right, but it is still possible to mess it up. (I will discuss ways of messing it up, in detail, later in this chapter.)

The Nib Owner

To use an outlet to capture a reference to an instance created from a nib, we need an outlet that runs from an object *outside* the nib to an object *inside* the nib. This seems metaphysically impossible — but it isn't. The nib editor permits such an outlet to be created, using the *nib owner object*. First, I'll tell you where to find the nib owner object in the nib editor; then I'll explain what it is:

- In a storyboard scene, the nib owner is the top-level view controller. It is the first object listed for that scene in the document outline, and the first object shown in the scene dock.

- In a *.xib* file, the nib owner is a proxy object. It is the first object shown in the document outline or dock, and is listed under Placeholders as the File's Owner.

The nib owner object in the nib editor represents an instance that *already* exists *outside* the nib at the time that the nib is loaded. When the nib is loaded, the nib-loading mechanism *doesn't* instantiate this object; it is *already* an instance. Instead, the nib-loading mechanism substitutes the real, already existing instance for the nib owner object, using it to fulfill any connections that involve the nib owner.

But wait! How does the nib-loading mechanism know *which* real, already existing instance to substitute for the nib owner object in the nib? It knows because it is told, in one of two ways, at nib-loading time:

- If your code loads the nib either by calling `loadNibNamed:owner:options:` or by calling `instantiateWithOwner:options:`, you specify an owner object as the `owner:` argument.

- If a view controller instance loads a nib automatically in order to obtain its main view, the view controller instance specifies *itself* as the owner object.

For example, return to our Dog object and Person object. Suppose there is a Person nib object in our nib, but *no* Dog nib object. Instead, the *nib owner object* is a Dog. A Dog has a `master` instance property. We configure an outlet in the nib from the Dog nib owner object to the Person object — an outlet called `"master"`. We then load the nib *with an existing Dog instance as owner*. The nib-loading mechanism will match the Dog nib owner object with this already existing actual Dog instance, and will set the newly instantiated Person instance as that Dog instance's `master` (Figure 7-10).

Return now to Empty View, and let's reconfigure things to demonstrate this mechanism. We're already loading the View nib in code in *ViewController.swift*. This code is running inside a ViewController instance. So we'll use that instance as the nib owner. This will

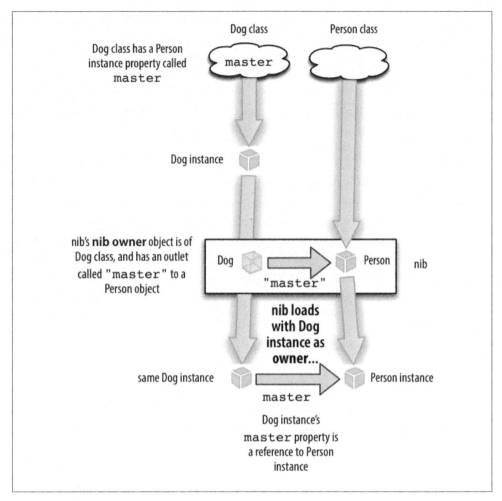

Dog class has a Person instance property called `master`

Dog class

Person class

`master`

Dog instance

nib's **nib owner** object is of Dog class, and has an outlet called `"master"` to a Person object

Dog

Person

nib

`"master"`

nib loads with Dog instance as owner...

same Dog instance

`master`

Person instance

Dog instance's `master` property is a reference to Person instance

Figure 7-10. An outlet from the nib owner object

be a little tedious to configure, but bear with me, because understanding how to use this mechanism is crucial. Here we go:

1. First, we need an instance property in ViewController. At the start of the body of the ViewController class declaration, insert the property declaration, like this:

```
class ViewController: UIViewController {
    @IBOutlet var coolview : UIView!
```

The `var` declaration you already understand; we're making an instance property called `coolview`. It is declared as an Optional because it won't have a "real" value when the ViewController instance is created; it's going to get that value through the

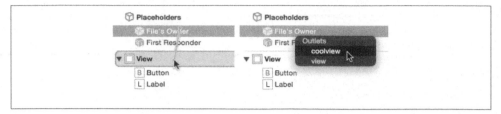

Figure 7-11. Creating an outlet

loading of the nib, later. The @IBOutlet attribute is a hint to Xcode to allow us to create the outlet in the nib editor.

2. Edit *View.xib*. Our first step must be to ensure that the nib owner object is designated as a ViewController instance. Select the File's Owner proxy object and switch to the Identity inspector. In the first text field, under Custom Class, set the Name value as ViewController. Tab out of the text field and save.

3. Now we're ready to make the outlet! In the document outline, hold down the Control key and drag from the File's Owner object to the View; a little line follows the mouse as you drag. Release the mouse. A little HUD (heads-up display) appears, listing possible outlets we are allowed to create (Figure 7-11). There are two of them: coolview and view. Click coolview (*not* view!).

4. Finally, we need to modify our nib-loading code. We no longer need to capture the top-level array of instantiated objects. That's the whole point of this exercise! Instead, we're going to load the nib *with ourself as owner*. This will cause our coolview instance property to be set automatically, so we can proceed to use it immediately:

```
NSBundle.mainBundle().loadNibNamed("View", owner: self, options: nil)
self.view.addSubview(self.coolview)
```

Build and run. It works! The first line loaded the nib *and set our coolview instance property* to the view instantiated from the nib. Thus, the second line can display self.coolview in the interface, because self.coolview now *is* that view.

Let's sum up what we just did. Our preparatory configuration was a little tricky, because it was performed in two places — in code, and in the nib:

- In code, there must be an instance property in the class whose instance will act as owner when the nib loads. (Not only did we create the property, but we also marked it as @IBOutlet.)

- In the nib editor, the class of the nib owner object must be set to the class whose instance will act as owner when the nib loads.

- In the nib editor, an outlet must be created, with the same name as the property, from the nib owner to some nib object. (This will be possible only if the other two configurations were correctly performed.)

If all those things are true, then, when the nib loads, *if* it is loaded with an owner of the correct class, that owner's instance property will be set to the outlet destination.

 New in Xcode 7, when you configure an outlet to an object in the nib, that object's name as listed in the document outline ceases to be generic (e.g. "View") and takes on the name of the outlet (e.g. "coolview"). This name is still just a label — it has no effect on the operation of the outlet — and you can change it in the Identity inspector.

Automatically Configured Nibs

In some situations, the configuration of the owner class and the nib is performed for us. Now that we've gone through the work of configuring the owner and the nib manually, we can understand and appreciate those automatic configurations.

An important example is how a view controller gets its main view. A view controller has a view property. The actual view will typically come from a nib. So the view controller instance needs to act as owner when that nib loads, and there needs to be a view outlet from the nib owner object to that view. If you examine an actual nib that holds a view controller's main view, you'll see that this is, in fact, the case.

Look at our Empty Window project. Edit *Main.storyboard*. It has one scene, whose nib owner object is the View Controller object. Select the View Controller in the document outline. Switch to the Identity inspector. It tells us that the nib owner object's class is indeed ViewController!

Now, still with the View Controller in the document outline selected, switch to the Connections inspector. It tells us that there is indeed an outlet connection from the View Controller to the View object, and that this outlet is indeed named "view"! If you hover the mouse over that outlet connection, the View object in the canvas is highlighted, to help you identify it.

That explains completely how this view controller gets its main view! When the view controller needs its main view (because that view is about to be displayed in the interface), the view nib loads — with the view controller as owner. Thus, the view controller's view property is set to the view that we design here. The view is then displayed in the interface: it, and its contents as you have designed them, appear in the running app.

The same sort of thing is true in our Truly Empty project from Chapter 6. Edit *MyViewController.xib*. The nib owner object is the File's Owner proxy object. Select the

File's Owner object. Switch to the Identity inspector. It tells us that the nib owner object's class is indeed MyViewController! Switch to the Connections inspector. It tells us that there is indeed an outlet connection to the View object, called "view"!

That explains how *this* view controller gets its main view. We told this view controller where to find its nib when we instantiated it by saying MyViewController(nibName:"My-ViewController", bundle:nil). But the nib itself was already correctly configured, because Xcode set it up that way when we created the MyViewController class and checked the "Also create XIB file" checkbox. The view controller loads the nib with itself as owner, and the outlet works: the view from the nib file becomes the view controller's view, and appears in the interface.

Misconfigured Outlets

Setting up an outlet to work correctly involves several things being true at the same time. I guarantee that at some point in the future you will fail to get this right, and your outlet won't work properly. Don't be offended, and don't be afraid; be prepared! This happens to everyone. The important thing is to recognize the symptoms so that you know what's gone wrong. We're deliberately going to make things go wrong, so that we can explore the main ways that an outlet can be incorrectly configured:

Outlet name doesn't match a property name in the source class
Start with our working Empty Window example. Run the project to prove that all is well. Now, in *ViewController.swift*, change the property name to badview:

```
@IBOutlet var badview : UIView!
```

In order to get the code to compile, you'll also have to change the reference to this property in viewDidLoad:

```
self.view.addSubview(self.badview)
```

The code compiles just fine. But when you run it, the app crashes with this message in the console: "This class is not key value coding-compliant for the key coolview."

That message is just a technical way of saying that the name of the outlet in the nib (which is still coolview) doesn't match the name of a property of the nib's owner when the nib loads — because we changed the name of that property to badview and thus wrecked the configuration. In effect, we had everything set up correctly, but then we went behind the nib editor's back and removed the corresponding instance property from the outlet source's class. When the nib loads, the runtime can't match the outlet's name with any property in the outlet's source — the View-Controller instance — and we crash.

There are other ways to bring about this same misconfiguration. For example, you could change things so that the nib owner is an instance of *the wrong class*:

```
NSBundle.mainBundle().loadNibNamed("View", owner: NSObject(), options: nil)
```

We made the owner a generic NSObject instance. The effect is the same: the NSObject class has no property with the same name as the outlet, so the app crashes when the nib loads, complaining about the owner not being "key value coding-compliant." Another common way to make that same mistake is to make the nib owner class *in the nib* the wrong class.

No outlet in the nib

Fix the problem from the previous example by changing both references to the property name from badview back to coolview in *ViewController.swift*. Run the project to prove that all is well. Now we're going to mess things up at the other end! Edit *View.xib*. Select the File's Owner and switch to the Connections inspector, and disconnect the coolview outlet by clicking the X at the left end of the second cartouche. Run the project. We crash with this error message in the console: "Fatal error: unexpectedly found nil while unwrapping an Optional value."

We removed the outlet from the nib. So when the nib loaded, our ViewController instance property coolview, which is typed as an implicitly unwrapped Optional wrapping a UIView (UIView!), was *never set to anything*. Thus, it kept its initial value, which is nil. We then tried to *use* the implicitly unwrapped Optional by putting it into the interface:

```
self.view.addSubview(self.coolview)
```

Swift tries to obey by unwrapping the Optional for real, but you can't unwrap nil, so we crash.

No view outlet

For this one, you'll have to use the Truly Empty example from Chapter 6, where we load a view controller's main view from a *.xib* file; I can't demonstrate the problem using a *.storyboard* file, because the storyboard editor guards against it. In the Truly Empty project, edit the *MyViewController.xib* file. Select the File's Owner object, switch to the Connections inspector, and disconnect the view outlet. Run the project. We crash at launch time: "Loaded the 'MyViewController' nib but the view outlet was not set."

The console message says it all. A nib that is to serve as the source of a view controller's main view *must* have a connected view outlet from the view controller (the nib owner object) to the view.

Deleting an Outlet

Deleting an outlet coherently — that is, without causing one of the problems described in the previous section — involves working in several places at once, just as creating an outlet does. I recommend proceeding in this order:

1. Disconnect the outlet in the nib.

2. Remove the outlet declaration from the code.

3. Attempt compilation and let the compiler catch any remaining issues for you.

Let's suppose, for example, that you decide to delete the `coolview` outlet from the Empty Window project. You would follow the same three-step procedure that I just outlined:

1. Disconnect the outlet in the nib. To do so, edit *View.xib*, select the source object (the File's Owner proxy object), and disconnect the `coolview` outlet in the Connections inspector by clicking the X.

2. Remove the outlet declaration from the code. To do so, edit *ViewController.swift* and delete or comment out the `@IBOutlet` declaration line.

3. Remove other references to the property. The easiest way is to attempt to build the project; the compiler issues an error on the line referring to `self.coolview` in *ViewController.swift*, because there is now no such property. Delete or comment out that line, and build again to prove that all is well.

More Ways to Create Outlets

Earlier, we created an outlet by first declaring an instance property in a class file, and then, in the nib editor, by control-dragging from the source (an instance of that class) to the destination in the document outline and choosing the desired outlet property from the HUD (heads-up display). Xcode provides many other ways to create outlets — too many to list here. I'll survey some of the most interesting.

We'll continue to use the Empty Window project and the *View.xib* file. Keep in mind that all of this works exactly the same way for a *.storyboard* file.

To prepare, delete the outlet in *View.xib* using the Connections inspector (if you haven't already done so). In *ViewController.swift*, create (or uncomment) the property declaration, and save:

```
@IBOutlet var coolview : UIView!
```

Now we're ready to experiment!

Drag from source Connections inspector

You can drag from a circle in the Connections inspector in the nib editor to connect the outlet. In *View.xib*, select the File's Owner and switch to the Connections inspector. The `coolview` outlet is listed here, but it isn't connected: the circle at its right is open. Drag from the circle next to `coolview` to the UIView object in the nib. You can drag to the view in the canvas or in the document outline. You don't need to hold the Control key as you drag from the circle, and there's no HUD because you're dragging from a specific outlet, so Xcode knows which one you mean.

Drag from destination Connections inspector

Now let's make that same move the other way round. Delete the outlet in the nib. Select the View and look at the Connections inspector. We want an outlet that has this view as its destination: that's a "referencing outlet." Drag from the circle next to New Referencing Outlet to the File's Owner object. The HUD appears: click `coolview` to make the outlet connection.

Drag from source HUD

You can summon a HUD that effectively is the same as the Connections inspector. Let's start with that HUD. Again delete the outlet in the Connections inspector. Control-click the File's Owner. A HUD appears, looking a lot like the Connections inspector! Drag from the circle at the right of `coolview` to the UIView.

Drag from destination HUD

Again, let's make that same move the other way round. Delete the outlet in the Connections inspector. Either in the canvas or in the document outline, Control-click the view. There's the HUD showing its Connections inspector. Drag from the New Referencing Outlet circle to the File's Owner. A second HUD appears, listing possible outlets; click `coolview`.

Again, delete the outlet. Now we're going to create the outlet by dragging *between the code and the nib editor*. This will require that you work in two places at once: you're going to need an assistant pane. In the main editor pane, show *ViewController.swift*. In the assistant pane, show *View.xib*, in such a way that the view is visible.

Drag from property declaration to nib

Next to the property declaration in the code, in the gutter, is an empty circle. What do you think it's for? Drag from it *right across the barrier* to the View in the nib editor (Figure 7-12). The outlet connection is formed in the nib; you can see this by looking at the Connections inspector, and also because, back in the code, the circle in the gutter is now filled in. Hover over the filled circle, or click it, to learn what the outlet in the nib is connected to. You can click the little menu that appears when you click in the filled circle to navigate to the destination object.

Here's one more way — the most amazing of all. Keep the two-pane arrangement from the preceding example. Again, delete the outlet (you will probably need to use the Connections inspector or HUD in the nib editor pane to do this). Also delete the `@IBOutlet` line from the code! We're going to create the property declaration and connect the outlet, *all in a single move!*

Drag from nib to code

Control-drag from the view in the nib editor across the pane boundary to just inside the body of the `class ViewController` declaration. A HUD offers to Insert Outlet

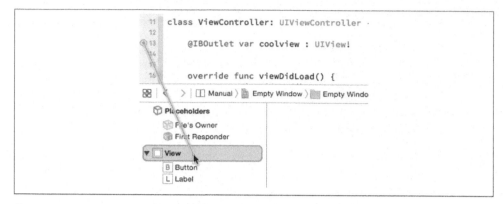

Figure 7-12. Connecting an outlet by dragging from code to nib editor

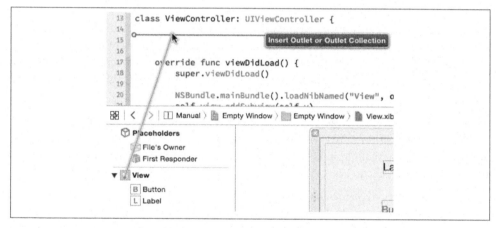

Figure 7-13. Creating an outlet by dragging from nib editor to code

or Outlet Collection (Figure 7-13). Release the mouse. A popover appears, where you can configure the declaration to be inserted into your code. Configure it as shown in Figure 7-14: you want an outlet, and this property should be named `coolview`. Click Connect. The property declaration is inserted into your code, and the outlet is connected in the nib, in a single move.

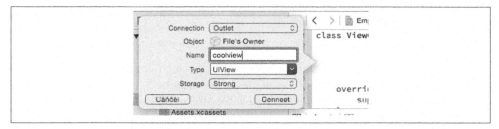

Figure 7-14. Configuring a property declaration

 Making an outlet by connecting directly between code and the nib editor is extremely cool and convenient, but don't be fooled: there's no such direct connection. There are always, if an outlet is to work properly, *two distinct and separate things* — an instance property in a class, and an outlet in the nib, *with the same name* and *coming from an instance of that class*. It is the identity of the names and classes that allows the two to be matched at runtime when the nib loads. Xcode tries to help you get everything set up correctly, but it is *not* in fact magically connecting the code to the nib.

Outlet Collections

An *outlet collection* is an array instance property (in code) matched (in a nib) by multiple connections to objects of the same type.

For example, suppose a class contains this property declaration:

```
@IBOutlet var coolviews: [UIView]!
```

The outcome is that, in the nib editor, with an instance of this class selected, the Connections inspector lists `coolviews` — not under Outlets, but under Outlet Collections. This means that you can form *multiple* `coolviews` outlets, each one connected to a different UIView object in the nib. When the nib loads, those UIView instances become the elements of the array `coolviews`; the order in which the outlets are formed is the order of the elements in the array.

The advantage of this arrangement is that your code can refer to multiple interface objects instantiated from the nib by number (the index into the array) instead of your having to devise and manipulate a separate name for each one. This turns out to be particularly useful when forming outlets to such things as autolayout constraints and gesture recognizers.

Action Connections

An action connection, like an outlet connection, is a way of giving one object in a nib a reference to another. It's not a property reference; it's a message-sending reference.

An *action* is a message emitted automatically by a Cocoa UIControl interface object (a *control*), and sent to another object, when the user does something to it, such as tapping the control. The various user behaviors that will cause a control to emit an action message are called *events*. To see a list of possible events, look at the UIControl class documentation, under "Control Events." For example, in the case of a UIButton, the user tapping the button corresponds to the `UIControlEvents.TouchUpInside` event.

For this architecture to work, the control object must know three things:

- What control event to respond to
- What message to send (method to call) when that control event occurs (the *action*)
- What object to send that message to (the *target*)

An action connection in a nib builds the knowledge of those three things into itself. It has the control object as its source; its destination is the target; and you tell the action connection, as you form it, what the control event and action message should be. To form the action connection, you need first to configure the class of the *destination* object so that it has a method suitable as an action message.

To experiment with action connections, we'll need a UIControl object in a nib, such as a button. You may already have such a button in the Empty Window project's *Main.storyboard* file. However, it's probable that, when the app runs, we've been covering the button with the view that we're loading from *View.xib*. So first clear out the `ViewController` class declaration body in *ViewController.swift*, so that there is no outlet property and no manual nib-loading code; this should be all that's left:

```
class ViewController: UIViewController {
}
```

Now let's arrange to use the view controller in our Empty Window project as a target for an action message emitted by the button's `UIControlEvents.TouchUpInside` event (meaning that the button was tapped). We'll need a method in the view controller that will be called by the button when the button is tapped. To make this method dramatic and obvious, we'll have the view controller put up an alert window. Insert this method into the *ViewController.swift* declaration body:

```
class ViewController: UIViewController {
    @IBAction func buttonPressed(sender:AnyObject) {
        let alert = UIAlertController(
            title: "Howdy!", message: "You tapped me!", preferredStyle: .Alert)
        alert.addAction(
```

```
                    UIAlertAction(title: "OK", style: .Cancel, handler: nil))
            self.presentViewController(alert, animated: true, completion: nil)
    }
}
```

The @IBAction attribute is like @IBOutlet: it's a hint to Xcode itself, asking Xcode to make this method available in the nib editor. And indeed, if we look in the nib editor, we find that it *is* now available: edit *Main.storyboard*, select the View Controller object and switch to the Connections inspector, and you'll find that buttonPressed: is now listed under Received Actions.

In *Main.storyboard*, in the single scene that it contains, the top-level View Controller's View should contain a button. (We created it earlier in this chapter: see Figure 7-5.) If it doesn't, add one, and position it in the upper left corner of the view. Our goal now is to connect that button's Touch Up Inside event, as an action, to the buttonPressed: method in ViewController.

As with an outlet connection, there is a source and a destination. The source here is the button; the destination is View Controller, the ViewController instance acting as owner of the nib containing the button. There are many ways to form this outlet connection, all of them completely parallel to the formation of an action connection. The difference is that we must configure *both* ends of the connection. At the button (source) end, we must specify that the control event we want to use is Touch Up Inside; fortunately, this is the default for a UIButton, so we might be able to skip this step. At the view controller (destination) end, we must specify that the action method to be called is button-Pressed:.

Let's form the action connection by simply Control-dragging from the button to the view controller in the nib editor:

1. Control-drag from the button (in the canvas or in the document outline) to the View Controller listing in the document outline (or to the view controller icon in the scene dock above the view in the canvas).

2. A HUD listing possible connections appears (Figure 7-15); it lists mostly segues, but it also lists Sent Events, and buttonPressed: in particular.

3. Click the buttonPressed: listing in the HUD.

The action connection has now been formed. This means that when the app runs, any time the button gets a Touch Up Inside event — meaning that it was tapped — it will send the action message buttonPressed: to the target, which is the view controller instance. We know what that method should do: it should put up an alert. Try it! Build and run the app, and when the app appears in the Simulator, tap the button. It works!

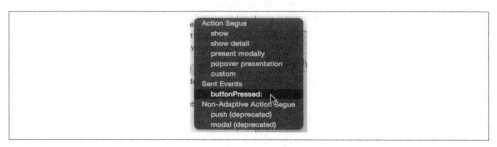

Figure 7-15. A HUD showing an action method

More Ways to Create Actions

Other ways in which you can form the action connection in the nib, having created the action method in *ViewController.swift*, include the following:

- Control-click the view controller. A HUD appears, similar to the Connections inspector. Drag from `buttonPressed:` (under Received Actions) to the button. Another HUD appears, listing possible control events. Click Touch Up Inside.

- Select the button and use the Connections inspector. Drag from the Touch Up Inside circle to the view controller. A HUD appears, listing the known action methods in the view controller; click `buttonPressed:`.

- Control-click the button. A HUD appears, similar to the Connections inspector. Proceed as in the previous case.

- Arrange to see *ViewController.swift* in one pane and the storyboard in the other. The `buttonPressed:` method in *ViewController.swift* has a circle to its left, in the gutter. Drag from that circle across the pane boundary to the button in the nib.

As with an outlet connection, the most impressive way to make an action connection is to drag from the nib editor to your code, inserting the action method and forming the action connection in the nib *in a single move*. To try this, first delete the `button-Pressed:` method in your code and delete the action connection in the nib. Arrange to see *ViewController.swift* in one pane and the storyboard in the other. Now:

1. Control-drag from the button in the nib editor to an empty area in the View-Controller class declaration's body. A HUD offering to create an outlet *or an action* appears in the code. Release the mouse.

2. The popover view appears. This is the tricky part. By default, the popover view is offering to create an outlet connection. That isn't what you want; you want an action connection! Change the Connection pop-up menu to Action. Now you can enter

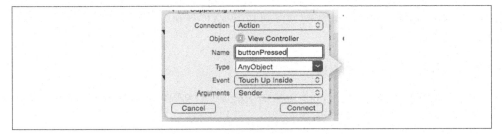

Figure 7-16. Configuring an action method declaration

the name of the action method (`buttonPressed`) and configure the rest of the declaration (the defaults are probably good enough: see Figure 7-16).

Xcode forms the action connection in the nib, and inserts a stub method into your code:

```
@IBAction func buttonPressed(sender: AnyObject) {
}
```

The method is just a stub (Xcode can't read your mind and guess what you want the method to do), so in real life, at this point, you'd insert some functionality between those curly braces. As with an outlet connection, the filled circle next to the code in an action method tells you that Xcode believes that this connection is correctly configured, and you can click the filled circle to learn, and navigate to, the object at the source of the connection.

Misconfigured Actions

As with an outlet connection, configuring an action connection involves setting things up correctly at both ends (the nib and the code) so that they match. Thus, you can wreck an action connection's configuration and crash your app. The typical misconfiguration is that the name of the action method as embedded in the action connection in the nib no longer matches the name of the action method in the code.

To see this, change the name of the function in the code from `buttonPressed` to something else, like `buttonPushed`. Now run the app and tap the button. Your app crashes, displaying in the console the dreaded error message, "Unrecognized selector sent to instance." A selector is a message — the name of a method. The runtime tried to send a message to an object, but that object turned out to have no corresponding method (because we renamed it). If you look a little earlier in the error message, it even tells you the name of this method:

```
-[Empty_Window.ViewController buttonPressed:]
```

The runtime is telling you that it tried to call the `buttonPressed:` method in your Empty Window module's ViewController class, but the ViewController class has no `button-Pressed:` method.

Connections Between Nibs — Not!

You cannot draw an outlet connection or an action connection between an object in one nib and an object in another nib. For example:

- You can't open nib editors on two different *.xib* files and Control-drag a connection from one to the other.
- In a *.storyboard* file, you cannot Control-drag a connection between an object in one scene and an object in another scene.

If you expect to be able to do this, you haven't understood what a nib is (or what a scene is, or what a connection is).

The reason is simple: objects in a nib together will become instances together, at the moment when the nib loads, so it makes sense to connect them in the nib, because we know what instances we'll be talking about when the nib loads. The two objects may both be instantiated from the nib, or one of them may be a proxy object (the nib owner), but they must both be represented *in the same nib*, so that the actual instances can be configured in relation to one another on a particular occasion when this nib loads.

If an outlet connection or an action connection were drawn from an object in one nib to an object in another nib, there would be no way to understand what actual future instances the connection is supposed to connect, because they are different nibs and will be loaded at different times (if ever). The problem of communicating between an instance generated from one nib and an instance generated from another nib is a special case of the more general problem of how to communicate between instances in a program, discussed in Chapter 13.

Additional Configuration of Nib-Based Instances

By the time a nib finishes loading, its instances are fully fledged; they have been initialized and configured with all the attributes dictated through the Attributes and Size inspectors, and their outlets have been used to set the values of the corresponding instance properties. Nevertheless, you might want to append your own code to the initialization process as an object is instantiated from a loading nib. This section describes some ways you can do that.

A common situation is that a view controller, functioning as the owner when a nib containing its main view loads (and therefore represented in the nib by the nib owner object), has an outlet to an interface object instantiated from the nib. In this architecture, the view controller can perform further configuration on that interface object, because it has a reference to it after the nib loads — the corresponding instance property. The earliest place where it can perform such configuration is its viewDidLoad method. At the time viewDidLoad is called, the view controller's view has loaded — that is, the view controller's view property has been set to its actual main view, instantiated from the nib — and all outlets have been connected; but the view is not yet in the visible interface.

Another possibility is that you'd like the nib object to configure itself, over and above whatever configuration has been performed in the nib. Often, this will be because you've got a custom subclass of a built-in interface object class — in fact, you might want to create a custom class, just so you have a place to put this self-configuring code. The problem you're trying to solve might be that the nib editor doesn't let you perform the configuration you're after, or that you have many objects that need to be configured in some identical, elaborate way, so that it makes more sense for them to configure themselves by virtue of sharing a common class than to configure each one individually in the nib editor.

One approach is to implement awakeFromNib in your custom class. The awakeFrom-Nib message is sent to all nib-instantiated objects just after they are instantiated by the loading of the nib: the object has been initialized and configured and its connections are operational.

For example, let's make a button whose background color is always red, regardless of how it's configured in the nib. (This is a nutty example, but it's dramatically effective.) In the Empty Window project, we'll create a button subclass, RedButton:

1. In the Project navigator, choose File → New → File. Specify iOS → Source → Cocoa Touch Class. Click Next.

2. Call the new class RedButton. Make it a subclass of UIButton. Click Next.

3. Make sure you're saving into the project folder, with the Empty Window group, and make sure the Empty Window app target is checked. Click Create. Xcode creates *RedButton.swift*.

4. In *RedButton.swift*, inside the body of the RedButton class declaration, implement awakeFromNib:

```
override func awakeFromNib() {
    super.awakeFromNib()
    self.backgroundColor = UIColor.redColor()
}
```

We now have a UIButton subclass that turns itself red when it's instantiated from a nib. But we have no instance of this subclass in any nib. Let's fix that. Edit the storyboard, select the button that's already in the main view, and use the Identity inspector to change this button's class to RedButton.

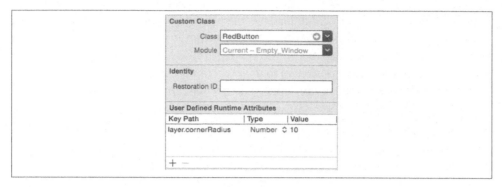

Figure 7-17. Rounding a button's corners with a runtime attribute

Now build and run the project. Sure enough, the button is red!

A further possibility is to take advantage of the User Defined Runtime Attributes in the nib object's Identity inspector. This can allow you to configure, in the nib editor, aspects of a nib object for which the nib editor itself provides no built-in interface. What you're actually doing here is sending the nib object, at nib-loading time, a `setValue:forKey-Path:` message; key paths are discussed in Chapter 10. Naturally, the object needs to be prepared to respond to the given key path, or your app will crash when the nib loads.

For example, one of the disadvantages of the nib editor is that it provides no way to configure layer attributes. Let's say we'd like to use the nib editor to round the corners of our red button. In code, we would do that by setting the button's `layer.corner-Radius` property. The nib editor gives no access to this property. Instead, we can select the button in the nib editor and use the User Defined Runtime Attributes in the Identity inspector. We set the Key Path to `layer.cornerRadius`, the Type to Number, and the Value to whatever value we want — let's say 10 (Figure 7-17). Now build and run; sure enough, the button's corners are now rounded.

You can also configure a custom property of a nib object by making that property *inspectable*. To do so, add the `@IBInspectable` attribute to the property's declaration in your code. This causes the property to be listed in the nib object's Attributes inspector.

For example, let's make it possible to configure our button's border in the nib editor. At the start of the RedButton class declaration body, add this code:

```
@IBInspectable var borderWidth : CGFloat {
    get {
        return self.layer.borderWidth
    }
    set {
        self.layer.borderWidth = newValue
    }
}
```

Figure 7-18. An inspectable property in the nib editor

That code declares a RedButton property, `borderWidth`, and makes it a façade in front of the layer's `borderWidth` property. It also causes the nib editor to display that property in the Attributes inspector for any button that is an instance of the RedButton class (Figure 7-18). The result is that when we give this property a value in the nib editor, that value is sent to the setter for this property at nib-loading time, and the button border appears with that width.

To intervene with a nib object's initialization even earlier, if the object is a UIView (or a UIView subclass), you can implement `init(coder):`. Note that, for a UIView, `init(frame:)` is *not called* during instantiation by the loading of a nib — `init(coder:)` is called instead. (Implementing `init(frame:)`, and then wondering why your code isn't called when the view is instantiated from a nib, is a common beginner mistake.) A minimal implementation would look like this:

```
required init?(coder aDecoder: NSCoder) {
    super.init(coder:aDecoder)
    // your code here
}
```

CHAPTER 8

Documentation

*Knowledge is of two kinds. We know a subject
ourselves, or we know where we can find
information upon it.*

—Samuel Johnson, *Boswell's Life of Johnson*

No aspect of iOS programming is more important than a fluid and nimble relationship with the documentation. There is a huge number of built-in Cocoa classes, with many methods and properties and other details. Apple's documentation, whatever its flaws, is the definitive official word on how you can expect Cocoa to behave, and on the contractual rules incumbent upon you in working with this massive framework whose inner workings you cannot see directly.

The Xcode documentation installed on your machine comes in large chunks called *documentation sets* (or *doc sets*, also called *libraries*). You do not merely install a doc set; you subscribe to it, so that when Apple releases a documentation update, you can obtain the updated version.

When you first install Xcode, the bulk of the documentation is *not* installed on your machine; viewing the documentation in the documentation window (discussed in the next section) may require an Internet connection, so that you can see the online docs at Apple's site. This situation is untenable; you're going to want a copy of the documentation locally, on your own machine.

Therefore, you should start up Xcode immediately after installation to let it download and install your initial doc sets. The process can be controlled and monitored, to some extent, in the Downloads pane of the Preferences window (under Documentation); you can also specify here whether you want updates installed automatically or whether you prefer to click Check and Install Now manually from time to time. This is also where you specify which doc sets you want; I believe that the iOS 9 doc set and the Xcode 7 doc set are all you need for iOS development, but it can't hurt to install the OS X 10.11

doc set as well. You may have to provide your machine's admin password when a doc set is first installed. Doc sets are installed in your home *Library/Developer/Shared/Documentation/DocSets* directory.

The Documentation Window

Your primary access to the documentation is in Xcode, through the documentation window (Window → Documentation and API Reference, or Help → Documentation and API Reference, Command-Shift-0). Within the documentation window, the primary way into the documentation is to do a search; for example, press Command-Shift-0 (or Command-L if you're already in the documentation window), type NSString, and press Return to select the top hit, which is the NSString Class Reference. Click the magnifying glass icon to limit the results to the iOS-related doc sets if desired.

There are two ways to see the results of a search in the documentation window:

Pop-up results window
> If you're actively typing in the search field, a dozen or so primary results are listed in a pop-up window. Click with the mouse, or navigate with arrow keys and press Return, to specify which result you want to view. You can also summon and hide this pop-up window by pressing Esc whenever the search field has focus.

Full results page
> When the search field has focus and the pop-up results window is *not* showing, press Return to see a page listing *all* results of the search; these results are listed on four separate pages, by category: API Reference, SDK Guides, Tools Guides, and Sample Code.

You can also perform a documentation window search starting from *within your code*. You'll very often want to do this: you're looking directly at a symbol (a class name, a method name, a property name, and so on) at its point of use in your code, and you want to know more about it. Hold Option and hover the mouse over a term in your code until a blue dotted underline appears; then (still holding Option) double-click the term. The documentation window opens, and you are taken directly to the explanation of that term within its class documentation page, or to the full results page for a search on that term.

(Similarly, during code completion — discussed in Chapter 9 — you can click the More link to make this same move, jumping directly to the documentation on the current symbol.)

Alternatively, you can select text in your code (or anywhere else) and choose Help → Search Documentation for Selected Text (Command-Option-Control-/). This is the equivalent of typing that text into the search field in the documentation window and asking to see the full results page.

The documentation window behaves basically as a glorified web browser, because the documentation consists essentially of web pages. Multiple pages can appear simultaneously as tabs in the documentation window. To navigate to a new tab, hold Command as you navigate — for example, Command-click a link, or Command-click your choice in the pop-up results window — or choose Open Link in New Tab from the contextual menu. You can navigate between tabs (Window → Show Next Tab), and each tab remembers its navigation history (Navigate → Go Back, or use the Back button in the window toolbar, which is also a pop-up menu).

 You can open in your web browser the local page you're currently viewing in the documentation window: choose Editor → Share → Open in Browser.

A documentation page may be accompanied by a list of related items. The start of the list is shown in a pane above the page; the full list appears in a popover when you click the "More related items" link (Figure 8-1). For example, the related items pane for the NSString Class Reference page includes links to NSString's class inheritance and its adopted protocols, with further information and links in the popover. I'll talk more about a class's related items later in this chapter.

A documentation page may be accompanied by a table of contents, displayed in a pane to the left of the documentation page (Figure 8-1); to see it if it isn't showing, choose Editor → Show Table of Contents, or click the Table of Contents icon in the window toolbar. For example, the NSString Class Reference page has a table of contents pane linking to all the topics and methods listed within the page. Some documentation pages may use the table of contents to show the page's place within a larger group of pages; for example, the String Programming Guide consists of multiple pages, and when you're viewing one, the Table of Contents pane lists all the pages of the String Programming Guide along with each page's main topics.

A full hierarchical table of contents for all doc sets (the *library*) appears at the far left of the documentation window; to see it if it isn't showing, choose Editor → Show Library, or click the Navigator button in the window toolbar. The hierarchy shows all reference documents, along with guides and sample code, clumped together by subject. When viewing a documentation page, to show it in its place within the full hierarchical table of contents, choose Editor → Reveal in Library (or choose Reveal in Library from the contextual menu).

When you encounter a documentation page to which you're likely to want to return, make it a bookmark: choose Editor → Share → Add Bookmark, or click the Share button in the toolbar and choose Add Bookmark, or choose Add Bookmark from the contextual menu, or (easiest of all) click the bookmark icon in the left margin of the documentation page. Bookmarks are displayed at the left of the documentation window, sharing space in the navigator with the full hierarchical table of contents; to see the bookmarks pane if it isn't showing, choose Editor → Show Bookmarks. Icons at the top of the navigator let you switch between the library pane and the bookmarks pane. Click a bookmark in the bookmarks pane to jump to it in the documentation window. Bookmark management is simple but effective: you can rearrange bookmarks or delete a bookmark, and that's all.

To search for text *within* the current documentation page, use the Find menu commands. Find → Find (Command-F) summons a find bar, as in Safari.

A third-party documentation viewer application, such as Dash (*http://kapeli.com/dash*), may provide better searchability and a better view of your local doc sets than the documentation window does. Also, most of the documentation can be accessed using a real web browser at *http://developer.apple.com*, Apple's developer site; this web browser display allows sections to be shown and hidden, it includes an alphabetic searchable index of methods and properties, and it may even show information that the documentation window omits.

Class Documentation Pages

In the vast majority of cases, your target documentation page will be the documentation for a class. It's important to be comfortable and conversant with the typical features and information provided by a class documentation page, so let's pause to notice them (Figure 8-1).

You'll want to keep an eye on the related items information when you're studying a class (click the "More related items" link to see it):

Inherits from
> Lists, and links to, the chain of superclasses. One of the biggest beginner mistakes is failing to consult the documentation up the superclass chain. A class inherits from its superclasses, so the functionality or information you're looking for may be in a superclass. You won't find out about addTarget:action:forControlEvents: from the UIButton class page; that information is in the UIControl class page. You won't find out that a UIButton has a frame property from the UIButton class page; that information is in the UIView class page.

Conforms to
> Lists, and links to, the protocols adopted by this class. Failing to consult the documentation for adopted protocols is a serious beginner mistake. For example, you won't find out that UIViewController gets a viewWillTransitionToSize:with-TransitionCoordinator: event by looking at the UIViewController class documentation page: you have to look in the documentation for the UIContentContainer protocol, which UIViewController adopts.

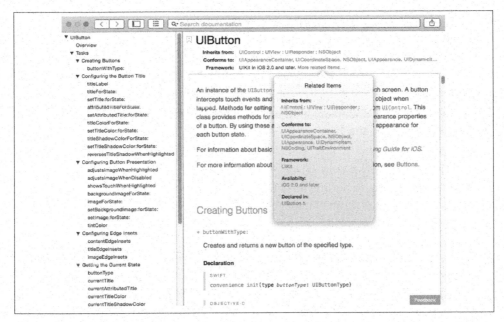

Figure 8-1. The start of the UIButton class documentation page

Framework

Tells what framework this class is part of. Your code must link to this framework, and import this framework's header, in order to use this class; in Swift, it will typically be sufficient to import the framework by its module name (see Chapter 6).

Availability

States the earliest version of the operating system where this class is implemented. For example, the UIView `layoutGuides` property is an array of UILayoutGuide objects. But the UILayoutGuide class wasn't invented until iOS 9. So if you want to use this feature in your app, you must make sure either that your app targets only iOS 9 or later, or that your code never uses this class when your app is running on an earlier system.

Declared in

The header file(s) where this class is declared. Unfortunately this is not a link; I have not found any quick way to view a header file starting from the documentation. That's a pity, as it can often be worth looking at the header file, which may contain helpful comments or other details. You can open the header file from the project window, as explained later in this chapter.

Related documents

If a class documentation page lists a related guide, you might want to click that link and read that guide. For example, the UIView class documentation page lists (and links to) the *View Programming Guide for iOS*. Guides are broad surveys of a topic; they provide important information (including, often, useful code examples), and they can serve to orient your thinking and make you aware of your options.

The body of the class documentation page is divided into sections, which are listed in the table of contents pane:

Overview

Some class pages provide extremely important introductory information in the Overview section, including links to related guides and further information. (See the UIView class documentation page for an example.)

Tasks

This section lists, clumped into categories, the properties and methods of this class.

Constants

Many classes define constants that accompany particular methods. For example, in the UIButton class documentation page, you'll find that, to create a UIButton instance in code, you can call the `init(type:)` initializer; the argument value will be listed under `UIButtonType` in the Constants section.

Finally, let's talk about how a class documentation page lists and explains individual properties and methods. In recent years, this part of the documentation has become quite splendid, with good hyperlinks. Note the following subsections, after the property or method name:

Description

A short summary of what the property or method does.

Declaration

Read this to learn things like the method's parameters and return type.

Parameters and Return Value

Precise information on the meaning and purpose of these.

Discussion

Often contains extremely important further details about how this method behaves. Always pay attention to this section!

Availability

An old class can acquire new methods as the operating system advances; if a newer method is crucial to your app, you might want to exclude your app from running on older operating systems that don't implement the method.

Links to related methods and properties. Very helpful for giving you a larger perspective on how this method fits into the overall behavior of this class.

 Methods injected into a class by a category (Chapter 10) are often *not* listed on that class's documentation page and can be very difficult to discover. For example, awake-FromNib (discussed in Chapter 7) isn't mentioned in the documentation for UIButton or for any of its superclasses or protocols. This is a major weakness in Apple's organization and display of the documentation.

Sample Code

Apple provides plenty of sample code projects, listed in the full table of contents in the documentation window (Editor → Show Library). You can view the code directly *in* the documentation window; sometimes this will be sufficient, but you can see only one file at a time, so it's difficult to get an overview. The alternative is to open the sample code project in Xcode; click the Open Project link at the top of a sample code page in the documentation window. If you're looking at the sample code in your browser at *http://developer.apple.com*, there's a Download Sample Code button. With the sample code project open as a project window, you can read the code, navigate it, edit it, and of course run the project.

As a form of documentation, sample code is both good and bad. It can be a superb source of working code that you can often copy and paste and use with very little alteration in your own projects. It is usually heavily commented, because the Apple folks are aware, as they write the code, that it is intended for instructional purposes. Sample code also illustrates concepts that users have difficulty extracting from the documentation. (Users who have not grasped UITouch handling, for instance, often find that the lightbulb goes on when they discover the MoveMe example.) But the logic of a project is often spread over multiple files, and nothing is more difficult to understand than someone else's code (except, perhaps, your own code). Moreover, what learners most need is not the *fait accompli* of a fully written project but the reasoning process that constructed the project, which no amount of commentary can provide.

My own assessment is that Apple's sample code is uneven. Some of it is a bit careless or even faulty, while some of it is astoundingly well-written. It is generally thoughtful and instructive, though, and is definitely a major component of the documentation; it deserves more appreciation and usage than it seems to get. But it is most useful, I think, after you've reached a certain level of competence and comfort.

Quick Help

Quick Help is a condensed rendering of the documentation on some single topic, usually a symbol name. It appears with regard to the current selection or insertion point automatically in the Quick Help inspector (Command-Option-2) if the inspector is showing. Thus, for example, if you're editing code and the insertion point or selection is within the term `CGPointMake`, documentation for `CGPointMake` appears in the Quick Help inspector if it is visible.

Quick Help is also available in the Quick Help inspector for interface objects selected in the nib editor, for build settings while editing a project or target, and so forth.

Quick Help documentation can also be displayed as a popover window, without the Quick Help inspector. Select a term and choose Help → Quick Help for Selected Item (Command-Control-Shift-?). Alternatively, hold down Option and hover the mouse over a term until the cursor becomes a question mark (and the term turns blue with a dashed underline); then Option-click the term.

 When you're developing Swift code, Quick Help is of increased importance. If you click in the name of a Swift variable whose type is inferred, Quick Help shows the inferred type (see Figure 3-1). This can help you understand compile errors and other surprises.

The Quick Help documentation contains links. For example, click the Reference link to open the full documentation in the documentation window.

You can inject documentation for your own code into Quick Help. To do so, precede a declaration with a comment enclosed in `/**...*/`. (Alternatively, use a sequence of single-line comments starting with `///`.) Within the comment, Markdown formatting can be used (see *http://daringfireball.net/projects/markdown/syntax*); this use of Markdown is new in Xcode 7. The comment becomes the Description field for Quick Help; certain list items (paragraphs beginning with * or - followed by space) are treated in a special way:

- Paragraphs beginning with "Parameter [paramname]:" are incorporated into the Parameters field.
- A paragraph beginning with "Throws:" becomes the Throws field.
- A paragraph beginning with "Returns:" becomes the Returns field.

For example, here's a function declaration with a preceding comment:

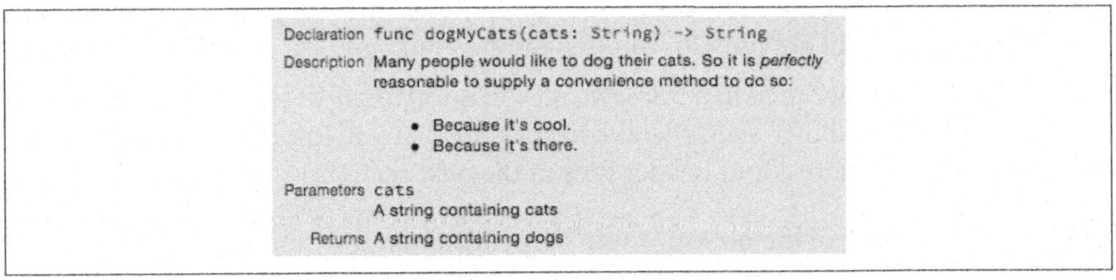

Figure 8-2. Custom documentation injected into Quick Help

```
/**
Many people would like to dog their cats. So it is *perfectly*
reasonable to supply a convenience method to do so:

* Because it's cool.
* Because it's there.

* Parameter cats: A string containing cats

* Returns: A string containing dogs
*/

func dogMyCats(cats:String) -> String {
    return "Dogs"
}
```

The double asterisk in the opening comment delimiter denotes that this is documentation, and the comment's location automatically associates it with the dogMyCats method whose definition follows. The word surrounded by asterisks is formatted as italics; the asterisked paragraphs become bulleted paragraphs; and the last two paragraphs become special fields. The outcome is that when dogMyCats is selected anywhere in my code, its documentation is displayed in Quick Help (Figure 8-2). The first paragraph of the description is also displayed as part of code completion (see Chapter 9).

Symbols

A *symbol* is a declared term, such as the name of a function, variable, or object type. If you can see the name of a symbol in your code in an editor in Xcode, you can jump quickly to the declaration of the symbol. Select text and choose Navigate → Jump to Definition (Command-Control-J). Alternatively, hold down Command and hover the mouse over a prospective term, until the cursor becomes a pointing finger (and the term becomes blue with a solid underline); Command-click the term to jump to the declaration for that symbol. When you do:

- If the symbol is declared in your code, you jump to that declaration in your code; this can be helpful not only for understanding your code but also for navigating it.
- If the symbol is declared in a framework, you jump to the declaration in the header file. If you started in a *.swift* file, the header file that you jump to is translated into Swift. (I'll talk more about header files in the next section.)

The precise meaning of the notion "jump" depends upon the modifier keys you use in addition to the Command key, and on your settings in the Navigation pane of Xcode's preferences. By default, Command-click jumps in the same editor, Command-Option-click jumps in an assistant pane, and Command-double-click jumps in a new window. Similarly, Command-Option-Control-J jumps in an assistant pane to the declaration of the selected term.

Another way to see a list of your project's symbols, and to navigate to a symbol declaration, is through the Symbol navigator (Chapter 6). If the second icon in the filter bar is highlighted, these are symbols declared in your project; if not, symbols from imported frameworks are listed as well.

To jump to the declaration of a symbol whose name you know, even if you don't see the name in the code before you, choose File → Open Quickly (Command-Shift-O). In the search field, type key letters from the name, which will be interpreted intelligently; for example, to search for `application:didFinishLaunchingWithOptions:`, you might type `appdidf`. Possible matches are shown in a scrolling list below the search field; you can navigate this list with the mouse or by keyboard alone. Besides declarations from the framework headers, declarations in your own code are listed as well, so this, too, can be a rapid way of navigating your code.

Header Files

Often, a header file can be a useful form of documentation — possibly the *most* useful form of documentation. The header is necessarily accurate, up-to-date, and complete; the class documentation is not. A header consists chiefly of declarations, but it may also contain comments with helpful information; this, too, can tell you things that the class documentation might not. Also, a single header file can contain declarations for multiple classes and protocols. So it can be an excellent quick reference.

The simplest way to reach a header file is to jump to the declaration of a symbol there. For example, to reach *NSString.h* — the `Foundation.NSString` header file — Command-click on the term `NSString` wherever it may appear in your code. See the previous section for the various ways of jumping to a symbol declaration; since most symbols are declared in header files, these are ways of reaching header files.

When you jump to a header file from your code, if the code that you started from was a Swift file, the header file, if it is written in Objective-C, is spontaneously translated into Swift. That's good because it tells you what you can say in Swift. But it's bad if you were hoping to get a look at the actual Objective-C header! New in Xcode 7, you can switch from a Swift translated (generated) header to the Objective-C original by choosing Navigate > Jump to Original Source (or choose Original Source from the Related Items menu at the left end of the jump bar).

You can learn a lot about the Swift language and the built-in library functions by examining the Swift header file. There are also special Swift header files for Core Graphics and Foundation.

 A useful trick is to write an `import` statement just so that you can Command-click it to reach a header. For example, if you `import Swift` at the top of a *.swift* file, the word `Swift` itself is a symbol that you can Command-click to jump to the Swift header.

Internet Resources

Programming has become a lot easier since the Internet came along and Google started indexing it. It's amazing what you can find out with a Google search. Your problem is very likely one that someone else has faced, solved, and written about on the Internet. Often you'll find sample code that you can paste into your project and adapt.

Apple's documentation resources are available at *http://developer.apple.com/library/*. These resources are updated before the changes are rolled into your doc sets for download. There are also some materials here that aren't part of the Xcode documentation on your computer. For example, you can download the videos for all WWDC 2015 sessions (as well as for some earlier years).

Apple also hosts some developer forums at *https://forums.developer.apple.com*. Some interesting discussions take place here, and they are patrolled by some very helpful Apple employees; but the interface remains extraordinarily clunky.

Other online resources have sprung up spontaneously as iOS programming has become more popular, and lots of iOS and Cocoa programmers blog about their experiences. I am particularly fond of Stack Overflow (*http://www.stackoverflow.com*); it isn't devoted exclusively to iOS programming, of course, but lots of iOS programmers hang out there, questions are answered succinctly and correctly, and the interface lets you focus on the right answer quickly and easily.

CHAPTER 9

Life Cycle of a Project

This chapter surveys some of the main stages in the life cycle of an Xcode project, from inception to submission at the App Store. This survey will provide an opportunity to discuss some additional features of the Xcode development environment: configuring your build settings and your *Info.plist*; editing, debugging, and testing your code; running your app on a device; profiling; localization; and final preparations for the App Store.

Device Architecture and Conditional Code

As you create a project (File → New → Project), after you pick a project template, in the screen where you name your project, the Devices pop-up menu offers a choice of iPad, iPhone, or Universal. You can change this setting later, using the Devices pop-up menu in the General tab when you edit the app target; but your life will be simpler if you decide correctly here, at the outset, because your decision can affect the details of the template on which your new project will be based. Your choice in the Devices pop-up menu also affects your project's Targeted Device Family build setting:

1 *(iPhone)*
> The app will run on an iPhone or iPod touch. It can also run on an iPad, but not as a native iPad app; it runs in a reduced enlargeable window, which I call the *iPhone Emulator* (Apple sometimes refers to this as "compatibility mode").

2 *(iPad)*
> The app will run only on an iPad.

1,2 *(Universal)*
> The app will run natively on both kinds of device.

Two additional project-level build settings determine what systems your device will run on:

Base SDK
The *latest* system your app can run on. As of this writing, in Xcode 7.0, you have just two choices, iOS 9.0 and Latest iOS (iOS 9.0). They sound the same, but the latter is better (and is the default for a new project). If you update Xcode to develop for a subsequent system, any existing projects that are already set to Latest iOS will automatically use that newer system's most recent SDK as their Base SDK, without you having to update their Base SDK setting manually.

iOS Deployment Target
The *earliest* system your app can run on: in Xcode 7, this can be any major iOS system all the way back to iOS 6.0. To change the project's iOS Deployment Target setting easily, edit the project and switch to the Info tab, and choose from the iOS Deployment Target pop-up menu.

Backward Compatibility

Writing an app whose Deployment Target differs from its Base SDK — that is, an app that is *backward compatible* to an earlier system — is something of a challenge. There are two chief problems:

Changed behavior
With each new system, Apple permits itself to change the way some features work. The result is that certain features that exist on different systems may work differently depending what system it is. An entire area of functionality may be handled differently on different systems, requiring you to implement or call a whole different set of methods or use a completely different set of classes. It is even possible that the very same method may do two quite different things, depending on what system the app runs on.

Unsupported features
With each new system, Apple adds new features. Your app will crash if execution encounters features not supported by the system on which it is actually running.

Changed behavior is terribly troublesome, and I have little advice to give you. Often the issue is one of sheer breakage, or breakage and repair. For example, code using UIProgressView's `progressImage` property works in iOS 7, doesn't work at all from iOS 7.1 through iOS 8.4, and works in iOS 9. You have no way of knowing this aside from trial and error, and working your way around it coherently is extremely tricky.

Less unpredictable but just as drastic, alert views are presented using UIAlertView in iOS 7 and before, but with UIAlertController in iOS 8 and later. Your simplest solution would be to keep using UIAlertView even in iOS 8 and later, but you cannot guarantee that this will always work, as UIAlertView is deprecated in iOS 9 and may eventually be dropped altogether — plus, you're robbing yourself of the chance to use UIAlertController, which is a significantly better API. The situation with popovers is similar

(UIPopoverController vs. UIPopoverPresentationController). In this way, improvements from one system to the next present the developer with a nasty paradox: they are desirable, but they make backward compatibility harder.

New in Xcode 7, however, the compiler will at least help you in one way that it never did before — by deliberately making it difficult for your code to use features not supported on the target system. Prior to Xcode 7, if you were to set the project's Deployment Target to an earlier system, *your code would compile* and your app would run on that earlier system, even if it contained features that didn't exist on that earlier system — and then your app would crash on that earlier system if any of those features were actually encountered. In Xcode 7, the compiler will prevent that situation from arising in the first place.

Thus, for example:

```
let arr = self.view.layoutGuides
```

The UIView `layoutGuides` property exists only on iOS 9.0 and later. Formerly, the compiler would permit that code to compile even if your deployment target was, say, iOS 8.0; realizing that that code must never actually *run* on iOS 8 was up to *you*. Now, however, the compiler will stop you with an error: "`layoutGuides` is only available on iOS 9.0 or newer." You cannot proceed until you acknowledge to the compiler that this code is to run only on iOS 9 or later. And Xcode's Fix-It feature will show you how to do that:

```
if #available(iOS 9.0, *) {
    let arr = self.view.layoutGuides
} else {
    // Fallback on earlier versions
}
```

The `#available` condition — an *availability check* — tests the current system against a set of requirements matching the actual availability of a feature as specified in its declaration. The `layoutGuides` property declaration is preceded (in Swift) with this annotation:

```
@available(iOS 9.0, *)
```

For the detailed meaning of that annotation, consult the documentation. But you don't really need to understand it! Your `#available` condition should match that annotation, and Xcode's Fix-It will make sure that it does. You can use `#available` either in an `if` condition or in a `guard` condition.

You can annotate your own type and member declarations with an `@available` attribute, and your code will then have to use an availability check. For example, if a method is declared `@available(iOS 9.0, *)`, then you can't call that method, when the deployment target is earlier than iOS 9, without an availability check. Within such a method, you don't need any `#available(iOS 9.0, *)` availability checks, because you've already guaranteed that this method won't run on a system earlier than iOS 9.

 To *test* your app on an earlier system, you'll need a device, real or simulated, *running* that earlier system. You can download an iOS 8 SDK through Xcode's Downloads preference pane (see Chapter 6), but to test on a system earlier than that, you'll need an older version of Xcode, or preferably an older device. Do not submit to the App Store an app that runs on a system for which you have not tested!

Device Type

It can be useful, in the case of a universal app, to react to whether your code is running on an iPad, on the one hand, or an iPhone or iPod, on the other. The current UIDevice, or the `traitCollection` of any UIViewController or UIView in the hierarchy, will tell you the current device's type as its `userInterfaceIdiom`, which will be a UIUserInterface-Idiom, either `.Phone` or `.Pad`.

You can load resources conditionally depending on the device type or screen resolution. In the case of images loaded from the top level of the app bundle, name suffixes can be used, such as `@2x` and `@3x` to indicate screen resolution, or `~iphone` and `~ipad` to indicate device type; but it is simpler wherever possible to use an asset catalog, and with Xcode 7 and iOS 9 you can do this for any kind of data resource (see "Resources in an asset catalog" on page 315).

Similarly, certain *Info.plist* settings come with name suffixes, so you can adopt one setting on one device type and another setting on another. It is quite common, for example, for a universal app to adopt one set of possible orientations on iPhone and another set on iPad: typically, the iPhone version permits a limited set of orientations and the iPad version permits all orientations. You can configure this in the General pane when you edit the target:

1. Switch the Devices pop-up menu to iPhone and check the desired Device Orientation checkboxes for the iPhone.
2. Switch the Devices pop-up menu to iPad and check the desired Device Orientation checkboxes for the iPad.
3. Switch the Devices pop-up menu to Universal.

Even though you're now seeing just one set of orientations, both sets are remembered. What you've really done is to configure two groups of "Supported interface orientations" settings in the *Info.plist*, a general set (`UISupportedInterfaceOrientations`) and an iPad-only set that overrides the general case when the app runs on an iPad (`UISupported-InterfaceOrientations~ipad`). Examine the *Info.plist* file to see that this is so.

In the same way, your app can load different nib files, and thus can display different interfaces, depending on the device type. For example, you can have two main storyboards, loading one of them at launch if this is an iPhone and the other if this is an iPad. Again, you can configure this in the General pane when you edit the target, and again, what you're really doing is telling the *Info.plist* setting "Main storyboard file base name" to appear twice, once for the general case (`UIMainStoryboardFile`) and once for iPad only (`UIMainStoryboardFile~ipad`). If your app loads a nib file by name, the naming of that nib file works like that of an image file: if there is an alternative nib file by the same name with `~ipad` appended, it will load automatically if we are running on an iPad.

However, you are less likely than in the past to need to distinguish one device type from another. In iOS 7 and before, entire interface object classes (such as popovers) were available only on the iPad; in iOS 8 and later, there are no iPad-only classes, and the interface classes themselves adapt if your code is running on an iPhone. Similarly, in iOS 7 and before, a universal app might need a completely different interface, and hence a different set of nib files, depending on the device type; in iOS 8 and later, size classes allow a single nib file to be configured conditionally depending on the device type. And in general the physical distinction between an iPad and an iPhone is not so sharp as in the past: thanks to the intermediate iPhone 6 and (especially) the iPhone 6 Plus, it's more of a continuum.

Version Control

Sooner rather than later in the life of any real app, you should consider putting your project under version control. Version control is a way of taking periodic snapshots (technically called *commits*) of your project. Its purpose might be:

Security
> Version control can help you store your commits in a repository offsite, so that your code isn't lost in case of a local computer glitch or some equivalent "hit by a bus" scenario.

Collaboration
> Version control affords multiple developers ready, rational access to the same code.

Freedom from fear
> A project is a complicated thing; often, changes must be made experimentally, sometimes in many files, possibly over a period of many days, before a new feature can be tested. Version control means that I can easily retrace my steps (to some previous commit) if things go badly; this gives me confidence to start down some tentative programmatic road whose outcome may not be apparent until much later. Also, if I'm confused about what programmatic road I seem to be taking, I can ask a version control system to list the changes I've made recently. If an ancillary bug

is introduced, I can use version control to pinpoint when it happened and help discover the cause.

Xcode provides various version control facilities, which are geared chiefly to git (*http:// git-scm.com*) and Subversion (*http://subversion.apache.org*, also called svn). This doesn't mean you can't use any other version control system with your projects; it means only that you can't use any other version control system in an integrated fashion from inside Xcode. That's no disaster; there are many other ways to use version control, and even with git and Subversion, it is perfectly possible to ignore Xcode's integrated version control and rely on the Terminal command line, or use a specialized third-party GUI front end such as svnX for Subversion (*http://www.lachoseinteractive.net/en/products*) or SourceTree for git (*http://www.sourcetreeapp.com*).

If you *don't* want to use Xcode's integrated version control, you can turn it off more or less completely. If you uncheck Enable Source Control in the Source Control preference pane, the only thing you'll be able to do is choose Check Out from the Source Control menu, to fetch code from a remote server. If you check Enable Source Control, three additional checkboxes let you select which automatic behaviors you want. Personally, I like to check Enable Source Control along with "Refresh local status automatically," so that Xcode displays a file's status in the Project navigator; I leave the other two checkboxes unchecked, because I'm a manual control kind of person.

When you create a new project, the Save dialog includes a checkbox that offers to place a git repository into your project folder from the outset. This can be purely local to your computer, or you can choose a remote server. If you have no reason to decide otherwise, I suggest that you check that checkbox!

When you open an existing project, if that project is already managed with Subversion or git, Xcode detects this and is ready instantly to display version control information in its interface. If a remote repository is involved, Xcode automatically enters information for it in the Accounts preference pane, which is the unified interface for repository management. To use a remote server without having a working copy checked out from it, enter its information manually in the Accounts preference pane.

Source control actions are available in two places: the Source Control menu and the contextual menu in the Project navigator. To check out and open a project stored on a remote server, choose Source Control → Check Out. Other items in the Source Control menu are obvious, such as Commit, Push, Pull (or Update), Refresh Status, and Discard Changes. Note particularly the first item in the Source Control menu, which lists all open working copies by name and branch; its hierarchical menu items let you perform rudimentary branch management.

Files in the Project navigator are marked with their status. For example, if you're using git, you can distinguish modified files (M), new untracked files (?), and new files added

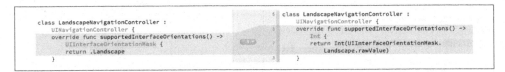

Figure 9-1. Version comparison

to the index (A). (If you've unchecked "Refresh local status automatically," those markings may not appear until you choose Source Control → Refresh Status.)

When you choose Source Control → Commit, you're shown a comparison view of all changes in all changed files. Each change can be excluded from this commit (or reverted entirely), so it's possible to group related file hunks into meaningful commits. A similar comparison view is available for any commit by choosing Source Control → History. (But Xcode has nothing like the visual branch representation of git's own `gitk` tool.) Merge conflicts are also presented in a useful graphical comparison interface.

You can also see a comparison view for the file being currently edited, at any time, through the Version editor; choose View → Version Editor → Show Version Editor, or click the third Editor button in the project window toolbar. The Version editor actually has three modes: Comparison view, Blame view, and Log view (choose from View → Version Editor, or use the pop-up menu from the third Editor button in the toolbar).

For example, in Figure 9-1, I can see that in the more recent version of this file (on the left) I've changed my `supportedInterfaceOrientations` implementation (because the Swift language changed). If I choose Editor → Copy Source Changes, the corresponding diff text (a patch file) is placed on the clipboard. If I switch to Blame view I can see my own commit message. The jump bar at the bottom of the Version editor permits me to view any commit's version of the current file in the editor.

Another way to learn how a line was changed is to select within that line (in the normal editor) and choose Editor → Show Blame For Line. A popover appears, describing the commit where this line changed to its current form; using buttons in that popover, you can switch to Blame view or Comparison view.

Editing and Navigating Your Code

Many aspects of Xcode's editing environment can be modified to suit your tastes. Your first step should be to pick a Source Editor font face and size you like in Xcode's Fonts & Colors preference pane. Nothing is so important as being able to read and write code comfortably! I like a largish size (13, 14 or even 16) and a pleasant monospaced font such as Menlo or Consolas, or the freeware Inconsolata (*http://levien.com/type/myfonts/*) or Source Code Pro (*https://github.com/adobe-fonts/source-code-pro*).

Xcode has some automatic formatting, autotyping, and text selection features. Their exact behavior depends upon your settings in the Editing and Indentation tabs of Xcode's Text Editing preference pane. I'm not going to describe these settings in detail, but I urge you to take advantage of them. Under Editing, I like to check just about everything, including Line Numbers; visible line numbers are useful when debugging. Under Indentation, I like to have just about everything checked too; I find the way Xcode lays out code to be excellent with these settings.

 If you like Xcode's smart syntax-aware indenting, but you find that once in a while a line of code isn't indenting itself correctly, choose Editor → Structure → Re-Indent (Control-I), which autoindents the current line or selection.

With "Enable type-over completions" checked, Xcode helps balance delimiters. For example, suppose I intend to make a UIView by calling its initializer init(frame:). I type as far as this:

```
let v = UIView(fr
```

Xcode automatically appends the closing right parenthesis, with the insertion point still positioned before it:

```
let v = UIView(fr)
// I have typed ^
```

That closing right parenthesis, however, is tentative; it's in gray. Now I finish typing the parameter; the right parenthesis is *still* gray:

```
let v = UIView(frame:r)
//       I have typed ^
```

I can now confirm the closing right parenthesis in any of several ways: I can actually type a right parenthesis, or I can type Tab or Right arrow. The tentative right parenthesis is replaced by a real right parenthesis, and the insertion point is now positioned after it, ready for me to continue typing. Xcode behaves similarly with double quotes, right curly braces, right square brackets, and so on.

Autocompletion

As you write code, you'll take advantage of Xcode's autocompletion feature. Cocoa type names and method names are astonishingly verbose, and whatever reduces your time and effort typing will be a relief. However, I personally do *not* check "Suggest completions while typing" under Editing; instead, I check "Use Escape key to show completion suggestions," and when I want autocompletion to happen, I ask for it manually, by pressing Esc.

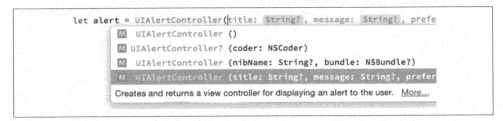

Figure 9-2. The autocompletion menu

For example, suppose I want my code to create an alert. I type as far as `UIAlert-Controller(` and press Esc. A menu pops up, listing the four initializers appropriate to a UIAlertController (Figure 9-2). You can navigate this menu, dismiss it, or accept the selection, using only the keyboard. So, if it were not already selected by default, I would navigate to `title:...` with the Down arrow key, and press Return to accept the selected choice.

When I choose from the autocompletion menu, the template for the method call is entered in my code (I've broken it into multiple lines here):

```
let alert = UIAlertController(
    title: <#String?#>,
    message: <#String?#>,
    preferredStyle: <#UIAlertControllerStyle#>)
```

The expressions in `<#...#>` are *placeholders*, showing the type of each parameter. They appear in Xcode as cartouche-like "text tokens" (see Figure 9-2) to prevent them from being edited accidentally. You can select the next placeholder with Tab or by choosing Navigate → Jump to Next Placeholder (Control-/). Thus I can select a placeholder and type over it, entering the actual argument I wish to pass, select the next placeholder and type that argument, and so forth. To convert a placeholder to a normal string without the delimiters, select it and press Return, or double-click it.

Autocompletion and its contextual intelligence works for object type names, method calls, and property names. It also works when you're entering a declaration for a function that's inherited or defined in an adopted protocol. You don't need to type even the initial `func`; just type the first few letters of the method's name. For example, in my app delegate class I might type:

```
applic
```

If I then press Esc, I see a list of methods such as `application:didFinishLaunchWith-Options:`; these are methods that might be sent to my app delegate (by virtue of its being the app delegate, as discussed in Chapter 11). When I choose one, the entire declaration is filled in for me, including the curly braces:

```
func application(application: UIApplication,
    didFinishLaunchingWithOptions launchOptions: [NSObject : AnyObject]?)
    -> Bool {
        <#code#>
}
```

A placeholder for the code appears between the curly braces, and it is selected, ready for me to start entering the body of the function. If a function needs an override designation, Xcode's code completion provides it.

Snippets

Code autocompletion is supplemented by code snippets. A code snippet is a bit of text with an abbreviation. Code snippets are kept in the Code Snippet library (Command-Option-Control-2), but a code snippet's abbreviation is globally available to code completion, so you can use a snippet without showing the library: you type the abbreviation and the snippet's name is included among the possible completions.

For example, to enter a class declaration at the top level of a file, I would type class and press Esc, to get autocompletion, and select "Swift Class" or "Swift Subclass." When I press Return, the template appears in my code: the class name and superclass name are placeholders, the curly braces are provided, and the body of the declaration (between the curly braces) is another placeholder.

To learn a snippet's abbreviation, you must open its editing window — double-click the snippet in the Code Snippet library — and click Edit. If learning a snippet's abbreviation is too much trouble, simply drag the snippet from the Code Snippet library into your text. The filter bar (Edit → Filter → Filter in Library, Command-Option-L) helps you reach a snippet by name quickly.

You can add your own snippets, which will be categorized as User snippets; the easiest way is to drag text into the Code Snippet library. Edit to suit your taste, providing a name, a description, and an abbreviation; the Completion Scopes pop-up menu lets you narrow the contexts in which the snippet will be available through code completion. In the text of the snippet, use the <#...#> construct to form any desired placeholders.

For example, I've created an outlet snippet defined like this:

```
@IBOutlet var <#name#> : <#type#>!
```

And I've created an action snippet defined like this:

```
@IBAction func <#name#> (sender:AnyObject!) {
    <#code#>
}
```

My other snippets constitute a personal library of utility functions that I've developed. For example, my delay snippet inserts my dispatch_after wrapper function (see "Delayed Performance" on page 501).

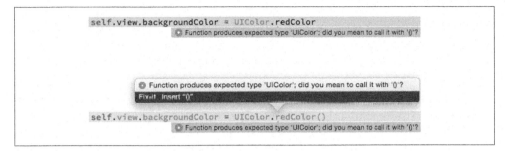

Figure 9-3. A compile error with a Fix-it suggestion

Fix-it and Live Syntax Checking

Xcode's Fix-it feature can make *and implement* positive suggestions on how to avert a problem. To summon it, click on an issue badge in the gutter. Such an issue badge will appear after compilation if there's a problem.

For instance, Figure 9-3, at the top, shows that I've accidentally forgotten the parentheses after a method call. This causes a compile error, because the backgroundColor property that I'm trying to set is a UIColor, not a function. But the stop-sign icon next to the error tells me that Fix-it has a suggestion. I click the stop-sign icon, and Figure 9-3, at the bottom, shows what happens: a Fix-It dialog pops up, telling me how it proposes to fix the problem — by inserting the parentheses. Moreover, Xcode is showing me what my code would look like if Fix-It *did* fix the problem in this way. If I press Return, or double-click the "Fix-it" suggestion in the dialog, Xcode *really* inserts the parentheses — and the error vanishes, because the problem is solved.

 If you're confident that Xcode will do the right thing, choose Editor → Fix All in Scope (Command-Option-Control-F), and Xcode will implement *all* nearby Fix-it suggestions without your even having to show the dialog.

Live syntax checking is like a form of continual compilation. Even if you don't compile or save, live syntax checking can detect the presence of a problem, and can suggest the solution with Fix-it. This feature can be toggled on or off using the "Show live issues" checkbox in the General preference pane.

Personally, I find live syntax checking intrusive. My code is almost never valid while I'm in the middle of typing, because the terms and parentheses are always half-finished; that's what it means to be typing! For example, merely typing the first letter of let will instantly cause the syntax checker to complain of an unresolved identifier; I hate that. So I've got "Show live issues" unchecked.

Navigation

Developing an Xcode project involves editing code in many files at once. Fortunately, Xcode provides numerous ways to navigate your code, many of which have been mentioned in previous chapters. Here are some of Xcode's chief forms of navigation:

The Project navigator
> If you know something about the name of a file, you can find it quickly in the Project navigator (Command-1) by typing into the search field in the filter bar at the bottom of the navigator (Edit → Filter → Filter in Navigator, Command-Option-J). For example, type story to see just your *.storyboard* files. Moreover, after using the filter bar, you can press Tab and then the Up or Down arrow key to navigate the Project navigator; thus you can reach the desired file with the keyboard alone.

The Symbol navigator
> If you highlight the first two icons in the filter bar (the first two are blue, the third is dark), the Symbol navigator lists your project's object types and their members. Click on a symbol to navigate to its declaration in the editor. As with the Project navigator, the filter bar's search field can help get you where you want to go.

The jump bar
> Every path component of the code editor's jump bar is a menu:

> *The bottom level*
> > At the bottom level (farthest right) in the jump bar is a list of your file's object and member declarations, in the order in which they appear (hold Command while choosing the menu to see them in alphabetical order); choose one to navigate to it.

> > You can inject bold section titles into this bottom-level menu using a comment whose first word is MARK:. For example, try modifying *ViewController.swift* in our Empty Window project:

> > ```
> > // MARK: - view lifecycle
> > override func viewDidLoad() {
> >     super.viewDidLoad()
> > }
> > ```

> > The result is that the viewDidLoad item in the bottom-level menu is preceded by view lifecycle. To make a divider line in the menu, type a MARK: comment whose value is a hyphen; in the preceding example, both a hyphen (to make a divider line) and a title (to make a bold title) are used. Similarly, comments starting with TODO: and FIXME: will appear in the bottom-level menu.

> *Higher levels*
> > Higher-level path components are hierarchical menus; thus you can use any of them to work your way down the file hierarchy.

History

Each editor pane remembers the names of files you've edited in it. The Back and Forward triangles are both buttons and pop-up menus (or choose Navigate → Go Back and Navigate → Go Forward, Command-Control-Left and Command-Control-Right).

Related items

The leftmost button in the jump bar summons the Related Items menu, a hierarchical menu of files related to the current file, such as superclasses and adopted protocols. This list even includes functions that call or are called by the currently selected function.

 A path component menu in the jump bar can be filtered! Start typing while a jump bar menu is open, to filter what the menu displays. This filtering uses an "intelligent" search, not a strict text containment search; for example, typing "adf" will find `application:didFinishLaunchingWithOptions:` (if it's present in the menu).

The Assistant pane

The Assistant pane lets you be in two places at once (see Chapter 6). Hold Option while navigating to open something in an Assistant pane instead of the primary editor pane. The Tracking menu in an Assistant pane's jump bar sets its automatic relationship to the main pane.

Tabs and windows

You can also be in two places at once by opening a tab or a separate window (again, see Chapter 6).

Jump to definition

Navigate → Jump to Definition (Command-Control-J) lets you jump to the declaration of the symbol already selected in your code.

Open quickly

File → Open Quickly (Command-Shift-O) opens a dialog where you can search for a symbol in your code and in the framework headers.

Breakpoints

The Breakpoint navigator lists all breakpoints in your code. Xcode lacks code bookmarks, but you can misuse a disabled breakpoint as a bookmark. Breakpoints are discussed later in this chapter.

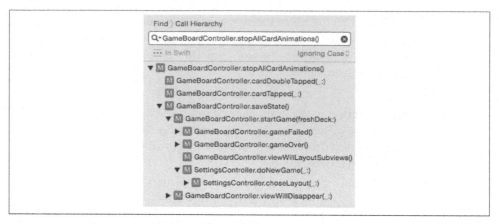

Figure 9-4. A call hierarchy in the Find navigator

Finding

Finding is a form of navigation. Xcode has both a global find (Find → Find in Project, Command-Shift-F), which is the same as using the Find navigator, and an editor-level find (Find → Find, Command-F); don't confuse them.

Find options are all-important. For editor-level find, click the magnifying glass icon in the search field to get the Edit Find Options item. You can search for word middles or word starts, case sensitive or insensitive — you can even find using regular expressions. There's a lot of power lurking here! The global find options appear above and below the search field, and include a scope, allowing you to specify in sophisticated ways which files will be searched: click the current scope to see the Search Scopes panel, where you can select a different scope or create a custom scope.

Global find options above the search field include Text, Regular Expression, Definitions (where a symbol is defined), and References (where a symbol is used). New in Xcode 7 is the Call Hierarchy find option, which allows you to trace the nests of calls backwards through your code. Click the second item in the search bar to summon the pop-up menu, and choose Call Hierarchy; alternatively, select a term in your code and choose Find → Find Call Hierarchy (Shift-Control-Command-H). The call hierarchy is displayed inverted in the Find navigator (Figure 9-4).

To replace text, click the word Find at the left end of the search bar to summon the pop-up menu, and choose Replace. You can replace all occurrences (Replace All), or select particular find results in the Find navigator and replace only those (Replace); you can also *delete* find results from the Find navigator, to protect them from being affected by Replace All. The Find navigator's Preview button summons a dialog that shows you the effect of each possible replacement, and lets you accept or reject particular replacements in advance of performing the replacement. For editor-level find, hold Option before clicking Replace All, to find-and-replace within only the current selection.

A sophisticated form of editor-level find is Editor → Edit All In Scope, which finds simultaneously all occurrences of the currently selected term within the same scope; you can use this to change the name of a variable or function throughout its scope, or just to survey how the name is used.

Running in the Simulator

When you build and run with the Simulator as the destination, you run in the iOS Simulator application. The Simulator window represents a device. Depending on your app target's Base SDK, Deployment Target, and Targeted Device Family build settings, and on what SDKs you have installed, you may have choices about the device and system to be represented by the Simulator as you choose your destination before running (see Chapter 6).

The Simulator window can be displayed at various sizes: choose from Window → Scale. This is a matter of display merely, comparable to zooming the window. For example, you might run a double-resolution device in the Simulator at full size to see every pixel, or at half size to save space.

You can interact with the Simulator in some of the same basic ways as you would a device. Using the mouse, you can tap on the device's screen; hold Option to make the mouse represent two fingers moving symmetrically around their common center, and Option-Shift to represent two fingers moving in parallel. To click the Home button, choose Hardware → Home (Command-Shift-H). Items in the Hardware menu also let you perform hardware gestures such as rotating the device, shaking it, and locking its screen; you can also test your app by simulating certain rare events, such as a low-memory situation.

 Clicking the Home button to switch from the app you're running in Xcode to the home screen does *not* stop your app running, in Xcode or the Simulator. To quit your app in the Simulator, quit the Simulator, or switch to Xcode and choose Product → Stop.

The Debug menu in the Simulator is useful for detecting problems with animations and drawing. Toggle Slow Animations makes animations unfold in slow motion so that you can see in detail what's happening. The next four menu items (their names begin with Color) are similar to features available when running using Instruments, under the Core Animation instrument, revealing possible sources of inefficiency in screen drawing.

The Debug menu also lets you open the log in the Console application, and lets you set the simulated device's location (useful when testing a Core Location app).

Debugging

Debugging is the art of figuring out what's wrong with the behavior of your app as it runs. I divide this art into two main techniques: caveman debugging and pausing your running app.

Caveman Debugging

Caveman debugging consists of altering your code, usually temporarily, typically by adding code to dump informative messages into the console. You can view the console in the Debug pane; Chapter 6 describes a technique for displaying the console in a tab of its own.

The standard Swift command for sending a message to the console is the `print` function. Using Swift's string interpolation and the CustomStringConvertible protocol (which requires a `description` property; see Chapter 4), you can pack a lot of useful information into a `print` call. Cocoa objects generally have built-in `description` property implementations. For example:

```
print(self.view)
```

The output in the console reads something like this (I've formatted it for clarity here):

```
<UIView: 0x79121d40;
    frame = (0 0; 320 480);
    autoresize = RM+BM;
    layer = <CALayer: 0x79121eb0>>
```

We learn the object's class, its address in memory (useful for confirming whether two instances are in fact the same instance), and the values of some additional properties.

If you're importing Foundation — and in real life iOS programming, you are — you also have access to the `NSLog` C function. It takes an NSString which operates as a format string, followed by the format arguments. A *format string* is a string containing symbols called *format specifiers*, for which values (the format arguments) will be substituted at runtime. All format specifiers begin with a percent sign (%), so the only way to enter a literal percent sign in a format string is as a double percent sign (%%). The character(s) following the percent sign specify the type of value that will be supplied at runtime. The most common format specifiers are `%@` (an object reference), `%d` (an int), `%ld` (a long), and `%f` (a double). For example:

```
NSLog("the view: %@", self.view)
```

In that example, `self.view` is the first (and only) format argument, so its value will be substituted for the first (and only) format specifier, `%@`, when the format string is printed in the console:

```
2015-01-26 10:43:35.314 Empty Window[23702:809945]
   the view: <UIView: 0x7c233b90;
      frame = (0 0; 320 480);
      autoresize = RM+RM;
      layer = <CALayer: 0x7c233d00>>
```

I like `NSLog`'s output because it provides the current time and date, along with the process name, process ID, and thread ID (useful for determining whether two logging statements are called on the same thread). Also, `NSLog` is thread-safe, whereas it appears that `print` is not.

For the complete repertory of format specifiers available in a format string, read Apple's document *String Format Specifiers* (in the *String Programming Guide*). The format specifiers are largely based on those of the C `printf` standard library function.

The main ways to go wrong with `NSLog` (or any format string) are to supply a different number of format arguments from the number of format specifiers in the string, or to supply an argument value different from the type declared by the corresponding format specifier. I often see beginners claim that logging shows a certain value to be nonsense, when in fact it is their `NSLog` call that is nonsense; for example, a format specifier was `%d` but the value of the corresponding argument was a float. Another common mistake is treating an NSNumber as if it were the type of number it contains; an NSNumber isn't any kind of number — it's an object (`%@`). Problems with signed vs. unsigned integers, or 32-bit vs. 64-bit numbers, can be tricky as well.

C structs are not objects, so they cannot provide a `description`. But Swift extends some of the most common C structs as Swift structs, and thus allows them to be printed with `print`. Thus, for example, this works:

```
print(self.view.frame) // (0.0,0.0,320.0,480.0)
```

However, you can't do the same thing with `NSLog`. For this reason, common Cocoa structs are usually accompanied by convenience functions that render them as strings. For example:

```
NSLog("%@", NSStringFromCGRect(self.view.frame)) // {{0, 0}, {320, 480}}
```

 Swift defines four special literals, particularly useful when logging because they describe their own position in the surrounding file: __FILE__, __LINE__, __COLUMN__, and __FUNCTION__.

Figure 9-5. Defining a Swift flag

You will probably want to remove your logging calls before shipping your app, as you won't want your finished app to dump unnecessary messages into the console. A useful trick is to put your own global function in front of Swift's `print` function:

```
func print(object: Any) {
    Swift.print(object)
}
```

When it's time to stop logging, just comment out the second line:

```
func print(object: Any) {
    // Swift.print(object)
}
```

If you prefer this to be automatic, you can use *conditional compilation*. Swift's conditional compilation is rudimentary, but it's sufficient for this task. For example, we can make the body of our function depend upon a `DEBUG` flag:

```
func print(object: Any) {
    #if DEBUG
        Swift.print(object)
    #endif
}
```

That code depends upon a `DEBUG` flag that doesn't actually exist. To make it exist, create it in your target's build settings, under Other Swift Flags. The value that defines a flag called `DEBUG` is `-D DEBUG`. If you define this for the Debug configuration but not for the Release configuration (Figure 9-5), then a debug build (build and run in Xcode) will log with `print`, but a release build (archive and submit to the App Store) will not.

Another useful form of caveman debugging is deliberately aborting your app because something has gone seriously wrong. See the discussion of `assert`, `precondition`, and `fatalError` in Chapter 5. `precondition` and `fatalError` work even in a Release build. By default, `assert` never fails in a Release build, so it is safe to leave it in your code when your app is ready to ship; by that time, of course, you should be confident that the bad situation your `assert` was intended to detect has been debugged and will never actually occur.

Purists may scoff at caveman debugging, but I use it heavily: it's easy, informative, and lightweight. And sometimes it's the only way. Unlike the debugger, console logging

Figure 9-6. A breakpoint

works with any build configuration (Debug or Release) and wherever your app runs (in the Simulator or on a device). It works when pausing is impossible (because of threading issues, for example). It even works on someone else's device, such as a tester to whom you've distributed your app. It's a little tricky for a tester to get a look at the console so as to be able to report back to you, but it can be done: for example, the tester can connect the device to a computer and view its log in Xcode's Devices window.

The Xcode Debugger

When you're building and running in Xcode, you can pause in the debugger and use Xcode's debugging facilities. The important thing, if you want to use the debugger, is that the app should be built with the Debug build configuration (the default for a scheme's Run action). The debugger is not very helpful against an app built with the Release build configuration, not least because compiler optimizations can destroy the correspondence between steps in the compiled code and lines in your code.

Breakpoints

There isn't a strong difference between running and debugging in Xcode; the main distinction is whether breakpoints are effective or ignored. The effectiveness of breakpoints can be toggled at two levels:

Globally (active vs. inactive)
> Breakpoints as a whole are either *active or inactive*. If breakpoints are inactive, we won't pause at any breakpoints.

Individually (enabled vs. disabled)
> A given breakpoint is either *enabled or disabled*. Even if breakpoints are active, we won't pause at this one if it is disabled. Disabling a breakpoint allows you to leave in place a breakpoint that you might need later without pausing at it every time it's encountered.

To create a breakpoint (Figure 9-6), select in the editor the line where you want to pause, and choose Debug → Breakpoints → Add Breakpoint at Current Line (Command-\). This keyboard shortcut toggles between adding and removing a breakpoint for the current line. The breakpoint is symbolized by an arrow in the gutter. Alternatively, a simple click in the gutter adds a breakpoint; to remove a breakpoint gesturally, drag it out of the gutter.

Figure 9-7. A disabled breakpoint

To disable a breakpoint at the current line, click on the breakpoint in the gutter to toggle its enabled status. Alternatively, Control-click on the breakpoint and choose Disable Breakpoint in the contextual menu. A dark breakpoint is enabled; a light breakpoint is disabled (Figure 9-7).

To toggle the active status of breakpoints as a whole, click the Breakpoints button in the bar at the top of the Debug pane, or choose Debug → Activate/Deactivate Breakpoints (Command-Y). The active status of breakpoints as a whole doesn't affect the enabled or disabled status of any breakpoints; if breakpoints are inactive, they are simply ignored *en masse*, and no pausing at breakpoints takes place. Breakpoint arrows are blue if breakpoints are active, gray if they are inactive.

Once you have some breakpoints in your code, you'll want to survey and manage them. That's what the Breakpoint navigator is for. Here you can navigate to a breakpoint, enable or disable a breakpoint by clicking on its arrow in the navigator, and delete a breakpoint.

You can also edit a breakpoint's behavior. Control-click on the breakpoint, in the gutter or in the Breakpoint navigator, and choose Edit Breakpoint; or Command-Option-click the breakpoint. This is a very powerful facility: you can have a breakpoint pause only under a certain condition or after it has been encountered a certain number of times, and you can have a breakpoint perform one or more actions when it is encountered, such as issuing a debugger command, logging, playing a sound, speaking text, or running a script.

A breakpoint can be configured to continue automatically after performing its action when it is encountered. This can be an excellent alternative to caveman debugging: instead of inserting a print or NSLog call, which must be compiled into your code and later removed when the app is released, you can set a breakpoint that logs and continues. By definition, such a breakpoint operates only when you're actively debugging the project; it won't dump any messages into the console when the app runs on a user's device, because there are no breakpoints on a user's device.

Certain special kinds of breakpoint can be created in the Breakpoint navigator — click the Plus button at the bottom of the navigator and choose from its pop-up menu — or by choosing from the Debug → Breakpoints hierarchical menu:

Exception breakpoint
> An exception breakpoint causes your app to pause at the time an exception is thrown or caught, without regard to whether the exception would crash your app later. I recommend that you create an exception breakpoint to pause on all exceptions

when they are thrown, because this gives the best view of the call stack and variable values at the moment of the exception (rather than later when the crash actually occurs); you can see where you are in your code, and you can examine variable values, which may help you understand the cause of the problem. If you do create such an exception breakpoint, I also suggest that you use the contextual menu to say Move Breakpoint To → User, which makes this breakpoint permanent and global to all your projects.

 Sometimes Apple's code will throw an exception and catch it, deliberately. This isn't a crash, and nothing has gone wrong; but if you've created an exception breakpoint, your app will pause at it, which can be confusing.

Symbolic breakpoint

A symbolic breakpoint causes your app to pause when a certain method or function is called, regardless of what object called it or to what object the message is sent. A method may be specified in one of two ways:

Using Objective-C notation

The instance method or class method symbol (- or +) followed by square brackets containing the class name and the method name. For example:

```
-[UIApplication beginReceivingRemoteControlEvents]
```

By method name

The method name alone. The debugger will resolve this for you into all possible class–method pairs, as if you had entered them using the Objective-C notation that I just described. For example:

```
beginReceivingRemoteControlEvents
```

If you enter the method name (or class name) incorrectly, the symbolic breakpoint won't do anything. In general, you'll know if you got it right, because you'll see the resolved breakpoint listed hierarchically below yours.

Paused at a breakpoint

When the app runs with breakpoints active and an enabled breakpoint is encountered (and assuming its conditions are met, and so on), the app pauses. In the active project window, the editor shows the file containing the point of execution, which will usually be the file containing the breakpoint. The point of execution is shown as a green arrow; this is the line that is *about* to be executed (Figure 9-8). Depending on the settings for Running → Pauses in the Behaviors preference pane, the Debug navigator and the Debug pane may also appear.

Here are some things you might like to do while paused at a breakpoint:

Figure 9-8. Paused at a breakpoint

See where you are

One common reason for setting a breakpoint is to make sure that the path of execution is passing through a certain line. Functions listed in the call stack in the Debug navigator with a User icon, with the text in black, are yours; click one to see where you are paused in that function. (Listings with the text in gray are functions and methods for which you have no source code, so there would be little point clicking one unless you know something about assembly language.) You can also view and navigate the call stack using the jump bar at the top of the Debug pane.

Study variable values

In the Debug pane, variable values for the current scope (corresponding to what's selected in the call stack) are visible in the variables list. You can see additional object features, such as collection elements, properties, and even some private information, by opening triangles. (Local variable values are shown even if, at the point where you are paused, those variables have not yet been initialized; *such values are meaningless,* so ignore them.)

You can use the search field to filter variables by name or value. If a formatted summary isn't sufficiently helpful, you can send `description` (or, if this object adopts CustomDebugStringConvertible, `debugDescription`) to an object variable and view the output in the console: choose Print Description of [Variable] from the contextual menu, or select the variable and click the Info button below the variables list.

You can also view a variable's value graphically: select the variable and click the Quick Look button (an eye icon) below the variables list, or press Spacebar. For example, in the case of a CGRect, the graphical representation is a correctly proportioned rectangle. You can make instances of your own custom class viewable in the same way; declare the following method and return an instance of one of the permitted types (see Apple's *Quick Look for Custom Types in the Xcode Debugger*):

```
@objc func debugQuickLookObject() -> AnyObject {
    // ... create and return your graphical object here ...
}
```

You can also inspect a variable's value in place in your code, by examining its data tip. To see a data tip, hover the mouse over the name of a variable in your code. The data tip is much like the display of this value in the variables list: there's a flippy triangle that you can open to see more information, plus an Info button that displays

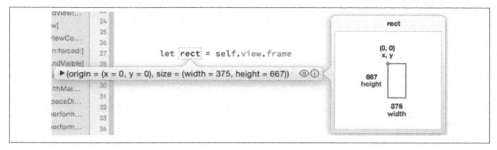

Figure 9-9. A data tip

the value description here and in the console, and a Quick Look button for showing
a value graphically (Figure 9-9).

Inspect your view hierarchy

You can study the view hierarchy while paused in the debugger. Click the Debug
View Hierarchy button in the bar at the top of the Debug pane, or choose Debug
→ View Debugging → Capture View Hierarchy. Views are listed in an outline in
the Debug navigator. The editor displays your views; this is a three-dimensional
projection that you can rotate. The Object inspector and Size inspector display
information about the currently selected view.

Manage expressions

An expression is code to be added to the variables list and evaluated every time we
pause. Choose Add Expression from the contextual menu in the variables list. The
expression is evaluated within the current context in your code, so be careful of side
effects.

Talk to the debugger

You can communicate directly with the debugger through the console. Xcode's debugger interface is a front end to the *real* debugger, LLDB (*http://lldb.llvm.org*); by
talking directly to LLDB, you can do everything that you can do through the Xcode
debugger interface, and more. Common commands are:

`fr v` *(short for* `frame variable`*)*

Alone, prints out all variables locally in scope, similar to the display in the
variables list. Alternatively, can be followed by the name of a variable you want
to examine.

`po` *(meaning "print object")*

Followed by the name of an object variable in scope, similar to Print Description: displays the object variable's value in accordance with its `description` or
`debugDescription`.

p (*or* expression, expr, *or simply* e)
Evaluates, in the current context, *any* expression in the current language.

Fiddle with breakpoints

You are free to create, destroy, edit, enable and disable, and otherwise manage breakpoints dynamically even while your app is running, which is useful because where you'd like to pause next might depend on what you learn while you're paused here. Indeed, this is one of the main advantages of breakpoints over caveman debugging. To change your caveman debugging, you have to stop the app, edit it, rebuild it, and start running the app all over again. But to fiddle with breakpoints, you don't have to be stopped; you don't even have to be paused! An operation that went wrong, if it doesn't crash your app, can probably be repeated in real time; so you can just add a breakpoint and try again. For example, if tapping a button produces the wrong results, you can add a breakpoint to the action handler and tap the button again; you pass through the same code, and this time you can work out what the trouble is.

Step or continue

To proceed with your paused app, you can either resume running until the next breakpoint is encountered (Debug → Continue) or take one step and pause again. Also, you can select in a line and choose Debug → Continue to Current Line (or Continue to Here from the contextual menu), which effectively sets a breakpoint at the chosen line, continues, and removes the breakpoint. The stepping commands (in the Debug menu) are:

Step Over
Pause at the next line.

Step Into
Pause in your function that the current line calls, if there is one; otherwise, pause at the next line.

Step Out
Pause when we return from the current function.

You can access these commands through convenient buttons in the bar at the top of the Debug pane. Even if the Debug pane is collapsed, the bar containing the buttons appears while running.

Start over, or abort

To kill the running app, click Stop in the toolbar (Product → Stop, Command-Period). Clicking the Home button in the Simulator (Hardware → Home) or on the device does *not* stop the running app in the multitasking world of iOS 4 and later. To kill the running app and relaunch it without rebuilding it, Control-click Run in the toolbar (Product → Perform Action → Run Without Building, Command-Control-R).

You can make changes to your code while the app is running or paused, but those changes are not magically communicated to the running app; there are programming milieus where that sort of thing is possible, but Xcode is not among them. You must stop the app and run in the normal way (which includes building) to see your changes in action.

Testing

A *test* is code that isn't part of your app target; its purpose is to make sure that your app works as expected. Tests can be of two kinds:

Unit tests
A unit test exercises your app target *internally*, from the point of view of its *code*. For example, a unit test might call some method in your app target code, handing it various parameters and looking to see if the expected result is returned each time, not just under normal conditions but also when incorrect or extreme inputs are supplied.

Interface (UI) tests
An interface test (new in Xcode 7) exercises your app *externally*, from the point of view of a *user*. Such a test guides your app through use case scenarios by effectively tapping buttons with a ghost finger, watching to make sure that the interface behaves as expected.

Tests should ideally be written and run constantly as you develop your app. It can even be useful to write unit tests *before* writing the real code, as a way of developing a working algorithm. Having initially ascertained that your code passes your tests, you continue to run those tests to detect whether a bug has been introduced during the course of development.

Tests are bundled in a separate target of your project (see Chapter 6). The application templates give you an opportunity to add a test target at the time you create your project: in the second dialog ("Choose options"), where you name your project, you can check Include Unit Tests or Include UI Tests, or both. Alternatively, you can easily create a new test target at any time: make a new target and specify iOS → Test → iOS Unit Testing Bundle or iOS UI Testing Bundle. Your tests do not run until you explicitly run them. Tests can be managed and run easily from the Test navigator (Command-5) as well as from within a test class file.

A test class is a subclass of XCTestCase (which is itself a subclass of XCTest). A test method is an instance method of a test class, returning no value and taking no parameters, whose name starts with `test`. The test target depends upon the app target, meaning that before a test class can be compiled and built, the app target must be compiled and built. Running a test also runs the app; the test target's product is a bundle, which is loaded into the app as it launches.

A test method may call one or more test asserts; in Swift, these are global functions whose names begin with XCTAssert. For a list of these functions, see Apple's document *Testing With Xcode*, in the "Writing Test Classes and Methods" chapter, under "Assertions Listed by Category." Unlike the corresponding Objective-C macros, the Swift test assert functions do *not* take format strings (the way NSLog does); each takes a single, simple message string. Test assert functions marked as being "for scalars" are not really for scalars in Swift, because in Swift there are no scalars (as opposed to objects): they apply to any types that adopt Equatable or Comparable.

A test class may also contain utility methods that are called by the test methods. In addition, you can override any of four special methods inherited from XCTestCase:

setUp *class method*
> Called once before *all* test methods in the class.

setUp *instance method*
> Called before *each* test method.

tearDown *instance method*
> Called after *each* test method.

tearDown *class method*
> Called once after *all* test methods in the class.

The test target is a target, and what it produces is a bundle, with build phases like an app target. This means that resources, such as test data, can be included in the bundle. You might use setUp to load such resources; you can get a reference to the bundle by way of the test class, as NSBundle(forClass: self.dynamicType).

The test target is also a module, just as the app target is a module. In order to see into the app target, therefore, the test target must import the app target as a module. To overcome privacy restrictions, the import statement should be preceded by the @testable attribute; this attribute, new in Xcode 7, temporarily changes internal (explicit or implicit) to public throughout the app target.

As an example of writing and running a unit test method, let's use our Empty Window project. Give the ViewController class a (nonsensical) instance method dogMyCats:

```
func dogMyCats(s:String) -> String {
    return ""
}
```

The method dogMyCats is supposed to receive any string and return the string "dogs". At the moment, though, it doesn't; it returns an empty string instead. That's a bug. Now we'll write a test method to ferret out this bug.

In the Empty Window project, choose File → New → Target and specify iOS → Test → iOS Unit Testing Bundle. Call the product *EmptyWindowTests*; observe that the target to be tested is the app target. Click Finish. In the Project navigator, a new group has been created, EmptyWindowTests, containing a single test file, *EmptyWindow-Tests.swift*. It contains a test class EmptyWindowTests, including stubs for two test methods, `testExample` and `testPerformanceExample`; comment out those two methods. We're going to replace them with a test method that calls `dogMyCats` and makes an assertion about the result:

1. At the top of *EmptyWindowTests.swift*, where we are importing XCTest, we must also import the app target:

   ```
   @testable import Empty_Window
   ```

2. Prepare an instance property in the declaration of the EmptyWindowTests class to store our ViewController instance:

   ```
   var viewController = ViewController()
   ```

3. Write the test method. Its name must start with `test`! Let's call it `testDogMyCats`. It has access to the ViewController instance as `self.viewController`:

   ```
   func testDogMyCats() {
       let input = "cats"
       let output = "dogs"
       XCTAssertEqual(output,
           self.viewController.dogMyCats(input),
           "Failed to produce \(output) from \(input)")
   }
   ```

 If you add a unit test to an older project, you may need some additional configuration. To ensure that the app target is capable of being imported with the @testable attribute, find Enable Testability in its build settings and make sure it is set to Yes for the Debug configuration. Also, edit the scheme and make sure that the Build action builds the test target only for the Test action.

We are now ready to run our test! There are many ways to do this. Switch to the Test navigator, and you'll see that it lists our test target, our test class, and our test method. Hover the mouse over any name, and a button appears to its right. By clicking the appropriate button, you can thus run all tests in every test class, all tests in the Empty-WindowTests class, or just the `testDogMyCats` test. But wait, there's more! Back in *EmptyWindowTests.swift*, there's also a diamond-shaped indicator in the gutter to the left of the class declaration and the test method name; you can also click one of those to run, respectively, all tests in this class or an individual test. Or, to run all tests, you can choose Product → Test.

So now let's run `testDogMyCats`. The app target is compiled and built; the test target is compiled and built. (If any of those steps fails, we can't test, and we'll be back on familiar ground with a compile error or a build error.) The app launches in the Simulator, and the test runs.

The test fails! (Well, we knew that was going to happen, didn't we?) The error is described in a banner next to the assert that failed in our code, as well as in the Issue navigator and the Report navigator. Moreover, red X marks appear everywhere — in the Test navigator next to testDogMyCats, in the Issue navigator, in the Report navigator, and in *EmptyWindowTests.swift* next to the class declaration and the first line of testDogMy-Cats.

Now let's fix our code. In *ViewController.swift*, modify dogMyCats to return "dogs" instead of an empty string. Now run the test again. It passes!

Recently run tests are listed in the Report navigator. When you select one, the editor displays two panes. The Tests pane lists in simple outline form what tests passed and failed, including the text of any assertion failure messages. The Logs pane goes into much more detail; by expanding transcripts, you can see the full console output from the test run, including any caveman debugging messages (print) that you may have sent from your test code.

When a test failure occurs, you might like to pause at the point where the assertion is about to fail. To do so, in the Breakpoint navigator, click the Plus button at the bottom and choose Add Test Failure Breakpoint. This is like an Exception breakpoint, pausing on the assert line in your test method just before it reports failure. You could then switch to the method being tested, for example, and debug it, examining its variables and so forth, to work out the reason for the impending failure.

There's a helpful feature allowing you to navigate between a method and a test that calls it: when the selection is within a method, the Related Items menu in the jump bar includes Test Callers. The same is true of the Tracking menu in an assistant pane.

In our example, we made a new ViewController instance in order to initialize Empty-WindowTests's self.viewController. But what if our test required us to get a reference to the *existing* ViewController instance? This is the same general problem of getting a reference to an instance that crops up so often in iOS programming (see "Instance References" on page 127, and Chapter 13). The test code runs inside a bundle that is effectively injected into your running app. This means that it can see app globals such as UIApplication.sharedApplication(). From there, you can work your way to the desired reference:

```
if let viewController =
    (UIApplication.sharedApplication().delegate as? AppDelegate)?
        .window?.rootViewController as? ViewController {
            // ...
}
```

Organization of your test methods into test targets (suites) and test classes is largely a matter of convenience; it dictates the layout of the Test navigator and which tests will be run together, plus each test class has its own properties, its own `setUp` method, and so on. To make a new test target or a new test class, click the Plus button at the bottom of the Test navigator.

In addition to simple unit tests of the type I've just illustrated, there are two other forms of unit test:

Asynchronous testing

Allows a test method to be called back after a time-consuming operation. In your test method, you create an XCTestExpectation object by calling `expectationWith-Description`; then you initiate an operation that takes a completion handler, and call `waitForExpectationsWithTimeout:handler:`. One of two things will happen:

The operation completes

The completion handler is called. In the completion handler, you perform any asserts having to do with the result of the operation, and then call `fulfill` on the XCTestExpectation object. This causes the timeout `handler` to be called.

The operation times out

The timeout `handler` is called. Thus, the timeout `handler` is called either way, allowing you to clean up as necessary.

Performance testing

Allows you to test that the speed of an operation has not fallen off. In your test method, you call `measureBlock` and, in the block, do something (possibly many times, so as to get a reasonable time measurement sample). If the block involves setup and teardown that you don't want included in the measurement, call `measure-Metrics:automaticallyStartMeasuring:forBlock:` instead, and wrap the heart of the block with calls to `startMeasuring` and `stopMeasuring`.

The performance test runs your block several times, recording how long each run takes. The first time you run a performance test, it fails, but you establish a baseline measurement. On subsequent runs, it fails if the standard deviation of the runs is too far from the baseline, or if the average time has grown too much.

Now let's experiment with interface testing. I'm going to assume that you still have (from Chapter 7) a button in the Empty Window interface with an action method hooked to a ViewController method that summons an alert. We'll write a test that taps that button and makes sure that the alert is summoned. Add an iOS UI Testing Bundle to the project; call it *EmptyWindowUITests*.

Interface test code is based on *accessibility*, a feature that allows the screen interface to be described verbally and to be manipulated programmatically. It revolves around three classes: XCUIElement, XCUIApplication (an XCUIElement subclass), and

XCUIElementQuery. To a large extent, you can avoid learning anything about these classes, because accessibility actions are *recordable*. This means that you can generate your code by performing the actual actions that constitute the test. Let's try it:

1. In the `testExample` stub method, create a new empty line and leave the insertion point within it.

2. Choose Editor → Start Recording UI Test. (Alternatively, there's a Record button at the bottom of the project window, in the debug bar.) The app launches in the Simulator.

3. Tap the button in the interface. When the alert appears, tap OK to dismiss it.

4. Return to Xcode and choose Editor → Stop Recording UI Test. Also choose Product → Stop to stop running in the Simulator.

The following code has been generated (assuming that your interface button's title is "Hello"):

```
let app = XCUIApplication()
app.buttons["Hello"].tap()
app.alerts["Howdy!"].collectionViews.buttons["OK"].tap()
```

The `app` object, obviously, is an XCUIApplication instance. Properties such as `buttons` and `alerts` return XCUIElementQuery objects. Subscripting such an object returns an XCUIElement, which can then be sent action methods such as `tap`.

Now run the test by clicking in the diamond in the gutter at the left of the `test-Example` declaration. The app launches in the Simulator, and a ghost finger performs the same actions we performed, tapping first the button in the interface and then, when the alert appears, the OK button that dismisses it. The test ends and the app stops running in the simulator. The test passes!

The important thing, however, is that if the interface stops looking and behaving as it does now, the test will *not* pass. For example, in *Main.storyboard*, select the button and, under Control in the Attributes inspector, uncheck Enabled. The button is still there, but it can't be tapped; we've broken the interface. Run the test. As desired, the test fails, and the Report navigator explains why: when we came to the Tap the "OK" Button step, we first had to perform Find the "OK" Button, and after two retries, we failed because there was no alert. Ingeniously, the report also incorporates screen shots so that we can inspect the state of the interface during the test. Hover the mouse over Tap the "OK" Button, and an Eye icon appears. Click it, and a screen shot shows the screen at that moment, displaying clearly the disabled interface button (and no alert).

Fix the bug by enabling the button once again. If you now choose Product → Test, all tests in all test suites are run, both the unit tests and the interface tests, and they all pass. Our app may be trivially simple, but it's definitely working!

As I've already said, interface testing depends upon accessibility. Standard interface objects are accessible, but other interface that you create might not be. Select an interface element in the nib editor to view its accessibility characteristics in the Identity inspector. Run the app in the Simulator and choose Xcode → Open Developer Tool → Accessibility Inspector to explore in real time the accessibility characteristics of whatever is under the cursor. For more about adding useful accessibility to your interface objects, see Apple's *Accessibility Programming Guide for iOS*.

Clean

From time to time, during repeated testing and debugging, and before making a different sort of build (switching from Debug to Release, or running on a device instead of the Simulator), it is a good idea to *clean* your target. This means that existing builds will be removed and caches will be cleared, so that all code will be considered to be in need of compilation and you can build your app from scratch.

Cleaning removes the cruft, quite literally. For example, suppose you have been including a certain resource in your app, and you decide it is no longer needed. You can remove it from the Copy Bundle Resources build phase (or from your project as a whole), but that doesn't remove it from your built app. This sort of leftover resource can cause all kinds of mysterious trouble. The wrong version of a nib may seem to appear in your interface; code that you've edited may seem to behave as it did before the edit. Cleaning removes the built app, and very often solves the problem.

I think of cleaning as having several levels or degrees:

Shallow clean
Choose Product → Clean, which removes the built app and some of the intermediate information in the build folder.

Deeper clean
Hold Option and choose Product → Clean Build Folder, which removes the entire build folder.

Complete clean
Close the project. Open the Projects window (Window → Projects). Find your project listed at the left side; click it. On the right, click Delete. This removes the project's entire folder in your user *Library/Developer/Xcode/DerivedData* folder.

Insanely clean
Quit Xcode. Open your user *Library/Developer/Xcode/DerivedData* folder and move all its contents to the trash. This is a complete clean for every project you've opened recently — plus the module cache. Removing the module cache can reset Swift itself, thus causing occasional mysterious compilation, code-completion, or syntax coloring issues to go away.

In addition to cleaning your project, you should also remove your app from the Simulator. This is for the same reason as cleaning the project: when the app is built and copied to the Simulator, existing resources inside the built app may not be removed (in order to save time), and this may cause the app to behave oddly. To clean out the Simulator while running the Simulator, choose iOS Simulator → Reset Content and Settings.

Running on a Device

Sooner or later, you'll want to progress from running and testing and debugging in the Simulator to running and testing and debugging on a real device. The Simulator is nice, but it's only a simulation; there are many differences between the Simulator and a real device. The Simulator is really your computer, which is fast and has lots of memory, so problems with memory management and speed won't be exposed until you run on a device. User interaction with the Simulator is limited to what can be done with a mouse: you can click, you can drag, you can hold Option to simulate use of two fingers, but more elaborate gestures can be performed only on an actual device. And many iOS facilities, such as the accelerometer and access to the music library, are not present on the Simulator at all, so that testing an app that uses them is possible *only* on a device.

 Don't even think of developing an app without testing it on a device. You have no idea how your app *really* looks and behaves until you run it on a device. Submitting to the App Store an app that you have not run on a device is asking for trouble.

Running an app on a device is a remarkably complicated business. You will need to *sign* the app as you build it. An app that is not properly signed for a device will not run on that device (assuming you haven't jailbroken the device). Signing an app requires two things:

An identity
> An identity represents Apple's permission for a given team to develop, on a particular computer, apps that can run on a device. It consists of two parts:
>
> *A private key*
>> The private key is stored in the keychain on your computer. Thus, it identifies a computer where this team can *potentially* develop device-targeted apps.
>
> *A certificate*
>> A certificate is a virtual permission slip from Apple. It contains the public key matching the private key (because you told Apple the public key when you asked for the certificate). With a copy of this certificate, any machine holding the private key can *actually* be used to develop device-targeted apps under the name of this team.

A provisioning profile
A provisioning profile is a virtual permission slip from Apple, uniting four things:

- An identity.
- An app, identified by its bundle id.
- A list of eligible devices, identified by their UDIDs (unique device identifiers).
- A list of entitlements. An *entitlement* is a special privilege that not every app needs, such as the ability to talk to iCloud. You won't concern yourself with entitlements unless you write an app that needs one.

Thus, a provisioning profile is sufficient for signing an app as you build it. It says that on *this* Mac it is permitted to build *this* app such that it will run on *these* devices.

There are two types of identity, and hence two types of certificate, and hence two types of provisioning profile: *development* and *distribution* (a distribution certificate is also called a *production* certificate). We are concerned here with the development identity, certificate, and profile; I'll talk about the distribution side later in this chapter.

Apple is the ultimate keeper of all information: your certificates, your provisioning profiles, what apps and what devices you've registered. Your communication with Apple, when you need to verify or obtain a copy of this information, will take place through one of two means:

The Member Center
A set of web pages at *https://developer.apple.com/membercenter*. If you have a Developer Program membership, you can click Certificates, Identifiers, & Profiles to access all features and information to which you are entitled by your membership type and role. (This is the area of Apple's site formerly referred to as the Portal.)

Xcode
Except for obtaining a distribution provisioning profile, just about everything you would need to do at the Member Center can be done through Xcode instead. When all goes well, using Xcode is a lot simpler! If there's a problem, you can head for the Member Center to iron it out.

Running Without a Developer Program Membership

In the past, it was necessary to have an iOS Developer Program membership — meaning that it cost you an annual fee — just to test your app on your own device. New in Xcode 7, however, you can configure your app to run on your device *without* a Developer Program membership. All you need is an Apple ID, which you surely have already.

Therefore, before describing in full what running on a device *really* entails, I'll explain the steps needed to run your app on your device with no preparations whatever: you have no Developer Program membership, you have entered no account information in Xcode, and you have never run any app on a device before:

1. Edit the app target, switch to the General pane, and look at the Team pop-up menu. Assuming there is no team listed, your first move is to create one. Choose Add an Account from the Team pop-up menu; this brings up the Xcode Accounts preference pane, in the same state as if you had pressed the Plus button and chosen Add Apple ID. Enter your Apple ID and password. The result is a *free account*. Dismiss the Accounts preference pane. Back in the Team pop-up menu, choose the team you just created.

2. Under the Team pop-up menu, you'll see a warning that you have no code signing identities. Click Fix Issue. Xcode communicates online with the Member Center. The issue will be partly fixed, but you will see a dialog: "Unable to create a provisioning profile because your team has no devices registered in the Member Center…" Click Done.

3. Attach your device to the computer. Wait while the symbol files are processed (you can track this by choosing Window → Devices and selecting the device, or you can just go get a cup of coffee and come back in five minutes).

4. The device is now ready to use for development. Select the device as destination in the Scheme pop-up menu and attempt to run the project! You'll see a dialog, "Failed to code sign…" Click Fix Issue. Xcode will communicate online with the Member Center once again — and your app will then build and run on the device.

Behind the scenes, Xcode has performed several necessary steps:

- It has created a Developer identity in your keychain (use the Keychain Access application to see it).

- It has registered your device with the Member Center (even though, without a Developer Program membership, you cannot actually log in to the Member Center to see this registration).

- It has created and downloaded a Team Provisioning Profile uniting those two things — that is, it allows your app to be run on this device from this computer.

Obtaining a Developer Program Membership

Sooner or later, you'll likely want a Developer Program membership. Go to the iOS Developer Program web page (*http://developer.apple.com/programs/ios*) to initiate the enrollment process. When you're starting out, the Individual program is sufficient. The Organization program costs no more, but adds the ability to privilege additional developers in various roles. You do *not* need the Organization program merely in order to distribute your built app to other users for testing.

Your iOS Developer Program membership involves two things:

An Apple ID

> The user ID that identifies you at Apple's site (along with the corresponding password). You'll use your Developer Program Apple ID for all kinds of things. In addition to letting you prepare an app to run on a device, this same Apple ID lets you post on Apple's development forums, download Xcode beta versions, and so forth.

A team name

> You, under the same Apple ID, can belong to more than one *team*. On each team, you will have a *role* dictating your privileges. If you are the head (or sole member) of the team, your role is Agent, meaning that you can do everything: you can develop apps, run them on your device, submit apps to the App Store, and receive the money for any paid apps that sell any copies there.

Having established your Developer Program Apple ID, you should enter it into the Accounts preference pane in Xcode. Click the Plus button at the bottom left and choose Add Apple ID. Provide the Apple ID and password. From now on, Xcode will identify you through the team name(s) associated with this Apple ID; you shouldn't need to tell Xcode this password again.

Obtaining a Certificate

Setting up an identity and obtaining a certificate is something you only have to do once (or, perhaps, once a year at most; you might have to do it again when your annual Developer Program membership approaches expiration and needs to be renewed). The certificate, you remember, depends upon a private–public key pair. The private key will live in your keychain; the public key will be handed over to Apple, to be built into the certificate. The way you give Apple your public key is through a *request* for the certificate. Ideally, you'll be able to do this easily through Xcode:

1. Open Xcode's Accounts preference pane.
2. If you haven't entered your developer Apple ID and password, do so now.
3. On the left, select your Apple ID. On the right, select your team. Click View Details.
4. If you had a certificate and it was revoked from the Member Center but is still valid, you may see a dialog offering to request and download the certificate. Click Request. Otherwise, click the Create button to the right of iOS Development.

Everything then happens automatically: the private–public key pair is generated in your keychain, and the certificate is requested from the Member Center, generated at the Member Center, downloaded from the Member Center, stored in your keychain, and listed under Signing Identities in the View Details dialog of Xcode's Accounts preference pane. Moreover, a universal team development provisioning profile may also be gen-

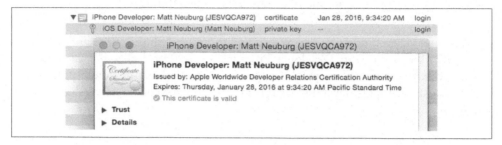

Figure 9-10. A valid development certificate, as shown in Keychain Access

erated, as shown in Figure 9-11. Thus you may now have everything you need to run any app on a device.

It can be useful to know also the more elaborate procedure for generating the private–public key pair and the certificate request manually. Instructions are also available at the Member Center as you initiate the process (go to the Certificates page and click the Plus button at the top right):

1. You launch Keychain Access and choose Keychain Access → Certificate Assistant → Request a Certificate from a Certificate Authority. Using your name and email address as identifiers, you generate and save to disk a 2048-bit RSA certificate request file. Your private key is stored in your keychain then and there; the certificate request containing your public key has been saved temporarily onto your computer. (For example, you might save it to the desktop.)

2. At the Member Center, you are presented with an interface allowing you to upload the saved certificate request file. You upload it, and the certificate is generated; click its listing at the Member Center to expose the Download button, and click Download.

3. Locate and double-click the file you just downloaded; Keychain Access automatically imports the certificate and stores it in your keychain, where Xcode is able to see it from now on.

You do not need to keep the certificate request file or the downloaded certificate file; your keychain now contains all the needed credentials. If this has worked, you can see the certificate in your keychain, read its details, and observe that it is valid and linked to your private key (Figure 9-10). Moreover, you should be able to confirm that Xcode now knows about this certificate: in the Accounts preference pane, click your Apple ID on the left and your team name on the right, and click View Details; a dialog opens where you should see an iOS Development signing identity listed at the top, with a Valid status.

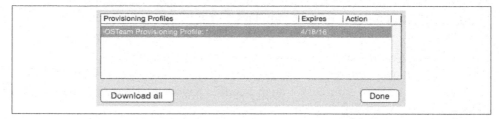

Figure 9-11. A universal development profile

 If this is your very, very first time obtaining any certificate from the Member Center, you will need *another* certificate: the WWDR Intermediate Certificate. This is the certificate that certifies that certificates issued by WWDR (the Apple Worldwide Developer Relations Certification Authority) are to be trusted. (You can't make this stuff up.) Xcode should automatically install this in your keychain; if not, you can obtain a copy of it manually by clicking a link at the bottom of the page at the Member Center where you begin the process of adding a certificate.

Obtaining a Development Provisioning Profile

A provisioning profile, as I've already mentioned, unites an identity, a device, and an app bundle id. If things go well, in the simplest case, you'll be able to obtain a development provisioning profile in a single step from within Xcode. If an app doesn't require special entitlements or capabilities, a single development profile associated with your team is sufficient for all your apps, so you might only have to do this step once.

You already have a development identity, from the previous section. You may also have a universal team development provisioning profile, from the previous section! If not, the simplest solution is to connect your device to your computer with Xcode running and, after passing through any necessary delays (such as telling the device to trust the computer), choose the device as a destination and try to run your project on it. Xcode will register the device at the Member Center for you, and will create and download a universal team provisioning profile for this device.

To confirm that the device has been added to the Member Center, go there in your browser and click Devices. To confirm that you have the universal team development provisioning profile, click View Details in the Accounts preference pane (for the appropriate team). Certificates and profiles are listed here. The universal team development profile, in addition to the title "iOS Team Provisioning Profile," will have a nonspecific app bundle id associated with it, indicated by an asterisk (Figure 9-11).

The universal development profile allows you to run *any* app on the targeted device for testing purposes, provided that the app doesn't require special entitlements (such as using iCloud).

It is also possible to register a device manually at the Member Center. Under Devices, click the Plus button and enter a name for this device along with its UDID. You can copy the device's UDID from its listing in Xcode's Devices window. Alternatively, you can submit a tab-delimited text file of UDIDs and names.

If necessary, you can make a provisioning profile for a specific app at the Member Center:

1. Make sure your app is registered at the Member Center under Identifiers → App IDs. If it isn't, add it, as follows: Click Plus. Enter a name for this app. Don't worry about the nonsense letters and numbers that the Member Center adds as a prefix to your bundle identifier; use the Team ID. Enter the bundle identifier under Explicit App ID exactly as shown in Xcode, in the Bundle Identifier field under General when you edit the app target.

2. Under Provisioning Profiles, click Plus. Ask for an iOS App Development profile. On the next screen, choose the App ID. On the next screen, check your development certificate. On the next screen, select the device(s) you want to run on. On the next screen, give this profile a name, and click Generate. Click the Download button.

3. Find the downloaded profile, and double-click it to open it in Xcode. You can then throw the downloaded profile away; Xcode has made a copy.

Running the App

Once you have a development profile applicable to an app and a device (or, in the case of the universal team profile, all apps and all registered devices), connect the device, choose it as the destination in the Scheme pop-up menu, and build and run the app. If you're asked for permission to access your keychain, grant it. If necessary, Xcode will install the associated provisioning profile onto the device.

The app is built, loaded onto your device, and runs there. As long as you launch the app from Xcode, everything is just as when running in the Simulator: you can run, or you can debug, and the running app is in communication with Xcode, so that you can stop at breakpoints, read messages in the console, and so on. The outward difference is that to interact physically with the app, you use the device (tethered physically to your computer), not the Simulator.

Running the app from Xcode on the device can also be used simply as a way of copying the current version of the app to the device. You can then stop the app (in Xcode), disconnect the device from your computer, and launch the app on the device and play with it. This is a good way of testing. You are not debugging, so you can't get any feedback in Xcode, but messages are written to the console internally and can be retrieved later.

Profile and Device Management

The central location for surveying identities and provisioning profiles is Xcode's Accounts preference pane.

An important feature of the Accounts preference pane is the ability to export account information. You'll need this if you want to be able to develop on a different computer. Select an Apple ID and use the Gear menu at the bottom of the pane to choose Export Developer Accounts. You'll be asked for a file name and a place to save, along with a password; this password is associated solely with this file, and is needed only to open the file later on another computer. On the other computer, to which you have copied the exported file, run Xcode and double-click the exported file; Xcode asks for its password. When you provide it, like magic the entire suite of teams and identities and certificates and provisioning profiles springs to life in that other copy of Xcode, including the entries in your keychain.

Alternatively, you might need to export just an identity, without any provisioning profiles. You can do that with the contextual menu in the Accounts preference pane's View Details dialog.

If the provisioning profiles listed in the Accounts preference pane's View Details dialog get out of sync with the Member Center, click the Download All button at the bottom left. If that doesn't help, quit Xcode and, in the Finder, open your user *Library/Mobile-Device/Provisioning Profiles* folder, and delete everything that's in there. Relaunch Xcode. In Accounts, your provisioning profiles are gone! *Now* click the Download All button. Xcode will download fresh copies of all your provisioning profiles, and you'll be back in sync with the Member Center.

When a device is attached to the computer, it appears in Xcode's Devices window. Click its name to access information on the device. You can see (and copy) the device's UDID. You can see (and delete) apps that have been installed for development using Xcode. You can view the device's console log in real time. (The interface for this is a little obscure: click the tiny up-arrow at the bottom left of the main pane of the Devices window.) Using the Gear menu, you can see provisioning profiles that have been installed on the device. You can see log reports for crashes that took place on the device. And you can take screenshots that image your device's screen; you'll need to do this for your app when you submit it to the App Store.

Profiling

Xcode provides tools for probing the internal behavior of your app graphically and numerically, and you should keep an eye on those tools. The gauges in the Debug navigator allow you to monitor key indicators, such as CPU and memory usage, any time you run your app. And Instruments, a sophisticated and powerful utility application, collects profiling data that can help track down problems and provide the numeric information you need to improve your app's performance and responsiveness. You'll probably want to spend some time with Instruments as your app approaches completion (optimizing prematurely is notoriously a waste of time and effort).

Gauges

The gauges in the Debug navigator are operating whenever you build and run your app. Click on a gauge to see further detail displayed in the editor. The gauges do not provide highly detailed information, but they are extremely lightweight and always active, so they provide an easy way to get a general sense of your running app's behavior at any time. In particular, if there's a problem, such as a prolonged period of unexpectedly high CPU usage or a relentless unchecked increase in memory usage, you can spot it in the gauges and then use Instruments to help track it down.

There are four basic gauges: CPU, Memory, Disk, and Network. Depending on the circumstances, you may see additional gauges. For example, new in Xcode 7, an Energy Impact gauge appears when running on a device, and for certain devices, a GPU gauge may appear as well. If your app is iCloud-enabled, you'll also see an iCloud gauge.

In Figure 9-12, I've been heavily exercising my app for a few moments, repeatedly performing the most memory-intensive actions I expect the user to perform. These actions do cause some spikes in memory usage, but my app's memory usage then always settles back down and levels off, so I don't suspect any memory issues.

 Note that Figure 9-12 is the result of running *on a device*. Running in the Simulator gives completely different — and therefore misleading — results.

Instruments

You can use Instruments on the Simulator or the device. The device is where you'll do your ultimate testing, for maximum verisimilitude.

To get started with Instruments, set the desired destination in the Scheme pop-up menu in the project window toolbar, and choose Product → Profile. Your app builds using the Profile action for your scheme; by default, this uses the Release build configuration, which is probably what you want. If you're running on a device, you may see some validation warnings, but you can safely ignore them. Instruments launches; if your scheme's Instrument pop-up menu for the Profile action is set to Ask on Launch (the default), Instruments presents a dialog where you choose a trace template.

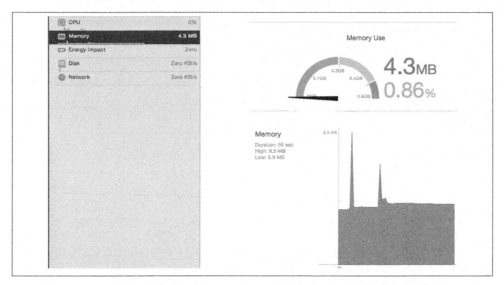

Figure 9-12. The Debug navigation gauges

Alternatively, click Profile In Instruments in a Debug navigator gauge editor; this is convenient when the gauges have suggested a possible problem, and you want to reproduce that problem under the more detailed monitoring of Instruments. Instruments launches, selecting the appropriate trace template for you. A dialog offers two options: Restart stops your app and relaunches it with Instruments, whereas Transfer keeps your app running and hooks Instruments into it.

When the Instruments main window appears, it can be further customized to profile the kind of data that particularly interests you, and you can save the structure of the Instruments window as a custom template. You may have to click the Record button, or choose File → Record Trace, to get your app running. Now you should interact with your app like a user; Instruments will record its statistics.

 If you've archived or distributed your app (as explained later in this chapter) with the Code Signing Identity build setting for the Release configuration set to iOS Distribution, you won't be able to profile in Instruments on a device. You must set that build setting to iOS Developer instead.

Use of Instruments is an advanced topic, which is largely beyond the scope of this book. Indeed, an entire book could (and really should) be written about Instruments alone. For proper information, you should read Apple's documents, especially the *Instruments User Reference* and *Instruments User Guide*. Also, many WWDC videos from current and prior years are about Instruments; look particularly for sessions with "Instruments"

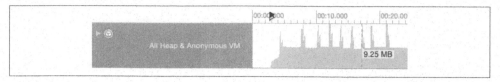

Figure 9-13. Instruments graphs memory usage over time

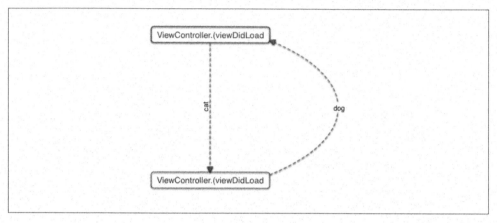

Figure 9-14. Instruments describes a retain cycle

or "Performance" in their names. Here, I'll just demonstrate, without much explanation, the sort of thing Instruments can do.

Figure 9-13 shows me doing much the same thing in Instruments that I did with the Debug navigator gauges in Figure 9-12. I've set the destination to my device. I choose Product → Profile; when Instruments launches, I choose the Allocations trace template. With my app running under Instruments, I exercise it for a while and then pause Instruments, which meanwhile has charted my memory usage. Examining the chart, I find that there are spikes up to about 10MB, but the app in general settles down to a much lower level (less than 4MB). Those are very gentle and steady memory usage figures, so I'm happy.

Another field of Instruments expertise is the ability to detect memory leaks. In Figure 9-14, I've run the retain cycle code from Chapter 5: I have a Dog class instance and a Cat class instance with persisting references to one another. There are no other references to either instance, so they are both leaking. I've profiled the app using the Leaks trace template. Instruments has detected the leak, and has even drawn me a diagram showing me the structure of my mistake!

In this final example, I'm curious as to whether I can shorten the time it takes my Diabelli's Theme app to load a photo image. I've set the destination to a device, because

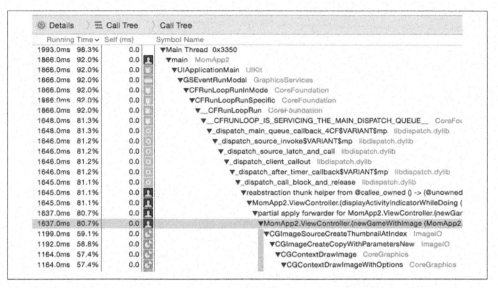

Running Time ⌄	Self (ms)		Symbol Name
1993.0ms 98.3%	0.0		▼Main Thread 0x3350
1866.0ms 92.0%	0.0		▼main MomApp2
1866.0ms 92.0%	0.0		▼UIApplicationMain UIKit
1866.0ms 92.0%	0.0		▼GSEventRunModal GraphicsServices
1866.0ms 92.0%	0.0		▼CFRunLoopRunInMode CoreFoundation
1866.0ms 92.0%	0.0		▼CFRunLoopRunSpecific CoreFoundation
1866.0ms 92.0%	0.0		▼__CFRunLoopRun CoreFoundation
1648.0ms 81.3%	0.0		▼__CFRUNLOOP_IS_SERVICING_THE_MAIN_DISPATCH_QUEUE__ CoreFou
1648.0ms 81.3%	0.0		▼_dispatch_main_queue_callback_4CF$VARIANT$mp libdispatch.dylib
1646.0ms 81.2%	0.0		▼_dispatch_source_invoke$VARIANT$mp libdispatch.dylib
1646.0ms 81.2%	0.0		▼_dispatch_source_latch_and_call libdispatch.dylib
1646.0ms 81.2%	0.0		▼_dispatch_client_callout libdispatch.dylib
1646.0ms 81.2%	0.0		▼_dispatch_after_timer_callback$VARIANT$mp libdispatch.dylib
1645.0ms 81.1%	0.0		▼_dispatch_call_block_and_release libdispatch.dylib
1645.0ms 81.1%	0.0		▼reabstraction thunk helper from @callee_owned () -> (@unowned
1645.0ms 81.1%	0.0		▼MomApp2.ViewController.(displayActivityIndicatorWhileDoing (
1637.0ms 80.7%	0.0		▼partial apply forwarder for MomApp2.ViewController.(newGar
1637.0ms 80.7%	0.0		▼MomApp2.ViewController.(newGameWithImage (MomApp2.
1199.0ms 59.1%	0.0		▼CGImageSourceCreateThumbnailAtIndex ImageIO
1192.0ms 58.8%	0.0		▼CGImageCreateCopyWithParametersNew ImageIO
1164.0ms 57.4%	0.0		▼CGContextDrawImage CoreGraphics
1164.0ms 57.4%	0.0		▼CGContextDrawImageWithOptions CoreGraphics

Figure 9-15. Drilling down into the time profile

that's where speed matters and needs to be measured. I choose Product → Profile. Instruments launches, and I choose the Time Profiler trace template. When the app launches under Instruments on the device, I load new images repeatedly to exercise this part of my code.

In Figure 9-15, I've paused Instruments, and am looking at what it's telling me. Opening the triangles in the lower portion of the window, I can drill down to my own code, indicated by the appearance of my module name, MomApp2 (so called because I originally wrote this app as a birthday present for my mother).

By double-clicking the listing of that line, I can see my own code, time-profiled (Figure 9-16). The profiler is drawing my attention to the call to `CGImageSourceCreate-ThumbnailAtIndex`; this is where we're spending most of our CPU time. That call is in the ImageIO framework; it isn't my code, so I can't make it run any faster. It may be, however, that I could load the image another way; for example, at the expense of some temporary memory usage, perhaps I could load the image at full size and scale it down by redrawing myself. If I'm concerned about speed here, I could spend a little time experimenting. The point is that now I know *what* the experiment should be. This is just the sort of focused, fact-based numerical analysis at which Instruments excels.

Localization

A device can be set by the user to prefer a certain language as its primary language. You might like the text in your app's interface to respond to this situation by appearing in

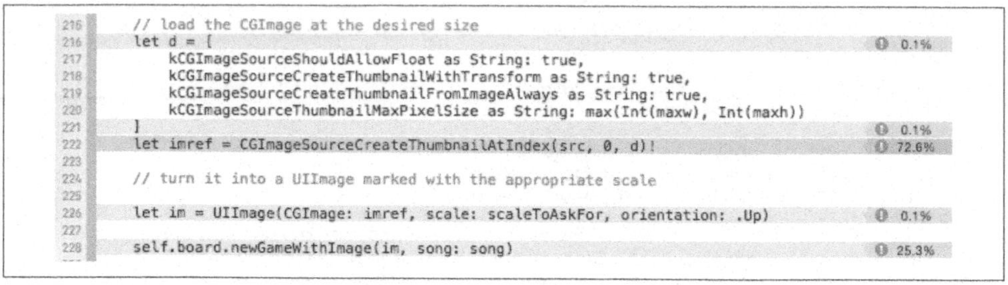

```
215       // load the CGImage at the desired size
216       let d = [                                                                    ① 0.1%
217           kCGImageSourceShouldAllowFloat as String: true,
218           kCGImageSourceCreateThumbnailWithTransform as String: true,
219           kCGImageSourceCreateThumbnailFromImageAlways as String: true,
220           kCGImageSourceThumbnailMaxPixelSize as String: max(Int(maxw), Int(maxh))
221       ]                                                                            ① 0.1%
222       let imref = CGImageSourceCreateThumbnailAtIndex(src, 0, d)!                   ① 72.6%
223
224       // turn it into a UIImage marked with the appropriate scale
225
226       let im = UIImage(CGImage: imref, scale: scaleToAskFor, orientation: .Up)      ① 0.1%
227
228       self.board.newGameWithImage(im, song: song)                                  ① 25.3%
```

Figure 9-16. My code, time-profiled

that language. This is achieved by *localizing* the app for that language. You will probably want to implement localization relatively late in the lifetime of the app, after the app has achieved its final form, in preparation for distribution.

Localization operates through *localization folders* in your project folder and in the built app bundle. Let's say that a resource in one of these localization folders has a counterpart in the other localization folders. Then, when your app goes to load such a resource, it automatically loads the one appropriate to the user's preferred language.

Any type of resource can live in these localization folders; for example, you can have one version of an image to be loaded for one language, and another version of that image for another language. You will be most concerned, however, with *text* that is to appear in your interface. Such text must be maintained in specially formatted *.strings* files, with special names. For example:

- To localize your *Info.plist* file, use *InfoPlist.strings*.
- To localize your *Main.storyboard*, use *Main.strings*.
- To localize your code strings, use *Localizable.strings*.

You don't have to create or maintain these files manually. Instead, you can work with exported XML files in the standard *.xliff* format. Xcode will generate these files automatically, based on the structure and content of your project; it will also read them and will turn them automatically into the various localized *.strings* files.

To help you understand how the *.xliff* export and import process works, I'll start by explaining what you would have to do in order to create and maintain your *.strings* files manually. Then I'll describe how to do the same thing using *.xliff* files. I'll use our good old Empty Window project as the basis for the examples.

Localizing the Info.plist

I'll begin by localizing the string that appears in the Springboard under the app's icon — the visible title of the app. This string is the value of the CFBundleDisplayName key in our *Info.plist* file. If our *Info.plist* file doesn't have a `CFBundleDisplayName` key, the first step is to make one:

1. Edit the *Info.plist* file.
2. Select "Bundle name" and click the Plus button that appears to its right.
3. A new entry appears. From the pop-up menu of key names, choose "Bundle display name."
4. For the value, enter "Empty Window" and save.

Now we're going to localize that string: we're going to make a different string appear in the Springboard when the device's language is French. How is the *Info.plist* file localized? It depends on another file, which by default is not created by the app template — *InfoPlist.strings*. So we need to create that file:

1. Choose File → New → File.
2. Select iOS → Resource → Strings File. Click Next.
3. Make sure this file is part of our app target, and name it *InfoPlist*. Get the name and capitalization exactly right! Click Create.
4. A file called *InfoPlist.strings* has appeared in the project navigator. Select it and, in the File inspector, click Localize.
5. A dialog appears offering us a choice of initial languages. The default is Base, which is fine. Click Localize.

We are now ready to add a language! Here's how to do it:

1. Edit the project. Under Info, the Localizations table lists our app's localizations. We are initially localized only for the development language (English in my case).
2. Click the Plus button under the Localizations table. From the pop-up menu that appears, choose French.
3. A dialog appears, listing files that are currently localized for English (because they came that way as part of the app template). We're dealing here with just *Info-Plist.strings*, so leave it checked but uncheck any other files that appear here. Click Finish.

We have now set up *InfoPlist.strings* to be localized for both English and French. In the Project navigator, the listing for *InfoPlist.strings* has acquired a flippy triangle. Open the triangle to reveal that our project now contains *two* copies of *InfoPlist.strings*, one for Base (namely English) and one for French. Thus we can now edit either one individually.

Now let's edit our *InfoPlist.strings* files. A *.strings* file is a collection of key–value pairs in the following format:

```
/* Optional comments are C-style comments */
"key" = "value";
```

In the case of *InfoPlist.strings*, the key is the key name from *Info.plist* — the raw key name, not the English-like name. So the English *InfoPlist.strings* should look like this:

```
"CFBundleDisplayName" = "Empty Window";
```

The French *InfoPlist.strings* should look like this:

```
"CFBundleDisplayName" = "Fenêtre Vide";
```

That's all there is to it! Now let's try it out:

1. Build and run Empty Window in the Simulator.

2. In Xcode, stop the running project. In the Simulator, the home screen is revealed.

3. Examine the name of our app, as displayed in the Simulator home screen (the Springboard). It is Empty Window (perhaps truncated).

4. In the Simulator, launch the Settings app and change the language to French (General → Language & Region → iPhone Language → Français). Click Done. An action sheet asks to confirm that we want to Change to French. Do so.

5. After a pause, the language changes. Quit the Settings app and look at our app in the Springboard again. Its name is now displayed as Fenêtre Vide!

Is this fun or what? When you're done marveling at your own cosmopolitanism, change the Simulator's language back to English.

Localizing a Nib File

Now let's talk about how nib files are localized. Once upon a time, it was necessary to localize a copy of the entire nib. So, for example, if you wanted a French version of a nib file, you were constantly maintaining two separate nib files. If you created a button in one nib file, you had to create the same button in the other — except that in one, the title was in English, while in the other, the title was in French. And so on, for every interface object and every localization language. It doesn't sound like fun, does it?

Nowadays, happily, there's a better way. If a project uses base internationalization, then a correspondence can be created between a nib file in a *Base.lproj* folder and a *.strings* file in a localization folder. Thus the developer has just one copy of the nib file to maintain. If the app runs on a device that's localized for a language for which a *.strings* file exists, the strings in the *.strings* file are substituted for the strings in the nib file.

By default, our Empty Window project does use base internationalization, and its *Main.storyboard* file is in a *Base.lproj* folder. So we're ready to localize the storyboard file for French. You're going to need something in the storyboard file to localize:

1. Edit *Main.storyboard* and make sure that the initial main view contains a button whose title is "Hello". If there isn't one, add one. Make the button about 100 pixels wide, and save (that's important).

2. Still editing *Main.storyboard*, look at the File inspector. Under Localization, Base should be checked already. In addition, check French.

3. In the Project navigator, examine the listing for *Main.storyboard*. It now has a flippy triangle. Flip it open. Sure enough, there is now a base-localized *Main.storyboard* and a French-localized *Main.strings*.

4. Edit the French *Main.strings*. It has been created automatically, with keys corresponding to every interface item in *Main.storyboard* that has a title. You have to deduce, from comments and the key names, how this correspondence works. In our case, there's just one interface item in *Main.storyboard*, and anyway it's pretty easy to guess what interface item the key represents. It looks something like this:

   ```
   /* Class = "UIButton"; normalTitle = "Hello"; ObjectID = "PYn-zN-WlH"; */
   "PYn-zN-WlH.normalTitle" = "Hello";
   ```

5. In the second line, containing the key–value pair, change the value to "Bonjour". *Don't change the key!* It has been generated automatically, and correctly, so as to specify the correspondence between this value and the title of the button.

Run the project and view the interface. As we are now looking at our own app in action, there's a faster way to view it in any language for which it is localized: instead of switching the *device* language, you can change the *app* language. To do so, edit the scheme and, in the Run action's Options tab, change the Application Language pop-up menu. Sure enough, the button's title appears as "Bonjour" when the app runs in French!

What happens if we now modify the nib? Suppose, for example, we add another button to the view in *Main.storyboard*. There's no automatic change to any *.strings* files corresponding to nibs; such files must instead be regenerated manually. (That's why, in real life, it's a good idea not to start localizing your nib files until your interface is pretty much finished.) But all is not lost:

1. Select *Main.storyboard* and choose File → Show in Finder.

2. Run Terminal. Type xcrun ibtool --export-strings-file output.strings followed by a space, and drag *Main.storyboard* from the Finder into the Terminal window. Press Return.

The result is that a new file called *output.strings* based on *Main.storyboard* is generated in your home directory (or whatever the current directory is). Merging this information with the existing localized *.strings* files based on *Main.storyboard* is up to you.

In that example, I made you widen the "Hello" button in advance, to make room for a longer localized title, "Bonjour". In real life, you'll probably use autolayout; this allows buttons and labels to grow and shrink automatically, while shifting other parts of the interface to compensate.

To test your interface under different localizations, you can also *preview* your localized nib files within Xcode, without running the app. Edit a *storyboard* or *.xib* file and open an assistant pane, and switch the Tracking menu to Preview. A menu at the lower right lists localizations; choose from the menu to switch between them. A "double-length pseudolanguage" stress-tests your interface with really long localized replacement text.

 New in iOS 9, the runtime will automatically reverse (mirror) the *entire interface and its behavior* when the app runs in a right-to-left language. For example, a push transition will slide the old view out to the right and bring the new view in from the left. If you're already using autolayout and leading-and-trailing constraints, your interface will reverse correctly, but if you have code that depends upon assumptions about left-to-right directionality you will need to adopt some new UIView API.

Localizing Code Strings

What about localizing strings whose value is generated in code? In the Empty Window app, an example would be the alert summoned by tapping the button. It displays text — the title and message of the alert, and the title of the button that dismisses it:

```
@IBAction func buttonPressed(sender:AnyObject) {
    let alert = UIAlertController(
        title: "Howdy!", message: "You tapped me!", preferredStyle: .Alert)
    alert.addAction(
        UIAlertAction(title: "OK", style: .Cancel, handler: nil))
    self.presentViewController(alert, animated: true, completion: nil)
}
```

How is that text to be localized? The approach is the same — a *.strings* file — but your code must be modified to use it explicitly. Your code calls the global NSLocalized-String function; the first parameter is a key into a *.strings* file, and the comment parameter provides an explanatory comment, such as the original text to be translated. NSLocalizedString takes several additional, optional parameters; if you omit them, the default is to use a file called *Localizable.strings*.

So, for example, we might modify our buttonPressed: method to look like this:

```
@IBAction func buttonPressed(sender:AnyObject) {
    let alert = UIAlertController(
        title: NSLocalizedString("ATitle", comment:"Howdy!"),
        message: NSLocalizedString("AMessage", comment:"You tapped me!"),
        preferredStyle: .Alert)
    alert.addAction(
```

```
        UIAlertAction(title: NSLocalizedString("Accept", comment:"OK"),
            style: .Cancel, handler: nil))
        self.presentViewController(alert, animated: true, completion: nil)
    }
```

Our code is now broken, of course, because there is no *Localizable.strings* file. Let's make one. The procedure is just as before:

1. Choose File → New → File.

2. Select iOS → Resource → Strings File. Click Next.

3. Make sure this file is part of our app target, and name it *Localizable*. Get the name and capitalization exactly right! Click Create.

4. A file called *Localizable.strings* has appeared in the project navigator. Select it and, in the File inspector, click Localize.

5. A dialog appears offering us a choice of initial languages. The default is Base, which is fine. Click Localize.

6. In the File inspector, check French.

The *Localizable.strings* file now exists in two localizations, Base (meaning English) and French. We must now provide these files with content. Just as we did with `ibtool` earlier, we can generate the initial content automatically using the `genstrings` tool. For example, on my machine I would now, in the Terminal, type `xcrun genstrings` followed by space. Then I drag *ViewController.swift* from the Finder into the Terminal window, and press Return. The result is a file *Localizable.strings* in the current directory, reading as follows:

```
/* OK */
"Accept" = "Accept";

/* You tapped me! */
"AMessage" = "AMessage";

/* Howdy! */
"ATitle" = "ATitle";
```

Now you copy and paste that content into the English and French versions of our project's *Localizable.strings* files, and go through those pairs, changing the value in each pair so that it reads correctly for the given localization. For example, in the English *Localizable.strings* file:

```
/* Howdy! */
"ATitle" = "Howdy!";
```

And in the French *Localizable.strings* file:

```
/* Howdy! */
"ATitle" = "Bonjour!";
```

And so forth.

Localizing With XML Files

Since Xcode 6, there's been another way do everything we just did. The surface mechanics of text localization can be made to revolve around the exporting and importing of *.xliff* files. This means that you typically won't actually have to press any Localize buttons or edit any *.strings* files! Instead, you edit the target and choose Editor → Export For Localization; when you save, a folder is created containing *.xliff* files for your various localizations. You then edit these files (or get a translation house to edit them for you) and import the edited files: edit the target and choose Editor → Import Localizations. Xcode reads the edited *.xliff* files and does the rest, automatically creating localizations and generating or modifying *.strings* files as needed.

To demonstrate, let's add another language — namely, Spanish — to our localizations:

1. Edit the target and choose Editor → Export For Localization.

2. We are offered a chance to export strings in our existing localizations as well as our base language. If we were planning to edit our French localization further, we would export it, but I'm not going to do that in this example. Instead, switch the Include pop-up menu to Development Language Only.

3. Specify a good place to save (such as the Desktop). You're creating a folder, so don't use the name of an existing folder in the same place. For example, if you're saving to the same folder that contains the project folder, you might call it *Empty Window Localizations*. Click Save.

4. In the Finder, open the folder you just created. It contains an *.xliff* file in your project's base language. For example, my file is called *en.xliff* because my development language is English.

Examine this *.xliff* file, and you will see that Xcode has done for us everything that we did manually. No *.strings* files need be present initially! Xcode does all the work:

- For every *Info.plist* file in your project, Xcode has created a corresponding `<file>` element. When imported, these elements will be turned into localized *Info-Plist.strings* files.

- For every *.storyboard* and *.xib* file, Xcode has run `ibtool` to extract the text, and has created a corresponding `<file>` element. When imported, these elements will be turned into eponymous localized *.strings* files.

- For every code file containing a call to `NSLocalizedString`, Xcode has run `genstrings`, and has created a corresponding `<file>` element. When imported, these elements will be turned into localized *Localizable.strings* files.

We now proceed to translate some or all of the strings in this file into some other language, save the edited *.xliff* file, and import it:

1. Open the *.xliff* file in a decent text editor (or an XML editor if you have one).

2. Just for the sake of this example, I'm going to localize only the "Hello" button in the storyboard. So delete (carefully, so as not to mess up the XML) all the `<file>...</file>` element groups except the one whose original attribute is "Empty Window/Base.lproj/Main.storyboard". And delete (carefully) all the `<trans-unit>...</trans-unit>` elements except the one whose `<source>` is "Hello".

3. To specify Spanish as the target language, add an attribute to the `<file>` element: `target-language="es"`.

4. To provide an actual translation, add a `<target>` element after the `<source>` element, and give it some text, such as "Hola". Save. The file should now look something like this:

```
<?xml version="1.0" encoding="UTF-8" standalone="no"?>
<xliff xmlns="urn:oasis:names:tc:xliff:document:1.2"
  xmlns:xsi="http://www.w3.org/2001/XMLSchema-instance" version="1.2"
  xsi:schemaLocation="urn:oasis:names:tc:xliff:document:1.2
  http://docs.oasis-open.org/xliff/v1.2/os/xliff-core-1.2-strict.xsd">
  <file original="Empty Window/Base.lproj/Main.storyboard"
  source-language="en" target-language="es" datatype="plaintext">
    <header>
      <tool tool-id="com.apple.dt.xcode" tool-name="Xcode"
      tool-version="6.2" build-num="6C107a"/>
    </header>
    <body>
      <trans-unit id="PYn-zN-WlH.normalTitle">
        <source>Hello</source>
        <target>Hola</target>
        <note>Class = "UIButton"; normalTitle = "Hello";
          ObjectID = "PYn-zN-WlH";</note>
      </trans-unit>
    </body>
  </file>
</xliff>
```

5. Back in Xcode, edit the target and choose Editor → Import Localizations. In the Open dialog, select the edited *en.xliff* and click Open.

6. Xcode complains that we didn't translate everything there was to translate. Ignore that complaint and click Import.

Amazing things have now happened! With no visible prompting, Xcode has added Spanish to our localizations, and has created an additional *InfoPlist.strings* file, an additional *Main.strings* file, and an additional *Localizable.strings* file, all localized to Spanish. If you examine *Main.strings*, you'll see that it looks just as it would have looked if we had edited it manually:

```
/* Class = "UIButton"; normalTitle = "Hello"; ObjectID = "PYn-zN-WlH"; */
"PYn-zN-WlH.normalTitle" = "Hola";
```

Clearly, the round-trip to and from an *.xliff* file is an extremely convenient way to create and maintain your localizations. The *structure* of the localization within your project is exactly the same as I described earlier in this section, but the *.xliff* file externalizes that same information in a format that can be readily edited in a single file. The *.xliff* export process runs `ibtool` and `genstrings` for you, so your localized content is easy to maintain as you add interface and code.

Archiving and Distribution

By *distribution* is meant providing to others who are not developers on your team your built app for running on their devices. There are two kinds of distribution:

Ad Hoc distribution
> You are providing a copy of your app to a limited set of known users so that they can try it on their specific devices and report bugs, make suggestions, and so forth.

App Store distribution
> You are providing the app to the App Store so that anyone can download it (possibly for a fee) and run it.

To create a copy of your app for distribution, you need first to build an *archive* of your app. It is this archive that will subsequently be exported for Ad Hoc or App Store distribution. An archive is basically a preserved build. It has three main purposes:

Distribution
> An archive will serve as the basis for an Ad Hoc distribution or an App Store distribution.

Reproduction
> Every time you build, conditions can vary, so the resulting app might behave slightly differently. But an archive preserves a specific built binary; every distribution from a particular archive is guaranteed to contain an identical binary, and thus will behave the same way. This fact is important for testing: if a bug report comes in based on an app distributed from a particular archive, you can Ad Hoc distribute that archive to yourself and run it, knowing that you are testing exactly the same app.

Symbolication
> The archive includes a *.dSYM* file which allows Xcode to accept a crash log and report the crash's location in your code. This allows you to deal with crash reports from users.

Here's how to build an archive of your app:

1. Set the destination in the Scheme pop-up menu in the project window toolbar to iOS Device. Until you do this, the Product → Archive menu item will be disabled. You do *not* have to have a device connected; you are not building to run on a *particular* device, but saving an archive that will run on *some* device.

2. If you like, edit the scheme to confirm that the Release build configuration will be used for the Archive action. This is the default, but it does no harm to double-check.

3. Choose Product → Archive. The app is compiled and built. The archive itself is stored in a date folder within your user *Library/Developer/Xcode/Archives* folder. Also, it is listed in Xcode's Organizer window (Window → Organizer) under Archives; this window may open spontaneously to show the archive you've just created. You can add a comment here; you can also change the archive's name (this won't affect the name of the app).

To perform any kind of distribution based on your archive, you will also need a distribution identity (a private key and a distribution certificate in your computer's keychain) and a distribution profile for this app. If you're doing an Ad Hoc distribution and an App Store distribution, you'll need a separate distribution profile for each. Only a Developer Program member can obtain a distribution identity and profile.

 If you see a note in the Organizer window, "Distribution requires enrollment in the Apple Developer Program," you must have postponed signing up for a Developer Program membership. Well, now is the moment! Without a membership, your Organizer window is a Roach Motel: archives check in, but they can't check out.

You can obtain a distribution identity from within Xcode in exactly the same way as I described obtaining a development identity: in the Accounts preference pane, in the View Details dialog for your team, click the Create button to the right of iOS Distribution. If that doesn't work, obtain the distribution certificate manually, just as I described for a development certificate.

In theory, Xcode can also create an appropriate distribution profile for you when you export your archive. However, I have never found this to work reliably; I always create my distribution profiles manually, at the Member Center, in a web browser. Here's how to do that:

1. If this is to be an Ad Hoc distribution profile, collect the UDIDs of all the devices where this build is to run, and add each of them at the Member Center under Devices. (For an App Store distribution profile, omit this step.)

2. Make sure that the app is registered at the Member Center, as I described earlier in this chapter.

3. At the Member Center, under Provisioning Profiles, click the Plus button to ask for a new profile. In the Add iOS Provisioning Profile form, specify an Ad Hoc profile or an App Store profile. On the next screen, choose your app from the pop-up menu. On the next screen, choose your distribution certificate. On the next screen, for an Ad Hoc profile only, specify the devices you want this app to run on. On the next screen, give the profile a name.

   Be careful about the profile's name, as you will need to be able to recognize it later from within Xcode! My own practice is to assign a name containing the term "Ad-Hoc" or "AppStore" and the name of the app.

4. Click Generate to generate the profile. To obtain the profile, either click Download and then find the downloaded profile and double-click it to get Xcode to see it, or else open the View Details dialog in Xcode's Accounts preference pane and click the Download All button at the bottom left to make Xcode download it.

Ad Hoc Distribution

Apple's docs say that an Ad Hoc distribution build should include an icon that will appear in iTunes, but my experience is that this step, though it does work, is unnecessary. If you want to include this icon, it should be a PNG or JPEG file, 512×512 pixels in size, and its name should be *iTunesArtwork*, with *no file extension*. Make sure the icon is included in the build, being present in the Copy Bundle Resources build phase.

Here are the steps for creating an Ad Hoc distribution file (I'm assuming that you have a distribution identity, as described in the previous section):

1. If necessary, create, download, and install an Ad Hoc distribution profile for this app, as described in the previous section.

2. If necessary, create an archive of your app, as described in the previous section. Just before creating the archive, double-check your Code Signing build settings: your Code Signing Identity for a Release build (or whatever build configuration your scheme uses for an Archive action) should be iOS Distribution, and your Provisioning Profile should be Automatic. (It is possible to specify these settings more precisely, but I find that nowadays these general settings work well.)

3. In the Organizer window, under Archives, select the archive and click the Export button at the upper right of the window. A dialog appears. Here, you are to specify a method; choose Save for Ad Hoc Deployment. Click Next.

4. You are now asked to select a Development Team. Select the correct team and click Choose.

5. New in Xcode 7, you may see a dialog asking whether you want the exported app *thinned*, meaning that it will contain resources appropriate only to one type of

device, simulating what the App Store will do when the user downloads the app to a device. You probably don't, though it might be interesting to learn the size of your thinned app.

6. The archive is prepared, and a summary window is displayed. The name of the provisioning profile is shown, so you can tell that the right thing is happening. Click Next.

7. The file is saved to the Desktop inside a uniquely named folder. It will have the suffix *.ipa* ("iPhone app").

8. Locate in the Finder the file you just saved. Provide this file to your users with instructions.

A user should copy the *.ipa* file to a safe location, such as the Desktop, and then launch iTunes and drag the *.ipa* file from the Finder onto the iTunes icon in the Dock (or double-click the *.ipa* file). Then the user should connect the device to the computer, make certain the app is present in the list of apps for this device *and that it will be installed on the next sync*, and finally sync the device to cause the app to be copied to it. (If this isn't the first version of your app that you've distributed to your Ad Hoc testers, the user might need to delete the current version from the device beforehand; otherwise, the new version might not be copied to the device when syncing.)

If you listed your own device as one of the devices for which this Ad Hoc distribution profile was to be enabled, you can obey these instructions yourself to make sure the Ad Hoc distribution is working as expected. First, remove from your device any previous copies of this app (such as development copies) and any profiles that might be associated with this app (you can do that through the Devices window in Xcode). Then copy the app onto your device by syncing with iTunes as just described. The app should run on your device, and you should see the Ad Hoc distribution profile on your device. Because you are not privileged over your other Ad Hoc testers, what works for you should work for them.

There is a registration limit of 100 devices per year per developer (not per app), which limits your number of Ad Hoc testers. Devices used for development are counted against this limit. You can work around this limit, and provide your betas more conveniently to testers, by using TestFlight beta testing instead.

TestFlight beta testing lifts the limit of 100 devices to a limit of 1000 testers, and is more convenient than Ad Hoc distribution because your users download and install prelease versions of your app directly from the App Store onto their devices through the Test-Flight app (acquired by Apple in 2014 by buying Burstly). Configuration is performed at the iTunes Connect site; a prerelease version uploaded to iTunes Connect must be archived as if for App Store distribution (see the discussion of App Store submission later in this chapter). See the "TestFlight Beta Testing" chapter of Apple's *iTunes Connect Developer Guide.*

Prerelease versions of your app intended for distribution to beta testers (as opposed to internal testers who have direct access to your iTunes Connect account) require review by Apple.

Final App Preparations

As the big day approaches when you're thinking of submitting your app to the App Store, don't let the prospect of huge fame and massive profits hasten you past the all-important final stages of app preparation. Apple has a lot of requirements, and failure to meet them can cause your app to be rejected. Take your time. Make a checklist and go through it carefully. See Apple's *App Distribution Guide* as well as the "Icon and Image Design" chapter of the *Human Interface Guidelines* for full details.

Icons in the App

The simplest way to provide your app with icons is to use the asset catalog. If you're not using an asset catalog for icons and you'd like to switch to using one, edit the target and, in the General pane, under App Icons and Launch Images, next to App Icons Source, click the Use Asset Catalog button. The Use Asset Catalog button then changes to a pop-up menu listing the asset catalog's name and the name of the image set within the catalog to be used for icons.

The image sizes needed are listed in the asset catalog itself. Select an image slot and look in the Attributes inspector. Confusingly, "2x" or "3x" means that the image should be double or triple the listed dimensions for an icon; thus, for example, an iPhone app icon listed as "60pt" or "60×60," but also with "3x," means that you should provide an image measuring 180×180. To determine which slots should be displayed, use the checkboxes in the Attributes inspector when you select an icon set or launch image set (Figure 9-17). To add an image, drag it from the Finder into the appropriate slot.

An icon file must be a PNG file, without alpha transparency. It should be a full square; the rounding of the corners will be added for you. Apple seems nowadays to prefer simple, cartoony images with a few bright colors and possibly a gentle gradient background.

When your app is built and the asset catalog is processed, the icons are written out to the top level of the app bundle and are given appropriate names (Figure 6-15); at the same time, an appropriate entry is written into the app's *Info.plist*, enabling the system to find and display the icon on a device. The details are complicated, but you won't have to worry about them — that is exactly why you're using the asset catalog!

App icon sizes have changed over the years. If your app is to be backward-compatible to earlier systems, you may need additional icons in additional sizes, corresponding to

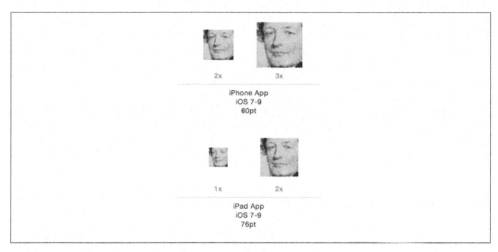

Figure 9-17. Icon slots in the asset catalog

the expectations of those earlier systems. Again, this is exactly the sort of thing the asset catalog will help you with.

Optionally, you may elect to include smaller versions of your icon to appear when the user does a search on the device, as well as in the Settings app if you include a settings bundle. However, I never include those icons.

Other Icons

When you submit an app to the App Store, you will be asked to supply a 1024×1024 PNG or high-quality JPEG icon to be displayed at the App Store. Apple's guidelines say that it should not merely be a scaled-up version of your app's icon; but it must not differ perceptibly from your app's icon, either, or your app will be rejected (I know this from bitter experience).

The App Store icon does *not* need to be built into your app; indeed, it should not be, as it will merely swell the built app's size unnecessarily. On the other hand, you will probably want to keep it in your project (and in your project folder) so that you can find and maintain it easily. So I recommend that you import it into your project and copy it into your project folder, but do *not* add it to any target.

If you created an *iTunesArtwork* icon for Ad Hoc distribution, you may wish to delete it from the Copy Bundle Resources build phase now.

Launch Images

There is a delay between the moment when the user taps your app's icon to launch it and the moment when your app is up and running and displaying its initial window. To cover this delay and give the user a visible indication that something is happening, a launch image needs to be displayed during that interval.

The launch image needn't be detailed. It might be just a blank depiction of the main elements or regions of the interface that will be present when the app has finished launching. In this way, when the app *does* finish launching, the transition from the launch image to the real app will be a matter of those elements or regions being filled in.

In iOS 7 and before, the launch image was literally an image (a PNG file). It had to be included in your app bundle, and it had to obey certain naming conventions. As the variety of screen sizes and resolutions of iOS devices proliferated, so did the number of required launch images. The asset catalog, introduced in iOS 7, was helpful in this regard. But with the introduction of the iPhone 6 and iPhone 6 Plus, the entire situation threatened to become unmanageable.

For this reason, iOS 8 introduced a better solution. Instead of a set of launch images, you now provide a *launch nib file* — a single *.xib* or *.storyboard* file containing a single view to be displayed as a launch image. You construct this view using subviews and autolayout. Thus, the view is automatically reconfigured to match the screen size and orientation of the device on which the app is launching.

By default, a new app project comes with a *LaunchScreen.storyboard* file. This is where you design your launch image. The *Info.plist* points to this file as the value of its "Launch screen interface file base name" key (`UILaunchStoryboardName`). You can configure the *Info.plist*, if necessary, by editing the target and setting the Launch Screen File field (under App Icons and Launch Images).

You should take advantage of this feature — and not merely because it is convenient. The presence of a "Launch screen interface file base name" key in your *Info.plist* tells the system that your app runs natively on newer device types, such as the iPhone 6 and iPhone 6 Plus. Without it, your app will be displayed zoomed, as if the iPhone 6 were just a big iPhone 5S — in effect, you won't be getting all the pixels you're entitled to (and the display will be somewhat fuzzy).

Another reason for using a launch nib file is that it is localizable! As with any *.xib* or *.storyboard* file, strings displayed in a base-localized launch screen *.xib* or *.storyboard* file can be localized through individual *.strings* files.

As far as I can tell, custom fonts included in your app bundle cannot be displayed in a launch nib file. This is evidently because they have not yet been loaded at the time the launch screen needs to be displayed.

The bad news is that if your app is to be backward-compatible to earlier systems, you'll have to supply old-fashioned launch images *in addition to* the launch nib file. The requirements for launch images in iOS 7 and before are complicated — and are made more complicated by the fact that the rules have changed over the years, so that the more systems you want to be compatible with, the more requirements you'll have to satisfy. I have covered these requirements in earlier editions of this book, and I'm not going to repeat them here.

 Apple provides an extremely helpful sample code project called Application Icons and Launch Images for iOS. It provides icons and launch images of all sizes and demonstrates the proper naming conventions.

Screenshots and Video Previews

When you submit your app to the App Store, you will be asked for one or more screenshots of your app in action to be displayed at the App Store. You should take these screenshots beforehand and be prepared to provide them during the app submission process. You must provide at least one screenshot corresponding to the screen size of every device on which your app can run, in the corresponding resolution.

You can obtain screenshots either from the Simulator or from a device connected to the computer:

Simulator
> Run the app in the Simulator, first setting the destination to get the desired device type. Choose File → Save Screen Shot.

Device
> In Xcode, in the Devices window, locate your connected device under Devices and click Take Screenshot. Alternatively, choose Debug → View Debugging → Take Screenshot of [Device].

In both cases, the screenshot file is saved to wherever screenshots are normally saved on your computer (usually the Desktop).

You can also take a screenshot on a device by clicking the screen lock button and the Home button simultaneously. Now the screenshot is in the Camera Roll in the Photos app, and you can communicate it to your computer in any convenient way (such as by emailing it to yourself).

You can also submit to the App Store a video preview showing your app in action. It can be up to 30 seconds long, in H.264 or Apple ProRes format. Your computer can capture video of your device if it is running OS X 10.10 ("Yosemite") or later. Your device must be sufficiently modern to have a Lightning connector:

1. Connect the device to the computer and launch QuickTime Player. Choose File → New Movie Recording.
2. If necessary, set the Camera and Microphone to the device, using the pop-up menu from the down-pointing chevron button next to the Record button that appears when you hover the mouse over the QuickTime Player window.
3. Start recording, and exercise the app on the device. When you're finished, stop recording and save.

The resulting movie file can be edited in iMovie or Final Cut Pro to prepare it for submission to the App Store. For example, in iMovie:

1. After importing the movie file, choose File → New App Preview.
2. Edit! When you're done editing, choose File → Share → App Preview. This ensures the correct resolution and format.

For more details, see the "App Preview" section of the "First Steps" chapter of Apple's *iTunes Connect Developer Guide*.

Property List Settings

A number of settings in the *Info.plist* are crucial to the proper behavior of your app. You should peruse Apple's *Information Property List Key Reference* for full information. Most of the required keys are created as part of the template, and are given reasonable default values, but you should check them anyway. The following are particularly worthy of attention:

Bundle display name (CFBundleDisplayName)
> The name that appears under your app's icon on the device screen; this name needs to be short in order to avoid truncation. I talked earlier in this chapter about how to localize the display name.

Supported interface orientations (UISupportedInterfaceOrientations)
> This key designates the totality of orientations in which the app is ever permitted to appear. You can perform this setting with checkboxes in the General tab of the target editor. But you may also need to edit the *Info.plist* manually to rearrange the order of possible orientations, because on an iPhone the *first* orientation listed may be the one into which the app will actually launch.

Required device capabilities (`UIRequiredDeviceCapabilities`)
> You should set this key if the app requires capabilities that are not present on all devices. But don't use this key unless it makes no sense for your app to run *at all* on a device lacking the specified capabilities.

Bundle version (`CFBundleVersion`)
> Your app needs a version number. The best place to set it is the General tab of the target editor. Things are a little confusing here because there are two fields:

> *Version*
>> Corresponds in the *Info.plist* to "Bundle versions string, short" (`CFBundleShort-VersionString`).

> *Build*
>> Corresponds in the *Info.plist* to "Bundle version" (`CFBundleVersion`).

> As far as I can determine, Apple will pay attention to the former if it is set, and otherwise will fall back on the latter. In general I play it safe and set both to the same value when submitting to the App Store. The value needs to be a version string, such as `"1.0"`. The version string will be displayed at the App Store, distinguishing one release from another. Failure to increment the version string when submitting an update will cause the update to be rejected. It is legal, however, to increment the Build number without incrementing the Version number, and you will need to do so if you submit several successive builds of the same prospective release (during the course of TestFlight testing, or because you found a bug and had to withdraw a submitted binary before it appeared on the App Store).

Submission to the App Store

When you're satisfied that your app works well, and you've installed or collected all the necessary resources, you're ready to submit your app to the App Store for distribution. To do so, you'll need to make preparations at the iTunes Connect web site. You can find a link to it on the iOS developer pages when you've logged in at Apple's site. You can go directly to *http://itunesconnect.apple.com*, but you'll still need to log in with your iOS Developer username and password.

 The first time you visit iTunes Connect, you should go to the Contracts section and complete submission of your contract. You can't offer any apps for sale until you do, and even free apps require completion of a contractual form.

I'm not going to recite all the steps you have to go through to tell iTunes Connect about your app, as these are described thoroughly in Apple's *iTunes Connect Developer*

Guide, which is the final word on such matters. But here are some of the main pieces of information you will sooner or later have to supply:

Your app's name
>This is the name that will appear at the App Store; it need not be identical to the short name that will appear under the app's icon on the device, dictated by the "Bundle display name" setting in your *Info.plist* file. Apple recommends that this be 25 characters or fewer, though it can be longer. You can get a rude shock when you submit your app's information to iTunes Connect and discover that the name you wanted is already taken. There is no reliable way to learn this in advance, and such a discovery can necessitate a certain amount of last-minute scrambling on your part.

Description
>You must supply a description of fewer than 4,000 characters; Apple recommends fewer than 580 characters, and the first paragraph is the most important, because this may be all that users see at first when they visit the App Store. It must be pure text, without HTML and without character styling.

Keywords
>This is a comma-separated list shorter than 100 characters. These keywords will be used, in addition to your app's name, to help users discover your app through the Search feature of the App Store.

Support
>This the URL of a web site where users can find more information about your app; it's good to have the site ready in advance.

Copyright
>Do not include a copyright symbol in this string; it will be added for you at the App Store.

SKU number
>This is arbitrary, so don't get nervous about it. It's just a unique identifier, unique within the world of your own apps. It's convenient if it has something to do with your app's name. It needn't be a number; it can actually be any string.

Price
>You don't get to make up a price. You have to choose from a list of pricing "tiers."

Availability Date
>There's an option to make the app available as soon as it is approved, and this will typically be your choice.

As you submit information, click Save often! If the connection goes down and you haven't explicitly saved, all your work can be lost. (Can you guess how I know that?)

When you're ready to upload the app for which you've already submitted the information at iTunes Connect, you can perform the upload using Xcode. You should have an iOS Development identity. Your app should already have been archived with the Code Signing Identity build setting for the Release configuration set to iOS Distribution (presumably, this will be an archive you've already created and tested using Ad Hoc or TestFlight distribution). Select the archived build in the Organizer and click Upload to App Store. The upload will be performed, and the app will be validated at the far end.

Alternatively, you can use Application Loader. Export the archive as an *.ipa* file, as for an Ad Hoc distribution, but when selecting a method for export, choose Save for iOS App Store Deployment. Launch Application Loader by choosing Xcode → Open Developer Tool → Application Loader, and hand it the *.ipa* file.

After uploading the archive, you have one final step to perform. Wait about five or ten minutes for the binary to be processed at Apple's end. Then return to iTunes Connect, where you submitted your app information. You will now be able to select the binary, save, and submit the app for review.

You will subsequently receive emails from Apple informing you of your app's status as it passes through various stages: "Waiting For Review," "In Review," and finally, if all has gone well, "Ready For Sale" (even if it's a free app). Your app will then appear at the App Store.

PART III

Cocoa

The Cocoa Touch frameworks provide the general capabilities needed by any iOS application. Buttons can be tapped, text can be read, screens of interface can succeed one another, because Cocoa makes it so. To use the framework, you must learn to let the framework use you. You must put your code in the right place so that it will be called at the right time. You must fulfill certain obligations that Cocoa expects of you. You master Cocoa by being Cocoa's obedient servant. In this part of the book, that's what you'll learn to do.

- Chapter 10 describes how Cocoa is organized and structured through such Objective-C language features as subclassing, categories, and protocols. Then some important built-in Cocoa object types are introduced. The chapter concludes with a description of Cocoa key–value coding and a look at how the root NSObject class is organized.

- Chapter 11 presents Cocoa's event-driven model of activity, along with its major design patterns and event-related features — notifications, delegation, data sources, target–action, the responder chain, and key–value observing. The chapter concludes with some words of wisdom about managing the barrage of events Cocoa will be throwing at you, and how to escape that barrage momentarily with delayed performance.

- Chapter 12 is about Cocoa memory management. I'll explain how memory management of reference types works. Then some special memory management situations are described: autorelease pools, retain cycles, notifications and timers, nib loading, and CFTypeRefs. The chapter concludes with a discussion of Cocoa property memory management, and advice on how to debug memory management issues.

- Chapter 13 discusses the question of how your objects are going to see and communicate with one another within the confines of the Cocoa-based world. It concludes with some advice about adhering to the model–view–controller architecture.

Finally, don't forget to read Appendix A for more detail about how Objective-C and Swift interact and cooperate.

CHAPTER 10

Cocoa Classes

When you program iOS, you're programming Cocoa. So you need to be acquainted with Cocoa; you have to know, as it were, who you're talking to when you talk to Cocoa, and what sort of behavior Cocoa is likely to expect from you. Cocoa is a big framework, subdivided into many smaller frameworks, and it takes time and experience to become reasonably familiar with it. Nevertheless, Cocoa has certain chief conventions and primary components that can serve as guideposts from the outset.

The Cocoa API is written mostly in Objective-C, and Cocoa itself consists mostly of Objective-C classes, derived from the root class, NSObject. When programming iOS, you'll be using mostly the built-in Cocoa classes. Objective-C classes are comparable to and compatible with Swift classes, but the other two Swift object type flavors, structs and enums, are not matched by anything in Objective-C. Structs and enums declared originally in Swift cannot generally be handed across the bridge from Swift to Objective-C and Cocoa. Fortunately, some of the most important native Swift object types are also bridged to Cocoa classes. (See Appendix A for more details about the Objective-C language and how communications work between Swift and Objective-C.)

This chapter introduces Cocoa's class structure. It discusses how Cocoa is conceptually organized, in terms of its underlying Objective-C features, and then surveys some of the most commonly encountered Cocoa utility classes, concluding with a discussion of the Cocoa root class and its features, which are inherited by all Cocoa classes.

Subclassing

Cocoa effectively hands you a large repertory of objects that already know how to behave in certain desirable ways. A UIButton, for example, knows how to draw itself and how to respond when the user taps it; a UITextField knows how to display editable text, how to summon the keyboard, and how to accept keyboard input.

Often, the default behavior or appearance of an object supplied by Cocoa won't be quite what you're after, and you'll want to customize it. This does *not* necessarily mean that you need to subclass! Cocoa classes are heavily endowed with methods that you can call, and properties that you can set, precisely in order to customize an instance, and these will be your first resort. Always study the documentation for a Cocoa class to see whether instances can already be made to do what you want. For example, the class documentation for UIButton shows that you can set a button's title, title color, internal image, background image, and many other features and behaviors, without subclassing.

Nevertheless, sometimes setting properties and calling methods won't suffice to customize an instance the way you want to. In such cases, Cocoa may provide methods that are called internally as an instance does its thing, and whose behavior you can customize by subclassing and overriding (Chapter 4). You don't have the source code for any of Cocoa's built-in classes, but you can still subclass them, creating a new class that acts just like a built-in class except for the modifications you provide.

Certain Cocoa Touch classes are subclassed routinely. For example, a plain vanilla UIViewController, not subclassed, is very rare, and an iOS app without at least one UIViewController subclass would be practically impossible.

Another case in point is UIView. Cocoa Touch is full of built-in UIView subclasses that behave and draw themselves as needed (UIButton, UITextField, and so on), and you will rarely need to subclass any of them. On the other hand, you might create your *own* UIView subclass, whose job would be to draw itself in some completely new way. You don't actually draw a UIView; rather, when a UIView needs drawing, its `drawRect:` method is called so that the view can draw itself. So the way to draw a UIView in some completely custom manner is to subclass UIView and implement `drawRect:` in the subclass. As the documentation says, "Subclasses that ... draw their view's content should override this method and implement their drawing code there." The documentation is saying that you *need* to subclass UIView in order to draw content that is completely your own.

For example, suppose we want our window to contain a horizontal line. There is no horizontal line interface widget built into Cocoa, so we'll just have to roll our own — a UIView that draws itself as a horizontal line. Let's try it:

1. In our Empty Window example project, choose File → New → File and specify iOS → Source → Cocoa Touch Class, and in particular a subclass of UIView. Call the class MyHorizLine. Xcode creates *MyHorizLine.swift*. Make sure it's part of the app target.

2. In *MyHorizLine.swift*, replace the contents of the class declaration with this (without further explanation):

```
    required init?(coder aDecoder: NSCoder) {
        super.init(coder:aDecoder)
        self.backgroundColor = UIColor.clearColor()
    }
    override func drawRect(rect: CGRect) {
        let c = UIGraphicsGetCurrentContext()!
        CGContextMoveToPoint(c, 0, 0)
        CGContextAddLineToPoint(c, self.bounds.size.width, 0)
        CGContextStrokePath(c)
    }
```

3. Edit the storyboard. Find UIView in the Object library (it is called simply "View"), and drag it into the View object in the canvas. You may resize it to be less tall.

4. With the UIView that you just dragged into the canvas still selected, use the Identity inspector to change its class to MyHorizLine.

Build and run the app in the Simulator. You'll see a horizontal line corresponding to the location of the top of the MyHorizLine instance in the nib. Our view has drawn itself as a horizontal line, because we subclassed it to do so.

In that example, we started with a bare UIView that had no drawing functionality of its own. That's why there was no need to call super; the default implementation of UIView's drawRect: does nothing. But you might also be able to subclass a built-in UIView subclass to modify the way it already draws itself. For example, the UILabel documentation shows that two methods are present for exactly this purpose. Both drawTextInRect: and textRectForBounds:limitedToNumberOfLines: explicitly tell us: "This method should only be overridden by subclasses that want to [modify how the label is drawn]." The implication is that these are methods that will be called for us, automatically, by Cocoa, as a label draws itself; thus, we can subclass UILabel and implement these methods in our subclass to modify how a particular type of label draws itself.

Here's an example from one of my own apps, in which I subclass UILabel to make a label that draws its own rectangular border and has its content inset somewhat from that border, by overriding drawTextInRect:. As the documentation tells us: "In your overridden method, you can configure the current context further and then invoke super to do the actual drawing [of the text]." Let's try it:

1. In the Empty Window project, make a new class file, a UILabel subclass; call the class MyBoundedLabel.

2. In *MyBoundedLabel.swift*, insert this code into the body of the class declaration:

```
    override func drawTextInRect(rect: CGRect) {
        let context = UIGraphicsGetCurrentContext()!
        CGContextStrokeRect(context, CGRectInset(self.bounds, 1.0, 1.0))
        super.drawTextInRect(CGRectInset(rect, 5.0, 5.0))
    }
```

3. Edit the storyboard, add a UILabel to the interface, and change its class in the Identity inspector to MyBoundedLabel.

Build and run the app, and you'll see how the rectangle is drawn and the label's text is inset within it.

Oddly enough, however (and you might be particularly surprised by this if you've used another object-oriented application framework), subclassing is one of the rarer ways in which your code will relate to Cocoa. Knowing when to subclass can be somewhat tricky, but the general rule is that you probably *shouldn't* subclass unless you're explicitly invited to do so. Most built-in Cocoa Touch classes will never need subclassing (and some, in their documentation, downright forbid it).

One reason why subclassing is rare in Cocoa is that so many built-in classes use *delegation* (Chapter 11) as the preferred way of letting you customize their behavior. For example, you wouldn't subclass UIApplication (the class of the singleton shared application instance) just in order to respond when the application has finished launching, because the delegate mechanism provides a way to do that (`application:didFinish-LaunchingWithOptions:`). That's why the templates give us an AppDelegate class, which is *not* a UIApplication subclass, but which does adopt the UIApplicationDelegate protocol.

On the other hand, if you needed to perform certain tricky customizations of your app's fundamental event messaging behavior, you might subclass UIApplication in order to override `sendEvent:`. The documentation has a special "Subclassing Notes" section that tells you this, and also tells you, rightly, that doing so would be "very rare." (See Chapter 6 on how to ensure that your UIApplication subclass is instantiated as the app launches.)

Categories and Extensions

A *category* is an Objective-C language feature that allows code to reach right into an existing class and inject additional methods. This is comparable to a Swift extension (see Chapter 4). Using a Swift extension, you can add class or instance methods to a Cocoa class; the Swift headers make heavy use of extensions, both as a way of organizing Swift's own object types and as a way of modifying Cocoa classes. In the same way, Cocoa uses categories to organize its own classes.

 Objective-C categories have names, and you may see references to these names in the headers, the documentation, and so forth. However, the names are effectively meaningless, so don't worry about them.

How Swift Uses Extensions

If you look in the main Swift header, you'll see that many native object type declarations consist of an initial declaration followed by a series of extensions. For example, after declaring the generic struct Array<Element>, the header proceeds to declare no fewer than seven extensions on the Array struct. Some of these add protocol adoptions; most of them don't. All of them add declarations of properties or methods to Array; that's what extensions are for.

These extensions are not, of themselves, functionally significant; the header *could* have declared the Array struct with all of those properties and methods within the body of a single declaration. Instead, it breaks things up into multiple extensions. The extensions are simply a way of clumping related functionality together, organizing this object type's members so as to make them easier for human readers to understand.

In the Swift Core Graphics header, just about *everything* is an extension. Here Swift is adapting types defined elsewhere — adapting Swift numeric types for use with Core Graphics and the CGFloat numeric type, and adapting Cocoa structs such as CGPoint and CGRect as Swift object types. CGRect, in particular, is provided with numerous additional properties, initializers, and methods so that you can work with it directly as a Swift struct rather than having to call the Cocoa Core Graphics C utility functions that manipulate a CGRect.

How You Use Extensions

Swift permits you to write global functions, and there is nothing formally wrong with doing so. Nevertheless, for the sake of object-oriented encapsulation, you will often want to write a function as part of an existing object type. It will often be simplest and most sensible for you to inject such functions, as methods, into an existing object type with an extension. Subclassing merely to add a method or two is heavy-handed — and besides, it often wouldn't help you do what you need to do. (Also, extensions work on all three flavors of Swift object type, whereas you can't subclass a Swift enum or struct.)

For example, suppose you wanted to add a method to Cocoa's UIView class. You could subclass UIView and declare your method, but then it would be present only in your UIView subclass and in subclasses of that subclass: it would *not* be present in UIButton, UILabel, and all the other built-in UIView subclasses — because they are subclasses of UIView, not of *your* subclass, and you can't do anything to change that! An extension, on the other hand, solves the problem beautifully: you inject your method into UIView, and it is inherited by all built-in UIView subclasses as well.

New in Swift 2.0, you can use protocol extensions to inject functionality into classes in a selective but unified manner. Suppose I want UIButton and UIBarButtonItem — which is not a UIView, but does have button-like behavior — to share a certain method. I can declare a protocol with a method, implement that method in a protocol extension, and then use extensions to make UIButton and UIBarButtonItem adopt that protocol and thus acquire that method:

```
protocol ButtonLike {
    func behaveInButtonLikeWay()
}
extension ButtonLike {
    func behaveInButtonLikeWay() {
        // ...
    }
}
extension UIButton : ButtonLike {}
extension UIBarButtonItem : ButtonLike {}
```

Chapter 4 provides some examples of extensions I've written in my real iOS programming life (see "Extensions" on page 197). Also, as I explain there, I often use extensions in the same way as the Swift headers do, organizing my code for a single object type into multiple extensions simply for clarity.

How Cocoa Uses Categories

Cocoa uses categories as an organizational tool very much as Swift uses extensions. The declaration of a class will often be divided by functionality into multiple categories, and these will often appear in separate header files.

A good example is NSString. NSString is defined as part of the Foundation framework, and its basic methods are declared in *NSString.h*. Here we find that NSString itself, aside from its initializers, has just two methods, `length` and `characterAtIndex:`, because these are regarded as the minimum functionality that a string needs in order to be a string.

Additional NSString methods — those that create a string, deal with a string's encoding, split a string, search in a string, and so on — are clumped into categories. These are shown in the Swift translation of the header as extensions. So, for example, after the declaration for the String class itself, we find this in the Swift translation of the header:

```
extension NSString {
    func substringFromIndex(from: Int) -> String
    func substringToIndex(to: Int) -> String
    // ...
}
```

That, as it turns out, is actually Swift's translation of this Objective-C code:

```
@interface NSString (NSStringExtensionMethods)
- (NSString *)substringFromIndex:(NSUInteger)from;
- (NSString *)substringToIndex:(NSUInteger)to;
// ...
@end
```

That notation — the keyword @interface, followed by a class name, followed by another name in parentheses — is an Objective-C category.

Moreover, although the declarations for some of Cocoa's NSString categories appear in this same file, *NSString.h*, many of them appear elsewhere. For example:

- A string may serve as a file pathname, so we also find a category on NSString in *NSPathUtilities.h*, where methods and properties such as pathComponents are declared for splitting a pathname string into its constituents and the like.

- In *NSURL.h*, which is primarily devoted to declaring the NSURL class (and *its* categories), there's also another NSString category, declaring methods for dealing with percent-escaping in a URL string, such as stringByAddingPercentEscapes-UsingEncoding.

- Off in a completely different framework (UIKit), *NSStringDrawing.h* adds two further NSString categories, with methods like drawAtPoint: having to do with drawing a string in a graphics context.

This organization won't matter to you as a programmer, because an NSString is an NSString, no matter how it acquires its methods. But it can matter when you consult the documentation! The NSString methods declared in *NSString.h*, *NSPathUtilities.h*, and *NSURL.h* are documented together in the NSString class documentation page. But the NSString methods declared in *NSStringDrawing.h* are not; instead, they appear in a separate document, *NSString UIKit Additions Reference*. (Presumably, this is because because they originate in a different framework.) As a result, the string drawing methods can be difficult to discover, especially as the NSString class documentation page doesn't link to the other document. I regard this as a major flaw in the structure of the Cocoa documentation.

Protocols

Objective-C has protocols, and these are generally comparable to and compatible with Swift protocols (see Chapter 4). Since classes are the only Objective-C object type, all Objective-C protocols are seen by Swift as class protocols. Conversely, Swift protocols marked as @objc (which are implicitly class protocols) can be seen by Objective-C. Cocoa makes extensive use of protocols.

For example, let's talk about how Cocoa objects are copied. Some objects can be copied; some can't. This has nothing to do with an object's class heritage. Yet we would like a uniform method to which any object that *can* be copied will respond. So Cocoa defines a protocol named NSCopying, which declares just one required method, copyWith-Zone:. Here's how the NSCopying protocol is declared in Objective-C (in *NSObject.h*):

```
@protocol NSCopying
- (id)copyWithZone:(nullable NSZone *)zone;
@end
```

That's translated into Swift as follows:

```
protocol NSCopying {
    func copyWithZone(zone: NSZone) -> AnyObject
}
```

The NSCopying protocol declaration in *NSObject.h*, however, is not a statement that NSObject conforms to NSCopying. Indeed, NSObject does *not* conform to NSCopying! This doesn't compile:

```
let obj = NSObject().copyWithZone(nil) // compile error
```

But this does compile, because NSString *does* conform to NSCopying (the literal "hello" is implicitly bridged to NSString):

```
let s = "hello".copyWithZone(nil)
```

A typical Cocoa pattern is that Cocoa wants to say: "An instance of any class will do here, provided it implements the following methods." That, obviously, is a protocol. For example, consider how a protocol is used in connection with a table view (UITableView). A table view gets its data from a data source. For this purpose, UITableView declares a dataSource property, like this:

```
@property (nonatomic, weak, nullable) id <UITableViewDataSource> dataSource;
```

That's translated into Swift as follows:

```
weak var dataSource: UITableViewDataSource?
```

UITableViewDataSource is a protocol. The table view is saying: "I don't care what class my data source belongs to, but whatever it is, it should conform to the UITableView-DataSource protocol." Such conformance constitutes a promise that the data source will implement at least the required instance methods `tableView:numberOfRowsIn-Section:` and `tableView:cellForRowAtIndexPath:`, which the table view will call when it needs to know what data to display. When you use a UITableView, and you want to provide it with a data source object, the class of that object *will* adopt UITableView-DataSource and *will* implement its required methods; otherwise, your code won't compile:

```
let obj = NSObject()
let tv = UITableView()
tv.dataSource = obj // compile error
```

Far and away the most pervasive use of protocols in Cocoa is in connection with the delegation pattern. I'll discuss this pattern in detail in Chapter 11, but you can readily see an example in our handy Empty Window project: the AppDelegate class provided by the project template is declared like this:

```
class AppDelegate: UIResponder, UIApplicationDelegate { // ...
```

AppDelegate's chief purpose on earth is to serve as the shared application's delegate. The shared application object is a UIApplication, and UIApplication's `delegate` property is declared like this:

```
unowned(unsafe) var delegate: UIApplicationDelegate?
```

(I'll explain the `unsafe` modifier in Chapter 12.) The `UIApplicationDelegate` type is a protocol. This is how the shared UIApplication object knows that its delegate might be capable of receiving messages such as `application:didFinishLaunchingWith-Options:`. So the AppDelegate class officially announces its role by explicitly adopting the UIApplicationDelegate protocol.

A Cocoa protocol has its own documentation page. When the UIApplication class documentation tells you that the `delegate` property is typed as a UIApplicationDelegate, it's implicitly telling you that if you want to know what messages a UIApplication's delegate might receive, you need to look in the UIApplicationDelegate protocol documentation. You won't find `application:didFinishLaunchingWithOptions:` mentioned anywhere on the UIApplication class documentation page! It's documented in the UIApplicationDelegate protocol documentation page.

This separation of information can be particularly confusing when a class adopts a protocol. When a class's documentation mentions that the class conforms to a protocol, don't forget to examine that protocol's documentation! The latter might contain important information about how the class behaves. To learn what messages can be sent to an object, you need to look upward through the superclass inheritance chain; you also need to look at any protocols that this object's class (or superclass) conforms to. For example, as I already mentioned in Chapter 8, you won't find out that UIViewController gets a `viewWillTransitionToSize:withTransitionCoordinator:` event by looking at the UIViewController class documentation page: you have to look in the documentation for the UIContentContainer protocol, which UIViewController adopts.

Informal Protocols

You may occasionally see, online or in the documentation, a reference to an *informal protocol*. An informal protocol isn't really a protocol at all; it's just a way of providing the compiler with a method signature so that it will allow a message to be sent without complaining.

There are two complementary ways to implement an informal protocol. One is to define a category on NSObject; this makes any object eligible to receive the messages listed in the category. The other is to define a protocol to which no class formally conforms; instead, messages listed in the protocol are sent only to objects typed as `id` (AnyObject), thus suppressing any possible objections from the compiler (see "Suppressing type checking" on page 206).

These techniques were widespread before protocols could declare methods as optional; now they are largely unnecessary, and are also mildly dangerous. In iOS 9, very few informal protocols remain — but they do exist. For example, NSKeyValueCoding (discussed later in this chapter) is an informal protocol; you may see the term NSKeyValueCoding in the documentation and elsewhere, but there isn't actually any such type: it's a category on NSObject.

Optional Methods

Objective-C protocols, and Swift protocols marked as @objc, can have optional members (see "Optional Protocol Members" on page 179). The question thus arises: How, in practice, is an optional method feasible? We know that if a message is sent to an object and the object can't handle that message, an exception is raised and your app will likely crash. But a method declaration is a contract suggesting that the object *can* handle that message. If we subvert that contract by declaring a method that might or might not be implemented, aren't we inviting crashes?

The answer is that Objective-C is both dynamic and introspective. Objective-C can ask an object whether it can really deal with a message without actually sending it that message. The key method here is NSObject's respondsToSelector: method, which takes a selector parameter and returns a Bool. (A selector is basically a method name expressed independently of any method call; see Appendix A.) Thus it is possible to send a message to an object only if it would be safe to do so.

Demonstrating respondsToSelector: in Swift is generally a little tricky, because it's hard to get Swift to throw away its strict type checking long enough to let us send an object a message to which it might not respond. In this artificial example, I start by defining, at top level, *two* classes: one that derives from NSObject, because otherwise we can't send respondsToSelector: to it, and another to declare the message that I want to send conditionally:

```
class MyClass : NSObject {
}
class MyOtherClass {
    @objc func woohoo() {}
}
```

Now I can say this:

```
let mc = MyClass()
if mc.respondsToSelector("woohoo") {
    (mc as AnyObject).woohoo()
}
```

Note the cast of mc to AnyObject. This causes Swift to abandon its strict type checking (see "Suppressing type checking" on page 206); we can now send this object any message that Swift knows about, provided it is susceptible to Objective-C introspection — that's why I marked my woohoo declaration as @objc to start with. As you know, Swift provides a shorthand for sending a message conditionally — append a question mark to the name of the message:

```
let mc = MyClass()
(mc as AnyObject).woohoo?()
```

Behind the scenes, those two approaches are exactly the same; the latter is syntactic sugar for the former. In response to the question mark, Swift is calling respondsTo-Selector: for us, and will refrain from sending woohoo to this object if it *doesn't* respond to this selector.

That explains also how optional protocol members work. It is no coincidence that Swift treats optional protocol members like AnyObject members. Here's the example I gave in Chapter 4:

```
@objc protocol Flier {
    optional var song : String {get}
    optional func sing()
}
```

When you call sing?() on an object typed as a Flier, respondsToSelector: is called behind the scenes to determine whether this call is safe.

You wouldn't want to send a message optionally, or call respondsToSelector: explicitly, before sending just any old message, because it isn't generally necessary except with optional methods, and it slows things down a little. But Cocoa does in fact call responds-ToSelector: on your objects as a matter of course. To see that this is true, implement respondsToSelector: on AppDelegate in our Empty Window project and instrument it with logging:

```
override func respondsToSelector(aSelector: Selector) -> Bool {
    print(aSelector)
    return super.respondsToSelector(aSelector)
}
```

The output on my machine, as the Empty Window app launches, includes the following (I'm omitting private methods and multiple calls to the same method):

```
application:handleOpenURL:
application:openURL:sourceApplication:annotation:
application:openURL:options:
applicationDidReceiveMemoryWarning:
applicationWillTerminate:
applicationSignificantTimeChange:
application:willChangeStatusBarOrientation:duration:
application:didChangeStatusBarOrientation:
application:willChangeStatusBarFrame:
application:didChangeStatusBarFrame:
application:deviceAccelerated:
application:deviceChangedOrientation:
```

```
applicationDidBecomeActive:
applicationWillResignActive:
applicationDidEnterBackground:
applicationWillEnterForeground:
application:didResumeWithOptions:
application:handleWatchKitExtensionRequest:reply:
application:shouldSaveApplicationState:
application:supportedInterfaceOrientationsForWindow:
application:performFetchWithCompletionHandler:
application:didReceiveRemoteNotification:fetchCompletionHandler:
application:willFinishLaunchingWithOptions:
application:didFinishLaunchingWithOptions:
```

That's Cocoa, checking to see which of the optional UIApplicationDelegate protocol methods (including a couple of undocumented methods) are actually implemented by our AppDelegate instance — which, because it is the UIApplication object's delegate and formally conforms to the UIApplicationDelegate protocol, has explicitly agreed that it *might* be willing to respond to any of those messages. The entire delegate pattern (Chapter 11) depends upon this technique. Observe the policy followed here by Cocoa: it checks all the optional protocol methods once, when it first meets the object in question, and presumably stores the results; thus, the app is slowed a tiny bit by this one-time initial bombardment of `respondsToSelector:` calls, but now Cocoa knows all the answers and won't have to perform any of these same checks on the same object later.

Some Foundation Classes

The Foundation classes of Cocoa provide basic data types and utilities that will form the basis of your communication with Cocoa. Obviously I can't list all of them, let alone describe them fully, but I can survey those that you'll probably want to be aware of before writing even the simplest iOS program. For more information, start with Apple's list of the Foundation classes in the *Foundation Framework Reference*.

Useful Structs and Constants

NSRange is a C struct (see Appendix A) of importance in dealing with some of the classes I'm about to discuss. Its components are integers, `location` and `length`. For example, an NSRange whose `location` is 1 starts at the second element of something (because element counting is always zero-based), and if its `length` is 2 it designates this element and the next.

Cocoa supplies various convenience functions for dealing with an NSRange; for example, you can create an NSRange from two integers by calling `NSMakeRange`. (Note that the name, `NSMakeRange`, is backward compared to names like `CGPointMake` and `CGRect-Make`.) Swift helps out by bridging NSRange as a Swift struct, and you can convert between an NSRange and a Swift Range whose endpoints are Ints: Swift gives NSRange an initializer that takes a Swift Range, along with a toRange method.

NSNotFound is a constant integer indicating that some requested element was not found. The true numeric value of NSNotFound is of no concern to you; always compare against NSNotFound itself, to learn whether a result is meaningful. For example, if you ask for the index of a certain object in an NSArray and the object isn't present, the result is NSNotFound:

```
let arr = ["hey"] as NSArray
let ix = arr.indexOfObject("ho")
if ix == NSNotFound {
    print("it wasn't found")
}
```

Why does Cocoa resort to an integer value with a special meaning in this way? Because it has to. The result could not be 0 to indicate the absence of the object, because 0 would indicate the first element of the array. Nor could it be -1, because an NSArray index value is always positive. Nor could it be nil, because Objective-C can't return nil when an integer is expected (and even if it could, it would be seen as another way of saying 0). Contrast Swift, whose indexOf method returns an Int wrapped in an Optional, allowing it to return nil to indicate that the target object wasn't found.

If a search returns a range and the thing sought is not present, the location component of the resulting NSRange will be NSNotFound. As I mentioned in Chapter 3, Swift will sometimes do some clever automatic bridging for you, thus saving you the trouble of comparing with NSNotFound. The canonical example is NSString's rangeOfString: method. As defined in Cocoa, it returns an NSRange; Swift reconfigures it to return a Swift Range (of String.Index) wrapped in an Optional, returning nil if the NSRange's location is NSNotFound:

```
let s = "hello"
let r = s.rangeOfString("ha") // nil; an Optional wrapping a Swift Range
```

That's great if what you wanted is a Swift Range, suitable for further slicing a Swift String; but if you wanted an NSRange, suitable for handing back to Cocoa, you'll need to cast your original Swift String to an NSString to start with — thus causing the result to remain in the Cocoa world:

```
let s = "hello" as NSString
let r = s.rangeOfString("ha") // an NSRange
if r.location == NSNotFound {
    print("it wasn't found")
}
```

NSString and Friends

NSString is the Cocoa object version of a string. NSString and Swift String are bridged to one another, and you will often move between them without thinking, passing a Swift String to Cocoa where an NSString is expected, calling Cocoa NSString methods on a Swift String, and so forth. For example:

```
let s = "hello"
let s2 = s.capitalizedString
```

In that code, s is a Swift String and s2 is a Swift String, but the `capitalizedString` property actually belongs to Cocoa. In the course of that code, a Swift String has been bridged to NSString and passed to Cocoa, which has processed it to get the capitalized string; the capitalized string is an NSString, but it has been bridged back to a Swift String. In all likelihood, you are not conscious of the bridging; `capitalizedString` feels like a native String property, but it isn't — as you can readily prove by trying to use it in an environment where Foundation is not imported (you can't do it).

In some cases, you will need to cross the bridge yourself by casting explicitly. Swift may fail to cross the bridge implicitly for you; for example, if s is a Swift string, you can't call `stringByAppendingPathExtension:` on it directly:

```
let s = "MyFile"
let s2 = s.stringByAppendingPathExtension("txt") // compile error
```

You have to cast explicitly to NSString:

```
let s2 = (s as NSString).stringByAppendingPathExtension("txt")
```

Also, trouble can arise where you need to provide an index on a string. For example:

```
let s = "hello"
let s2 = s.substringToIndex(4) // compile error
```

The problem here is that the bridging is in your way. Swift has no objection to your calling the `substringToIndex:` method on a Swift String, but then the index value must be a `String.Index`, which is rather tricky to construct (see Chapter 3):

```
let s2 = s.substringToIndex(s.startIndex.advancedBy(4))
```

If you don't want to talk that way, you must cast the String to an NSString beforehand; now you are in Cocoa's world, where string indexes are integers:

```
let s2 = (s as NSString).substringToIndex(4)
```

As I explained in Chapter 3, however, those two calls are not equivalent: they can give different answers! The reason is that String and NSString have fundamentally different notions of what constitutes an element of a string (see "The String–NSString Element Mismatch" on page 90). A String must resolve its elements into characters, which means that it must walk the string, coalescing any combining codepoints; an NSString behaves as if it were an array of UTF-16 codepoints. On the Swift side, each increment in a

`String.Index` corresponds to a true character, but access by index or range requires walking the string; on the Cocoa side, access by index or range is extremely fast, but might not correspond to character boundaries. (See the "Characters and Grapheme Clusters" chapter of Apple's *String Programming Guide*.)

Another important difference between a Swift String and a Cocoa NSString is that an NSString is immutable. This means that, with NSString, you can do things such as obtain a new string based on the first — as `capitalizedString` and `substringToIndex:` do — but you can't change the string *in place*. To do that, you need another class, a subclass of NSString, NSMutableString. NSMutableString has many useful methods, and you'll probably want to take advantage of them; but Swift String isn't bridged to NSMutable-String, so you can't get from String to NSMutableString merely by casting. To obtain an NSMutableString, you'll have to make one. The simplest way is with NSMutableString's initializer `init(string:)`, which expects an NSString — meaning that you can pass a Swift String. Coming back the other way, you can cast all the way from NSMutableString to a Swift String in one move:

```
let s = "hello"
let ms = NSMutableString(string:s)
ms.deleteCharactersInRange(NSMakeRange(ms.length-1,1))
let s2 = (ms as String) + "ion" // now s2 is a Swift String
```

As I said in Chapter 3, native Swift String methods are thin on the ground. All the real string-processing power lives over on the Cocoa side of the bridge. So you're going to be crossing that bridge a lot! And this will not be only for the power of the NSString and NSMutableString classes. Many other useful classes are associated with them.

For example, suppose you want to search a string for some substring. All the best ways come from Cocoa:

- An NSString can be searched using various `rangeOfString:...` methods, with numerous options such as ignoring diacriticals, ignoring case, starting at the end, and insisting that the substring occupy the start or end of the searched string.

- Perhaps you don't know exactly what you're looking for: you need to describe it structurally. NSScanner lets you walk through a string looking for pieces that fit certain criteria; for example, with NSScanner (and NSCharacterSet) you can skip past everything in a string that precedes a number and then extract the number.

- By specifying the option `.RegularExpressionSearch`, you can search using a regular expression. Regular expressions are also supported as a separate class, NSRegularExpression, which in turn uses NSTextCheckingResult to describe match results.

- More sophisticated automated textual analysis is supported by some additional classes, such as NSDataDetector, an NSRegularExpression subclass that efficiently finds certain types of string expression such as a URL or a phone number, and

NSLinguisticTagger, which actually attempts to analyze text into its grammatical parts of speech.

In this example, our goal is to replace all occurrences of the word "hell" with the word "heaven." We don't want to replace mere occurrences of the *substring* "hell" — for example, "hello" should be left intact. Thus our search needs some intelligence as to what constitutes a word boundary. That sounds like a job for a regular expression. Swift doesn't have regular expressions, so everything has to be done by Cocoa:

```
let s = NSMutableString(string:"hello world, go to hell")
let r = try! NSRegularExpression(
    pattern: "\\bhell\\b",
    options: .CaseInsensitive)
r.replaceMatchesInString(
    s, options: [], range: NSMakeRange(0,s.length),
    withTemplate: "heaven")
// s is "hello world, go to heaven"
```

NSString also has convenience utilities for working with a file path string, and is often used in conjunction with NSURL, which is another Foundation class worth looking into. In addition, NSString — like some other classes discussed in this section — provides methods for writing out to a file's contents or reading in a file's contents; the file can be specified either as an NSString file path or as an NSURL.

An NSString carries no font and size information. Interface objects that display strings (such as UILabel) have a font property that is a UIFont; but this determines the *single* font and size in which the string will display. If you want styled text — where different runs of text have different style attributes (size, font, color, and so forth) — you need to use NSAttributedString, along with its supporting classes NSMutableAttributedString, NSParagraphStyle, and NSMutableParagraphStyle. These allow you to style text and paragraphs easily in sophisticated ways. The built-in interface objects that display text can display an NSAttributedString.

String drawing in a graphics context can be performed with methods provided through the NSStringDrawing category on NSString (see the *String UIKit Additions Reference*) and on NSAttributedString (see the *NSAttributedString UIKit Additions Reference*).

NSDate and Friends

An NSDate is a date and time, represented internally as a number of seconds (NSTimeInterval) since some reference date. Calling NSDate's initializer init() — i.e., saying NSDate() — gives you a date object for the current date and time. Many date operations will also involve the use of NSDateComponents, and conversions between NSDate and NSDateComponents require that you pass through an NSCalendar. Here's an example of constructing a date based on its calendrical values:

```
let greg = NSCalendar(calendarIdentifier:NSCalendarIdentifierGregorian)!
let comp = NSDateComponents()
comp.year = 2016
comp.month = 8
comp.day = 10
comp.hour = 15
let d = greg.dateFromComponents(comp) // Optional wrapping NSDate
```

Similarly, NSDateComponents provides the correct way to do date arithmetic. Here's how to add one month to a given date:

```
let d = NSDate() // or whatever
let comp = NSDateComponents()
comp.month = 1
let greg = NSCalendar(calendarIdentifier:NSCalendarIdentifierGregorian)!
let d2 = greg.dateByAddingComponents(comp, toDate:d, options:[])
```

You will also likely be concerned with dates represented as strings. If you don't take explicit charge of a date's string representation, it is represented by a string whose format may surprise you. For example, if you simply print an NSDate, you are shown the date in the GMT timezone, which can be confusing if that isn't where you live. A simple solution is to call descriptionWithLocale:; the locale comprises the user's current time zone, language, region format, and calendar settings:

```
print(d)
// 2016-08-10 22:00:00 +0000
print(d.descriptionWithLocale(NSLocale.currentLocale()))
// Wednesday, August 10, 2016 at 3:00:00 PM Pacific Daylight Time
```

For exact creation and parsing of date strings, use NSDateFormatter, which uses a format string similar to NSLog (and NSString's stringWithFormat:). In this example, we surrender completely to the user's locale by generating an NSDateFormatter's format with dateFormatFromTemplate:options:locale: and the current locale. The "template" is a string listing the date components to be used, but their order, punctuation, and language are left up to the locale:

```
let df = NSDateFormatter()
let format = NSDateFormatter.dateFormatFromTemplate(
    "dMMMMyyyyhmmaz", options:0, locale:NSLocale.currentLocale())
df.dateFormat = format
let s = df.stringFromDate(NSDate())
```

The result is the date shown in the user's time zone and language, using the correct linguistic conventions. It involves a combination of region format and language, which are two separate settings. Thus:

- On my device, the result might be "July 16, 2015, 7:44 AM PDT."

- If I change my device's *region* to France, it might be "16 July 2015 7:44 AM GMT-7."

- If I also change my device's *language* to French, it might be "16 juillet 2015 7:44 AM UTC−7."

NSNumber

An NSNumber is an object that wraps a numeric value. The wrapped value can be any standard Objective-C numeric type (including BOOL, the Objective-C equivalent of Swift Bool). It comes as a surprise to Swift users that NSNumber is needed. But an ordinary number in Objective-C is not an object (it is a scalar; see Appendix A), so it cannot be used where an object is expected. Thus, NSNumber solves an important problem, converting a number into an object and back again.

Swift does its best to shield you from having to deal directly with NSNumber. It bridges Swift numeric types to Objective-C in two different ways:

- If an ordinary number is expected, a Swift number is bridged to an ordinary number (a scalar).

- If an object is expected, a Swift number of a basic numeric type is bridged to an NSNumber. A basic numeric type is Int, UIInt, Float, or Double — and also Bool, because NSNumber can wrap an Objective-C BOOL.

Here's an example:

```
let ud = NSUserDefaults.standardUserDefaults()
let i = 0
ud.setInteger(i, forKey: "Score") ❶
ud.setObject(i, forKey: "Score") ❷
```

The third and fourth lines look alike, but Swift treats the Int value of i differently:

❶ `setInteger:forKey:` expects an integer (a scalar) as its first parameter, so Swift turns the Int struct value of i into an ordinary Objective-C number.

❷ `setObject:forKey:` expects an object as its first parameter, so Swift turns the Int struct value of i into an NSNumber.

Naturally, if you need to cross the bridge explicitly, you can. You can cast a Swift number (of a basic numeric type) to an NSNumber:

```
let n = 0 as NSNumber
```

For more control over what numeric type an NSNumber will wrap, you can call one of NSNumber's initializers:

```
let n = NSNumber(float:0)
```

Coming back from Objective-C to Swift, a value will typically arrive as an AnyObject and you will have to cast down. NSNumber comes with properties for accessing the wrapped value by its numeric type. Recall this example from Chapter 5, involving an NSNumber extracted as a value from an NSNotification's `userInfo` dictionary:

```
if let prog = (n.userInfo?["progress"] as? NSNumber)?.doubleValue {
    self.progress = prog
}
```

An NSNumber can also be cast down to a basic Swift numeric type. Therefore, so can an AnyObject wrapping an NSNumber. Thus, the same example can be rewritten like this, without explicitly mentioning NSNumber:

```
if let prog = n.userInfo?["progress"] as? Double {
    self.progress = prog
}
```

In the second version, Swift is actually doing behind the scenes exactly what we did in the first version — treating an AnyObject as an NSNumber and getting its `double-Value` property to extract the wrapped number.

An NSNumber object is just a wrapper and no more. It can't be used directly for numeric calculations; it isn't a number. It *wraps* a number. One way or another, if you want a number, you have to extract it from the NSNumber.

An NSNumber subclass, NSDecimalNumber, on the other hand, *can* be used in calculations, thanks to a bunch of arithmetic methods:

```
let dec1 = NSDecimalNumber(float: 4.0)
let dec2 = NSDecimalNumber(float: 5.0)
let sum = dec1.decimalNumberByAdding(dec2) // 9.0
```

NSDecimalNumber is useful particularly for rounding, because there's a handy way to specify the desired rounding behavior.

Underlying NSDecimalNumber is the NSDecimal struct (it is an NSDecimalNumber's `decimalValue`). NSDecimal comes with C functions that are faster than NSDecimal-Number methods.

NSValue

NSValue is NSNumber's superclass. It is used for wrapping nonnumeric C values, such as C structs, where an object is expected. The problem being solved here is parallel to the problem solved by NSNumber: a Swift struct is an object, but a C struct is not, so a struct cannot be used in Objective-C where an object is expected.

Convenience methods provided through the NSValueUIGeometryExtensions category on NSValue (see the *NSValue UIKit Additions Reference*) allow easy wrapping and unwrapping of CGPoint, CGSize, CGRect, CGAffineTransform, UIEdgeInsets, and UIOffset; additional categories allow easy wrapping and unwrapping of NSRange, CATransform3D, CMTime, CMTimeMapping, CMTimeRange, MKCoordinate, and MKCoordinateSpan. You are unlikely to need to store any other kind of C value in an NSValue, but you can if you need to.

Swift will *not* magically bridge any of these C struct types to or from an NSValue. You must manage them explicitly, exactly as you would do if your code were written in Objective-C. In this example from my own code, we use Core Animation to animate the movement of a button in the interface from one position to another; the button's starting and ending positions are each expressed as a CGPoint, but an animation's from-Value and toValue must be objects. A CGPoint is not an Objective-C object, so we must wrap the CGPoint values in NSValue objects:

```
let ba = CABasicAnimation(keyPath:"position")
ba.duration = 10
ba.fromValue = NSValue(CGPoint:self.oldButtonCenter)
ba.toValue = NSValue(CGPoint:goal)
self.button.layer.addAnimation(ba, forKey:nil)
```

Similarly, you can make an array of CGPoint in Swift, because CGPoint becomes a Swift object type (a Swift struct), and a Swift Array can have elements of any type; but you can't hand such an array to Objective-C, because an Objective-C NSArray must have objects as its elements, and a CGPoint, in Objective-C, is not an object. Thus you must wrap the CGPoints in NSValue objects first. This is another animation example, where I set the values array (an NSArray) of a keyframe animation by turning an array of CGPoints into an array of NSValues:

```
anim.values = [oldP,p1,p2,newP].map{NSValue(CGPoint:$0)}
```

NSData

NSData is a general sequence of bytes; basically, it's just a buffer, a chunk of memory. It is immutable; the mutable version is its subclass NSMutableData.

In practice, NSData tends to arise in two main ways:

- When downloading data from the Internet. For example, NSURLConnection and NSURLSession supply whatever they retrieve from the Internet as NSData. Transforming it from there into (let's say) a string, specifying the correct encoding, would then be up to you.

- When storing an object as a file or in user preferences (NSUserDefaults). For example, you can't store a UIColor value directly into user preferences. So if the user has made a color choice and you need to save it, you transform the UIColor into an NSData (using NSKeyedArchiver) and save that:

```
let ud = NSUserDefaults.standardUserDefaults()
let c = UIColor.blueColor()
let cdata = NSKeyedArchiver.archivedDataWithRootObject(c)
ud.setObject(cdata, forKey: "myColor")
```

Equality and Comparison

In Swift, the equality and comparison operators can be overridden for an object type that adopts Equatable and Comparable ("Operators" on page 265). But Objective-C operators can't do that; they are applicable only to scalars.

To permit determination of whether two objects are "equal" — whatever that may mean for this object type — an Objective-C class must implement isEqual:, which is inherited from NSObject. Swift will help out by treating NSObject as Equatable and by permitting the use of the == operator, implicitly converting it to an isEqual: call. Thus, if a class does implement isEqual:, ordinary Swift comparison will work. For example:

```
let n1 = NSNumber(integer:1)
let n2 = NSNumber(integer:2)
let n3 = NSNumber(integer:3)
let ok = n2 == 2 // true ❶
let ok2 = n2 == NSNumber(integer:2) // true ❷
let ix = [n1,n2,n3].indexOf(2) // Optional wrapping 1 ❸
```

That code seems to do three impossible things before breakfast:

❶ We directly compare an Int to an NSNumber, and we get the right answer, as if we were comparing the Int to the integer wrapped by that NSNumber.

❷ We directly compare two NSNumber objects to one another, and we get the right answer, as if we were comparing the integers that they wrap.

❸ We treat an array of NSNumber objects as an array of Equatables and call the indexOf method, and we successfully determine which NSNumber object is "equal" to an actual number.

There are two parts to this apparent magic:

- The numbers are being wrapped in NSNumber objects for us.
- The == operator (also used behind the scenes by the indexOf method) is being converted to an isEqual: call.

NSNumber implements isEqual: to compare two NSNumber objects by comparing the numeric values that they wrap; therefore the equality comparisons all work correctly.

If an NSObject subclass *doesn't* implement isEqual:, it inherits NSObject's implementation, which compares the two objects for identity (like Swift's === operator). For example, these two Dog objects can be compared with the == operator, even though Dog does not adopt Equatable, because they derive from NSObject — but Dog doesn't implement isEqual:, so == defaults to NSObject's identity comparison:

```
class Dog : NSObject {
    var name : String
    init(_ name:String) {self.name = name}
}
let d1 = Dog("Fido")
let d2 = Dog("Fido")
let ok = d1 == d2 // false
```

A number of classes that implement isEqual: also implement more specific and efficient tests. The usual Objective-C way to determine whether two NSNumber objects are equal (in the sense of wrapping identical numbers) is by calling isEqualToNumber:. Similarly, NSString has isEqualToString:, NSDate has isEqualToDate:, and so forth. However, these classes do *also* implement isEqual:, so I don't think there's any reason not to use the Swift == operator.

Similarly, in Objective-C it is up to individual classes to supply ordered comparison methods. The standard method is called compare:, and returns one of three NSComparisonResult cases:

.OrderedAscending
    The receiver is less than the argument.

.OrderedSame
    The receiver is equal to the argument.

.OrderedDescending
    The receiver is greater than the argument.

Swift comparison operators (< and so forth) do *not* magically call compare: for you. You can't compare two NSNumber values directly:

```
let n1 = NSNumber(integer:1)
let n2 = NSNumber(integer:2)
let ok = n1 < n2 // compile error
```

You will typically fall back on calling compare: yourself, exactly as in Objective-C:

```
let n1 = NSNumber(integer:1)
let n2 = NSNumber(integer:2)
let ok = n1.compare(n2) == .OrderedAscending // true
```

NSIndexSet

NSIndexSet represents a collection of unique whole numbers; its purpose is to express element numbers of an ordered collection, such as an NSArray. Thus, for instance, to retrieve multiple objects simultaneously from an array, you specify the desired indexes as an NSIndexSet. It is also used with other things that are array-like; for example, you pass an NSIndexSet to a UITableView to indicate what sections to insert or delete.

To take a specific example, let's say you want to speak of elements 1, 2, 3, 4, 8, 9, and 10 of an NSArray. NSIndexSet expresses this notion in some compact implementation that can be readily queried. The actual implementation is opaque, but you can imagine that this NSIndexSet might consist of two NSRange structs, {1,4} and {8,3}, and NSIndexSet's methods actually invite you to think of an NSIndexSet as composed of ranges.

An NSIndexSet is immutable; its mutable subclass is NSMutableIndexSet. You can form a simple NSIndexSet consisting of just one contiguous range directly, by passing an NSRange to indexSetWithIndexesInRange:; but to form a more complex index set you'll need to use NSMutableIndexSet so that you can append additional ranges:

```
let arr = ["zero", "one", "two", "three", "four", "five",
    "six", "seven", "eight", "nine", "ten"]
let ixs = NSMutableIndexSet()
ixs.addIndexesInRange(NSRange(1...4))
ixs.addIndexesInRange(NSRange(8...10))
let arr2 = (arr as NSArray).objectsAtIndexes(ixs)
```

To walk through (enumerate) the index values specified by an NSIndexSet, you can use for...in; alternatively, you can walk through an NSIndexSet's indexes or ranges by calling enumerateIndexesUsingBlock: or enumerateRangesUsingBlock: or their variants.

NSArray and NSMutableArray

NSArray is Objective-C's array object type. It is fundamentally similar to Swift Array, and they are bridged to one another. But NSArray elements must be objects (classes and class instances), and they don't have to be of a single type. For a full discussion of how to bridge back and forth between Swift Array and Objective-C NSArray, implicitly and by casting, see "Swift Array and Objective-C NSArray" on page 222.

 New in iOS 9, if an NSArray object has a single element type, Objective-C can mark up its declaration to say what that type is. Swift 2.0 can read this markup. This means that you will not receive an [AnyObject] — and be compelled to cast it down to its actual type — as often as in the past. The same is true for NSSet and, to a lesser degree, for NSDictionary.

An NSArray's length is its count, and a particular object can be obtained by index number using objectAtIndex:. The index of the first object, as with a Swift Array, is zero, so the index of the last object is count minus one.

Instead of calling `objectAtIndex:`, you can use subscripting with an NSArray. This is not because NSArray is bridged to Swift Array, but because NSArray implements `object-AtIndexedSubscript:`. This method is the Objective-C equivalent of a Swift `subscript` getter, and Swift knows this. In fact, by a kind of trickery, when you examine the NSArray header file translated into Swift, this method is shown as a `subscript` declaration! Thus, the Objective-C version of the header file shows this declaration:

```
- (ObjectType)objectAtIndexedSubscript:(NSUInteger)idx;
```

But the Swift version of the same header file shows this:

```
subscript (idx: Int) -> AnyObject { get }
```

(For the meaning of `ObjectType` in the Objective-C declaration, see Appendix A).

You can seek an object within an array with `indexOfObject:` or `indexOfObject-IdenticalTo:`; the former's idea of equality is to call `isEqual:`, whereas the latter uses object identity (like Swift's `===`). As I mentioned earlier, if the object is not found in the array, the result is `NSNotFound`.

Unlike a Swift Array, and like an Objective-C NSString, an NSArray is immutable. This doesn't mean you can't mutate any of the objects it contains; it means that once the NSArray is formed you can't remove an object from it, insert an object into it, or replace an object at a given index. To do those things while staying in the Objective-C world, you can derive a new array consisting of the original array plus or minus some objects, or use NSArray's subclass, NSMutableArray. Swift Array is not bridged to NSMutable-Array; if you want an NSMutableArray, you must create it. The simplest way is with the NSMutableArray initializers, `init()` or `init(array:)`.

Once you have an NSMutableArray, you can call methods such as NSMutableArray's `addObject:` and `replaceObjectAtIndex:withObject:`. You can also assign into an NSMutableArray using subscripting. Again, this is because NSMutableArray implements a special method, `setObject:atIndexedSubscript:`; Swift recognizes this as equivalent to a `subscript` setter.

Coming back the other way, you cannot cast directly from NSMutableArray to a Swift Array of any type other than [AnyObject]; the usual approach is to cast up from NSMutableArray to NSArray and then down to a specific type of Swift Array:

```
let marr = NSMutableArray()
marr.addObject(1) // an NSNumber
marr.addObject(2) // an NSNumber
let arr = marr as NSArray as! [Int]
```

Cocoa provides ways to search or filter an array using a block. You can also derive a sorted version of an array, supplying the sorting rules in various ways, or if it's a mutable array, you can sort it directly. You might prefer to perform those kinds of operation in the Swift Array world, but it can be useful to know how to do them the Cocoa way. For example:

```
let pep = ["Manny", "Moe", "Jack"] as NSArray
let ems = pep.objectsAtIndexes(
    pep.indexesOfObjectsPassingTest {
        obj, idx, stop in
        return (obj as! NSString).rangeOfString(
            "m", options:.CaseInsensitiveSearch
        ).location == 0
    }
) // ["Manny", "Moe"]
```

NSDictionary and NSMutableDictionary

NSDictionary is Objective-C's dictionary object type. It is fundamentally similar to Swift Dictionary, and they are bridged to one another. But NSDictionary keys and values must be objects (classes and class instances), and they don't have to be of a single type; the keys must conform to NSCopying and be hashable. See "Swift Dictionary and Objective-C NSDictionary" on page 227 for a full discussion of how to bridge back and forth between Swift Dictionary and Objective-C NSDictionary, including casting.

An NSDictionary is immutable; its mutable subclass is NSMutableDictionary. Swift Dictionary is not bridged to NSMutableDictionary; you can most easily make an NSMutableDictionary with an initializer, init() or init(dictionary:).

The keys of an NSDictionary are distinct (using isEqual: for comparison). If you add a key–value pair to an NSMutableDictionary, then if that key is not already present, the pair is simply added, but if the key is already present, then the corresponding value is replaced. This is parallel to the behavior of Swift Dictionary.

The fundamental use of an NSDictionary is to request an entry's value by key (using objectForKey:); if no such key exists, the result is nil. In Objective-C, nil is not an object, and thus cannot be a value in an NSDictionary; the meaning of this response is thus unambiguous. Swift handles this by treating the result of objectForKey: as an Any-Object? — that is, an Optional wrapping an AnyObject.

Subscripting is possible on an NSDictionary or an NSMutableDictionary for similar reasons to why subscripting is possible on an NSArray or an NSMutableArray. NSDictionary implements objectForKeyedSubscript:, and Swift understands this as equivalent to a subscript getter. In addition, NSMutableDictionary implements setObject:forKeyedSubscript:, and Swift understands this as equivalent to a subscript setter.

You can get from an NSDictionary a list of keys (allKeys), a list of values (allValues), or a list of keys sorted by value. You can also walk through the key–value pairs together using a block, and you can even filter an NSDictionary by a test against its values.

NSSet and Friends

An NSSet is an unordered collection of distinct objects. "Distinct" means that no two objects in a set can return `true` when they are compared using `isEqual:`. Learning whether an object is present in a set is much more efficient than seeking it in an array, and you can ask whether one set is a subset of, or intersects, another set. You can walk through (enumerate) a set with the `for...in` construct, though the order is of course undefined. You can filter a set, as you can an NSArray. Indeed, much of what you can do with a set is parallel to what you can do with an array, except that of course you can't do anything with a set that involves the notion of ordering.

To escape even that restriction, you can use an ordered set. An ordered set (NSOrdered-Set) is *very* like an array, and the methods for working with it are very similar to the methods for working with an array — you can even fetch an element by subscripting (because it implements `objectAtIndexedSubscript:`). But an ordered set's elements must be distinct. An ordered set provides many of the advantages of sets: for example, as with an NSSet, learning whether an object is present in an ordered set is much more efficient than for an array, and you can readily take the union, intersection, or difference with another set. Since the distinctness restriction will often prove no restriction at all (because the elements were going to be distinct anyway), it is worthwhile to use NSOrderedSet instead of NSArray wherever possible.

 Handing an array over to an ordered set *uniques* the array, meaning that order is maintained but only the first occurrence of an equal object is moved to the set.

An NSSet is immutable. You can derive one NSSet from another by adding or removing elements, or you can use its subclass, NSMutableSet. Similarly, NSOrderedSet has its mutable counterpart, NSMutableOrderedSet (which you can insert into by subscripting, because it implements `setObject:atIndexedSubscript:`). There is no penalty for adding to a set an object that the set already contains; nothing is added (and so the distinctness rule is enforced), but there's no error.

NSCountedSet, a subclass of NSMutableSet, is a mutable unordered collection of objects that are *not* necessarily distinct (this concept is often referred to as a *bag*). It is implemented as a set plus a count of how many times each element has been added.

Swift Set is bridged to NSSet. But NSSet elements must be objects (classes and class instances), and they don't have to be of a single type. For details, see "Swift Set and Objective-C NSSet" on page 233. Nothing in Swift is bridged to NSMutableSet, NSCountedSet, NSOrderedSet, or NSMutableOrderedSet, but they are easily formed by coercion from a set or an array using an initializer. Coming back the other way, you can cast an NSMutableSet or NSCountedSet up to NSSet and down to a Swift Set (similar to an NSMutableArray). NSOrderedSet comes with "façade" properties that present it as an array or a set. Because of their special behaviors, however, you are much more likely to leave an NSCountedSet or an NSOrderedSet in its Objective-C form for as long you're working with it.

NSNull

The NSNull class does nothing but supply a pointer to a singleton object, NSNull(). This singleton object is used to stand for nil in situations where an actual Objective-C object is required and nil is not permitted. For example, you can't use nil as the value of an element of an Objective-C collection (such as NSArray, NSSet, or NSDictionary), so you'd use NSNull() instead.

You can test an object for equality against NSNull() using the ordinary equality operator (==), because it falls back on NSObject's isEqual:, which is identity comparison. This is a singleton instance, and therefore identity comparison works.

Immutable and Mutable

Beginners sometimes have difficulty with the Cocoa Foundation notion of class pairs where the superclass is immutable and the subclass is mutable. This notion is itself reminiscent of the Swift distinction between a constant (let) and a true variable (var), and has similar consequences. For example, the fact that NSArray is "immutable" means much the same thing as the fact that a Swift Array is referred to with let: you can't append or insert into this array, or replace or delete an element of this array, but if its elements are reference types — and of course, for an NSArray, they *are* reference types — you can mutate an element in place.

The reason why Cocoa needs these immutable/mutable pairs is to prevent unauthorized mutation. These are ordinary classes, so an NSArray object, say, is an ordinary class instance — a reference type. If a class has an NSArray property, and if this array were mutable, the array could be mutated by some other object, behind this class's back. To prevent that from happening, a class will work internally and temporarily with a mutable instance but then store and vend to other classes an immutable instance, thus protecting the value from being changed accidentally or behind its own back. (Swift doesn't face the same issue, because its fundamental built-in object types such as String, Array, and Dictionary are structs, and therefore are value types, which cannot be mutated in place; they can be changed only by being replaced, and that is something that can be guarded against or detected through a setter observer.)

The documentation may not make it completely obvious that the mutable classes obey and, if appropriate, override the methods of their immutable superclasses. For example, dozens of NSMutableArray methods are not listed on NSMutableArray's class documentation page, because they are inherited from NSArray. And when such methods are inherited by the mutable subclass, they may be overridden to fit the mutable subclass. For example, NSArray's init(array:) generates an immutable array, but NSMutableArray's init(array:) — which isn't even listed on the NSMutableArray documentation page, because it is inherited from NSArray — generates a mutable array.

That fact also answers the question of how to make an immutable array mutable, and *vice versa*. If init(array:), sent to the NSArray class, yields a new immutable array containing the same objects in the same order as the original array, then the same initializer, init(array:), sent to the NSMutableArray class, yields a *mutable* array containing the same objects in the same order as the original. Thus this single method can transform an array between immutable and mutable in either direction. You can also use copy (produces an immutable copy) and mutableCopy (produces a mutable copy), both inherited from NSObject; but these are not as convenient because they yield an AnyObject which must then be cast.

 These immutable/mutable class pairs are all implemented as *class clusters*, which means that Cocoa uses a secret class, different from the documented class you work with. You may discover this by peeking under the hood; for example, saying NSStringFromClass(s.dynamicType), where s is an NSString, might yield a mysterious value "__NSCFString". You should not spend any time wondering about this secret class. It is subject to change without notice and is none of your business; you should never have looked at it in the first place.

Property Lists

A *property list* is a string (XML) representation of data. The Foundation classes NSString, NSData, NSArray, and NSDictionary are the only classes that can be converted into a property list. Moreover, an NSArray or NSDictionary can be converted into a property list only if the only classes it collects are these classes, along with NSDate and NSNumber. (This is why, as I mentioned earlier, you must convert a UIColor into an NSData in order to store it in user defaults; the user defaults *is* a property list.)

The primary use of a property list is to store data as a file. It is a way of *serializing* a value — saving it to disk in a form from which it can be reconstructed. NSArray and NSDictionary provide convenience methods writeToFile:atomically: and writeToURL:atomically: that generate property list files given a pathname or file URL, respectively; conversely, they also provide initializers that create an NSArray object or an NSDictionary object based on the property list contents of a given file. For this very reason, you are likely to start with one of these classes when you want to create a property list. (NSString and NSData, with their methods writeToFile:... and writeToURL:..., just write the data out as a file directly, not as a property list.)

When you reconstruct an NSArray or NSDictionary object from a property list file in this way, the collections, string objects, and data objects in the collection are all immutable. If you want them to be mutable, or if you want to convert an instance of one of the other property list classes to a property list, you'll use the NSPropertyListSerialization class (see the *Property List Programming Guide*).

Accessors, Properties, and Key–Value Coding

An Objective-C instance variable is structurally similar to a Swift instance property: it's a variable that accompanies each instance of a class, with a lifetime and value associated with that particular instance. An Objective-C instance variable, however, is usually private, in the sense that instances of other classes can't see it (and Swift can't see it). If an instance variable is to be made public, an Objective-C class will typically implement *accessor methods*: a getter method and (if this instance variable is to be publicly writable) a setter method. This is such a common thing to do that there are naming conventions:

The getter method
> A getter should have the same name as the instance variable (without an initial underscore if the instance variable has one). Thus, if the instance variable is named myVar (or _myVar), the getter method should be named myVar.

The setter method
> A setter method's name should start with set, followed by a capitalized version of the instance variable's name (without an initial underscore if the instance variable has one). The setter should take one parameter — the new value to be assigned to the instance variable. Thus, if the instance variable is named myVar (or _myVar), the setter should be named setMyVar:.

This pattern — a getter method, possibly accompanied by an appropriately named setter method — is so common that there's a shorthand: an Objective-C class can declare a *property*, using the keyword @property and a name. Here, for example, is a line from the UIView class declaration:

```
@property(nonatomic) CGRect frame;
```

(Ignore the material in parentheses.) Within Objective-C, this declaration constitutes a promise that there is a getter accessor method frame returning a CGRect, along with a setter accessor method setFrame: that takes a CGRect parameter.

When Objective-C formally declares a @property in this way, Swift sees it as a Swift property. Thus, UIView's frame property declaration is translated directly into a Swift declaration of an instance property frame of type CGRect:

```
var frame: CGRect
```

An Objective-C property name is mere syntactic sugar. When you set a UIView's `frame` property, you are actually calling its `setFrame:` setter method, and when you get a UIView's `frame` property, you are actually calling its `frame` getter method. In Objective-C, use of the property is optional; Objective-C code can, and often does, call the `setFrame:` and `frame` methods *directly*. In Swift, however, you can't do that. If an Objective-C class has a formal `@property` declaration, *the accessor methods are hidden from Swift*.

An Objective-C property declaration can include the word `readonly` in the parentheses. This indicates that there is a getter but no setter. So, for example (ignore the other material in the parentheses):

```
@property(nonatomic,readonly,strong) CALayer *layer;
```

Swift will reflect this restriction with `{get}` after the declaration, as if this were a computed read-only property; the compiler will not permit you to assign to such a property:

```
var layer: CALayer { get }
```

An Objective-C property and its accompanying accessor methods have a life of their own, independent of any underlying instance variable. Although accessor methods may literally be ways of accessing an invisible instance variable, they don't have to be. When you set a UIView's `frame` property and the `setFrame:` accessor method is called, you have no way of knowing what that method is really doing: it might be setting an instance variable called `frame` or `_frame`, but who knows? In this sense, accessors and properties are a façade, hiding the underlying implementation. This is similar to how, within Swift, you can set a variable without knowing or caring whether it is a stored variable or a computed variable; what setting the variable *really* does is unimportant (and possibly unknown) to the code that sets it.

Swift Accessors

Just as Objective-C properties are actually a shorthand for accessor methods, so Objective-C treats Swift properties as a shorthand for accessor methods — even though no such methods are formally present. If you, in Swift, declare that a class has a property `prop`, Objective-C can call a `prop` method to get its value or a `setProp:` method to set its value, *even though you have not implemented such methods*. Those calls are routed to your property through *implicit* accessor methods.

In Swift, you should *not* write *explicit* accessor methods for a property; the compiler will stop you if you attempt to do so. If you need to implement an accessor method explicitly and formally, use a computed property. Here, for example, I'll add to my UIViewController subclass a computed `color` property with a getter and a setter:

```
class ViewController: UIViewController {
    var color : UIColor {
        get {
            print("someone called the getter")
```

```
            return UIColor.redColor()
        }
        set {
            print("someone called the setter")
        }
    }
}
```

Objective-C code can now call explicitly the implicit `setColor:` and `color` accessor methods — and when it does, the computed property's setter and getter methods are in fact called:

```
ViewController* vc = [ViewController new];
[vc setColor:[UIColor redColor]]; // "someone called the setter"
UIColor* c = [vc color]; // "someone called the getter"
```

This proves that, in Objective-C's mind, you *have* provided `setColor:` and `color` accessor methods. You can even change the Objective-C names of these accessor methods! To do so, add an `@objc(...)` attribute with the Objective-C name in parentheses. You can add it to a computed property's setter and getter methods, or you can add it to a property itself:

```
@objc(hue) var color : UIColor?
```

Objective-C code can now call `hue` and `setHue:` accessor methods directly.

If all you want to do is add functionality to the setter, use a setter observer. For example, to add functionality to the Objective-C `setFrame:` method in your UIView subclass, you can override the `frame` property and write a `didSet` observer:

```
class MyView: UIView {
    override var frame : CGRect {
        didSet {
            print("the frame setter was called: \(super.frame)")
        }
    }
}
```

Key–Value Coding

Cocoa can dynamically call an accessor — and thus can access a Swift property — based on a string name specified at runtime, through a mechanism called *key–value coding* (KVC). (This resembles, and is related to, the ability to use a selector name for introspection with `respondsToSelector:`.) The string name is the *key*; what is passed to or returned from the accessor is the *value*. The basis for key–value coding is the NSKey-ValueCoding protocol, an informal protocol; it is actually a category injected into NSObject. A Swift class, to be susceptible to key–value coding, must therefore be derived from NSObject.

The fundamental key–value coding methods are `valueForKey:` and `setValue:for-Key:`. When one of these methods is called on an object, the object is introspected. In simplified terms, first the appropriate accessor is sought; if it doesn't exist, the instance variable is accessed directly. Another useful pair of methods is `dictionaryWithValues-ForKeys:` and `setValuesForKeysWithDictionary:`, which allow you to get and set multiple key–value pairs by way of an NSDictionary with a single command.

The value in key–value coding must be an Objective-C object, and is typed in Swift as AnyObject. When calling `valueForKey:`, you'll receive an Optional wrapping an Any-Object; you'll want to cast this down safely to its expected type.

A class is *key–value coding compliant* (or *KVC compliant*) on a given key if it provides the accessor methods, or possesses the instance variable, required for access through that key. An attempt to access a key for which a class is *not* key–value coding compliant will cause an exception at runtime. It is useful to be familiar with the message you'll get when such a crash occurs, so let's cause it deliberately:

```
let obj = NSObject()
obj.setValue("hello", forKey:"keyName") // crash
```

The console says: "This class is not key value coding-compliant for the key keyName." The last word in that error message, despite the lack of quotes, is the key string that caused the trouble.

What would it take for that method call *not* to crash? The class of the object to which it is sent would need to have a `setKeyName:` setter method (or a `keyName` or `_keyName` instance variable). In Swift, as I demonstrated in the previous section, an instance property implies the existence of accessor methods. Thus, we can use key–value coding on an instance of any NSObject subclass that has a declared property, provided the key string is the string name of that property. Let's try it! Here is such a class:

```
class Dog : NSObject {
    var name : String = ""
}
```

And here's our test:

```
let d = Dog()
d.setValue("Fido", forKey:"name") // no crash!
print(d.name) // "Fido" - it worked!
```

Uses of Key–Value Coding

Key–value coding allows you, in effect, to decide at runtime, based on a string, what accessor to call. In the simplest case, you're using a string to access a dynamically specified property. That's useful in Objective-C code; but such unfettered introspective dynamism is contrary to the spirit of Swift, and in translating my own Objective-C code into Swift I have found myself accomplishing the same effect in other ways

Here's an example. In a flashcard app, I have a class Term, representing a Latin word. It declares many properties. Each card displays one term, with its various properties shown in different text fields. If the user taps any of three text fields, I want the interface to change from the term that's currently showing to the next term whose value is different for the particular property that this text field represents. Thus this code is the same for all three text fields; the only difference is *which property* to consider as we hunt for the next term to be displayed. In Objective-C, by far the simplest way to express this parallelism is through key–value coding:

```
NSInteger tag = g.view.tag; // the tag tells us which text field was tapped
NSString* key = nil;
switch (tag) {
    case 1: key = @"lesson"; break;
    case 2: key = @"lessonSection"; break;
    case 3: key = @"lessonSectionPartFirstWord"; break;
}
// get current value of corresponding instance variable
NSString* curValue = [[self currentCardController].term valueForKey: key];
```

In Swift, however, it's easy to implement the same dynamism using an array of anonymous functions:

```
let tag = g.view!.tag - 1
let arr : [(Term) -> String] = [
    {$0.lesson}, {$0.lessonSection}, {$0.lessonSectionPartFirstWord}
]
let f = arr[tag]
let curValue = f(self.currentCardController().term)
```

Nevertheless, key–value coding remains valuable in programming iOS, especially because a number of built-in Cocoa classes permit you to use key–value coding in special ways. For example:

- If you send valueForKey: to an NSArray, it sends valueForKey: to each of its elements and returns a new array consisting of the results, an elegant shorthand. NSSet behaves similarly.

- NSDictionary implements valueForKey: as an alternative to objectForKey: (useful particularly if you have an NSArray of dictionaries). Similarly, NSMutableDictionary treats setValue:forKey: as a synonym for setObject:forKey:, except that value: can be nil, in which case removeObject:forKey: is called.

- NSSortDescriptor sorts an NSArray by sending valueForKey: to each of its elements. This makes it easy to sort an array of dictionaries on the value of a particular dictionary key, or an array of objects on the value of a particular property.

- NSManagedObject, used in conjunction with Core Data, is guaranteed to be key–value coding compliant for attributes you've configured in the entity model. Thus, it's common to access those attributes with valueForKey: and setValue:forKey:.

- CALayer and CAAnimation permit you to use key–value coding to define and retrieve the values for *arbitrary* keys, as if they were a kind of dictionary; they are, in effect, key–value coding compliant for *every key*. This is extremely helpful for attaching identifying and configuration information to an instance of one of these classes. That, in fact, is my own most common way of using key–value coding in Swift.

KVC and Outlets

Key–value coding lies at the heart of how outlet connections work (Chapter 7). The name of the outlet in the nib is a string. It is key–value coding that turns the string into a hunt for a matching property at nib-loading time.

Suppose, for example, that you have a class Dog with an @IBOutlet property master, and you've drawn a "master" outlet from that class's representative in the nib to a Person nib object. When the nib loads, the outlet name "master" is translated though key–value coding to the accessor method name setMaster:, and your Dog instance's setMaster: implicit accessor method is called with the Person instance as its parameter — thus setting the value of your Dog instance's master property to the Person instance (Figure 7-9).

If something goes wrong with the match between the outlet name in the nib and the name of the property in the class, then at runtime, when the nib loads, Cocoa's attempt to use key–value coding to set a value in your object based on the name of the outlet will fail, and will generate an exception, complaining that the class is not key–value coding compliant for the key (the outlet name) — that is, your app will crash at nib-loading time. A likely way for this to happen is that you form the outlet correctly but then later change the name of (or delete) the property in the class (see "Misconfigured Outlets" on page 344).

Key Paths

A *key path* allows you to chain keys in a single expression. If an object is key–value coding compliant for a certain key, and if the value of that key is itself an object that is key–value coding compliant for another key, you can chain those keys by calling valueForKeyPath: and setValue:forKeyPath:. A key path string looks like a succession of key names joined using dot-notation. For example, valueForKeyPath("key1.key2") effectively calls valueForKey: on the message receiver, with "key1" as the key, and then takes the object returned from that call and calls valueForKey: on that object, with "key2" as the key.

To illustrate this shorthand, imagine that our object myObject has an instance property theData which is an array of dictionaries such that each dictionary has a name key and a description key:

```
var theData = [
    [
        "description" : "The one with glasses.",
        "name" : "Manny"
    ],
    [
        "description" : "Looks a little like Governor Dewey.",
        "name" : "Moe"
    ],
    [
        "description" : "The one without a mustache.",
        "name" : "Jack"
    ]
]
```

We can use key–value coding with a key path to drill down into that array of dictionaries:

```
let arr = myObject.valueForKeyPath("theData.name") as! [String]
```

The result is an array consisting of the strings "Manny", "Moe", and "Jack". If you don't see why, review what I said earlier about how NSArray and NSDictionary implement valueForKey:.

 Recall also the discussion of user-defined runtime attributes, in Chapter 7. This feature uses key–value coding! The string you're entering in the first column when you define a runtime attribute in an object's Identity inspector in a nib is a key path.

Array Accessors

Key–value coding is a powerful technology with many additional ramifications. (See Apple's *Key-Value Coding Programming Guide* for full information.) I'll illustrate just one of them. Key–value coding allows an object to synthesize a key whose value appears to be an array (or a set), even if it isn't. You implement specially named accessor methods; key–value coding sees them when you try to use the corresponding key.

To illustrate, I'll add these methods to the class of our object myObject:

```
func countOfPepBoys() -> Int {
    return self.theData.count
}
func objectInPepBoysAtIndex(ix:Int) -> AnyObject {
    return self.theData[ix]
}
```

By implementing `countOf...` and `objectIn...AtIndex:`, I'm telling the key–value coding system to act as if the given key — `"pepBoys"`, in this case — exists and is an array. An attempt to fetch the value of the key `"pepBoys"` by way of key–value coding will succeed, and will return an object that can be treated as an NSArray, though in fact it is a proxy object (an NSKeyValueArray). Thus we can now say things like this:

```
let arr : AnyObject = myObject.valueForKey("pepBoys")!
let arr2 : AnyObject = myObject.valueForKeyPath("pepBoys.name")!
```

In that code, `arr` is the array proxy, and `arr2` is the same array of the names of the three Pep Boys as before. The example seems pointless: the underlying implementation is *already* an array, so how does saying `"pepBoys"` here differ from saying `"theData"`, as we did before? It doesn't. But it could! Imagine that there is no simple actual array — that the result of `countOfPepBoys` and `objectInPepBoysAtIndex:` is obtained through some completely different sort of operation. In effect, we have created a key that *poses* as an NSArray; we could have anything at all hiding behind it.

The Secret Life of NSObject

Because every Objective-C class inherits from NSObject, it's worth taking some time to explore NSObject. NSObject is constructed in a rather elaborate way:

- It defines some native class methods and instance methods having mostly to do with the basics of instantiation and of method sending and resolution. (See the *NSObject Class Reference*.)

- It adopts the NSObject protocol. This protocol declares instance methods having mostly to do with memory management, the relationship between an instance and its class, and introspection. Because all the NSObject protocol methods are required, the NSObject class implements them all. (See the *NSObject Protocol Reference*.) In Swift, the NSObject protocol is called NSObjectProtocol, to avoid name clash.

- It implements convenience methods related to the NSCopying, NSMutable-Copying, and NSCoding protocols, without formally adopting those protocols. NSObject intentionally doesn't adopt these protocols because this would cause all other classes to adopt them, which would be wrong. But thanks to this architecture, if a class *does* adopt one of these protocols, you can call the corresponding convenience method. For example, NSObject implements the copy instance method, so you can call `copy` on any instance, but you'll crash unless the instance's class also adopts the NSCopying protocol and implements `copyWithZone:`.

- A large number of methods are injected into NSObject by more than two dozen categories on NSObject, scattered among various header files. For example, awake-

FromNib (see Chapter 7) comes from the UINibLoadingAdditions category on NSObject, declared in *UINibLoading.h*.

- A class object is an object. Therefore all Objective-C classes, which are objects of type Class, inherit from NSObject. Therefore, *any method defined as an instance method by NSObject can be called on a class object as a class method!* For example, respondsToSelector: is defined as an instance method by NSObject, but it can (therefore) be treated also as a class method and sent to a class object.

The problem for the programmer is that Apple's documentation is rather rigid about classification. When you're trying to work out what you can say to an object, you don't care where that object's methods come from; you just care what you can say. But the documentation differentiates methods by where they come from. As a result, even though NSObject is the root class, the most important class, from which all other classes inherit, *no single page* of the documentation provides a conspectus of all its methods. Instead, you have to look at both the *NSObject Class Reference* and the *NSObject Protocol Reference* simultaneously, plus the pages documenting the NSCopying, NSMutable-Copying, and NSCoding protocols (in order to understand how they interact with methods defined by NSObject), plus you have to supply mentally a class method version of every NSObject instance method!

Then there are the methods injected into NSObject by categories. Some that are general in nature are documented on the NSObject class documentation page itself; for example, awakeAfterUsingCoder: comes from a category declared in a separate header, but it is documented under NSObject, quite rightly, since this is a class method, and therefore effectively a global method, that you might want to send at any time. Others are delegate methods used in restricted situations (so that these are really informal protocols), and do not need centralized documentation; for example, animationDidStart: is documented under the CAAnimation class, quite rightly, because you need to know about it only and exactly when you're working with CAAnimation. However, every object responds to awakeFromNib, and it's likely to be crucial to every app you write; yet you must learn about it outside of the NSObject documentation, sitting all by itself in the *NSObject UIKit Additions Reference* page, where you're extremely unlikely to discover it! The same goes, it might be argued, for all the key–value coding methods (see earlier in this chapter) and key–value observing methods (Chapter 11).

Once you've collected, by hook or by crook, all the NSObject methods, you can see that they fall into a certain natural classification:

Creation, destruction, and memory management
Methods for creating an instance, such as alloc and copy, along with methods for learning when something is happening in the lifetime of an object, such as initialize and dealloc, plus methods that manage memory.

Class relationships

Methods for learning an object's class and inheritance, such as superclass, isKind-OfClass:, and isMemberOfClass:.

Object introspection and comparison

Methods for asking what would happen if an object were sent a certain message, such as respondsToSelector:, for representing an object as a string (description), and for comparing objects (isEqual:).

Message response

Methods for meddling with what does happen when an object is sent a certain message, such as doesNotRecognizeSelector:. If you're curious, see the *Objective-C Runtime Programming Guide*.

Message sending

Methods for sending a message dynamically. For example, performSelector: takes a selector as parameter, and sending it to an object tells that object to perform that selector. This might seem identical to just sending that message to that object, but what if you don't know what message to send until runtime? Moreover, variants on performSelector: allow you to send a message on a specified thread, or send a message after a certain amount of time has passed (performSelector:with-Object:afterDelay: and similar).

 The performSelector... methods are newly available in Swift 2.0. Previously, they could not be called from Swift; I used them often in Objective-C, but translating my code into Swift forced me to find other ways of accomplishing the same goals, and I discovered that I could manage quite well without them.

CHAPTER 11

Cocoa Events

All of your app's executable code lies in its functions. The impetus for a function being called must come from somewhere. One of your functions may call another, but who will call the first function in the first place? How, ultimately, will *any* of your code *ever* run? As I said in Chapter 6, after your app has launched, "UIApplicationMain is just sitting there, watching for the user to do something, maintaining the *event loop*, which will respond to user actions as they occur."

The event loop is the key. The runtime is watching and waiting for certain things to happen, such as the user making a gesture on the screen, or some specific stage arriving in the lifetime of your app. When such things do happen, the runtime calls your code. But the runtime can call your code only if your code is there to be called. Your code is like a panel of buttons, waiting for Cocoa to press one. If something happens that Cocoa feels your code needs to know about and respond to, it presses the right button — if the right button is there.

The art of Cocoa programming lies in knowing what Cocoa wants to do. You organize your code, right from the start, with Cocoa's behavior in mind. Cocoa makes certain promises about how and when it will dispatch messages to your code. These are Cocoa's *events*. You know what these events are, and you arrange for your code to be ready when Cocoa delivers them.

The specific events that you can receive are listed in the documentation. The overall architecture of how and when events are dispatched and the ways in which your code arranges to receive them is the subject of this chapter.

Reasons for Events

Broadly speaking, the reasons you might receive an event may be divided informally into four categories. These categories are not official; I made them up. Often it isn't completely clear which of these categories an event fits into; an event may well appear to fit two categories. But they are still generally useful for visualizing how and why Cocoa interacts with your code:

User events

> The user does something interactive, and an event is triggered directly. Obvious examples are events that you get when the user taps or swipes the screen, or types a key on the keyboard.

Lifetime events

> These are events notifying you of the arrival of a stage in the life of the app, such as the fact that the app is starting up or is about to go into the background, or of a component of the app, such as the fact that a UIViewController's view has just loaded or is about to be removed from the screen.

Functional events

> Cocoa is about to do something, and turns to you in case you want to supply additional functionality. I would put into this category UIView's `drawRect:` (your chance to have a view draw itself) and UILabel's `drawTextInRect:` (your chance to modify the look of a label), with which we experimented in Chapter 10.

Query events

> Cocoa turns to you to ask a question; its behavior will depend upon your answer. For example, the way data appears in a table (a UITableView) is that whenever Cocoa needs a cell for a row of the table, it turns to you and asks for the cell.

Subclassing

A built-in Cocoa class may define methods that Cocoa itself will call and that you are invited (or required) to override in a subclass, so that your custom behavior, and not (merely) the default behavior, will take place.

An example I gave in Chapter 10 was UIView's `drawRect:`. This is what I call a functional event. By overriding `drawRect:` in a UIView subclass, you dictate the full procedure by which a view draws itself. You don't know exactly when this method will be called, and you don't care; when it is, you draw, and this guarantees that the view will always appear the way you want it to. (You *never* call `drawRect:` yourself; if some underlying condition has changed and you want the view to be redrawn, you call `setNeedsDisplay` and let Cocoa call `drawRect:` in response.)

Built-in UIView subclasses may have other functional event methods you'll want to customize through subclassing. Typically this will be in order to change the way the view is drawn, without taking command of the entire drawing procedure yourself. In Chapter 10 I gave an example involving UILabel and its `drawTextInRect:`. A similar case is UISlider, which lets you customize the position and size of the slider's "thumb" by overriding `thumbRectForBounds:trackRect:value:`.

UIViewController is a class meant for subclassing. Of the methods listed in the UIView-Controller class documentation, just about all are methods you might have reason to override. If you create a UIViewController subclass in Xcode, you'll see that the template already includes a couple of method overrides to get you started. For example, `viewDidLoad` is called to let you know that your view controller has obtained its main view (its `view`), so that you can perform initializations; it's an obvious example of a lifetime event. And UIViewController has many other lifetime events that you can and will override in order to get fine control over what happens when. For example, `viewWillAppear:` means that your view controller's view is about to be placed into the interface; `viewDidAppear:` means that your view controller's view *has* been placed into the interface; `viewDidLayoutSubviews` means that your view has been positioned within its superview; and so on.

A UIViewController method like `supportedInterfaceOrientations` is what I call a query event. Your job is to return a bitmask telling Cocoa what orientations your view can appear in at this moment — whenever that may be. You trust Cocoa to call this method at the appropriate moments, so that if the user rotates the device, your app's interface will or won't be rotated to compensate, depending on what value you return.

When looking for events that you can receive through subclassing, be sure to look upward though the inheritance hierarchy. For example, if you're wondering how to be notified when your custom UILabel subclass is embedded into another view, you won't find the answer in the UILabel class documentation; a UILabel receives the appropriate event by virtue of being a UIView. In the UIView class documentation, you'll learn that you can override `didMoveToSuperview` to be informed when this happens. By the same token, look upward through adopted protocols as well. If you're wondering how to be notified when your view controller's view is about to undergo app rotation, you won't find out by looking in the UIViewController class documentation; a UIViewController receives the appropriate event by virtue of adopting the UIContentContainer protocol. In the UIContentContainer protocol documentation, you'll learn that you can override `viewWillTransitionToSize:withTransitionCoordinator:`.

Nevertheless, as I said in Chapter 10, subclassing and overriding is far from being the most important or commmon way of arranging to receive events. Aside from UIViewController, it is hard to think of *any* built-in Cocoa class that you will *regularly* subclass for this purpose. So what are the *other* ways in which your code receives events? That's what the rest of this chapter is about.

Notifications

Cocoa provides your app with a single instance of NSNotificationCenter, informally called the *notification center*. This instance, available by calling `NSNotificationCenter.defaultCenter()`, is the basis of a mechanism for sending messages called *notifications.* A notification is an instance of NSNotification. The idea is that any object can be registered with the notification center to receive certain notifications. Another object can hand the notification center a notification to send out (this is called *posting* the notification). The notification center will then send that notification to all objects that are registered to receive it.

The notification mechanism is often described as a dispatching or broadcasting mechanism, and with good reason. It lets an object send a message without knowing or caring what object or how many objects receive it. This relieves your app's architecture from the formal responsibility of somehow hooking up instances just so a message can pass from one to the other (which can sometimes be quite tricky or onerous, as discussed in Chapter 13). When objects are conceptually "distant" from one another, notifications can be a fairly lightweight way of permitting one to message the other.

An NSNotification instance has three pieces of information associated with it, which can be retrieved by instance methods:

name
> An NSString which identifies the notification's meaning.

object
> An instance associated with the notification; typically, the instance that posted it.

userInfo
> Not every notification has a userInfo; it is an NSDictionary, and can contain additional information associated with the notification. What information this NSDictionary will contain, and under what keys, depends on the particular notification; you have to consult the documentation. For example, the documentation tells us that UIApplication's UIApplicationDidChangeStatusBarOrientation-Notification includes a userInfo dictionary with a key UIApplicationStatus-BarOrientationUserInfoKey whose value is the status bar's previous orientation. When you post a notification yourself, you can put anything you like into the user-Info for the notification's recipient(s) to retrieve.

Cocoa itself posts notifications through the notification center, and your code can register to receive them. You'll find a separate Notifications section in the documentation for a class that provides them.

Receiving a Notification

To register to receive a notification, you send one of two messages to the notification center. One is addObserver:selector:name:object:. The parameters are as follows:

observer:

> The instance to which the notification is to be sent. This will typically be `self`; it would be quite unusual for one instance to register a different instance as the receiver of a notification.

selector:

> The message to be sent to the observer instance when the notification occurs. The designated method should return no result (`Void`) and should take one parameter, which will be the NSNotification instance (so the parameter should be typed as `NSNotification` or `AnyObject`). In Swift, you specify the selector by giving the name of the method as a string.
>
> Don't get the string name of this method wrong, and don't forget to implement the method! If the notification center sends a notification by trying to call the method specified as the `selector:`, and if that exact method doesn't exist, *your app will crash*. See Appendix A for the rules about how to turn a method name into a string name.
>
> The method named by this selector cannot be called unless it is exposed to Objective-C. If the notification center sends a notification by trying to call the method specified as the `selector:`, and if Objective-C can't *see* that method, *your app will crash*. Objective-C can see the method if the class is a subclass of NSObject, or if the method is marked `@objc` (or `dynamic`).

name:

> The string `name` of the notification you'd like to receive. If this parameter is `nil`, you're asking to receive *all* notifications associated with the object designated in the `object:` parameter. A built-in Cocoa notification's name is usually a constant. This is helpful, because if you flub the name of a constant, the compiler will complain, whereas if you enter the name of the notification directly as a string literal and you get it wrong, the compiler won't complain but you will mysteriously fail to get any notifications (because no notification has the name you actually entered) — a very difficult sort of mistake to track down.

object:

> The `object` of the notification you're interested in, which will usually be the object that posted it. If this is `nil`, you're asking to receive *all* notifications with the name designated in the `name:` parameter. (If both the `name:` and `object:` parameters are `nil`, you're asking to receive all notifications!)

For example, in one of my apps I want to change the interface whenever the device's music player starts playing a different song. The API for the device's built-in music player belongs to the MPMusicPlayerController class; this class provides a notification to tell me when the built-in music player changes what song is being played, listed under

Notifications in the MPMusicPlayerController class documentation as `MPMusicPlayer-ControllerNowPlayingItemDidChangeNotification`.

It turns out, looking at the documentation, that this notification won't be posted at all unless I first call MPMusicPlayerController's `beginGeneratingPlayback-Notifications` instance method. This architecture is not uncommon; Cocoa saves itself some time and effort by not sending out certain notifications unless they are switched on, as it were. So my first job is to get an instance of MPMusicPlayerController and call this method:

```
let mp = MPMusicPlayerController.systemMusicPlayer()
mp.beginGeneratingPlaybackNotifications()
```

Now I register myself to receive the desired playback notification:

```
NSNotificationCenter.defaultCenter().addObserver(self,
    selector: "nowPlayingItemChanged:",
    name: MPMusicPlayerControllerNowPlayingItemDidChangeNotification,
    object: nil)
```

As a result, whenever an `MPMusicPlayerControllerNowPlayingItemDidChange-Notification` is posted, my `nowPlayingItemChanged:` method will be called:

```
func nowPlayingItemChanged (n:NSNotification) {
    self.updateNowPlayingItem()
    // ... and so on ...
}
```

For `addObserver:selector:name:object:` to work properly, you must get the selector right and make sure you implement the corresponding method. Heavy use of `add-Observer:selector:name:object:` means that your code ends up peppered with methods that exist solely in order to be called by the notification center. There is nothing about these methods that tells you what they are for — you will probably want to use explicit comments in order to remind yourself — and the methods are separate from the registration call, all of which makes your code rather confusing.

This problem is solved by using the *other* way of registering to receive a notification — by calling `addObserverForName:object:queue:usingBlock:`. It returns a value, whose purpose I'll explain in a moment. The `queue:` will usually be `nil`; a non-`nil` `queue:` is for background threading. The `name:` and `object:` parameters are just like those of `add-Observer:selector:name:object:`. Instead of an observer and a selector, you provide a Swift function consisting of the actual code to be executed when the notification arrives. This function should take one parameter — the NSNotification itself. If you use an anonymous function, your response to the notification you're registering for is visible as part of the registration:

```
let ob = NSNotificationCenter.defaultCenter()
    .addObserverForName(
        MPMusicPlayerControllerNowPlayingItemDidChangeNotification,
        object: nil, queue: nil) {
            _ in
            self.updateNowPlayingItem()
            // ... and so on ...
    }
```

 Use of addObserverForName:... can impose some additional memory management complications that I'll talk about in Chapter 12.

Unregistering

It is up to you, for every object that you register as a recipient of notifications, to unregister that object before it goes out of existence. If you fail to do this, and if the object
does go out of existence, and if a notification for which that object is registered is posted,
the notification center will attempt to send the appropriate message to that object, which
is now missing in action. The result will be a crash at best, and chaos at worst.

To unregister an object as a recipient of notifications, send the notification center the
removeObserver: message. (Alternatively, you can unregister an object for just a specific
set of notifications with removeObserver:name:object:.) The object passed as the
observer: argument is the object that is no longer to receive notifications. What object
that is depends on how you registered in the first place:

You called addObserver:...
> You supplied an observer originally; that is the observer you must now unregister.

You called addObserverForName:...
> The call to addObserverForName:... returned an observer token object typed as
> an NSObjectProtocol (its real class and nature are no concern of yours); that is the
> observer you must now unregister.

The trick is finding the right moment to unregister. The fallback solution is the registered
instance's deinit method, this being the last lifetime event an instance is sent before it
goes out of existence.

If you're calling addObserverForName:... multiple times from the same class, you're
going to end up receiving from the notification center multiple observer tokens, which
you need to preserve so that you can unregister all of them later. If your plan is to
unregister everything at once, one way to handle this situation is through an instance
property that is a mutable collection. My favored approach is a Set property:

```
var observers = Set<NSObject>()
```

Each time I register for a notification using addObserverForName..., I capture the result and add it to the set:

```
let ob = NSNotificationCenter.defaultCenter().addObserverForName(/*...*/)
self.observers.insert(ob as! NSObject)
```

When it's time to unregister, I enumerate the set and empty it:

```
for ob in self.observers {
    NSNotificationCenter.defaultCenter().removeObserver(ob)
}
self.observers.removeAll()
```

 NSNotificationCenter cannot be introspected: you cannot ask an NSNotification-Center what objects are registered with it as notification recipients. This is a major gap in Cocoa's functionality, and can make it difficult to track down bugs if you make a mistake such as unregistering an observer prematurely (as usual, I know this from bitter experience).

Posting a Notification

Although you'll mostly be interested in receiving notifications from Cocoa, you can also take advantage of the notification mechanism as a way of communicating between your own objects. One reason for doing this might be that two objects are conceptually distant or independent from one another. You should probably avoid using notifications too freely, or as an excuse for not bothering to devise proper lines of communication between objects; but they are certainly appropriate in some circumstances. (I'll raise this point again in Chapter 13.)

To use notifications in this way, your objects must play both roles in the communication chain. One of your objects (or more than one) will register to receive a notification, identified by name or object or both, as I've already described. Another of your objects will post a notification, identified in the same way. The notification center will then pass the message along from the poster to the registered recipient(s).

To post a notification, send to the notification center the message postNotification-Name:object:userInfo:.

For example, one of my apps is a simple card game. The game needs to know when a card is tapped. But a card knows nothing about the game; when it is tapped, it simply emits a virtual shriek by posting a notification:

```
NSNotificationCenter.defaultCenter().postNotificationName(
    "cardTapped", object: self)
```

The game object has registered for the "cardTapped" notification, so it hears about this and retrieves the notification's object; now it knows what card was tapped and can proceed correctly.

NSTimer

A timer (NSTimer) is not, strictly speaking, a notification; but it behaves very similarly. It is an object that gives off a signal (*fires*) after the lapse of a certain time interval. The signal is a message to one of your instances. Thus you can arrange to be notified when a certain time has elapsed. The timing is not perfectly accurate, but it's pretty good.

Timer management is not exactly tricky, but it is a little unusual. A timer that is actively watching the clock is said to be *scheduled*. A timer may fire once, or it may be a *repeating* timer. To make a timer go out of existence, it must be *invalidated*. A timer that is set to fire once is invalidated automatically after it fires; a repeating timer repeats until *you* invalidate it by sending it the invalidate message. An invalidated timer should be regarded as off-limits: you cannot revive it or use it for anything further, and you should probably not send any messages to it.

The straightforward way to create a timer is with the NSTimer class method scheduled-TimerWithTimeInterval:target:selector:userInfo:repeats:. This both creates the timer and schedules it, so that it begins watching the clock immediately. The target and selector determine what message will be sent to what object when the timer fires; the method in question should take one parameter, which will be a reference to the timer. The userInfo is just like the userInfo of a notification.

 The same cautions apply to a Timer's target: and selector: as for NSNotifications. At the time that a timer fires, the target must *exist*, and it must have a method corresponding *exactly* to the action selector, and Objective-C must be able to *see* that method. Otherwise, bad things will happen.

An NSTimer has a tolerance property, which is a time interval signifying how long after the timer *would* fire you're willing to grant before it really *does* fire. The documentation suggests that you can improve device battery life and app responsiveness by supplying a value of at least 10 percent of the timeInterval.

For example, one of my apps is a game with a score; I want to penalize the user, by diminishing the score, for every ten seconds that elapses after each move without the user making a further move. So each time the user makes a move, I create a repeating timer whose time interval is ten seconds (and I also invalidate any existing timer); in the method that the timer calls, I diminish the score.

Timers have some memory management implications that I'll discuss in Chapter 12, along with a block-based alternative to a timer.

Delegation

Delegation is an object-oriented design pattern, a relationship between two objects, in which a primary object's behavior is customized or assisted by a secondary object. The secondary object is the primary object's *delegate*. No subclassing is involved, and indeed the primary object is agnostic about the delegate's class.

As implemented by Cocoa, here's how delegation works. A built-in Cocoa class has an instance property, usually called `delegate` (it will certainly have `delegate` in its name). For some instance of that Cocoa class, you set the value of this property to an instance of one of *your* classes. At certain moments in its activity, the Cocoa class promises to turn to its delegate for instructions by sending it a certain message: if the Cocoa instance finds that its delegate is not `nil`, and that its delegate is prepared to receive that message, the Cocoa instance sends the message to the delegate.

Recall the discussion of protocols from Chapter 10. Delegation is one of Cocoa's main uses of protocols. In the old days, delegate methods were listed in the Cocoa class's documentation, and their method signatures were made known to the compiler through an informal protocol (a category on NSObject). Now, though, a class's delegate methods are usually listed in a genuine protocol with its own documentation. There are over 70 Cocoa delegate protocols, showing how heavily Cocoa relies on delegation. Most delegate methods are optional, but in a few cases you'll discover some that are required.

Cocoa Delegation

To customize a Cocoa instance's behavior through delegation, you start with one of your classes, which adopts the relevant delegate protocol. When the app runs, you set the Cocoa instance's `delegate` property (or whatever its name is) to an instance of your class. You might do this in code; alternatively, you might do it in a nib, by connecting an instance's `delegate` outlet (or whatever it's called) to an appropriate instance that is to serve as delegate. Your delegate class will probably do other things besides serving as this instance's delegate. Indeed, one of the nice things about delegation is that it leaves you free to slot delegate code into your class architecture however you like; the delegate type is a protocol, so the actual delegate can be an instance of *any* class.

In this simple example, I want to ensure that my app's root view controller, a UINavigationController, doesn't permit the app to rotate — the app should appear only in portrait orientation when this view controller is in charge. But UINavigation-Controller isn't my class; it belongs to Cocoa. My own class is a *different* view controller, a UIViewController subclass, which acts as the UINavigationController's child. How can the child tell the parent how to rotate? Well, UINavigationController has a `delegate` property, typed as UINavigationControllerDelegate (a protocol). It promises to send this delegate the `navigationControllerSupportedInterfaceOrientations` message when it needs to know how to rotate. So my view controller, in response to a very early lifetime event, sets itself as the UINavigationController's delegate. It also implements the `navigationControllerSupportedInterfaceOrientations` method. Presto, the problem is solved:

```
class ViewController : UIViewController, UINavigationControllerDelegate {
    override func viewDidLoad() {
        super.viewDidLoad()
        self.navigationController?.delegate = self
    }
    func navigationControllerSupportedInterfaceOrientations(
        nav: UINavigationController) -> UIInterfaceOrientationMask {
            return .Portrait
    }
}
```

An app's shared application instance, `UIApplication.sharedApplication()`, has a delegate that serves such an important role in the life of the app that the Xcode app templates automatically supply one — a class called AppDelegate. I described in Chapter 6 how an app gets started by calling `UIApplicationMain`, which instantiates the AppDelegate class and makes that instance the delegate of the shared application instance (which it has also created). As I pointed out in Chapter 10, AppDelegate formally adopts the UIApplicationDelegate protocol, signifying that it is ready to serve in this role; `respondsToSelector:` is then sent to the app delegate to see what UIApplicationDelegate protocol methods it implements. Thereafter, the application delegate instance is sent messages letting it know of major events in the lifetime of the app. That is why the UIApplicationDelegate protocol method `application:didFinishLaunchingWith-Options:` is so important; it is one of the earliest opportunities for *your* code to run.

 The UIApplication delegate methods are also provided as notifications. This lets an instance other than the app delegate hear conveniently about application lifetime events, by registering for them. A few other classes provide duplicate events similarly; for example, UITableView's `tableView:didSelectRowAtIndexPath:` delegate method is matched by a notification `UITableViewSelectionDidChange-Notification`.

By convention, many Cocoa delegate method names contain the modal verbs `should`, `will`, or `did`. A `will` message is sent to the delegate just before something happens; a `did` message is sent to the delegate just after something happens. A `should` method is special: it returns a Bool, and you are expected to respond with `true` to permit something or false to prevent it. The documentation tells you what the default response is; you don't have to implement a should method if the default response is always acceptable.

In many cases, a property will control some overall behavior, while a delegate method lets you modify that behavior based on circumstances at runtime. For example, whether the user can tap the status bar to make a scroll view scroll quickly to the top is governed by the scroll view's scrollsToTop property; but even if this property's value is true, you can prevent this behavior for a *particular* tap by returning false from the scroll view delegate's scrollViewShouldScrollToTop:.

When you're searching the documentation for how you can be notified of a certain event, be sure to consult the corresponding delegate protocol, if there is one. You'd like to know when the user taps in a UITextField to start editing it? You won't find anything relevant in the UITextField class documentation; what you're after is textFieldDid- BeginEditing: in the UITextFieldDelegate protocol. And so on.

Implementing Delegation

The Cocoa pattern of a delegate whose responsibilities are described by a protocol is one that you will want to imitate in your own code. Setting up this pattern takes some practice, and can be a little time-consuming, but it is often the correct approach, because it appropriately assigns knowledge and responsibility to the various objects involved.

Consider an actual case. In one of my apps I present a view controller whose view contains three sliders that the user can move to choose a color. Appropriately, this view controller is a UIViewController subclass called ColorPickerController. When the user taps Done or Cancel, the view should be dismissed; but first, the code that presented this view needs to hear about what color the user chose. So I need to send a message from the ColorPickerController instance *back to the instance that presented it*.

Here is the declaration for the message that I want the ColorPickerController to send before it goes out of existence:

```
func colorPicker (picker:ColorPickerController,
    didSetColorNamed theName:String?,
    toColor theColor:UIColor?)
```

The question is: where and how should this method be declared?

Now, it happens that in my app I know the class of the instance that will in fact present the ColorPickerController: it is a SettingsController. So I could simply declare this method in SettingsController. But this, if it is all I do, means that the ColorPicker- Controller, in order to send this message to the SettingsController, must *know* that the view that presented it *is* a SettingsController. But surely it is merely a *contingent* fact that the instance being sent this message is a SettingsController; it should be open to *any* class to present and dismiss a ColorPickerController, and thus to be eligible to receive this message.

Therefore we want ColorPickerController *itself* to declare the method that *it itself is going to call*; and we want it to send the message blindly to some receiver, without regard to the class of that receiver. That's what a protocol is for! The solution, then, is for ColorPickerController to define a protocol, with this method as part of that protocol, and for the class that presents a ColorPickerController to conform to that protocol. ColorPickerController also has an appropriately typed delegate property; this provides the channel of communication, and tells the compiler that sending this message is legal:

```
protocol ColorPickerDelegate : class {
    // color == nil on cancel
    func colorPicker (picker:ColorPickerController,
        didSetColorNamed theName:String?,
        toColor theColor:UIColor?)
}
class ColorPickerController : UIViewController {
    weak var delegate: ColorPickerDelegate?
    // ...
}
```

(On the meaning of and reasons for the weak attribute, see Chapter 5.) When my SettingsController instance creates and configures a ColorPickerController instance, it also sets itself as that ColorPickerController's delegate — which it can do, because it adopts the protocol:

```
extension SettingsController : ColorPickerDelegate {
    func showColorPicker() {
        let colorName = // ...
        let c = // ...
        let cpc = ColorPickerController(colorName:colorName, andColor:c)
        cpc.delegate = self
        self.presentViewController(cpc, animated: true, completion: nil)
    }
    func colorPicker (picker:ColorPickerController,
        didSetColorNamed theName:String?,
        toColor theColor:UIColor?) {
            // ...
    }
}
```

Now, when the user picks a color, the ColorPickerController *knows* to whom it should send colorPicker:didSetColorNamed:toColor: — namely, its delegate! And the compiler allows this, because the delegate has adopted the ColorPickerDelegate protocol:

```
@IBAction func dismissColorPicker(sender : AnyObject?) { // user tapped Done
    let c : UIColor? = self.color
    self.delegate?.colorPicker(
        self, didSetColorNamed: self.colorName, toColor: c)
}
```

Data Sources

A *data source* is like a delegate, except that its methods supply the data for another object to display. The chief Cocoa classes with data sources are UITableView, UICollection-View, UIPickerView, and UIPageViewController. In each case, the data source must formally adopt a data source protocol with required methods.

It comes as a surprise to some beginners that a data source is necessary at all. Why isn't a table's data just part of the table? Or why isn't there at least some fixed data structure that contains the data? The reason is that such an architecture would violate generality. Use of a data source separates the object that displays the data from the object that manages the data, and leaves the latter free to store and obtain that data however it likes (see on model–view–controller in Chapter 13). The only requirement is that the data source must be able to supply information quickly, because it will be asked for it in real time when the data needs displaying.

Another surprise is that the data source is different from the delegate. But this again is only for generality; it's an option, not a requirement. There is no reason why the data source and the delegate should not be the same object, and most of the time they probably will be. Indeed, in most cases, data source methods and delegate methods will work closely together; you won't even be conscious of the distinction.

In this example from one of my apps, I implement a UIPickerView that allows the user to configure a game by saying how many stages it should consist of ("1 Stage," "2 Stages", and so on). The first two methods are UIPickerView data source methods; the third method is a UIPickerView delegate method. It takes all three methods to supply the picker view's content:

```
extension NewGameController: UIPickerViewDelegate, UIPickerViewDataSource {
    func numberOfComponentsInPickerView(pickerView: UIPickerView) -> Int {
        return 1
    }
    func pickerView(pickerView: UIPickerView,
        numberOfRowsInComponent component: Int) -> Int {
            return 9
    }
    func pickerView(pickerView: UIPickerView,
        titleForRow row: Int, forComponent component: Int) -> String? {
            return "\(row+1) Stage" + ( row > 0 ? "s" : "")
    }
}
```

Actions

An *action* is a message emitted by an instance of a UIControl subclass (a *control*) reporting a significant user event taking place in that control. The UIControl subclasses are all simple interface objects that the user can interact with directly, such as a button (UIButton) or a segmented control (UISegmentedControl).

The significant user events (*control events*) are listed under UIControlEvents in the Constants section of the UIControl class documentation. Different controls implement different control events: for example, a segmented control's Value Changed event signifies that the user has tapped to select a different segment, but a button's Touch Up Inside event signifies that the user has tapped the button. Of itself, a control event has no external effect; the control responds visually (for example, a tapped button looks tapped), but it doesn't automatically share the information that the event has taken place. If you want to know when a control event takes place, so that you can respond to it in your code, *you* must arrange for that control event to trigger an *action message*.

Here's how it works. A control maintains an internal dispatch table: for each control event, there can be any number of target–action pairs, in each of which the *action* is a message selector (the name of a method) and the *target* is the object to which that message is to be sent. When a control event occurs, the control consults its dispatch table, finds all the target–action pairs associated with that control event, and sends each action message to the corresponding target (Figure 11-1).

There are two ways to manipulate a control's action dispatch table:

Action connection
> You can configure an action connection in a nib. I described in Chapter 7 how to do this, but I didn't completely explain the underlying mechanism. Now all is revealed: an action connection formed in the nib editor is a visual way of configuring a control's action dispatch table.

Code
> You can use code to operate directly on the control's action dispatch table. The key method here is the UIControl instance method `addTarget:action:forControl-Events:`, where the `target:` is an object, the `action:` is a selector (in Swift, a string), and the `controlEvents:` are designated by a bitmask (see "Option sets" on page 231). Unlike a notification center, a control also has methods for introspecting the dispatch table.

 The same cautions apply to a UIControl's `target:` and `action:` as for NSNotifications, earlier in this chapter. At the time that a control event fires, the target must *exist*, and it must have a method corresponding *exactly* to the action selector, and Objective-C must be able to *see* that method. Otherwise, bad things will happen.

Recall the example of a control and its action from Chapter 7. We have a `button-Pressed:` method:

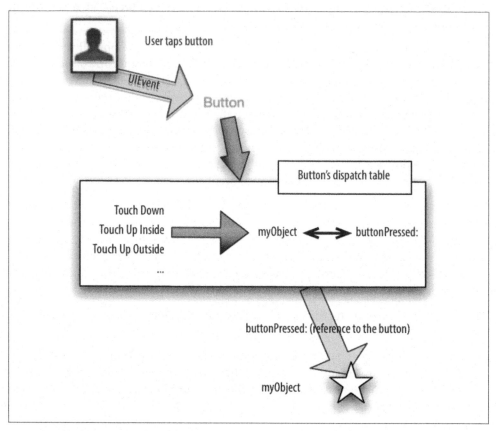

Figure 11-1. The target–action architecture

```
@IBAction func buttonPressed(sender:AnyObject) {
    let alert = UIAlertController(
        title: "Howdy!", message: "You tapped me!", preferredStyle: .Alert)
    alert.addAction(
        UIAlertAction(title: "OK", style: .Cancel, handler: nil))
    self.presentViewController(alert, animated: true, completion: nil)
}
```

The purpose of this method is to be called when the user taps a certain button in the interface. In Chapter 7, we arranged for that to happen by setting up an action connection in the nib: we connected the button's Touch Up Inside event to the ViewController `buttonPressed:` method. In reality, we were forming a target–action pair and adding that target–action pair to the button's dispatch table for the Touch Up Inside control event.

Instead of making that arrangement in the nib, we could have done the same thing in code. Suppose we had *never* drawn that action connection. And suppose that, instead, we have an outlet connection from the view controller to the button, called `button`. Then the view controller, after the nib loads, can configure the button's dispatch table like this:

```
self.button.addTarget(self,
    action: "buttonPressed:",
    forControlEvents: .TouchUpInside)
```

 A control event can have multiple target–action pairs. You might configure it this way intentionally, but it is also possible to do so accidentally. Unintentionally giving a control event a target–action pair without removing its *existing* target-action pair is an easy mistake to make, and can cause some very mysterious behavior. For example, if we had formed an action connection in the nib *and* configured the dispatch table in code, a tap on the button would cause `button-Pressed:` to be called *twice*.

The signature for the action selector can be in any of three forms:

- The fullest form takes two parameters:
  - The control, usually typed as `AnyObject`.
  - The UIEvent that generated the control event.
- A shorter form, the one most commonly used, omits the second parameter. `button-Pressed:` is an example; it takes one parameter, `sender`. When `buttonPressed:` is called through an action message emanating from the button, `sender` will be a reference to the button.
- There is a still shorter form that omits both parameters.

What is the UIEvent, and what is it for? Well, a *touch event* is generated whenever the user does something with a finger (sets it down on the screen, moves it, raises it from the screen). UIEvents are the lowest-level objects charged with communication of touch events to your app. A UIEvent is basically a timestamp (a Double) along with a collection (Set) of touch events (UITouch). The action mechanism deliberately shields you from the complexities of touch events, but by electing to receive the UIEvent, you can still deal with those complexities if you want to.

 Curiously, none of the action selector parameters provide any way to learn *which* control event triggered the current action selector call! Thus, for example, to distinguish a Touch Up Inside control event from a Touch Up Outside control event, their corresponding target–action pairs must specify two different action handlers; if you dispatch them to the same action handler, that handler cannot discover which control event occurred.

The Responder Chain

A *responder* is an object that knows how to receive UIEvents directly (see the previous section). It knows this because it is an instance of UIResponder or a UIResponder subclass. If you examine the Cocoa class hierarchy, you'll find that just about any class that has anything to do with display on the screen is a responder. A UIView is a responder. A UIWindow is a responder. A UIViewController is a responder. Even a UIApplication is a responder. Even the app delegate is a responder!

A UIResponder has four low-level methods for receiving touch-related UIEvents:

- `touchesBegan:withEvent:`
- `touchesMoved:withEvent:`
- `touchesEnded:withEvent:`
- `touchesCancelled:withEvent:`

These methods — the *touch methods* — are called to notify a responder of a touch event. No matter how your code ultimately hears about a user-related touch event — indeed, even if your code *never* hears about a touch event (because Cocoa reacted in some automatic way to the touch, without your code's intervention) — the touch was initially communicated to a responder through one of the touch methods.

The mechanism for this communication starts by deciding which responder the user touched. The UIView methods `hitTest:withEvent:` and `pointInside:withEvent:` are called until the correct view (the *hit-test view*) is located. Then UIApplication's `sendEvent:` method is called, which calls UIWindow's `sendEvent:`, which calls the correct touch method of the hit-test view (a responder).

The responders in your app participate in a *responder chain*, which essentially links them up through the view hierarchy. A UIView can sit inside another UIView, its *superview*, and so on until we reach the app's UIWindow (a UIView that has no superview). The responder chain, from bottom to top, looks like this:

1. The UIView that we start with (here, the hit-test view).
2. If this UIView is a UIViewController's `view`, that UIViewController.
3. The UIView's superview.
4. Go back to step 2 and repeat! Keep repeating until we reach…
5. The UIWindow.
6. The UIApplication.
7. The UIApplication's delegate.

Deferring Responsibility

The responder chain can be used to let a responder defer responsibility for handling a touch event. If a responder receives a touch event and can't handle it, the event can be passed up the responder chain to look for a responder that *can* handle it. This can happen in two main ways:

- The responder doesn't implement the relevant touch method.
- The responder implements the relevant touch method to call super.

For example, a plain vanilla UIView has no native implementation of the touch methods. Thus, by default, even if a UIView is the hit-test view, the touch event effectively falls through the UIView and travels up the responder chain, looking for someone to respond to it. In certain situations, it might make sense for you to defer responsibility for this touch to the main background view, or even to the UIViewController that controls it.

Here's an example from one of my apps. The app is a game that's a simple jigsaw puzzle: a rectangular photo is divided into smaller pieces, and the pieces are shuffled. The user's job is to tap two pieces in succession to swap them. The background view is a UIView subclass called Board; the puzzle pieces are generic UIView objects, and are subviews of the Board. Knowledge of how a piece should respond when tapped resides in the Board, which knows the overall layout of the pieces; thus, I don't need a puzzle piece to contain any tap detection logic. Therefore I take advantage of the responder chain to defer responsibility: the puzzle pieces don't implement any touch methods, and a tap on a puzzle piece falls through to the Board, which *does* perform touch detection and handles the tap, and tells the tapped piece what to do. The user, of course, knows nothing about that: outwardly, you touch a piece and the piece responds.

Nil-Targeted Actions

A *nil-targeted action* is a target–action pair in which the target is nil. There is no designated target object, so the following rule is used: starting with the hit-test view (the view with which the user is interacting), Cocoa walks up the responder chain, one responder at a time, looking for an object that can respond to the action message:

- If a responder is found that handles this message, that method is called on that responder, and that's the end.
- If we get all the way to the top of the responder chain without finding a responder to handle this message, the message goes unhandled (with no penalty) — in other words, nothing happens.

Suppose, for example, that we were to configure a button in code, like this:

```
self.button.addTarget(nil,
    action: "buttonPressed:",
    forControlEvents: .TouchUpInside)
```

That's a nil-targeted action. So what happens when the user taps the button? First, Cocoa looks in the UIButton itself to see whether it responds to buttonPressed:. If not, it looks in the UIView that is its superview. And so on, up the responder chain. If self is the view controller that owns the view that contains the button, and if the class of this view controller does in fact implement buttonPressed:, tapping the button will cause the view controller's buttonPressed: to be called!

It's obvious how to construct a nil-targeted action in code: you set up a target–action pair where the target is nil, as in the preceding example. But how do you construct a nil-targeted action in a nib? The answer is: you form a connection to the First Responder proxy object (in the dock). This is what the First Responder proxy object is for! The First Responder isn't a real object with a known class, so before you can connect an action to it, you have to define the action message within the First Responder proxy object, like this:

1. Select the First Responder proxy in the nib, and switch to the Attributes inspector.

2. You'll see a table (probably empty) of user-defined nil-targeted First Responder actions. Click the Plus button and give the new action a signature; it must take a single parameter (so that its name will end with a colon).

3. Now you can Control-drag from a control, such as a UIButton, to the First Responder proxy to specify a nil-targeted action with the signature you specified.

Key–Value Observing

Key–value observing, or *KVO*, is a notification mechanism that doesn't use the NSNotificationCenter. It allows one object to be registered *directly with a second object* so as to be notified when a value in the second object changes. Moreover, the second object — the observed object — doesn't actually have to *do* anything; it needn't even be conscious of the fact that this registration has taken place. When the value in the observed object changes, the registered object — the observer — is automatically notified. (Perhaps a better architectural analogy would be with the target–action mechanism; this is a target–action mechanism that works between *any* two objects.)

When you use KVO, the observer will be *your* object; you will write the code that will respond when the observer is notified of the change for which it has registered. But the observed object, the one with which you register to hear about changes, needn't be your object at all; in fact, it often will not be. Many Cocoa objects promise to behave in a KVO compliant way, and you are invited and expected to use KVO on them. Typically, KVO is used in place of delegation or notifications.

The process of using KVO may be broken down into three stages:

Registration

> To hear about a change in a value belonging to the observed object, we must be registered with the observed object. This typically involves calling the observed object's `addObserver:forKeyPath:options:context:` method. (All objects derived from NSObject have this method, because it is injected into NSObject by the informal protocol NSKeyValueObserving, which is actually a set of categories on NSObject and other classes.)

Change

> The change takes place in the value belonging to the observed object, and it must take place in a special way — a KVO compliant way. Typically, this means using a key–value coding compliant accessor to make the change. Setting a property passes through a key–value coding compliant accessor.

Notification

> The observer is automatically notified that the value in the observed object has changed: its `observeValueForKeyPath:ofObject:change:context:` method, which we have implemented for exactly this purpose, is called by the runtime.

It is also necessary, sooner or later, to unregister with the observed object when we no longer want to receive this notification, by sending it `removeObserver:forKeyPath:` (or `removeObserver:forKeyPath:context:`). This is important for the same reason that unregistering for an NSNotification is important: if we don't, the app can crash if the notification is sent to an observer that has gone out of existence. You must explicitly unregister the observer for every key path for which it is registered; you can't use `nil` as the second argument to mean "all key paths." The last possible moment to unregister is the observer's `deinit`; obviously, this requires that the observer have a reference to the observed object.

But there's more. All observers must be unregistered from an observed object before *the observed object* goes out of existence! If an object goes out of existence with observers still registered with it, your app will crash, with a helpful message in the console: "An instance … was deallocated while key value observers were still registered with it."

Here's an example from my actual code. An AVPlayerViewController is a view controller whose view displays video content. When the view first appears, there can be a nasty flash, because the view is black until the video content is ready, which may take a little time. The solution is to make the view initially invisible, until the video content *is* ready. Thus, we want to be notified when the video content is ready. AVPlayerViewController has a `readyForDisplay` property — so we want to be notified when that property becomes `true`. But AVPlayerViewController has no delegate, and provides no notifications. The solution is to use KVO: we register ourself with the AVPlayerViewController to hear about changes in its `readyForDisplay` property. Here's the part of my code that configures and shows an AVPlayerViewController's view:

```
func setUpChild() {
    // ...
    let av = AVPlayerViewController()
    av.player = player
    av.view.frame = CGRectMake(10,10,300,200)
    av.view.hidden = true // looks nicer if we don't show until ready
    av.addObserver(self,
        forKeyPath: "readyForDisplay", options: [], context: nil) ❶
    // ...
}
override func observeValueForKeyPath(keyPath: String?,
    ofObject object: AnyObject?, change: [String : AnyObject]?,
    context: UnsafeMutablePointer<()>) { ❷
        if keyPath == "readyForDisplay" {
            if let obj = object as? AVPlayerViewController {
                dispatch_async(dispatch_get_main_queue(), {
                    self.finishConstructingInterface(obj)
                })
            }
        }
}
func finishConstructingInterface (vc:AVPlayerViewController) {
    if !vc.readyForDisplay {
        return
    }
    vc.removeObserver(self, forKeyPath:"readyForDisplay") ❸
    vc.view.hidden = false
}
```

❶ The AVPlayerViewController's view starts out invisible (`hidden` is `true`). We register to hear about any change in its `readyForDisplay` property.

❷ The AVPlayerViewController's `readyForDisplay` property changes, and we hear about it because our `observeValueForKeyPath:...` is called. We make sure this is the right notification; if it is, we proceed to finish constructing the interface. Note that the observed object (the AVPlayerViewController) arrives as the `object` parameter; this not only helps us identify the notification, but also allows us to communicate with that object. There are no guarantees about the thread on which `observeValueForKeyPath:...` will be called, so we step out to the main thread before doing anything that would affect the interface.

❸ After one final check to make sure that `readyForDisplay` actually changed from `false` to `true`, we unregister — we only need to hear about this change once — and proceed to make the view visible (`hidden` is `false`).

The `options:` argument is a bitmask (NSKeyValueObservingOptions). One of the things it lets us do is ask for the new value of the changed property to be sent to us in the `change:` dictionary. Thus, we can rewrite our code so as to move the check for whether `readyForDisplay` is now `true` into our implementation of `observeValueForKeyPath....` We now register like this:

```
av.addObserver(
    self, forKeyPath: "readyForDisplay", options: .New, context: nil)
```

And here's the rest of the code; as I suggested in Chapter 5, a sequence of guard statements reads nicely here:

```
override func observeValueForKeyPath(keyPath: String?,
    ofObject object: AnyObject?, change: [String : AnyObject]?,
    context: UnsafeMutablePointer<()>) {
        guard keyPath == "readyForDisplay" else {return}
        guard let obj = object as? AVPlayerViewController else {return}
        guard let ok = change?[NSKeyValueChangeNewKey] as? Bool else {return}
        guard ok else {return}
        dispatch_async(dispatch_get_main_queue(), {
            self.finishConstructingInterface(obj)
        })
}
func finishConstructingInterface (vc:AVPlayerViewController) {
    vc.removeObserver(self, forKeyPath:"readyForDisplay")
    vc.view.hidden = false
}
```

You're probably wondering about the `context:` parameter in `addObserver:...` and `observeValueForKeyPath:....` On the whole, I recommend against using this parameter, but I'll tell you about it anyway. It is said to represent "arbitrary data" that is handed into `addObserver:...` and retrieved in `observeValueForKeyPath:....` You have to be careful with its value, however, because it is typed as `UnsafeMutablePointer<Void>`. This means that its memory is not managed while the runtime has hold of it; *you* must manage its memory by keeping a persistent reference to the value elsewhere. The usual approach is to use a global variable (a variable declared at the top level of a file); to prevent it from being *too* global, you can declare it `private`, like this:

```
private var con = "ObserveValue"
```

When you call `addObserver:...`, you pass the address of this variable, `&con`, as the `context:` argument. When you are notified in `observeValueForKeyPath:...`, you can use the `context:` parameter as an identifier by comparing it to `&con`:

```
override func observeValueForKeyPath(keyPath: String?,
    ofObject object: AnyObject?, change: [String : AnyObject]?,
    context: UnsafeMutablePointer<Void>) {
        if context != &con {
```

```
                return // wrong notification
        }
        // ...
    }
```

In that code, the *value* stored in the global variable is irrelevant; we are using its *address* as an identifier. If you want to *use* the value stored in the global variable, coerce the UnsafeMutablePointer to another UnsafeMutablePointer specified as the underlying type. Now you can access the underlying value as the UnsafeMutablePointer's `memory` property. In our example, con is a String:

```
override func observeValueForKeyPath(keyPath: String?,
    ofObject object: AnyObject?, change: [String : AnyObject]?,
    context: UnsafeMutablePointer<Void>) {
        let c = UnsafeMutablePointer<String>(context)
        let s = c.memory // "ObserveValue"
        // ...
    }
```

Key–value observing is a deep mechanism; consult Apple's *Key-Value Observing Guide* for full information. (For example, it is possible to observe a mutable NSArray, but the mechanism is more elaborate than I have described here.) KVO also has some unfortunate shortcomings. For one thing, all notifications arrive by calling the same bottleneck method; that's a pity. And keeping track of who's observing whom, and making sure both observer and observed have appropriate lifetimes and that unregistration takes place in a timely fashion, can be tricky. But in general, KVO is useful for keeping values coordinated in different objects; and, as I've already said, certain parts of Cocoa will expect you to use it.

 Both the observed and the observer in KVO must derive from NSObject. Moreover, if the property to be observed is declared in Swift, it *must* be marked `dynamic` — otherwise, KVO won't work. (The reason is that KVO works by swizzling the accessor methods; Cocoa needs to be able to reach right in and change your object's code, and it can't do that unless the property is `dynamic`.)

Swamped by Events

Your code runs only because Cocoa sends an event and you had previously set up a method ready to receive it. Cocoa has the potential to send *lots* of events, telling you what the user has done, informing you of each stage in the lifetime of your app and its objects, asking for your input on how to proceed. To receive the events that you need to hear about, your code is peppered with methods that are *entry points* — methods that you have written with just the right name and in just the right class so that they can be called by Cocoa through events. In fact, it is easy to imagine that in many cases your code for a class will consist almost entirely of entry points.

Arranging all those entry points is one of your primary challenges as an iOS programmer. You know what you want to do, but you don't get to "just do it." You have to divide up your app's functionality and allocate it in accordance with when and how Cocoa is going to call into your code. Before you've written a single line of your own code, the skeleton structure of a class is likely to have been largely mapped out for you by the need to be prepared to receive the events that Cocoa is going to want to send you.

Suppose, for example, that your iPhone app presents an interface consisting of a table view. (This is in fact an extremely probable scenario.) You're likely to have a corresponding UITableViewController subclass; UITableViewController is a built-in UIViewController subclass, and an instance of your UITableViewController subclass will own and control the table view, plus you'll probably use this same class as the table view's data source and delegate. In this single class, then, you're likely to want to implement *at a minimum* the following methods:

`initWithCoder:` *or* `initWithNibName:bundle:`
UIViewController lifetime method, where you perform instance initializations.

`viewDidLoad`
UIViewController lifetime method, where you perform view-related initializations.

`viewDidAppear:`
UIViewController lifetime method, where you set up states that need to apply only while your view is onscreen. For example, if you're going to register for a notification or set up a timer, this is a likely place to do it.

`viewDidDisappear:`
UIViewController lifetime method, where you reverse what you did in `viewDid-Appear:`. For example, this would be a likely place to unregister for a notification or invalidate a repeating timer that you set up in `viewDidAppear:`.

`supportedInterfaceOrientations`
UIViewController query method, where you specify what device orientations are allowed for this view controller's main view.

`numberOfSectionsInTableView:`
`tableView:numberOfRowsInSection:`
`tableView:cellForRowAtIndexPath:`
UITableView data source query methods, where you specify the contents of the table.

`tableView:didSelectRowAtIndexPath:`
UITableView delegate user action method, where you respond when the user taps a row of the table.

```
deinit
```
Swift class instance lifetime method, where you perform end-of-life cleanup.

Suppose, further, that you did in fact use `viewDidAppear:` to register for a notification and to set up a timer. Then that notification has a selector (unless you used a block), and the timer has a selector; you must therefore also implement the methods specified by those selectors.

We already have, then, about a dozen methods whose presence is effectively a matter of boilerplate. These are not *your* methods; *you* are never going to call them. They are *Cocoa's* methods, which you have placed here so that each can be called at the appropriate moment in the life story of your app.

The logic of a program laid out in this fashion is by no means easy to understand! I'm not criticizing Cocoa here — indeed, it's hard to imagine how else an application framework could work — but, purely as an objective matter of fact, the result is that a Cocoa program, even your own program, even *while you're developing it*, is hard to read, because it consists of numerous disconnected entry points, each with its own meaning, each called at its own set moment which is not in any way obvious from looking at the program. To understand what our hypothetical class does, you have to know *already* such things as when `viewDidAppear:` is called and how it is typically used; otherwise, you don't even know where to look to find the program's logic and behavior, let alone how to interpret what you see when you do look there. And this difficulty is greatly compounded when you try to read someone else's code (this is one reason why, as I mentioned in Chapter 8, sample code is not all that helpful to a beginner).

Looking at the code of an iOS program — even your own code — your eyes can easily glaze over at the sight of all these methods called automatically by Cocoa under various circumstances. To be sure, experience will teach you about such things as the overridden UIViewController methods and the table view delegate and data source methods. On the other hand, no amount of experience will tell you that a certain method is called as a button's action or through a notification. Comments really help, and I strongly advise you, as you develop any iOS app, to comment every method, quite heavily if need be, saying what that method does and under what circumstances you expect it to be called — especially if it is an entry point, where it is Cocoa itself that will do the calling.

Perhaps the most common kind of mistake in writing a Cocoa app is not that there's a bug in your code itself, but that you've put the code *in the wrong place*. Your code isn't running, or it's running at the wrong time, or the pieces are running in the wrong order. I see questions about this sort of thing all the time on the various online user forums (these are all actual examples that appeared over the course of just two days):

- *There's a delay between the time when my view appears and when my button takes on its correct title.*

  That's because you put the code that sets the button's title in `viewDidAppear:`. That's *too late*; your code needs to run earlier, perhaps in `viewWillAppear:`.

- *My subviews are positioned in code and they're turning out all wrong.*

  That's because you put the code that positions your subviews in `viewDidLoad`. That's *too early*; your code needs to run later, when your view's dimensions have been determined.

- *My view is rotating even though my view controller's `supportedInterface-Orientations` says not to.*

  That's because you implemented `supportedInterfaceOrientations` in the *wrong class*; it needs to be implemented in the UINavigationController that contains your view controller (or by using the delegate's `navigationControllerSupported-InterfaceOrientations`, as I described earlier in this chapter).

- *I set up an action connection for Value Changed on a text field, but my code isn't being called when the user edits.*

  That's because you connected the *wrong control event*; a text field emits Editing Changed, not Value Changed.

Adding to your challenges is that fact that you can't really know *precisely when* an entry point will be called. The documentation may give you a general sense, but in most cases there are no guarantees about when events will arrive and in what order. What you think is going to happen, and even what the documentation leads you to believe is going to happen, might not be quite what really does happen. Your own code can trigger unintended events. The documentation might not make it clear just when a notification will be sent. There could even be a bug in Cocoa such that events are called in a way that seems to contradict the documentation. And you have no access to the Cocoa source code, so you can't work out the underlying details. Therefore I also recommend that as you develop your app, you instrument your code heavily with caveman debugging (`print` and `NSLog`; see Chapter 9). As you test your code, keep an eye on the console output and check whether the messages make sense. You may be surprised at what you discover.

Delayed Performance

Your code is executed in response to some event; but your code in turn may trigger a new event or chain of events. Sometimes this causes bad things to happen: there might be a crash, or Cocoa might appear not to have done what you said to do. To solve this problem, sometimes you just need to step outside Cocoa's own chain of events for a moment and wait for everything to settle down before proceeding.

The technique for doing this is called *delayed performance*. You tell Cocoa to do something, not right this moment, but in a little while, when things have settled down. Perhaps you need only a very short delay, possibly even as short as zero seconds, just to let Cocoa finish doing something, such as laying out the interface. Technically, you're allowing the current run loop to finish, completing and unwinding the entire current method call stack, before proceeding further with your own code.

When you program iOS, you're likely to be using delayed performance a lot more than you might expect. With experience, you'll develop a kind of sixth sense for when delayed performance might be the solution to your difficulties.

The main way to get delayed performance in iOS programming is by calling `dispatch_after`. It takes a block (a function) stating what should happen after the specified time has passed. Calling `dispatch_after` is a bit elaborate, though, especially in Swift where there's a lot of coercing to do; so I've written a utility function that simplifies things and calls `dispatch_after` for me:

```
func delay(delay:Double, closure:()->()) {
    dispatch_after(
        dispatch_time(
            DISPATCH_TIME_NOW,
            Int64(delay * Double(NSEC_PER_SEC))
        ),
        dispatch_get_main_queue(), closure)
}
```

That utility function is so important that I routinely paste it at the top level of the AppDelegate class file in every app I write. It's going to come in handy, I know! To use it, I call `delay` with a delay time (usually a very small number of seconds such as `0.1`) and an anonymous function saying what to do after the delay. Note that what you propose to do in this anonymous function will be done later on; you're deliberately breaking out of your own code's line-by-line sequence of execution. So a delayed performance call will be the last call in its own surrounding function, and cannot return any value.

In this actual example from one of my own apps, the user has tapped a row of a table, and my code responds by creating and showing a new view controller:

```
override func tableView(tableView: UITableView,
    didSelectRowAtIndexPath indexPath: NSIndexPath) {
        let t = TracksViewController(
            mediaItemCollection: self.albums[indexPath.row])
        self.navigationController!.pushViewController(
            t, animated: true)
}
```

Unfortunately, the innocent-looking call to my TracksViewController initializer init(mediaItemCollection:) can take a moment to complete, so the app comes to a stop with the table row highlighted — very briefly, but just long enough to startle the user. To cover this delay with a sense of activity, I've rigged my UITableViewCell subclass to show a spinning activity indicator when it's selected:

```
override func setSelected(selected: Bool, animated: Bool) {
    if selected {
        self.activityIndicator.startAnimating()
    } else {
        self.activityIndicator.stopAnimating()
    }
    super.setSelected(selected, animated: animated)
}
```

But there's a problem: the spinning activity indicator never appears and never spins. The reason is that the events are stumbling over one another here. UITableViewCell's setSelected:animated: isn't called until the UITableView delegate method table-View:didSelectRowAtIndexPath: has finished. But the delay we're trying to paper over is *during* tableView:didSelectRowAtIndexPath:; the whole problem is that it *doesn't* finish fast enough.

Delayed performance to the rescue! I'll rewrite tableView:didSelectRowAtIndex-Path: so that it finishes immediately — thus triggering setSelected:animated: immediately and causing the activity indicator to appear and spin — and I'll use delayed performance to call init(mediaItemCollection:) later on, when the interface has ironed itself out:

```
override func tableView(tableView: UITableView,
    didSelectRowAtIndexPath indexPath: NSIndexPath) {
        delay(0.1) { // let spinner start spinning
            let t = TracksViewController(
                mediaItemCollection: self.albums[indexPath.row])
            self.navigationController!.pushViewController(
                t, animated: true)
        }
}
```

CHAPTER 12

Memory Management

Class instances, both in Swift and in Objective-C, are reference types (see "Value Types and Reference Types" on page 140). Behind the scenes, Swift and Objective-C memory management for reference types works essentially the same way. Such memory management, as I pointed out in Chapter 5, can be a tricky business.

Fortunately, Swift uses ARC (automatic reference counting), so that you don't have to manage the memory for every reference type object explicitly and individually, as was once necessary in Objective-C. Thanks to ARC, you are far less likely to make a memory management mistake, and more of your time is liberated to concentrate on what your app actually does instead of dealing with memory management concerns.

But even with ARC it is still possible to make a memory management mistake, or to be caught unawares by Cocoa's memory management behavior. A memory management mistake can lead to runaway excessive memory usage, crashes, or mysterious misbehavior of your app, and even in Swift it is possible to make such a mistake. Cocoa memory management can be surprising in individual cases, and you need to understand, and prepare for, what Cocoa is going to do.

Principles of Cocoa Memory Management

The reason why reference type memory must be managed at all is that references to reference type objects are merely pointers. The real object pointed to occupies a hunk of memory that must be explicitly set aside when the object is brought into existence and that must be explicitly freed up when the object goes out of existence. The memory is set aside when the object is instantiated, but how is this memory to be freed up, and when should it happen?

At the very least, an object should certainly go out of existence when no other objects exist that have a pointer to it. An object without a pointer to it is useless; it is occupying memory, but no other object has, or can ever get, a reference to it. This is a *memory leak*. Many computer languages solve this problem through a policy called *garbage collection*. Simply put, the language prevents memory leaks by periodically sweeping through a central list of all objects and destroying those to which no pointer exists. But garbage collection would be an expensive strategy on an iOS device, where memory is strictly limited and the processor is relatively slow (and may have only a single core). Thus, memory in iOS must be managed more or less manually, on an individual basis; each object needs to go out of existence exactly when it is no longer needed.

The hard part in that sentence is the word "exactly." An object must go out of existence neither too late nor too soon. Multiple objects can have a pointer (a reference) to the very same object. If both the object Manny and the object Moe have a pointer to the object Jack, and if Manny somehow tells Jack to go out of existence now, poor old Moe is left with a pointer to nothing (or worse, to garbage). A pointer whose object has been destroyed behind the pointer's back is a *dangling pointer*. If Moe subsequently uses that dangling pointer to send a message to the object that it thinks is there, the app will crash.

To prevent both dangling pointers and memory leakage, there is a policy of manual memory management based on a number, maintained by every reference type object, called its *retain count*. The rule is that other objects can increment or decrement an object's retain count — and that's all they are allowed to do. As long as an object's retain count is positive, the object will persist. No object has the direct power to tell another object to be destroyed; rather, as soon as an object's retain count is decremented to zero, it is destroyed automatically.

By this policy, every object that needs Jack to persist should increment Jack's retain count, and should decrement it once again when it no longer needs Jack to persist. As long as all objects are well-behaved in accordance with this policy, the problem of manual memory management is effectively solved:

- There cannot be any dangling pointers, because any object that has a pointer to Jack has incremented Jack's retain count, thus ensuring that Jack persists.

- There cannot be any memory leaks, because any object that no longer needs Jack decrements Jack's retain count, thus ensuring that eventually Jack will go out of existence (when the retain count reaches zero, indicating that no object needs Jack any longer).

Rules of Cocoa Memory Management

An object is well-behaved with respect to memory management as long as it adheres to certain very simple, well-defined rules in conformity with the basic concepts of memory management. The underlying ethic is that *each* object that has a reference to a reference type object is responsible solely for *its own* memory management of that object, in accordance with these rules. If *all* objects that *ever* get a reference to this reference type object behave correctly with respect to these rules, the object's memory will be managed correctly and it will go out of existence exactly when it is no longer needed.

Consider three objects: Manny, Moe, and Jack. Poor old Jack is going to be the victim here: we're going to manage his memory, and if Jack's memory is managed correctly, Jack will go out of existence correctly. Manny and Moe are going to participate in managing in Jack's memory. How will they do that? Everything will be fine as long as Manny and Moe follow these rules:

- If Manny or Moe *explicitly instantiates* Jack — by directly calling an initializer — then the initializer *increments* Jack's retain count.

- If Manny or Moe *makes a copy* of Jack — by calling `copy` or `copyWithZone:` or `mutableCopy` or any other method with `copy` in its name — then the copy method *increments* the retain count of this new, duplicate Jack.

- If Manny or Moe *acquires* a reference to Jack (not through explicit instantiation or copying), and needs Jack to *persist* — long enough to work with Jack in code, or long enough to be the value of an instance property — then he himself *increments* Jack's retain count. (This is called *retaining* Jack.)

- If and only if Manny or Moe, himself, has done any of those things — that is, if Manny or Moe has ever directly or indirectly caused Jack's retain count to be incremented — then when he himself no longer needs his reference to Jack, before letting go of that reference, he *decrements* Jack's retain count to balance exactly all previous increments that he himself has performed. (This is called *releasing* Jack.) Having released Jack, Manny or Moe should then assume that Jack no longer exists, because if this causes Jack's retain count to drop to zero, Jack *will* no longer exist. This is the *golden rule of memory management* — the rule that makes memory management work coherently and correctly.

A general way of understanding the golden rule of memory management is to think in terms of *ownership*. If Manny has created, copied, or retained Jack — that is, if Manny has ever incremented Jack's retain count — Manny has asserted ownership of Jack. Both Manny and Moe can own Jack at once, but each is responsible only for managing his own ownership of Jack correctly. It is the responsibility of an owner of Jack eventually to decrement Jack's retain count — to release Jack, thus resigning ownership of Jack. The owner thus says: "Jack may or may not persist after this, but as for me, I'm done with Jack, and Jack can go out of existence as far as I'm concerned." At the same time, a nonowner of Jack must *never* release Jack. As long as all objects behave this way with respect to Jack, Jack will not leak nor will any pointer to Jack be left dangling.

What ARC Is and What It Does

Once upon a time, retaining and releasing an object was a matter of you, the programmer, literally sending `retain` and `release` messages to it. NSObject still implements `retain` and `release`, but under ARC (and in Swift) you can't call them. That's because ARC is calling them for you! That's ARC's job — to do for you what you would have had to do if memory management were still up to the programmer.

ARC is implemented as part of the compiler. The compiler is literally modifying your code by inserting `retain` and `release` calls behind the scenes. Thus, for example, when you receive a reference type object by calling some method, ARC immediately retains it so that it will persist for as long as this same code continues to run; then ARC releases it when the code comes to an end. Similarly, when you create or copy a reference type object, ARC knows that its retain count has been incremented, and releases it when the code comes to an end.

ARC is very conservative, but also very accurate. In effect, ARC retains at every juncture that might have the slightest implications for memory management: it retains when an object is received as an argument, it retains when an object is assigned to a variable, and so forth. It may even insert temporary variables, behind the scenes, to enable it to refer sufficiently early to an object so that it can retain it. But of course it eventually also releases to match.

How Cocoa Objects Manage Memory

Built-in Cocoa objects will take ownership of objects that you hand to them, by retaining them, if it makes sense for them to do so, and will of course then balance that retain with a release later. Indeed, this is so generally true that if a Cocoa object is *not* going to retain an object you hand it, there will be a note to that effect in the documentation.

A collection, such as an NSArray or an NSDictionary, is a particularly obvious case in point (see Chapter 10 for a discussion of the common collection classes). An object can hardly be an element of a collection if that object can go out of existence at any time; so when you add an element to a collection, the collection asserts ownership of the object by retaining it. Thereafter, the collection acts as a well-behaved owner. If this is a mutable collection, then if an element is removed from it, the collection releases that element. If the collection object goes out of existence, it releases all its elements.

Prior to ARC, removing an object from a mutable collection constituted a potential trap. Consider the following Objective-C code:

```
id obj = myMutableArray[0];
[myMutableArray removeObjectAtIndex: 0]; // bad idea in non-ARC code!
// ... could crash here by referring to obj ...
```

As I just said, when you remove an object from a mutable collection, the collection releases it. So the commented line of code in the previous example involves an implicit release of the object that used to be element 0 of `myMutableArray`. If this reduces the object's retain count to zero, it will be destroyed. The pointer `obj` will then be a dangling pointer, and a crash may be in our future when we try to use it as if it were a real object.

With ARC, however, that sort of danger doesn't exist. Assigning a reference type object to a variable retains it! Thus that code is perfectly safe, and so is its Swift equivalent:

```
let obj = myMutableArray[0]
myMutableArray.removeObjectAtIndex(0)
// ... safe to refer to obj ...
```

The first line retains the object. The second line releases the object, but that release balances the retain that was placed on the object when the object was placed in the collection originally. Thus the object's retain count is still more than zero, and it continues to exist for the duration of this code.

Autorelease Pool

When a method creates an instance and returns that instance, some memory management hanky-panky has to take place. For example, consider this simple code:

```
func makeImage() -> UIImage? {
    if let im = UIImage(named:"myImage") {
        return im
    }
    return nil
}
```

Think about the retain count of `im`, the UIImage we are returning. This retain count has been incremented by our call to the UIImage initializer `UIImage(named:)`. According to the golden rule of memory management, as we pass `im` out of our own control by returning it, we should decrement the retain count of `im`, to balance the increment and surrender ownership. But when can we possibly do that? If we do it *before* the line `return im`, the retain count of `im` will be zero and it will vanish in a puff of smoke; we will be returning a dangling pointer. But we can't do it *after* the line `return im`, because when that line is executed, our code comes to an end.

Clearly, we need a way to vend this object without decrementing its retain count *now* — so that it stays in existence long enough for the caller to receive and work with it — while ensuring that at some future time we *will* decrement its retain count, so as to balance our `init(named:)` call and fulfill our own management of this object's memory. The solution is something midway between releasing the object and not releasing it — ARC *autoreleases* it.

Figure 12-1. Memory usage grows during a loop

Here's how autoreleasing works. Your code runs in the presence of something called an *autorelease pool*. When ARC autoreleases an object, that object is placed in the autorelease pool, and a number is incremented saying how many times this object has been placed in this autorelease pool. From time to time, when nothing else is going on, the autorelease pool is automatically *drained*. This means that the autorelease pool releases each of its objects, the same number of times as that object was placed in this autorelease pool, and empties itself of all objects. If that causes an object's retain count to be zero, so be it; the object is destroyed in the usual way. So autoreleasing an object is just like releasing it, but with a proviso, "later, not right this second."

In general, autoreleasing and the autorelease pool are merely an implementation detail. You can't see them; they are just part of how ARC works. So why am I telling you about them? It's because sometimes, on very rare occasions, you might want to drain the autorelease pool yourself. Consider the following code (it's slightly artificial, but that's because demonstrating the need to drain the autorelease pool isn't easy):

```
func test() {
    let path = NSBundle.mainBundle().pathForResource("001", ofType: "png")!
    for j in 0 ..< 50 {
        for i in 0 ..< 100 {
            let im = UIImage(contentsOfFile: path)
        }
    }
}
```

That method does something that looks utterly innocuous; it loads an image. But it loads it repeatedly in a loop. As the loop runs, memory climbs constantly (Figure 12-1); by the time our method comes to an end, our app's memory usage has reached almost 34MB. This is not because the images aren't being released each time through the loop; it's because a lot of *intermediate* objects — things you've never even heard of, such as NSPathStore2 objects — are secondarily generated by our call to `init(contentsOfFile:)` *and are autoreleased*, and are all sitting there, piling up in the autorelease pool by the tens of thousands, waiting for the pool to be drained. When our code finally comes to an end, the autorelease pool *is* drained, and our memory usage drops precipitately back down to almost nothing.

Granted, 34MB isn't exactly a massive amount of memory. But you may imagine that a more elaborate inner loop might generate more and larger autoreleased objects, and that our memory usage could potentially rise quite significantly. Thus, it would be nice

1.75 MB

Figure 12-2. Memory usage holds steady with an autorelease pool

to have a way to drain the autorelease pool *manually* now and then during the course of a loop with many iterations. Swift provides such a way — the global `autoreleasepool` function, which takes a single argument that you'll supply as a trailing anonymous function. Before the anonymous function is called, a special temporary autorelease pool is created, and is used for all autoreleased objects thereafter. After the anonymous function exits, the temporary autorelease pool is drained and goes out of existence. Here's the same method with an `autoreleasepool` call wrapping the inner loop:

```
func test() {
    let path = NSBundle.mainBundle().pathForResource("001", ofType: "png")!
    for j in 0 ..< 50 {
        autoreleasepool {
            for i in 0 ..< 100 {
                let im = UIImage(contentsOfFile: path)
            }
        }
    }
}
```

The difference in memory usage is dramatic: memory holds roughly steady at less than 2MB (Figure 12-2). Setting up and draining the temporary autorelease pool probably involves some overhead, so if possible you may want to divide your loop into an outer and an inner loop, as shown in the example, so that the autorelease pool is not set up and torn down on every iteration.

Memory Management of Instance Properties

Before ARC, managing memory for instance properties (Objective-C instance variables, Chapter 10) was one of the trickiest parts of Cocoa programming. The correct behavior is to retain a reference type object when you assign it to a property, and then release it when either of these things happens:

- You assign a different value to the same property.
- The instance whose instance property this is goes out of existence.

In order to obey the golden rule of memory management, the object taking charge of this memory management — the owner — clearly needs to be the object whose instance property this is. The only way to ensure that memory management of a property is handled correctly, therefore, is to implement it *in the setter method* for that property. The setter must release whatever object is currently the value of the property, and must retain whatever object is being assigned to that property. The exact details can be quite tricky (what if they are the same object?), and before ARC it was easy for programmers to get them wrong. And that, of course, is not the *only* memory management needed; to prevent a leak when the owner goes out of existence, the owner's `dealloc` method (the Objective-C equivalent of `deinit`) had to be implemented to release every object being retained as the value of a property.

Fortunately, ARC understands all that, and the memory of instance properties, like the memory of all variables, is managed correctly for you.

This fact also gives us a clue as to how to release an object on demand. This is a valuable thing to be able to do, because an object may be using a lot of memory. You don't want to put too great a strain on the device's memory, so you want to release the object as soon as you're done with it. Also, when your app goes into the background and is suspended, the Watchdog process will terminate it in the background if it is found to be using too much memory; so you might want to release this object when you are notified that the app is about to be backgrounded. (I talked about that problem in Chapter 3.)

You can't (and mustn't) call `release` explicitly, so you need another way to do it, some way that is consonant with the design and behavior of ARC. The solution is to assign something else — something small — to this property. That causes the object that was previously the value of this property to be released. A commonly used approach is to type this property as an Optional — possibly, to simplify matters, an implicitly unwrapped Optional. This means that `nil` can be assigned to it, purely as a way of releasing the current wrapped value.

Retain Cycles and Weak References

As I explained in Chapter 5, you can get yourself into a retain cycle where two objects have references to one another — for example, each is the value of the other's instance property. If such a situation is allowed to persist until no other objects have a reference to either of these objects, then neither can go out of existence, because each has a retain count greater than zero and neither will "go first" and release the other. Since these two objects, *ex hypothesi*, can no longer be referred to by any object except one another, this situation can now never be remedied — these objects are leaking.

The solution is to step in and modify how the memory is managed for one of these references. By default, a reference is a *persisting* reference (what ARC calls a *strong* or *retain* reference): assigning to it retains the assigned value. In Swift, you can declare a reference type variable as weak or as unowned to change the way its memory is managed:

weak

A weak reference takes advantage of a powerful ARC feature. When a reference is weak, ARC does *not* retain the object assigned to it. This seems dangerous, because it means that the object might go out of existence behind our backs, leaving us with a dangling pointer and leading to a potential crash later on. But ARC is very clever about this. It keeps track of all weak references and all objects assigned to them. When such an object's retain count drops to zero and the object is about to be destroyed, ARC sneaks in and assigns nil to the reference — that's why a weak reference in Swift must be an Optional declared with var, so that ARC can do that. Thus, provided you handle the Optional coherently, nothing bad can happen.

unowned

An unowned reference is a different kettle of fish. When you mark a reference as unowned, you're telling ARC to take its hands off completely: it does no memory management at all when something is assigned to this reference. This really *is* dangerous — if the object referred to goes out of existence, you really *can* be left with a dangling pointer and you really *can* crash. That is why you must never use unowned unless you know that the object referred to will *not* go out of existence: unowned is safe, provided the object referred to will outlive the object that refers to it. That is why an unowned object should be some single object, assigned only once, without which the referrer cannot exist at all.

In real life, a weak reference is most commonly used to connect an object to its delegate (Chapter 11). A delegate is an independent entity; there is usually no reason why an object needs to claim ownership of its delegate, and indeed an object is usually its delegate's servant, not its owner. Ownership, if there is any, often runs the other way; Object A might create *and retain* Object B, and make itself Object B's delegate. That's potentially a retain cycle. Therefore, most delegates should be declared as weak references:

```
class ColorPickerController : UIViewController {
    weak var delegate: ColorPickerDelegate?
    // ...
}
```

Unfortunately, properties of built-in Cocoa classes that keep weak references are sometimes *non-ARC* weak references (because they are old and backward-compatible, whereas ARC is new). Such properties are declared using the keyword assign. For example, AVSpeechSynthesizer's delegate property is declared like this:

```
@property(nonatomic, assign, nullable)
    id<AVSpeechSynthesizerDelegate> delegate;
```

In Swift, that declaration is translated like this:

```
unowned(unsafe) var delegate: AVSpeechSynthesizerDelegate?
```

```
libobjc.A.dylib`objc_retain:
    0x110706d00 <+0>:   xorl    %eax, %eax
    0x110706d02 <+2>:   testq   %rdi, %rdi
    0x110706d05 <+5>:   je      0x110706d0c              ; <+12>
    0x110706d07 <+7>:   jns     0x110706d0d              ; <+13>
    0x110706d09 <+9>:   movq    %rdi, %rax
    0x110706d0c <+12>:  retq
    0x110706d0d <+13>:  movq    (%rdi), %rax
->  0x110706d10 <+16>:  testb   $0x2, 0x20(%rax)    Thread 1: EXC_BAD_ACCESS (code=1, address=0x24)
    0x110706d14 <+20>:  jne     0x110706d25             ; <+37>
```

Figure 12-3. A crash from messaging a dangling pointer

The Swift term unowned and the Objective-C term assign are synonyms; they tell you that there's no ARC memory management here. The unsafe designation is a further warning inserted by Swift; unlike your own code, where you won't use unowned unless it is safe, Cocoa's unowned is potentially dangerous and you need to exercise caution.

Even though *your* code is using ARC, the fact that Cocoa's code is *not* using ARC means that memory management mistakes can still occur. A reference such as an AVSpeech-Synthesizer's delegate can end up as a dangling pointer, pointing at garbage, if the object to which that reference was pointing has gone out of existence. If anyone (you or Cocoa) tries to send a message by way of such a reference, the app will then crash — and, since this typically happens long after the point where the real mistake occurred, figuring out the cause of the crash can be quite difficult. The typical sign of such a crash is that EXC_BAD_ACCESS is reported in connection with memory management activity (Figure 12-3). (This is the sort of situation in which you might need to turn on zombies in order to debug, as I'll describe later in this chapter.)

Defending against this kind of situation is up to you. If you assign some object to a non-ARC unsafe reference, such as an AVSpeechSynthesizer's delegate, and if that object is about to go out of existence at a time when this reference still exists, *you* have a duty to assign nil (or some other object) to that reference, thus rendering it harmless.

Unusual Memory Management Situations

If you are using NSNotificationCenter to register for notifications (Chapter 11), and if you registered with the notification center using addObserver:selector:name:object:, you handed the notification center a reference to some object (usually self) as the first argument; the notification center's reference to this object is a non-ARC unsafe reference, and there is a danger that after this object goes out of existence the notification center will try to send a notification to whatever is referred to, which will be garbage. That is why you must unregister before that can happen. This is similar to the situation with delegates that I was talking about a moment ago.

If you registered with the notification center using `addObserverForName:object:queue:usingBlock:`, memory management can be even more tricky, because:

- The observer token returned from the call to `addObserverForName:object:queue:usingBlock:` is retained by the notification center until you unregister it.

- The observer token may also be retaining you (`self`) through the block (a function, probably anonymous), if it refers to `self`. If so, then until you unregister the observer token from the notification center, the notification center is retaining you. This means that you will leak until you unregister. But you cannot unregister from the notification center in `deinit`, because `deinit` isn't going to be called so long as you are registered.

- In addition, if you also retain the observer token, then if the observer token is retaining you, you have a retain cycle on your hands.

Thus, use of `addObserverForName:object:queue:usingBlock:` can put you into the same situation that I described in "Weak and Unowned References in Anonymous Functions" on page 278. And the solution is the same: mark `self` as `weak` or (preferably) `unowned` in the anonymous function that you pass in as the `block:` argument.

Consider, for example, this (artificial) code, in which we, a view controller, register for a notification and assign the observer token to an instance property:

```
var observer : AnyObject!
override func viewWillAppear(animated: Bool) {
    super.viewWillAppear(animated)
    self.observer = NSNotificationCenter.defaultCenter().addObserverForName(
        "woohoo", object:nil, queue:nil) {
            _ in
            self.description
    }
}
```

Our intention is eventually to unregister the observer; that's why we're keeping a reference to it. It's natural to do this in `viewDidDisappear::`:

```
override func viewDidDisappear(animated: Bool) {
    super.viewDidDisappear(animated)
    NSNotificationCenter.defaultCenter().removeObserver(self.observer)
}
```

This works in the sense that the observer is unregistered; but the view controller itself is leaking. We can see this by logging on `deinit`:

```
deinit {
    print("deinit")
}
```

In a situation where this view controller should be destroyed — for example, it was a presented view controller, and now it is being dismissed — deinit is never called. We have a retain cycle! The simplest solution is to mark self as unowned as it enters the anonymous function; this is safe because self will not outlive the anonymous function:

```
self.observer = NSNotificationCenter.defaultCenter().addObserverForName(
    "woohoo", object:nil, queue:nil) {
        [unowned self] _ in // fix the leak
        self.description
}
```

Another unusual case is NSTimer (Chapter 10). The NSTimer class documentation says that "run loops maintain strong references to their timers"; it then says of scheduled-TimerWithTimeInterval:target:... that "The timer maintains a strong reference to target until it (the timer) is invalidated." This should set off alarm bells in your head: "Danger, Will Robinson, danger!" The documentation is warning you that as long as a repeating timer has not been invalidated, the target is being retained by the run loop; the only way to stop this is to send the invalidate message to the timer. (With a non-repeating timer, the problem arises less starkly, because the timer invalidates itself immediately after firing.)

When you called scheduledTimerWithTimeInterval:target:..., you probably supplied self as the target: argument. This means that you (self) are being retained, and cannot go out of existence until you invalidate the timer. You can't do this in your deinit implementation, because as long as the timer is repeating and has not been sent the invalidate message, deinit won't be called. You therefore need to find another appropriate moment for sending invalidate to the timer. There's no good way out of this situation; you simply have to find such a moment, and that's that. For example, you could balance creation and invalidation of the timer by doing them in viewDid-Appear: and viewWillDisappear::

```
var timer : NSTimer!
override func viewWillAppear(animated: Bool) {
    super.viewWillAppear(animated)
    self.timer = NSTimer.scheduledTimerWithTimeInterval(
        1, target: self, selector: "dummy:", userInfo: nil, repeats: true)
    self.timer.tolerance = 0.1
}
func dummy(t:NSTimer) {
    print("timer fired")
}
override func viewDidDisappear(animated: Bool) {
    super.viewDidDisappear(animated)
    self.timer?.invalidate()
}
```

A more flexible solution is to use the block-based alternative to a repeating timer, available through GCD. You must still take precautions to prevent the timer's block from retaining self and causing a retain cycle, just as with notification observers; but this is easy to do, and the result is that there is no retain cycle, so you can invalidate the timer in deinit if you want to. The timer "object" is a dispatch_source_t, and must be retained, typically as an instance property (which ARC will manage for you, even though it's a pseudo-object). The timer will fire repeatedly after you initially "resume" it, and will stop firing when it is released, typically by setting the instance property to nil.

To generalize this approach, I've created a CancelableTimer class that can be used as an NSTimer replacement. It is basically a combination of a Swift closure and a GCD timer dispatch source. The initializer is init(once:handler:). The handler: is called when the timer fires. If once: is false, this will be a repeating timer. It obeys two methods, startWithInterval: and cancel:

```
class CancelableTimer: NSObject {
    private var q = dispatch_queue_create("timer",nil)
    private var timer : dispatch_source_t!
    private var firsttime = true
    private var once : Bool
    private var handler : () -> ()
    init(once:Bool, handler:()->()) {
        self.once = once
        self.handler = handler
        super.init()
    }
    func startWithInterval(interval:Double) {
        self.firsttime = true
        self.cancel()
        self.timer = dispatch_source_create(
            DISPATCH_SOURCE_TYPE_TIMER,
            0, 0, self.q)
        dispatch_source_set_timer(self.timer,
            dispatch_walltime(nil, 0),
            UInt64(interval * Double(NSEC_PER_SEC)),
            UInt64(0.05 * Double(NSEC_PER_SEC)))
        dispatch_source_set_event_handler(self.timer, {
            if self.firsttime {
                self.firsttime = false
                return
            }
            self.handler()
            if self.once {
                self.cancel()
            }
        })
        dispatch_resume(self.timer)
    }
    func cancel() {
        if self.timer != nil {
```

```
                dispatch_source_cancel(timer)
        }
    }
}
```

And here's how to use it in a view controller; observe that we can cancel the timer in deinit, provided our handler: anonymous function avoids a retain cycle:

```
var timer : CancelableTimer!
override func viewDidLoad() {
    super.viewDidLoad()
    self.timer = CancelableTimer(once: false) {
        [unowned self] in // avoid retain cycle
        self.dummy()
    }
    self.timer.startWithInterval(1)
}
func dummy() {
    print("timer fired")
}
deinit {
    print("deinit")
    self.timer?.cancel()
}
```

Other Cocoa objects with unusual memory management behavior will usually be called out clearly in the documentation. For example, the UIWebView documentation warns: "Before releasing an instance of UIWebView for which you have set a delegate, you must first set its delegate property to nil." And a CAAnimation object *retains its delegate*; this is exceptional and can cause trouble if you're not conscious of it.

Unfortunately, there are also situations where the documentation fails to warn of any special memory management considerations, but you can wind up with a retain cycle anyway. Discovering the problem can be tricky. Areas of Cocoa that have given me trouble include UIKit Dynamics (a UIDynamicBehavior's action handler) and WebKit (a WKWebKit's WKScriptMessageHandler).

Three Foundation collection classes — NSPointerArray, NSHashTable, and NSMap-Table — are similar respectively to NSMutableArray, NSMutableSet, and NSMutable-Dictionary, except that (among other things) their memory management policy is up to you. An NSHashTable created with the class method weakObjectsHashTable, for example, maintains ARC-weak references to its elements, meaning that they are replaced by nil if the retain count of the object to which they were pointing has dropped to zero. You may find uses for these classes as a way of avoiding retain cycles.

Nib Loading and Memory Management

When a nib loads, it instantiates its nib objects (Chapter 7). What happens to these instantiated objects? A view retains its subviews, but what about the top-level objects, which are not subviews of any view? The answer is, in effect, that they do not have elevated retain counts; if someone doesn't immediately retain them, they'll simply vanish in a puff of smoke.

If you don't want that to happen — and if you did, why would you be loading this nib in the first place? — you need to capture a reference to the top-level objects instantiated from the nib. There are two mechanisms for doing this. When a nib is loaded by calling NSBundle's `loadNibNamed:owner:options:` or UINib's `instantiateWithOwner:options:`, an NSArray is returned consisting of the top-level objects instantiated by the nib-loading mechanism. So it's sufficient to retain this NSArray, or the objects in it.

In some cases, this happens without your even being aware of it. For example, when a view controller is automatically instantiated from a storyboard, it is actually loaded from a nib with just one top-level object — the view controller. So the view controller ends up as the sole element of the array returned from `instantiateWithOwner:options:`. The view controller is then extracted from this array and is retained by the runtime — by assigning it a place in the view controller hierarchy.

The other possibility is to configure the nib owner with outlets that will retain the nib's top-level objects when they are instantiated. We did that in Chapter 7 when we set up an outlet like this:

```
class ViewController: UIViewController {
    @IBOutlet var coolview : UIView!
```

We then loaded the nib manually, with this view controller as owner:

```
NSBundle.mainBundle().loadNibNamed("View", owner: self, options: nil)
self.view.addSubview(self.coolview)
```

The first line instantiates the top-level view from the nib, and the nib-loading mechanism assigns it to `self.coolview`. Since `self.coolview` is a strong reference, it retains the view. Thus, the view is still there when we insert it into the interface in the second line.

The same thing happens when a view controller loads the nib containing its main view. The view controller has a `view` outlet, and is the owner of the nib. Thus, the view is instantiated and is assigned by the nib-loading mechanism to the view controller's `view` property — which retains it.

It is common, however, for `@IBOutlet` properties that you declare to be marked `weak`. This is not obligatory, and it probably does no harm to omit the `weak` designation. The reason such outlets work properly even when they *are* designated `weak` is that you use this designation only when this is an outlet to an object that you know will be retained by someone else — for example, it's a subview of your view controller's main view. A view is retained by its superview, so unless you're going to be removing this view from its superview later, you know that it will persist and there is no need for your @IBOutlet property to retain it as well.

Memory Management of CFTypeRefs

A CFTypeRef is a pure C analog to an Objective-C object. It is a pointer to an opaque C struct (see Appendix A), where "opaque" means that the struct has no directly accessible components. This struct acts as a pseudo-object; a CFTypeRef is analogous to an object type. It is *not* an object type, however, and code that works with a CFTypeRef is not object-oriented; a CFTypeRef has no properties or methods, and you do not send any messages to it. You work with CFTypeRefs entirely through global functions, which are actually C functions.

In Objective-C, CFTypeRef types are distinguished by the suffix Ref at the end of their name. In Swift, however, this Ref suffix is dropped.

Here's some Swift code for drawing a gradient:

```
let con = UIGraphicsGetCurrentContext()!
let locs : [CGFloat] = [ 0.0, 0.5, 1.0 ]
let colors : [CGFloat] = [
    0.8, 0.4, // starting color, transparent light gray
    0.1, 0.5, // intermediate color, darker less transparent gray
    0.8, 0.4, // ending color, transparent light gray
]
let sp = CGColorSpaceCreateDeviceGray()
let grad =
    CGGradientCreateWithColorComponents (sp, colors, locs, 3)
CGContextDrawLinearGradient (
    con, grad, CGPointMake(89,0), CGPointMake(111,0), [])
```

In that code, con is a CGContextRef, known in Swift as a CGContext; sp is a CGColorSpaceRef, known in Swift as a CGColorSpace; and grad is a CGGradientRef, known in Swift as a CGGradient. They are all CFTypeRefs. The code is not object-oriented; it is a sequence of calls to global C functions.

Nevertheless, a CFTypeRef pseudo-object genuinely *is* a pseudo-object. This means that the thing pointed to — the C struct at the far end of the pointer — is effectively the same sort of thing that you'd find at the far end of a reference to a class instance. And that, in turn, means that memory for CFTypeRefs must be managed. In particular, a CFTypeRef pseudo-object has a retain count! And this retain count works exactly as for a true object, in accordance with the golden rule of memory management. A CFTypeRef must be retained when it comes within the sphere of influence of an owner who wants it to persist, and it must be released when that owner no longer needs it.

In Objective-C, the golden rule, as applied to CFTypeRefs, is that if you obtained a CFTypeRef object through a function whose name contains the word `Create` or `Copy`, its retain count has been incremented. In addition, if you are worried about the object persisting, you'll retain it explicitly by calling the `CFRetain` function to increment its retain count. To balance your `Create`, `Copy`, or `CFRetain` call, you must eventually release the object. By default, you'll do that by calling the `CFRelease` function; some CFType-Refs, however, have their own dedicated object release functions — for example, for CGPath, there's a dedicated `CGPathRelease` function.

In Swift, however, you will never need to call `CFRetain`, or any form of `CFRelease`; indeed, you cannot. Swift will do it for you, behind the scenes, automatically.

Think of CFTypeRefs as living in two worlds: the CFTypeRef world of pure C, and the memory-managed object-oriented world of Swift. When you obtain a CFTypeRef pseudo-object, it *crosses the bridge* from the CFTypeRef world into the Swift world. From that moment on, until you are done with it, it needs memory management. Swift is aware of this, and for the most part, Swift itself will use the golden rule and will apply correct memory management. Thus, for example, the code I showed earlier for drawing a gradient is in fact memory-management complete. In Objective-C, we would have to release sp and grad, because they arrived into our world through `Create` calls; if we failed to do this, they would leak. In Swift, however, there is no need, because Swift will do it for us.

Working with CFTypeRefs in Swift is thus much easier than in Objective-C. In Swift, you can treat CFTypeRef pseudo-objects as actual objects! For example, you can assign a CFTypeRef to a property in Swift, or pass it as an argument to a Swift function, and its memory will be managed correctly; in Objective-C, those are tricky things to do.

It is possible, however, that you may receive a CFTypeRef through some API that lacks memory management information. Such a value will come forcibly to your attention, because it will arrive into Swift, not as a CFTypeRef, but as an Unmanaged generic wrapping the actual CFTypeRef. This is a form of warning that Swift does not know how to proceed with the memory management of this pseudo-object. You will in fact be *unable* to proceed until you unwrap the CFTypeRef by calling the Unmanaged object's `takeRetainedValue` or `takeUnretainedValue` method. You will call whichever method tells Swift how to manage the memory for this object correctly. For a CFTypeRef obtained from a built-in function with `Create` or `Copy` in its name, call `takeRetained-Value`; otherwise, call `takeUnretainedValue`.

Property Memory Management Policies

In Objective-C, a `@property` declaration (see Chapter 10) includes a statement of the memory management policy that is followed by the corresponding setter accessor method. It is useful to be aware of this and to know how such policy statements are translated into Swift.

For example, earlier I said that a UIViewController retains its `view` (its main view). How do I know this? Because the `@property` declaration tells me so:

```
@property(null_resettable, nonatomic, strong) UIView *view;
```

The term `strong` means that the setter retains the incoming UIView object. The Swift translation of this declaration doesn't add any attribute to the variable:

```
var view: UIView!
```

The default in Swift is that a variable referring to a reference object type *is* a strong reference — a persisting reference. This means that it retains the object. Thus, you can safely conclude from this declaration that UIViewController retains its `view`.

The possible memory management policies for a Cocoa property are:

`strong`, `retain` *(no Swift equivalent)*
> The default. The two terms are pure synonyms of one another; `retain` is the term inherited from pre-ARC days. Assignment to this property retains the incoming value and releases the existing value.

`copy` *(no Swift equivalent, or* `@NSCopying`*)*
> The same as `strong` or `retain`, except that the setter copies the incoming value by sending `copy` to it; the incoming value must be an object of a type that adopts NSCopying, to ensure that this is possible. The copy, which has an increased retain count already, becomes the new value.

`weak` *(Swift* weak*)*
> An ARC-weak reference. The incoming object value is not retained, but if it goes out of existence behind our back, ARC will magically substitute `nil` as the value of this property, which must be typed as an Optional declared with `var`.

`assign` *(Swift* unowned(unsafe)*)*
> No memory management. This policy is inherited from pre-ARC days, and is inherently unsafe (hence the additional `unsafe` warning in the Swift translation of the name): if the object referred to goes out of existence, this reference will become a dangling pointer and can cause a crash if you subsequently try to use it.

You'd probably like to hear more about the `copy` policy, as I haven't mentioned it until now. This policy is used by Cocoa particularly when an immutable class has a mutable subclass (such as NSString and NSMutableString, or NSArray and NSMutableArray; see Chapter 10). The idea is to deal with the danger of the setter's caller passing in an object of the mutable subclass. A moment's thought will reveal that this is possible, because, in accordance with the substitution principle of polymorphism (Chapter 4), wherever an instance of a class is expected, an instance of its subclass can be passed. But it would be bad if this were to happen, because now the caller might keep a reference to the incoming value and, since it is in fact mutable, could later mutate it behind our back. To prevent this, the setter calls `copy` on the incoming object; this creates a new instance, separate from the object provided — and belonging to the immutable class.

In Swift, this problem is unlikely to arise with strings and arrays, because on the Swift side these are value types (structs) and are effectively copied when assigned, passed as an argument, or received as a return value. Thus, Cocoa's NSString and NSArray property declarations, when translated into Swift as String and Array property declarations, don't show any special marking corresponding to Objective-C copy. But Cocoa types that are *not* automatically bridged from Swift structs *do* show a marking: `@NSCopying`. For example, the declaration of the `attributedText` property of a UILabel appears like this in Swift:

```
@NSCopying var attributedText: NSAttributedString?
```

NSAttributedString has a mutable subclass, NSMutableAttributedString. You've probably configured this attributed string as an NSMutableAttributedString, and now you're assigning it as the UILabel's `attributedText`. UILabel doesn't want you keeping a reference to this mutable string and mutating it in place, since that would change the value of the property without passing through the setter. Thus, it copies the incoming value to ensure that what it has is a separate immutable NSAttributedString.

You can do exactly the same thing in your own code, and you will want to do so. If your class has an NSAttributedString instance property, you'll mark it as `@NSCopying` — and similarly for other members of immutable/mutable pairs, such as NSIndexSet, NSParagraphStyle, NSURLRequest, and so on. Merely providing the `@NSCopying` designation is sufficient; Swift will enforce the `copy` policy and will take care of the actual copying for you when code assigns to this property.

If, as is sometimes the case, your own class wants the internal ability to mutate the value of this property while preventing a mutable value from arriving from outside, put a private computed property façade in front of it that transforms it to the corresponding mutable type:

```
class StringDrawer {
    @NSCopying var attributedString : NSAttributedString!
    private var mutableAttributedString : NSMutableAttributedString! {
        get {
            if self.attributedString == nil {return nil}
            return NSMutableAttributedString(
                attributedString:self.attributedString)
        }
        set {
            self.attributedString = newValue
        }
    }
}
```

`@NSCopying` can be used *only* for instance properties of classes, not of structs or enums — and only in the presence of Foundation, because that is where the NSCopying protocol is defined, which the type of a variable marked as `@NSCopying` must adopt.

Debugging Memory Management Mistakes

Though far less likely to occur under ARC (and Swift), memory management mistakes still *can* occur, especially because a programmer is prone to suppose (wrongly) that they can't. Experience suggests that you should use every tool at your disposal to ferret out possible mistakes. Here are some of those tools (and see Chapter 9):

- The memory gauge in the Debug navigator charts memory usage whenever your app runs, allowing you to observe possible memory leakage or other unwarranted heavy memory use. Note that memory management in the Simulator is not necessarily indicative of reality! Always observe the memory gauge with the app running on a device before making a judgment.

- Instruments (Product → Profile) has excellent tools for noticing leaks and tracking memory management of individual objects.

- Good old caveman debugging can help confirm that your objects are behaving as you want them to. Implement `deinit` with a `print` call. If it isn't called, your object is not going out of existence. This technique can reveal problems that even Instruments will not directly expose.

- Dangling pointers are particularly difficult to track down, but they can often be located by "turning on zombies." This is easy in Instruments with the Zombies template. Alternatively, edit the Run action in your scheme, switch to the Diagnostics tab, and check Enable Zombie Objects. The result is that an object that goes out of existence is replaced by a "zombie" that will report to the console if a message is sent to it ("message sent to deallocated instance"). Be sure to turn zombies back off when you've finished tracking down your dangling pointers. Don't use zombies with the Leaks instrument: zombies *are* leaks.

Even these tools may not help you with every possible memory management issue. For example, some objects, such as a UIView containing a large image, are themselves small (and thus may not cause the memory gauge or Instruments to register large memory use) but require a large backing store nevertheless; maintaining references to too many such objects can cause your app to be summarily killed by the system. This sort of issue is not easy to track down.

CHAPTER 13

Communication Between Objects

As soon as an app grows to more than a few objects, puzzling questions can arise about how to send a message or communicate data between one object and another. The problem is essentially one of architecture. It may require some planning to construct your code so that all the pieces fit together and information can be shared as needed at the right moment. This chapter presents some organizational considerations that will help you arrange for one object to be able to communicate with another.

The problem of communication often comes down to one object being able to *see* another: the object Manny needs to be able to find the object Jack repeatedly and reliably over the long term so as to be able to send Jack messages.

One obvious solution is an instance property of Manny whose value *is* Jack. This is appropriate particularly when Manny and Jack share certain responsibilities or supplement one another's functionality. The application object and its delegate, a table view and its data source, a view controller and the view that it controls — these are cases where the former must have an instance property pointing at the latter.

This does not necessarily imply that Manny needs to assert ownership of Jack as a matter of memory management policy (see Chapter 12) — but it might. An object does not typically retain its delegate or its data source; similarly, an object that implements the target–action pattern, such as a UIControl, does not retain its target. By using a weak reference and typing the property as an Optional, and then treating the Optional coherently and safely, Manny can avoid owning Jack while coping with the possibility that his supposed reference to Jack will turn out to be `nil`. On the other hand, a view controller is useless without a view to control; once it has a view, it will retain it, releasing it only when it itself goes out of existence.

Objects can perform two-way communication without both of them holding references to one another. It may be sufficient for *one* of them to have a reference to the other — because the former, as part of a message to the latter, can include a reference to himself.

For example, Manny might send a message to Jack where one of the parameters is a reference to Manny; this might merely constitute a form of identification, or an invitation to Jack to send a message back to Manny if Jack needs further information while doing whatever this method does. Manny thus makes himself, as it were, momentarily visible to Jack; Jack should not wantonly retain Manny (especially since there's an obvious risk of a retain cycle). Again, this is a common pattern. The parameter of the delegate message `textFieldShouldBeginEditing:` is a reference to the UITextField that sent the message. The first parameter of a target–action message is a reference to the control that sent the message.

But how is Manny to obtain a reference to Jack in the first place? That's a very big question. Much of the art of iOS programming, and of object-oriented programming generally, lies in one object *getting a reference* to some other object (see "Instance References" on page 127). Every case is different and must be solved separately, but certain general patterns emerge, and this chapter will outline some of them.

There are also ways for Manny to send a message that Jack *receives* without having to send it directly *to* Jack — possibly without even knowing or caring who Jack is. Notifications and KVO are examples, and I'll mention them in this chapter as well.

Finally, the chapter ends with a section on the larger question of what kinds of objects *need* to see one another, within the general scope of a typical iOS program.

Visibility by Instantiation

Every instance comes from somewhere and at someone's behest: some object sent a message commanding this instance to come into existence in the first place. The commanding object therefore has a reference to the instance at that moment. When Manny creates Jack, Manny has a reference to Jack.

That simple fact can serve as the starting point for establishing future communication. If Manny creates Jack and knows that he (Manny) will need a reference to Jack in the future, Manny can keep the reference that he obtained by creating Jack in the first place. Or, it may be that what Manny knows is that Jack will need a reference to Manny in the future; Manny can supply that reference immediately after creating Jack, and Jack will then keep it.

Delegation is a case in point. Manny may create Jack and immediately make himself Jack's delegate, as in my example code in Chapter 11:

```
let cpc = ColorPickerController(colorName:colorName, andColor:c)
cpc.delegate = self
```

Indeed, if this crucial, you might endow Jack with an initializer so that Manny can create Jack and hand Jack a reference to himself *at the same time*, to help prevent any slip-ups. Compare the approach taken by UIBarButtonItem, where three different initializers, such as `init(title:style:target:action:)`, require as a parameter the `target` to which future messages will be sent by the UIBarButtonItem.

When Manny creates Jack, it might not be a reference to Manny himself that Jack needs, but to something that Manny knows or has. You will presumably endow Jack with a method so that Manny can hand that information across; again, it might be reasonable to make that method Jack's initializer, if Jack simply cannot live without the information.

Recall this example from Chapter 11. It comes from a table view controller. The user has tapped a row of the table. We create a secondary table view controller, a Tracks-ViewController instance, handing it the data it will need, and display the secondary table view. I have deliberately devised TracksViewController to have a designated initializer `init(mediaItemCollection:)`, making it virtually obligatory for a Tracks-ViewController to have access, from the moment it comes into existence, to the data it needs:

```
override func tableView(tableView: UITableView,
    didSelectRowAtIndexPath indexPath: NSIndexPath) {
        delay(0.1) { // let spinner start spinning
            let t = TracksViewController(
                mediaItemCollection: self.albums[indexPath.row])
            self.navigationController!.pushViewController(
                t, animated: true)
        }
}
```

In that example, `self` does not keep a reference to the new TracksViewController instance, nor does the TracksViewController acquire a reference to `self`. But `self` does create the TracksViewController instance, and so, for one brief shining moment, it has a reference to it. Therefore `self` takes advantage of that moment to hand the Tracks-ViewController instance the information it needs. There will be no better moment to do this. Knowing the moment, and taking care not to miss it, is part of the art of data communication.

Nib-loading is also a case in point. The loading of a nib is a way of instantiating objects from the nib. Proper preparation is essential in order to ensure that there's a reference for those objects, so that they don't simply vanish in a puff of smoke ("Nib Loading and Memory Management" on page 519). The moment of the nib loading is the moment when the nib's owner or the code that loads the nib is in contact with those objects; it takes advantage of that moment to secure those references.

Beginners are often puzzled by how two objects are to get a reference to one another if they will be instantiated from *different* nibs — either different *.xib* files or different scenes in a storyboard. It is frustrating that you can't draw a connection between an object in nib A and an object in nib B; it's particularly frustrating when you can see both objects sitting right there in the same storyboard. But, as I explained earlier ("Connections Between Nibs — Not!" on page 354), such a connection would be meaningless, which is why it's impossible. These are different nibs, and they will load at different times. However, some object (Manny) is going to be the owner when nib A loads, and some object (Jack) is going to be the owner when nib B loads. Perhaps they (Manny and Jack) can then see each other, in which case, given all the necessary outlets, the problem is solved. Or perhaps some third object (Moe) can see both of them and will provide a communication path for them.

For example, when a segue in a storyboard is triggered, the segue's destination view controller is instantiated, and the segue has a reference to it. At the same time, the segue's source view controller already exists, and the segue has a reference to it as well. So the segue sends the source view controller the `prepareForSegue:sender:` message, containing a reference to itself (the segue). The segue is Moe; it is bringing Manny (the source view controller) and Jack (the destination view controller) together. This is the source view controller's chance (Manny's moment) to obtain a reference to the newly instantiated destination view controller (a reference to Jack), by asking the segue for it — and now the source view controller can make itself the destination view controller's delegate, hand it any needed information, and so forth.

Visibility by Relationship

Objects may acquire the ability to see one another automatically by virtue of their position in a containing structure. Before worrying about how to supply one object with a reference to another, consider whether there may *already* be a chain of references leading from one to the other.

For example, a subview can see its superview, through its `superview` property. A superview can see all its subviews, through its `subviews` property, and can pick out a specific subview through that subview's `tag` property, by calling `viewWithTag:`. A subview in a window can see its window, through its `window` property. Thus, by working your way up or down the view hierarchy by means of these properties, it may be possible to obtain the desired reference.

Similarly, a responder (Chapter 11) can see the next object up the responder chain, through the `nextResponder` method — which also means, because of the structure of the responder chain, that a view controller's main view can see the view controller. In this code from one of my apps, I work my way up from a view some way down the view hierarchy to obtain a reference to the view controller that's in charge of this whole scene (and there are similar examples in Chapter 5):

```
var r = sender as! UIResponder
repeat { r = r.nextResponder()! } while !(r is UIViewController)
```

Similarly, view controllers are themselves part of a hierarchy and therefore can see one another. If a view controller is currently presenting a view through a second view controller, the latter is the former's `presentedViewController`, and the former is the latter's `presentingViewController`. If a view controller is the child of a UINavigation-Controller, the latter is its `navigationController`. A UINavigationController's visible view is controlled by its `visibleViewController`. And from any of these, you can reach the view controller's view through its `view` property, and so forth.

All of these relationships are public. So if you can get a reference to just one object within any of these structures or a similar structure, you can effectively navigate the whole structure through a chain of references and lay your hands on any other object within the structure.

Global Visibility

Some objects are globally visible — that is, they are visible to all other objects. Object types themselves are an important example. As I pointed out in Chapter 4, it is perfectly reasonable to use a Swift struct with static members as a way of providing globally available namespaced constants ("Struct As Namespace" on page 139).

Classes sometimes have class methods that vend singleton instances. Some of these singletons, in turn, have properties pointing to other objects, making those other objects likewise globally visible. For example, any object can see the singleton UIApplication instance by calling `UIApplication.sharedApplication()`. So any object can also see the app's primary window, because that is the singleton UIApplication instance's `key-Window` property, and any object can see the app delegate, because that is its `delegate` property. And the chain continues: any object can see the app's root view controller, because that is the primary window's `rootViewController` — and from there, as I said in the previous section, we can navigate the view controller hierarchy and the view hierarchy.

You, too, can make your own objects globally visible by attaching them to a globally visible object. For example, a public property of the app delegate, which you are free to create, is globally visible by virtue of the app delegate being globally visible (by virtue of the shared application being globally visible).

Another globally visible object is the shared defaults object obtained by calling `NSUser-Defaults.standardUserDefaults()`. This object is the gateway to storage and retrieval of user defaults, which is similar to a dictionary (a collection of values named by keys). The user defaults are automatically saved when your application quits and are automatically available when your application is launched again later, so they are one of the ways in which your app maintains information between launches. But, being globally visible, they are also a conduit for communicating values within your app.

For example, in one of my apps there's a setting I call `HazyStripy`. This determines whether a certain visible interface object (a card in a game) is drawn with a hazy fill or a stripy fill. This is a setting that the user can change, so there is a preferences interface allowing the user to make this change. When the user displays this preferences interface, I examine the HazyStripy setting in the user defaults to configure the interface to reflect it in a segmented control (called self.hazyStripy):

```
func setHazyStripy () {
    let hs = NSUserDefaults.standardUserDefaults()
        .objectForKey(Default.HazyStripy) as! Int
    self.hazyStripy.selectedSegmentIndex = hs
}
```

Conversely, if the user interacts with the preferences interface, tapping the hazy-Stripy segmented control to change its setting, I respond by changing the actual Hazy-Stripy setting in the user defaults:

```
@IBAction func hazyStripyChange(sender:AnyObject) {
    let hs = self.hazyStripy.selectedSegmentIndex
    NSUserDefaults.standardUserDefaults().setObject(
        hs, forKey: Default.HazyStripy)
}
```

But here's the really interesting part. The preferences interface is not the only object that uses the HazyStripy setting in the user defaults; the drawing code that actually draws the hazy-or-stripy-filled card also uses it, so as to know how the card should draw itself! When the user leaves the preferences interface and the card game reappears, the cards are redrawn — consulting the HazyStripy setting in NSUserDefaults in order to do so:

```
override func drawRect(rect: CGRect) {
    let hazy : Bool = NSUserDefaults.standardUserDefaults()
        .integerForKey(Default.HazyStripy) == HazyStripy.Hazy.rawValue
    CardPainter.sharedPainter().drawCard(self.card, hazy:hazy)
}
```

Thus there is no need for the card object and the view controller object that manages the preferences interface to be able to see one another, because they can both see this common object, the HazyStripy user default. NSUserDefaults becomes, in itself, a global conduit for communicating information from one part of my app to another.

Notifications and KVO

Notifications (Chapter 11) can be a way to communicate between objects that are conceptually distant from one another without bothering to provide *any* way for one to see the other. All they really need to have in common is a knowledge of the name of the notification. Every object can see the notification center — it is a globally visible object — so every object can arrange to post or receive a notification.

Using a notification in this way may seem lazy, an evasion of your responsibility to architect your objects sensibly. But sometimes one object doesn't need to know, and indeed shouldn't know, what object (or objects) it is sending a message to.

Recall the example I gave in Chapter 11. In a simple card game app, the game needs to know when a card is tapped. A card, when it is tapped, knowing nothing about the game, simply emits a virtual shriek by posting a notification; the game object has registered for this notification and takes over from there:

```
NSNotificationCenter.defaultCenter().postNotificationName(
    "cardTapped", object: self)
```

Here's another example, taking advantage of the fact that notifications are a broadcast mechanism. In one of my apps, the app delegate may detect a need to tear down the interface and build it back up again from scratch. If this is to happen without causing memory leaks (and all sorts of other havoc), every view controller that is currently running a repeating NSTimer needs to invalidate that timer (Chapter 12). Rather than my having to work out what view controllers those might be, and endowing every view controller with a method that can be called, I simply have the app delegate shout "Everybody stop timers!", by posting a notification. *All* my view controllers that run timers have registered for this notification, and they know what to do when they receive it.

Similarly, KVO (Chapter 11) can be used to keep two conceptually distant objects synchronized with one another: a property of one object changes, and the other object hears about the change.

Model–View–Controller

In Apple's documentation and elsewhere, you'll find references to the term *model–view–controller*, or *MVC*. This refers to an architectural goal of maintaining a distinction between three functional aspects of a program where the user can view and edit information — meaning, in effect, a program with a graphical user interface. The notion goes back to the days of Smalltalk, and much has been written about it since then, but informally, here's what the terms mean:

Model
> The data and its management, often referred to as the program's "business logic;" the hard-core stuff that the program is really all about.

View
> What the user sees and interacts with.

Controller
> The mediation between the model and the view.

Consider, for example, a game where the current score is displayed to the user:

- A UILabel that shows the user the current score for the game in progress is *view*; it is effectively nothing but a pixel-maker, and its business is to know how to draw

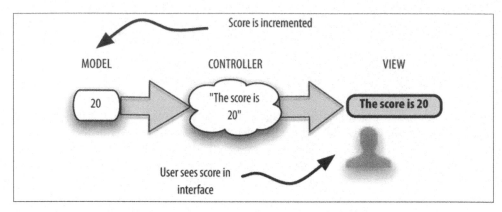

Figure 13-1. Model–view–controller

itself. The knowledge of *what* it should draw — the score, and the fact that this *is* a score — lies elsewhere.

A rookie programmer might try to use the score displayed by the UILabel as the actual score: to increment the score, read the UILabel's string, turn that string into a number, increment the number, turn the number back into a string, and present that string in place of the previous string. That is a gross violation of the MVC philosophy! The view presented to the user should *reflect* the score; it should not *store* the score.

- The score is data being maintained internally; it is *model*. It could be as simple as an instance property along with a public `increment` method or as complicated as a Score object with a raft of methods.

  The score is numeric, whereas a UILabel displays a string; this alone is enough to show that the view and the model are naturally different.

- Telling the score when to change, and causing the updated score to be reflected in the user interface, is the work of the *controller*. This will be particularly clear if we imagine that the model's numeric score needs to be transformed in some way for presentation to the user.

  For example, suppose the UILabel that presents the score reads: "The score is 20." The model is presumably storing and providing the number 20, so what's the source of the phrase "The score is…"? Whoever is causing this phrase to precede the score in the presentation of the score to the user is a controller.

Even this simplistic example (Figure 13-1) illustrates very well the advantages of MVC. By separating powers in this way, we allow the aspects of the program to evolve with a great degree of independence. Do you want a different font and size in the presentation of the score? Change the view; the model and controller need know nothing about it, but will just go on working exactly as they did before. Do you want to change the phrase that precedes the score? Change the controller; the model and view are unchanged.

Adherence to MVC is particularly appropriate in a Cocoa app, because Cocoa itself adheres to it. The very names of Cocoa classes reveal the MVC philosophy that underlies them. A UIView is a view. A UIViewController is a controller; its purpose is to embody the logic that tells the view what to display. In Chapter 11 we saw that a UIPickerView does not hold the data it displays; it gets that data from a data source. So the UIPicker-View is a view; the data maintained by the data source is model.

A further distinction, found in Apple's documentation, is this: true model material and true view material should be quite reusable, in the sense that they can be transferred wholesale into some other app; controller material is generally not reusable, because it is concerned with how *this* app mediates between the model and the view.

In one of my own apps, for example, we download an XML (RSS) news feed and present the article titles to the user as a table. The storage and parsing of the XML are pure model material, and are so reusable that I didn't even write this part of the code (I used some code called FeedParser, by Kevin Ballard). The table is a UITableView, which is obviously reusable, seeing as I obtained it directly from Cocoa. But when the UITableView turns to my code and asks what to display in this cell, and my code turns to the XML and asks for the title of the article corresponding to this row of the table, that's controller code, and is applicable only to this app.

MVC helps to provide answers about what objects need to be able to see what other objects in your app. A controller object will usually need to see a model object and a view object. A model object, or a group of model objects, usually won't need to see outside itself. A view object typically doesn't need to see outside itself *specifically*, but structural devices such as delegation, data source, and target–action allow a view object to communicate agnostically with a controller.

C, Objective-C, and Swift

You are an iOS programmer, and you've chosen to adopt Apple's new language, Swift. And this means that you'll never have to concern yourself with Apple's *old* language, Objective-C, right? Wrong.

Objective-C is not dead. Far from it. *You* may be using Swift, but Cocoa is not. Programming iOS involves communicating with Cocoa and its supplementary frameworks. The APIs for those frameworks are written in Objective-C — or in its underlying base language, C. Messages that you send to Cocoa using Swift are being translated for you into Objective-C. Objects that you send and receive back and forth across the Swift/Objective-C bridge are Objective-C objects. Some objects that you send from Swift to Objective-C are even being translated for you into other object types, or into nonobject types.

You need to understand what Objective-C expects from you when you are sending messages across the language bridge. You need to know what Objective-C is going to *do* with those messages. You need to know what is coming *from* Objective-C, and how it will be represented in Swift. Your app may include some Objective-C code as well as Swift code, so you need to know how the parts of your own app will communicate.

This appendix summarizes certain linguistic features of C and Objective-C, and describes how Swift interfaces with those features. I do not explain here how to write Objective-C! For example, I'll talk about Objective-C methods and method declarations, because you need to know how to call an Objective-C method from Swift; but I'm not going to explain how to call an Objective-C method *in Objective-C*. Earlier editions of this book teach C and Objective-C systematically and in detail, and I recommend consulting one for information about those languages.

The C Language

Objective-C is a superset of C; to put it another way, C provides the linguistic under-pinnings of Objective-C. Everything that is true of C is true also of Objective-C. It is possible, and often necessary, to write long stretches of Objective-C code that are, in effect, pure C. Some of the Cocoa APIs are written in C. Therefore, in order to know about Objective-C, it is necessary to know about C.

C statements, including declarations, must end in a semicolon. Variables must be declared before use. Variable declaration syntax is: a data type name followed by the variable name, optionally followed by assignment of an initial value:

```
int i;
double d = 3.14159;
```

The C typedef statement starts with an existing type name and defines a new synonym for it:

```
typedef double NSTimeInterval;
```

C Data Types

C is not an object-oriented language; its data types are not objects (they are *scalars*). The basic built-in C data types are all numeric: char (one byte), int (four bytes), float and double (floating-point numbers), and varieties such as short (short integer), long (long integer), unsigned short, and so on. Objective-C adds NSInteger, NSUInteger (unsigned), and CGFloat. The C bool type is actually a numeric, with zero representing false; Objective-C adds BOOL, which is also a numeric. The C native text type (string) is actually a null-terminated array of char.

Swift explicitly supplies numeric types that interface directly with C numeric types, even though Swift's types are objects and C's types are not. Swift type aliases provide names that correspond to the C type names: a Swift CBool is a C bool, a Swift CChar is a C char (a Swift Int8), a Swift CInt is a C int (a Swift Int32), a Swift CFloat is a C float (a Swift Float), and so on. Swift Int interchanges with NSInteger; Swift UInt interchanges with NSUInteger. Swift Bool interchanges with Swift ObjCBool, which represents Objective-C BOOL. CGFloat is adopted as a Swift type name.

A major difference between C and Swift is that C (and therefore Objective-C) implicitly coerces when values of different numeric types are assigned, passed, or compared to one another; Swift doesn't, so you must coerce explicitly to make types match exactly.

The native C string type, a null-terminated array of char, is typed in Swift, for reasons that will be clear later, as UnsafePointer<Int8> (recall that Int8 is CChar). A C string can't be formed as a literal in Swift, but you can pass a Swift String where a C string is expected:

```
let q = dispatch queue create("MyQueue", nil)
```

If you need to create a C string variable, the NSString UTF8String property and cString-UsingEncoding: method can be used to form a C string. Alternatively, you can use the Swift String withCString instance method; the syntax is a little tricky. In this example, I cycle through the "characters" of the C string until I reach the null terminator (I'll explain the memory property a bit later):

```
let _ : Void = "hello".withCString {
    var cs = $0
    while cs.memory != 0 {
        print(cs.memory)
        cs = cs.successor()
    }
}
```

In the other direction, a C string can be rendered into a Swift String (wrapped in an Optional) by way of the Swift String static method fromCString.

C Enums

A C enum is numeric; values are some form of integer, and can be implicit (starting from 0) or explicit. Enums arrive in various forms into Swift, depending on exactly how they are declared. Let's start with the simplest (and oldest) form:

```
enum State {
    kDead,
    kAlive
};
typedef enum State State;
```

(The typedef in the last line allows C programs to use the term State as the name of this type instead of the more verbose enum State.) The C enumerand names kDead and kAlive are not "cases" of anything; they are not namespaced. They are constants, and as they are not explicitly initialized, they represent 0 and 1 respectively. An enum declaration can specify the integer type further; this one doesn't, so the values are typed in Swift as UInt32.

In Swift 2.0, this old-fashioned sort of C enum arrives as a Swift struct adopting the RawRepresentable protocol. This struct is used automatically as a medium of interchange wherever a State enum arrives from or is expected by C. Thus, if a C function setState takes a State enum parameter, you can call it with one of the State names:

```
setState(kDead)
```

In this way, Swift has done its best to import these names helpfully and usefully, trying to represent State as a type even though, in C, it really isn't one. If you are curious about what integer is represented by the name kDead, you have to take its rawValue. You can also create an arbitrary State value by calling its init(rawValue:) initializer — there is no compiler or runtime check to see whether this value is one of the defined constants. But you aren't expected to do either of those things.

Starting in Xcode 4.4, a new C enum notation was introduced, based on the NS_ENUM macro:

```
typedef NS_ENUM(NSInteger, UIStatusBarAnimation) {
    UIStatusBarAnimationNone,
    UIStatusBarAnimationFade,
    UIStatusBarAnimationSlide,
};
```

That notation explicitly specifies the integer type and associates a type name with this enum as a whole. Swift imports an enum declared this way *as a Swift enum* with the name and raw value type intact. This is a true Swift enum, so the enumerand names become namespaced case names. Moreover, Swift automatically subtracts the common prefix from the case names:

```
enum UIStatusBarAnimation : Int {
    case None
    case Fade
    case Slide
}
```

Going the other way, a Swift enum with an Int raw value type can be exposed to Objective-C using the @objc attribute. Thus, for example:

```
@objc enum Star : Int {
    case Blue
    case White
    case Yellow
    case Red
}
```

Objective-C sees that as an enum with type NSInteger and enumerand names Star-Blue, StarWhite, and so on.

There is another variant of C enum notation, based on the NS_OPTIONS macro, suitable for bitmasks:

```
typedef NS_OPTIONS(NSUInteger, UIViewAutoresizing) {
    UIViewAutoresizingNone               = 0,
    UIViewAutoresizingFlexibleLeftMargin  = 1 << 0,
    UIViewAutoresizingFlexibleWidth       = 1 << 1,
    UIViewAutoresizingFlexibleRightMargin = 1 << 2,
    UIViewAutoresizingFlexibleTopMargin   = 1 << 3,
    UIViewAutoresizingFlexibleHeight      = 1 << 4,
    UIViewAutoresizingFlexibleBottomMargin = 1 << 5
};
```

An enum declared this way arrives into Swift as a struct adopting the OptionSetType protocol. The OptionSetType protocol adopts the RawRepresentable protocol, so this is a struct with a `rawValue` instance property holding the underlying integer. The C enum case names are represented by static properties, each of whose values *is an instance of this struct*; the names of these static properties are imported with the common prefix subtracted:

```
struct UIViewAutoresizing : OptionSetType {
    init(rawValue: UInt)
    static var None: UIViewAutoresizing { get }
    static var FlexibleLeftMargin: UIViewAutoresizing { get }
    static var FlexibleWidth: UIViewAutoresizing { get }
    static var FlexibleRightMargin: UIViewAutoresizing { get }
    static var FlexibleTopMargin: UIViewAutoresizing { get }
    static var FlexibleHeight: UIViewAutoresizing { get }
    static var FlexibleBottomMargin: UIViewAutoresizing { get }
}
```

Thus, for example, when you say `UIViewAutoresizing.FlexibleLeftMargin`, it *looks* as if you are initializing a case of a Swift enum, but in fact this is an instance of the UIViewAutoresizing *struct*, whose `rawValue` property has been set to the value declared by the original C enum — which, for `.FlexibleLeftMargin`, is 1<<0. Because a static property of this struct *is* an instance of the same struct, you can, as with an enum, omit the struct name when supplying a static property name where the struct is expected:

```
self.view.autoresizingMask = .FlexibleWidth
```

Moreover, because this is an OptionSetType struct, set-like operations can be applied — thus permitting you to manipulate the bitmask by working with instances as if this were a Set:

```
self.view.autoresizingMask = [.FlexibleWidth, .FlexibleHeight]
```

 Where an `NS_OPTIONS` enum is expected in Objective-C, you pass 0 to indicate that no options are provided. In Swift 2.0, where a corresponding struct is expected, you pass [] (an empty set).

Many common lists of alternatives, unfortunately, are not implemented as enums in the first place. This is not problematic, but it is inconvenient. For example, the names of the AVFoundation audio session categories are just NSString constants:

```
NSString *const AVAudioSessionCategoryAmbient;
NSString *const AVAudioSessionCategorySoloAmbient;
NSString *const AVAudioSessionCategoryPlayback;
// ... and so on ...
```

Even though this is a list of alternatives with an obvious common prefix, Swift cannot (and does not) magically transform it into an AVAudioSessionCategory enum or struct with abbreviated names. When you want to specify the Playback category, you have to use the whole name, `AVAudioSessionCategoryPlayback`.

C Structs

A C struct is a compound type whose elements can be accessed by name using dot-notation after a reference to the struct. For example:

```
struct CGPoint {
    CGFloat x;
    CGFloat y;
};
typedef struct CGPoint CGPoint;
```

After that declaration, it becomes possible to talk like this in C:

```
CGPoint p;
p.x = 100;
p.y = 200;
```

A C struct arrives wholesale into Swift as a Swift struct, which is thereupon endowed with Swift struct features. Thus, for example, CGPoint in Swift has x and y CGFloat instance properties, as you would expect; but it also magically acquires the implicit memberwise initializer! In addition, a zeroing initializer with no parameters is injected; thus, saying CGPoint() makes a CGPoint whose x and y are both 0. Extensions can supply additional features, and the Swift CoreGraphics header adds a few to CGPoint:

```
extension CGPoint {
    static var zeroPoint: CGPoint { get }
    init(x: Int, y: Int)
    init(x: Double, y: Double)
}
```

As you can see, a Swift CGPoint has additional initializers accepting Int or Double arguments, along with another way of making a zero CGPoint, CGPoint.zeroPoint. CGSize is treated similarly. CGRect is particularly well endowed with added methods and properties in Swift; these do not allow you to do anything that you couldn't do with the built-in C functions provided by the Core Graphics framework for manipulating a CGRect, but they do allow you to do those things in a Swiftier way.

The fact that a Swift struct is an object, while a C struct is not, does not pose any problems of communication. You can assign or pass a Swift CGPoint, for example, where a C CGPoint is expected, because CGPoint came from C in the first place. The fact that Swift has endowed CGPoint with object methods and properties doesn't matter; C doesn't see them. All that C cares about are the x and y elements of this CGPoint, which are communicated from Swift to C without difficulty.

C Pointers

A C pointer is an integer designating the location in memory (the *address*) where the real data resides. Allocating and disposing of that memory is a separate matter. The declaration for a pointer to a data type is written with an asterisk after the data type name; a space can appear on either or both sides of the asterisk. These are equivalent declarations of a pointer-to-int:

```
int *intPtr1;
int* intPtr2;
int * intPtr3;
```

The type name itself is int* (or, with a space, int *). Objective-C, for reasons that I'll explain later, uses C pointers heavily, so you're going to be seeing that asterisk a lot if you look at any Objective-C.

A C pointer arrives into Swift as an UnsafePointer or, if writable, an UnsafeMutable-Pointer; this is a generic, and is specified to the actual type of data pointed to. (A pointer is "unsafe" because Swift isn't managing the memory for, and can't even guarantee the integrity of, what is pointed to.)

For example, here's a C function declaration; I haven't discussed C function syntax yet, but just concentrate on the types which precede each parameter name:

```
void CGRectDivide(CGRect rect,
    CGRect *slice,
    CGRect *remainder,
    CGFloat amount,
    CGRectEdge edge)
```

The term void means that this function returns no value. CGRect and CGRectEdge are C structs; CGFloat is a basic numeric type. The phrases CGRect *slice and CGRect *remainder, despite the position of the space, state that slice and remainder are both CGRect* — that is, pointer-to-CGRect. The Swift translation of that declaration looks like this:

```
func CGRectDivide(rect: CGRect,
    _ slice: UnsafeMutablePointer<CGRect>,
    _ remainder: UnsafeMutablePointer<CGRect>,
    _ amount: CGFloat,
    _ edge: CGRectEdge)
```

UnsafeMutablePointer in this context is used like a Swift inout parameter: you declare and initialize a var of the appropriate type beforehand, and then pass its address as argument by way of the & prefix operator. When you pass the address of a reference in this way, you are in fact creating and passing a pointer:

```
var arrow = CGRectZero
var body = CGRectZero
CGRectDivide(rect, &arrow, &body, Arrow.ARHEIGHT, .MinYEdge)
```

In C, to access the memory pointed to by a pointer, you use an asterisk before the pointer's name: *intPtr is "the thing pointed to by the pointer intPtr." In Swift, you use the pointer's memory property.

In this example, we receive a `stop` parameter typed originally as a `BOOL*`, a pointer-to-BOOL; in Swift, it's an `UnsafeMutablePointer<ObjCBool>`. To set the BOOL at the far end of this pointer, we set the pointer's `memory` (`mas` is an NSMutableAttributedString):

```
mas.enumerateAttribute("HERE", inRange: r, options: []) {
    value, r, stop in
    if let value = value as? Int where value == 1 {
        // ...
        stop.memory = true
    }
}
```

The most general type of C pointer is pointer-to-void (`void*`), also known as the *generic pointer*. The term `void` here means that no type is specified; it is legal in C to use a generic pointer wherever a specific type of pointer is expected, and *vice versa*. In effect, pointer-to-void casts away type checking as to what's at the far end of the pointer. This will appear in Swift as a pointer generic specified to `Void` — typically, `UnsafeMutable-Pointer<Void>`, or its equivalent `UnsafeMutablePointer<()>`. In general, when you encounter pointers of this type, if you need to access the underlying data, you'll start by coercing to an UnsafeMutablePointer generic specified to the underlying type.

C Arrays

A C array contains a fixed number of elements of a certain data type. Under the hood, it is a block of memory sized to accommodate this number of elements of this data type. For this reason, the name of an array in C is the name of a pointer — to the first element of the array. For example, if `arr` has been declared as an array of int, the term `arr` can be used wherever a value of type `int*` (a pointer-to-int) is expected. The C language will indicate an array type either by appending square brackets to a reference or as a pointer.

(This also explains why string methods involving C strings type those C strings in Swift as an unsafe pointer to Int8: a C string is an array of char, and an Int8 is a char.)

For example, the C function `CGContextStrokeLineSegments` is declared like this:

```
void CGContextStrokeLineSegments(CGContextRef c,
    const CGPoint points[],
    size_t count
);
```

The second parameter is a C array of CGPoints; that's what the square brackets tell you. A C array carries no information about how many elements it contains, so to pass this C array to this function, you must also *tell* the function how many elements the array contains; that's what the third parameter is for. A C array of CGPoint is a pointer to a CGPoint, so this function's declaration is translated into Swift like this:

```
func CGContextStrokeLineSegments(c: CGContext?,
    _ points: UnsafePointer<CGPoint>,
    _ count: Int)
```

To call this function and pass it a C array of CGPoints, it would appear that you need to *make* a C array of CGPoints. A C array is not, by any stretch of the imagination, a Swift array; so how on earth will you do this? Surprise! You don't have to. Even though a Swift array is not a C array, you can pass a pointer to a Swift array here. In fact, you don't even need to pass a pointer; you can pass a reference to a Swift array *itself*. And since this is not a mutable pointer, you can declare the array with `let`; indeed, you can even pass a Swift array literal! No matter which approach you choose, Swift will convert to a C array for you as the argument crosses the bridge from Swift to C:

```
let c = UIGraphicsGetCurrentContext()!
let arr = [CGPoint(x:0,y:0),
    CGPoint(x:50,y:50),
    CGPoint(x:50,y:50),
    CGPoint(x:0,y:100),
]
CGContextStrokeLineSegments(c, arr, 4)
```

However, you *can* form a C array if you really want to. To do so, you must first set aside the block of memory yourself: declare an UnsafeMutablePointer of the desired type, calling the static method `alloc` with the desired number of elements. You can then initialize the memory by writing the elements directly into it with subscripting. Finally, since the UnsafeMutablePointer *is* a pointer, you pass *it*, not a pointer to it, as argument:

```
let c = UIGraphicsGetCurrentContext()!
let arr = UnsafeMutablePointer<CGPoint>.alloc(4)
arr[0] = CGPoint(x:0,y:0)
arr[1] = CGPoint(x:50,y:50)
arr[2] = CGPoint(x:50,y:50)
arr[3] = CGPoint(x:0,y:100)
CGContextStrokeLineSegments(c, arr, 4)
```

The same convenient subscripting is available when you *receive* a C array. For example:

```
let col = UIColor(red: 0.5, green: 0.6, blue: 0.7, alpha: 1.0)
let comp = CGColorGetComponents(col.CGColor)
```

After that code, `comp` is typed as an UnsafePointer to CGFloat. This really means that it's a C array of CGFloat — and so you can access its elements by subscripting:

```
if let sp = CGColorGetColorSpace(col.CGColor) {
    if CGColorSpaceGetModel(sp) == .RGB {
        let red = comp[0]
        let green = comp[1]
        let blue = comp[2]
        let alpha = comp[3]
        // ...
    }
}
```

C Functions

A C function declaration starts with the return type (which might be void, meaning no returned value), followed by the function name, followed by a parameter list, in parentheses, of comma-separated pairs consisting of the type followed by the parameter name. The parameter names are purely internal; you won't use them when calling a C function.

Here's the C declaration for CGPointMake, which returns an initialized CGPoint:

```
CGPoint CGPointMake (
    CGFloat x,
    CGFloat y
);
```

And here's how to call it in Swift:

```
let p = CGPointMake(50,50)
```

In Objective-C, where CGPoint is not an object, CGPointMake is the *main* way to create a CGPoint. Swift, as I've already mentioned, supplies initializers — though I personally still prefer CGPointMake.

In C, a function has a type based on its signature, and the name of a function is a reference to the function, and so it is possible to pass a function — sometimes referred to as a *pointer-to-function* — by using the function's name where a function of that type is expected. In a declaration, a pointer-to-function may be symbolized by an asterisk in parentheses.

For example, here's the declaration for a C function from the Audio Toolbox framework:

```
extern OSStatus
AudioServicesAddSystemSoundCompletion(SystemSoundID inSystemSoundID,
    CFRunLoopRef __nullable inRunLoop,
    CFStringRef __nullable inRunLoopMode,
    AudioServicesSystemSoundCompletionProc inCompletionRoutine,
    void * __nullable inClientData)
```

(Ignore for now the terms __nullable, which I'll explain later, and extern, which I won't.) A SystemSoundID is just a UInt32. But what's an AudioServicesSystemSound-CompletionProc? It's this:

```
typedef void (*AudioServicesSystemSoundCompletionProc)(SystemSoundID ssID,
    void* __nullable clientData);
```

A SystemSoundID is a UInt32, so that tells you, in the rather tortured syntax that C uses for these things, that an AudioServicesSystemSoundCompletionProc is a pointer to a function taking two parameters (typed UInt32 and pointer-to-void) and returning no result.

In Swift 1.2 and before, the only way to call AudioServicesAddSystemSound-Completion was to form the AudioServicesSystemSoundCompletionProc *in Objective-*

C. This C function parameter was typed as a CFunctionPointer, an opaque generic struct that you couldn't create within Swift.

In Swift 2.0, however, you can pass a Swift function where a C pointer-to-function is expected! As always when passing a function, you can define the function separately and pass its name, or you can form the function inline as an anonymous function. If you're going to define the function separately, it must be a *function* — meaning that it cannot be a method. A function defined at the top level of a file is fine; so is a function defined locally within a function.

So here's my AudioServicesSystemSoundCompletionProc, declared at the top level of a file:

```
func soundFinished(snd:UInt32, _ c:UnsafeMutablePointer<Void>) -> Void {
    AudioServicesRemoveSystemSoundCompletion(snd)
    AudioServicesDisposeSystemSoundID(snd)
}
```

And here's my code for playing a sound file as a system sound, including a call to Audio-ServicesAddSystemSoundCompletion:

```
let sndurl =
    NSBundle.mainBundle().URLForResource("test", withExtension: "aif")!
var snd : SystemSoundID = 0
AudioServicesCreateSystemSoundID(sndurl, &snd)
AudioServicesAddSystemSoundCompletion(snd, nil, nil, soundFinished, nil)
AudioServicesPlaySystemSound(snd)
```

Objective-C

Objective-C is built on the back of C. It adds some syntax and features, but it continues to use C syntax and data types, and remains C under the hood.

Unlike Swift, Objective-C has no namespaces. For this reason, different frameworks distinguish their contents by starting their names with different prefixes. The "CG" in "CGFloat" stands for Core Graphics, because it is declared in the Core Graphics framework. The "NS" in "NSString" stands for NeXTStep, a historical name for the framework that later became Cocoa. And so on.

Objective-C Objects and C Pointers

All the data types and syntax of C are part of Objective-C. But Objective-C is also object-oriented, so it needs a way of adding objects to C. It does this by taking advantage of C pointers. C pointers accommodate having anything at all at the far end of the pointer; management of whatever is pointed to is a separate matter, and that's just what Objective-C takes care of. Thus, Objective-C object types are expressed using C pointer syntax.

For example, here's the Objective-C declaration for the addSubview: method:

```
- (void)addSubview:(UIView *)view;
```

I haven't discussed Objective-C method declaration syntax yet, but focus on the type declaration for the `view` parameter, in parentheses: it is `UIView*`. This appears to mean "a pointer to a UIView." It does mean that — and it doesn't. *All* Objective-C object references are pointers. Thus, the fact that this is a pointer is merely a way of saying it's an object. What's at the far end of the pointer is a UIView instance.

The Swift translation of this method declaration, however, doesn't appear to involve any pointers:

```
func addSubview(view: UIView)
```

In general, in Swift, you will simply pass a reference to a class instance where Objective-C expects a class instance; the fact that an asterisk is used in the Objective-C declaration to express the fact that this is an object won't matter. What you pass as argument when calling the `addSubview:` method from Swift is a UIView instance. There is a sense in which you *are* passing a pointer when you pass a class instance — because class instances are reference types. Thus, a class instance is actually seen the same way by both Swift and Objective-C. The difference is that Swift doesn't use pointer *notation*.

Objective-C's `id` type is a general pointer to an object — the object equivalent of pointer-to-void. Any object type can be assigned or cast to or from an `id`. (Swift's AnyObject is parallel.) Because `id` is itself a pointer, a reference declared as `id` doesn't use an asterisk; you will probably never see an `id*`.

Objective-C Objects and Swift Objects

Objective-C objects are classes and instances of classes. They arrive into Swift more or less intact. You won't have any trouble subclassing Objective-C classes or working with instances of Objective-C classes.

The same is true in reverse. If Objective-C expects an object, it expects a class, and Swift can provide it. In the most general case, where Objective-C expects an `id`, you can pass any instance whose type adopts AnyObject — that is, whose type is a class. Moreover, Swift will convert certain nonclass types to their Objective-C class equivalents for you. The following structs can be cast to AnyObject, and are automatically bridged to Objective-C class types where Objective-C expects an object:

- String to NSString
- Int, UInt, Double, Float, and Bool to NSNumber
- Array to NSArray
- Dictionary to NSDictionary
- Set to NSSet

Swift's automatic bridging thus makes working with numeric types *easier* than in Objective-C. A Swift Int can be used where an Objective-C object is expected, because Swift will wrap it in an NSNumber for you; in Objective-C, you would have had to remember to wrap an integer in an NSNumber yourself.

 A Swift collection (Array, Dictionary, or Set) can be bridged to an Objective-C collection only if the types of its elements are class types or are bridged to class types (they can be cast to AnyObject) and only if they are not Optionals (because an Objective-C collection cannot contain nil).

Swift can see just about all aspects of an Objective-C class type (for how Swift sees Objective-C properties and accessors, see Chapter 10). But much of Swift, while not problematic for Objective-C, is simply invisible to it. Objective-C can't see any of the following types:

- Swift enums, except for an @objc enum with an Int raw value
- Swift structs, except for structs that are bridged or that come ultimately from C
- Swift classes not derived from NSObject
- Nested types, generics, and tuples

Even if Objective-C can see a Swift type, therefore, it cannot see within it any property whose type is a type that it can't see, and it cannot see any method that takes a parameter or returns a value of a type that it can't see. You are perfectly free to use such properties and methods, even in a subclass or extension of an Objective-C class type; they won't give Objective-C any difficulty, because as far as Objective-C is concerned, they won't be present at all.

 If Objective-C can see a type, it can see an Optional wrapping that type — *except for numeric types*. For example, Objective-C can't see a property typed as an Int?. This is presumably because Int is not *directly* bridged to Objective-C; it has to be *wrapped* in an NSNumber, and that doesn't happen through a mere type declaration.

The @objc attribute exposes to Objective-C something that it normally would not be able to see, provided it is legal for Objective-C to see it. And it has another purpose: when you mark something with @objc, you can add parentheses containing the name by which you want Objective-C to see this thing. You are free to do this even for a class or a class member that Objective-C can see already, as in this example:

```
@objc(ViewController) class ViewController : UIViewController { // ...
```

That code demonstrates something that is in fact useful to do. By default, Objective-C sees your class's name as being namespaced (prefixed) by the module name (typically, the project name). Thus, this ViewController class might be seen by Objective-C as MyCoolApp.ViewController. This can wreck the association between the class name and something else. For example, when you're translating an existing Objective-C project into Swift, you may want to use @objc(...) syntax to prevent a nib object or an NSCoding archive from losing track of its associated class.

Objective-C Methods

In Objective-C, method parameters can have names, and the name of a method as a whole is not distinct from the names of the parameters. The parameter names are *part* of the method name, with a colon appearing where each parameter would need to go. For example, the UIViewController class has an instance method called presentView-Controller:animated:completion:. That name contains three colons, so this method takes three parameters. Here's a typical example of calling it in Objective-C:

```
SecondViewController* svc = [SecondViewController new];
[self presentViewController:svc animated:YES completion:nil];
```

The declaration for an Objective-C method has three parts:

- Either + or -, meaning that the method is a class method or an instance method, respectively.

- The data type of the return value, in parentheses. It might be void, meaning no returned value.

- The name of the method, split after each colon so as to make room for the parameters. Following each colon is the data type of the parameter, in parentheses, followed by a placeholder name for the parameter.

So, for example, the Objective-C declaration for the UIViewController instance method presentViewController:animated:completion: is:

```
- (void)presentViewController: (UIViewController *)viewControllerToPresent
    animated: (BOOL)flag
    completion: (void (^ __nullable)(void))completion;
```

(That mysterious-looking third parameter type is a *block*; I'll discuss blocks later.)

Recall that Swift methods, by default, externalize all their parameter names *except the first*. So an Objective-C method declaration is translated into Swift as follows:

- The stuff before the *first* colon becomes the *name* of the function.

- The stuff before each of the *other* colons becomes an *external parameter name*. The *first* parameter has *no* external name.

- The names after the parameter types become internal (local) parameter names. If an external parameter name would be the same as the internal (local) name, there is no need to repeat it.

Thus, the Swift translation of that Objective-C method declaration looks like this:

```
func presentViewController(viewControllerToPresent: UIViewController,
    animated flag: Bool,
    completion: (() -> Void)?)
```

When you *call* a method in Swift, the internal parameter names don't come into play:

```
let svc = SecondViewController()
self.presentViewController(svc, animated: true, completion: nil)
```

When you *implement* a method declared in Objective-C, it will be to conform to an adopted protocol or to override an inherited method. The internal parameter names are supplied for you by Xcode's code completion feature — but you are free to change them. The external parameter names, however, must *not* be changed; they are part of the name of this method!

Thus, if you were to override `presentViewController:animated:completion:` (though you probably wouldn't), this would be legal:

```
override func presentViewController(vc: UIViewController,
    animated anim: Bool,
    completion handler: (() -> Void)?) {
        // ...
}
```

Unlike Swift, Objective-C does not permit overloading of methods. Two ViewController instance methods called `myMethod:` returning no result, one taking a CGFloat parameter and one taking an NSString parameter, would be illegal in Objective-C. Therefore, two such Swift methods, though legal as far as Swift is concerned, would be illegal if they were both visible to Objective-C. New in Swift 2.0, you can use the `@nonobjc` attribute to *hide* from Objective-C something that it would normally be able to see. Thus, marking one of the methods `@nonobjc` solves the problem.

Objective-C has its own version of a variadic parameter. For example, the NSArray instance method `arrayWithObjects:` is declared like this:

```
+ (id)arrayWithObjects:(id)firstObj, ... ;
```

Unlike Swift, such methods must somehow be told explicitly how many arguments are being supplied. Many such methods, including `arrayWithObjects:`, use a `nil` terminator; that is, the caller supplies `nil` after the last argument, and the callee knows when it has reached the last argument because it encounters `nil`. A call to `arrayWithObjects:` in Objective-C would look something like this:

```
NSArray* pep = [NSArray arrayWithObjects: manny, moe, jack, nil];
```

Objective-C cannot call (or see) a Swift method that takes a variadic parameter. Swift, however, *can* call an Objective-C method that takes a variadic parameter, provided that it is marked `NS_REQUIRES_NIL_TERMINATION`. `arrayWithObjects:` *is* marked in this way, so you can say `NSArray(objects:1, 2, 3)` and Swift will supply the missing `nil` terminator.

Objective-C Initializers and Factories

Objective-C initializer methods are instance methods; actual instantiation is performed using the NSObject class method `alloc`, for which Swift has no equivalent (and doesn't need one), and the initializer message is sent to the instance that results. For example, this is how you create a UIColor instance by supplying red, green, blue, and alpha values in Objective-C:

```
UIColor* col = [[UIColor alloc] initWithRed:0.5 green:0.6 blue:0.7 alpha:1];
```

The name of that initializer, in Objective-C, is `initWithRed:green:blue:alpha:`. It's declared like this:

```
- (UIColor *)initWithRed:(CGFloat)red green:(CGFloat)green
    blue:(CGFloat)blue alpha:(CGFloat)alpha;
```

In short, an initializer method, to all outward appearances, is just an instance method like any other in Objective-C.

Swift, nevertheless, is able to detect that an Objective-C initializer *is* an initializer, because the name is special — it starts with `init`! Therefore, Swift is able to translate an Objective-C initializer into a Swift initializer.

This translation is performed in a special way. Unlike an ordinary method, an Objective-C initializer is translated into Swift with *all* the parameter names appearing as external names inside the parentheses. At the same time, the external name of the *first* parameter is subject to some automatic shortening: the word `init` is stripped from the start of the first parameter name, and the word `With`, if it appears, is stripped as well. Thus, the external name of the first parameter of this initializer in Swift is `red:`. If the external names are the same as the internal names, there's no need to repeat them. Thus, Swift translates Objective-C `initWithRed:green:blue:alpha:` into the Swift initializer `init(red:green:blue:alpha:)`, which is declared like this:

```
init(red: CGFloat, green: CGFloat, blue: CGFloat, alpha: CGFloat)
```

And you'd call it like this:

```
let col = UIColor(red: 0.5, green: 0.6, blue: 0.7, alpha: 1.0)
```

There is a second way to create an instance in Objective-C. Very commonly, a class will supply a class method that is a *factory* for an instance. For example, the UIColor class has a class method `colorWithRed:green:blue:alpha:`, declared as follows:

```
+ (UIColor*) colorWithRed: (CGFloat) red green: (CGFloat) green
                    blue: (CGFloat) blue alpha: (CGFloat) alpha;
```

Swift detects a factory method of this kind by some pattern-matching rules — a class method that returns an instance of the class, and whose name begins with the name of the class, stripped of its prefix — and translates it *as an initializer*, stripping the class name (and the With) from the start of the first parameter name.

If the resulting initializer exists already, as it does in this example, then Swift treats the factory method as superfluous and suppresses it completely! Thus, the Objective-C class method colorWithRed:green:blue:alpha: isn't callable from Swift, because it would be identical to the init(red:green:blue:alpha:) that already exists.

The same name munging operates also in reverse: for example, a Swift initializer init(value:) is visible to and callable by Objective-C under the name initWithValue:.

Selectors

An Objective-C method will sometimes expect as parameter the name of a method to be called later. Such a name is called a *selector*. For example, the addTarget:action:for-ControlEvents: method can be called as a way of telling a button in the interface, "From now on, whenever you are tapped, send this message to this object." The message, the action: parameter, is a selector.

You may imagine that, if this were a Swift method, you'd be passing a function here. A selector, however, is not the same as a function. It's just a name. Objective-C, unlike Swift, is so dynamic that it is able, at runtime, to construct and send an arbitrary message to an arbitrary object based on the name alone.

But even though it is just a name, a selector is not a string, either. It is, in fact, a separate object type, designated in Objective-C declarations as SEL and in Swift declarations as Selector. In most cases, however, Swift will permit you, as a shortcut, to pass a string where a selector is expected! For example:

```
b.addTarget(self, action: "doNewGame:", forControlEvents: .TouchUpInside)
```

Once in a while, you may have to form an actual Selector object, which you can do by coercing a string to a Selector. In this example, a Selector arrives as a parameter and we need to identify it by comparison. We can't compare a Selector to a string, so we coerce a string to a Selector so that we can compare two Selectors:

```
override func canPerformAction(action: Selector,
    withSender sender: AnyObject!) -> Bool {
        if action == Selector("undo:") { // ...
```

Now please pretend that I am banging on the table with a large stick and screaming at you: you *must* get the name of a selector right when you supply it! If you call a method like addTarget:action:forControlEvents: and if you get the method name wrong when you supply the action: argument, there will be no error or warning at compile time, but Objective-C will later attempt to send this wrong message to your target *and your app will crash,* along with the dreaded "unrecognized selector" message in the console. This is one of the few situations in which Swift opens itself to the sort of disastrous Objective-C programmer error that, on the whole, it is designed to prevent. (I regard this as a major flaw in the Swift language.)

To get the name right, you need to translate from a Swift method declaration to the Objective-C name of that method. This translation is simple and follows rules that are completely mechanical, but you will be entering the name as a literal string and it is all too easy to make a typing mistake, so be careful:

1. The name starts with everything that precedes the left parenthesis in the method name.

2. If the method takes *no parameters,* stop. That's the end of the name.

3. If the method takes any parameters, add a colon.

4. If the method takes more than one parameter, add the *external* names of all parameters *except the first parameter,* with a colon after each external parameter name.

Observe that this means that if the method takes any parameters, its Objective-C name *will end with a colon.* Capitalization counts, and the name should contain no spaces or other punctuation except for the colons.

To illustrate, here are three Swift method declarations, with their Objective-C names given as a string in a comment:

```
func sayHello() -> String // "sayHello"

func say(s:String) // "say:"

func say(s:String, times n:Int) // "say:times:"
```

If you are so contrary as to externalize the name of a Swift method's first parameter, Objective-C adds "With" and a capitalized version of the external parameter name to the first part of the method name. For example:

```
func say(string s:String) // "sayWithString:"
```

It is possible to crash even though your selector name corresponds correctly to a declared method. For example, here's a small test class that creates an NSTimer and tells it to call a certain method once per second:

```
class MyClass {
    var timer : NSTimer?
    func startTimer() {
        self.timer = NSTimer.scheduledTimerWithTimeInterval(1,
            target: self, selector: "timerFired:",
            userInfo: nil, repeats: true)
```

```
    }
    func timerFired(t:NSTimer) {
        print("timer fired")
    }
}
```

There's nothing wrong with that class structurally; it compiles, and can be instantiated when the app runs. But when we call startTimer, we crash. The problem is not that timerFired doesn't exist, or that "timerFired:" is not its name; the problem is that Cocoa can't *find* timerFired. This, in turn, is because our class MyClass is a pure Swift class; therefore it lacks the Objective-C introspection and message-sending machinery that would permit Cocoa to see and call timerFired. Any of the following solutions will solve the problem:

- Declare MyClass as a subclass of NSObject.

- Declare timerFired with the @obc attribute.

- Declare timerFired with the dynamic keyword. (But this would be overkill; you should reserve use of dynamic for situations where it is needed, namely where Objective-C needs the ability to *alter* the implementation of a class member.)

CFTypeRefs

CFTypeRef functions are global C functions, and are generally easy to call. The resulting code will usually appear almost as if Swift were C.

For CFTypeRef pseudo-objects and their memory management, see Chapter 12. A CFTypeRef is a pointer, so it is interchangeable with C pointer-to-void. And because it is a pointer to a pseudo-object, it is interchangeable with Objective-C id and Swift AnyObject.

Many CFTypeRefs are *toll-free bridged* to corresponding Objective-C object types. For example, CFString and NSString, CFNumber and NSNumber, CFArray and NSArray, CFDictionary and NSDictionary are all toll-free bridged (and there are many others). Such pairs are interchangeable by casting, and sometimes you'll need to do so. Again, this is much easier in Swift than in Objective-C. In Objective-C, you must perform a *bridging cast*, to tell Objective-C how to manage this object's memory as it crosses between the memory-managed world of Objective-C objects and the unmanaged world of C and CFTypeRefs. But in Swift, CFTypeRefs are memory-managed, and so there is no need for a bridging cast; you can just cast, plain and simple. In fact, in many cases, Swift will know about the toll-free bridging, and will cast for you, automatically!

For example, in this code from one of my apps, I'm using the ImageIO framework. This framework has a C API and uses CFTypeRefs. CGImageSourceCopyPropertiesAt-Index returns a CFDictionary whose keys are CFStrings. The easiest way to obtain a value from a dictionary is by subscripting, but you can't do that with a CFDictionary, because it isn't an object — so I cast it to a Swift Dictionary. The key kCGImageProperty-PixelWidth is a CFString, which is not a Hashable (it isn't a true object at all, and can't adopt protocols), and hence cannot be used as a Swift dictionary key; but when I try to use it directly in a subscript, Swift allows me to do so, because it casts it for me to an NSString:

```
let result =
    CGImageSourceCopyPropertiesAtIndex(src, 0, nil)! as [NSObject:AnyObject]
let width = result[kCGImagePropertyPixelWidth] as! CGFloat
```

Similarly, in this code, I form a dictionary d using CFString keys and pass it to the CGImageSourceCreateThumbnailAtIndex function where a CFDictionary is expected. I don't need to cast anything explicitly! But I do need to type the dictionary in order to get Swift to cast all the keys and values to Objective-C objects for me:

```
let d : [NSObject:AnyObject] = [
    kCGImageSourceShouldAllowFloat : true,
    kCGImageSourceCreateThumbnailWithTransform : true,
    kCGImageSourceCreateThumbnailFromImageAlways : true,
    kCGImageSourceThumbnailMaxPixelSize : w
]
let imref = CGImageSourceCreateThumbnailAtIndex(src, 0, d)!
```

Blocks

A *block* is a C language feature introduced by Apple starting in iOS 4. It is very like a C function, but it is not a C function; it behaves as a closure and can be passed around as a reference type. A block, in fact, is parallel to and compatible with a Swift function, and indeed the two are interchangeable: you can pass a Swift function where a block is expected, and when a block is handed to you by Cocoa it appears as a function.

In C and Objective-C, a block declaration is signified by the caret character (^), which appears where a function name (or an asterisk in parentheses) would appear in a C function declaration. For example, the NSArray instance method sortedArrayUsing-Comparator: takes an NSComparator parameter, which is defined through a typedef like this:

```
typedef NSComparisonResult (^NSComparator)(id obj1, id obj2);
```

To read that declaration, it helps to start in the middle and work your way outwards; it says: "NSComparator is the type of a block taking two id parameters and returning an NSComparisonResult." In Swift, therefore, that typedef is translated like this:

```
typealias NSComparator = (AnyObject, AnyObject) -> NSComparisonResult
```

In many cases, there won't be a typedef, and the type of the block will appear directly in a method declaration. Here's the Objective-C declaration for a UIView class method that takes two block parameters:

```
+ (void)animateWithDuration:(NSTimeInterval)duration
    animations:(void (^)(void))animations
    completion:(void (^ __nullable)(BOOL finished))completion;
```

In that declaration, `animations:` is a block taking no parameters (`void`) and returning no value, and `completion:` is a block taking one parameter, a BOOL, and returning no value. Here's the Swift translation:

```
class func animateWithDuration(duration: NSTimeInterval,
    animations: () -> Void,
    completion: ((Bool) -> Void)?)
```

Those are examples of methods that you would call, passing a function as argument where a block parameter is expected. Here's an example of a method that you would implement, where a function is passed *to you*. This is the Objective-C declaration:

```
- (void)webView:(WKWebView *)webView
    decidePolicyForNavigationAction:(WKNavigationAction *)navigationAction
    decisionHandler:(void (^)(WKNavigationActionPolicy))decisionHandler;
```

You implement this method, and it is called when the user taps a link in a web view, so that you can decide how to respond. The third parameter is a block that takes one parameter — a WKNavigationActionPolicy, which is an enum — and returns no value. The block is passed to you as a Swift function, and you respond by *calling* the function to report your decision:

```
func webView(webView: WKWebView,
    decidePolicyForNavigationAction navigationAction: WKNavigationAction,
    decisionHandler: ((WKNavigationActionPolicy) -> Void)) {
        // ...
        decisionHandler(.Allow)
}
```

In Objective-C, a block can be cast to an `id`. A Swift function, however, cannot readily be cast to an AnyObject. Nevertheless, there are situations where, in Objective-C, you would have supplied a block where an `id` is expected, and you may wish to do the same thing in Swift, supplying a Swift function where an AnyObject is expected. For example, some object types, such as CALayer and CAAnimation, permit the use of key–value coding to attach an arbitrary key–value pair and to retrieve it later; it is perfectly reasonable to want to attach a function as the value.

A simple solution is to declare an NSObject subclass consisting of a single property of our function type:

```
typealias MyStringExpecter = (String) -> ()
class StringExpecterHolder : NSObject {
    var f : MyStringExpecter!
}
```

We can now wrap a function in an instance of our class:

```
func f (s:String) {print(s)}
let holder = StringExpecterHolder()
holder.f = f
```

We can then pass that instance where an AnyObject is expected:

```
let lay = CALayer()
lay.setValue(holder, forKey:"myFunction")
```

It is then a simple matter, at some future time, to extract the instance, cast it down from AnyObject, and call the function that it wraps:

```
let holder2 = lay.valueForKey("myFunction") as! StringExpecterHolder
holder2.f("testing")
```

A C function is not a block, but, new in Swift 2.0, you can also use a Swift function where a C function is expected, as I demonstrated earlier. Going in the other direction, to declare a type as a C pointer-to-function, mark the type as @convention(c). For example, here are two Swift method declarations:

```
func blockTaker(f:()->()) {}
func functionTaker(f:@convention(c)() -> ()) {}
```

Objective-C sees the first as taking an Objective-C block, and the second as taking a C pointer-to-function.

API Markup

As soon as Swift was first introduced to the programming public in June of 2014, it was evident that Swift's strict, specific typing was a poor match for Objective-C's dynamic, loose typing. The chief problems were:

- In Objective-C, any object instance reference can be nil. But in Swift, only an Optional can be nil. The default solution was to use implicitly unwrapped Optionals as the medium of object interchange between Objective-C and Swift. But this was a blunt instrument, especially because most objects arriving from Objective-C were never *in fact* going to be nil.

- In Objective-C, a collection type such as NSArray can contain elements of multiple object types, and the collection itself is agnostic as to what types of elements it may contain. But a Swift collection type can contain elements of just one type, and is itself typed according that element type. The default solution was for every collection to arrive from Objective-C typed in the most general way; it then had to be cast down explicitly on the Swift side. It was particularly galling to ask for a view's subviews, for example, and get back an [AnyObject] which had to be cast down to a [UIView] — when nothing could be more obvious than that a view's subviews would in fact all be UIView objects.

These problems have subsequently been solved by modifying the Objective-C language to permit *markup* of declarations in such a way as to communicate to Swift a more specific knowledge of what to expect.

An Objective-C object type can be marked as nonnull or nullable, to specify, respectively, that it will never be nil or that it might be nil. In the same way, C pointer types can be marked __nonnull or __nullable. Using these markers obviates all need for implicitly unwrapped Optionals as a medium of interchange; every type can be either a normal type or a normal Optional. Thus, implicitly unwrapped Optionals are a rare sight in the Cocoa APIs nowadays.

If you're writing an Objective-C header file and you don't mark up any of it as to nullability, you'll return to the bad old days: Swift will see your types as implicitly unwrapped Optionals. For example, here's an Objective-C method declaration:

```
- (NSString*) badMethod: (NSString*) s;
```

In the absence of markup, Swift sees that as follows:

```
func badMethod(s: String!) -> String!
```

As soon as your header file contains any markup, the Objective-C compiler will complain until it is completely marked up. To help you with this, you can mark an entire stretch of your header file with a default nonnull setting; you will then need to mark up only the exceptional nullable types:

```
NS_ASSUME_NONNULL_BEGIN
- (NSString*) badMethod: (NSString*) s;
- (nullable NSString*) goodMethod: (NSString*) s;
NS_ASSUME_NONNULL_END
```

Swift sees that with no implicitly unwrapped Optionals:

```
func badMethod(s: String) -> String
func goodMethod(s: String) -> String?
```

This sort of markup also allows the Swift compiler to be stricter than in the past about whether your declaration of an inherited or protocol-based Objective-C method is correct. In the past, you could change the optionality of a type; now the compiler will slap your hand if you don't get it right. For example, you can't declare a type as String if Objective-C declares it as nullable NSString*; you *must* say String? to match.

To mark a collection type as containing a certain type of element, put the element type in angle brackets (<>) after the name of the collection type but before the asterisk. This is an Objective-C method that returns an array of strings:

```
- (NSArray<NSString*>*) pepBoys;
```

Swift sees the return type of that method as [String], and there will be no need to cast it down.

In the declaration of an actual Objective-C collection type, a placeholder name stands for the type in angle brackets. For example, the declaration for NSArray starts like this:

```
@interface NSArray<ObjectType>
- (NSArray<ObjectType> *)arrayByAddingObject:(ObjectType)anObject;
// ...
```

The first line says that we're going to use ObjectType as the placeholder name for the element type. The second line says that the `arrayByAddingObject:` method takes an object of the element type and returns an array of the element type. If a particular array is declared as `NSArray<NSString*>*`, the ObjectType placeholder would be resolved to `NSString*`. (You can see why Apple refers to this as a "lightweight generic.")

Bilingual Targets

It is legal for a target to be a *bilingual target* — one that contains both Swift files and Objective-C files. A bilingual target can be useful for various reasons. You might want to take advantage of Objective-C language features. You might want to incorporate third-party code written in Objective-C. You might want to incorporate your own *existing* code written in Objective-C. Your app itself may have been written in Objective-C originally, and now you want to migrate part of it (or all of it, in stages) into Swift.

The key question is how, within a single target, Swift and Objective-C hear about one another's code in the first place. Recall that Objective-C, unlike Swift, has a visibility problem already: Objective-C files cannot automatically see one another. Instead, each Objective-C file that needs to see another Objective-C file must be instructed explicitly to see that file, usually with an `#import` directive at the top of the first file. In order to prevent unwanted exposure of private information, an Objective-C class declaration is conventionally spread over *two* files: a header file (*.h*) containing the `@interface` section, and a code file (*.m*) containing the `@implementation` section. Also conventionally, only *.h* files are ever imported. Thus, if declarations of class members, constants, and so forth are to be public, they are placed in a *.h* file.

Visibility of Swift and Objective-C to one another depends upon this convention: it works through *.h* files. There are two directions of visibility, and they operate separately:

How Swift sees Objective-C

When you add a Swift file to an Objective-C target, or an Objective-C file to a Swift target, Xcode offers to create a *bridging header*. This is a *.h* file *in the project*. Its default name is derived from the target name — for example, *MyCoolApp-Bridging-Header.h* — but the name is arbitrary and can be changed, provided you change the target's Objective-C Bridging Header build setting to match. (Similarly, if you decline the bridging header and you decide later that you want one, create a *.h* file manually and point to it in the target's Objective-C Bridging Header build setting.)

An Objective-C *.h* file will then be visible to Swift provided you #import it in this bridging header.

How Objective-C sees Swift

If you have a bridging header, then when you build your target, the appropriate top-level declarations of *all* your Swift files are *automatically* translated into Objective-C and are used to construct a *hidden* bridging header inside the *Intermediates* build folder for this target, deep inside your *DerivedData* folder. The easiest way to see this is with the following Terminal command:

```
$ find ~/Library/Developer/Xcode/DerivedData -name "*Swift.h"
```

This will reveal the name of the hidden bridging header. For example, for a target called MyCoolApp, the hidden bridging header is called *MyCoolApp-Swift.h*. The name may involve some transformation; for example, a space in the target name is translated into an underscore. Alternatively, examine (or change) the target's Product Module Name build setting; the hidden bridging header's name is derived from this. Your Objective-C files will be able to see your Swift declarations, provided you #import this hidden bridging header into each Objective-C file that needs to see it.

For simplicity, I will refer to these two bridging headers as the *visible* and *invisible* bridging headers, respectively.

For example, let's say that I've added to my Swift target, called MyCoolApp, a Thing class written in Objective-C. It is distributed over two files, *Thing.h* and *Thing.m*. Then:

- For Swift code to see the Thing class, I need to #import "Thing.h" in the *visible* bridging header (*MyCoolApp-Bridging-Header.h*).
- For Thing class code to see my Swift declarations, I need to import the *invisible* bridging header (#import "MyCoolApp-Swift.h") at the top of *Thing.m*.

On that basis, here's the procedure I use for turning my own Objective-C apps into Swift apps:

1. Pick a *.m* file to be translated into Swift. Objective-C cannot subclass a Swift class, so if you have defined both a class and its subclass in Objective-C, start with the subclass. Leave the app delegate class for last.

2. Remove that *.m* file from the target. To do so, select the *.m* file and use the File inspector.

3. In every Objective-C file that #imports the corresponding *.h* file, remove that #import statement and import in its place the invisible bridging header (if you aren't importing it in this file already).

4. If you were importing the corresponding *.h* file in the visible bridging header, remove the #import statement.

5. Create the *.swift* file for this class. Make sure it is added to the target.

6. In the *.swift* file, declare the class and provide stub declarations for all members that were being made public in the *.h* file. If this class needs to adopt Cocoa protocols, adopt them; you may have to provide stub declarations of required protocol methods as well. If this file needs to refer to any other classes that your target still declares in Objective-C, import their *.h* files in the visible bridging header.

7. The project should now compile! It doesn't work, of course, because you have not written any real code in the *.swift* file. But who cares about that? Time for a beer!

8. Now fill out the code in the *.swift* file. My technique is to translate more or less line-by-line from the original Objective-C code, even though the outcome is not particularly idiomatic (Swifty).

9. When the code for this *.m* file is completely translated into Swift, build and run and test. If the runtime complains (probably accompanied by crashing) that it can't find this class, find all references to it in the nib editor and reenter the class's name in the Identity inspector (and press Tab to set the change). Save and try again.

10. On to the next *.m* file! Repeat all of the above steps.

11. When all of the other files have been translated, translate the app delegate class. At this point, if there are no Objective-C files left in the target, you can delete the *main.m* file (replacing it with a `@UIApplicationMain` attribute in the app delegate class declaration) and the *.pch* (precompiled header) file.

Your app should now run, and is now written in pure Swift (or is, at least, as pure as you intend to make it). Now go back and think about the code, making it more Swifty and idiomatic. You may well find that things that were clumsy or tricky in Objective-C can be made much neater and clearer in Swift.

Note also that you can do a *partial* conversion of an Objective-C class by extending it in Swift. This can be useful as a stage along the path to total conversion, or you might quite reasonably write only one or two methods of an Objective-C class in Swift, just because Swift makes it so much easier to say or understand certain kinds of thing. However, Swift cannot see the Objective-C class's members unless they are made public, so methods and properties that you were previously keeping private in the Objective-C class's *.m* file may have to be declared in its *.h* file.

Index

We'd like to hear your suggestions for improving our indexes. Send email to index@oreilly.com.

protocols, 173–183, 443
  adopter, 186
  adopting, 174
  associated type, 186
  associated type, chaining, 191
  associated type, constraining, 194
  casting, 177
  class, 180
  conforming to, 174
  declaration, 177
  delegate, 486
  documentation, 445
  extensions, 200, 442
  extensions, constraining associated type, 205
  generic, 186
  generic, constraining associated type, 194
  implicitly required initializers, 181
  informal, 445
  literal convertible, 183
  memory management, 281
  Objective-C, 443
  optional members, 179, 446
  testing type, 177
provisioning profile, 403
provisioning profile, development, 407
provisioning profile, distribution, 423
provisioning profile, exporting, 409
provisioning profile, universal, 407
proxy objects, 329, 340
public, 269

Q

query events, 476
question mark, 99, 107, 166, 180, 242, 247, 248
Quick Help, 295, 366
Quick Look a variable, 392

R

Range struct, 93
range, indexing with, 94, 214
range, modifying, 94, 216
range, string, 88
raw value, 130
RawRepresentable, 202
read-only variables, 69
recursion, 44
recursive references, 145
reduce, 220

Refactoring (book), 26
reference types, 140
reference types, memory management, 273
reference, getting, 127, 525
reference, persisting, 275
reference, recursive, 145
reference, strong, 275
reference, unowned, 277, 513
reference, unsafe, 514
reference, weak, 275, 513
references to class types, 209
references to object types, 168
references to object types, Objective-C, 545
references to same object, 143, 208
registering for a notification, 478
regular expressions, 451
Related Items menu, 296
releasing a property, 512
removeAtIndex, 92, 218
removeFirst, 218
removeLast, 218
removeRange, 94
removeValueForKey, 226
renaming a project or target, 324
REPL, xv
replaceRange, 94
replacing, 385
Report navigator, 294, 398
required initializers, 156, 170, 181
resolution of generics, 184, 186, 190
resolution, screen, 315, 374
resources, 313
resources in an asset catalog, 315
resources in the app bundle, 314
resources, on-demand, 316
responder, 492
responder chain, 492
respondsToSelector:, 446
result of a function, 27
retain count, 506
retain cycles, 274, 512
  anonymous functions, 278
  notifications, 515
  timers, 516
retains, unusual, 518
rethrows, 259
return function from function, 56
return statement, 28
return value of function, 28

About the Author

Matt Neuburg started programming computers in 1968, when he was 14 years old, as a member of a literally underground high school club, which met once a week to do timesharing on a bank of PDP-10s by way of primitive teletype machines. He also occasionally used Princeton University's IBM-360/67, but gave it up in frustration when one day he dropped his punch cards. He majored in Greek at Swarthmore College, and received his PhD from Cornell University in 1981, writing his doctoral dissertation (about Aeschylus) on a mainframe. He proceeded to teach Classical languages, literature, and culture at many well-known institutions of higher learning, most of which now disavow knowledge of his existence, and to publish numerous scholarly articles unlikely to interest anyone. Meanwhile he obtained an Apple IIc and became hopelessly hooked on computers again, migrating to a Macintosh in 1990. He wrote some educational and utility freeware, became an early regular contributor to the online journal *TidBITS*, and in 1995 left academe to edit *MacTech* magazine. In August 1996 he became a freelancer, which means he has been looking for work ever since. He is the author of *Frontier: The Definitive Guide*, *REALbasic: The Definitive Guide*, and *AppleScript: The Definitive Guide*, as well as *Programming iOS 7* (all for O'Reilly Media), and *Take Control of Using Mountain Lion* (TidBITS Publishing).

Colophon

The animal on the cover of *iOS 9 Programming Fundamentals with Swift* is a harp seal (*Pagophilus groenlandicus*), a Latin name that translates to "ice-lover from Greenland." These animals are native to the northern Atlantic and Arctic Oceans, and spend most of their time in the water, only going onto ice packs to give birth and molt. As earless ("true") seals, their streamlined bodies and energy-efficient swimming style make them well-equipped for aquatic life. While eared seal species like sea lions are powerful swimmers, they are considered semiaquatic because they mate and rest on land.

The harp seal has silvery-gray fur, with a large black marking on its back that resembles a harp or wishbone. They grow to be 5–6 feet long, and weigh 300–400 pounds as adults. Due to their cold habitat, they have a thick coat of blubber for insulation. A harp seal's diet is very varied, including several species of fish and crustaceans. They can remain underwater for an average of 16 minutes to hunt for food, and are able to dive several hundred feet.

Harp seal pups are born without any protective fat, but are kept warm by their white coat, which absorbs heat from the sun. After nursing for 12 days, the seal pups are abandoned, having tripled their weight due to their mother's high-fat milk. In the subsequent weeks until they are able to swim off the ice, the pups are very vulnerable to predators and will lose nearly half of their weight. Those that survive reach maturity after 4–8 years (depending on their gender), and have an average lifespan of 35 years.

Harp seals are hunted commercially off the coasts of Canada, Norway, Russia, and Greenland for their meat, oil, and fur. Though some of these governments have regulations and enforce hunting quotas, it is believed that the number of animals killed every year is underreported. Public outcry and efforts by conservationists have resulted in a decline in market demand for seal pelts and other products, however.

The cover image is from Wood's *Animate Creation*. The cover fonts are URW Typewriter and Guardian Sans. The text font is Adobe Minion Pro; the heading font is Adobe Myriad Condensed; and the code font is Dalton Maag's Ubuntu Mono.

Get even more for your money.

Join the O'Reilly Community, and register the O'Reilly books you own. It's free, and you'll get:

- $4.99 ebook upgrade offer
- 40% upgrade offer on O'Reilly print books
- Membership discounts on books and events
- Free lifetime updates to ebooks and videos
- Multiple ebook formats, DRM FREE
- Participation in the O'Reilly community
- Newsletters
- Account management
- 100% Satisfaction Guarantee

Signing up is easy:

1. Go to: oreilly.com/go/register
2. Create an O'Reilly login.
3. Provide your address.
4. Register your books.

Note: English-language books only

To order books online:
oreilly.com/store

For questions about products or an order:
orders@oreilly.com

To sign up to get topic-specific email announcements and/or news about upcoming books, conferences, special offers, and new technologies:
elists@oreilly.com

For technical questions about book content:
booktech@oreilly.com

To submit new book proposals to our editors:
proposals@oreilly.com

O'Reilly books are available in multiple DRM-free ebook formats. For more information:
oreilly.com/ebooks

WITHDRAWN

$49.99   3/29/16.

LONGWOOD PUBLIC LIBRARY
800 Middle Country Road
Middle Island, NY 11953
(631) 924-6400
mylpl.net

LIBRARY HOURS

Monday-Friday	9:30 a.m. - 9:00 p.m.
Saturday	9:30 a.m. - 5:00 p.m.
Sunday (Sept-June)	1:00 p.m. - 5:00 p.m.

CPSIA information can be obtained at www.ICGtesting.com
Printed in the USA
BVOW09s2349240116

434066BV00008B/46/P

9 781491 936771